IMPORTANT:

HERE IS YOUR REGISTRATION CODE TO ACCESS
YOUR PREMIUM McGRAW-HILL ONLINE RESOURCES.

MCGRAW-HILL
ONLINE RESOURCES

For key premium online resources you need THIS CODE to gain access. Once the code is entered, you will be able to use the Web resources for the length of your course.

If your course is using **WebCT** or **Blackboard**, you'll be able to use this code to access the McGraw-Hill content within your instructor's online course.

Access is provided if you have purchased a new book. If the registration code is missing from this book, the registration screen on our Website, and within your WebCT or Blackboard course, will tell you how to obtain your new code.

Registering for McGraw-Hill Online Resources

TO gain access to your McGraw-Hill web
resources simply follow the steps b⌐¹

1. USE YOUR WEB BROWSER TO GO TO: **www.mhhe.com/west2**

2. CLICK ON **FIRST TIME USER**.

3. ENTER THE REGISTRATION CODE* PRINTED ON THE TEAR-OFF BOOKMARK ON THE RIGHT.

4. AFTER YOU HAVE ENTERED YOUR REGISTRATION CODE, CLICK **REGISTER**.

5. FOLLOW THE INSTRUCTIONS TO SET-UP YOUR PERSONAL UserID AND PASSWORD.

6. WRITE YOUR UserID AND PASSWORD DOWN FOR FUTURE REFERENCE.
   KEEP IT IN A SAFE PLACE.

TO GAIN ACCESS to the McGraw-Hill content in your instructor's **WebCT** or **Blackboard** course simply log in to the course with the UserID and Password provided by your instructor. Enter the registration code exactly as it appears in the box to the right when prompted by the system. You will only need to use the code the first time you click on McGraw-Hill content.

Thank you, and welcome
to your McGraw-Hill
online Resources!

Mc Graw Hill **Higher Education**

REGISTRATION CODE

3DCV-7KA0-Q7WF-JMEU-RY7Q

D1306947

Mc Graw Hill | **Higher Education**

* YOUR REGISTRATION CODE CAN BE USED ONLY ONCE TO ESTABLISH ACCESS. IT IS NOT TRANSFERABLE.

0-07-293704-1 WEST: INTRODUCING COMMUNICATION THEORY: ANALYSIS AND APPLICATION, 2/E

Introducing Communication Theory

Introducing Communication Theory

ANALYSIS AND APPLICATION

Second Edition

Richard West
University of Southern Maine

Lynn H. Turner
Marquette University

Boston   Burr Ridge, IL   Dubuque, IA   Madison, WI   New York
San Francisco   St. Louis   Bangkok   Bogotá   Caracas   Kuala Lumpur
Lisbon   London   Madrid   Mexico City   Milan   Montreal   New Delhi
Santiago   Seoul   Singapore   Sydney   Taipei   Toronto

INTRODUCING COMMUNICATION THEORY: ANALYSIS AND APPLICATION, SECOND EDITION
Published by McGraw-Hill, a business unit of The McGraw-Hill Companies, Inc., 1221 Avenue of the Americas, New York, NY 10020. Copyright © 2004 by The McGraw-Hill Companies, Inc. All rights reserved. Previous edition © 2000 by Mayfield Publishing Company. No part of this publication may be reproduced or distributed in any form or by any means, or stored in a database or retrieval system, without the prior written consent of The McGraw-Hill Companies, Inc., including, but not limited to, any network or other electronic storage or transmission, or broadcast for distance learning.

Some ancillaries, including electronic and print components, may not be available to customers outside the United States.

2 3 4 5 6 7 8 9 0 FGR/FGR 0 9 8 7 6 5 4

Vice president and editor-in-chief: *Thalia Dorwick*
Publisher: *Phil Butcher*
Sponsoring editor: *Nanette Kauffman Giles*
Development editors: *Gabrielle Goodman, Nancy Lubars*
Marketing manager: *Sally Constable*
Production services manager: *Jennifer Mills*
Production service: *Strawberry Field Publishing*
Manuscript editor: *Jan McDearmon*
Art director: *Jeanne M. Schreiber*
Design manager: *Gino Cieslik*
Cover designer: *Mary L. Spanburg*
Interior designer: *Elise Lansdon*
Art manager: *Robin Mouat*
Illustrators: *Joan Carol, John and Judy Waller, Robin Mouat*
Production supervisor: *Carol Bielski*

The text was set in 10/12 Sabon by G & S Typesetters, Inc. and printed on acid-free, 45# New Era Matte by Quebecor World, Fairfield.

Library of Congress Cataloging-in-Publication Data

West, Richard
   Introducing communication theory : analysis and application / Richard West, Lynn H. Turner.—2nd ed.
      p. cm.
   Includes bibliographical references and indexes.
   ISBN 0-7674-3034-4
      1. Information theory.   2. Communication.   I. Turner, Lynn H.   II. Title.

Q360.W47 2003
003'.54—dc21
2003046369

www.mhhe.com

Brief Contents

Contents

Preface

Introducing Communication Theory: Analysis and Application explores the practical, engaging, and relevant ways in which theory operates in our lives. The text is written for students who have little or no background in communication theory. We originally wrote the book because we felt that students needed to know how theorizing helps us understand ourselves, our experiences, our environment, and our culture.

Specifically, our original objectives included:

- Familiarizing students with the principles and central ideas of important theories they are likely to encounter in the communication discipline
- Demystifying the concept of theory and helping students see the application of theory in their everyday activities
- Helping students become more systematic and thoughtful critical thinkers
- Providing students with an overview and brief history of how the communication discipline came into focus
- Introducing students to the research process and the place of theory within this process

The second edition of the book maintains its original focus of introducing communication theory to students in an accessible, appealing, and memorable way. Our hope is that students will take away a basic knowledge of and appreciation for communication theory from reading our text. Over the course of more than thirty combined years of teaching communication theory, we have learned that students understand material best when it is explained in a simple, direct way through a number of realistic and applicable examples. *Introducing Communication Theory: Analysis and Application* adapts and applies all that we as teachers have learned from our students. We continue to be indebted to both students and colleagues whose suggestions and comments have greatly influenced this second edition.

Because of the interdisciplinary nature of communication theory, we include not only the unique contributions of communication theorists but also theories that originated in other fields, such as psychology, business, sociology, biology, and philosophy. We do not presume to speak for the theorists; our goal is to frame their words and illustrate their theories with real-world examples and applications so that they become accessible for our students.

The Challenges of Teaching and Learning Communication Theory

Instructors teaching communication theory face a number of challenges. Because many students think of theory as distant, abstract, and obscure, teachers must overcome these potentially negative connotations. Negative feelings toward the subject can be magnified in classrooms where students represent a variety of ages and socioeconomic, ethnic, cultural, and linguistic backgrounds. *Introducing Communication Theory* addresses this challenge by offering a readable and practical guide that integrates content with examples, capturing the essence and elegance of theory in a straightforward manner.

A second challenge is that instructors often must overcome preconceived ideas about scholarship, which students may view as difficult or remote. This book demonstrates to students that they already possess many of the characteristics of researchers, such as curiosity and ambition. Students will be pleasantly surprised to know that they operate according to many personal theories every day. Once students begin to revise their misconceptions about research and theory, they are in a position to become critical thinkers and learners.

A third challenge of teaching and learning communication theory is capturing the complexity of a theory in an approachable way without oversimplifying the theoretical process. To address this problem, instructors often present a skeletal version of a theory and then fill in the missing pieces with personal materials. By providing a variety of real-life examples and applications reflecting a wide range of classroom demographics, *Introducing Communication Theory* facilitates such an approach.

Special Features and Learning Aids

To accomplish our goals and address the challenges of teaching communication theory, we have incorporated a number of special features and learning aids into the second edition:

"The first four chapters of the book give students a solid foundation for studying the theories that follow. This guidework is essential in order to understand how theorists conceptualize and test their theories."

- *Part I, Setting the Stage.* The first four chapters of the book continue to give students a solid foundation for studying the theories that follow. This groundwork is essential in order to understand how theorists conceptualize and test their theories. Chapters 1 and 2 define communication and provide a brief history of the discipline. We also present the prevailing contexts in which theory is customarily categorized. Chapters 3 and 4 cover the basics of theory and research as well as the relationship between them.

- *Coverage of twenty-five theories.* Discrete chapters on each of twenty-five theories provide accessible, thorough coverage for students and offer flexibility to instructors. We kept the original theories from the first edition, but have added two **NEW** theories to this edition: Chapter 13, Communication Privacy Management Theory (Sandra Petronio), and Chapter 25, Medium Theory (Marshall McLuhan).

- **NEW** *section openers*. The theory chapters in Part II, Understanding the Dialogue, are organized into six sections. In this edition, we have written new section openers to introduce these groups of chapters. The overviews provide students with an explanation for our choices, placing the theories in context and allowing students to see the connections between and among theories.

- *Chapter opening vignettes*. Each chapter begins with an extended vignette, which is then integrated throughout the chapter, providing examples to illustrate the theoretical concepts and claims. These stories help students understand how communication theory plays out in the everyday lives of ordinary people. Students' comments have affirmed the value of these opening stories.

- *A structured approach to each theory*. Every theory chapter has a consistent format that includes a vignette, an introduction, a summary of assumptions, a description of core concepts, and a critique (using the criteria established in Part I). This consistency provides continuity for students and ensures a balanced presentation of the theories.

- *Tables and Figures*. To increase conceptual organization and enhance the visual presentation of content, we have added numerous **NEW** tables and figures throughout the text. Nearly every chapter has a new visual aid for students to consider, helping them to understand the material. These visuals provide a clearer sense of the conceptual organization of the theories, and they support those students who best retain information visually.

- *Theory into Practice (TIP) boxes*. These boxes, featured in every theory chapter, come from popular media and demonstrate how theory (or its components) relates to real life. For example, in Chapter 8 on Expectancy Violations Theory, the TIP box examines how space variations affect the flirting process. Ten **NEW** TIP boxes have been added to the second edition to keep the material current. Further, we have added a **NEW** follow-up question to each TIP so that students can apply the information to both theory and their life experiences.

- *Research Note boxes*. These boxes present abstracts of research articles and essays that are relevant to the chapter and, like TIP boxes, appear in every theory chapter. Research Note boxes demonstrate how theories or theoretical principles are utilized in research studies; they also serve to familiarize students with the content and conventions of original research. Updated in many chapters for the second edition, the feature reflects the breadth and depth of the research being conducted in the discipline today.

- **NEW** *Running Glossary*. Throughout each chapter, a new running glossary gives students immediate access to unfamiliar terms and their meanings.

- **NEW** *The Theory Chronicles*. These new, unique journal assignments appear in each chapter and demonstrate the usefulness of theory in our

> "Every theory chapter has a consistent format that includes a vignette, an introduction, a summary of assumptions, a description of core concepts, and a critique (using the criteria established in Part I). This consistency provides continuity for students and ensures a balanced presentation of the theories."

"We ask students to look at how two theories from different contexts relate to each other. We also consider how some theories may deal with similar contexts but approach them in very different ways."

surroundings. For instance, in Chapter 12, Relational Dialectics Theory, students are asked to detail the extent to which the conclusions on dialectics would differ if the research had been set in Africa or Asia.

- **NEW** *The Theory Connection.* We believe that many theories cut across multiple contexts. Therefore, we ask students to look at how two theories from different contexts relate to each other. We also consider how some theories may deal with similar contexts but approach them in very different ways. The Theory Connection, feature asks students to think about these contrasts. For instance, in Chapter 14, Groupthink, we ask students to consider the role of silence in both Groupthink and Muted Group Theory (Chapter 28).

- **NEW** *Theory Application in Groups (TAG).* Working with others can help students better appreciate the material. We developed this feature to encourage collaborate learning and to foster critical thinking across different learning styles. In Chapter 15, Adaptive Structuration Theory, for instance, we ask small groups to think about ethical lapses in judgment from organizational leaders and how Adaptive Structuration Theory can inform their thinking about this issue.

- *Discussion Starters* conclude each chapter. These thought-provoking questions prompt students to critically examine the chapter and focus on critical issues.

Supplemental Resources

The Online Learning Center at www.mhhe.com/west2 provides interactive resources to address the needs of a variety of teaching and learning styles. For every chapter, students and instructors can access chapter outlines, sample quizzes with feedback, crossword puzzles using key terms, and Internet activities. For instructors specifically, the Online Learning Center offers an online Instructor's Resource Manual with general guidelines for teaching the basic theory course, sample syllabi for quarter and semester courses, chapter outlines, and classroom activities.

In addition, a computerized test bank with multiple-choice and short-answer questions for every chapter is available in both Windows and Macintosh versions. The computerized format allows instructors to edit the test bank and incorporate their own questions.

Organization

Part I, Setting the Stage, provides a conceptual foundation for the discrete theory chapters in Part II. Chapter 1 begins by introducing the discipline and describing the process of communication. It then explores the dark side of communication, which looks at how people use negative communication to impair human interaction (to deceive, hurt, verbally abuse, and so forth). We conclude the chapter with a discussion of ethics. Chapter 2 gives a brief history of the communication field by examining research pioneers and the establishment of the largest communication association: the National Communication Association. In this chapter, we focus both on the roots of communication theory in ancient Greece and on current trends. The chapter then turns to the primary contexts of communication (intrapersonal, interpersonal, small group, organizational, public, mediated, intercultural), which frame the study of communication in most academic settings across the country. Chapter 3 explores the nature of theory, providing definitions and characteristics of theories in general. The chapter also discusses perspectives that guide communication research and outlines criteria for evaluating theories. Chapter 4 explores the relationship between theory and research. Our goal in this chapter is to familiarize students with the research process, explaining its direct relationship with theory and practice. We present four common research methodologies (surveys, experiments, depth interviews, and textual analysis) to illustrate how communication research is conducted.

With this foundation established in Part I, Part II, Understanding the Dialogue, introduces students to twenty-five different theories, each in a discrete, concise chapter. Many of these theories cut across communication contexts. For example, Relational Dialectics Theory can be understood and applied in an organizational context as well as in an interpersonal context. However, to facilitate understanding, we have grouped theories into six sections according to primary focus: The Self and Messages, Relationship Development, Groups and Organizations, The Public, The Media, and Culture and Diversity.

It was not easy for us to decide which theories to include because there are so many from which to choose. In making our selections, we were guided by four broad criteria: (1) whether the theory was significant in the history of the field, (2) whether it reflects the interdisciplinary nature of the field, (3) whether it is important in the context of current thinking in the field, and (4) whether it contributes to a balance of pioneering and contemporary theories in the book. In addition, we were sensitive to the need to include theories developed by a diverse group of scholars.

Finally, in Part III, Beyond the Curtain Call, Chapter 30 describes the constant evolution of theory and theory building based on new societal trends. To show students that the communication major provides practical knowledge leading to employment, we conclude with a focus on career paths that make use of communication theory. We also make suggestions for becoming more adept in a communication career.

Acknowledgments

Any book owes its existence to efforts made by others in addition to the listed authors, and some people who have helped with this book may not even realize the debt we acknowledge here. We would like to thank all those who have helped us as we worked our way through this large project. First, our work rests on the shoulders of the theorists whose creations we profile in this book. We are grateful for their creative thinking, which allows us to understand and predict the complexities of the communication process. Second, our insights represent the discussions that we have had with our communication theory students over the years. Several parts of this book are based upon student input at both of our universities. Students have contributed to this book in both direct and indirect ways. Our families, too, contributed in ways both large and small in helping us complete this project. For providing us with patience, support, and food, we cannot thank them enough.

Our chosen family of friends and colleagues have helped with this project. Rich would like to thank Beverly, his mother, for eager attempts to understand not only this book and its contents, but also his other texts and research with which she is unfamiliar. She remains by far his best communication theory student. Although his 15-year-old wonderful dog, Roger, passed away during the writing of this edition, his extraordinary love continues to be felt in Rich's life. Finally, he'd like to thank his colleagues in the Department of Communication: Russ Kivatisky, Rebecca Lockridge, Lenny Shedletsky, Erika Andersen, Julie Zink, Dan Panici, Kathryn Lasky, David Pierson, and Cathy Bourgeois for helping him develop as a scholar, teacher, and colleague.

Lynn would like to thank her family: her husband, Ted; her daughter's family, the Spitznagles—Sabrina, Billy, Sophie; her stepdaughter's family, the Kissels—Leila, Russ, Zoe, Dylan; and her stepson's family, the Feldshers—Ted, Sally, and Ely for invaluable lessons in communication theory and practice. Further, she is indebted to her parents and her brother and his family, as well as all of her extended family members who helped in ways great and small as this project continued over time. Friends and colleagues, especially Pat Sullivan and Patrice Buzzanell, provided great support and have taught her many valuable lessons about scholarship and communication theory. She also owes a significant debt to her research assistant, Jaime Leick, for tracking down those elusive sources and for a great deal of helpful copyediting.

We wish to thank the University of Southern Maine and Marquette University. They continue to offer supportive climates that allowed us to finish this project in a timely manner. We are grateful for the secretarial help, the research assistance, and the general tenor of encouragement fostered by the administration, faculty, and staff.

In addition, we would like to thank Justin LaBerge who, as a top student of communication theory, was instrumental in creating the Instructor's Manual and Test Bank. He has been unrelenting in ensuring that the information remains applicable to students' lives. He will be our valued colleague in the near future.

We also thank those people who worked hard to put this book into production. We need to first thank Nanette Kauffman Giles, Senior Sponsoring Editor at McGraw-Hill. Her patience, thoughtfulness, and sense of calm was appreciated as we completed this project. She served as an excellent resource as we worked through ideas for this edition. In addition to Nanette, several other people gave their time, talent, and expertise to make this a book of which we are proud. They include developmental editors Nancy Lubars and Gabrielle Goodman, marketing manager Sally Constable, media producer Jessica Bodie, project managers Jen Mills and Melanie Field, designer Elise Lansdon, and supplement producer Marc Mattson. We thank each of these individuals for their contributions to the second edition of the text. Their determination in making this an outstanding product is deeply appreciated.

Finally, we thank the manuscript reviewers who gave their time and expertise to keep us on track in our interpretation of the ideas of others. We are grateful for their careful reading and insightful suggestions, which expanded and clarified our thinking in many ways. The errors in this book are our own, but the strengths were established through their help. Our text is a much more useful product because of the comments and suggestions of the following:

First edition reviewers

John R. Baldwin,
Illinois State University

Holly H. Bognar,
Cleveland State University

Sheryl Bowen,
Villanova University

Cam Brammer,
Marshall University

Jeffrey D. Brand,
North Dakota State University

Randy K. Dillon,
Southwest Missouri State University

Kent Drummond,
University of Wyoming

James Gilchrist,
Western Michigan University

Laura Jansma,
University of California–Santa Barbara

Madeline M. Keaveney,
California State University–Chico

Joann Keyton,
University of Kansas

Debra Mazloff,
University of St. Thomas

Elizabeth M. Perse,
University of Delaware

Linda M. Pledger,
University of Arkansas

Mary Ann Renz,
Central Michigan University

Patricia Rockwell,
University of Southwestern Louisiana

Deborah Smith-Howell,
University of Nebraska

Denise Solomon,
University of Wisconsin

Tami Spry,
St. Cloud State University

Rebecca W. Tardy,
University of Louisville

Ralph Thompson,
Cornell University

Second edition reviewers

Sue Barnes,
Fordham University

Jack Baseheart,
University of Kentucky

Jamie Byrne,
Millersville University

Thomas Feeley,
State University of New York, Geneseo

Amy Hubbard,
University of Hawaii at Manoa

Matthew McAllister,
Virginia Tech

Janet Skupien,
University of Pittsburgh

Jon Smith,
Southern Utah University

Katy Wiss,
Western Connecticut State University

Kevin Wright,
University of Memphis

About the Authors

Richard West is a professor in the Department of Communication at the University of Southern Maine in Portland. He received his B.A. and M.A from Illinois State University, and his Ph.D. from Ohio University. Rich has been teaching since 1984, and his teaching and research interests range from family diversity to teacher–student communication. He began teaching communication theory as a graduate student and currently teaches the course in lecture format to more than 100 students. Rich is the recipient of various teaching and research awards at USM, including the College of Arts and Sciences Outstanding Teacher-Scholar and the Faculty Senate Award in Communication Research. He is a past recipient of the Outstanding Alumni Award in Communication at Illinois State University and Ohio University. He is also co-author (with Lynn Turner) of *Gender and Communication* and *Perspectives on Family Communication*. He dedicates this book to his golden retriever/ridgeback mix, Roger.

Lynn H. Turner is an associate professor in Communication Studies at Marquette University in Milwaukee, Wisconsin. She received her B.A. from the University of Illinois–Chicago, her M.A. from the University of Iowa, and her Ph.D. from Northwestern University. She teaches communication theory and research methods to first-year communication studies majors. Lynn began teaching at Marquette in 1985, and prior to that taught at Iowa State University. Her research interests include family communication and gender and communication. She is the recipient of several awards, including Marquette's College of Communication Research Excellence Award and the Book of the Year award from the Organization for the Study of Communication, Language, and Gender for her book with Patricia Sullivan, *From the Margins to the Center*. She lives with her husband, Ted, and looks forward to visits from their children and grandchildren.

PART One

Setting the Stage
Communication, Theory, and Research

YOU MIGHT NOT HAVE THOUGHT ABOUT THIS, BUT each day, the decisions we make, the media we consume, and the relationships we experience are all guided and explained by communication theory. Communication theory helps us to understand other people and their communities, the media, and our associations with families, friends, roommates, co-workers, and companions. Perhaps most important, communication theory makes it easier to understand ourselves.

We begin our discussion of communication theory by asking you to consider the experiences of Morgan and Alex. After randomly being assigned as roommates, the two met on "move-in day" at Scott Hall. They were both pretty nervous; yet, because they had e-mailed each other and talked on the phone a few times, they knew a little bit about each other. Once they met, they started talking. They went out for coffee the first few weeks of school, getting to know each other better. They spent a lot of time telling stories about their families and friends, and talking about what they look for in a partner. They both loved television, especially the "reality shows," because they loved to see how other people dealt with their lives in times of stress. After several weeks, Morgan and Alex became closer and felt that they'd be able to live with each other. They were going to have to balance their desire to hang out with each other with their need to be alone. And it was going to be give-and-take because their schedules were completely opposite. Eventually, the two became great friends.

What you just read is an exercise in theory building. To illustrate the various ways in which communication theory functions in the lives of Morgan and Alex, let's

1

identify the various issues and see how theory played itself out. First, these roommates no doubt supported the research of Uncertainty Reduction Theory (Chapter 9) through their need to reduce their uncertainty about each other. They also probably self-disclosed some personal information to each other, underscoring a central feature of Social Penetration Theory (Chapter 10). Next, they discovered that they both watch television and use it to see how others live their lives, highlighting the essence of Uses and Gratifications Theory (Chapter 23). Balancing the need to be together with the need to remain private encompasses Relational Dialectics Theory (Chapter 12). Morgan and Alex also told personal stories to each other; storytelling is at the heart of The Narrative Paradigm (Chapter 20). In sum, at least five communication theories could help explain the experiences of the two roommates.

We are not suggesting that communication theory can explain all of life's events. Rather, it is a start to help us understand most of life's events. We therefore set the stage by presenting you an important backdrop, a proscenium, for understanding this intriguing area known as communication theory.

The first four chapters provide you an important foundation for discussing each communication theory. These chapters give you a general introduction to communication and to theory. First, in order to give you an idea about the communication discipline, in Chapter 1 we present our definition of communication, the prevailing models of communication, and other important issues such as ethics and negative communication. Chapter 2 begins with a brief discussion of the history of the largest communication association in the field. This is followed by a detailed analysis of the six primary contexts of communication that serve as an organizing scheme for the rest of the book.

We prepare you directly for discussing each theory in the text in Chapter 3. In this chapter, we define theory and its relationship to our lives. We also present several ways to evaluate the theories you will read about. Finally, Chapter 4 identifies the role of doing research in theory. As you will learn, when scholars develop a theory, it's a result of a great deal of research. We introduce several research tools used by theorists to test and retest their theories.

Thinking about communication theory may not be at the top of your priority list right now, but as in the example of Morgan and Alex, communication theory is an important part of our lives, regardless of our awareness of how it affects us. One of your authors once heard communication theory described this way: "It's like a sleeping dog."

CHAPTER 1

What Is Communication?

The McLeans

Jimmy and Angie McLean have been married for almost thirty years, and they are the parents of three children. The three kids have been out of the house for years, but a recent layoff at the company where their son Eddy worked has forced the 24-year-old to return home until he can get another job.

At first, Eddy's return was viewed quite favorably by his parents. His father was proud of the fact that Eddy felt comfortable returning home, and his mom was happy to help Eddy with some of the mundane tasks of life, such as laundry and cooking.

But the good times associated with Eddy's return soon ended. The McLeans' once serene breakfasts were marred by Eddy's blaring radio. Jimmy and Angie's walks at night were complicated because Eddy often wanted to join them. The couple's privacy was inevitably interrupted by Eddy all through the day.

When Eddy's parents thought about communicating their frustration and disappointment, they quickly recalled Eddy's situation. They didn't want to upset him any further. The McLeans tried to figure out a way to communicate to their son that although they love him, they wish that he would get a job and leave the house. They simply wanted some peace, privacy, and freedom, and their son was preventing this.

Recently, the couple's frustration with the situation took a turn for the worse. Returning from one of their long walks, they discovered Eddy on the couch, a bit intoxicated from a party at his friend's house. When Jimmy and Angie confronted him about his demeanor, Eddy shouted, "Don't start lecturing me now. Is it any wonder that none of your other kids call you? It's because you don't know when to stop!" Jimmy snapped, "Get out of my house. Now!" Eddy left the home, slamming the front door behind him. Angie stared out of the window, wondering whether they would ever hear from their son again. ∎

Communication depends on our ability to understand one another. Although our communication can be ambiguous ("Thanks for the present—it's just what I would have expected from you!"), one primary goal is understanding. Our daily activities are wrapped in conversations with others. Yet, as we see with Jimmy and Angie McLean, we may be unsure about how to express our thoughts. Therefore, effective communication is often sacrificed.

For years, self-help books have proclaimed communication to be the panacea for all relational ills. To be sure, being able to communicate effectively is highly valued in the United States. Corporations in particular have recognized the importance of communication. In the health care industry, for instance, Andrew Lum and Mark Zuiderveen (2002) observed that communication plays a crucial role in clinician–patient relationships. They note that patients "deserve to be listened to, heard, cared about, and involved in decisions about their health care—not only to have satisfying care experiences but also to achieve optimum health" (www.kaiserpermanente.org). They note that communication mishaps in organizations are "extremely costly" to the company.

Stephanie Armour (1998) agrees. She writes in *USA Today* that problems in communication have led to loss of organizational profits. She concludes: "Communication mishaps are eroding productivity and leaving employers at a competitive disadvantage . . . the blunders can crush morale, especially during times of widespread change" (p. B1). Clearly, whether in the classroom or on the job, we must be able to articulate our thoughts carefully and incisively.

As a student of communication, you are uniquely positioned to determine your potential for effective communication. To do so, however, you must have a basic understanding of the communication process and of how communication theory functions in your life. We need to be able to talk effectively to a number of very different types of people during an average day: teachers, ministers, salespeople, family members, friends, automobile mechanics, and healthcare providers. Communication opportunities fill our lives each day. However, we need to understand the whys and hows of our conversations with others. For instance, why do two people in a relationship feel a simultaneous need for togetherness and independence? Why do some women feel ignored or devalued in conversations with men? Why does language often influence the thoughts of others? These and many other questions are at the root of why communication theory is so important in our society and so critical to understand.

Defining Communication

Before venturing further into a discussion of the communication process, we need to define what we mean by the term *communication*. Defining *communication* can be challenging. Sarah Trenholm (1991), for example, notes that although the study of communication has been around for centuries, that does not mean communication is well understood. In fact, Trenholm provocatively illustrates the dilemma when defining the term. She states: "Communication has become a sort of 'portmanteau' term. Like a piece of luggage, it is overstuffed with all manner of odd ideas and meanings. The fact that some of these do fit, resulting in a conceptual suitcase much too heavy for anyone to carry, is often overlooked" (p. 4).

We should note that there are dozens of definitions of *communication*—a result of the complexity and richness of the communication discipline. Imagine, for instance, taking this course from two different professors. Each would have his or her own way of presenting the material, and each classroom of students would approach communication theory in a unique manner. The result would be an exciting and distinctive approach to studying the same topic.

This uniqueness holds true with defining *communication*. Scholars tend to see human phenomena from their own perspectives. In some ways, they establish boundaries when they try to explain phenomena to others. Communication scholars may approach the interpretation of communication differently because of differences in scholarly values. As you read this book, try to develop your personal definition of *communication*. Various theories may influence your definition along the way. Nonetheless, we offer the following definition of *communication* to get us pointed in the same direction: Communication is a social process in which individuals employ symbols to establish and interpret meaning in their environment.

Before we discuss this definition in detail, we need to be clear in stating that our view of communication necessarily includes both face-to-face and mediated communication. With that in mind, let's define five key terms in our perspective: social, process, symbols, meaning, and environment.

First, we believe that communication is a social process. When interpreting communication as social, we mean to suggest that it involves people and interactions. This necessarily includes two people, a sender and a receiver. Both play an integral role in the communication process. When communication is social, it involves people who come to an interaction with various intentions, motivations, and abilities. To suggest that communication is a process means that it is ongoing and unending. Communication is also dynamic, complex, and continually changing. With this view of communication, we emphasize the dynamics of making meaning. Therefore, communication has no definable beginning and ending. For example, although Jimmy and Angie McLean may end up telling their son that he must leave the house, their discussions with him and about him will continue well after he leaves. In fact, the conversation that they will have with Eddy today will most likely affect their communication with him tomorrow. Similarly, our past communications with people have been stored in their minds and have affected their conversations with us.

The process nature of communication also means that much can happen from the beginning of a conversation to the end. People may end up at a very different place once a discussion begins. This is exemplified by the frequent conflicts that roommates, spouses, and siblings experience. Although a conversation may begin with absolute and inflexible language, the conflict may be resolved with compromise. All of this can occur in a matter of minutes.

There are also individual and cultural changes that affect communication. Conversations between siblings, for example, were very different in 1987 than they are right now. People do not remain static, and as siblings grow, they change. Culture changes as well. For instance, the climate of the 1950s was very different from today's. The 1950s was an era of postwar euphoria and conventional values; the traditional nuclear family was the norm. Conversations in the 1950s were contextualized by this atmosphere. Today, however, the traditional nuclear family makes up very little of the U.S. population. And the terrorist attacks on September 11, 2001, have prompted a renewed patriotic commitment not seen since World War II. Prior to the attacks, the country was rather complacent and somewhat cynical. Today, however, red, white, and blue seems to pervade even the most pessimistic community. As you can see, perceptions and feelings in the United States can change and remain in flux.

Some of you may be thinking that because the communication process is dynamic and unique, it is virtually impossible to study. However, C. Arthur

communication
a social process in which individuals employ symbols to establish and interpret meaning in their environment

social
the notion that people and interactions are part of the communication process

process
ongoing, dynamic, and unending occurrence

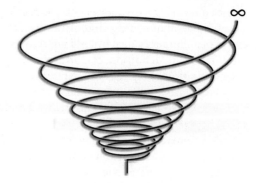

Figure 1.1
Communication Process as a Helix
Source: Adapted from Dance, 1967.

VanLear (1996) argues that because the communication process is so dynamic, researchers and theorists can look for patterns over time. He concludes that "if we recognize a pattern across a large number of cases, it permits us to 'generalize' to other unobserved cases" (p. 36). Or, as Paul Watzlawick, Janet Beavin, and Don Jackson (1967) suggest, the interconnectedness of communication events is critical and pervasive. Thus, it *is* possible to study the dynamic communication process.

To help you visualize this process, imagine a continuum where the points are unrepeatable and irreversible. Frank Dance (1967) depicts the communication process by using a spiral, or helix (Figure 1.1). He believes that communication experiences are cumulative and are influenced by the past. He notes that present experiences inevitably influence a person's future, and so he emphasizes a nonlinear view of the process. Communication, therefore, can be considered a process that changes over time and among interactants.

A third term associated with our definition of communication is *symbols*. A **symbol** is an arbitrary label or representation of phenomena. Words are symbols for concepts and things—for example, the word *love* represents the idea of love; the word *chair* represents the thing we sit on. Labels may be ambiguous, may be both verbal and nonverbal, and may occur in face-to-face and mediated communication. Symbols are usually agreed on within a group but may not be understood outside of the group. In this way, their use is often arbitrary. For instance, most college students understand the phrase "this course has no prereqs"; those outside of college may not understand its meaning. Further, there are both **concrete symbols** (the symbol represents the object) and **abstract symbols** (the symbol stands for a thought or idea). The concrete symbol of a computer, for example, is understood more easily than the abstract symbolic phrase "Your mind is like a computer." One person may interpret this statement to mean that you are able to remember details and specific events (a compliment). Another person may interpret the statement to mean that you are robotic or unfeeling in your interactions with others (an insult). Our interpretation of that phrase will be based on our experiences with, and feelings toward, computers, and therefore we will probably assign various meanings to it.

In addition to process and symbols, meaning is central to our definition of communication. Meaning is what people extract from a message. In communication episodes, messages can have more than one meaning and even multiple

symbol
arbitrary label given
to a phenomenon

concrete symbol
symbol representing
an object
abstract symbol
symbol representing
an idea or thought

layers of meaning, as Chapter 6 indicates. Without sharing some meanings, we would all have a difficult time speaking the same language or interpreting the same event. Judith Martin and Tom Nakayama (2000) point out that meaning has cultural consequences. For instance, people in the United States typically dislike Mondays, the first day of the workweek, and enjoy Fridays. Many Muslims, however, dislike Saturdays, which is their first day of the week, after Friday, the holy day. Martin and Nakayama note, therefore, that cultural expressions, such as TGIF, may not communicate the same meaning to everyone.

Of course, not all meaning is shared, and people do not always know what others mean. In these situations, we must be able to explain, repeat, and clarify. For example, if the McLeans want to tell Eddy to move out, they will probably need to go beyond explaining that they simply want to be left alone. Clear communication may not always be welcomed by others. Eddy, for instance, may feel better if his parents are indirect and if the idea of moving seems to be his. Nonetheless, without sharing the same meaning, communicators will have a challenging time getting their messages across to one another.

The final key term in our definition of communication is *environment*. Environment is the situation or context in which communication occurs. The environment includes a number of elements, including time, place, historical period, relationship, and a speaker's and listener's cultural backgrounds. Bank loan officers, for instance, must consider environmental influences that others bring to conversations. People seeking a loan may have been rejected several times, may not trust banks, and may have little or no experience applying for money. These are important environmental features to consider as loan officers process both the loan application and the communication taking place.

The environment can also be mediated. By that, we mean that communication can take place with technological assistance. It's likely that each of you has communicated in some sort of mediated environment, namely through e-mail, electronic chat rooms, or the Internet. These mediated environments necessarily influence the communication between two people in that when developing electronic relationships, we are not able to observe another's eye behavior, listen to his or her vocal characteristics, or watch the person's body movement. This mediated environment is an important (and relatively new) area in communication theory, but one that influences the communication process directly and indirectly.

environment
situation or context in which communication occurs

The Intentionality Debate: Did You Mean That?

Before we close our discussion on defining *communication*, we need to address the important issue of intentionality. Is all behavior communication? For example, suppose that Eric and his landlady, Martha, are talking about renewing his lease for the upcoming year. In this scenario, the two engage in a rather heated discussion because Martha claims she has to raise the rent due to higher heating costs. As the two speak, Eric notices that Martha cannot seem to look him in the eye as she explains the $75 increase. He begins to wonder whether Martha is telling the truth, thinking that her shifting eyes and constant throat

clearing must signify something deceptive. Can Martha's shifting eyes and throat clearing be considered communication? Are these behaviors within the boundaries of our definition of *communication*? Or is Eric's perception simply Eric's perception? What if Martha never intended to communicate anything other than that she needs the money to offset the cost of heating the apartment?

Some communication researchers have strongly favored the view that only intentional behaviors are communicative. For instance, Gerald Miller and Mark Steinberg (1975) interpret the communication process this way:

> We have chosen to restrict our discussion of communication to intentional symbolic transactions: those in which at least one of the parties transmits a message to another with the intent of modifying the other's behavior. . . . By our definition, intent to communicate and intent to influence are synonymous. If there is no intent, there is no message. (p. 15)

Despite this perspective, researchers have debated whether messages that are sent unintentionally—or mistaken meanings that people make ("I didn't mean *that*—you misunderstood me")—fit the definition of *communication*. Those who say that these sorts of messages are not communication (Miller and Steinberg) argue that only intentionally sent and accurately received messages can be called communication. However, other researchers believe that the latter approach narrows the definition too much.

This tension in interpreting what constitutes a communication event was a primary discussion point of researchers many years ago. In the early 1950s, a group of scholars met in Palo Alto, California, to collaborate on a new approach to human communication. These researchers represented a variety of disciplines, including psychiatry, anthropology, and communication. Among the many findings emanating from a series of scholarly papers was the assumption that "you cannot not communicate" (Watzlawick, Beavin, & Jackson, 1967). This thinking reflects the notion that all things can be considered communication. According to the **Palo Alto team,** when two people are together, they constantly communicate because they cannot escape behavior. Even silence and avoidance of eye contact are communicative. So, using our earlier example of Eric and Martha, Eric's perception of distrust would be legitimized under the Palo Alto rubric: One can say nothing and still say something. The Palo Alto group believed that anything we do, including ignoring or refusing to speak to another, is communication. This greatly broadens the definition of *communication*, making it virtually synonymous with *behavior*.

Palo Alto team
a group of scholars who believed that a person "cannot not communicate"

Although this line of thinking has enjoyed much popular support, it is potentially problematic for those of us interested in communication theory. In fact, Michael Motley (1990) reasons that "not all behavior is communication, only interactive behavior is; so in noninteractive situations one can indeed 'not communicate,' but in interactive situations one indeed cannot not communicate" (p. 619). In other words, Motley believes that one *can* not communicate. To be fair, one of the original proponents of the "you cannot not communicate" argument later recanted her original thinking by concluding that "all behavior is not communicative, although it may be informative" (Beavin-Bavelas, 1990, p. 599).

If everything can be thought of as communication—our verbal and nonverbal unintended expressions—then studying communication in a systematic manner is not only challenging but nearly impossible. As we discussed earlier in this chapter, setting boundaries on behavior in conversations or relationships is necessary in theory building. By defining everything as communication, we inevitably undermine the field we wish to study. Defining communication requires both that we draw boundaries and that we still acknowledge some overlap. Definitions can be somewhat subjective, and you will soon discover as you review and understand communication theory that once you've defined communication, your understanding of communication and theory will necessarily guide your thinking. This happens with communication researchers and theorists as well. Each approaches his or her research with a personal way of looking at the communication process, and these views influence who and what is studied, and when and how the study is executed. We encourage you to consider the theories in this book and the theorists' views of communication before you make up your mind.

Models of Understanding:
Communication as Action, Interaction, and Transaction

Communication theorists create **models, or simplified representations of complex interrelationships among elements in the communication process, which allow us to visually understand a sometimes complex process.** Although there are many communication models, we discuss the three most prominent ones

models
simplified representations of the communication process

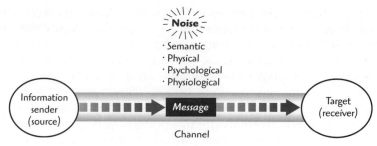

Figure 1.2
Linear Model of Communication
Source: Adapted from Shannon & Weaver, 1949.

here. In discussing these models and their underlying approaches, we wish to demonstrate the manner in which communication has been conceptualized over the years. As you will learn in Chapter 2, the communication discipline has a rich history.

Communication as Action: The Linear Model

In 1949, Claude Shannon, a Bell Laboratories scientist and professor at the Massachusetts Institute of Technology, and Warren Weaver, a consultant on projects at the Sloan Foundation, described communication as a linear process. They were concerned with radio and telephone technology and wanted to develop a model that could explain how information passed through various channels. The result was the conceptualization of the **linear model of communication.**

This approach to human communication comprises several key elements, as Figure 1.2 demonstrates. A **source,** or transmitter of a message, sends a **message** to a **receiver,** the recipient of the message. The receiver is the person who makes sense out of the message. All of this communication takes place in a **channel,** which is the pathway to communication. Channels frequently correspond to the visual, tactile, olfactory, and auditory senses. Thus, you use the visual channel when you see your roommate, and you use the tactile channel when you hug your parent.

Communication also involves **noise,** which is anything not intended by the informational source. There are four types of noise. First, **semantic noise** pertains to the slang, jargon, or specialized language used by individuals or groups. For instance, when one of your authors received a medical report from his ophthalmologist, the physician's letter included phrases such as "ocular neuritis," "dilated funduscopic examination," and "papillary conjunctival changes." This is an example of semantic noise because outside of the medical community, these words have limited (or no) meaning. **Physical, or external, noise** exists outside of the receiver. **Psychological noise** refers to a communicator's prejudices, biases, and predispositions toward another or the message. To exemplify these two types, imagine listening to participants at a Ku Klux Klan rally. You may experience psychological noise listening to the views of a KKK member, but you may also experience physical noise due to the people nearby

linear model of communication
one-way view of communication that assumes a message is sent by a source to a receiver through a channel

source
originator or transmitter of message

message
words, sounds, actions, or gestures in an interaction

receiver
recipient of message

channel
pathway to communication

noise
distortion in channel not intended by the source

semantic noise
linguistic influences on reception of message

physical (external) noise
bodily influences on reception of message

psychological noise
cognitive influences on reception of message

who are protesting the Klan's presence. Finally, **physiological noise** refers to the biological influences on the communication process. Physiological noise, then, exists if you or a speaker is ill, fatigued, or hungry.

Although this view of the communication process was highly respected many years ago, the approach is very limited for several reasons. First, the model presumes that there is only one message in the communication process. We all can point to a number of circumstances in which we send several messages at once. Second, as we have previously noted, communication does not have a definable beginning and ending. Shannon and Weaver's model presumes this mechanistic orientation. Further, to suggest that communication is simply one person speaking to another oversimplifies the complex communication process. Listeners are not so passive, as we can all confirm when we are in heated arguments with others. Clearly, communication is more than a one-way effort.

Communication as Interaction: The Interactional Model

The linear model suggests that a person is only a sender or a receiver. That is a narrow view of the participants in the communication process. Wilbur Schramm (1954), therefore, proposed that we also examine the relationship between a sender and a receiver. He conceptualized the **interactional model of communication,** which emphasizes the two-way communication process between communicators (Figure 1.3). In other words, communication goes in two directions: from sender to receiver and from receiver to sender. This circular process suggests that communication is ongoing. The interactional view illustrates that a person can perform the role of either sender or receiver during an interaction, but not both roles simultaneously.

One element essential to the interactional model of communication is **feedback,** or the response to a message. Feedback may be verbal or nonverbal,

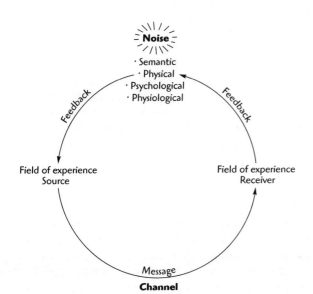

Figure 1.3
Interactional Model of Communication

intentional or unintentional. Feedback also helps communicators to know whether or not their message is being received and the extent to which meaning is achieved. In the interactional model, feedback takes place after a message is received, not during the message itself.

To illustrate the critical nature of feedback and the interactional model of communication, consider our opening example of the McLean family. When Eddy's parents find him on the couch drunk, they proceed to tell Eddy how they feel about his behavior. Their outcry prompts Eddy to argue with his parents, who in turn, tell him to leave their house immediately. This interactional sequence shows that there is an alternating nature in the communication between Eddy and his parents. They see his behavior and provide their feedback on it, Eddy listens to their message and responds, then his father sends the final message telling his son to leave. We can take this even further by noting the door slam as one additional feedback behavior in the interaction.

field of experience
overlap of sender's
and receiver's culture,
experiences, and
heredity in
communication

A final feature of the interactional model is a person's **field of experience**, or how a person's culture, experiences, and heredity influence his or her ability to communicate with another. Each person brings a unique field of experience to each communication episode, and these experiences frequently influence the communication between people. For instance, when two people come together and begin dating, the two inevitably bring their fields of experience into the relationship. Whereas one person may have been raised in a large family with several siblings, the other may be an only child. Further, one may have been raised by a grandparent while the other was raised by two men. These experiences (and others) will necessarily influence how the two come together and will most likely affect how they maintain their relationship.

Like the linear view, the interactional model has been criticized. First, the interactional model suggests that one person acts as sender while the other acts as receiver in a communication encounter. As you have experienced, people communicate as both senders and receivers in a single encounter. The prevailing criticism of the interactional model, however, pertains to the issue of feedback. What occurs when a person sends a nonverbal message during an interaction? Smiling, frowning, or simply moving away from the conversation during an interaction between two people happens all the time. For example, in an interaction between a mother and her daughter, the mother may be reprimanding her child while simultaneously "reading" the child's nonverbal behavior. Is the girl laughing? Is she upset? Is she even listening to her mother? Each of these behaviors will inevitably prompt the mother to modify her message as she speaks to her daughter. The interactional view assumes two people speaking and listening, but not at the same time. It was this criticism that inspired a third model of communication to be developed.

Communication as Transaction: The Transactional Model

**transactional
model of
communication**
view of
communication as the
simultaneous sending
and receiving of
messages

The **transactional model of communication** (Barnlund, 1970) underscores the simultaneous sending and receiving of messages in a communication episode, as Figure 1.4 shows. To say that communication is transactional means that the process is cooperative; the sender and the receiver are mutually responsible for

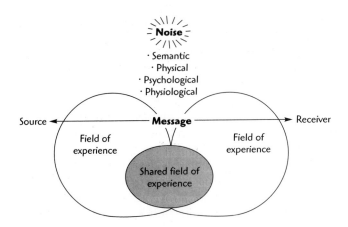

Figure 1.4
Transactional Model
of Communication

the effect and the effectiveness of communication. In the linear model of communication, meaning is sent from one person to another. In the interactional model, meaning is achieved through the feedback of a sender and a receiver. In the transactional model, people build shared meaning. Further, what people say during a transaction is greatly influenced by their past experience. So, for instance, at a college fair, it is likely that a college student will have a great deal to say to a high school senior because of the college student's experiences in class and around campus. A college senior will, no doubt, have a different view of college than, say, a college sophomore, due in large part to his or her past college experiences.

Transactional communication requires us to recognize the influence of one message on another. One message builds on the previous message; therefore, there is an interdependency between and among the components of communication. A change in one causes a change in others. Further, the transactional model presumes that as we simultaneously send and receive messages, we attend to both a message's verbal and its nonverbal elements. In a sense, communicators negotiate meaning. For instance, if a friend asks you about your family background, you may use some private jargon that your friend doesn't understand. Your friend may make a face while you are presenting your message, indicating some sort of confusion with your language. As a result, you will most likely back up and define your terms and then continue with the conversation. This example highlights the degree to which two people are actively involved in a communication encounter. The nonverbal communication is just as important as the verbal message in such a transactional process.

Earlier we noted that the field of experience functions in the interactional model. In the transactional model, the fields of experience exist, but overlap occurs. That is, rather than person A and person B having separate fields of experience, eventually the two fields merge (see Figure 1.4). This was an important addition to the understanding of the communication process because it demonstrates an active process of understanding. That is, for communication to take place, individuals must build shared meaning. For instance, in our earlier example of two people with different childhoods, the interactional model suggests that they would come together with an understanding of their backgrounds. The transactional model, however, requires each of them to understand and incorporate the other's field of experience into his or her life. For example, it's not enough for Julianna to know that Paul has a prior prison record; the transactional view holds that she must figure out a way to put his past into perspective. Will it affect their current relationship? How? If not, how will Julianna discuss it with Paul? The transactional model takes the meaning-making process one step further than the interactional model. It assumes reciprocity, or shared meaning.

You now have a basic understanding of how we define communication, and we have outlined the basic elements and a few communication models. Recall this definition as you read the book and interpret the various theories. It is likely that you will interpret communication differently from one theory to another. Remember that theorists set boundaries in their discussions about human behavior, and, consequently, they often define *communication* according to their view. One of our goals in writing this book is that after you have read it, you will be able to articulate how communication functions in a number of different theories.

The Dark Side of Communication

At this point, you may have the impression that communication can solve most of the problems in our society. It is no wonder. National best-sellers have made millions of dollars advancing the idea that communication is the magic potion for life's ailments. Researchers, too, have centered their work on healthy and satisfying relationships, at times neglecting the fact that some relationships are simply unhealthy and unpleasant (Cupach & Spitzberg, 1994).

dark side of communication
negative communication that can undermine the communication process

In recent years, communication researchers and theorists have begun referring to the **dark side of communication**. Researchers began focusing on this dark side of communication because obviously not all relationships are exciting and rewarding undertakings. As Steve Duck (1994) notes, particularly in relational development, we may be disappointed, betrayed, and distressed.

Suggesting that communication has a dark side generally means that communication has a negative component. Negative communication can be manipulative, sarcastic, abusive, and humiliating. It can also take the form of seemingly less harmful behaviors, such as name-calling and teasing, which are common among teenagers. Still, such badgering can be harassing and tormenting. For instance, some people believe that the shootings at Columbine High School in Littleton, Colorado, in 1999 were the result of years of verbal heckling of the killers. The dark side of communication also includes verbal and psychological abuse and racist, ageist, and homophobic remarks. The murder of gay University of Wyoming student Matthew Shepard in 1998 illustrates the most dangerous consequence of homophobia. The men who were prosecuted for the murder would later note that they were disgusted with the victim's sexuality and lured him to a farm field where they killed him. What has been even more distressing is the homophobic language spoken by some religious leaders who lambasted the student because he was gay.

When framing negative communication within the transactional model of communication, the complexity of the model becomes apparent. As one person sends supportive messages, the other may be simultaneously sending disparaging messages. For instance, a wife may be prepared to sit down and talk over marital problems, whereas her husband would rather revisit the name-calling that precipitated the problems in the first place. People often engage in conversations with an agenda in mind (Mortensen, 1997), making miscommunication (and negative communication) possible.

So, how does the dark side of communication relate to a course on communication theory? We include this discussion of the dark side of communication because you will encounter some theories that rest on an optimistic view of human relationships (Spitzberg & Cupach, 1998). In Part II, for instance, you will learn that Social Penetration Theory and Uncertainty Reduction Theory rely on rational communication. Yet, we all know that not all people communicate rationally. In addition, when studying theories associated with interpersonal relationships, some writers believe that the communication field has not been as inclusive and comprehensive as it could be. Duck (1994) concludes that "the relational significance of the unpleasant in the real lives of everyday mortals has been seriously underrepresented in theory and research" (p. 4). As you learn about the theories, try to sense whether theorists make efforts to explain all types of human interaction, including the unpleasant ones.

Finally, learning about negative communication will help you personally in your conversations with others. Being knowledgeable about negative communication may allow you to understand and detect it when it occurs, and that can be empowering. Also, you should realize that some conversations go wrong, regardless of how much of your communication is supportive.

Our discussion of the dark side of communication suggests that people behave and communicate according to their ethical standards. What are the ethical values of those who engage in dark communication? We discuss the interaction of ethics and the communication process next.

Ethics and Communication

In the movie *Erin Brockovich*, which was based on a true story, the title character is a single mom with no money who is in desperate need of a job. She finds a job as a research assistant for an attorney and, in her research, discovers that a disproportionate amount of cancer exists in her area. As she starts investigating a large corporation—Pacific Gas and Electric Company—she finds that the company has been knowingly releasing toxins into the local environment.

Erin pursues a civil case against the company on behalf of the 600 local community members who have been afflicted by the toxins. She unearths concealed documents that help her in her zealous pursuit of the company. She is driven even further in her civil suit when she discovers that the company tried to cover up the toxic waste dumped near the town. On behalf of those with various illnesses, Erin managed to facilitate a settlement of over $300 million for the plaintiffs. Erin clearly believed that saving lives was the right and only thing to do, and she made her actions fit her beliefs: She acted on her ethics.

ethics
perceived rightness or wrongness of an action or behavior

Simply put, **ethics** is the perceived rightness or wrongness of an action or behavior. Ethics is a type of moral decision making, and determining what is right or wrong is influenced by a society with its rules and laws. U.S. society is built on standards of moral conduct, and these standards are central to a number of institutions and relationships (Conrad, 1993). Because societal standards shift over time, ethics often shift as well. A number of influences affect ethical standards. As William Howell (1986) notes, the timing and time of the conversation, the environment, and the human relationships all affect the application of ethical standards.

From a communication perspective, ethical issues surface whenever messages potentially influence others (Johannesen, 2000). Consider, for instance, the ethics associated with persuasion. What ethics are involved when one teenager tries to persuade others to smoke marijuana? Yet, persuasion can also be used to help a friend stop drinking. Ethical issues also involve revealing information. In 2002, the United States was besieged with the corporate abuses of WorldCom, Enron, and Global Crossing and the creative ways these companies presented their financial health to their stockholders and to the public at large. Paul Davidson (2002) of *USA Today* notes that these and other companies were found to hide company costs, engage in creative accounting, and commit fraud, trying to turn losses into profits. Although the media and the vast majority of the public felt at the time that these corporations should be held to a standard of accountability, others felt that the companies had no ethical obligation to inform the public unless something illegal was going on. In other words, a company is not breaking the law by being unethical. Finally, ethics are a consideration with regard to messages on television. Television can be used constructively if children are sent messages that promote racial harmony and tolerance; however, portrayals of ethnic and cultural groups in stereotypical and offensive ways have obvious ethical implications. Religion, the entertainment industry, higher education, medicine, and technology are just five of the many fields immersed in discussions of ethics and communication (see Table 1.1). We continue our discussion of ethics by identifying some of the institutions whose ethical standards have been the subject of much conversation.

Table 1.1 Examples of Ethical Decision Making in the United States

INSTITUTION	EXAMPLES OF ETHICAL ISSUES
Religion	Should Catholic priests be allowed to marry? Are same-sex marriages moral?
Entertainment	Does viewing violence in movies prompt violence in society? Should Hollywood develop a morality code?
Higher Education	Should students be allowed credit for "life experience" (jobs)? Should student fees pay for student political groups?
Medicine	Can pharmaceutical companies be held responsible for sample medicines? Should medical professionals be given license to end the life of a patient?
Technology	Should Internet sites be held accountable for their content? Who should monitor websites targeting children?

Religion

Both Eastern and Western civilizations have stressed ethics in their moral traditions. For instance, according to Taoism, no one exists in isolation, and, therefore, empathy and insight will lead to truth. For the Buddhist, being moral requires that one use words that elicit peace and avoid gossip, self-promotion, anger, argument, and lying. From a Western perspective, many ethical issues derive from early Greek civilization. Aristotle first articulated the principle of the Golden Mean. He believed that a person's moral virtue stands between two vices, with the middle, or the mean, being the foundation for a rational society. For instance, when the McLeans are deciding what to say to their son Eddy about overstaying his welcome, their Golden Mean might look like this:

EXTREME	GOLDEN MEAN	EXTREME
lying	truthful comments	disclose everything

The Judeo-Christian religions are centered as well on questions of ethics. Christianity, for instance, is founded on the principle of good example—that is, live according to God's laws and set an example for others. However, some believe that such moral standards are not uniquely religious. For those not affiliated with organized religion, the secular values of fairness and justice and working toward better relationships are important as well. Affiliating with a religion may also pose some ethical difficulty if a person does not subscribe to a number of its philosophies or orientations. For instance, people who believe that gay men and lesbians should be able to marry may be challenged because most religions reject such ceremonies.

The Entertainment Industry

The entertainment industry has also been intimately involved in dialogues about ethics and communication. Often, a circular argument surfaces with respect to Hollywood: Does Hollywood reflect society or does Hollywood shape society? Many viewpoints are raised in these arguments, but three seem to dominate. One belief is that Hollywood has a responsibility to show the moral side of an immoral society; movies should help people escape a difficult reality, not relive it. A second opinion is that Hollywood should create more nonviolent and nonsexual films so that all family members can watch a movie. Unfortunately, critics note, films like *Collateral Damage* and *Gangs of New York* only exacerbate violent tendencies in young people. A third school of thought is that Hollywood is in show *business*, and therefore making money is what moviemaking is all about. Regardless of whether you agree with any of these orientations, the entertainment industry will continue to reflect *and* influence changing moral climates in the United States. Consequently, Hollywood is at the center of many ethical debates concerning communication.

Higher Education

A third cultural institution interested in ethics and communication is higher education. Colleges and universities across the United States teach introductory courses in ethics, and they are required courses in many schools. Evidently, faculty and administrators believe that ethics permeates all aspects of a complex society and want students to learn the importance of ethical decision making.

Interestingly, ethical issues concerning communication pervade higher education. For instance, colleges and universities face an ethical choice about reporting crime statistics on their campus. Fearing bad publicity, schools may keep this information private. Another ethical decision arises when schools are required to identify the enrollment patterns for legislative and financial support. Frequently, schools will report statistical increases in enrollment over a number of years when in reality the school system has simply adopted a new way of counting heads.

Medicine

A fourth institution concerned with ethics and communication is the medical community. Specifically, with advances in science changing the cultural landscape, bioethical issues are topics of conversation around the dinner table. Physician-assisted suicide is one example of medicine at the center of ethical controversy. To some, the decision to prolong life should be a private one, made by the patient and his or her doctor. To others, society should have a say in such a decision.

Medical decisions can become publicly debated issues, far from the hospital bedside. Whether the U.S. Senate discusses late-term abortions, politicians decry human cloning, or the U.S. attorney general lashes out against legalizing medicinal marijuana, ethics, politics, and medicine are all interrelated.

Technology

Technology is at the center of many ethical debates today. Armed with a copy of the First Amendment, proponents of free speech say the Internet, for example, should not be censored. Free speech advocates stress that what is considered inappropriate can vary tremendously from one person to another, and consequently, censorship is arbitrary. Consider, for instance, the U.S. Supreme Court decision in 2002 protecting "virtual" child pornography on the Internet. Noting that the Child Pornography Protection Act was overly broad, the justices felt that banning computer-generated images of young people was unjustified. In fact, Thomas Tedford and Dale Herbeck (2000) observe that the Supreme Court has held that "speech on the Internet was entitled to the highest degree of First Amendment protection" (p. 391).

As we become more and more reliant on technology, particularly the Internet, in the United States, ethical decisions will likely continue. To a large extent, technology and ethics pervade our national culture. In the future, we will be faced with electronic voting and watching executions on the Internet, and the Internet will become the new means of interpersonal communication (Selnow, 2000). These issues and others will become part of our national dialogue in the foreseeable future.

Some Guidelines

The relationship between communication and ethics is intricate and complex. Public discourse requires responsibility. We presume that political leaders will tell the truth and that spiritual leaders will guide us by their example. Yet, we know that not all elected officials are honest and that not all religious leaders set a spiritual standard. Organizations are especially prone to ethical dilemmas. For instance, whistle-blowing, or revealing ethically suspicious behavior in a company, can have lasting implications. Although some may view whistle-blowing as courageous and morally sound, others may view it as a violation of trust. This difference in perception usually rests on whether a whistle-blower is perceived as a disgruntled employee who may have been passed over for a promotion or as someone who is genuinely concerned about a company's ethical practices. Unethical practices do little to garner trust in people. As J. Michael

---

Theory Application in Groups (TAG)

In this chapter, we noted that ethics is an important element in our discussion of the communication process. Each communication encounter has both explicit and implicit ethical standards. In small groups, construct a list of ethical guidelines that are followed in your classroom. Then compare these ethical practices with the ethical behaviors on the job. Discuss the various kinds of jobs held by group members. What differences and similarities exist? What conclusions can you draw?

Sproule (1980) concludes, "When people are misled they distrust the sources that have deceived them. If the majority of a society's information sources behave without concern for honest communication, then all communication is weakened" (p. 282).

There is an ethical dimension to listening as well. As listeners (or readers) we have a responsibility to give a fair hearing to the ideas of others. This responsibility extends to such ideas as the communication theories presented in this book. Rob Anderson and Veronica Ross (2002) point out six important ethical strategies to consider when reading communication theory:

1. Remain open to being persuaded by the statements of others.

2. Remain willing to try out new ideas that may be seen by others as mistakes, and invite others to experiment also.

3. Accept that multiple perspectives on reality are held as valid by different people, especially in different cultural contexts.

4. Attempt to test any tentatively held knowledge.

T*I*P

*Theory * Into * Practice*

Stephanie Armour in *USA Today* writes about the complication of being able to communicate what you wish while on the job. She notes that particularly after the September 11, 2001 terrorist attacks, employers have begun to regulate free speech much more. Armour writes about a history professor who stated that "anyone who can blow up the Pentagon has my vote" and a university librarian who sent out a mass e-mail message criticizing the foreign policy of the United States. And then there is the ABC News president who told a group of college students that as journalists, it is important to remain objective and not have an opinion on whether the Pentagon was a legitimate target. These comments, Armour points out, "are raising new questions about how far employers should go in regulating free speech" (p. C1). She notes that employers cannot limit what employees talk about, but they can prevent them from using company resources to present personal views.

Armour also states that some employees have been in trouble because of nonverbal communication as well. For instance, a United Parcel Service driver was fired for refusing to remove a red, white, and blue pin, although he was later reinstated because he agreed to wear a pin provided by UPS. Armour quotes a UPS spokesperson who states that symbols of patriotism must conform to company policies; "otherwise, you have 85,000 employees who each are deciding what they're going to do to show patriotism" (p. C1).

Source: Armour, 2001.

TIP Follow-up
Do you believe that communication should have limitations like those expressed above? What would you say to the employers of schools and corporations who try to regulate free speech?

5. Live with ambiguity, but become less tolerant of contradiction.

6. Evaluate knowledge claims against personal experience and the everyday concrete pragmatics of what works. (p. 15)

In addition to these suggestions, we add one more: If a theory is a bit difficult to understand at first, don't gloss over it. Delve into the explanation once more to gain a clearer picture of the theorists' intentions.

You may feel inexperienced or unprepared to challenge these theories. Yet, we offer the theories for review, application, and comment and want you to ask questions about them. Although we would like to think that all theorists are open and receptive to multiple ways of knowing, the reality remains that theory construction is bound by culture, personality, time, circumstance, and the availability of resources. As students of communication theory, you must be willing to ask some difficult questions and probe some confusing areas.

Conclusion

In this chapter, we introduced you to the communication process. We presented our definition of *communication* and reviewed the intentionality debate as a point of controversy in the communication field. In addition, we identified three prevailing models of communication: the linear model, the interactional model, and the transactional model. We also explored the dark side of the communication process. Finally, we discussed ethics and its relationship to communication theory.

You now have an understanding of the communication process and some sense of how complex it can be. As you read about the many theories in this book, you will be able to view communication from a variety of perspectives. You will also gain valuable information that will help you understand human behavior and give you a new way to think about our society. We continue this examination in Chapter 2 when we present a brief overview of the communication field and the significant contexts in which communication takes place.

Discussion Starters

1. What miscommunications led to the blowup between Eddy McLean and his parents? Do you believe that Eddy and his parents were trying to handle his situation in an ethical way? Why or why not?

2. Do you believe that all slips of the tongue, conversational faux pas, and unintentional nonverbal behaviors should be considered communicative? Why or why not? What examples can you provide to justify your thoughts?

3. Explain why you believe that the linear model of communication was so appealing years ago. Explain the appeal of the transactional model using current societal events.

4. Now that you have some information on the dark side of communication, what types of strategies would you use to manage those who engage in this kind of communication? Is negative communication ever appropriate? What examples can you offer?

5. What are some recent ethical dilemmas related to communication? How was each dilemma resolved, if it was?

6. Comment on why so many definitions of communication exist.

Terms for Review

communication
social
process
symbol
concrete symbol
abstract symbol
environment
Palo Alto team
models
linear model of communication
source
message
receiver
channel

noise
semantic noise
physical (external) noise
psychological noise
physiological noise
interactional model of
    communication
feedback
field of experience
transactional model of
    communication
dark side of communication
ethics

Online Learning Center

Visit the Online Learning Center at www.mhhe.com/west2. Use the multiple-choice and true/false quizzes to help you prepare for exams, and the glossary, crossword puzzles, and flashcards to further your knowledge of key terms.

CHAPTER 2

Framing Our Past and Present

Lee and Jenny Yamato

As the 18-year-old daughter of a single parent, Lee Yamato knew that life could be difficult. She is the only child of Jenny Yamato, a Japanese American woman whose husband died from a heart attack several years ago. Jenny raised her daughter in Lacon, a small rural town in the South. It was stressful being a single mom, and single moms were sometimes the targets of overt racist jokes. As a waitress, Jenny knew that college would be the way to a better life for her daughter. She saved every extra penny and worked at the children's library for several months to bring in extra income. Jenny knew that Lee would get financial aid in college, but she also wanted to be able to help her only child with college finances.

As Lee finished her senior year in high school, she knew that before too long she would be leaving to attend a public university. Unfortunately, the closest college was over 200 miles from Lacon. Lee had mixed feelings about her move. She was very excited to get away from the small-town gossip, but she also knew that leaving Lacon meant that her mom would have to live by herself. Being alone could be devastating to her mom, Lee thought. Still, Lee recognized that her education was her first priority and that in order to get into veterinary

school, she would have to stay focused. Thinking about her mom would only make the transition more difficult and could sour her first year as a college student.

Jenny, too, felt ambivalent about Lee leaving. When Jenny's husband died, she didn't think that she could raise a 13-year-old by herself. However, her own tenacity and determination had paid off, and she was extremely proud that her child was going away to college. Like her daughter, though, Jenny felt sad about Lee's departure. She felt as if her best friend was leaving her, and she couldn't imagine her life without her daughter. She knew that they would talk on the phone, but it couldn't replace the hugs, the laughter, and the memories.

On the day that Lee was to leave, Jenny gave her a box with chocolate chip cookies, some peanut butter cups (Lee's favorite), a photo album of Lee and Jenny during their camping trip to Arizona, and a shoe box. Inside the shoe box were old letters that Jenny and her husband had written to each other during their courtship. Jenny wanted Lee to have the letters to remind her that her dad's spirit lives on in her. When Lee looked at the first letter, she put it down, hugged her mom, and cried. She then got into her car and slowly drove away, leaving her house and her only true friend behind. ∎

Chapter 1 provided a foundation for conceptualizing what communication is and understanding the complexity of the communication process. In this chapter, we introduce you to a brief history of the communication field and also explore the contexts in which communication takes place. The communication discipline has a rich history, and its depth is reflected in the lives of people across the United States, people like Lee and Jenny Yamato. As Molefe Kete Asante (1997) concludes, "Communication is the defining characteristic of contemporary life" (p. ix).

A Brief History

To paraphrase author Willa Cather, communication begins in the heart of every man and woman. Although many scholars trace the communication discipline back to early Greek and Roman days, the modern version begins around 1900. Much of the story is written in very personal ways (Gray, 1964; O'Neill, 1915; Schramm, 1997; Weaver, 1959), and the information forms the skeleton of what is today known as the communication field.

This chapter begins by tracing the development of one of the oldest professional organizations dedicated to communication study: the National Communication Association. Rather than discuss the evolution of the communication discipline (that information is available elsewhere; see Boileau & Friedrich, 1999; Rogers, 1994; Rogers & Chaffee, 1983), we focus our efforts on the largest organization dedicated to studying the communication process in the broadest sense. We then identify several influential scholars in the discipline. We finally explore the predominant way to interpret the discipline and provide the contexts in which communication takes place. This chapter gives you a basis from which to draw as you review the theories in the text.

What's in a Name? Associations and Tensions

Present-day communication courses were taught in departments of English in the early 1900s. Public speaking courses dominated the curriculum at that time. Well-trained teachers of English were assigned to teach students public speaking skills. The prevailing thinking was that the discipline of English had proprietary rights over any communication; speaking and writing were considered to be synonymous.

At that time, many public speaking scholars (now considered communication scholars) protested this reductionist thinking. These scholars believed that there were significant and important differences between written and oral communication. What was especially appalling to the public speaking teachers was that the English teachers felt they understood the speaking process when in reality their training was severely limited.

A turning point came in 1913, when the National Council of Teachers of English held its annual conference in Chicago. After a closed-door meeting with public speaking teachers (they met at an English conference because they had no independent outlet for their own research), the following motion was made: "That a National Association of Academic Teachers of Public Speaking (NAATPS) be organized." Seventeen individuals from thirteen different schools voted unanimously to adopt the resolution and establish an association for their own research and theory.

Some of you may be wondering why so much energy was expended on this. First, it is important to understand that many of these teachers felt that if there were national recognition of their existence (via an association), then they could demonstrate the need to establish their own departments "back home." In addition, many speech teachers argued that placing them in English departments was absurd, considering that the principles of public speaking were taught for centuries before an English language even existed. Also, affiliating with an English association permitted no independent authority for public speaking teachers. Finally, the establishment of an association was critical for thinking through theoretical issues specifically related to oral communication in an academic environment.

In 1915, the NAATPS included members from thirty-one states and Canada. Because of this group, departments of public speaking gained momentum in colleges and universities across the country. The *Quarterly Journal of Public Speaking* (now the *Quarterly Journal of Speech*) became the first published periodical of the association. It published research, reviews, discussions, and news items of interest to public speaking teachers. The *Journal* was viewed as both a way to link various interest groups and a way to keep informed those who could not attend the annual conference sponsored by the association.

Despite the need for independence from English, the first president pledged cooperation with English teachers (O'Neill, 1915). In 1945, the members voted to change their name to the Speech Association of America (SAA), reflecting the name of many of the departments of speech across the country as well as the varied interests of the membership. Membership records indicate that in 1945, over 3,500 individuals were members of the SAA. In 1970, the name changed again, to the Speech Communication Association (SCA). The group had representation on a number of boards and in twenty-one scholarly areas, including finance, research, and educational policies. Finally, in 1997, the SCA membership voted to change its name to the National Communication Association (NCA). Currently, the name remains, with over forty interest groups, fifteen standing committees, and over 8,000 members. For an example of the depth and breadth of the National Communication Association, see Table 2.1.

Although the National Communication Association is among the oldest of the professional associations, it is not the only organization dedicated to the study of communication. Today communication teachers and researchers have a number of other associations with which to affiliate. For instance, at the global level, the International Communication Association (ICA) and World Communication Association (WCA) hold yearly conferences in countries across the world. For those specifically interested in mass communication, the Association for Education in Journalism and Mass Communication and the Broadcast Education Association are possible outlets. Each region of the country is also represented by independent associations (Eastern Communication Association, Southern States Communication Association, Central States Communication Association, and Western States Communication Association). In addition to holding yearly conferences, each association publishes journals that allow scholars to share their ideas with colleagues in the discipline.

Table 2.1 Divisions of the National Communication Association

African American Communication and Culture	International and Intercultural Communication
Applied Communication	Interpersonal Communication
Argumentation and Forensics	Language and Social Interaction
Asian Pacific American Communication Studies	Latina/Latino Communication Studies
Basic Course	Mass Communication
Critical and Cultural Studies	Organizational Communication
Ethnography	Performance Studies
Family Communication	Political Communication
Feminist and Women Studies	Public Address
Freedom of Expression	Public Relations
Gay, Lesbian, Bisexual, Transgender Studies	Rhetorical and Communication Theory
Group Communication	Small Group Communication
Health Communication	Theatre
Instructional Development	Training and Development

Source: www.natcom.org.

The Theory Chronicles

In this chapter, we noted that the National Communication Association is a large academic group with a variety of intellectual interest areas. Looking at the divisions of the NCA listed in Table 2.1, write your views about an organization such as NCA and the value of being so large and diverse. Then discuss the potential shortcomings of having so many divisions. Use examples from both your personal life and popular culture as you write your opinions.

In fact, many of the theories that you will read about later in this book had their beginnings in these journals. As you can see, the primary outlets for discussing research and theory—the journals and the associations—have a rich history and continue to shape the future in research and theory.

Before moving on to the structure of the communication field, let's briefly discuss a few individuals who were considered pioneers in the field's development. These five have been influential in inspiring others to start many of the associations we described previously and in helping to carve out several areas of study in the communication field. Further, these individuals have inspired many of the theories you will encounter in the book.

Establishing Communication Theory: The Founders

In December 1987, Stanford University professor Wilbur Schramm, widely considered to be a pioneer in the study of the communication process, died in his home. Many weeks later, when friends came to sort through his personal belongings, they found a manuscript for a book that he was completing on the beginnings of the communication field (Chaffee & Rogers, 1997). His writing focused on the four individuals who were responsible for centering communication in the social sciences: Harold Lasswell, Paul Lazarsfeld, Kurt Lewin, and

Carl Hovland. They came from different academic backgrounds with diverse research and theoretical experiences. All four were original in their research and warrant brief mention.

Lasswell's early work on propaganda was viewed as groundbreaking in that he saw propaganda as a daily event in modern society. Lasswell felt that propaganda is inescapable in life and that all democracies must learn to handle it in some way. Lasswell's most enduring contribution to communication studies is his description of the communication process: Who says what to whom through what channel with what effect? Lazarsfeld was instrumental in studying voting and the effects that the media have upon voter preferences. (Today, we clearly recognize such a fact, but many years ago, this was innovative research.) Lewin was primarily interested in small groups and the way that they function. To this end, he conceptualized what is called **lifespace,** which is a group member's psychological environment. This includes a person's goals, values, needs, memories, beliefs, and other forces that may influence behavior. Finally, as a Yale psychologist, Hovland examined attitude change and investigated the extent to which long- and short-term recall influence an individual's attitudes and beliefs. In the 1950s—before computers were popular—Hovland also was the first to experiment with computer simulations and the learning process. These four men and their research are respected today for their innovative methods and relevant findings. As Schramm (1997) wrote, "They brought to the study of communication a sense of urgency and challenge that had not been there before them" (p. 20).

Although Schramm believed that these four were instrumental in advancing the communication discipline, some scholars and historians believe that it is Schramm himself who should be considered the founder of the field of communication (Chaffee & Rogers, 1997). As director of the Institute of Communications Research at the University of Illinois, Schramm was instrumental in building a communication program, and established the first doctoral program in communication studies. In fact, many of his students became communication theorists themselves, and throughout this book, you will read about their contributions in several theories. Schramm is also credited with bringing research money to the study of communication, further establishing credibility for the discipline and its research. Steve Chaffee and Everett Rogers (1997) note that at age 64, Schramm became the director of the East-West Communication Institute in Hawaii to fulfill his interest in bringing international graduate students to the United States. He encouraged these students to return to their countries as communication professors, and this contributed greatly to the field.

In addition to the five individuals we have mentioned here, a number of others have also been important contributors to the field of communication. We showcase several of them as we discuss their theories.

Where Are We Now?

Near the end of the 1950s, Bernard Berelson (1959) wrote a provocative essay entitled "The State of Communication Research." Berelson believed that the communication field was "withering away" and that "no ideas of comparable

lifespace
group member's
psychological
environment

scope and generating power [were] emerging" (p. 4). His autopsy on the discipline was a bit premature. Today, the field is flourishing. The National Communication Association (www.natcom.org) reports that there are over 118,000 undergraduates in communication and 16,000 graduate students. Approximately 50,000 students a year receive a degree in communication, and about 250 doctoral students—the future researchers, theorists, and professors—receive their degree. While researchers study the communication process, employers are eager to hire students with backgrounds in communication. We explore some potential pathways to careers in communication later in the book.

Research and theory in communication at this point in the discipline's history is complex and diverse. At the associations' meetings each year, scholars have a number of outlets to which they can submit their scholarship. These outlets range in perspective from the Political Communication Division to the Asian/Pacific American Caucus to the Spiritual Communication Commission. Each unit provides a forum for particular research. For instance, members of the Family Communication Division would be interested in the mother–daughter relationship of the Yamato family. Scholars in the International and Intercultural Communication Division may also find the Yamatos' heritage to be worthy of study. And scholars in a number of other divisions would be interested in both individuals' thoughts and experiences.

As disciplines grow, they mature. Philosopher Thomas Kuhn (1970), the author of a classic work on philosophy and science called *The Structure of Scientific Revolutions,* commented that one mark of a mature discipline is the establishment of a universal model, or paradigm. In the communication field, however, no such universal model exists. The diversity in research and theory represents great diversity in perspective. As you read and think about the theories in the coming chapters, recall that each is a result of not only years of work but also multiple ways of viewing human behavior. For the communication discipline, then, establishing one core communication theory is not only inappropriate; it is virtually impossible.

Although the discipline of communication is broad and encompasses diversity in perspective, scholars have traditionally divided the field into several areas. The following section details one way of dividing the discipline.

Contexts of Communication

To make the communication field and the communication process more understandable and manageable, let's take a look at the various contexts of communication. First, what is a context? **Contexts** are environments in which communication takes place. Contexts provide a backdrop against which researchers and theorists can analyze phenomena. Contexts also provide clarity. Our discussion of context focuses on **situational contexts.** To suggest that a context is situationally based means that the communication process is limited by a number of factors—namely, the number of people, the degree of space between interactants, the extent of feedback, and the available channels (Miller, 1978).

Earlier we noted that the communication field is very diverse and offers various research opportunities. This can be a bit cumbersome, and at times even

contexts
environments in
which communication
takes place
situational
contexts
environments limited
by a number of issues,
including people,
space, and feedback

CONTEXT

INTRAPERSONAL
Communication with one's self

INTERPERSONAL
Face-to-face communication

SMALL GROUP
Communication with a group
of people

ORGANIZATIONAL
Communication within and among
large and extended environments

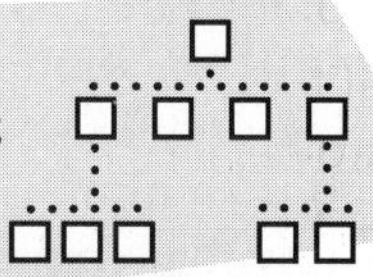

PUBLIC/RHETORICAL
Communication to a large
group of listeners (audience)

MASS
Communication to a very
large audience through
mediated forms

INTERCULTURAL
Communication between
and among members of different
cultural backgrounds

SOME THEORETICAL CONCERNS

Impression formation and decision
making; symbols and meaning;
observations and attributions; ego
involvement and persuasion

Relationship maintenance strategies;
relational intimacy; relationship control;
interpersonal attraction

Gender and group leadership; group
vulnerability; groups and stories; group
decision making; task difficulty

Organizational hierarchy and power;
culture and organizational life; employee
morale; opinions and worker satisfaction

Communication apprehension; delivery
effectiveness; speech and text criticism;
ethical speechmaking; popular culture
analysis

Use of media; affiliation and television
programming; television and values;
media and need fulfillment

Culture and rule-setting; culture and
anxiety; hegemony; ethnocentrism

**Figure 2.1
Contexts of
Communication**

communication scholars lament the wide array of options. Still, there seems to
be some universal agreement on the fundamental contexts of communication.
In fact, most communication departments are built around some or all of the
following seven communication contexts: intrapersonal, interpersonal, small
group, organizational, public, mass, and intercultural. Keep in mind, however,
that communication departments across the United States divide themselves
uniquely. Some, for instance, include mass communication in a Department of
Communication whereas others may have a separate Department of Mass
Communication. Some schools have a Department of Interpersonal Communication and include every context therein. This diversity underscores that the
discipline is permeable, that boundary lines among the contexts are not absolute. In a similar fashion, theories frequently cut across several contexts. We
have outlined these seven contexts in Figure 2.1.

Intrapersonal Communication

intrapersonal communication communication with one's self

Intrapersonal communication is communication with oneself. It is kind of an internal dialogue and may take place even in the presence of another individual. For instance, when you are with someone, what goes on inside your head is intrapersonal communication. Intrapersonal communication theorists frequently study the role that cognition plays in human behavior. Intrapersonal communication is usually more repetitive than other communication. This context is also unique from other contexts in that it includes those times when you imagine, perceive, daydream, and solve problems in your head. Lance Morrow in *Time* (1998) notes that "most talking to oneself involves a low order of business—pettiness, self-justification, improvised rants" (p. 98). Joan Aitken and Leonard Shedletsky (1997) tell us that intrapersonal communication is much more than that. It also includes the many attributions you may make about another person's behavior. For instance, an employer may want to know why an employee arrives late and disheveled to work each day. The supervisor may believe that the worker's tardiness and demeanor are a result of some domestic problems. In reality, the employee may have another job in order to pay for his or her child's college tuition. We all have internal dialogues, and these internalized voices can vary tremendously from one person to another.

In addition to making attributions about others, intrapersonal communication is distinguished from other contexts in that it allows communicators to make attributions about themselves. People have the ability to assess themselves. From body image to work competencies, people are always making self-attributions. You may have thought seriously about your own strengths and shortcomings in a number of situations. For example, do you find that you are an excellent parent but not so excellent as a statistics student? Are there times when you feel that you are a trusted friend but not so trusted in your own family? Communicating with oneself often results in self-judgments.

self-esteem the positive orientation a person has of himself or herself

Although some people may believe that talking to oneself is a bit peculiar, Virginia Satir (1988) believes that these internal dialogues may help individuals bolster their **self-esteem**—the degree of positive orientation people have about themselves. Often, intrapersonal communication is difficult; it requires individuals to accept their accomplishments and confront their fears and anxieties. Looking in a mirror can be both enlightening and frightening. Of course, mirrors can also be distorting. Jenny Yamato, for example, may think that her world is over once her daughter leaves for college. The reality for the vast majority of parents, however, is that they survive the "loss." As a single parent, Jenny may think that she is incapable of moving on without Lee. Once Lee leaves, however, Jenny may find that she is more empowered living alone.

Our discussion of intrapersonal communication has focused on the role of the self in the communication process. Recall that as individuals communicate with themselves, the process may be either intentional (such as telling oneself "I've got pretty good decorating sense") or unintentional (such as telling oneself "I'm such a klutz" after falling down the stairs). Intrapersonal communication is at the heart of a person's communication activities. Without recognizing one's self, it is difficult to recognize another.

Interpersonal Communication

Interpersonal communication refers to face-to-face communication between people. Several theories that you will read about in this book have their origins in the interpersonal context. This context is rich with research and theory and is perhaps the most expansive of all of the contexts. Investigating how relationships begin, the maintenance of relationships, and the dissolution of relationships (Berger, 1979; Dainton & Stafford, 2000) characterizes much of the interpersonal context.

One reason that researchers and theorists study relationships is that relationships are so complex and diverse. For instance, you may find yourself in dozens of relationship types right now, including physician–patient, teacher–student, parent–child, supervisor–employee, and so forth. Interacting within each of these relationships affords communicators a chance to maximize the number of channels (visual, auditory, tactile, olfactory) used during an interaction. In this context, these channels function simultaneously for both interactants: A child may scream for his mom, for instance, and as she is able to calm him with her caress, she touches the child, looks in his eyes, and listens to his whimpering subside.

The interpersonal context itself comprises many related contexts. Interpersonal communication researchers have studied the family (Pawlowski, Thilborger, & Cieloha-Meekins, 2001), friendships (Chen, Drzewiecka, & Sias, 2001), marital relationships (Graham, 1997), physician–patient relationships (Richmond, Smith, Heisel, & McCroskey, 2001), and relationships in the workplace (Hinkle, 2001). Further, researchers are interested in a host of issues and themes (for example, competence, self-disclosure, power, gossip, liking, attraction, emotions, and so forth) associated with these relationships. Researchers have also examined the link between interpersonal communication and mass media, organizations, and the classroom (Frymier & Houser, 2002; Meyer, 1995; Rubin & Rubin, 1992). Finally, relationships that have not been studied enough, including gay and lesbian relationships, cohabiting relationships, and computer network relationships, are gaining researchers' attention (Heinz, 2002; Wright, 2002). As you can see, researchers have framed some very diverse and exciting work within the interpersonal communication context, and studying relationships and what takes place within them has broad appeal.

Small Group Communication

A third context of communication is the **small group.** Small groups are composed of a number of people who work together to achieve some common purpose. Small group research focuses on task groups as opposed to friendship and family groups, which are found in the interpersonal context. There is disagreement by researchers about how many people make up a small group. Some scholars argue that the optimal number for a small group is five to seven members, whereas others put no limit on the maximum number of members. Nearly all agree, however, that there must be at least three people for a small group to exist (Schultz, 1996).

interpersonal communication
face-to-face communication between people

small group
individuals who come together for a common purpose

31

The number in a group, however, is not as important as the implications of that number. For instance, as the number increases in a small group, there is less opportunity for individual contributions. In addition, the more people, the greater the opportunity for more personal relationships to develop. This may influence whether small groups stay focused on their goals and whether group members are satisfied with their experiences (Shaw, 1981). A classic study (Kephart, 1950) revealed that as the size of the group increases, the number of relationships increases substantially. With a three-person group, then, the number of potential relationships is 6; with a seven-person group, there are 966 possible relationships! When there are too many group members, there is a tendency for cliques to form (Mamali & Paun, 1982). However, large numbers of group members may result in additional resources that were not present in smaller groups.

People are influenced by the presence of others. For example, some small groups are very **cohesive,** or have a high degree of togetherness and a common bond. This cohesiveness may influence whether the group functions effectively and efficiently. In addition, the small group context affords individuals a chance to gain multiple perspectives on an issue. That is, in the intrapersonal context, an individual views events from his or her own perspective; in the interpersonal context there are more perspectives. In the small group context, many more people have the potential to contribute to the group's goals. In problem-solving groups or task groups in particular, many perspectives may be advantageous. The benefit small groups derive from this exchange of multiple perspectives is called **synergy** and explains why small groups may be more effective than an individual at achieving goals.

Networking and role behavior are two important components of small group behavior. **Networks** are communication patterns through which information flows, and networks in small groups answer the following question: Who speaks to whom and in what order? The patterns of interaction in small groups may vary significantly. For instance, in some groups the leader may be included in all deliberations, whereas in other groups members may speak to one another without the leader. The small group context is made up of individuals who take on various **roles,** or the positions of group members and their relationship to the group. These roles may be very diverse, including task leader, passive observer, active listener, recorder, and so forth.

Before we close our discussion of small groups, we should point out that as with the interpersonal communication context, research on small groups spans a variety of areas. Researchers have studied power in small groups (Boulding, 1990), group hate (Sorensen, 1981), juries (Burnett & Badzinski, 2000), decision making (Gouran, Hirokawa, & Martz, 1986), leadership (Hackman & Johnson, 1996), creativity (Sabatine, 1989), and ethnic and racial culture (Chen & Starosta, 2000). Much research and theory today continues to underscore the fact that groups exist to meet important human needs (Brilhart, Galanes, & Adams, 2001).

Working in small groups seems to be a fact of life in society. At times, it may seem as if we cannot go anywhere without some sort of small group forming. From peer groups to task groups to support groups, the small group expe-

cohesive
sense of togetherness in a group

synergy
process that allows for multiple perspectives to be given on issues or events

networks
communication patterns through which information flows

roles
positions of group members and their relationship to the group

rience is a ubiquitous one. Very few students can receive their degree without working in small groups. From study groups to presentations, you may feel as if you are immersed in small group activities. Company supervisors relish team approaches to problem solving. Some families have weekly or monthly family meetings, at which the group discusses such issues as vacations, sibling rivalry, and curfew.

The United States will continue to rely on small groups, even as we increase our reliance on technology. Although we have reached a point at which 50 percent of all U.S. homes have at least one computer, it appears that person-to-person contact will never go out of style. Computers may crash and break down, but people will continue to function and communicate in small groups.

Organizational Communication

To discuss our fifth context of communication, it is important to distinguish between small group communication and organizational communication. **Organizational communication** pertains to communication within and among large, extended environments. This communication is extremely diverse in that organizational communication necessarily entails interpersonal encounters (supervisor–subordinate conversations), public speaking opportunities (presentations by company executives), small group situations (a task group preparing a report), and mediated experiences (internal memos, e-mail, and teleconferencing). Organizations, then, comprise groups that are goal directed.

What distinguishes this context from others is that a clearly defined hierarchy exists in most organizations. **Hierarchy** is an organizing principle whereby things or persons are ranked one above the other. For an example of the hierarchy in many colleges and universities, see Figure 2.2. Does your

organizational communication communication within and among large, extended environments

hierarchy organizing principle demonstrating rankings

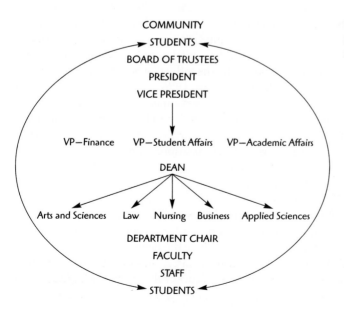

**Figure 2.2
Example of Hierarchy
in Higher Education**

school follow the same hierarchy? Tom Daniels, Barry Spiker, and Michael Papa (1997) point out that most Western organizations are traditionally hierarchical in that there are clear ideas about "division of labor, unity of command, and unity of direction" (p. 45). Organizations are unique in that much of the communication taking place is highly structured, and role playing is often specialized and predictable. Employees and employers alike are clear in their chain of command. Unlike in the interpersonal context, several modes of communication can substitute for face-to-face interaction, namely the use of memos, e-mail, and teleconferencing.

The uniqueness of organizational communication is also represented by the research and theory conceptualized in this context. Many of the present-day organizational communication theories had their origins in a series of studies conducted in the mid-1920s to early 1930s. These studies, known as the **Hawthorne experiments,** were significant influences on modern theory in that they inaugurated the human relations approach to organizations. Researchers at the Western Electric Hawthorne Plant in suburban Chicago were interested in determining the effect of lighting levels on employee productivity. Interestingly, results of this research indicated that not only did the environmental conditions influence employee output but so did the interpersonal relationships with other employees and supervisors. One conclusion arising from these studies was that organizations should be viewed as social entities; to speed up production, employers must consider workers' attitudes and feelings. These studies were among the first to put a human face on the impersonal corporate world (Roethlisberger & Dickson, 1939).

Although the human relations approach has enjoyed a great deal of research and theoretical attention, today there are a number of additional organizational orientations—for instance, cultural systems and scientific management. Further, organizational communication research and theory today address a number of eclectic issues, including the *Challenger* disaster (Gouran et al., 1986), ethics (King & Hermodson, 2000), whistle-blowing (Stewart, 1992), rumor (Rosnow, 1992), job training (Waldron & Lavitt, 2000), sexual harassment (Keyton, Ferguson, & Rhodes, 2001), and grapevines (Hellweg, 1992). In addition, as with other contexts, the influence of ethnic and racial culture has also been examined (Nkomo & Cox, 1996).

What is important to glean from this discussion is that, like other contexts, the organizational context has a rich tradition. The Hawthorne studies of human behavior on the job have led today's researchers and theorists to expand their perspectives of organizations and organizational life.

Public Communication

The fifth context is known as the **public communication** context, or the dissemination of information from one person to a large group. This is not a new context; speech presentations have existed since the beginning of time and continue today. Tony Robbins, Bill Clinton, Bill Gates, Oprah Winfrey, and Bono are just a few of the contemporary public figures who are in high demand as public speakers.

Hawthorne experiments
research studies that found workplace productivity increased when changes in environment occurred

public communication
dissemination of information from one person to a large group

In public speaking, speakers usually have three primary goals in mind: to inform, to entertain, or to persuade. This latter goal—persuasion—is at the core of rhetorical communication. Many of the principles of persuasion—including audience analysis, speaker credibility, and delivery of message—are necessarily part of the persuasive process. As you reflect upon your own public speaking experiences, you may be surprised to learn that in actuality, you have been following rhetorical strategies rooted in early Greek and Roman days. How people have constructed their persuasive speeches has been the focus of study for more than 2,500 years.

Effective public speakers owe their success to early rhetorical principles, a topic that we will discuss further in Chapter 18. **Rhetoric** is defined as a speaker's available means of persuading his or her audience. This definition was advanced many years ago by Aristotle. Rhetoric has been described as an art that brings together both speakers and audience (Hart, 1997); the study of rhetoric has evolved from studying texts of speeches, such as presidential inaugural addresses, to rhetorical analyses of cultural themes and issues, including AIDS (Foss, 1994), the Catholic Church (Lamoureux, 1994), Hollywood movies (McMullen, 1996), and politics (Moore, 1997).

rhetoric
speaker's available means of persuasion

One area that has received considerable attention from communication researchers is **communication apprehension (CA)**, or the fear of speaking before an audience. Research by James McCroskey, Virginia Richmond, and their colleagues has helped shape what people study in the public communication context. You will recall that the boundaries among contexts are often blurred. The CA research is one example of that blurring. Although communication apprehension is a public speaking concern, CA focuses on intrapersonal issues. Further, CA has been studied with a number of different populations, including at-risk children (Ayres, Ayres, & Hopf, 1995), small groups (Daly, McCroskey, & Richmond, 1977) and families (Beatty & Dobos, 1993), and across cultures (McCroskey, Burroughs, Daun, & Richmond, 1990). Ways to reduce this apprehension have also been investigated for years (Ayres & Hopf, 1989, 1991, 1992). Clearly, the public communication context addresses both theory and skills and includes research that overlaps other contexts.

communication apprehension
fear of speaking before an audience

Mass Communication

The sixth context is the mass communication context, which targets large audiences. First, we need to define a few terms. **Mass media** refers to the channels, or delivery modes, for mass messages. Mass media include newspapers, videos, CD-ROMs, computers, radios, and so forth. **Mass communication** refers to communication to a large audience via these channels of communication. The mass communication context, therefore, encompasses the channel and the audience. Although mass communication traditionally refers to newspapers, videos, CD-ROMs, and radios, we expand our discussion to include **new media**, which encompass computer-related technology, everything from e-mail to the Internet to digital cable television to video technology such as DVDs. As of now, however, *mass communication* is being defined and redefined and simultaneously, so is new media. For our purposes, then, we identify mass communication as communication to a large audience via multiple channels of communication,

mass media
channels or delivery modes for mass messages
mass communication
communication to a large audience via mass media
new media
electronic media (notably computer-related technology) such as the Internet, e-mail, and digital cable

including radio, television, newspapers, and computers. The mass communication context, therefore, includes both the channel and the audience.

Like each of the preceding five contexts, the mass communication context is distinctive. First, the mass communication context allows both senders and receivers to exercise control. Sources such as a newspaper editor or a television broadcaster make decisions about what information should be sent, and receivers have control over what they decide to read, listen to, watch, or review. Suppose, for instance, that you are an advertiser who has slotted an expensive television commercial featuring Tiger Woods. You've paid Woods handsomely, and yet, to determine whether his endorsement has made a difference in sales, you have to wait for the numbers to come in. You have control over the choice of the endorser, but the audience also has control over what they watch and what they buy.

Finally, the mass communication context distinguishes itself from other contexts in that communication is often more constrained and restricted. That is, the communication is influenced by costs, by politics, and by other concerns. Key decision makers usually use profit-loss margins to determine whether messages will continue to be heard. For instance, the decision to cancel a television show or to run a personal interest story in a newspaper is often based on the bottom line: money.

Some, like theorist Stuart Hall, suggest that mass media inherently serve the interests of the elite, especially big business and multinational corporations, who, Hall suggests, fund much of the research in mass communication. Many studies, however, are not underwritten by corporate sponsorship, but rather reflect the growing diversity of mass communication researchers. Among the topics investigated are online support communities (Wright, 2000), heroes in the movie *The Matrix* (Stroud, 2001), audience involvement in television talk shows (McKenzie, 2000), and an analysis of such quiz shows as *Who Wants to Be a Millionaire* (Hetsroni, 2001). As you see, a diverse research agenda characterizes mass communication research.

Although some scholars (such as Postman, 1992) believe that unprecedented developments in new mediated technologies can be harmful for society, we have witnessed tremendous growth in accessing and receiving information. As we watch television news in the United States, we simultaneously receive live satellite images from the war in the Middle East. Satellites also allow us to see the Olympics in Greece, the Tour de France, and the running of the bulls in Pamplona, Spain. Computer modems help a Polish American woman in New York interested in her family history to immediately link up with a distant relative in Poland. Without doubt, we are a society reliant upon mass communication and new media.

As we write this, we fear that our comments may already be out of date. Mass communication is rapidly changing, and what was promised as a marvelous advance today is often considered outdated tomorrow. Because of the pervasiveness and availability of mass media in our society, media theorists will have to deal with the impact of media on the communication process itself. Some researchers (for instance, Turkle, 1998) suggest that computers may redefine the way we conceive of ourselves. This redefinition may have an inevitable impact on the communication process. Further, although a large number of homes and businesses subscribe to new technologies, a gap will always exist between those who have the resources and those who do not. Consequently, future mass communication theorists may have to rethink the universality of their theories.

Intercultural Communication

The final communication context we wish to examine is intercultural communication. To begin, we should define what we mean by *culture*. There are many definitions of *culture*. John Baldwin and S. L. Lindsley (1994), for instance, provided over 200 definitions! For our purposes, **culture** can be viewed as a "community of meaning and a shared body of local knowledge" (Gonzalez, Houston, & Chen, 2000, p. xv). **Intercultural communication,** therefore, refers to communication between individuals whose cultural backgrounds differ. These individuals do not necessarily have to be from different countries. In a diverse country such as the United States, we can experience intercultural communication within one state, one community, and even one block. It is not uncommon in many parts of this society, for instance, to see two people from different cultural backgrounds speaking to each other. Urban centers, in particular, can be exciting cultural arenas where communication takes place between members of different co-cultures. **Co-cultures** are groups of individuals who are part of the same larger culture but who—through unity and individual identification around such attributes as race, ethnicity, sexual orientation, religion, and so forth—create opportunities of their own. The word *co-culture* is now widely accepted in the academic community as a replacement for *subculture,* a term suggesting that one culture has dominance over another culture.

Intercultural communication is a relatively young academic context, with its beginnings traced back only to the 1950s (Leeds-Hurwitz, 1990). However, much exciting work has been done since then. The growth of this area of study can be attributed to the growth of the global market, with more U.S. companies doing business abroad. In addition, technological availability, population shifts, and genuine efforts to understand other cultures contribute to the growing interest in this context. Yet, the United States has a long way to go before harmonious communication exists between and among all cultures and co-cultures. Still, we are beginning to witness progress in recognizing and appreciating today's cultural diversity.

The intercultural context differentiates itself from other contexts in a few ways. First, as you may have determined, this context is the only context that specifically addresses culture. Although some contexts, such as the organizational context, comprise research on racial and ethnic cultures, this work is often ancillary, with culture being examined for its effects on the context. In the intercultural context, however, researchers and theorists purposely explore the interactions and events between and among people of different cultures. Second, study in the intercultural communication context means that researchers inherently accept the fact that human behavior is culturally based. In other words, culture structures how we act.

To give you an indication of the type of research and thinking going on in the intercultural communication context, consider the following research titles:

culture
community of meaning and a shared body of knowledge

intercultural communication
communication between individuals with different cultural backgrounds

co-cultures
cultural groups that are part of the larger (national) culture

"Breaking into Silence: Technology Transfer and Mythical Knowledge Among the Acomas of Nuevo Mexico" (Gonzalez & Bradley, 1990), "*De Que Colores:* A Critical Examination of Multicultural Children's Books" (Willis-Rivera & Melker, 2002), "Buddhist Preaching" (Ishii, 1992), "Illusive Reflections: African American Women on Prime Time Television" (Merritt, 1997), and "Conceptual Foundations for Teaching About Whiteness" (Martin & Davis, 2001). This context is filled with opportunities to study areas that have not received a lot of attention in the past. Investigating culture and cultural groups holds continued promise as the United States grows more diverse.

Although this research derives from a number of different cultural perspectives, you should be aware that much of what we know and how we relate is a result of a Western model of thinking—that is, many of us interpret events and behaviors through a European (American) lens (Asante, 1987). We need to remember that peoples' beliefs often reflect the media's beliefs, and the mass media often "speak for cultural communities to which they are unrelated" (Gonzalez et al., 2000, p. xii).

Putting It All Together

In discussing these seven contexts, we hope to have provided you with a basic category system for dividing the broad field of communication. These seven categories help us discuss the communication process more clearly and specifically. Yet, the system is not perfect, and as you have probably noted in our discussion, there is often overlap among the categories. For instance, when people belong to a cancer support group online, their communication has elements of at least four contexts: intrapersonal, interpersonal, small group, and mass communication. Thus, we caution you against viewing these categories as completely exclusive and distinctive from one another.

Conclusion

This chapter has provided a brief historical overview of the beginnings of the communication field. We first discussed how various communication associations were conceptualized and developed, and then identified five pioneers who carved out the beginnings of the modern communication discipline. We next examined the primary contexts of communication: intrapersonal, interpersonal, small group, organizational, public, mass, and intercultural. As you read the

Theory * Into * Practice

T*I*P

When John Daly, former president of the National Communication Association, addressed the membership in 1998 in New York City, he noted that the communication field has a long and rich history, with the annual conventions evolving into a vast and complex undertaking. In 1973, Daly recalled, the index listing convention participants was three and a half pages; in 1998, the index of participants was almost thirty pages. Daly noted that although the field has changed, the constant in the communication profession that cuts across contexts and research areas is the scholars and teachers working together to better understand the communication process.

Daly then illustrated the importance of communication skills in job employment and offered a number of examples demonstrating how communication pervades U.S. society. In reference to the "bountiful harvest of discoveries" (Daly, 1999, p. 12) in the research process, Daly pointed out how the communication field has shaped our knowledge:

- We understand ways to reduce stage fright, and communication research has helped people reduce their fear of public speaking.
- We understand how persuasive campaigns undertaken in the health sciences can be more effective.
- We help teachers improve their effectiveness with their students and help students better understand their own potential.
- We know strategies for handling conflict in relationships.
- We can challenge people's unethical behavior.
- We know how language can be used both to empower and to disenfranchise others.
- We can caution policymakers about the dangers of the media.
- We understand how culture affects communication and how communication affects culture.

These conclusions represent a number of different contexts, including interpersonal, organizational, mass, and intercultural communication.

Daly challenged the National Communication Association to be careful in its thinking, thorough in its analysis, and willing to share knowledge with others. With new technologies, the communication discipline also must be prepared to adapt to the developments.

Daly concluded by noting that communication scholars should be bolder about offering advice to others. Many researchers have been leery of offering advice, given the complexity of human behavior. Yet, Daly believes that those less informed—newspaper columnists, pundits, and talk show hosts—are telling others how to behave and they are not trained to offer such guidance. The communication discipline—its diversity represented by its various contexts—is uniquely qualified to offer guidance on real-life issues.

Source: Daly, 1999.

TIP Follow-up
Daly's comments suggest that communication scholars—because of their education and training—should be at the forefront of offering insights into communication-related issues. Such issues may include presidential rhetoric, interpreting divorce statistics, decisions regarding child discipline, sexual identity topics, and language associated with dealing with terrorists. Why do you believe communication scholars are rarely on the evening news interpreting world events?

theories in this book, you will see that many of them fall neatly into these divisions; some, however, cut across several contexts.

You should now be able to discern the uniqueness of the communication discipline. As you read the next few chapters on theory building, you will begin to link the communication process with the theoretical process. These preliminary chapters offer important foundations to draw on as you encounter the theories presented later in the book.

Discussion Starters

1. Lee and Jenny Yamato's experiences fall across several of the contexts we identified in this chapter. In your own words, complete their story using the remaining contexts. Identify how their experiences relate to these contexts.

2. Are the name changes pertaining to the national associations "much ado about nothing"? Explain and use examples.

3. Which context of communication most appeals to you? Why? What types of examples—other than those provided—can you think of to illustrate the context?

4. If you had to add another context of communication based on your experiences, what context would it be? How would you interpret the context for others? What examples illustrate the context?

5. Why is it important to understand the history of a discipline? Use examples to support your views.

6. Explain how politics can influence each of the communication contexts.

Terms for Review

lifespace
contexts
situational contexts
intrapersonal communication
self-esteem
interpersonal communication
small group
cohesive
synergy
networks
roles
organizational communication

hierarchy
Hawthorne experiments
public communication
rhetoric
communication apprehension (CA)
mass media
mass communication
new media
culture
intercultural communication
co-cultures

Online Learning Center

Visit the Online Learning Center at www.mhhe.com/west2. Use the multiple-choice and true/false quizzes to help you prepare for exams, and the glossary, crossword puzzles, and flashcards to further your knowledge of key terms.

CHAPTER 3

Thinking About Theory

Emile and Irene Hirsch

Emile Hirsch and his wife, Irene, have been married for fifty-five years. For fifty years, they have lived in the small town of Antigo, Wisconsin, on a dairy farm. Together they raised two daughters and four sons and successfully managed their farm business. Now they have retired from the active life of running the farm and turned it over to one of their daughters and her family. But they continue to live in the old farmhouse where they shared fifty years of experiences both joyful and sorrowful.

One night at supper, Emile suggested to Irene that they should think about moving to a warmer climate. He observed that they were both getting on in years and that Geoff, one of their sons, who lives in Florida, had mentioned how nice it would be to have his parents come to live nearby in a retirement village.

Irene was startled by Emile's comments. She had absolutely no desire to leave Antigo, the farm, their church, their friends, or the rest of their children, who had all settled in Wisconsin. Further,

she had never gotten along with Geoff's wife, and she couldn't foresee how that relationship would improve if they lived closer. She was also dumbfounded that Emile would entertain thoughts of leaving their happy life in Antigo. She had always believed that the two of them were so alike in the way they approached new situations and problems. She almost started to cry thinking that at this late date they might differ on such a fundamental issue. She put down her coffee cup and cleared her throat before speaking.

Emile looked at her with some concern. She had been silent so long he was getting nervous because he thought that she didn't like the idea or that she was angry at him for discussing it with Geoff before the two of them had a chance to talk. He knew that all major decisions had to be made by the two of them together; that was the way their marriage always had worked. It was just chance that Geoff had called him with this idea at the same time that Emile himself had been wondering if he and Irene needed to make a move.

The Hirsches, like all of us, continually experience complex communication interactions such as those described above. Often people wonder to themselves, or even ask each other, Why do we act the way we do? Why do we argue about some things and not others? Why are we successful in communicating sometimes and not at other times? How can we be better communicators? Researchers believe that we can provide answers to these kinds of questions with theory, a type of framework that helps us sort out the separate bits of our behavior and quilt them together in some meaningful way. Sir Karl Popper, a philosopher who significantly shaped many researchers' approach to theoretical thinking, captured this notion eloquently stating: "Theories are nets cast to catch what we call 'the world'" (1959, p. 48). Popper's point, that theories shape our sense of reality, is one we consider throughout this text.

For the Hirsches, a theory might be able to offer a general pattern that would help Emile understand Irene's silence or that would explain why, even after fifty-five years of marriage, there are still elements of unpredictability in their relationship. Theories may help them satisfy questions about their interactions and clarify what is happening between them.

Emile and Irene are primarily interested in explaining each other's behavior, and they will probably be satisfied with the first compelling explanation they discover. Communication researchers, however, have larger goals. They want to explain communication behavior in general or to explain specific behaviors in a rich, in-depth manner. Theories can help both everyday interactors and communication researchers in reaching satisfactory explanations.

In this book we are discussing theory as professional researchers use it in their work; yet, all of us in daily life think like researchers, using implicit theories to help us understand those questions we mentioned previously. Fritz Heider (1958) referred to everyday interactors engaging in theoretical thinking as "naive psychologists." Whenever we pose an answer to one of our questions (for example, if we suggest that maybe we are really fighting over power and control and not what color to paint the living room), we are engaging in theoretical thinking. Studying theory can be challenging, yet remember that we are all intuitive theorists trying to find explanations for our communication interactions.

In many ways, this text points out the similarities and differences between thinking as a "naive" theorist and thinking as a professional theorist. First, as we have just mentioned, they are similar because both puzzle over questions encountered through observations and both seek answers for these questions. Both also set up certain criteria that define what an acceptable answer might be. For instance, when Ely wonders why his roommate talks so much more than what is comfortable for him, he might decide on the following criteria for an answer: The answer has to apply to all communication contexts (phone, face-to-face, and so forth); and the answer has to make sense (Ely wouldn't accept an answer such as his roommate comes from another planet where talk is more highly valued than here on Earth). When Ely (and social scientists) find an answer that satisfies their criteria, they generalize from it and may apply it to other situations that are similar. If Ely concludes that his roommate is insecure and talks to cover up his insecurity, he may determine that others he meets who talk more than he does are also insecure.

In all those processes, everyday communicators follow the basic outline advanced by social science. However, there are very clear differences apparent in this description as well. First, social scientists systematically test theories while nonscientists test selectively. Ely will accept evidence that agrees with his theory about the relationship of insecurity and talking and tend to ignore evidence that contradicts it. Researchers are more rigorous in their testing and more willing to amend theories, incorporating information pointing to inconsistencies in the original formulation of the theory. In the text, many of the theories we present (e.g., Uncertainty Reduction Theory) have undergone extensive revisions as testing has indicated problems with the original theoretical principles or a need for expansion of them.

Defining Theory: What's in a Name?

theory
an abstract system of concepts and their relationships that help us to understand a phenomenon

Generally speaking, a **theory** is an abstract system of concepts with indications of the relationships among these concepts that help us to understand a phenomenon. Stephen Littlejohn (2000) suggests this abstract system is derived through systematic observation. In 1986, Jonathan H. Turner defined *theory* as "a process of developing ideas that can allow us to explain how and why events occur" (p. 5). This definition focuses on the nature of theoretical thinking without specifying exactly what the outcome of this thinking might be. William Doherty and his colleagues (1993) have elaborated on Turner's definition by conveying the notion that theories are both process and product: "Theorizing is the process of systematically formulating and organizing ideas to understand a particular phenomenon. A theory is the set of interconnected ideas that emerge from this process" (p. 20). In this definition, the authors attempt to be inclusive. They do not use Turner's word *explain* because the goals of theory can be more numerous than simply explanation, a point we explore later in this chapter.

In this brief discussion, you have probably noticed that different theorists approach the definition of *theory* somewhat differently. The search for a universally accepted definition of *theory* is a difficult, if not impossible, task. In part, the difficulty in defining *theory* is due to the many ways in which a theory can be classified or categorized. Here we will review two ways to categorize theories in an effort to clarify our definition: level of generality and focus. In Chapter 4 we will review three different approaches to knowing that also provide a classification system for distinguishing among theories.

A common means of classifying theories pertains to their level of generality. Theories are often seen as being grand (or universal), mid-range (or general), and narrow (or very specific). **Grand theories** purport to explain all of communication behavior in a manner that is universally true. Outside the discipline of communication, Marxism is an example of a grand theory. A grand theory would have the ability to unify all the knowledge we have about communication into one integrated theoretical framework. This may or may not be a worthy goal (Craig, 1999), but most would agree that no grand theory of communication exists. There are too many instances where communication differs from group to group or when communication behavior is modified by changes in context or time to create a grand theory.

grand theory
theory that attempts to explain all of a phenomenon such as communication

mid-range theory
theory that attempts to explain a specified aspect of a phenomenon such as communication

A **mid-range theory** explains the behavior of a specific group of people rather than everyone, as a grand theory would do, or tries to explain the behavior of all people within a specified time or context. Uncertainty Reduction Theory (URT) falls into the mid-range theory category because although its claims initially covered only a small amount of relational time (initial encounters), these claims were forwarded as a general explanation for people in all initial encounters.

DILBERT reprinted by permission of United Features Syndicate, Inc.

Finally, a **narrow theory** "concerns only certain people in certain situations—for example, the communication rules pertinent to standing in an elevator" (Stacks, Hickson, & Hill, 1991, p. 284). Often theories are criticized for claiming to be grander than they really are. For instance, some critics of Standpoint Theory (Chapter 27) argue that its assertions about women have to be modified by other identifiers such as class and race. In sum, knowing the level of generality helps us sort through different theories and understand the term better.

Theories may also be classified by their difference in focus, or what they try to explain. Some theories focus on the entire communication process (e.g., Symbolic Interaction Theory), while others focus more specifically on a given aspect of the process, such as the message or the sender (e.g., Rhetorical Theory). Still others attend to communication as a means for relationship development (e.g., Social Penetration Theory). Knowing how to classify theories helps us see how very dissimilar works (such as URT, Medium, and Muted Group Theory) can all be defined as theory.

However, when defining the term *theory,* as D. C. Phillips (1992) observes, "there is no divinely ordained *correct* usage, but we can strive to use the word consistently and to mark distinctions that we feel are important" (p. 121). The distinctions we think are important include (1) an explanation of the key components of theories, (2) an examination of the goals of theory, (3) a discussion of the relationship between theory and experience, and (4) an investigation of the paradigms and metatheoretical foundations that shape researchers' approaches to and uses of theory. We address these elements in this chapter.

narrow theory
theory that attempts
to explain a very limited aspect of a
phenomenon such as
communication

Components of Theory

concepts
labels for the most important elements in a theory

Theories are composed of several key parts, the two most important of which are called concepts and relationships. **Concepts** are words or terms that label the most important elements in a theory. Concepts in some of the theories we will discuss include cohesiveness (Groupthink), dissonance (Cognitive Dissonance Theory), self (Symbolic Interaction Theory), and scene (Dramatism). As you can see, sometimes theories are named using one of their key concepts, although this is not always the case.

A concept often has a specific definition that is unique to its use in a theory, which differs from how we would define the word in everyday conversation. For example, the concept "cultivation" used in Cultivation Analysis (see Chapter 22) refers specifically to the way media, especially television, create a picture of social reality in the minds of media consumers. This use of the term differs somewhat from using it to mean hoeing your garden or developing an interest, skill, or friendship. In the theory, cultivation has a unique and relatively narrow definition. It is always the task of the theorist to provide a clear definition of the concepts used in the theory.

nominal concepts
concepts that are not directly observable
real concepts
concepts that are observable

Concepts may be nominal or real. **Nominal concepts** are those that are not observable, such as democracy or love. **Real concepts** are observable, such as noise or spatial distance. As we discuss in Chapter 4, when researchers use theory in their studies, they must turn both nominal and real constructs into something concrete so that they can be observed. It is much easier to do this for real concepts than for nominal ones.

relationships
the ways in which the concepts of a theory are combined

Relationships specify the ways in which the concepts in the theory are combined. For example, in Chapter 1 we presented three different models of the process of communication. In each model, the concepts are very similar. What is different is the relationship specified among them. In the first model, the relationship is a linear one where one concept relates to the second, which then relates to the next, and so forth. In the second model, the posited relationship is interactive, or two-way. The third model illustrates mutual influence (transaction), where all the concepts are seen as affecting one another simultaneously.

Goals of Theory

In a broad, inclusive sense, the goals of theory can include explanation, understanding, prediction, and social change; we are able to *explain* something (Emile's request to Irene about moving, for example) because of the concepts and their relationships specified in a theory. We are able to *understand* something (Irene's increased uncertainty) because of theoretical thinking. Additionally, we are able to *predict* something (how Emile and Irene will negotiate their differences about moving) based on the patterns suggested by a theory. Finally, we are able to effect *social change* or empowerment (altering the institution of marriage so that it more completely empowers both partners, for example) through theoretical inquiry.

Although some theories try to reach all these goals, most feature one goal over the others. Rhetorical theories, some media theories, and many inter-

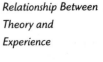

personal theories seek primarily to provide explanation or understanding. Others—for example, traditional persuasion and organizational theories—focus on prediction. Still others—for instance, some feminist and other critical theories—have as their central goal to change the structures of society. For critical theorists, this means effecting social change, not simply improving individual lives. For instance, a theory about conflict management may help people understand how to engage in conflict more productively, thus enriching their lives. Yet it may do nothing to change the underlying structures that promoted the conflict in the first place. We will discuss this critical approach further in Chapter 4.

Theories, then, help us answer why and how questions about our communication experiences. From this, you can see that experience and theory are related, although experience is concrete and theory is abstract.

Relationship Between Theory and Experience

In 1952, Carl Hempel compared a scientific theory to a complex spatial network, saying that "its terms are represented by the knots, while the threads connecting the latter correspond, in part, to the definitions and, in part, to the fundamental and derivative hypotheses included in the theory" (p. 36). Hempel then noted that this theory/network

> floats, as it were, above the plane of observation and is anchored to it by rules of interpretation. These might be viewed as strings which are not part of the network but link certain points of the latter with specific places in the plane of observation. . . . From certain observational data, we may ascend, via an interpretive string, to some point in the theoretical network, then proceed, via definitions and hypotheses, to other points, from which another interpretive string permits a descent to the plane of observation. (p. 36)

Hempel suggests that although a theory is abstract, it enables us to understand concrete experiences and observations, and that a theory itself is capable of being modified by observations. In addition, his statement asserts that our concrete experiences and observations are interpreted by us through the lens offered by the theory we are using.

If we applied Uncertainty Reduction Theory (Berger & Calabrese, 1975), a theory we discuss in Chapter 9, to an analysis of the Hirsches' dinner table

The Theory Chronicles

In your journal, note for one week the theoretical thinking that you engage in. Observe how systematic and rigorous you are in testing your theoretical propositions.

conversation, we might attribute Emile and Irene's halting contributions to a high degree of uncertainty suddenly presenting itself in their relationship. We would reach this conclusion because the theory suggests that uncertainty and intimacy are negatively related. Yet, if we applied a dialectic approach (Baxter, 1988, 1990; Montgomery, 1984; Rawlins, 1992; Yerby, 1995), discussed in Chapter 12, we might interpret their conversation differently, seeing it instead as a strategic means of negotiating tensions between simultaneous desires for closeness and individuality.

Janet Yerby (1995), commenting on the notion that theories act as a lens, allowing us to see some things while ignoring others, refers to theories as "the stories we have developed to explain our view of reality" (p. 362). The strings of interpretation that Hempel mentions can be seen as the elements in the story we have chosen as satisfactory explanations for communication behaviors. In taking this approach, we have to be aware, as Yerby suggests, that theories, like stories, change and evolve over time as new information modifies and refines them.

Paradigms: How Do You See the World?

One explanation for why theories may change and for why scholars have different perspectives about the definition of theory itself has to do with the fact that individual theories are grounded in intellectual traditions that involve different assumptions. By an intellectual tradition, we mean a way of viewing the world, or "a general way of thinking that has been shared in common by a community of scholars" (Klein & White, 1996, p. 10). Intellectual traditions affect the values, goals, and scholarly style of researchers, and they greatly influence the work that researchers do. It is critical to understand the intellectual traditions, or **paradigms,** that ground the theories we read and use. Thus, paradigms offer general ways of viewing human communication; theories are the more specific explanations of a particular aspect of communication behavior.

paradigms
intellectual traditions that ground specific theories

Thomas Kuhn (1970) notes that paradigms tend to become entrenched over time until they are dislodged by newer ways of organizing the world that seem to make better sense to researchers. Kuhn refers to this process as a scientific revolution. In the natural sciences, for example, Newtonian physics was replaced by Einsteinian relativism.

In the communication discipline, modern communication theory originated with information processing and the notion of cybernetic tradition (Wiener, 1948). This perspective epitomizes the linear model we pictured in Chapter 1 and sometimes has been described as a mechanistic approach. Theorizing communication from an information processing perspective was the dominant paradigm from the 1950s through the 1980s. Although it has not disappeared from communication research, it has been removed from its dominant position. Now communication researchers are just as likely to theorize from a social constructivist or phenomenological perspective as from an information processing model.

In fact, several paradigms guide researchers working today. Some researchers are influenced by feminism, constructivism, or Marxism. These paradigms guide researchers' beliefs about the world. For example, researchers who operate within a feminist paradigm believe that women are subjugated and that this status should be changed (Cirksena & Cuklanz, 1992). Those working within a constructivist paradigm suggest that people continuously create social structure through their actions and interactions; thus, there is no abstract truth or reality because reality exists only as people create it together (Yerby, 1995). Researchers subscribing to a Marxist paradigm believe that social behavior is best understood as a process of conflict, specifically, the conflict between different economic classes (Marx, 1963). We can theorize from more than one paradigm as some are compatible with one another. Of course, not all researchers subscribe to the same paradigm at a given time. Although one paradigm may be very popular, it is only natural that different people see the world differently. When we discuss Standpoint Theory in Chapter 27, we explore a theoretical explanation for this very phenomenon.

Paradigms revolve around three areas, representing three philosophical questions concerning the research enterprise: **ontology**, questions about the nature of reality; **epistemology**, questions about how we know things; and **axiology**, questions about what is worth knowing.

ontology
questions about the
nature of reality
epistemology
questions about how
we know things
axiology
questions about what
is worth knowing

Ontology

Ontological questions focus on the nature of reality and on what we should be studying. The decisions that scholars come to about ontology form the background for their theorizing. Ontological questions have provided many ongoing debates, and we cannot address them all here. However, we wish to map some of the most important characteristics of the notion of ontology as it has been developed in the philosophy of science and adapted for the social sciences.

Ontology is the study of being and nonbeing, or in other words, it is the study of reality. The word *ontology* comes from the Greek and means the science of beings or the general principles of being.

The What Is Ontology? website (www.formalontology.it/section_4.htm) provides the following definition for ontology: "a science or study of being: specifically, a branch of metaphysics relating to the nature and relations of being: a particular system according to which problems of the nature of being are investigated; first philosophy." This definition focuses on the idea that ontology gives us a certain vision of the world and on what constitutes its important features. It is called the first philosophy because it is not possible to philosophize until the nature of reality is determined.

Epistemology

The questions that cluster in the domain of epistemology focus on how we go about knowing and what counts as knowledge. We discuss this area in greater detail in Chapter 4 when we examine research methods—the specific ways that scholars gather and analyze information in their attempt to generate and expand knowledge about communication phenomena. We raise the issue here, however, because it is intimately related to ontology. How researchers see the world, truth, and human nature necessarily influences how they believe they should try to learn about these things. As with ontology, epistemology has generated a great many debates, and our discussion here will only touch the tip of the iceberg. Two epistemologies are worthy of note: the objectivist position and the subjectivist position.

The objectivist epistemology holds that it is possible to explain the world (because there is some type of objective truth that exists apart from our knowing of it) and that as researchers study the world, they accumulate small pieces of information about the truth. The way in which we ultimately learn the truth about social life is through social scientists combining all these small pieces of information. This is why scholars publish their findings and gather at conventions to share their research. In contrast, the subjectivist epistemology rejects the notion that truth exists apart from the knower of truth. Subjectivists believe that the social world is relativistic and "can only be understood from the point of view of the individuals who are directly involved in the activities which are to be studied" (Burrell & Morgan, 1979, p. 5). Thus, objectivists could study the Hirsches by observing them and comparing them to other couples who are similar to them in age, ethnicity, and so forth. Yet, subjectivists would argue that the way to know about the Hirsches is to ask them to explain themselves; subjectivists would want the insiders' viewpoint to permeate anything they conclude about the Hirsch family.

The objectivist approach suggests that theories be sufficiently general to explain many different specific observations or experiences. The subjectivist approach suggests that theories be sufficiently general to guide multiple investigations, allowing different researchers to apply them to a variety of texts for study.

Axiology

The final set of considerations involves axiology, or questions about the place of values in theory and research. Like epistemology, this is a topic that we will return to in Chapter 4 when we address research methods. The traditional scientific position on axiology is that science must be value-free. This position fits with the objectivist epistemology we discussed previously. However, most researchers do not take this extreme position and accept that some subjectivity, in the form of values, informs the research process. The question that is still debated concerns not *whether* values should permeate theory and research but *how* they should.

Here we briefly present three positions on this debate: avoiding values that influence verification, recognizing how values influence the entire research process, and advocating that values should be closely intertwined with scholarly work. The first stance argues that the research process consists of many stages and that values should inform some of these stages but not others. For example, the part of the research enterprise that focuses on theory choice and paradigm considerations must be informed by the values of the researcher. Scholars choose to view a research problem through the lens that they believe accurately describes the world. Thus, some researchers choose theoretical frameworks that are consistent with an ontology of free choice, whereas others choose frameworks that are more lawlike and deterministic. Yet, when they test these theories (the verification stage), then they must eliminate "extra-scientific values from scientific activity" (Popper, 1976, p. 97). As you can see, this stance proposes a very limited role for values.

The second position argues that it is not possible to eliminate values from any part of theorizing and research. In fact, some values are so embedded in researchers' culture that researchers are unconscious that they even hold them. Sandra Bem (1993), for instance, observes that much of the research on differences between women and men was influenced by biases existing at the time. Many feminist scholars argue that social science itself suffers from a male bias (Harding, 1987). Some African American scholars make the same observations about the European American biases that exist in much social scientific research (Houston, 1992). Thomas Nakayama and Robert Krizek (1995) point out that communication researchers often take White for granted as the default race. Thus, the values and assumptions held by those with a European American perspective are never highlighted, questioned, or acknowledged; they simply inform a scholar's process.

The final position argues that not only are values unavoidable, but they are a desirable aspect of the research process. Earlier in this chapter we referred to the goals of theory as including social change. Those who embrace this goal are called critical theorists. In Chapter 4 we discuss this approach further. For now, we wish to clarify that critical theorists support an axiology that advocates seeing theory and research as political acts that call upon scholars to change the status quo. Thus, scholars must contribute to changing conditions rather than simply reporting conditions.

Metatheory

A researcher's paradigm, or worldview, shapes much of the research process. In particular, it affects how communication researchers develop theory. When researchers seek to create theory, they are guided by **metatheory**, or theories about theory. We will review three traditional metatheories: covering law, rules, and systems. The covering law approach and the rules approach represent two extremes, whereas the systems approach provides an intermediate position between the extremes. We must caution that few scholars take the extreme positions sketched out here. Rather, these positions form benchmarks from which researchers anchor their own stances on questions of truth and human nature.

The extremes focus on questions of free will, and they provide us with two different ways to approach theory creation. The **covering law approach** seeks to explain an event in the real world by referring to a general law. Researchers applying a covering law approach believe that communication behavior is governed by forces that are predictable and generalizable. The **rules approach**, at the other end of the ontological continuum, holds that communication behavior is rule governed, not lawlike. The rules approach differs from the covering law approach in that researchers holding the rules approach admit the

metatheory
theory about how to develop theory
covering law approach
a metatheoretical framework suggesting that theories should follow if-then formats and should be universal, invariant statements
rules approach
a metatheoretical framework suggesting that theories should follow a format that lists rules in given contexts and should acknowledge variability across situations, cultures, and time

Table 3.1 Ontological Approaches to Communication

APPROACH	DESCRIPTION/EXAMPLE
Covering Law	Covering law theorists hold that there are fixed relationships between two or more events or objects. Example: Whenever A occurs, B occurs; this is a lawlike statement that expresses a relationship between A and B. These statements are commonly referred to as if-then statements.
Rules	Rules theorists contend that much of human behavior is a result of free choice. People pick the social rules that govern their interactions. Example: In an interaction between co-workers, much of their conversation will be guided by rules of politeness, turn taking, and so on.
Systems	Systems theorists hold that human behavior is part of a system. Example: Think of a family as a system of family relationships rather than individual members. This illuminates the complexity of communication patterns within the family.

cause
an antecedent condition that determines an effect

effect
a condition that inevitably follows a causative condition

systems approach
a metatheoretical framework suggesting that theories should follow a format that maps the systemic properties of a phenomenon; takes the position that people have free will, which is sometimes constrained by systemic factors

possibility that people are free to change their minds, to behave irrationally, to have idiosyncratic meanings for behaviors, and to change the rules. Ultimately, their differences focus on the concept of choice. The covering law model explains human choices by seeking an antecedent condition (usually a **cause**) that determines the choice that is made (usually an **effect**). From the rules model, rule following results from a choice made by the follower but does not necessarily involve antecedent conditions or any aspect of the cause-effect logic of the covering law approach.

A third view, the **systems approach**, subscribes somewhat to the beliefs of the rules approach while also suggesting that people's free will may be constrained by the system in which they operate. Further, this approach acknowledges the impossibility of achieving what the covering law approach requires: laws about human communication that are invariant and general. The systems approach proposes assumptions that are more easily met than those of the covering law approach (Monge, 1973). We now examine each of the three approaches in more detail and provide an overview in Table 3.1.

Covering Law Approach

This term was first introduced by William Dray (1957), a historian who defined *covering law* as that "explanation is achieved, and only achieved, by *subsuming what is to be explained under a general law*" (p. 1 [emphasis in original]). Carl Hempel (1952) expanded the notion by distinguishing three types of covering law explanations: deductive-nomological (D-N), deductive-statistical (D-S), and inductive-statistical (I-S).

D-N explanations refer to universal laws that state all x is y. These laws are not restricted by time or space. However, as new information comes to light, even laws have to be modified. Hempel suggests that if the truth of a law is in doubt, the term *lawlike* should be used.

D-N explanations do not always have to be cause-effect. They may also specify relationships of coexistence. A causal relationship is specified when we say that self-disclosures by one person cause reciprocal self-disclosures from a relational partner. A claim of coexistence merely asserts that two things go together—that is, when one person self-discloses, the other does too—but it does not claim that the first self-disclosure causes the second. It's possible that social norms of reciprocity cause the second self-disclosure or that both disclosures are caused by the environment (an intimate, smoky bar or more alcohol than usual).

Critical attributes of D-N explanations are that they provide an explicit statement of a boundary condition and that they allow **hypotheses,** testable predictions of relationships, of varying levels of specificity to be generated within this boundary condition. Further, because the system is deductive, complete confirmation of theories is never possible. There will always be unexamined instances of the hypothesis.

Deductive-statistical explanations are similar to D-N explanations except that they specify the probability of the relationship in a statistical manner. Where D-N explanations state all x is y, D-S explanations state the probability that x is y. For example, as Berger (1977) asserts, "We can predict with a certain probability that if males and females with certain eye colors have large numbers of children, a certain proportion of those children will have a certain eye color. However, we are *not* in a position to predict what the eye color of a *particular* child will be" (p. 10).

The third type of covering law is the inductive-statistical explanation. This type explains a particular event by employing statistical laws as inductive support for the event. For example, let's assume that high levels of conflict between two people have a high probability of producing a high level of negative feelings between the two people. If we further assume that Mark and Brian have high levels of conflict between them, then we can conclude that Mark and Brian will likely have a high level of negative feelings as well. In this example, the negative feelings between Mark and Brian (that which is to be explained) does not follow with deductive certainty from the statistical law that high levels of conflict produce high levels of negative feelings and does not follow from the statement that Mark and Brian engage in high levels of conflict. Rather, we must use the explanation as inductive support for the phenomenon.

Overall, a covering law approach instructs researchers to search for lawlike generalizations and regularities in human communication. These lawlike generalizations may be culturally bound or may have some other complex relationship with culture. Covering law offers a theory-generating option that aims for complete explanation of a phenomenon. The law, in effect, governs the relationship among phenomena. Figure 3.1 provides a diagram of relationships within the covering law approach.

Rules Approach

This approach assumes that people are typically engaged in intentional, goal-directed behavior and are capable of acting rather than simply being acted upon. We can be restricted by previous choices we have made, by the choices

hypotheses
testable predictions of relationships between concepts that follow the general predictions made by a theory

$$\boxed{\text{D-N}} \quad \text{All } X = Y$$

$$\boxed{\text{D-S}} \quad P(X,Y) = r$$

$$\boxed{\text{I-S}} \quad P(X,Y) = r$$

$$\frac{X_P}{Y_P} = r$$

P = probability
X_P = probability of a particular instance of X
Y_P = probability of a particular instance of Y

Figure 3.1
Covering Law
Relationships

of others, and by cultural and social conditions, but we are conscious and active choice makers. Further, human behavior can be classified into two categories: activities that are stimulus-response behaviors (termed **movements**) and activities that are intentional choice responses (termed **actions**) (Cushman & Pearce, 1977). Rules theorists contend that studying actions is most relevant to theorists.

movements
stimulus-response
behaviors
actions
intentional choice
responses

Rules theorists look inside communities or cultures to get a sense of how people regulate their interaction with others (Shimanoff, 1980). Rules do not require people to act in a certain way; rather, rules refer to the standards or criteria that people use when acting in a particular setting (Cushman & Cahn, 1985). For example, when two people meet, they normally do not begin at an intimate level of exchange. Rather, there is an agreed-upon starting point, and they will delve further into intimacy if the two see the relationship as having a future. The process of meeting another is guided by rules, although these rules are rarely verbally identified by either person. Don Cushman and Barnett Pearce (1977) believe that if the relationship evolves, the rules guiding interactions change. Rules, then, are important benchmarks for the direction of an interaction. Table 3.2 illustrates how rules guide initial encounters of peers in the United States.

Several researchers (Lull, 1982; Wolf, Meyer, & White, 1982) have used a rules-based theoretical framework to study family television viewing behaviors. James Lull (1982) identified three types of rules that govern family television watching. First are **habitual rules,** which are nonnegotiable and are usually instituted by the authority figures in the family. When Roger and Marie tell their children that there can be no television until all homework is checked over by one of them and declared finished for the night, they are establishing a habitual rule. **Parametric rules** are also established by family authority figures, but they are more negotiable than habitual rules. For example, the Marsh family may have a rule that members can engage in extended talk only during commercial

habitual rules
rules that are set by
an authority and are
nonnegotiable
parametric rules
rules that are set by
an authority but are
negotiable

Table 3.2   Rules Governing Initial Peer Encounters

In the first fifteen minutes of an encounter:	*In the second fifteen minutes:*
Politeness should be observed.	Politeness should be observed.
Demographics should be exchanged.	Likes and dislikes can be discussed.
Partners should speak in rough equivalence to each other.	One partner can speak more than another, but avoid dominance.
Interruptions and talk-overs should be minimal.	More interruptions can be tolerated, but avoid dominance.

Theory Application in Groups (TAG)

In small groups, create a theoretical statement that follows covering law, one that follows rules, and one that follows the systems ontology.

range. The thermostat provides a common example illustrating this process. Home heating is usually set at a certain temperature, say 65 degrees. The thermostat will allow a temperature range around 65 before changing anything. Therefore, if the thermostat is set for 65 and the temperature is 65 plus or minus 3 degrees, nothing happens. If the temperature drops below 62 degrees, the heat goes on; if it rises above 68 degrees, the furnace shuts off. In this way, the heating system remains stable. However, if conditions change in the house (for example, the family insulates the attic), the thermostat may need to be recalibrated or set at a slightly lower temperature to accommodate the change. After insulating, the house can be comfortable if the temperature is set at 63 degrees.

Changing the standard (moving the temperature from 65 to 63 degrees) is accomplished through feedback. Feedback, in systems thinking, is positive when it produces change (the thermostat is set differently) and negative when it maintains the status quo (the thermostat remains at 65). When systems change they are called **morphogenic,** and when they stay the same they are called **homeostatic.**

Equifinality Open systems are characterized by the ability to achieve the same goals through different means, or **equifinality** (von Bertalanffy, 1968). This principle applies to human groups in two ways. First, a single group can achieve a goal through many different routes. For example, if a manager wants to increase productivity, he can raise wages, threaten the workers with firing, hire a consultant, or do some combination of the above. There are several ways the manager can reach the goal. Additionally, equifinality implies that different groups can achieve the same goal through multiple pathways. For instance, Dell Computers may achieve profitability by adopting a casual organizational culture, whereas Gateway may achieve profitability by demanding a more formal workplace.

Overall, a systems approach instructs researchers to search for holistic explanations for communication behavior. Systems metatheory offers a theory-generating option that aims to model the phenomenon as a whole, admitting the possibility for change from a variety of outside sources.

morphogenic
a term for changing systems
homeostatic
a term for stable systems
equifinality
a property of systems theory stating that systems can achieve the same goals through different means

Evaluating Communication Theory:
Look Closely, Very Closely

As you read the communication theories in the following chapters, you need some standards for judging their worth. The following criteria are generally accepted as useful measures for evaluating communication theory: scope, logical consistency, parsimony, utility, testability, heurism, and the test of time. We will discuss each of them briefly, and as you read through the book, refer back to this section to judge the theories we present.

Scope

scope
a criterion for evaluating theories; refers to the breadth of communication behaviors covered in the theory

Scope refers to the breadth of communication behaviors covered by the theory. Boundaries are the demarcations of a theory's scope. Although theories should explain enough of communication to be meaningful, they should also have clear boundaries specifying the limits of their scope. Some theories cover a relatively narrow range of behaviors, whereas others try for much larger scope. Uncertainty Reduction Theory (URT), which we discuss in Chapter 9, originally was bounded by initial encounters between strangers. In some ways this suggests a rather limited scope for the theory. However, although the duration of initial encounters is short, it is true that people spend a great deal of time throughout their lives meeting and conversing with new people. Thus, the scope of the theory may seem a bit broader upon reflection. Additionally, since URT was first proposed in 1975, other researchers have expanded the theory to cover developed relationships such as dating and friendship (Planalp & Honeycutt, 1985; Planalp & Rivers, 1988; Planalp, Rutherford, & Honeycutt, 1988) and marriage (Turner, 1992). As the theory has been used by researchers, its scope and boundaries have expanded.

Logical Consistency

logical consistency
a criterion for evaluating theories; refers to the internal logic in the theoretical statements

Simply put, theories should make sense and have an internal **logical consistency** that is clear and not contradictory. Theories should provide us with good explanations that show us how the concepts work together and what results follow from their interactions. Additionally, the claims made by the theory should be consistent with the assumptions of the theory. If a theory is constructed using the covering law approach, it would be inconsistent for the theory to focus on people's choices and idiosyncratic activities.

Parsimony

parsimony
a criterion for evaluating theories; refers to the simplicity of the explanation provided by the theory

Parsimony refers to the simplicity of the explanation provided by the theory. Theories should contain only the number of concepts necessary to explain the phenomenon under consideration. However, because theories of communication and social behavior are dealing with complex phenomena, they may have to be complex themselves. Parsimony requires simplicity without sacrificing completeness.

Utility

utility
a criterion for evaluating theories; refers to the theory's usefulness or practical value

This criterion refers to the theory's usefulness, or practical value. A good theory has **utility** in that it tells us a great deal about communication and human behavior. It allows us to understand some element of communication that was previously unclear. It weaves together pieces of information in such a way that we are able to see a pattern that was previously unclear to us. In so doing, theories can shape and change our behavior.

Testability

Testability refers to our ability to investigate a theory's accuracy. One of the biggest issues involved in testability concerns the specificity of the concepts that are central to the theory. For example, as we discuss in Chapter 11, Social Exchange Theory is predicated on the concepts of costs and rewards. The theory predicts that people will engage in behaviors that they find rewarding and avoid behaviors that are costly to them. However, the theory does not clearly define costs and rewards. In fact, they are defined in a circular fashion: Behaviors that people engage in repeatedly are rewarding, and those that they avoid are costly. You can see how difficult it is to test the central prediction of Social Exchange Theory given this circular definition. This criterion is more useful in theories framed from an objectivist epistemology than those from a subjectivist epistemology.

testability
a criterion for evaluating theories; refers to our ability to test the accuracy of a theory's claims

Heurism

Heurism refers to the amount of research and new thinking that is stimulated by the theory. Theories are judged to be good to the extent that they generate insights and new research. Although not all theories produce a great deal of research, an effective theory prompts some research activity. For example, the theory we discuss in Chapter 21, Cultural Studies, came from many diverse disciplines and has stimulated research programs in English, anthropology, social psychology, and communication.

heurism
a criterion for evaluating theories; refers to the amount of research and new thinking stimulated by the theory

Test of Time

The final criterion, the **test of time,** can be used only after some time has passed since the theory's creation. Are these theories still generating research or have they been discarded as outmoded? Deciding whether a theory has withstood the test of time is often arbitrary. For instance, if a theory was conceptualized and tested in the 1970s but has remained dormant in the literature for over a decade and is now being reintegrated into research, has this theory satisfied the test of time? Judging this criterion is often a subjective process. Further, it is not a criterion that can be used to assess a new theory.

test of time
a criterion for evaluating theories; refers to the theory's durability over time

Conclusion

This chapter introduced the concept of theory and its usefulness for examining communication behaviors. We have provided an initial definition of *theory* as well as explored some of the goals of theory and the relationship between theory and experience. We discussed the frameworks for theories,

T*I*P

Theory * Into * Practice

Silvia Cardoso, a behavioral biologist, has been researching laughter. Some of her findings were reported in a recent issue of the *Utne Reader*. Cardoso found that women smile more than they laugh. She also affirmed that the old adage "laughter is the best medicine" is true. For example, she observes that laughing is exercise that activates the cardiovascular system and releases brain endorphins. Further, she asserts that laughter acts as a social lubricant. She found that only 10 to 20 percent of laughter is a response to humor. The rest of the time, laughter is communication sending messages of happiness and social bonding.

Cardoso also discovered that laughter transcends cultural boundaries. For example, in all cultures "socially dominant individuals, from bosses to tribal chiefs, use laughter to control their subordinates. . . . Laughter might be a form of asserting power by controlling the emotional climate of the group, and it also has a dark side. There are theories that laughter and aggression have common origins; some kinds of laughter in primates apparently are threatening—just look at the way they bare their teeth. That may explain why being laughed at is so unpleasant" (p. 24).

Source: Petit-Zerman, 2002.

TIP Follow-up
How is theoretical thinking exhibited in this example? What concepts and relationships are specified in outlining the theoretical aspects of Cardoso's research on laughter?

which consist of intellectual traditions and paradigms. We detailed three metatheoretical perspectives, and we provided criteria for evaluating the theories that you will encounter in this book. As we seek to understand communication, we need to turn to theory to help us organize the information that research provides.

Yet, we must realize the limitations of theory. Communication interactions consist of multiple perspectives, and theories are, at best, only partial explanations of the multiplicity of social life. We can overcome this limit to an extent by acknowledging the partiality of our theories and opening ourselves to diverse points of view. As Yerby (1995) states, our ability to listen to the perspectives of others while at the same time voicing our own perspectives ultimately contributes to our ability to understand how we are connected to others.

Discussion Starters

1. Do you think that a theory can help us understand the communication behavior of Emile and Irene Hirsch? Why or why not? Use examples in your response.

2. Provide some examples of ways you think like a theorist in your daily life.

3. How would you distinguish between covering laws and systems approaches to theory building? Try to be specific and provide examples in your answer.

4. Do you see communication behavior as being lawlike or rule governed? Explain your answer.

5. How do your own paradigm and metatheory affect your thinking? Be specific.

6. Why is it important to evaluate communication theory? Can you think of any other criteria for evaluating theory besides those listed in the chapter?

Terms for Review

theory
grand theory
mid-range theory
narrow theory
concepts
nominal concepts
real concepts
relationships
paradigms
ontology
epistemology
axiology
metatheory
covering law approach
rules approach
cause
effect
systems approach
hypotheses
movements
actions
habitual rules

parametric rules
tactical rules
wholeness
interdependence
subsystems
suprasystems
hierarchy
boundaries
openness
calibration
feedback
morphogenic
homeostatic
equifinality
scope
logical consistency
parsimony
utility
testability
heurism
test of time

 ## Online Learning Center

Visit the Online Learning Center at www.mhhe.com/west2. Use the multiple-choice and true/false quizzes to help you prepare for exams, and the glossary, crossword puzzles, and flashcards to further your knowledge of key terms.

CHAPTER 4

Understanding the Research Process

Rolanda Nash

Rolanda Nash had to hurry to class from work. She seemed always to be running late these days. She had a lot on her mind since she had decided to divorce Anton and move from Sheridan, Wyoming to Chicago. She was pretty sure Anton was finally going to leave her alone now and just cooperate with the divorce. After her relationship with him, she felt she would never trust another man again. Meanwhile, she had to complete six credits in order to graduate and keep the new job she had secured in Chicago. In addition to doing her schoolwork, Rolanda was working thirty hours a week for one of her professors, Dr. Stevens. Dr. Stevens was testing a theory about communication behaviors, and so far it had been a fun job for Rolanda. Stevens was interested in examining Communication Accommodation Theory in an organizational setting. The professor had sent Rolanda into two different organizations with a tape recorder. Rolanda's task was to tape naturally occurring conversations between subordinates and managers. Stevens called it water cooler conversations, but so far Rolanda had not seen a single water cooler!

Rolanda thought it was very challenging to capture natural conversations. Although Stevens had obtained permission for her to record conversations in the organizations, some people recognized Rolanda and were self-conscious about talking around her. Additionally, neither of the two organizations employed many African Americans. Rolanda felt she stuck out as she walked through the hallways. But she was used to that. In most of her university classes she was the only African American woman. At first, it really bothered her, but she was used to it by now. She was hoping Chicago would be a better experience.

Now, if she could only get enough conversations to satisfy Dr. Stevens, she could go home to tackle her English assignment. Stevens hadn't really told her how many conversations she needed. Rolanda was hoping ten would be enough. That's all she had gotten in five days of taping. Dr. Stevens had mentioned last week that when Rolanda was finished taping, she would probably be sending her back to the organizations to do some follow-up interviews with the people she had taped. Rolanda wondered how that would work out. She hoped she could get what Dr. Stevens wanted.

Like all of us, Rolanda experiences the effects of theorizing in many aspects of her life. First, her job is one of collecting data for theory testing. In this, Rolanda (and her boss, Dr. Stevens) are following the traditional scientific model. This model begins with Dr. Stevens's interest in the phenomenon of communication accommodation in the workplace. In other words, the traditional model begins with theory. Communication Accommodation (CA), a theory we profile in Chapter 29 refers to the process of conforming one's speaking style to that of one's partner. Communication Accommodation is the theoretical framework from which Dr. Stevens begins to speculate. Because the theory suggests certain relationships and the existence of certain behaviors, Stevens has a guide for these speculations. The theory supports a series of specific guesses, or hypotheses, that can be tested by Stevens's work. As we commented in Chapter 3, the theory is general, whereas the observations Stevens makes and her hypotheses are specific. For example, the theory is not bounded by the context of the workplace; it generalizes to communication accommodation in all contexts. Yet, Stevens narrows her study to the specific area of communication accommodation in organizational life.

After Stevens has hypothesized about what she will find in the workplace regarding accommodations between workers and managers based on the theory, she then must **operationalize** all the concepts. This means she needs to specify how she will measure the concepts that are important to her study. In this process, Dr. Stevens turns the abstract concepts of the theory into concrete variables that can be observed and measured. For example, status difference is a critical notion in the theoretical framework, so Stevens specifies to Rolanda how she should measure this. In this case, measurement will be based on job title. Rolanda has to discover the job title for each of the people she observes and then compare those titles to a chart Stevens has given her classifying job titles into the two categories of "supervisor" and "subordinate." This seems like a fairly straightforward means to operationalize the notion of status, but there may be instances where it is not a perfect operationalization. For instance, a lower-level employee who has worked for the company for many years might hold more status than a middle manager who has only recently arrived and is just learning the corporate culture. Additionally, women managers often report some problems with achieving the status expected from their job title. You can see how concepts that are more complex and abstract, like love and intimacy, for example, would be even more difficult to operationalize than occupational status.

The next step in the traditional scientific model sends Rolanda into the two organizations to make **observations** and collect **data** (in this case, the conversations and the job titles). When Rolanda returns with the tapes, Dr. Stevens will have to **code** the conversations, again using operationalizations for terms such as *convergence* (making your speech similar to your partner's) and *divergence* (making your speech patterns dissimilar to your partner's). Some types of data do not need extensive coding to analyze. For example, if Dr. Stevens operationalized status based on income and then provided respondents with a survey asking them to indicate the category for their salary, these data would not need the same type of coding required in the Communication Accommodation study. The income categories could simply be numbered consecutively. In contrast, the conversations have to be listened to repeatedly in order to determine whether a given comment converges with or diverges from the comment preceding it.

In the example of Dr. Stevens's study, the coded data are used to test Stevens's hypotheses about communication accommodation in the workplace. Dr. Stevens will see if the speculations she made based on the theory's logic hold true in the conversations that Rolanda taped. This traditional process, known

operationalize
making an abstract concept measurable and observable

observations
focused examination within a context of interest; may be guided by hypotheses and/or research questions

data
the raw materials collected by the researcher to answer the questions posed in the research and/or to test a hypothesis

code
converting raw data to a category system

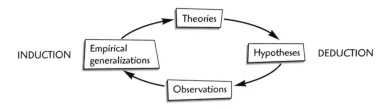

Figure 4.1
The Wheel of Science
Source: Loosely adapted from several conceptual drawings, and reduced from the concept on page18
of Walter L. Wallace, THE LOGIC OF SCIENCE IN SOCIOLOGY (New York: Aldine de Gruyter, 1971).
Copyright © 1971 by Walter L. Wallace. Renewed 1999.

scientific method
the traditional
method for doing
research involving
controlled observa-
tions and analysis to
test the principles of
a theory

deductive logic
moving from the gen-
eral to the specific

inductive logic
moving from the
specific to the general

grounded theory
theory induced from
data collection and
analysis in a study

as the **scientific method,** follows **deductive logic** in that Stevens moved from the general (the theory) to specific instances (the actual conversations gathered in two workplaces). If Stevens had used **inductive logic,** she would have asked Rolanda to record many more conversations. Stevens would have refrained from hypothesizing, or guessing, about what she might find in advance of the data collection. Then she and Rolanda would have listened to their tapes, trying to find some type of pattern that best explained what they heard. Finally, Stevens would have generalized based on her observations.

The deductive approach allows Stevens to test a specific prediction, or hypothesis, generated from a generalization, or theory. The results of this testing allow modifications and corrections to the theory. The inductive approach enables Stevens to gather many specific instances in the hopes of being able to generalize, or create, theory. This approach is called **grounded theory.** The grounded theory approach does not seek to test hypotheses to support theory; instead, "it is discovered, developed, and provisionally verified through systematic data collection and analysis of data" (Young, 1998, p. 26) relating to the phenomenon of interest. In this manner, the components of the research process (theory, data collection, and data analysis) are in reciprocal relationship with one another.

Although some researchers approach their work strictly as hypothesis testers and some approach it more as theory generators, in practice most weave back and forth between the two. Walter Wallace (1971) suggests that the research process is circular, moving continuously between induction and deduction. Researchers refer to this as the wheel of science (Figure 4.1). Additionally, as Wallace noted elsewhere (1983), this process is endless. "Each step presupposes that all the others have been taken before it—presumably at lower levels of understanding and control. Thus, although one may *consciously* start a given analysis by making certain predictions, one always has in mind (as largely unconscious background assumptions) certain prior explanations, empirical generalizations, tests, outcomes, implementations, and so on" (p. 358).

Further, Wallace (1983) has expanded this wheel of science to include two types of research: pure and applied (Figure 4.2). In **pure research,** researchers are guided by knowledge-generating goals. They are interested in testing or generating theory for its own sake and for the sake of advancing our knowledge

pure research
research to generate
knowledge

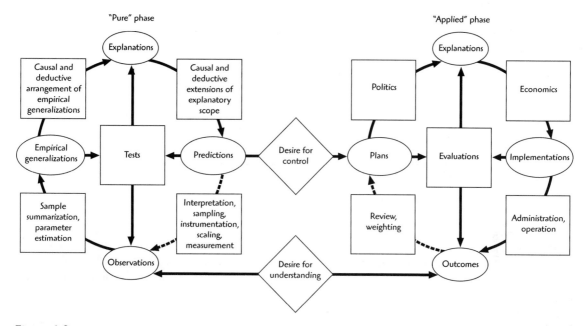

Figure 4.2
The Procedures of Scientific Analysis
Source: Reprinted with permission from Walter L. Wallace, PRINCIPLES OF SCIENTIFIC SOCIOLOGY
(New York: Aldine de Gruyter, 1983), page 359. Copyright © 1983 by Walter L. Wallace.

in an area. In **applied research,** researchers wish to solve specific problems with the knowledge they or other researchers have generated. Figure 4.2 illustrates the relationship between these two types of research goals and processes. In our example of Dr. Stevens's research, we see her performing pure research. If a specific organization hired Dr. Stevens to consult with them to improve employee morale, however, her research would become applied.

In the example of Rolanda and Dr. Stevens, we have seen how Rolanda's job utilizes theory and how theory and research relate in Dr. Stevens's study. Additionally, just as we discussed in Chapter 3, Rolanda operates as an intuitive or naive scientist in her daily life. An intuitive scientist follows many of the same processes and reasoning patterns that trained scientists do, just not in as explicit or rigorous a fashion. Usually, intuitive scientists follow inductive logic: They experience something and then generalize from that. So when Rolanda concludes that all men are untrustworthy, she is inducing a general statement about all men from her experiences with one man, Anton. This is similar to the process a researcher might follow; however, a social scientist would not make hasty generalizations, or move to theory, on the basis of one observation.

Intuitive science proceeds on the basis of deductive logic as well, as Rolanda's theory about cities demonstrates. She believes that larger cities are more diverse than smaller ones. As she moves from Sheridan to Chicago, she will test that theory with her observations about life in Chicago. Here again, the issue of numbers of observations is important. How long does Rolanda have to live in Chicago before she can be satisfied that her theory is correct? Does

applied research
research to solve a
problem or create a
policy

she have to sample life in other large cities to substantiate her theory, or is Chicago alone a sufficient observation? This is very similar to Dr. Stevens's concerns in her study. When Rolanda wonders about the number of conversations that she is collecting for Dr. Stevens, she focuses on a key point: How many instances do you need to observe before you can come to a conclusion? There are no absolute answers to this question although there are some standards that are often accepted by practicing researchers. Ultimately, social science depends on the arguments that researchers are able to muster to convince readers that they have made good observations and used careful logic.

Observations and logic combine in many patterns beyond the deductive and inductive that we have outlined here. There are almost as many research methods as there are researchers, and there is room for a great deal of creativity in the research process. In this chapter we outline four of the standard methods used by communication researchers to test theoretical propositions or to generate theoretical statements. First, however, we discuss three general approaches to scholarly work that ground researchers' processes. As we described in Chapter 3, issues about *how* to gather data belong in the domain of epistemology. But as our discussion indicated, epistemological issues are intertwined with concerns about ontology and axiology.

Approaches to Knowing

The decisions about what theory to use in research, what type of logic to use, and what type of method to apply are conditional on the three philosophical questions that we reviewed in Chapter 3. The first question concerns ontology, or views of human nature. In Chapter 3, we concluded that a researcher's notion of how much choice and free will humans possess will influence the research process. The second question centers on epistemology, or how we know what we know. Whereas ontology addresses the question of what human nature is, epistemology approaches the question of what truth is and how to go about finding knowledge. The third question deals with issues of axiology, or what is worth knowing. This taps into the question of how much values should affect research, or to what degree should subjectivity enter into the research process?

In our discussion in Chapter 3, we noted that researchers' answers to these questions are based on their paradigm, or worldview. As you can guess, there are spirited disagreements among researchers about issues of worldview. David Klein and James White (1996) discuss three different philosophies of science that present three separate ontologic, epistemologic, and axiologic interpretations. Adherence to any one of these philosophies influences the way to approach theory and research in communication. Klein and White label these three philosophies positivistic, interpretive, and critical. These three philosophies conform to the three perspectives (empiricism, hermeneutics, and critical theory) that Arthur Bochner (1985) reviewed while discussing the study of interpersonal communication. As we mentioned in Chapter 3, these philosophies are presented in extreme form, and many researchers would not identify themselves as subscribing to the extremes. Most people find a comfortable middle ground based on these philosophies that represents their worldview.

The Positivistic, or Empirical, Approach

The **positivistic,** or **empirical, approach,** assumes that there are objective truths that can be uncovered and that the process of inquiry that discovers these truths can be, at least in part, value-neutral. This tradition advocates the methods of the natural sciences, with the goal of constructing general laws governing human interactions. The researcher in this intellectual tradition strives to be objective and works for **control,** or direction over the important concepts in the theory. In other words, when the researcher moves to the plane of observation, he or she carefully structures the situation so that only one element varies, enabling the researcher to make relatively definitive statements about that element. For instance, if Dr. Stevens worked in the positivistic tradition, she would institute many more controls than we described. Further, the number of observations would not be left to chance or to Rolanda's schedule. Dr. Stevens would have calculated the number of conversations she needed to support statistics testing relationships among status and communication accommodation.

positivistic (empirical) approach
an approach assuming the existence of objective reality and value-neutral research

control
the researcher's ability to direct the important concepts in the research process

The Interpretive, or Hermeneutic, Approach

The **interpretive,** or **hermeneutic, approach** views truth as subjective and co-created by the participants. And the researcher him- or herself is clearly one of the participants. There is less emphasis on objectivity because complete objectivity is seen as impossible. However, this does not mean that research in this tradition has to rely totally on what participants say with no outside judgment by the researcher. Martyn Hammersley (1992), for example, advocates a "subtle realism" that suggests that researchers "monitor [their] assumptions and the inferences [they] make on the basis of them" (p. 53). In this subtle realism, Hammersley suggests that research can find a way to be reasonably objective. In this tradition, the researcher believes that values are relevant in the study of communication and that researchers need to be aware of their own values and to clearly state them for readers, because values will naturally permeate the research. These researchers are not concerned with control and the ability to generalize across many people as much as they are interested in rich descriptions about the people they study. For example, if Dr. Stevens operated in this tradition, she would not be content with her own analysis of the conversations. She might invite the participants to read the transcripts of their conversations so that they could tell her whether they were trying to accommodate to their partners. Stevens would probably be interested in the participants' explanations for why they changed (or did not change) their speech patterns as they conversed with superiors or subordinates in the workplace. For researchers in this tradition, theory is best induced from the observations and experiences the researcher shares with the respondents.

interpretive (hermeneutic) approach
an approach viewing truth as subjective and stressing the participation of the researcher in the research process

The Critical Approach

Finally, Klein and White (1996) discuss the **critical approach,** where an understanding of knowledge relates to power. As Bochner (1985) notes, this tradition "assumes that science cannot exist without ideology" (p. 46). In this tradition,

critical approach
an approach stressing the researcher's responsibility to change the inequities in the status quo

researchers believe that those in power shape knowledge in ways that work to perpetuate the status quo. Thus, powerful people work at keeping themselves in power, which requires silencing minority voices questioning the distribution of power and the power holders' version of truth. Patricia Hill Collins (1991) speaks from this tradition when she says that "the tension between the suppression of Black women's ideas and our intellectual activism in the face of that suppression, comprises the politics of Black feminist thought" (pp. 5–6). Black feminists are not the only researchers who are comfortably rooted in the critical tradition; Marxists, postmodernists, and feminists of all types, among others, also work from this intellectual tradition. For critical researchers, it is generally important to change the status quo to resolve power imbalances and to give voice to those who have been silenced by the power structure.

Some critical theorists, notably Stuart Hall (1981), whose work we feature in Chapter 21, have commented that power imbalances may not always be the result of intentional strategies on the part of the powerful. Rather, ideology, or "those images, concepts, and premises which provide the frameworks through which we represent, interpret, understand and 'make sense' of some aspect of social existence" (Hall, 1981, p. 31), is often "produced and reproduced" accidentally. For example, this may come about when certain images of masculinity work to sell a product. When advertisers observe this success, they continue creating ads with these images. In this fashion, the images of masculinity become entrenched in society. Thus, although the powerful are interested and invested in staying in power, they may not be fully aware of what they do to silence minority voices.

Using a critical approach, Dr. Stevens might bring some of the following questions to her research: How is the relationship between workers of differing statuses communicatively constructed? Does convergence happen unequally based on status? Are there other status differences that impact communication accommodation besides occupation? How can we change the prevailing power structures to improve the inequities we observe in the workplace?

We can see that each tradition or philosophy suggests something different about the definition of *truth* and the best method for searching for truth. Additionally, there are other intellectual traditions we have not reviewed that entail different values, goals, and methods. Intellectual traditions influence how given researchers try to understand, explain, predict, or change communication. When researchers pick a theory to guide them that is rooted in one of these traditions, they also get all the intellectual trappings that come along with the tradition. As we have noted, people call the trappings a paradigm because they provide people with a lens for seeing and making sense of the world they inhabit.

Our views of the world—answers to questions about what is the nature of humans, what is the best way to gather knowledge, and what is the relationship between values and knowledge—together form a foundation to guide us as we think about the questions of our lives and strive to discover the answers. In other words, our paradigm shapes our choices of theories for explaining communication behavior and our choices of methods for investigating questions relevant to those theories. Yet, it is also true that the scholarly process itself

In small groups, create a research approach for studying the following question: What communication strategies do people engage in when initiating the breakup of a romantic relationship? Label your approach as either quantitative, qualitative, or a combination and explain what ontological and axiological assumptions guided your choices.

shapes our paradigm. As we think about communication and as we pursue the answers to our questions about it, we may modify our beliefs about the nature of truth, the utility of objectivity, or the necessity for social change. Thus, paradigms evolve and have a somewhat reciprocal relationship with the research process. We now turn our attention to the specific ways of gathering knowledge about communication, or research methods. You will see how some methods seem better suited to one worldview than to others.

Methods of Inquiry

Many researchers divide research methods into two main categories: quantitative and qualitative. Although that may be overly simplistic in light of what scholars actually do, it provides a starting point for our discussion. **Quantitative methods** require researchers to gather observations that can be quantified (converted to numbers) and then to analyze the numbers. The analysis provides the basis for an argument about the observations' meaning relative to a theoretical position. **Qualitative methods** ask researchers to analyze the topics of their study through sense-making tools like stories, myths, and themes. These tools help researchers understand how people make sense of their experiences. Qualitative methods do not depend on statistical analysis to support an interpretation but rather require researchers to make a rhetorical appeal or a reasoned argument for their findings. Quantitative methods are considered more appropriate for researchers who embrace a positivistic or empirical worldview and qualitative methods more appropriate for interpretive and critical researchers.

In practice, it is a bit more complicated than this, and occasionally researchers blend methodologies from both the quantitative and qualitative categories. This is referred to as **triangulation,** or approaching the question with more than one method. Although triangulating is useful, it is sometimes difficult to achieve for two reasons. First, researchers are usually trained in only one methodology, and it is difficult to learn a new set of methods on the job. But, perhaps more important, researchers believe that the two categories of methods represent different epistemologies, ontologies, and axiologies. Thus, it would be difficult for a researcher who believes in the utility of control and the possibility of discovering universal truth to adopt interpretive and critical methods that ignore issues of researcher control and support multiple truths. Conversely, a researcher who focuses on giving voice to her respondents would

quantitative methods
methods that require data to be converted to numbers and subjected to statistical analyses

qualitative methods
methods that require data to be interpreted through sense-making analyses

triangulation
an approach to research involving multiple methods

69

Calvin and Hobbes

by Bill Watterson

recoil at speaking for them by analyzing their words without concern for their
interpretations. Sometimes researchers employ multiple methods, or triangu-
late, without trying to merge ontological assumptions. For example, when
Stacy Young (1998) examined how communication networks in organizations
affect women employees, she used multiple data-gathering methods: direct conversation and interviews, unobtrusive observation, and participant observation. Yet, all these methods reflected the subjectivist perspective that Young
brought to the study.

To give you a brief glimpse at the range of research methods available, we
will review two popular quantitative methods—surveys and experiments—
and two well-regarded qualitative methods—depth interviews and textual
analysis. Keep in mind that there are many other methods for conducting
communication research; we are simply illustrating these four to get you started
in understanding the research process.

Surveys

Many researchers wishing to use quantitative methods opt for survey research.
Survey research is a form of data collection that uses some sort of questionnaire
administered to a sample of people. The responses given enable researchers to
draw conclusions about the entire population the respondents represent. For
example, when Dr. Stevens wants to find out how managers and employees
communicate, she is interested in the population of employed people. When she
chooses two specific organizations and a certain number of workers and managers from each, she is drawing a sample group from the entire population.

Surveys are a very old research technique. Earl Babbie notes that the Bible
contains a reference to God instructing Moses and Eleazar to "take a census of
all the congregation of the people of Israel, from twenty old and upward"
(Num. 26:1–2, cited in Babbie, 1995, p. 256). You probably have been a respondent in survey research and perhaps you have even constructed a survey of
your own at some time.

Typically, survey research consists of a researcher administering some type
of a standardized questionnaire to a sample of respondents. The questionnaires
may require directives from the researcher or they may be self-administered,

survey research
a specific research
method asking partic-
ipants to respond to
written questionnaires

meaning that once the researcher gets the questionnaire to the respondent, all the information is provided for the respondent to fill in without any guidance or instruction from the researcher. There are various types of questionnaires, including paper and pencil type; telephone interviews, which consist of a series of closed-ended questions similar to what you would find on the paper and pencil type; and face to face in a structured interview format. Surveys may be administered in classrooms or other public facilities to groups of people, or researchers may give surveys individually. Surveys may also be given to respondents to fill out in their own homes, to be returned to the researcher at a later time.

Self-administered surveys are often sent to the respondents through the mail. The researcher has to depend on the respondents to return the completed questionnaire. Researchers utilize a variety of clever ways to ensure a high return rate for mailed questionnaires. These include providing stamped, self-addressed envelopes, making the questionnaire a self-mailer so that envelopes are not needed, including a monetary incentive, and administering follow-up mailings to nonrespondents as needed.

Survey research is best suited to questions where the individual is the **unit of analysis**, or object of study. For example, Dr. Stevens's work focuses on a dyadic phenomenon, accommodation. This is true because accommodation can occur only when more than one person is present. Thus, Dr. Stevens chose to send Rolanda to observe the employees talking to each other. Rather than obtaining survey information from one person at a time, it was important for Dr. Stevens to get a sense of the dyad, because that was her unit of analysis. Although individuals can give information about groups to which they belong, such as families and organizations, researchers have to keep in mind that the data generated are from individuals, reflecting what one member reports about the family, not what the whole family reports about itself, for example.

unit of analysis
the specific object of study; may be an individual, a family, an organization, and so forth

Surveys are very useful for collecting data from a large population. When researchers are interested in information about a population that is too large to observe directly, surveys are useful methods for reflecting the population as a whole. Public opinion polls such as Gallup and Roper are able to sample carefully to determine the opinions of all people in the United States, for instance.

As an example of survey research, let's examine a study conducted by Kory Floyd and Mark Morman on the nature of communication in men's relationships with their sons (Floyd & Morman, 2001). The researchers were interested in positive interaction patterns between fathers and sons, specifically the exchange of affectionate communication within the relationship. The researchers were guided by two theories: Affection Exchange Theory and the Theory of Discriminative Parental Solicitude. Using these theoretical frames, they hypothesized the following: Men communicate more affection to biological sons than to stepsons; men communicate more affection to adopted sons than to stepsons; and affectionate communication between fathers and sons is directly related to their closeness, their satisfaction with their relationships, and their degree of positive involvement in each other's lives.

To come to their findings, the researchers had to analyze the responses that the 384 participants provided. They did this by using statistical tests to determine the relationships among the variables of interest to them. For example, to test the first hypothesis, they had to judge whether relationship type (biological, step, or adoptive) made a difference in affectionate communication. They found that it was a significant relationship for verbal and nonverbal affection.

To test these three hypotheses, the researchers conducted two studies involving 182 fathers of at least one son and 101 father–son dyads. The participants were relatively evenly distributed with regard to the types of relationships that Floyd and Morman hypothesized about (biological, step, adoptive). In the first study, the 182 men filled out questionnaires that were mailed to them with a postage-paid return envelope. In the second study, the same questionnaires were mailed to father–son dyads who were asked to fill them out separately and return them.

The questionnaires contained a variety of question sets that were geared toward measuring the concepts of interest: affectionate communication (measured by a 19-item Likert-type questionnaire including items like "we say I love you"), relational closeness (measured by a scale that depicts relationships with overlapping circles, each of which represents different degrees of overlap and participants choose the one that best illustrates their relationship), positive relational involvement (measured by a 15-item Likert-type scale including items that assess how much time the fathers and sons spend together), and father–son satisfaction (measured by a nine-item Likert-type scale with items such as "my relationship with my son is just the way I'd want it to be"). Likert-type scales ask respondents to indicate on a scale of 1 to 7 (or 1 to 5) their agreement with the statements.

Floyd and Morman found support for their hypotheses in the first study, providing confirmation for both of the theories they utilized. They conclude that their findings support the logic of Affection Exchange Theory and the Theory of Discriminative Parental Solicitude. If there were no relationship between affection and relationship type, we would expect the test of the relationship to show nothing (or a null relationship) at least 95 times out of 100. When the tests indicate that the relationship is greater than what we would expect to find 95 times out of 100, we say that it is **statistically significant** at the .05 level.

Survey research is a useful methodology that allows for a certain measure of researcher control because the researcher shapes the questions and each respondent receives the same questions in the same format. Additionally, self-administered surveys make large samples feasible. Thus, researchers in the positivist, or empiricist, tradition should feel comfortable with survey research because it fits rather well with many of their metatheoretical assumptions about the nature of people and the nature of truth. Perhaps researchers in qualitative traditions would feel more hesitant about utilizing surveys to answer their questions about communication behavior.

Experiments

Experimental research is a type of investigation that requires a researcher to systematically manipulate variables: the **independent variable,** a concept of interest that is presumed to have effects on another variable, and the **dependent variable,**

statistically significant
a finding indicating the presence of a relationship at a rate greater than chance

experimental research
a specific research method where researchers manipulate conditions; often done in a laboratory setting

independent variable
a concept of interest that is presumed to have effects on another variable

dependent variable
a concept of interest that is presumed to vary as a result of the independent variable

a concept that is presumed to vary because of the independent variable. Variables are concepts such as education, gender, communication apprehension, and deception. In Dr. Stevens's research, communication accommodation and occupation are variables.

Further, variables have levels (in other words, they vary). Communication apprehension, for instance, is usually measured on three levels: high, moderate, and low. Occupation is a variable with levels consisting of job titles such as teacher, attorney, contractor, plumber, and so forth. Sex (or gender) is a variable we measure on two levels: female and male. When we say variables are independent or dependent, we are postulating a relationship between them. If we use gender as the independent variable in an experiment and communication apprehension as the dependent variable, we are saying that fear of communicating varies depending on whether a person is male or female. The opposite would not be presumed to be true; people's gender does not depend on how apprehensive they are. In this example, gender is independent of communication apprehension, whereas communication apprehension depends on gender.

Experiments involve the researcher taking some type of action (the manipulation) and then observing the results of that action on the dependent variable. Research by Judee Burgoon and her colleagues on interpersonal deception illustrates the experimental approach (Burgoon, Buller, Guerrero, Afifi, & Feldman, 1996). These researchers were interested in how people specifically accomplish deception and in whether their targets, or receivers, recognize the changes that deceivers, or senders, make in order to deceive. They generated three hypotheses deduced from Interpersonal Deception Theory, which proposes that deceivers use five separate strategies to create credible but untrue messages. Their first hypothesis specified that deceivers would use these strategies, and their other two hypotheses referred to how receivers would hear deception compared to truthfulness. Hypothesis 2 asserted that receivers would respond more positively to the truth, and hypothesis 3 contended that receivers would notice and respond differently to the five strategies of deception.

The experiment to test the hypotheses involved forty adults (twenty-one men and nineteen women) from a metropolitan southwestern community who volunteered to come to a lab setting to participate in mock interviews. Six undergraduate students were employed to observe the interviews and rate the interviewees. The undergraduates were not aware of the experimenters' interests or of the instructions to the interviewees. Participants were asked to role play two interviews. In the first one they were instructed to be completely truthful, and in the second one they were told to be truthful in the first two answers but thereafter to engage in deception. The interviewers for all the interviews were pairs of men or pairs of women, so the participants had same-sex interviewers for both the truthful and the deceptive interviews. The interviewers were trained to control the interview and to be consistent across multiple interviews.

You can see that the researchers' goal was to keep everything constant except the deception/truthfulness variable. In this way they hoped to be able to measure whether participants were deceived in the ways predicted by the theory and whether observers were able to detect the strategies that deceivers used. Their results supported their contentions in the main, although the data did not confirm every hypothesis.

Experimental research is well suited to the ontology of covering law, objectivist epistemology, and axiology that advocates objectivity in some stages of the research process. Because experimental research relies on control and researcher manipulation without much concern for the qualitative input of the research participants, it is usually not the method chosen by proponents of the interpretive or critical traditions. Additionally, as you noticed in our description of Burgoon and her colleagues' study, experiments are often performed in a laboratory setting. In this fashion, researchers can exert more control over the environment. But many researchers believe that this is an artificial context for testing theory and theory building.

Depth Interviews

depth interviews
semistructured or un-structured interviews lasting at least one hour aimed at collecting rich descriptions from respondents

Depth interviews are, like surveys, a method that allows interviewers to question respondents in the hopes of obtaining information about a phenomenon of interest. However, they differ from surveys in many significant ways. First, depth interviews are, at most, semistructured by the interviewer. They are seen by researchers as a collaboration between interviewer and participant, wherein what the participant wants to discuss is at least as important as what the interviewer had expected to discuss. Researchers employing depth interviews are interested in the directions in which respondents wish to take the interview. They are not as concerned with testing hypotheses as they are in finding out about the experiences of the respondents.

Second, depth interviews typically last between one and three hours. Researchers are more interested in obtaining rich, thick description than they are in collecting information from hundreds of respondents. Further, depth interviews are generally conducted in person. It may be possible to conduct depth interviews on the Internet (Garner, 1999), but this is a new technique, and typically personal contact is preferred.

ethnography
a specific research method where re-searchers immerse themselves in participants' lives, aiming to describe people's culturally distinct patterns of communication

Depth interviews are often used together with or as a part of ethnographic research. Gerry Philipsen (1989) notes that **ethnography** is a description of people's culturally distinctive patterns of communication. He observes that this description is derived after the researcher has spent a great deal of time living among the people and observing and gathering information from them. Thus, depth interviews are useful tools in ethnography. In some senses, Rolanda's observations in the two organizations constitute ethnographic research, and Dr. Stevens's plans for the follow-up interviews may involve this in-depth approach. Although depth interviews and ethnography are not identical methods, the two are compatible and may work together.

Sandra Petronio, Lisa Flores, and Michael Hecht (1997) published an essay making use of depth interview data and using qualitative methods to analyze the data. Petronio and her colleagues engaged in depth interviews with thirty-eight children and adolescents (thirty-two girls and six boys), ranging in age from 7 to 18 years old. These children had all been sexually abused, and the researchers were interested in "how sexually abused children regulate their privacy boundaries when they are deciding to disclose to others" (p. 103).

The researchers examined the transcripts of the interviews and identified five categories that the children used to judge whether to disclose to another.

They found that children disclosed based on credibility, supportiveness, advocacy, strength, and protectiveness. After discussing these five categories, the authors concluded, "As adults, we need to hear these voices, to pay attention to their calls, and to acknowledge our own fears of involvement. . . . We need to let the children's logic prevail" (p. 111). Petronio and her colleagues are interested in giving voice to those who may have been silenced, and their article contains many quotes from the participants to substantiate their claims about the children's use of logic and voice to rebuild trust.

Given this brief description of Petronio and her colleagues' work and the explanation of depth interviews as a research method, you can see that they represent a different paradigm for theory and research activity than do surveys and experiments. Here, lived experiences are the priority, and the researchers are collaborators with the research participants.

Textual Analysis

Textual analysis requires a researcher to identify a specific text for scrutiny. Texts can be presidential speeches, television shows, advertisements, or any type of discourse that the researcher focuses on to illuminate. Researchers engaged in textual analysis must apply some type of analytic tool (often, but not always, rhetorical theory) in order to understand the messages embodied within the text.

textual analysis
a specific research method requiring researchers to analyze a particular text such as a presidential speech or a television series

Textual analysis differs from the other methods we have discussed in several ways. First, it is centered on messages more completely than the other methods. By this we mean that textual analysis focuses on the actual words or symbols that are used in some type of discourse. Researchers adopting this method use a very inclusive definition of *text*. It can mean anything from a book to a speech to a film to a piece of architecture. Second, this method is nonreactive in the sense that when we study transcripts of speeches, we do not have to be concerned with the reactions we might engender in the transcripts. When Rolanda observes and tapes people in the organization, she is concerned about how they might be changing their behavior because of her presence. Transcripts do not present this concern.

Finally, textual analysis does not require any manipulation or intervention, as surveys, experiments, and interviews do. In this way, they remain true to what the communication stated originally (Frey, Botan, Friedman, & Kreps, 1991). This does not mean that textual analysis is superior to the other methods but rather that it presents a different set of challenges and rewards. Textual analysis more closely fuses method and theory than the other methodologies we have reviewed because it is not interested in prediction or causality; rather, it focuses on insightful description and understanding of communication practices. Therefore, the analytic tool also may form the conceptual approach or theoretical framework for the analysis. The following example illustrates this assertion.

Trevor Parry-Giles and Shawn J. Parry-Giles (1996) explored political campaigning in the United States. They examined three presidential campaign films (their text) from the 1984, 1988, and 1992 campaigns to argue that campaigning is shifting toward a more intimate, self-disclosive style. The authors

Theory * Into * Practice

A recent article in the *New York Times* (Kotkin, 2002) speaks to the divisions among researchers with regard to methodological choices. In this article, Stephen Kotkin observes that it is difficult to find a political scientist from a top university in the United States whose specialty is the Middle East. Instead, he notes, the place to find expertise in this important area is in policy schools and research groups. In explaining the reasons behind this state of affairs, Kotkin asserts that methodological issues related to questions of ontology play a large role.

Kotkin states that "the absence of regional experts in political science departments of many elite universities goes back to a long-running rancorous debate over the best method for understanding the way the world works: Is it using statistics and econometrics to identify universal patterns that underlie all economic and political systems, or zeroing in on a particular area, and mastering its languages, cultures and institutions?" (p. A15). Kotkin labels the two sides in this debate "hard science" and "area studies" and comments that the hard science advocates wish to generate universal truths while the area studies researchers work for culturally specific knowledge.

Some researchers believe that the two extremes can be combined through triangulation of research methods. Kotkin notes that "many of today's younger researchers—like Ellen Lust-Okar, an assistant professor of political science at Yale University, whose work on Jordan and Morocco combines both modeling and Arabic— readily accept the double burden of mastering both regional expertise and social science tools" (p. A17).

Source: Kotkin, 2002.

TIP Follow-up
Make a case for and against triangulation when the methods involved originate in different ontological and axiological assumptions.

used a Freudian theory, scopophilia, as it has been applied in rhetorical theory to explain this shift. Scopophilia suggests that humans possess a need to gaze at others and that this gaze provides pleasure. The researchers examined the campaign films of Ronald Reagan, George Bush, and Bill Clinton, focusing on devices in each film that increased a sense of intimacy with the audience. They concluded with a discussion of the implications of this new "politics of intimacy" on life in the United States.

In this study, the assertions of the theory form the building blocks of the analysis, providing a close relationship between theory and its application to a research study. Textual analysis fits comfortably within the interpretive and the critical traditions because it allows the researcher to illuminate inequities and to give voice to silenced groups. Yet, because traditional rhetoricians may also apply this methodology, it also can fit within the positivist, or empirical, approach. With a text, researchers have complete control, and they can exercise an authoritative voice about its meaning without considering multiple interpretations.

The Theory Chronicles

In your journal, record instances of research projects that are reported in local news media such as newspapers or televised newscasts. Keep the record for two weeks and try to accumulate at least five entries. For each entry record the source completely, give a brief description of the study, and note the research methodology utilized.

Conclusion

In this chapter, we have introduced you to the overall logic of research, and we have discussed the relationship between theory and research. We have also presented you with some specific methods that communication researchers are currently using to investigate issues ranging from child sexual abuse to political campaigns to deception to father-son communication. As you read about the four different research studies done with four different methodologies, you were probably struck by some of the epistemological, axiological, and ontological differences in their approaches.

As you examine the theories in this book, think about how they might be applied to specific research questions and hypotheses. You may find that some of the theories and questions you wish to explore have different assumptions about the nature of truth, values, and human choice. Your evolving paradigm is an integral part of the process of becoming a critical thinker.

Discussion Starters

1. If you were interested in the question that Dr. Stevens is studying, which of the four methods that we described would you utilize for your study? Explain your choice.

2. What are your own epistemologic assumptions? What do you think is the nature of truth, and what is your ontological stance? How do you see these affecting the research process?

3. What is the difference between inductive and deductive logic? Give some examples of your everyday use of both induction and deduction.

4. Describe how you might approach a study of presidential apologies. What methods might be useful? What theoretical framework would help you in this effort?

5. If you wanted to study the communicative foundations of romantic attraction, how might you go about it? How might that study differ from an investigation of female and male managers' communication style?

6. What are some critiques you might lodge concerning the four studies described as exemplans of survey research, experimental research, depth

interviews, and textual analysis in this chapter? How confident would you be in their findings? Explain your reasoning.

Terms for Review

operationalize
observations
data
code
scientific method
deductive logic
inductive logic
grounded theory
pure research
applied research
positivistic (empirical) approach
control
interpretive (hermeneutic)
   approach

critical approach
quantitative methods
qualitative methods
triangulation
survey research
unit of analysis
statistically significant
experimental research
independent variable
dependent variable
depth interviews
ethnography
textual analysis

 ## Online Learning Center

Visit the Online Learning Center at www.mhhe.com/west2. Use the multiple-choice and true/false quizzes to help you prepare for exams, and the glossary, crossword puzzles, and flashcards to further your knowledge of key terms.

Understanding the Dialogue

The Self and Messages

ACHIEVING MEANING IS INSTRUMENTAL IN OUR LIVES. We can't get too far in our conversations unless we understand the messages of others and others understand our messages. Understanding messages is what the meaning-making process is all about. Meaning, therefore, requires us to assess our own thinking about messages and also be prepared to assess how others interpret our messages. So, through our conversations with others, we gain a better sense of our self and a clearer understanding of the messages we and others send and receive.

How we process meaning is the cornerstone of our first section of theories, which we have labeled "The Self and Messages." Four theories highlight the prominent role of intrapersonal communication in meaning making. First, Symbolic Interaction Theory explores the interplay between the self and the society in which we live. Symbolic interactionists argue that people act toward other people or events on the basis of meaning they assign to them. The Coordinated Management of Meaning is also concerned with achieving meaning; however, the theory goes a bit further. It states that people will apply a personal set of rules to try to understand a social situation. Cognitive Dissonance Theory also looks at the self's ability to manage meaning and the need for people to avoid listening to views opposite their own. Expectancy Violations Theory looks specifically at what happens when someone violates our expectations. The theory suggests that we will judge a violation as either good or bad and act accordingly in the conversation.

The theories associated with the self and with messages deal with the ways people work toward gaining clarity and comprehension. Before and during conversations with others, we process things cognitively to determine how best to achieve meaning. As you read about these theories, you will encounter a number of important topics, namely, the influence of society on attitudes, communicator credibility, decision making, conversational rules, attraction, and liking.

CHAPTER 5

Symbolic Interaction Theory

Roger Thomas

Roger Thomas stared in the mirror and straightened his tie. He gave his overall look a last glance and decided that he looked as good as he could. He was a little apprehensive about the new job, but he was excited too. He had just graduated from Carlton Tech with a degree in engineering, and he had landed a terrific job in Houston. This made for a lot of changes in his life. It was a bit overwhelming. He was born and raised in central Nebraska, and he had never really been in a city bigger than Omaha until he went on his job interviews. Now he was living in Houston! It had all happened so quickly that Roger could almost feel his head spin.

Some of Roger's concern centered on the fact that he was the first person in his family to graduate from college. As far back as he could recall, his family had been farmers, and although he knew that engineering was something he loved and excelled at, he felt a little confused about how to behave off the farm and in a completely new life. It also didn't help that he was so far from home. Whenever he had felt stressed at Carlton, he had gone home to see his family. That had usually made him feel better. He remembered one day in his first year at Carlton when he felt impossibly out of place and uncomfortable. He really didn't know how to act as a college student. He went home for the weekend, and being in a familiar place with his family instantly gave him confidence. When he re-

turned to Carlton on Monday, he felt much more self-assured.

Even though his parents had not attended college themselves, they respected education and communicated this to Roger. They expressed pride in him and his accomplishments. They also told him how his younger brothers looked up to him. This gave Roger confidence in himself, and he liked the idea that he was blazing a new trail for his family. Also, whenever he visited, he appreciated his parents' qualities; they were so calm and steady. As they went about their tasks, they demonstrated the peace and harmony that Roger wanted to find in his life's work. After seeing them, he always had a renewed sense of self.

Now Roger decided he would just have to carry their image in his mind, because he had to face his new office alone. Yet, even thinking about his family made him feel a little stronger. He was smiling when he got to the office. He was greeted warmly by the office assistant, who showed him into the conference room. He waited there for the other new hires to join him. By 9:05 A.M. they were all gathered, and their boss came in to give them an orientation speech. While the boss was talking, Roger looked around at his colleagues.

There were ten new employees in all, and they could not have been more different. Roger was the youngest person in the room by at least five years. He was a bit alarmed when he realized that he must be the one with the least experience. He tried to

---

This theory is based on the research of **George Herbert Mead.**

calm himself down. He thought of his parents' pride in him and how his brothers looked up to him. Then he remembered his favorite teacher telling him that he was one of the best engineering students to go through Carlton. This helped Roger, and after the boss was finished speaking, he felt prepared to face the challenge of the job. During the break, he even had the confidence to begin talking to one of his new colleagues. He introduced himself and discovered that he didn't have less experience than she did. Helen Underwood explained that she had lived in a small Texas farming town, where she worked for the government. After working there for a couple of years, she decided to go back to school and get a degree. Roger was amazed

to meet someone else who came from a farming background. Helen told Roger she was really impressed that he had graduated from Carlton. She knew it had a wonderful reputation, and its intern program was supposed to be the best in the country. Roger replied that he had been really lucky to go there and had loved working at his internship, where he had learned a great deal. Helen said she was a bit nervous at starting out at this firm, and Roger smiled and nodded.

This conversation made him feel much better about the challenges that were ahead of him. Even though Helen was in her forties, they had a great deal in common, and they were in the same situation at the firm. Roger thought they would be friends.

∎

As Roger goes through his preparations for the first day of his new job and as he speaks with his boss and his new colleagues, he is engaging in the dynamic exchange of symbols. George Herbert Mead, who is credited with originating the Theory of Symbolic Interaction, was fascinated with humans' ability to use symbols; he proposed that people act based on the symbolic meanings that arise in a given situation. In Chapter 1 we defined *symbols* as arbitrary labels or representations for phenomena. Symbols form the essence of Symbolic Interaction Theory. As its name suggests, Symbolic Interaction Theory (SI) centers on the relationship between symbols and interactions. Although Mead published very little during his academic career, after he died his students collaborated on a book based on his lectures. They titled the book *Mind, Self, and Society* (1934), and it contains the foundations of Symbolic Interaction Theory. Interestingly, the name, "Symbolic Interaction," was not a creation of Mead's. One of his students, Herbert Blumer, actually coined the term, but it was clearly Mead's work that began the theoretical movement. Blumer published his own articles on SI in a collection in 1969.

Ralph LaRossa and Donald C. Reitzes (1993) suggest that Symbolic Interaction is "essentially . . . a frame of reference for understanding how humans, in concert with one another, create symbolic worlds and how these worlds, in turn, shape human behavior" (p. 136). In this, we can see Mead's contention of the interdependency between the individual and society. In fact, SI forms a bridge between theories focusing attention on individuals and theories attending to social forces. As Kenneth J. Smith and Linda Liska Belgrave (1994) note, SI argues that society is made "real" by the interactions of individuals, who "live and work to make their social world meaningful" (p. 253). Further, in this contention we can see Mead's belief in individuals as active, reflective participants in their social context.

The ideas of SI have been very influential in communication studies. Gail McGregor (1995) employed the theory to critique gender representations in advertisements; Patricia Book (1996) examined family narrative influences on a person's ability to communicate about death; Linda Trevino, Robert Lengel, and Richard Daft (1987) examined managers' choices of face-to-face communication, written communication, and electronic communication in the workplace using an SI framework; and Richard Daft and Karl Weick (1984) studied organizations as interpretation systems that have been influenced by symbolic interaction. Several researchers observe, however, that Symbolic Interaction is a community of theories, rather than simply one theory. Many theorists refer to the Chicago School and the Iowa School as two of the branches of SI. Let's briefly examine the history of the theory to better understand Symbolic Interaction today.

History of Symbolic Interaction Theory

The intellectual ancestors of SI were the early-twentieth-century pragmatists, such as John Dewey and William James. The pragmatists believed that reality is dynamic, which was not a popular idea at that time. In other words, they had different ontological assumptions. They advanced the notion of an emerging social structure, and they insisted that meanings were created in interaction. They were activists who saw science as a way to advance knowledge and improve society.

Symbolic Interaction had its genesis at two different universities: the University of Iowa and the University of Chicago. At Iowa, Manford Kuhn and his students were instrumental in affirming the original ideas of SI and contributed to the theory as well. Additionally, the Iowa group was advancing some new ways of looking at the self, but their approach was viewed as eccentric; thus, most of SI's principles and developments stemmed from the Chicago School.

Both George Herbert Mead and his friend John Dewey were on the faculty at the University of Chicago (although Mead never did complete his doctorate). Mead had studied both philosophy and social science, and he lectured on the ideas that form the core of the Chicago School of SI. As a popular teacher who was widely respected, Mead played a critical role in establishing the perspective of the Chicago School, which focused on an approach to social theory emphasizing the importance of communication to life and social encounters.

The two schools diverged primarily on methodology. Mead and his student Herbert Blumer contended that the study of human beings could not be conducted using the same methods as the study of other things. They advocated the use of case studies and histories and nondirective interviews. The Iowa School adopted a more quantitative approach to their studies. Kuhn believed that the concepts of SI could be operationalized, quantified, and tested. To this end, Kuhn developed a technique called the twenty-statements self-attitudes questionnaire. A research respondent taking the twenty-statements test is asked to fill in twenty blank spaces in answer to the question, Who am I? Some of Kuhn's colleagues at Iowa became disenchanted with this view of the self, and they broke away to form the "new" Iowa School. Carl Couch was one of the leaders of this new school. Couch and his associates began studying interaction behavior through videotapes of conversations, rather than simply examining information extracted from the twenty-statements test.

In addition to these main schools of Symbolic Interaction, there are many variations. Many theories that emphasize slightly different aspects of human interaction owe some debt to the central concepts of SI. For example, Social Construction, Role Theory, and Self-Theory form branches of SI. Despite the diversity in ideas, Mead's central concepts remain relatively constant in most interpretations of SI. Consequently, we will examine the basic assumptions and the key concepts that Mead outlined and Blumer elaborated.

Themes and Assumptions of Symbolic Interaction Theory

Symbolic Interaction is based on ideas about the self and its relationship to society. Because this can be interpreted very broadly, we wish to spend some time detailing the themes of the theory and, in the process, reveal the assumptions framing the theory.

Ralph LaRossa and Donald C. Reitzes (1993) have examined Symbolic Interaction Theory as it relates to the study of families. They note that seven central assumptions ground SI and that these assumptions reflect three central themes:

- the importance of meanings for human behavior
- the importance of the self-concept
- the relationship between the individual and society

The Importance of Meanings for Human Behavior

Symbolic Interaction Theory holds that individuals construct meaning through the communication process because meaning is not intrinsic to any thing. It takes interpretive construction among people to make meaning. In fact, the goal of interaction, according to SI, is to create shared meaning. This is the case because without shared meaning communication is extremely difficult, if not impossible. Imagine trying to talk to a friend if you had to explain your own idiosyncratic meaning for every word you used, and your friend had to do the same. Of course, sometimes we assume that we and our conversational partner agree on a meaning only to discover we are mistaken ("I said get ready as fast as you can." "One hour was as fast as I could get ready." "But I meant for you to be ready in 15 minutes." "You didn't say that!"), but frequently we can count on people having common meanings in a conversation. According to LaRossa and Reitzes, this theme supports three main assumptions of SI, which are taken from Herbert Blumer's (1969) work. These assumptions are as follows:

- Humans act toward others on the basis of the meanings those others have for them.
- Meaning is created in interaction between people.
- Meaning is modified through an interpretive process.

Humans Act Toward Others on the Basis of the Meanings Those Others Have for Them This assumption explains behavior as a loop of conscious thought and behavior between stimuli and the responses people exhibit to those stim-

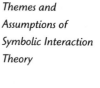

uli. SI theorists such as Herbert Blumer were concerned with the meaning behind behavior. They looked for meaning by examining psychological and sociological explanations for behavior. Thus, as SI researchers study the behaviors of Roger Thomas (from our beginning scenario), they see him making meanings that are congruent with the social forces that shape him. For instance, Roger assigns meaning to his new work experience by applying commonly agreed upon interpretations to the things he sees. When he sees the age of his co-workers, he believes that they have more experience than he does because we often equate age with expertise.

The meanings we assign to symbols are a product of social interaction and represent our agreement to apply certain meanings to specific symbols. For example, in the United States we generally associate wedding rings with love and commitment. The ring is a symbol of a legal and emotional bond, and thus most people invest the symbol with a positive connotation. However, some people see marriage as an oppressive institution. Those people will respond negatively to wedding rings and any other symbols of what they perceive as a degrading situation. The point that SI theorists make is that the ring itself has no specific meaning; it takes on meaning as people interact and invest it with importance. Further, SI researchers are interested in the meaning that Roger attaches to his encounter with Helen (for example, he is cheered up and believes they will become friends).

Meaning Is Created in Interaction Between People   Mead stresses the intersubjective basis of meaning. Meaning can exist, according to Mead, only when people share common interpretations of the symbols they exchange in interaction. Blumer (1969) explains that there are three ways of accounting for the origin of meaning. One approach regards meaning as being intrinsic to the thing. Blumer states, "Thus, a chair is clearly a chair in itself . . . the meaning emanates so to speak, from the thing and as such there is no process involved in its formation; all that is necessary is to recognize the meaning that is there in the thing" (pp. 3–4).

A second approach to the origin of meaning sees it as "brought to the thing by the person for whom the thing has meaning" (Blumer, 1969, p. 4). This position supports the popular notion that meanings are in people, not in things. In this perspective, meaning is explained by isolating the psychological elements within an individual that produce a meaning.

SI takes a third approach to meaning, seeing it as occurring between people. Meanings are "social products" or "creations that are formed in and

The Theory Chronicles

For one week, chronicle in your journal specific examples of symbols that have a shared cultural meaning at your school. Write about these shared meanings and how they contribute to a sense of identity among the students, faculty, and other school personnel.

through the defining activities of people as they interact" (Blumer, 1969, p. 5). Therefore, if Roger and Helen did not share a common language and did not agree on denotations and connotations of the symbols they exchanged, no shared meaning would result from their conversation. Further, the meanings created by Helen and Roger are unique to them and their relationship. See the Research Note for a study that examines this assumption of SI.

Meaning Is Modified Through an Interpretive Process   Blumer notes that this interpretive process has two steps. First, actors point out the things that have meaning. Blumer argues that this part of the process is different from a psychological approach and consists of people engaging in communication with themselves. Thus, as Roger gets ready for work in the morning, he communicates with himself about the areas that are meaningful to him. The second step involves actors selecting, checking, and transforming the meanings in the context in which they find themselves. When Roger talks with Helen, he listens for her remarks that are relevant to the areas he has decided are meaningful. Fur-

---

Research Note

Innes, M. (2002). Organizational communication and the symbolic construction of police murder investigations. *British Journal of Sociology, 53,* 67–87.

This study considers how murder investigations are symbolically constructed within police organizations and in the wider public. Innes begins by noting that police officers tend to agree that their job is primarily concerned with fighting crime and, as such, it is "an essentially benign and necessary form of state power" (p. 67). He then observes that other studies have shown that this symbolic construction of police work is not completely accurate because police are more focused on maintaining social order than on fighting crime. Yet, despite these studies and an acknowledgment of this "reality," the notion of policing continues to be symbolically constructed as crime fighting.

Innes uses symbolic interactionism, in particular the assumption that humans act toward others on the basis of the meanings those others have for them, to study "how organizations create and sustain a particular sense of meaningful reality" (p. 68). Innes observed police communication about murders in both formal (to the public) and informal (among one another) settings to determine how the police represented their organization.

He concludes that the police use a variety of communication strategies to validate their work as important, necessary, and moral. For instance, Innes observed that the police use distancing strategies such as joking among themselves in order to maintain a separation from victims and their families. Innes argues that distancing strategies provide impression management, allowing the officers to appear professional and expert. In this way, officers are seen as reassuring to those who have been traumatized and they are able to escape being traumatized themselves.

Innes asserts that his findings are consistent with a symbolic interaction framework because the crime of murder is symbolically constructed through the communication processes and strategies employed by the police and the public. Further, the organization is sustained, Innes found, through these strategies and communications that symbolically place "officers as acting on the side of good, protecting society, restoring order and achieving justice" (p. 84).

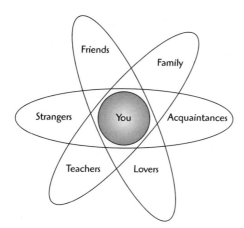

**Figure 5.1
How the Self-
Concept Develops**

ther, in his interpretation process, Roger depends on the shared social meanings that are culturally accepted. Thus, Roger and Helen are able to converse relatively easily because they both come from similar co-cultures.

The Importance of the Self-Concept

The second overall theme of SI focuses on the importance of the **self-concept**, or the relatively stable set of perceptions that people hold of themselves. When Roger (or any social actor) asks the question, Who am I? the answer relates to self-concept. The characteristics Roger acknowledges about his physical features, roles, talents, emotional states, values, social skills and limits, intellect, and so forth make up his self-concept. This notion is critical to Symbolic Interactionism. Further, SI is interested in the ways in which people develop self-concepts. SI pictures individuals with active selves, grounded in social interactions with others (see Figure 5.1). This theme suggests two additional assumptions, according to LaRossa and Reitzes (1993):

- Individuals develop self-concepts through interaction with others.
- Self-concepts provide an important motive for behavior.

Individuals Develop Self-Concepts Through Interactions with Others   This assumption suggests that it is only through contact with others that we develop a sense of self. People are not born with self-concepts; they learn them through interactions. According to SI, infants have no sense of an individuated self. During the first year of life, children begin to differentiate themselves from their surroundings. This is the earliest development of the self-concept. SI contends that this process continues through the child's acquisition of language and the ability to respond to others and internalize the feedback he or she receives. Roger has a sense of self because of his contacts with his parents and his teachers and his colleagues. Their interactions with him tell him who he is. Early family researchers such as Edgar Burgess (1926) reflect this assumption when they discuss the importance of the family as a socializing institution. Further, Burgess

self-concept
a relatively stable
set of perceptions
people hold about
themselves

notes that children and parents might conflict over children's self-concept or image.

Self-Concepts Provide an Important Motive for Behavior   The notion that beliefs, values, feelings, and assessments about the self affect behavior is a central tenet of SI. Mead argues that because human beings possess a self, they are provided with a mechanism for self-interaction. This mechanism is used to guide behavior and conduct. It is also important to note that Mead sees the self as a process, not as a structure. Having a self forces people to construct their actions and responses, rather than simply expressing them. So, for instance, if you feel great about your abilities in your communication theory course, then it is likely that you will do well in the course. In fact, it is likely that you will feel confident in all of your courses. This process is often called **self-fulfilling prophecy,** or the self-expectations that cause a person to behave in such a way that the expectations are realized. When Roger remembers his professor's praise of his engineering abilities, he is setting himself up to make a self-fulfilling prophecy about his performance at his new job.

**self-fulfilling
prophecy**
a prediction about
yourself causing you
to behave in such a
way that it comes true

The Relationship Between the Individual and Society

The final theme pertains to the relationship between individual freedoms and social constraint. Mead and Blumer took a middle position on this question. They tried to account for both order and change in social processes. Assumptions relating to this theme include:

- People and groups are influenced by cultural and social processes.
- Social structure is worked out through social interaction.

People and Groups Are Influenced by Cultural and Social Processes   This assumption recognizes that social norms constrain individual behavior. For instance, when Roger gets ready for his first day at his new job, he selects a navy suit, a white oxford shirt, and a burgundy and blue striped tie. His preferred mode of dress would be jeans and a flannel shirt, but he chooses clothing that he feels will be socially appropriate in the job context. Further, culture strongly influences the behaviors and attitudes that we value in our self-concepts. In the United States, people who see themselves as assertive are likely to be proud of this attribute and reflect favorably on their self-concept. This is the case because the United States is an individualistic culture that values assertiveness and individuality. Yet, in many Asian cultures, cooperation and community are highly valued. The collective is more important than the individual. Thus, an Asian who sees herself as assertive might feel ashamed of such a self-concept.

Mary Roffers (2002) notes that a college assignment to design a personal website was very difficult for a Hmong student in her class. The student explained that talking about one's self was not approved of in his culture and putting information about himself on the website felt inappropriate.

Social Structure Is Worked Out Through Social Interaction   This assumption mediates the position taken by the previous assumption. SI challenges the view that social structure is unchanging and acknowledges that individuals can modify social situations. For example, many U.S. workplaces have instituted "casual Fridays," when the employees wear casual clothing rather than the typical, socially prescribed office wear. In this way, the participants in the interaction modify the structure and are not completely constrained by it. In other words, SI theorists believe that humans are choice makers. In our opening scenario, Roger chooses to introduce himself to Helen; he is not bound to do so by forces outside his control. In making choices, Roger exerts his individuality and demonstrates that he is not completely constrained by culture or situation.

In review, we list the themes that ground SI and the assumptions they support:

THEMES

- the importance of meanings for human behavior
- the importance of the self-concept
- the relationship between the individual and society

ASSUMPTIONS

- Humans act toward others on the basis of the meanings those others have for them.
- Meaning is created in interaction between people.

- Meaning is modified through an interpretive process.
- Individuals develop self-concepts through interaction with others.
- Self-concepts provide an important motive for behavior.
- People and groups are influenced by cultural and social processes.
- Social structure is worked out through social interaction.

Key Concepts

Earlier we stated that the book outlining Mead's thinking was titled *Mind, Self, and Society.* The title of the book reflects the three key concepts of SI. We describe each concept here, noting how other important concepts relate to these basic three. It will become clear that the three concepts overlap to some extent, a consequence of describing a theory with global terminology that can be viewed in multiple ways.

Mind

mind
the ability to use symbols with common social meanings
language
a shared system of verbal and nonverbal symbols
significant symbols
symbols whose meaning is generally agreed upon by many people

Mead defines **mind** as the ability to use symbols that have common social meanings, and Mead believes that humans must develop minds through interaction with others. Infants cannot really interact with others until they learn **language,** or a shared system of verbal and nonverbal symbols organized in patterns to express thoughts and feelings. Language depends on what Mead calls **significant symbols,** or those symbols that evoke basically the same meaning for many people. Let's use the infant as an example to illustrate the concept of significant symbols. When parents coo and talk to their baby, the infant may respond, but she does not really understand the meanings of the words her parents use. As she learns language, the infant exchanges shared or significant symbols and can anticipate the responses of others to the symbols she uses. This, according to Mead, is how consciousness develops.

By using language and interacting with others, we develop what Mead calls mind, and this enables us to create an interior setting for the society that we see operating outside us. Thus, mind can be described as the way people internalize society. Yet, mind does not just depend on society. Mead suggests that they have a reciprocal relationship. Mind reflects and creates the social world. As people learn language, they learn the social norms and cultural mores that constrain them. But they also learn ways to shape and change that social world through interaction. When children learn to talk, they may learn to say "please" and "thank you" as cultural indicators of politeness. Yet, they may also create unique, personal ways of expressing politeness, like saying "mayberry" and "yes you," that become accepted idioms within a specific relationship.

thought
an inner conversation

Closely related to the concept of mind is the notion of **thought,** which Mead conceives of as an inner conversation. While Roger, in our opening story, prepares for his new job, he reviews all the experiences that brought him to that time and place. He thinks about his family's example and support, he remembers a favorite teacher, and he tells himself that he will be successful at this challenge. Through this intrapersonal conversation, Roger sorts out the meaning of his new situation. Mead holds that without social stimulation and interaction with others, people would not be capable of holding inner conversations or sustaining thought.

According to Mead, one of the most critical activities that people accomplish through thought is **role taking,** or the ability to symbolically place oneself in an imagined self of another person. This process is also called perspective taking because it requires that one suspend one's own perspective on an experience and instead view it from the imagined perspective of another. For example, if Helen thought about Roger after their meeting and reflected on how he must have felt to be new and so much younger than most of the other employees, then she would be role taking. Whenever we try to imagine how another person might view something or when we try to behave as we think another would, we are role taking. Mead suggests that role taking is a symbolic act that can help clarify our own sense of self even as it allows us to develop the capacity for empathy with others.

Self

Mead defines **self** as the ability to reflect on ourselves from the perspective of others. From this you can see that Mead does not believe that self comes from introspection or from simply thinking on one's own. For Mead, the self develops from a particular kind of role taking—that is, imagining how we look to another person. Borrowing a concept originated by the sociologist Charles Cooley in 1912, Mead refers to this as the **looking-glass self,** or our ability to see ourselves in the reflection of another's gaze. Cooley (1972) believes that three principles of development are associated with the looking-glass self: (1) we imagine how we appear to others, (2) we imagine their judgment of our appearance, and (3) we feel hurt or pride based on these self-feelings. A commercial for women's jeans has one character noting, "I feel beautiful when he looks at me like he did when we first met." This commercial provides an example of the looking-glass self. We learn about ourselves from the ways others treat us, view us, and label us. One of your authors once participated in the Great Bike Ride Across Iowa. She rode a three-speed bike 523 miles, from one end of the state to the other. The ride took one week, and after about three days, she felt she could not pedal a minute longer. But just as she was about to give up, a man biked up beside her and said, "You are amazing, going on this bike ride on a three-speed bike. You are just great. Keep it up." As he pedaled off, she straightened up and said to herself, "Well, I guess I am amazing. I can finish this ride!" The label the man gave her actually changed her feelings of exhaustion and made her see her accomplishments and herself differently and more positively.

Mead's notion of the looking-glass self implies the power that labels have on self-concept and behavior. This power represents a second type of self-fulfilling prophecy. Earlier in the chapter we spoke of self-fulfilling prophecies as being self-expectations that affect behaviors. For example, Roger tells himself repeatedly that he will succeed at his job and then engages in behaviors that are congruent with his expectations of success. In turn, these behaviors will

role taking
the ability to put oneself in another's place

self
imagining how we look to another person

looking-glass self
our ability to see ourself as another sees us

The Theory Connection

How does Mead's concept of the self relate to an understanding of self in Relational Dialectics Theory?

likely ensure that he will succeed. By the same token, negative self-talk can create situations where predictions of failure come true. This second type of self-fulfilling prophecy produced by labels is called the **Pygmalion effect,** and it refers to the expectations of others governing one's actions.

The name comes from the myth of Pygmalion, on which the play *My Fair Lady* was based. In *My Fair Lady,* the main character, Eliza, states that the difference between an upper-class lady and a poor flower girl is not in her behavior but in how others treat her. This phenomenon was tested in a classic study by Robert Rosenthal and Lenore Jacobson (1968). In their study, Rosenthal and Jacobson told elementary school teachers that 20 percent of their students were gifted. But the names of these "gifted" students were simply drawn at random. Eight months later these students showed significantly greater gains in IQ compared to the rest of the children in the class. Rosenthal and Jacobson concluded that this was the result of teachers' expectations (and behaviors based on these expectations) toward the "gifted" children.

As Mead theorizes about self, he observes that through language, people have the ability to be both subject and object to themselves. As subject, we act, and as object, we observe ourselves acting. Mead calls the subject, or acting self, the I and the object, or observing self, the **Me.** The I is spontaneous, impulsive, and creative, whereas the Me is more reflective and socially aware. The I might want to go out and party all night, whereas the Me might exercise caution and acknowledge the homework assignment that should be done instead of partying. Mead sees the self as a process that integrates the I and the Me.

Society

Mead argues that interaction takes place within a dynamic social structure—culture, society, and so forth. Individuals are born into already-existing social contexts. Mead defines **society** as the web of social relationships that humans create. Individuals engage in society through behaviors that they choose actively and voluntarily. Society thus features an interlocking set of behaviors that individuals continually adjust. Society exists prior to the individual but is also created and shaped by the individual, acting in concert with others.

Society, then, is made up of individuals, and Mead talks about two specific parts of society that affect the mind and the self. Mead's notion of **particular others** refers to the individuals in society who are significant to us. These people are usually family members, friends, and work colleagues and supervisors. We

Pygmalion effect
living up to or down to another's expectations of us

I
the spontaneous, impulsive, creative self
Me
the reflective, socially aware self

society
the web of social relationships humans create and respond to

particular others
individuals who are significant to us

look to particular others to get a sense of social acceptability and a sense of self. When Roger thinks of his parents' opinion of him, he is deriving a sense of self from particular others. The identity of the particular others and the context influence our sense of social acceptability and our sense of self. Often the expectations of some particular others conflict with those of others. For example, if Roger's family wants him to work hard and be successful, whereas his friends want him to party and ignore work, he will experience conflict.

The **generalized other** refers to the viewpoint of a social group or the culture as a whole. It is given to us by society, and "the attitude of the generalized other is the attitude of the whole community" (Mead, 1934, p. 154). The generalized other provides information about roles, rules, and attitudes shared by the community. The generalized other also gives us a sense of how other people react to us and of general social expectations. This sense is influential in developing a social conscience. The generalized other may help mediate conflicts generated by conflicting groups of particular others.

generalized other
the attitude of the whole community

Critique and Closing

Symbolic Interaction Theory has been a powerful theoretical framework for over sixty years. It provides striking insights about human communication behavior in a wide variety of contexts. The theory is logical in its development, beginning with the role of the self and progressing to an examination of the self in society. In this chapter we noted that the theory is heuristic, identifying its application in a variety of contexts, including media, organizational, and interpersonal. Yet, the theory is not without its critics.

The major objections raised in regard to SI tend to focus on the following areas: It is too broad, it places too much emphasis on personal behavior, it neglects other important variables, and it is not falsifiable. We briefly explore these criticisms below.

Some critics complain that SI is too broad to be useful. This criticism centers on the evaluation criterion of scope. SI covers too much ground, these critics assert, to fully explain specific meaning-making processes and communication behaviors. Related to this is the objection that the concepts that make up the theory are broadly drawn and rather vague. Additionally, due to this vagueness, SI is difficult to falsify. In response to this criticism, SI proponents explain that SI is not one unified theory; rather, it is a framework that can support many

Theory * Into * Practice

In a 1998 article in the magazine *Vanity Fair,* Michael Jordan writes about his life and basketball career. His comments reflect a Symbolic Interactionist framework. Jordan's thoughts about the relationship between his own sense of self and the self that fans and others saw in him illustrate the concepts of SI.

Jordan comments that his fame made him feel "like a fish in a fishbowl" (p. 124). He observes that his fame caused his fans to view him differently than he saw himself. He was a husband and a father in his home, but outside he was bigger than that. Jordan describes his outside self as some character he calls MICHAEL JORDAN. He says that everyone else had a sense of who that was, leading him to try to see himself from the fans' perspective. Jordan states, "Early in my career I really couldn't get a sense of who I was from the fan's perspective. I didn't feel as famous as people said I was" (p. 126). He also speculates that his own sense of himself may have contributed to his being well received by the public. He says he thought the fans knew that he was not acting or trying to be something he wasn't. Jordan notes that he felt comfortable in the spotlight because he was just being himself. Yet, Jordan concludes that it was lonely being put on a pedestal by his fans and that was one reason he took a break from basketball after the 1992–93 season.

Source: Jordan, 1998.

TIP Follow-up

How do Mead's notions of mind, self, and society apply to Michael Jordan's situation as described above? Be specific.

specific theories. In the more specific theories, like Role Theory, for example, the concepts are more clearly defined and are capable of falsification.

A second area of criticism concerns Mead's emphasis on the power of the actor to create reality. Critics observe that this ignores the extent to which people live in a world not of their own making. SI theorists regard a situation as real if the actors define it as real. But Erving Goffman (1974) comments that this notion, although true, ignores physical reality. For instance, if Roger and his parents agreed that he was an excellent engineer and that he was doing a wonderful job at his new firm, that would be reality for them. Yet, it would not acknowledge the fact that Roger's boss perceived his skills as inadequate and fired him. SI theorists counter by citing that they try to tread a middle ground between freedom of choice and external constraint. They recognize the validity of constraint, but they also emphasize the importance of shared meanings.

Another area of criticism suggests that there are important concepts that SI ignores, such as emotions and self-esteem. Critics observe that SI does not explain the emotional dimension of human interaction. Further, critics note that SI discusses how we develop a self-concept, but it does not have much to say about how we evaluate ourselves. With reference to the lack of attention to the emotional aspects of human life, SI theorists respond that although Mead does not emphasize these aspects, the theory itself can accommodate emotions.

In fact, some researchers have begun applying SI to emotions with success. For instance, James Forte, Anne Barrett, and Mary Campbell (1996) used a Symbolic Interaction perspective to examine grief. Their study examined the utility of a Social Interaction perspective in assessing and intervening in a bereavement group. The authors found that SI was a useful model. Regarding self-esteem, symbolic interactionists agree that it is not a focus of the theory. But they point out that this is not a flaw in the theory; it is simply beyond the bounds of what Mead chose to investigate.

In sum, Symbolic Interaction has critics, but it still remains a heuristic, enduring theory. It supports research in multiple contexts, and it is constantly being refined and extended. Further, it is one of the leading conceptual tools for interpreting social interactions, and its core constructs provide the foundation for many other theories that we discuss in this book, such as Dramatism, Muted Group Theory, Organizational Culture Theory, and Standpoint Theory. Thus, because Symbolic Interaction Theory has stimulated much conceptual thinking, it has accomplished much of what theories aim to do.

Discussion Starters

1. Discuss Roger Thomas's initial reactions to his new job in Houston. How do they specifically relate to his sense of self?

2. Do you believe Mead's argument that one cannot have a self without social interaction? Would a person raised by wolves have no sense of self? Explain your answers.

3. Has there been a time in your life when your sense of self changed dramatically? If so, what contributed to the change? Did it have anything to do with others in your life?

4. Do you agree with the emphasis that Mead places on language as a shared symbol system? Is it possible to interact with someone who uses a completely different language? Explain your position.

5. One of the criticisms of SI is that it puts too much emphasis on individual action and not enough emphasis on the constraints on individuals that they cannot think their way out of. What is your position on this criticism?

6. Explain the difference between the concepts self-fulfilling prophecy and Pygmalion effect. How are they similar?

Terms for Review

self-concept	significant symbols
self-fulfilling prophecy	thought
mind	role taking
language	self
looking-glass self	society

Pygmalion effect
I
Me

particular others
generalized other

 Online Learning Center

Visit the Online Learning Center at www.mhhe.com/west2. Use the multiple-choice and true/false quizzes to help you prepare for exams, and the glossary, crossword puzzles, and flashcards to further your knowledge of key terms.

CHAPTER 6

Coordinated Management of Meaning

The Taylor-Murphys

About two years ago, Jessie Taylor decided that she could not stay in her abusive marriage and left her husband, taking her two children—Megan, 13, and Melissa, 9—with her. They currently live in a small apartment, and Jessie knows that the place is too cramped for the three of them. Yet, with her upcoming marriage to Ben Murphy, Jessie realizes that her living situation will change very soon. Her work hours as a new law clerk, however, are quite long; at times, she must be in the office for twelve-hour days. As a result, Jessie's children frequently require adult supervision in the early evening. Although Jessie would rather be at home with her children, she realizes that she cannot count on her ex-husband's child support payments, and she must keep her job. She hopes that her approaching marriage to Ben will help ease the financial and familial challenges.

Ben Murphy's wife died a little over a year ago. He parents his 4-year-old son, Patrick, but gets a great deal of help from both his mother and his two sisters. He feels bad about leaving Patrick but is grateful that his family is there, because his job as a state trooper is frequently unpredictable. He never really knows when he is going to be called out for an emergency or when he will be asked to work overtime. Lately, however, his sisters have made some comments, and Ben worries that the baby-sitting may be turning into a burden for them and his mom. Ben is hoping that his marriage to Jessie will ease his reliance upon his mother and sisters.

One evening, as Ben and Jessie are discussing final wedding plans, the two begin to talk about their future family. Ben is very excited about raising three children and looks forward to his son, Patrick, having new siblings. Jessie, however, is nervous about the logistics of bringing new people into her children's lives. Megan and Melissa are not pleased about their upcoming blended family. They have already had disagreements with Ben about a number of issues, including computer use and after-school activities.

As Ben and Jessie sit in front of the fireplace, they openly talk about the challenges, obstacles, and frustrations that they know they will experience in just a few months. Ben admits, "First, I need to tell you that I love you and that should be the most important thing right now. And I really think that the kids will come around in time—probably after we've been together for a while. A lot of families in our situation start out like this. There's a lot of chaos and then things begin to settle down. Hey, we're not all that unusual."

Jessie agrees. "Yeah, I know we're not the first family arranged this way. And I know things will work out. But when? And how are we all going to keep from screaming at each other while we work it all out? Adjusting can take some time." Her words are greeted by a warm hug from Ben.

This theory is based on the research of **W. Barnett Pearce** and **Vernon Cronen**.

Many people take their conversations for granted. When individuals speak to one another, they often fall into predictable patterns of talk, and they rely on prescribed social norms. To understand what takes place during a conversation, Barnett Pearce and Vernon Cronen developed Coordinated Management of Meaning (CMM). For Pearce and Cronen, people communicate on the basis of rules. Rules figure prominently in this theory; the theorists contend that rules help us not only in our communication with others, but also in our interpretation of what others are communicating to us. CMM helps explain how individuals co-create the meaning in a conversation. Jessie Taylor and Ben Murphy, for instance, are beginning to forge rules and patterns that will govern their new family's interaction.

For our purposes, Coordinated Management of Meaning generally refers to how individuals establish rules for creating and interpreting meaning and how those rules are enmeshed in a conversation where meaning is constantly being coordinated. Cronen, Pearce, and Linda Harris's (1982) summary of CMM is informative here: "CMM theory describes human actors as attempting to achieve coordination by managing the ways messages take on meaning" (p. 68). As we discuss this theory in this chapter, we will underscore a number of issues associated with it.

All the World's a Stage

To describe life experiences, Pearce and Cronen (1980) use the metaphor "undirected theater" (p. 120). They believe that, in life as in theater, there are a number of actors who are following some sort of dramatic action and there are actors who produce "a cacophonous bedlam with isolated points of coherence" (p. 121). Pearce (1989) describes this metaphor in eloquent detail:

> Imagine a very special kind of theater. There is no audience: everyone is "on stage" and is a participant. There are many props, but they are not neatly organized: in some portions of the stage are jumbles of costumes and furniture; in others, properties have been arranged as a set for a contemporary office; in yet another, they depict a medieval castle. . . . Actors move about the stage, encountering sets, would-be directors, and other actors who might provide a supporting cast for a production of some play. (p. 48)

The theorists believe that in this theatrical world, there is no one grand director, but rather a number of self-appointed directors who manage to keep the chaos in check.

Conversational flow is essentially a theater production. Interactants direct their own dramas, and at times the plots thicken without any script. For many people, how they produce meaning is equivalent to their effectiveness as communicators. To continue the metaphor, when actors enter a conversation, they rely on their past acting experiences to achieve meaning. How they perceive the play is their reality, but the roles they play in the production are not known until the production begins. To this end, the actors are constantly coordinating their scripts with one another.

As you can imagine, this process is frequently chaotic. Pearce and Cronen indicate that the actors who are able to read another's script will attain conversational coherence. Those who are not will need to coordinate their meaning. Of course, even agreeing upon what conversational script to follow can be difficult. Jessie and Ben, for example, may agree that achieving family harmony is essential but may not agree on how to achieve that harmony. As Pearce (1989) observes, people may battle it out with respect to what script they will enact and then continue to argue about it.

This notion of a creative theatrical production was in stark contrast to the perspective held by other researchers at the time that CMM was conceptualized. Early discussions of CMM centered on the need to break away from the empirical tradition that characterized much theory building at that time. To shape their theory, Pearce and Cronen looked to a number of different disciplines, including philosophy (Wittgenstein), psychology (James), and education (Dewey). Before delving into the theory's central features, we first consider three assumptions of the Coordinated Management of Meaning.

Assumptions of Coordinated Management of Meaning

CMM focuses on the self and its relationship to others; it examines how an individual assigns meaning to a message. The theory is especially important because it focuses on the relationship between an individual and his or her society (Philipsen, 1995). Referring back to the theater metaphor, consider the fact that all actors must be able to improvise—using their personal repertoire of acting experiences—as well as reference the scripts that they bring into the drama.

Human beings, therefore, are capable of creating and interpreting meaning. There are a few other assumptions as well:

- Human beings live in communication.
- Human beings co-create a social reality.
- Information transactions depend on personal and interpersonal meaning.

The first assumption of CMM points to the centrality of communication. That is, human beings live *in* communication. At first glance, this premise suggests something peculiar about communication: the fact that people inhabit the communication process. Yet, Pearce (1989) claims that "communication is, and always has been, far more central to whatever it means to be a human being than had ever been supposed" (p. 3). That is, we live in communication. In adopting this claim, Pearce rejects traditional models of the communication process such as the linear model to which we referred in Chapter 2. Rather, CMM theorists propose a counterintuitive orientation in that they believe that social situations are created by interactions. Because individuals create their conversational reality, each interaction has the potential to be unique. This perspective requires CMM adherents to cast aside their preexisting views of what it means to be a communicator. Further, CMM theorists call for a reexamination of how individuals view communication because "Western intellectual history has tended to use communication as if it were an odorless, colorless, tasteless vehicle of thought and expression" (Pearce, 1989, p. 17). Pearce and Cronen contend that communication must be reconfigured and contextualized in order to begin to understand human behavior. When researchers begin this journey of redefinition, they start investigating the consequentiality of communication, not the behaviors or variables that accompany the communication process (Cronen, 1995).

To illustrate this assumption, consider our opening story. Although Jessie and Ben believe that they have covered most of the details associated with merging their families, many more issues will appear as the families come together. Family members will create new realities for themselves, and these realities will be based on communication. Conversations will frequently be determined by what the family knows as well as what the family does not know. That is, parents and children will work through unexpected as well as expected joys and sorrows. Like many families in their situation, they may stumble on areas about which they never thought. The two families will be working from different sets of conversation rules and therefore may arrive at very different conclusions as they discuss important issues.

A second assumption of CMM is that human beings co-create a social reality. Although we implied this assumption earlier, it merits delineation. **Social reality** refers to a person's beliefs about how meaning and action fit within his or her interpersonal encounters. When two people engage in a conversation, they each come with a host of past conversational experiences from previous social realities. Current conversations, however, elicit new realities because two people are arriving at the conversation from different vantage points. In this way, two people co-create a new social reality. Sometimes, these communication experiences are smooth; at other times they are cumbersome. As Gerry Philipsen (1995) concludes, "Many interactions are more messy than clean and more awkward than elegant" (p. 19).

Our opening example of Jessie and Ben illustrates this assumption. Although Jessie and Ben have been dating for some time and are preparing for their wedding, CMM theorists believe that they will continue to co-create a new social reality. For instance, the two will have to manage the issue of Jessie's daughters' reluctance to support the marriage. As Jessie and Ben discuss the matter in front of the fireplace, regardless of how they have previously discussed it, they create a new social reality. Perhaps some new issues will emerge—child support, Jessie's job, the age of the children, Jessie's ex-spouse, and so forth—or perhaps Jessie, Ben, or both will adopt new perspectives on their future family makeup. In any event, the social reality that the two experience will be a shared reality.

The third assumption guiding CMM relates to the manner in which people control conversations. Specifically, information transactions depend on personal and interpersonal meaning, as distinguished by Donald Cushman and Gordon Whiting (1972). **Personal meaning** is defined as the meaning achieved when a person interacts with another and brings into the interaction his or her unique experiences. Cushman and Whiting suggest that personal meaning is

social reality
a person's beliefs about how meaning and action fit within an interpersonal interaction

personal meaning
the meaning achieved when a person brings his or her unique experiences to an interaction

derived from the experiences people have with one another, and yet "it is improbable that two individuals will interpret the same experience in a similar manner . . . and equally improbable that they would select the same symbolic patterns to represent the experience" (p. 220). Personal meaning helps people in discovery; that is, it not only allows us to discover information about ourselves but also aids in our discovery about other people.

When two people agree on each other's interpretation, they are said to achieve **interpersonal meaning.** Cushman and Whiting (1972) argue that interpersonal meaning can be understood within a variety of contexts, including families, small groups, and organizations. They note that interpersonal meaning is co-constructed by the participants. Achieving interpersonal meaning may take some time because relationships are complex and deal with multiple communication issues. A family, for example, may be challenged with financial problems one day, child-raising concerns the next, and elderly care the next. Each of these scenarios may require family members to engage in unique communication pertaining to that particular family episode.

Personal and interpersonal meaning are achieved in conversations, frequently without much thought. Perceptive individuals recognize that they cannot engage in specialized personal meaning without explaining themselves to others. Cushman and Whiting (1972) tell us that interpersonal meaning must often be negotiated so that rules of meanings move from "in-house usage" to "standardized usage." Sharing meaning for particular symbols, however, is complicated by the fact that the meaning of many symbols is left unstated. For instance, consider a physician specializing in AIDS who discusses recent drug therapies with a group of college students. As the physician discusses AIDS, she must talk in layperson's terms so that audience members will understand. However, despite honest efforts at avoiding jargon, it may be nearly impossible to avoid it completely. That is, as much as the physician tries, time may not permit her to fully explain the meaning of all specialized terms.

These three assumptions form a backdrop for discussing Coordinated Management of Meaning. As these assumptions indicate, the theory rests primarily on the concepts of communication, social reality, and meaning. In addition, we can better understand the theory by examining a number of other issues in detail. Among these issues is the manner in which meaning is categorized.

interpersonal meaning
the result when two people agree on each other's interpretations of an interaction

The Hierarchy of Organized Meaning

According to CMM theorists, human beings organize meanings in a hierarchical manner. This is one of the core features of CMM, and so we will discuss this at length. First, we examine the meaning behind this claim, and then we look at the framework associated with the assumption. We have highlighted the hierarchy in Figure 6.1.

Suggesting that people organize meaning implies that they are able to determine how much weight to give to a particular message. In Chapter 1, you learned that people are constantly being bombarded with stimuli and that they must be able to organize that stimuli for communication to occur. This

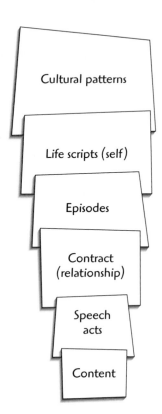

**Figure 6.1
Hierarchy of
Meaning**
Source: Adapted from
Pearce & Cronen, 1980.

thinking is relevant to CMM. Imagine, for instance, Ian arriving at his new job on Monday morning. Throughout the day he will be exposed to a number of messages. From understanding company policy on medical leaves to overtime pay to computer terminal safety, Ian must manage countless messages. As he returns home at the end of the day, he must organize the messages. In some way, he must try to coherently frame literally hundreds of messages from his day.

The process of organizing for Ian is similar to what many people experience when they speak to others. When people come together, they must try to handle not only the messages that are sent to them from others but also the messages that they send to others. This helps people understand the full meaning of the messages. Let's consider how Pearce and Cronen (1980) illustrate the management of meaning.

CMM theorists propose six levels of meaning: content, speech acts, contract, episodes, life scripts, and cultural patterns. As you read about the levels, keep in mind that higher levels help us to interpret lower-level meanings. That is, each type is embedded in the other. In addition, Pearce and Cronen (1980) prefer to use this hierarchy as a model, rather than as a true ordering system. They believe that no true ordering is appropriate because people differ in their interpretation of meaning at various levels. So, the theorists propose a hierarchy to help us understand the sequencing of meaning in different people.

Content

When information is presented to an individual, it is presented as **raw data**, or uninterpreted stimuli. Pearce and Forrest Conklin (1979) note that these raw data include movements, noises, and visual stimuli. The **content** level specifies the first step of converting raw data into some meaning. For instance, in class, as you take notes, you convert the symbols being sent into some type of meaning by its content. You may group all of the information about perception into one category and the material about self-concept into another category. For Ben Murphy in our chapter's opening, the words "I love you" convey information about Ben's reaction to Jessie, but the content of his words requires this additional level of meaning. Imagine the content level as a message without a context (Pearce, Cronen, & Conklin, 1979).

raw data
uninterpreted stimuli

content
the conversion of raw data into meaning

Speech Acts

In discussing the second level of meaning, Pearce (1994) describes **speech acts** as "actions that we perform by speaking . . . [including] compliments, insults, promises, threats, assertions, and questions" (p. 104). Speech acts communicate the intention of the speaker and indicate how a particular communication should be taken. Using our earlier example of Ben Murphy, when Ben states, "I love you," to Jessie, the phrase communicates more than an assertion. The phrase carries an affectional tone because of the speech act (Austin, 1975).

Further, Pearce (1994) notes that "speech acts are not things; they are configurations in the logic of meaning and action of conversations, and these configurations are co-constructed" (p. 119). Therefore, we should be aware that two people co-create the meaning of the speech act, a belief we alluded to in our earlier assumption of CMM. Frequently, the speech act is defined both by the sender and by the response to what others have said or done. As Pearce concludes, "You cannot be a 'victim' unless there is a 'victimizer'" (p. 119). In addition, the relational history must be taken into consideration when interpreting a speech act. It is difficult to figure out what a message means unless we have a sense of the dynamics between the participants.

speech acts
actions we perform by speaking (e.g., questioning, complimenting, or threatening)

Contract

The third level of meaning is the contract. Although the word *contract* sounds rather formal (and it can be), a tacit agreement exists between two people in a relationship. A **contract** can be defined as a relationship agreement whereby two people recognize their potential and limitations as relational partners. Contracts set guidelines and often prescribe behavior. In addition, contracts—like ongoing relationships—suggest a future. Few people would take the time to outline relational issues unless they were concerned about their future together.

Further, a contract communicates relational boundaries; it provides parameters for attitudes and behavior—for instance, how partners should speak

contract
relationship agreement and understanding between two people

to each other or what topics are considered taboo in their relationship. Pearce and Cronen (1980) note that boundaries distinguish between "we" and "they," or those people who are included in the contract and those who are not. The theorists use the term **enmeshment** to describe the extent to which people identify themselves as part of the relational system.

enmeshment
extent to which partners identify themselves as part of a system

A contract may prove invaluable as two people discuss issues that are especially challenging. For instance, there will certainly be some difficult discussions once the Murphy-Taylor family resides together. Knowing the relational boundaries and the expectations the family members hold for themselves as well as for one another will be important as they become a stepfamily. Although upcoming events will be trying for this family, they will be managed more effectively with an understanding of the contract.

Episodes

episodes
communication routines that have recognized beginnings, middles, and endings
punctuate
how individuls interpret or emphasize an episode

To interpret speech acts, Pearce and Cronen (1980) discuss **episodes,** or communication routines that have definable beginnings, middles, and endings. In a sense, episodes describe contexts in which people act. Individuals in an interaction may differ in how they **punctuate** or emphasize an episode. Pearce and Conklin (1979) clearly note that "coherent conversation requires some degree of coordinated punctuation" (p. 78). Different punctuation, however, may elicit different impressions of the episode, thereby creating "inside" and "outside" perspectives of the same episode. For example, Ben Murphy and Jessie Taylor may have punctuated differently their previous discussions about their future together. Ben may believe that dealing with the children will be better left until after their wedding, whereas Jessie may believe that the issue should be dealt with beforehand. Their subsequent episodes, therefore, will be partly determined by the way they handle their punctuation differences. Pearce (1976) believes that episodes are essentially imprecise because the actors in social situations find themselves in episodes that vary tremendously—from meeting someone for coffee to having an affair. He also notes that episodes are culturally based in that people bring to their interactions cultural expectations for how episodes should be executed.

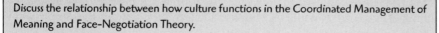

The Theory Connection

Discuss the relationship between how culture functions in the Coordinated Management of Meaning and Face-Negotiation Theory.

Life Scripts

Clusters of past and present episodes are defined as **life scripts.** Think of life scripts as interconnected with your sense of self. You are who you are because of the life scripts in which you have engaged. Imagine the differences between Ben Murphy's and Jessie Taylor's life scripts. Their past episodic experiences will be very informative as they try to deal with their future plans together. Ben comes from a very supportive and loving family, so he may expect conversations with Jessie to be characterized by these nurturing episodes. In fact, it is likely that his experiences as a single father and his perceptions of parenthood are less troubled because of past episodes co-created with his biological family. Jessie, however, did not have an affirming relationship with her ex-husband. Consequently, her past debilitating episodes influence how she now communicates with Ben. Moreover, in her interactions with Ben, she may expect something very different from what Ben expects from her. We should point out, though, that life scripts include those episodes that two people construct together. So, once Ben and Jessie begin to co-create their social reality, they will simultaneously co-create a life script.

life scripts
clusters of past or present episodes that create a system of manageable meanings with others

Cultural Patterns

When discussing cultural patterns, Pearce and Cronen (1980) contend that people identify with particular groups in particular cultures. **Cultural patterns,** or archetypes, can be described as "very broad images of world order and [a person's] relationship to that order" (Cronen & Pearce, 1981, p. 21). That is, an individual's relationship to the larger culture is relevant when interpreting meaning. This is even more paramount when two people from two different cultures try to understand the meaning of each other's words. For instance, Judith Martin and Thomas Nakayama (2000) point out that the U.S. culture puts a premium on **individualism,** or the notion that the interests of an individual are put before the interests of the group. Individualism focuses on independence and initiative. Other cultures (such as Colombia, Peru, and Taiwan) emphasize **collectivism,** or the notion that the interests of the group are put before the interests of the individual. Difficulty may arise when two people representing two different orientations interpret meaning from their particular vantage point. Culture, therefore, requires shared meanings and values.

cultural patterns
images of the world and a person's relationship to it

individualism
prioritizing personal needs or values over the needs or values of a group (I-identity)
collectivism
prioritizing group needs or values over the needs or values of an individual (we-identity)

107

The levels of meaning espoused by Pearce and Cronen are critical to consider when conversing with another. However, keep in mind that the theorists contend that their purpose is to model the way people process information, not to establish a true ordering. Also, remember that individuals vary in their past and present interactions. Therefore, some people will have highly complex hierarchies, and others will have simplified hierarchies. In addition, some people are able to interpret complex meaning, and others are not as proficient. The hierarchy of meaning is an important framework in helping us understand how meaning is coordinated and managed. We now turn our attention to the issue of coordination and examine the meaning of this feature in CMM.

The Coordination of Meaning: Making Sense of the Sequence

In his discussion of coordination, Pearce (1989) wisely notes that "coordination is more easily shown than described" (p. 37). That is, the best way to understand coordination is by watching people interact on a daily basis. Because people enter conversations with a variety of abilities and competencies, achieving coordination can be difficult at times. Further, coordination with others is challenging, in part, because others try to coordinate their actions with ours. **Coordination** exists when two people attempt to make sense out of the sequencing of messages in their conversation. Three outcomes are possible when two people converse: They achieve coordination, they do not achieve coordination, or they achieve some degree of coordination (Philipsen, 1995). Yet, Gerry Philipsen reminds us that because social reality is not perfectly coordinated, the most likely outcome is partially achieved coordination.

coordination
making sense of
message sequencing

Following, we present examples of perfect coordination, no coordination, and partial coordination by borrowing the experiences of Jessie Taylor and Ben Murphy. They are discussing an upcoming camping trip:

> BEN: We need to be straightforward with the girls now. I don't see any problem with sleeping in the same tent and letting the kids sleep in their tent. Patrick can sleep with us if he gets upset.
>
> JESSIE: I think you're right. He should have fun with the girls.
>
> BEN: Also, they love him, which makes it easier for all of us.
>
> JESSIE: The weekend should be a great bonding time for the families.

The two have coordinated their meanings of what to do with their children on the first family trip. Although each is entering the conversation with different experiences, Ben and Jessie have created a completed episode of meaning. Perfect coordination is attained.

However, things are not usually this smooth when discussing such complex issues. For instance:

> BEN: We need to be straightforward with the girls now. I don't see any problem with sleeping in the same tent and letting the kids sleep in their tent. Patrick can sleep with us if he gets upset.

JESSIE: My girls will not like that. Are you trying to say that our feelings are more important than our kids' feelings?

BEN: I didn't say that. . . .

JESSIE: Why would you even think that? Our first trip together shouldn't be spent trying to explain why Mom and Dad want their privacy.

BEN: All I was trying to do was to let the kids know that Mom and Dad need to have their own space.

JESSIE: And that they need to deal with their own problems?! I never knew I was marrying such a selfish man.

BEN: I'm sorry that I ever brought up the issue.

As you can see, the episode is quite different from the previous one. In fact, it appears that Ben and Jessie have different interpretations of what the other is saying, which prevents coordination from being achieved.

The following dialogue represents partial coordination of meaning:

BEN: We need to be straightforward with the girls now. I don't see any problem with sleeping in the same tent and letting the kids sleep in their tent. Patrick can sleep with us if he gets upset.

JESSIE: It's more complicated than that. This is the first time that we're all going to be together for a weekend.

BEN: Honey, if we don't try this right away, it'll be more difficult when we all move in together.

JESSIE: But the kids are still trying to get this situation all figured out. Separating things out this way may be more of a pain than we thought.

BEN: How about if we bought a larger tent and let the kids sleep on one side and we'll be on the other?

JESSIE: That's probably the best for now.

This partially coordinated dialogue closes the episode between the two parents. Both appear to be satisfied with the compromised sleeping arrangements.

Influences on the Coordination Process

Coordination is influenced by several issues, including a sense of morality and the availability of resources. In this section, we will examine both areas.

First, coordination requires that individuals be concerned with a higher moral order (Pearce, 1989). Many CMM theorists, like Pearce, explain morality as honor, dignity, and character. Moral order involves ethics, a topic we touched on in Chapter 1. Moral order is essentially an opportunity for individuals to assert an ethical stance in a conversation. CMM theorists contend that ethics is an inherent part of the conversational flow.

Each person brings various moral orders into a conversation to create and complete the episode. Pearce contends that people simultaneously perform various roles, such as sister, mother, lover, student, employee, friend, and citizen. He believes that each of these roles carries various rights and responsibilities that differ from one person to another. Difficulty arises, however, if

resources
stories, symbols, and
images that people
use to make sense
of their world

inconsistent moral obligations exist in conversations. For instance, in some cultures, men are identified as the sole decision makers and chief protectors of their family. This may conflict with women's obligations and may affect the coordination process in their conversations. These value differences may play themselves out throughout a relationship.

In addition to morality, coordination can be influenced by the resources available to an individual. When CMM theorists discuss **resources,** they refer to "the stories, images, symbols, and institutions that persons use to make their world meaningful" (Pearce, 1989, p. 23). Resources also include perceptions, memories, and concepts that help people achieve coherence in their social realities.

When there are incompatible or incommensurate resources in a conversation, coordination is challenged. To better understand this notion, consider the experiences of Loran and Wil. As a nineteen-year employee of a local steel mill, Loran is respected by the seven employees he supervises. Although he does not have a college degree, he relishes his seniority in a company that almost shut down a few years ago. Wil, however, has a college degree and an MBA. Because the company is interested in energizing its employees with fresh perspectives on management, it is hiring college graduates with management savvy. As a result, Wil became a new supervisor in Loran's department. These changes were marked by heated discussions and a great deal of disagreement between Loran and Wil. Loran's resources—his historical understanding of the factory, his relationships with his employees, the stories shared with others, the perceptions he has of the company's goals, and so forth—seem to be secondary to Wil's resources. Wil's resources are limited, because he has little understanding of the company's history, but he does bring his college education to his job, a credential shared by few at the factory. Because an incompatibility between resources exists, Loran and Wil may have difficulty coordinating their meaning. Two important, but incompatible, sets of resources exist between Loran and Wil, and each may threaten conversation coordination.

Coordinating conversations is critical to communication. At times, coordinating with others is simple, but at other times it is quite challenging. People bring different resources into conversations, prompting individuals to respond to others based on their own management of meaning. In addition to resources, coordination relies on the rules that conversationalists follow. We now explore rules and how they relate to CMM.

Rules and Unwanted Repetitive Patterns

One way that individuals manage and coordinate meaning is through the use of rules. Earlier in the chapter we mentioned that CMM follows a rules perspective. For CMM theorists, *rules* have a more specific definition than what we presented in Chapter 3. For Pearce and Cronen, rules provide people opportunities to choose between alternatives. Once rules are established in a dialogue, interactants will have a sufficiently common symbolic framework for communication (Cushman & Whiting, 1972). CMM theorists argue that rule usage in a conversation is more than an ability to use a rule; it also requires

"Let's stop this before we both say a lot of things we mean."

"flexible expanding abilities that cannot be reduced to technique" (Cronen, 1995, p. 224). Rules, therefore, are more than prescriptions for behavior. Interactants must understand the social reality and then incorporate rules as they decide how to act in a given situation.

Pearce and Cronen (1980) discuss two types of rules: constitutive and regulative. **Constitutive rules** refer to how behavior should be interpreted within a given context. Employing the meaning hierarchy described earlier in the chapter, we know that constitutive rules tell us how meanings at one level are interpreted on other meaning levels. In this case, we are able to understand another person's intention because of the constitutive rules in place. For example, saying "I love you" has different implications when you speak to a roommate, a lover, a family member, or even a co-worker. In each of these relationships, we adopt a rule that suggests that the relationship type (contract) and the episode will determine how the statement should be received. Clearly, constitutive rules help individuals assign meaning.

A second type of rule is the regulative rule. Whereas constitutive rules assist people in their interpretation of meaning, they do not provide people with guidelines for behavior. That is the function of regulative rules. **Regulative rules** refer to some sequence of action that an individual undertakes, and they communicate what happens next in a conversation.

To understand the interfacing of constitutive and regulative rules, consider the following situation. A couple married twenty years is having a crisis. The wife has discovered her husband's extramarital affair and must now decide

constitutive rules
organize behavior and
help us to understand
how meaning should
be interpreted

regulative rules
guidelines for people's
behavior

what constitutive and regulative rules to follow. She decides on a venting session because the constitutive rule tells her that such an affair is wrong in their marriage. In turn, her husband must determine how to interpret the venting (constitutive rule) and must construct some sequence of response (regulative rule). As the two engage in their discussion (and co-create their social reality), they will ultimately discover each other's rules systems. Although they have been married for two decades, this situation has not surfaced before, and consequently they may not know what the possibilities are in terms of constitutive and regulative rules. If they decide to continue in their dialogue, the two will discover each other's rules systems. Of course, as this discovery takes place, it is likely that the coordination of the conversation will be jeopardized. Each person, therefore, may enact different episodes along the way. They may not always agree on the rules enacted, but at least they are able to make sense out of their conversational experiences.

unwanted repetitive patterns (URPs)
recurring, undesirable conflicts in a relationship

    If the couple continue to have sustained conflict, they may engage in what Cronen, Pearce, and Linda Snavely (1979) identify as unwanted repetitive patterns (URPs). **Unwanted repetitive patterns** are sequential and recurring conflictual episodes that are considered unwanted by the individuals in the conflict. In their study, the researchers studied hostile workplace relationships and noted that although privately each worker communicated a genuine desire to be amicable and efficient, publicly their discussions were hostile and ego bruising. This verbal sparring seemed to be ripe for explanation using CMM. The researchers explained that URPs arise because two people with particular rules systems follow a structure that obligates them to perform specific behaviors, regardless of their consequences. It may seem peculiar that people believe they are obligated to act a certain way. Yet, Pearce (1989) reminds us that "persons find themselves in URPs . . . in which they report, with all sincerity, that 'I had no choice; I had to act this way'" (p. 39). Two people may continue to engage in unwanted repetitive patterns of behavior because they see no other available option. Our Research Note illustrates scholars' interest in URPs.

Charmed and Strange Loops

loop
the reflexiveness of levels in the hierarchy of meaning

The hierarchy of meaning presented earlier suggests that some lower levels can reflect back and affect the meaning of higher levels. Pearce and Cronen (1980) have termed this process of reflexivity a **loop**. Because the hierarchy cannot go

Research Note

Cronen, V. E., Pearce, W. B., & Snavely, L. M. (1979). A theory of rule-structure and types of episodes and a study of perceived enmeshment in undesired repetitive patterns (URPs). In D. Nimmo (Ed.), *Communication Yearbook 3* (pp. 225–240). New Brunswick, NJ: Transaction.

This article emphasizes the role that rules play in relational episodes. Cronen, Pearce, and Snavely extend the original thinking of CMM and emphasize how regulative rules function in conversation. The researchers utilize unwanted repetitive patterns (URPs) as one episode type and seek to develop an analytical schema using examples of these unwanted verbal fights.

In their study, thirty-four undergraduate students were asked to participate in two phases of the investigation. First, each person was asked to provide an account of a recent conversation. In order to get participants to focus on URPs, the interviewers stated the following: "You might be able to think of a conversation that seems to have a repetitive quality to it; that is, the same conversation seems to happen over and over whenever you and the other person discuss a certain topic. If not, you might be able to think of a conversation that proceeded well, in which you and the other person coordinated well. Sometimes our conversations can seem chaotic, and we don't know what will happen next" (p. 233). The subsequent discussions were taped and later transcribed by the researchers. Following their interviews, the participants were asked to complete a number of questions that pertained to speech acts and rule structure (earlier they had demonstrated no difficulty in labeling what a speech act is and what consequences existed when an act occurred).

To calculate how rules and URPs intersect, the researchers developed a formula for assessing how enmeshed—that is, how out of control—participants felt in URPs when certain rules were implemented in a conversation. The results of this study indicate that participants were enmeshed in their URPs a great deal of the time. In addition, the researchers contend that a number of conditions existed that accounted for over 50 percent of the reasons why these participants felt so enmeshed. These conditions included questioning whether the speech acts were necessary, the extent to which the rules constrained or facilitated conversations, and perceptions of whether the pattern was wanted or unwanted.

The researchers state that this study indicates the relationships of rules to URPs; they also acknowledge that their results clarify early conceptualizations of CMM. Further, Cronen and his colleagues agree that the results provide sufficient evidence for including rules in future research on conversations.

In addition, they note that future research should not ignore an individual's relationship to the rules in a conversation. They conclude that a "goodness of fit" may exist "between individuals and the rules of the systems of which they are members" (p. 239).

on forever, the theorists propose that some levels reflect back. This supports their view that communication is an ongoing, dynamic, and ever-changing process.

When loops are consistent throughout the hierarchy, Pearce and Cronen identify them as a **charmed loop.** Charmed loops occur when one part of the hierarchy confirms or supports another level. Consider the following example. You hired a painter to repaint the first floor of your home. You agreed to pay the painter by the hour, and when you receive the bill, you are shocked at the price. You confront the painter, stating that you observed a lot of "wasted" hours and that you are not going to pay the entire bill. The painter is prepared to challenge your judgment.

This encounter between painter and client exemplifies a charmed loop. In this case, the episode, or event, is the disagreement you both have over the costs of painting your home. Because your life script is your sense of self, your

charmed loop
rules of meaning are consistent throughout the loop

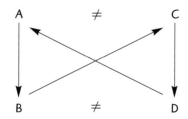

Figure 6.2
Strange Loops

life script in this encounter is consistent with your passion to stand up for what you believe. In this example, the cultural pattern suggests that the two of you—painter and client—enter the conflict with two different views of the situation. The painter wants to get paid for a service and the client wants to feel satisfied with the service. In this brief example, the loop is charmed in that there is consistency among the levels (episode, life script, cultural pattern) in the hierarchy. In other words, the encounter makes sense in that your willingness to challenge the bill is consistent with who you are, and the way you communicate with the painter is consistent with the cultural expectations of this type of relationship. The rules of meaning in this interaction are confirmed throughout the loop.

At times, however, some episodes are inconsistent with levels higher up in the hierarchy. Pearce and Cronen have called this a **strange loop**. We illustrate strange loops in Figure 6.2.

To exemplify strange loops, the theorists offer the case of an alcoholic whose bouts with sobriety are followed by bouts of drinking. We present this strange loop in Figure 6.3. In this strange loop, confusion sets in. The life script of an alcoholic, for instance, suggests that drinking is out of control, so the alcoholic refuses to drink. But once the drinking stops, an alcoholic may feel a sense of control, so drinking begins again. In this example, the life script is the person's alcoholism, which manages meaning (or drinking) in particular episodes. The episodes are part of the alcoholic's life script. It's apparent, then, that the strange loop will continue to repeat itself. We call this a vicious cycle.

strange loop
rules of meaning change within the loop

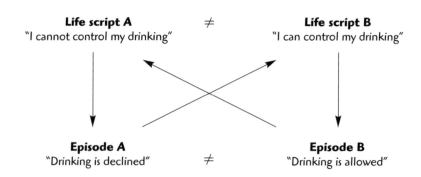

Figure 6.3
Example of a
Strange Loop
Source: Adapted from Branham & Pearce, 1985.

Critique and Closing

Coordinated Management of Meaning is one of the few theories to explicitly place communication as a cornerstone in its foundation. Because communication is central to the theory, many scholars have employed the theory in their writings. To this end, CMM is a heuristic effort. Researchers have incorporated the theory and its tenets to understand conflict (Pearce & Littlejohn, 1997), cultural communities (Narula & Pearce, 1986), conversations (Pearce & Conklin, 1979), groups (Pearce & Pearce, 2000), families (Cronen, Johnson, & Lannamann, 1982; Harris, 1980; Harris, Cronen, & McNamee, 1979), organizations (Cronen, Pearce, & Snavely, 1979), and public address (Branham & Pearce, 1985). In addition, the theory is broad in scope, in that it covers both the intrapersonal and interpersonal processes. Pearce and Cronen attempt to understand what takes place in the minds of communicators and how they manage meaning. Although some writers have criticized the theory because communication does not explicitly frame the CMM studies (Philipsen, 1995), the theory nonetheless consistently incorporates communication action. In terms of CMM's usefulness, the theorists claim that the theory is practical (Cronen, 1995). Considering that it tries to understand everyday conversations, we believe that the theory passes the test of utility.

Despite these strengths, CMM has been criticized by communication scholars. David Brenders (1987), for example, takes issue with Pearce and Cronen's belief that individuals introduce unique language systems into their conversations with others; for CMM theorists, meaning is an intrapersonal experience. Brenders disagrees. He argues that "we do share a language which is not our idiosyncratic production, but a medium of shared symbolic meanings" (1987, p. 342). For Brenders and others, the examples that Pearce and his associates use consistently underscore the fact that the rules inherent in a conversation may differ from one person to another. This is too broad a claim, says Brenders, and in fact "leaves unexplained the social nature of meaning" (1987, p. 342). The theory's validity, therefore, is suspect if one believes this claim.

Pearce and Cronen have attempted to respond to their critics over the years. First, they believe that many critics forget that they were trained within the empiricist tradition, something we explained in detail in Chapter 4. Therefore, their earlier discussions of the theory were rooted in this heritage. Pearce (1995) candidly admits that during "'the first phase of the CMM project,' [our writings] were confused because we used the language of interpretive social science. . . . Only as we continued to refine our thinking did we discover . . . that we *could not* say what we were doing in the language of . . . social science" (pp. 109, 110). Therefore, critics should interpret the theory within the spirit of change; even theorists change as they clarify the goals of their theory. Further, Cronen (1995) admits some early problems with the conceptualization of their theory by indicating that the way that he and Pearce discussed the creation of meaning was originally confusing and "wrong-headed." The theorists believe, however, that what they have produced is an ethical undertaking and do not believe that their theory should be discarded because of some past misjudgments. Pearce and Cronen, then, believe that those who levy indictments

Theory * Into * Practice

John Gottman and Nan Silver wrote an essay in *New Woman*. The two discuss how recurring conflict pervades a number of relationships. According to Gottman and Silver, conflict does not have to be the sounding call for the end of a relationship. Their article demonstrates that unwanted repetitive patterns emerge in both newly developed and established relationships. Although a couple recognizes that conflict can be damaging in their relationship, they nonetheless find themselves at odds over a number of issues. Their premise is clearly related to URPs: "Why do some couples get caught up in an endless cycle of arguments while others cope more gracefully" (p. 85)?

Gottman and Silver believe that "every couple, no matter how in sync, sometimes locks horns" (p. 85). With that, they note that couples experience unwanted recurring conflicts over seemingly benign issues ("how to hang the toilet paper roll") as well as more serious issues ("how often to socialize with others"). They trace the experiences of a few couples who the authors believe are functioning couples. For instance, one partner is prepared to quit his job and look for a new position while the other partner tries to finish a long-postponed college degree. Instead of having recurring conflicts over the consequences of getting a new job and not finishing college, the couple heads off serious conflict by devising a plan that meets the goals of both people. Gottman and Silver conclude, "Making decisions this way—with respect for each other's life goals—is what gives a relationship meaning" (p. 86).

The article continues by identifying several ways for couples to move beyond the cyclical nature of conflict. The prescriptions offered by the authors include: (1) defining the core areas on which you cannot yield; (2) defining your areas of flexibility; (3) devising a compromise that honors both perspectives; and (4) saying thank you.

Gottman and Silver acknowledge that relational partners are frequently at loggerheads over a number of topics. What is important as two people try to work out the conflict is not so much the source of the conflict, but rather what the conflict represents. Too many recurring and unwanted conflicts occur in a relationship when neither partner realizes the root of the disagreement. For instance, arguing about whether to go out to dinner every Sunday night may not have anything to do with Sunday or going out. Rather, the authors believe that it may reveal the fact that one partner used to do that with his family, "a ritual that made him feel special" (p. 85). As the authors conclude, "the conflict is not about where you eat, but about what makes each of you feel loved" (p. 85).

Gottman and Silver believe that in order for couples to remove themselves from future, unwanted, and unproductive conflict, they must be willing to suspend judgment, avoid rebuttals, and ask supportive questions. These sound fine in theory, say the authors, but in practice, they can be quite difficult.

Source: Gottman & Silver, 1999.

TIP Follow-up
How do communication rules influence what is being identified in this essay? Is it possible for both partners to have separate rules for the same relationship? How?

against their theory should understand the time period in which the theory was developed.

CMM proponents have responded to additional criticisms. For instance, some (Cronen, Pearce, & Changshen, 1989/1990) argue that critics such as Brenders fail to recognize that their interpretation of meaning is based on a view of communication not shared by their theoretical ancestors. Therefore, to suggest that meaning cannot be co-constructed and to claim that a "deficient notion of meaning" (Brenders, 1987, p. 341) exists within CMM is limiting and uninformed. Pearce and Karen Foss (1990) further believe that messages derive their meanings from a co-construction of the social interaction, not simply the meaning one brings into an interaction. Therefore, although Brenders's critique is aimed at the way Pearce and others interpret meaning, Pearce believes that CMM should not be reduced to a simplified view of what meaning is and is not.

The struggle to understand the dynamic interplay of intrapersonal and interpersonal communication will continue. Thanks in large part to CMM, we have a deeper understanding of how individuals co-create their meaning. Further, the theory has aided us in understanding the importance of rules in social situations. Critics may continue their critique of the theory, but few can deny that CMM positioned communication at the core of human experience. That makes Coordinated Management of Meaning one of the few communication theories that is "firmly in the world it describes" (Anderson, 1996, p. 209).

Discussion Starters

1. What types of coordination will the Taylor-Murphy family experience as they begin a life together? Try to identify stages that the family may experience and specific episodes of coordination.

2. How would you explain the reasoning behind Pearce and Cronen's hierarchy of meaning?

3. Discuss enmeshment and its relationship to conversations in your family. Be sure to define the term and apply it to your family relationships.

4. Chess and poker are games requiring coordination. Discuss some of life's games and how they require coordination. Be creative and give specific examples.

5. What types of meaning breakdowns have you experienced in your conversations with others? Be specific and identify the context, the situation, and the conversation topic.

6. Identify and explain a strange loop that exists in popular culture or in your interpersonal relationships.

Terms for Review

social reality
personal meaning
interpersonal meaning
raw data
content
speech acts
contract
enmeshment
episodes
punctuate
life scripts

cultural patterns
individualism
collectivism
coordination
resources
constitutive rules
regulative rules
unwanted repetitive patterns (URPs)
loop
charmed loop
strange loop

 ### Online Learning Center

Visit the Online Learning Center at www.mhhe.com/west2. Use
the multiple-choice and true/false quizzes to help you prepare for
exams, and the glossary, crossword puzzles, and flashcards to further
your knowledge of key terms.

CHAPTER 7

Cognitive Dissonance Theory

Ali Torres

Ali Torres shuffled through the papers on her desk and looked out the office window. She was really bored with this job. When she initially signed on to work with the Puerto Rican Alliance in Gary, Indiana, she was so excited. The job seemed to be a dream come true. First, it offered her a chance to give back to her community—both the city of Gary and the Puerto Rican community within the city. She had grown up in Gary, Indiana, and knew firsthand how difficult it was to get ahead for people of color, especially Latinos. Latinos were a minority among minorities in this city, and it was tough to make much progress. Despite that, Ali had gotten a lot from growing up in Gary. When she was in high school, a friendly guidance counselor had offered her a helping hand and suggested that Ali consider college. Without Ms. Martinez's support, she never would have thought about college, much less actually graduated. But Ali had finished college and now she felt strongly about giving something back. So, the job had seemed perfect; it would be a way for her to give back to the community and at the same time use her major in public relations.

Yet, in the six months Ali had worked in the Alliance office, her sole responsibilities had centered on typing and running errands. She felt like a gofer with no chance to do anything she considered important. Actually, she was beginning to question whether the Alliance itself was doing anything worthwhile. Sometimes she thought the whole operation was just a front so politicians could say something was being done to help the Latino population in the city.

Her co-workers didn't seem to mind that they didn't do much all day, so Ali wasn't getting much support from them. But it was her boss's attitude that bothered Ali the most. He was a respected leader in the Latino community; she remembered him from when she was growing up. When she found out she would be working for him, she had been delighted. But as far as Ali could tell, he hardly ever worked at all. He was rarely in the office, and when he did come in, he took long lunch hours and many breaks. He spoke to Ali very infrequently and never gave her assignments.

Ali was feeling extremely frustrated. She was on her own to develop projects or, more likely, simply to put in eight hours doing a lot of nothing. Ali had decided that she would quit this job and start looking for something where she could feel more useful, but she was having a hard time giving up on her dream of contributing to her community. She had begun this job with such high hopes. She had expected to work to persuade funding agencies to sponsor programs to strengthen opportunities for the Latino community. Ironically, now she found that the only person she was persuading was herself, as she wrestled with the decision of whether

This theory is based on the research of **Leon Festinger.**

to keep working or give up on this job. Ali spoke to some of her friends, who encouraged her to do what she thought was right and quit the Alliance if she wanted to. That made her feel better, but she couldn't completely shake her memories of the auspicious beginning of the job and all her high hopes.

Suppose you are Ali Torres's mother, and you are interested in knowing how she feels about her job. You notice that she seems a little depressed when she talks about work, and lately she hasn't brought up the subject at all. Her silence about her work is especially obvious to you compared to how enthusiastically she spoke about the position when she first started at the Alliance. You could ask Ali directly how she feels, but you wonder how honest she will be with you. You know Ali doesn't want you to worry about her. You also know that Ali cares a great deal about the ideals of the Alliance and that she might not want to tell you if she is disappointed. Your problem in this situation is inferring Ali's attitudes.

The problem faced by Ali's mother is a common one because people's attitudes cannot be directly observed; yet attitudes are believed to be excellent predictors of people's behaviors. As Susan Fiske and Shelley Taylor (1984) observe, "Attitudes have always been accorded star status in social explanations of human behavior by lay people and professionals alike" (p. 341). Because of their importance, many theories try to explain attitude formation, change, and the interlocking relationship among cognitions, attitudes, affect, and behavioral tendencies. Many psychologists (for example, Fiske and Taylor) assert that the most influential approaches to attitudes derive from cognitive consistency theories.

Consistency theories in general posit that the mind operates as an intermediary between stimulus and response. The theories assert that when people receive information (a stimulus), their minds organize it into a pattern with other previously encountered stimuli. If the new stimulus does not fit the pattern, or is inconsistent, then people feel discomfort. For example, if you believe that authority figures deserve respect and usually work in a moral, upright fashion, you would have found the publicity in 2002 about corporate accounting scandals such as Enron and insider trading allegations against Martha Stewart to be inconsistent with your beliefs. Ali Torres also feels this type of discomfort as she reflects on the discrepancy between her desire to respect her boss and her observations of his seeming indifference to the job. In these cases, consistency theorists note that there is a lack of balance among **cognitions,** or ways of knowing or beliefs, judgments, and so forth.

Leon Festinger called this feeling of imbalance **cognitive dissonance;** this is the feeling people have when they "find themselves doing things that don't fit with what they know, or having opinions that do not fit with other opinions they hold" (1957, p. 4). This concept forms the core of Festinger's Cognitive Dissonance Theory (CDT), a theory that argues that dissonance is an uncomfortable feeling that motivates people to take steps to reduce it (see Figure 7.1). As Roger

cognitions
ways of knowing, beliefs, judgments, and thoughts

cognitive dissonance
feeling of discomfort resulting from inconsistent attitudes, thoughts, and behaviors

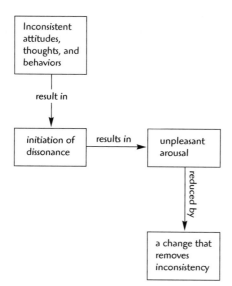

Figure 7.1
The Process of Cognitive Dissonance

Brown (1965) notes, the basics of the theory follow rather simple principles: "A state of cognitive dissonance is said to be a state of psychological discomfort or tension which motivates efforts to achieve consonance. *Dissonance* is the name for a disequilibrium and *consonance* the name for an equilibrium" (p. 584). Further, Brown points out that the theory allows for two elements to have three different relationships with each other: They may be consonant, dissonant, or irrelevant.

A **consonant relationship** exists between two elements when they are in equilibrium with one another. If you believed, for instance, that health and fitness were important goals and you worked out three to five times a week, then your beliefs about health and your own behaviors would have a consonant relationship with one another. Ali would have a consonant relationship if she believed that the Alliance was really making a difference in the Hispanic community and that her work was meaningful. A **dissonant relationship** means that elements are in disequilibrium with one another. An example of a dissonant relationship between elements would be a practicing Catholic who believed in a woman's right to choose abortion. In this case, the person's religious beliefs would be in conflict with her political beliefs about abortion. Ali Torres is experiencing a dissonant relationship.

An **irrelevant relationship** exists when elements imply nothing about one another. This type of relationship is illustrated by believing that the speed limit should be raised to 65 miles per hour on all freeways and believing that women should have equal rights in the workplace. Although the two beliefs may indicate a general view endorsing individual freedoms, they basically have no relationship to each other. When beliefs are consonant or irrelevant, there is no psychological discomfort. However, if beliefs are dissonant, discomfort results.

The importance of cognitive dissonance for communication researchers is Festinger's assertion that the discomfort caused by dissonance motivates

consonant relationship
two elements in equilibrium with one another

dissonant relationship
two elements in disequilibrium with one another

irrelevant relationship
two elements that have no meaningful relation to one another

Theory Application in Groups (TAG)

In small groups, create a role play that illustrates some of the ways dissonance can be increased and reduced.

change. As we see in our opening vignette, Ali Torres is feeling frustrated and uncomfortable in her job. Her initial belief about the opportunities for her to help others through this job and her prior high regard for her boss are inconsistent with her present situation. This is the point at which persuasion can occur. The theory suggests that to be persuasive, strategies should focus on the inconsistencies while providing new behaviors that allow for consistency or balance. Further, cognitive dissonance may motivate communication behavior as people seek to persuade others and as people strive to reduce their dissonant cognitions. For example, when Ali went to her friends to discuss her decision, she was seeking help in reducing dissonance. Her conversations with friends and her efforts at self-persuasion are instances of communication being used in the dissonance reduction process.

Assumptions of Cognitive Dissonance Theory

As we have indicated, Cognitive Dissonance Theory is an account of how beliefs and behavior change attitudes. Its focus is on the effects of inconsistency among cognitions. Our introductory material suggested a number of assumptions that frame Cognitive Dissonance Theory. Here we summarize four assumptions basic to the theory:

- Human beings desire consistency in their cognitions.
- Dissonance is created by psychological inconsistencies.
- Dissonance is an aversive state that drives people to actions with measurable effects.
- Dissonance motivates efforts to achieve consonance and efforts toward dissonance reduction.

The first assumption posits a model of human nature that is concerned with stability and consistency. When we discuss Uncertainty Reduction Theory in Chapter 9, you will see a similar conceptualization of human nature. Cognitive Dissonance Theory suggests that people do not enjoy inconsistencies in their thoughts and beliefs. Instead, they seek consistency. This is why Ali feels uncomfortable in her job and unhappy with her thoughts about quitting the job. She is seeking consistency, yet her perceptions of her job provide her with inconsistency.

The second assumption speaks to the kind of consistency that is important to people. The theory is not concerned with a strict logical consistency. Rather, it refers to the fact that cognitions must be psychologically inconsistent (as opposed to logically inconsistent) with one another to arouse cognitive dissonance. For example, if Ali Torres holds the cognition that "I want to contribute to my community," it is not logically inconsistent to also believe that the Alliance is not contributing much to the community. The two beliefs are not logically contradictory in the same way that simultaneously holding beliefs about the immorality of abortion and the validity of women's right to choose abortion would be. Yet, it is psychologically inconsistent for Ali to continue to work for the Alliance when she believes it is doing little to help Latinos in Gary, Indiana. That is, Ali will feel psychologically inconsistent by continuing to do nothing when she wishes to be of help. Ali also is stressed by her thoughts of quitting and her lingering hopes for what she might have accomplished in this job.

The third assumption of the theory suggests that when people experience psychological inconsistencies the dissonance that is created is aversive. Thus, people do not enjoy being in a state of dissonance; it is an uncomfortable state. Festinger asserted that dissonance is a drive state possessing arousal properties. Since Festinger's initial conceptualization of the theory, a significant amount of research has supported this assumption (Zanna & Cooper, 1976). Another study (Elkin & Leippe, 1986) found that physiological arousal was related to dissonance. Cognitive Dissonance Theory would assume that Ali would feel uncomfortable as a result of the psychological dissonance that she is experiencing.

Finally, the theory assumes that the arousal generated by dissonance will motivate people to avoid situations that create inconsistencies and strive toward situations that restore consistency. Thus, the picture of human nature that frames the theory is one of seeking psychological consistency as a result of the arousal caused by the aversive state of inconsistent cognitions.

Concepts and Processes of Cognitive Dissonance

As the theory developed, certain concepts were refined. For example, the following scenario illustrates a situation where dissonance would arise: If Juan believes that relationships should be completely harmonious (a cognition) and yet he argues a great deal with his partner (a conflicting cognition about his behavior), the theory predicts that Juan will become tense and suffer discomfort. When dissonance theorists seek to predict how much discomfort or dissonance Juan will suffer, they acknowledge the concept of magnitude of dissonance. **Magnitude of dissonance** refers to the quantitative amount of dissonance a person experiences. Magnitude of dissonance will determine actions people may take and cognitions they may espouse to reduce the dissonance. The theory differentiates between situations producing more dissonance and those producing less dissonance.

magnitude of dissonance
the quantitative amount of discomfort felt

Magnitude of Dissonance

There are three factors that influence the magnitude of dissonance a person will feel (Zimbardo, Ebbesen, & Maslach, 1977). First, the degree of **importance**, or how significant the issue is, affects the degree of dissonance felt. If, for

importance
a factor in determining magnitude of dissonance; refers to how significant the issue is

example, Juan has many friendships and activities outside his relationship and his partner is not critically important to him, the amount of dissonance will be much less than if he finds much of his identity and social interaction in his relationship with his partner. The same could be said for Ali Torres. If she does a great deal of volunteer work in the community and her job is not the main source of her identity, then the magnitude of her dissonance is not as great as if her job is critically important to her and the primary way in which she seeks to accomplish her goal of giving back to her community.

dissonance ratio
a factor in determining magnitude of dissonance; the amount of consonant cognitions relative to the dissonant ones

Second, the amount of dissonance is affected by the **dissonance ratio,** or the amount of dissonant cognitions relative to the amount of consonant cognitions. Given Juan's propensity to argue with his partner, he probably has many cognitions that are relevant to that behavior. Some of these cognitions are consonant with his behavior; for example, "It is good to get feelings out in the open." "It is positive to feel you can really be yourself with your partner." "Sometimes arguing allows you both to see problems in a creative way." Several of his cognitions are dissonant with conflict behavior, however; for example, "If we really loved each other, we wouldn't argue so much." "We spend so much time fighting, we never have any fun." "Our fights are so repetitive, we never solve anything." "My parents never argued with each other; we must not be very sensitive to each other." "I didn't picture my relationship like this." Because Juan has more dissonant cognitions than consonant ones, the ratio is negative. Thus, Juan is likely to feel that there is inconsistency, and dissonance will result. If the ratio were more balanced, Juan would feel less dissonance.

rationale
a factor in determining magnitude of dissonance; refers to the reasoning employed to explain the inconsistency

Finally, the magnitude of dissonance is affected by the rationale that an individual summons to justify the inconsistency. The **rationale** refers to the reasoning employed to explain why an inconsistency exists. The more reasons one has to account for the discrepancy, the less dissonance one will feel. For instance, if Juan and his partner have just moved, changed or lost a job, purchased a home, or experienced any other stressor, Juan may be able to justify the conflicts as being a result of the stress he is feeling and thus probably a temporary situation. In this case, it is likely that the dissonance he feels will be much less than if he is unable to come up with any rationale explaining his behaviors.

Coping with Dissonance

Although Cognitive Dissonance Theory explains that dissonance can be reduced through both behavioral and attitudinal changes, most of the research has focused on the latter. Many ways to increase consistency are cognitively based, and the theory suggests that there are several methods that Juan may use to reduce his dissonance. For example, Juan could add or subtract cognitions to change the ratio of consonant to dissonant cognitions. In Juan's case, this might mean adding the fact that his friends Jeff and Don fight a lot but seem to be happy, and subtracting the idea that he didn't picture his relationship as full of conflict. Juan might try to reduce the importance of the dissonant cognitions. He might think about the fact that children do not know much about their parents' relationship, so the fact that he did not think his parents fought a lot might not weigh too heavily in the equation. Juan could seek out information that advocates conflict in relationships and stresses the benefits of open communication between partners. Additionally, he might distort the information that suggests conflict is not good for a relationship by believing that it comes from an unrealistic, overly optimistic point of view.

Cognitive Dissonance and Perception

As Juan engages in any of these strategies to change his cognitions and reduce his feelings of dissonance, perceptual processes come into play. Specifically, Cognitive Dissonance Theory relates to the processes of selective exposure, selective attention, selective interpretation, and selective retention because the theory predicts that people will avoid information that increases dissonance. These perceptual processes are basic to this avoidance.

Selective exposure, or seeking consistent information not already present, helps to reduce dissonance. CDT predicts that people will avoid information that increases dissonance and seek out information that is consistent with their attitudes and behavior. In the example of the conflictual relationship, Juan might seek friends who also fight a great deal yet seem to be happy in their relationships.

Selective attention refers to looking at consistent information once it is there. People attend to information in their environment that conforms to their attitudes and beliefs while ignoring information that is inconsistent. Thus, Ali Torres might read positive articles about the Alliance in the newspaper while overlooking articles to the contrary.

Selective interpretation involves interpreting ambiguous information so that it becomes consistent. Utilizing selective interpretation, most people interpret close friends' attitudes as more congruent with their own than is actually true (Berscheid & Walster, 1978). Elaine Showalter (1997) discusses the seeming inconsistency of being a feminist critic while also loving to shop and wear feminine clothing and accessories. She interprets advice given to her by an academic about dressing conservatively as actually agreeing with her position that we should put "the *femme* back into feminist" (p. 80). People use selective interpretation to avoid potential dissonance.

Finally, **selective retention** refers to remembering and learning consistent information with much greater ability than we do inconsistent information. Cognitive Dissonance Theory predicts that if a couple were arguing about whether to spend a vacation camping or on a cruise, the partner who wished to camp would not remember the details of the cruise package and the one desiring the cruise would not remember much about the camping plans. If Juan heard a lecture once about how important conflict can be in close relationships, he may well remember that in his current situation of frequent fighting with his partner. Similarly, Ali might focus on stories she heard in the past about good works that the Alliance has done.

Attitudes seem to organize memory (Lingle & Ostrom, 1981). When thinking about someone as your teacher, you will remember her ability to lecture, her command of the subject, her ability to get a discussion started, and her

selective exposure
a method for reducing dissonance by seeking information that is consonant with current beliefs and actions

selective attention
a method for reducing dissonance by paying attention to information that is consonant with current beliefs and actions

selective interpretation
a method for reducing dissonance by interpreting ambiguous information so that it becomes consistent with current beliefs and actions

selective retention
a method for reducing dissonance by remembering information that is consonant with current beliefs and actions

accessibility to help you with assignments. If, on the other hand, you were thinking about the same person as an actor, you would recall her ability to project a character and to gain your interest. Once you have formed an attitude about someone as a teacher rather than an actor, that influences your recall about that person.

Minimal Justification

minimal justification
offering the least amount of incentive necessary to obtain compliance

One of the interesting and counterintuitive assertions that Festinger advances in this theory has to do with what he calls minimal justification. **Minimal justification** has to do with offering only the minimum incentive required to get someone to change. Festinger (1957) argues that "if one wanted to obtain private change in addition to mere public compliance, the best way to do this would be to offer just enough reward or punishment to elicit compliance" (p. 95).

The experiment that Festinger and his colleague James Carlsmith performed that established the principle of minimal justification is the now-famous one dollar/twenty dollars study. Festinger and Carlsmith (1959) recruited male students at Stanford University and assigned them to do a boring, repetitive task consisting of sorting spools into lots of twelve and giving square pegs a quarter turn to the right. At the end of an hour of this monotonous assignment, the experimenter asked the research participants to do him a favor. The researcher explained that they needed another person to continue doing this task and offered to pay the participants to recruit a woman in the waiting room by telling her how enjoyable the task was. This woman was actually a research assistant also, and she was helping the researchers examine how the men tried to persuade her. Some of the men were offered one dollar to recruit the woman, whereas others were offered twenty dollars for the same behavior. Remember, this was 1959, and both these sums were worth a great deal more than they are now. Twenty dollars then would be close to sixty dollars today. Festinger and Carlsmith found that the men engaged in this study differed in their attitudes at the end. Those who received twenty dollars for recruiting the woman said that they really thought the task was boring, whereas those who received only one dollar stated that they really believed the task was enjoyable.

From these results came the notion of minimal justification. Festinger and Carlsmith argue that doing something a person does not believe in for a minimal reward sets up more dissonance than doing that same thing for a larger re-

The Theory Chronicles

For the next week, chronicle in your journal examples of situations that provoke dissonance for you. Plot them using the concepts and processes of CDT from the chapter. At the end of the week, evaluate CDT using at least three criteria from Chapter 3.

ward. If people engage in deception for a lot of money, they will acknowledge that they did it for the money. If they engage in deception for only one dollar, they do not have a ready explanation that will make their attitudes and behaviors form a consonant relationship. In order to reduce their dissonance, they have to make some type of change to bring consistency to their cognitions. Therefore, they may change their opinion of the task to make sense of why they told the woman in the waiting room that it was fun. Now they believe they told her it was fun because, in fact, it *was* enjoyable. Thus, minimal justification sets up more cognitive dissonance and requires more change to reduce it than a more substantial justification would.

Cognitive Dissonance Theory and Persuasion

Much of the research following from Festinger's work focuses on persuasion, especially with regard to decision making. A large amount of research concentrates on cognitive dissonance as a postdecision phenomenon. Several studies examine **buyer's remorse**, which refers to the dissonance people often feel after deciding on a large purchase. An interesting study about buyer's remorse related to automobile purchases (Donnelly & Ivancevich, 1970). In their study, they located people who were waiting for delivery of cars they had signed contracts to buy. These people were divided into two groups. One group was contacted twice to reassure them about the wisdom of their purchase. Another group was not contacted between the contract signing and the delivery of the car. About twice as many in the group that was not contacted canceled the order for the car. This finding supported the theory that dissonance may be activated after making a large purchase. Further, the study showed that providing people with information about the wisdom of their decision can reduce the dissonance. This finding speaks to the importance of the decision and to manipulating the dissonance ratio, factors we discussed earlier in the chapter.

Another study (Knox & Inkster, 1968) investigated this regret period after a decision in a different context. This study had experimenters approach people either shortly before or shortly after they had placed a two-dollar bet at a Canadian racetrack. The bettors were asked how confident they felt about their horse's chances. Their findings indicated that people were more confident that their horse would win after they had placed the bet than they were before they placed the bet. They interpreted these findings as consistent with Cognitive Dissonance Theory because they reasoned that after the bet has been placed, people feel dissonance. The decision to choose one particular horse is dissonant with the belief that the horse has flaws that could prevent it from winning the race. A simple coping mechanism for reducing this dissonance is to increase the beliefs about the attractiveness of the horse that you bet on, or the chosen alternative. Thus, the theory would predict, and Knox and Inkster found, bettors expressing more confidence after making their decision than before. As Robert Wicklund and Jack W. Brehm (1976) point out, when a decision is irrevocable, as in a bet placed, people have to work quickly to reduce the inevitable dissonance that results.

buyer's remorse
postdecision dissonance related to a purchase

Festinger and two colleagues also examined postdecision dissonance in a pioneering case study (Festinger, Riecken, & Schachter, 1956). They followed the ethnographic method we discussed in Chapter 4. Festinger and his colleagues joined a doomsday cult based in Chicago in the 1950s. The group was led by a middle-aged man and woman. The woman, whom the researchers named Mrs. Keech, began to receive messages from spiritual beings who seemed to be predicting a great disaster, a flood that would end the world. Then the spiritual beings transmitted information to Mrs. Keech that the members of the cult would be saved before the flood. The group was instructed that spacemen would arrive and transport the believers to safety on another planet. The believers began to make preparations for the end of their world and their departure to another world. The appointed time for departure was midnight, and the group gathered in Mrs. Keech's living room to await the spaceship that would take them to safety. As the moments slipped by, it became apparent that no one was coming to rescue the believers, and, in fact, they did not need to be rescued because the world was not under water. At first, the cult seemed on the verge of disintegration as a result of the extreme dissonance everyone was feeling. Yet, the group was so committed to their beliefs that they found ways to reconcile the dissonance.

The group reconciled their dissonance in two specific ways. First, Mrs. Keech claimed a new message came from the spiritual beings telling the group that their faith had caused God to save the world from destruction. Thus, the group used selective interpretation and allowed new information through selective attention. Second, Mrs. Keech said she had received an additional message telling the group to publicize the situation. The group became energized again, reduced their dissonance, and confirmed themselves in their decision to be members of the group.

More recently, some researchers have examined the relationship of dissonance and communication strategies in situations other than decision making. Patrice Buzzanell and Lynn Turner (2003) examined family communication in families where the major wage earner had lost his or her job within the past eighteen months. Buzzanell and Turner interviewed family members to assess the communication issues created by the job loss.

Buzzanell and Turner observed that job loss did create feelings of dissonance in most family members, and the researchers argued that family members reduced their dissonance about job loss by using three interesting strategies. First, families adopted a tone of normalcy, telling the interviewers that nothing had really changed after the job loss. Second, families deliberately foregrounded positive themes and backgrounded negative ones. In doing this, families engaged in selective perceptual processes. Many times they reframed their situation by engaging in selective interpretation, suggesting that time off work was helpful to their family and that it allowed family members all to get back in touch with one another. Finally, families maintained gendered identity construction, working to assure the man who had lost his job that he was still the man of the family. In all of these strategies, family members worked to reduce the dissonance created by job loss.

In yet another context, Patricia Sullivan and Lynn Turner (1996) examined strategies used by female politicians to cope with assumptions about women in the public domain. Sullivan and Turner argue that women are somewhat restricted by old stereotypes that relegate them to the home and private sphere, reserving public life for men. To examine this assertion, Sullivan and Turner profiled several women in public life in the 1990s. One of their case studies was of Lani Guinier, who was nominated by President Clinton to be the Assistant Attorney General for Civil Rights. Guinier withdrew her nomination before the confirmation hearings after suffering scathing treatment in the press concerning her views on affirmative action and voting rights. One of Sullivan and Turner's main points about Guinier's abortive nomination was that Guinier maintained silence during the period when she was being savaged and misrepresented in the media. Sullivan and Turner argue that Guinier did not speak out because she believed that the truth would vindicate her. Sullivan and Turner imply that Guinier sought to play by the rules, because to do otherwise would have caused her too much dissonance. Her strategy for coping and keeping consistency ultimately cost her the chance to defend herself in confirmation hearings.

As this brief review indicates, CDT has been employed in countless studies examining decision making. Further, some recent studies have explored the processes of dissonance and dissonance reduction in contexts such as family and political communication. Thus, CDT continues to be a theoretical force for explaining communication behaviors.

Critique and Closing

Although researchers have been using and revising Festinger's theory since 1957, and some scholars point to the theory as the primary achievement of social psychology (Aron & Aron, 1989), the theory does have weaknesses and detractors.

One weakness that scholars point out relates specifically to our criterion of testability, discussed in Chapter 3. As you recall, testability refers to the theory's likelihood of ever being proven false. Theories that have a seeming escape clause against being falsified are not as strong as those that do not. Researchers have pointed out that because Cognitive Dissonance Theory asserts that dissonance will motivate people to act, when people do not act, proponents of the theory can say that the dissonance must not have been strong enough, rather than concluding that the theory is wrong. In this way it is difficult to disprove the theory.

The Theory Connection

Compare the scope of Cognitive Dissonance Theory to that of Symbolic Interaction Theory. Can you justify calling explanatory systems with such differences both "theories?" Explain your answer with examples.

Research Note

Gerard, H. B., & Mathewson, G. C. (1966). The effect of severity of initiation on liking for a group: A replication. *Journal of Experimental Social Psychology, 2,* 278–287.

This study was conducted to test Cognitive Dissonance Theory—specifically, to test a possible "afterglow" hypothesis that might threaten the logic of cognitive dissonance explanations. The afterglow hypothesis suggests that people who are happy about being admitted to groups that made them undergo difficult initiations might be so because of the excitement of getting in, rather than because of dissonance reduction.

This study involved telling the participants that in order to be admitted into a group, they would have to undergo a series of physiological tests, some involving electric shocks. Half the participants received mild shocks, and half received severe shocks. Half of the entire group was then told that they were admitted to the group, whereas half were told nothing. Then all the participants listened to a discussion that was supposedly held by the group the participants wanted to join. The discussion was staged to be very boring and uninvolving. Participants were asked to evaluate this group. The findings indicated that regardless of whether or not they had been told they were admitted to the group, participants who had received severe shocks evaluated the group more positively than those who had received mild shocks.

These findings provide support for cognitive dissonance and help rule out the afterglow hypothesis because the participants who believed they had been admitted to the group were not more likely to rate the group higher than those who did not know whether they were admitted to the group or not.

Further, some critics argue that dissonance may not be the most important concept to explain attitude change. For instance, some researchers believe that other theoretical frameworks can explain the attitude change that Festinger and Carlsmith (1959) found in the one dollar/twenty dollars experiment. The Research Note describes a study that tested CDT against a competing explanation. Irving Janis and Robert Gilmore (1965) argue that when people participate in an inconsistency, such as arguing a position they do not believe in, they become motivated to think up all the arguments in favor of the position while suppressing all the arguments against it. Janis and Gilmore call this process **biased scanning.** This biased scanning process should increase the chances of accepting the new position—for example, changing one's position from evaluating the spool-sorting task as dull to the position that it really was an interesting task.

Janis and Gilmore (1965) argue that when a person is overcompensated for engaging in biased scanning, suspicion and guilt are aroused. Thus, they are able to explain why the large incentive of twenty dollars does not cause the students in Festinger and Carlsmith's (1959) experiment to have an increased attitude change.

Other researchers (Cooper & Fazio, 1984) argue that the original theory of cognitive dissonance contains a great deal of "conceptual fuzziness." Some researchers note that the concept of dissonance is confounded by self-concept or impression management. **Impression management** refers to the activities people engage in to look good to themselves and others. For example, Elliot Aronson (1969) argues that people wish to appear reasonable to themselves

biased scanning
thinking of arguments in favor of a counter-attitudinal position while suppressing those against it

impression management
an alternative explanation to CDT; involves activities people engage in to look good to themselves and others

and suggests that in Festinger and Carlsmith's (1959) experiment, if "dissonance exists, it is because the individual's behavior is inconsistent with his self-concept" (p. 27). Aronson asserts that the Stanford students' dissonance resulted from seeing themselves as upright and truthful men contrasted with their behavior of deceiving someone else because they were being paid to do so.

In the study we discussed earlier by Patrice Buzzanell and Lynn Turner (2003) concerning family communication and job loss, we could conceive of the strategies the families adopted as employing impression management rather than reducing dissonance. When fathers reported that nothing had changed in their family despite the job loss, they may have been rationalizing to continue to seem reasonable to themselves, just as Aronson suggests.

In the preceding critiques, researchers disagree about what cognitive state is at work: dissonance, biased scanning, or impression management. Daryl Bem (1967) argues that the central concept of importance is not *any* type of cognition but, rather, is behavioral. Bem states that rather than dissonance in cognitions operating to change people, self-perception is at work. **Self-perception** simply means that people make conclusions about their own attitudes the same way others do—by observing their behavior. Bem's alternative explanation allows more simplicity in the theory as well.

In Bem's conceptualization, it is not necessary to speculate about the degree of cognitive dissonance that a person feels. People only need to observe what they are doing to calculate what their attitudes must be. For instance, if I am not working out regularly, but I believe fitness and health are important goals, I must not really believe working out is so important to good health. In our chapter opening story about Ali Torres, Bem would argue that the longer Ali works at the Alliance, the more likely she is to come to believe that she is doing something worthwhile. Bem's argument suggests that if Ali's mother asks her if she likes her job, she might reply, "I guess I do. I am still there."

Claude Steele's work (Steele, 1988; Steele, Spencer, & Lynch, 1993) also offers a behavioral explanation for dissonance effects: **Self-affirmation**. However, unlike Bem, Steele and his colleagues argue in Self-Affirmation Theory that dissonance is the result of behaving in a manner that threatens one's sense of moral integrity. You can see how this explanation might work quite well in Ali Torres's situation. Her discomfort might not be because she holds two contradictory beliefs but because she doesn't respect herself for staying in a job where she is not accomplishing anything of significance.

Finally, CDT has been critiqued for not having enough utility. These critics note that the theory does not provide a full explanation for how and when people will attempt to reduce dissonance. First, there is what has been called the "multiple mode" problem. This problem exists because, given a dissonance-producing situation, there are multiple ways to reduce the dissonance. As we discussed earlier in the chapter, there are several ways to bring about more consonance (such as changing your mind or engaging in selective exposure, attention, interpretation, or retention). The weakness in the theory is that it doesn't allow precise predictions.

This prediction problem is also apparent in the fact that the theory does not speak to the issue of individual differences. People vary in their tolerance for dissonance, and the theory fails to specify how this factors in to its explanation.

self-perception
an alternative explanation to CDT; involves making conclusions about your attitudes by observing your behavior

self-affirmation
an alternative explanation to CDT; involves creating dissonance by behaving in a manner that threatens one's sense of moral integrity

*Theory * Into * Practice*

In an article published in the *New York Times* in 1998, a judge in Florida is described as applying some of the principles of cognitive dissonance to the teens he is sentencing in his courtroom for underage smoking. The judge tries to generate a sense of dissonance within the youthful offenders in the hopes they will be motivated to change their behaviors. The article also points to the ways in which teens resist these efforts—employing other means, besides quitting smoking, to reduce dissonance.

Judge Steven G. Shutter of Broward County, Florida, holds a Teen Smoking Court once a month to deal with underage smoking. Underage teens who are caught smoking and their parents come into the courtroom to hear the judge's comments and those of others such as Earl G. Mogk, a survivor of larynx cancer. Mogk attributes his cancer to forty years as a smoker, and he speaks to the teens through an electronic device that has replaced his cancerous voice box and vocal cords. Mogk, 60, tells the teens, "When I was your age, there was nobody out there to tell me about the dangers of smoking. . . . The reason I'm here today is for a reality check" (p. A1).

Although there is total silence while Mogk speaks, the article suggests that Florida's approach is not altogether successful with the teen smokers. One high school student is quoted in the article as saying, "It's ridiculous. The bottom line is kids are going to smoke. It's my body and unless I have a desire to quit, I'm not going to" (p. A14). Some other students who were interviewed after the court session agreed, saying that they had no plans to quit. Some of the teens had difficulty explaining why they smoked even when they actually disapproved of the behavior themselves. One boy thought it was social pressures. One girl said it was something to do, "like biting your nails" (p. A14). The article observed that changing attitudes and behaviors is extremely difficult.

Source: Navarro, 1998.

TIP Follow-up
How would you utilize the concepts of importance, dissonance ratio, and rationale to explain why these teens aren't stopping smoking? Are there any ideas suggested by these concepts for making the stop-smoking efforts more successful?

Other scholars believe that Cognitive Dissonance Theory is basically useful and explanatory but needs some refinements. For example, Wicklund and Brehm (1976) argue that Cognitive Dissonance Theory is not clear enough about the conditions under which dissonance leads to change in attitudes. They believe that choice is the missing concept in the theory. Wicklund and Brehm posit that when people believe they have a choice about the dissonant relationship, they will be motivated to change that relationship. If people think they are powerless, then they will not be bothered by the dissonance, and they probably will not change. Regarding our beginning scenario about Ali Torres, Wicklund and Brehm would argue that we could predict whether she will leave her job based on how much choice she believes she has in the matter. If, for instance, she is tied to Gary, Indiana, because of family responsibilities or if she believes she would have trouble locating a new job in the city, she may not be motivated to act on her dissonant cognitions. On the other hand, if nothing really ties her to Gary, or there are plenty of other job opportunities, she will be motivated to change based on those same cognitions.

Another refinement is suggested by the work of Joel Cooper and Jeff Stone (2000). Cooper and Stone point out that in the more than 1,000 studies using Cognitive Dissonance Theory, only rarely has the group membership of the person experiencing dissonance been considered. Cooper and Stone believe that group membership plays an important role in how people experience and reduce dissonance. For example, they found that social identity derived from religious and political groups had an impact on how people responded to dissonance.

Although Cognitive Dissonance Theory has its shortcomings, it does offer us insight into the relationship among attitudes, cognitions, affect, and behaviors, and it does suggest routes to attitude change and persuasion. Social cognition researchers as well as communication scholars continue to use many of the ideas from CDT. As Steven Littlejohn (2002) observes, Festinger's theory is not only the most important consistency theory; it is one of the most significant theories in social psychology. CDT has been the framework for over a thousand research studies (Perloff, 1993), most of which have supported the theory. Additionally, numerous critiques and interpretations have refined and revised the theory. And some researchers (Harmon-Jones, 2000) believe that continuing to refine the theory by examining cognitions more specifically, for example, will yield rich theoretical insights. Cognitive Dissonance Theory has contributed greatly to our understanding of cognitions and their relationship to behaviors. The concept of dissonance remains a powerful one in the research literature, informing studies in psychology, cognitive psychology, communication, and other related fields.

Discussion Starters

1. Explain the relationship of selective attention, exposure, interpretation, and retention to cognitive dissonance. Provide examples where appropriate. How do you think Ali Torres might use these processes, given her situation?

2. Give an example of two attitudes you hold that have an irrelevant relationship to each other. Cite two consonant attitudes you hold. Do you have any attitudes that are dissonant with each other? If so, have you done anything about them? Explain how your actions fit with the theory.

3. What do you think about the problem of CDT's testability suggested in this chapter? Could the theory be revised to make it testable?

4. Suppose you want some friends to change their drinking and driving behaviors. What suggestions would you take from Cognitive Dissonance Theory? How could you apply the theory in persuading your friends?

5. Do you agree with the minimal justification notion that Cognitive Dissonance Theory advances? Provide an example in which minimal justification seemed to work to persuade someone.

6. How do you think group membership affects dissonance and what role do you believe it plays in dissonance reduction?

Terms for Review

cognitions
cognitive dissonance
consonant relationship
dissonant relationship
irrelevant relationship
magnitude of dissonance
importance
dissonance ratio
rationale
selective exposure

selective attention
selective interpretation
selective retention
minimal justification
buyer's remorse
biased scanning
impression management
self-perception
self-affirmation

Online Learning Center

Visit the Online Learning Center at www.mhhe.com/west2. Use the multiple-choice and true/false quizzes to help you prepare for exams, and the glossary, crossword puzzles, and flashcards to further your knowledge of key terms.

CHAPTER 8

Expectancy Violations Theory

Margie Russo

As she prepared for her interview with Ingraham Polling, Margie Russo felt confident that she would be able to handle any questions posed to her. As a 44-year-old mother of three young children, she felt that her life experiences alone would help her respond to any of the more difficult questions. She was a Girl Scout leader, served as treasurer of the Parent Teacher Association at the middle school, and worked part-time as an executive assistant. She knew these experiences would be invaluable as she answered questions in her interview.

Despite her confidence, Margie suddenly felt anxious about her interview with Janet Mueller, the polling company's human resources representative. When told by the office assistant that Ms. Mueller was ready to see her, Margie approached Janet's office, knocked on her door, and went into the room. When she was still more than 10 feet away from the big desk, Janet looked up and asked, "Are you Ms. Russo?" Margie responded, "I am." Janet replied, "Well, c'mon over here and sit down and let's chat a bit."

As Margie approached her interviewer, an uneasy feeling fell over her, a nervousness that she had never experienced before and had certainly not expected. Janet could sense Margie's anxiety and asked if she could get her some coffee or tea. "No, thank you," said Margie. "Well, why don't you sit down?" asked Janet.

Margie really wanted this job. She had been preparing for the interview with her husband, who asked her a number of different kinds of questions the night before. She didn't want to lose her chance at getting this job.

As the two sat and discussed the job and its responsibilities, Margie's mind began to wander. Why was she so nervous? She had been around people, and she knew that she had expertise for the job. Yet, Margie was very nervous, and she had butterflies in her stomach.

Janet focused on what duties Margie would be responsible for and to whom she would report. As she spoke, Janet walked around her office a bit, at times leaning on the side of her desk in front of Margie's chair. Janet had a number of different questions remaining but wanted Margie to speak. She asked her whether she had seen a good movie recently. "Oh, sorry, Janet," Margie replied. "I just don't have time for movies."

"I guess I should have figured that out," said Janet. "You really are a busy person. I'm very impressed by how you seem to manage so many things at one time. Your children are very lucky. How does your family do when you're so busy?"

"Oh, they're fine, thanks. I do get some free time, but I try to spend as much time as I can with my children." Margie was feeling more relaxed as she began to talk about how busy she was helping her two daughters sell Girl Scout cookies. She then talked about her ability to juggle several things at once.

This theory is based on the research of **Judee Burgoon.**

Janet responded, "That's great! Let's talk some more about how you handle deadlines."

It was apparent that as the two talked Margie became more comfortable speaking to Janet. Even-tually, she dismissed her nervousness and felt that she was well on her way to becoming employed with Ingraham Polling.

An important aspect of any discussion of communication is the role of non-verbal communication. What we do can be more important than what we say. To understand nonverbal communication and its effects on messages in a conversation, Judee Burgoon developed Expectancy Violations Theory (1978). Since that time, Burgoon and a number of her associates have studied various messages and the influence of nonverbal communication on message produc-tion. Burgoon (1994) discusses the intersection of nonverbal communication and message production when she states that "nonverbal cues are an inherent and essential part of message creation (production) and interpretation (pro-cessing)" (p. 239). The theory, following the positivistic, covering law ap-proach, was originally called the Nonverbal Expectancy Violations Theory, but Burgoon later dropped the word *nonverbal* because the theory now examines issues beyond the domain of nonverbal communication, something that we will explore a bit later in the chapter. Nonetheless, from its early beginnings in the late 1970s, Expectancy Violations Theory has been a leading theory in identi-fying the influence of nonverbal communication on behavior.

Our opening story of Margie Russo and Janet Mueller represents the na-ture of the theory. Margie entered the conversation with her interviewer with a sense of trepidation, and once their brief interaction was under way, she began to feel uneasy about the manner in which the space between them changed. Janet moved closer to Margie during the interview, causing Margie to feel un-comfortable. However, once the conversation centered on Margie's children, she did not view Janet or her closeness as a threat to her confidence.

Expectancy Violations Theory (EVT) suggests that people hold expecta-tions about the nonverbal behavior of others. Burgoon contends that un-expected changes in conversational distance between communicators are arousing and frequently ambiguous. Interpreting the meaning behind an ex-pectancy violation depends on how favorably the "violator" is perceived. Re-turning to our opening scenario, in many interviews, the interviewer is not expected to lean on a desk in front of the job candidate. When this occurred, Margie became uncomfortable. It was only after Janet began to talk about the movies that Margie began to feel more at ease. In other words, she started to view Janet in a more favorable light.

In our discussion thus far we have been using examples from nonverbal communication, primarily distance. Burgoon's (1978) early writing on EVT in-tegrated specific instances of nonverbal communication, namely personal space and people's expectations of conversational distance. Because personal space is a core concept of the theory, we will explore it in more detail. Further, because spatial violations constitute a primary feature of the theory, it is important to understand the various spatial distances before we delve further into the theory.

Giving Space

The study of a person's use of space is called **proxemics.** Proxemics includes the way people use space in their conversations as well as perceptions of another's use of space. Many people take spatial relations between communicators for granted, yet as Mark Knapp and Judith Hall (2002) conclude, people's use of space can seriously affect their ability to achieve desired goals. Spacial use can influence meaning and message. People's spaces have intrigued researchers for some time; Burgoon began her original work on EVT by studying interpretations of space violations.

Burgoon (1978) starts from the premise that humans have two competing needs: affiliation and personal space. **Personal space,** according to Burgoon (1978), can be defined as "an invisible, variable volume of space surrounding an individual which defines that individual's preferred distance from others" (p. 130). Burgoon and other Expectancy Violations writers believe that people simultaneously have the desire to stay in close proximity to others but also desire some distance. This is a perplexing but realistic dilemma for most of us. Few people can exist in isolation, and yet people prefer their privacy at times.

Proxemic Zones

Burgoon's Expectancy Violations Theory has been informed by the work of anthropologist Edward Hall (1966). After studying North Americans (in the Northeast), Hall claimed that four proxemic zones exist—intimate, personal, social, and public—and each zone is used for different reasons. Hall includes ranges of spatial distance and the behaviors that are appropriate for each zone. We have highlighted the proxemic zones in Figure 8.1.

Intimate Distance   This zone includes behaviors that exist in a range encompassing 0 to 18 inches. Hall (1966) notes that this includes behaviors that range from touch (for instance, making love) to being able to observe a person's facial characteristics. Whispers carried out in this **intimate distance** range have the ability to become extremely powerful. Hall finds it interesting that when U.S. citizens find themselves in intimate surroundings but are not with intimate partners, they often attempt to create a nonintimate experience. Consider what

proxemics
study of a person's use of space

personal space
individual's variable use of space and distance

intimate distance
very close spatial zone spanning 0–18 inches

Figure 8.1
Proxemic Zones
Source: Adapted from Hall, 1966.

Self

Intimate space

Personal space   Social space   Public space

0–18 in.   18 in.–4 ft   4–12 ft   12 ft +

happens in an elevator. People usually fix their eyes on the ceiling, the buttons, or the door as the elevator passes floor after floor. People keep their hands at their side or grasp some object. Hall finds it amusing that many people expend so much energy extracting themselves from intimate distances. Margie Russo may have been troubled by the intimate distance created by Janet. If she wasn't in an interview, she may have moved to remove herself from the situation. It's important to point out that invasions of personal space may be construed as sexual harassment, regardless of the intent. For this reason, we need to remain sensitive to the various perceptions of intimate distance.

Personal Distance   This zone includes those behaviors that exist in an area ranging from 18 inches to 4 feet. According to Hall (1966), **personal distance** encompasses being as close as holding another's hand to keeping someone at arm's length. You may have determined that most, if not all, of the intimate relationships you have are within the closest point of the personal distance zone. Personal distance is likely to be used for your family and friends. The farthest point—4 feet—is usually reserved for less personal relationships, such as sales clerks. Hall indicates that in the personal distance zone, the voice is usually moderate, body heat is detectable, and breath and body odor may be perceptible.

personal distance
spatial zone of 18 inches to 4 feet, reserved for family and friends

Social Distance   With a proxemic range spanning 4 to 12 feet, the **social distance** category characterizes many conversations in the U.S. culture, for instance, between and among co-workers. Hall (1966) contends that the closer social distance is usually reserved for those in a casual social setting, for example, a cocktail party. Although the distance seems a bit far, Hall reminds us that we are able to perceive skin and hair texture in the close phase of this category. The far phase is associated with individuals who have to speak louder than those in the close phase. In addition, the far phase can be considered to be more formal than the close phase. The far phase of social distance allows people to carry on simultaneous jobs. For instance, receptionists are able to carry on with their work while they converse with approaching strangers. It is possible, therefore, to monitor another person while completing a task.

social distance
spatial zone of 4– 12 feet, reserved for more formal relationships such as those with co-workers

Public Distance   The range encompassing 12 feet and beyond is considered to be **public distance**. The close phase of public distance is reserved for fairly formal discussions, for instance, in-class discussions between teachers and

public distance
spatial zone of 12 feet and beyond, reserved for very formal discussions such as between professor and students in class

The Theory Chronicles

Ask a friend if you can "shadow" him or her for an entire day. Pay particular attention to your friend's use of space in conversations with others. What variations in space did you notice among people? What similarities existed? Reflecting on your notes, write an analysis of how space and distance vary across individuals.

students. Public figures usually are at the far phase (around 25 feet or more). As you may have determined, it is difficult to read facial reactions at this point, unless media enhancements (for instance, large-screen projection) are used in the presentation. Whereas the close phase characterizes teachers in a classroom, the far phase includes teachers in a lecture hall. Also, actors use public distance in their performances. Consequently, their actions and words are exaggerated. Teachers and actors, however, are just two of the many types of people who use public distance in their lives.

Territoriality

Before we close our discussion of personal space, we explore an additional feature: **territoriality,** or a person's ownership of an area or object. Frequently, we lay claim to various spatial areas that we want to protect or defend. People decide that they want to erect fences, put on nameplates, or designate spaces as their own (Marissa's room, Mom's car, and so forth). Three types of territories exist: primary, secondary, and public (Altman, 1975). **Primary territories** signal an individual's exclusive domain. For instance, one's own workshop or computer are primary territories. In fact, many people put their names on their primary territories to further signify ownership. **Secondary territories** signal some sort of personal connection to an area or object. Secondary territories are not exclusive to an individual, but the individual feels some sort of association to the territory. For instance, many graduate students feel that a campus library is their secondary territory; they don't own the building, but they frequently occupy a space in the building. **Public territories** involve no personal affiliations and include those areas that are open to all people—for example, beaches, parks, movie theaters, and public transportation areas.

Territoriality is frequently accompanied by prevention and reaction (Knapp & Hall, 2002). That is, people may either try to prevent you from entering their territory or will respond once the territory is invaded. Some gangs will use territorial markers in a neighborhood to prevent other gangs from invading their turf. Knapp and Hall note that if prevention does not work in defending one's territory, a person may react in some way, including getting both physically and cognitively aroused. In sum, humans typically stake out their territory in four primary ways: markers (marking our spot), labels (identification symbols), offensive displays (demonstrating aggressive looks and behaviors), and tenure (being there first and staying the longest) (Knapp, 1978).

Our elaborated discussion of space has relevance to Expectancy Violations Theory not only because the theory is rooted in proxemics, but also because it has direct application to the distances previously discussed. EVT assumes that people will react to space violations. To this end, our expectations for behavior will vary from one distance to another. That is, people have a sense of where they want others to place themselves in a conversation. For instance, consider Margie and Janet from our opening story. Just as Margie has expectations for Janet's behavior in an interview, Janet, too, expects Margie to behave in a predictable way. Janet expects Margie to maintain a comfortable distance as well. She does not expect Margie to come into the office, put her briefcase on the desk, and pull a chair up next to Janet. According to EVT, if Margie's behavior

territoriality
person's ownership of an area or object

primary territories
signal a person's exclusive domain over an area or object
secondary territories
signal a person's affiliation with an area or object

public territories
signal open spaces for everyone, including beaches and parks

is unexpected and Janet evaluates her behavior negatively, Janet may become more concerned with the expectancy violation than with Margie's credentials. The proxemic zones proposed by Hall, then, are important frameworks to consider when interpreting another's behavior.

Thus far, we have introduced you to how personal space is associated with Expectancy Violations Theory. To further explore the theory, we will first provide the basic assumptions of the theory and then examine a number of issues associated with the theory.

Assumptions of Expectancy Violations Theory

Expectancy Violations Theory is rooted in how messages are presented to others and the kinds of behaviors others undertake during a conversation. In addition, three assumptions guide the theory:

- Human interaction is driven by expectations.
- Expectations for human behavior are learned.
- Evaluations of deviation are mediated by the reward value of the communicator.

expectations
thoughts and behaviors anticipated in conversations

The first assumption states that people carry expectations in their interactions with others. In other words, human interaction is expectancy driven. **Expectations** can be defined as the cognitions and behaviors anticipated and prescribed in a conversation with another person. Expectations, therefore, necessarily include individuals' nonverbal and verbal behavior. In her early writings of EVT, Burgoon (1978) notes that people do not view others' behaviors as random. People have various expectations of how others should think and behave. Consider, for instance, our story of Margie Russo and Janet Mueller. If you were the interviewer, what sort of expectations would you have for the nonverbal and verbal behavior of the interviewee? Many people conducting the interview would certainly expect a specific level of confidence, manifested by a warm handshake, a give-and-take conversational flow, and active listening skills. Interviewees would also be expected to keep a reasonable distance from the interviewer during the interview process. Many people in the United States do not want people whom they do not know to stand either too close or too far away from them. Whether it is in an interview situation or even

DILBERT reprinted by permission of United Feature Syndicate, Inc.

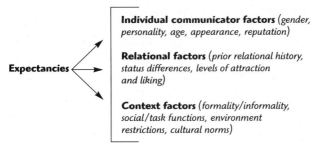

Figure 8.2
Influences on Expectancies
Adapted from Burgoon & Hale (1988).

a discussion between two people who have a prior relationship, Burgoon and other EVT writers argue that people enter interactions with a number of expectations about how a message should be delivered and how the messenger should deliver it. See Figure 8.2 for factors that influence a person's expectations.

Judee Burgoon and Jerold Hale (1988) contend that two types of expectations exist: pre-interactional and interactional. **Pre-interactional expectations** include a communicator's ability to carry out an interaction. In other words, what types of interactional knowledge and skills does a communicator possess *before* he or she enters a conversation? People do not always understand what it takes to enter and maintain a conversation. Some conversationalists may be very argumentative, for example, and others may be extremely passive. Most people do not expect such extreme behavior in their dialogues with others. **Interactional expectations** pertain to an individual's ability to carry out the interaction itself. Most people expect others to maintain appropriate conversational distance. In addition, in communicating with others, listening behaviors such as prolonged eye contact are frequently expected. These and a host of other behaviors are important to consider when examining the role of expectations before and during an interaction.

Of course, depending on the cultural background of communicators, these behaviors can vary tremendously from one person to another. In addition, whether or not our expectations are met will usually be influenced by the culture in which we live and by whether we have internalized cultural patterns for conversation expectations.

This leads us to our second assumption of EVT—that people learn their expectations from both the culture at large and the individuals in that culture. For instance, the U.S. culture teaches that a professor–student relationship is underscored by professional respect. Although not explicitly stated in most college classrooms, professors have more social status than students, and therefore certain expectations exist in their relationships with their students. For instance, we expect teachers to be knowledgeable about subject matter, to present it to students in a clear manner, and to be available if students are concerned or confused about a topic. We also expect professors to use touch in a thoughtful manner, since male and female students respond differently to a professor's touch behavior (Lannutti, Laliker, & Hale, 2001). The teacher–

**pre-interactional
expectations**
the knowledge
or skills a communicator brings to an
interaction

**interactional
expectations**
an individual's ability
to carry out the
interaction

student relationship is just one example of a culture teaching its citizens that expectations exist in a particular relationship. Any discussion between teachers and students, therefore, is laden with cultural expectations of how the two should relate to each other. A number of various societal institutions (the family, the media, business and industry, and so forth) are central in prescribing what cultural patterns to follow. These at-large cultural prescriptions ultimately may be followed by individuals in conversation with each other.

Individuals within a culture are also influential in communicating expectations. Burgoon and Hale (1988) remark that differences based on our prior knowledge of others, our relational history with them, and our observations are important to consider. For instance, Janet Mueller's past experiences with prospective employees influence how she perceives an interaction and her expectations of job candidates in an interview (relational history). In addition, expectations result from our observations. In one family, for instance, standing very close to one another is a family norm, and yet this norm is not shared in other families. Interesting scenarios occur in conversations between individuals with different norms; expectations for conversational distance vary and may influence perceptions of the interaction or have other consequences.

A third assumption of EVT pertains to what happens when our expectations are not met in a conversation with another. Burgoon believes that when people depart, or *deviate,* from expectations, how that deviation is received depends on the reward potential of others. Let's explain this a bit further. Burgoon, along with Deborah Coker and Ray Coker (1986), notes that not all violations of expected behavior necessarily yield negative perceptions. Specifically, the researchers offer the following: "In cases where behaviors are ambiguous or have multiple interpretations, acts committed by a high-reward communicator may be assigned positive meanings, and the same acts committed by a low-reward communicator may be assigned negative meanings" (p. 498). There are a number of rewards that communicators can offer each other, including smiles, head nods, physical attractiveness, attitude similarity, socioeconomic status, credibility, and competence. In our opening story, Janet Mueller's demeanor in asking about Margie's children was apparently viewed as reward behavior because Margie's nervousness immediately subsided. Burgoon thinks that people have the potential to either reward or punish in conversations and maintains that people bring both positive and negative characteristics to an interaction. She terms this **communicator reward valence.**

communicator reward valence
the sum of the positive and negative characteristics of a person and the potential for him or her to carry out rewards or punishments

Burgoon holds that the concept of reward encompasses a number of characteristics that allow a person to be viewed favorably. According to Expectancy Violations Theory, interpretations of violations frequently depend on the communicator and his or her value. So, for instance, Margie Russo may not view Janet's close proximity as a positive deviation from expected behavior in an interview. Yet, Janet's behavior was more positively received because of other characteristics, namely her courteous manner and interest in Margie's children.

Let's apply this assumption to eye behavior in a number of different contexts. A prolonged stare from a person on public transportation is probably not going to be received favorably, but it may be received favorably from one's romantic partner. If a keynote speaker at a dinner banquet looked above the listeners' heads, many people would be bewildered by this lack of eye contact. But when strangers pass on the street, lack of eye contact is expected. Or think about your response to receiving a constant stare from your supervisor or a co-worker. Finally, cultural differences influence perceptions of eye contact. A wife who avoids eye contact while telling her husband that she loves him may elicit a different evaluation than if she had direct eye contact, but this interpretation varies across cultural groups. Some (e.g., Irish Americans) would expect another to look directly at them when saying something very personal, such as "I love you." Others (e.g., Japanese Americans), however, do not place such value on eye contact. In each of these contexts, violations of expected eye behavior may be interpreted differently according to how we receive the communicator.

Arousal

Deviations from expectations have consequences. These deviations, or violations, have what Burgoon (1978) calls "arousal value" (p. 133). By this she means that when a person's expectations are violated, the person's interest or attention is aroused, and he or she uses a particular mechanism to cope with the violation. **Arousal** causes one to pay less attention to the message and more attention to the source of the arousal (LaPoire & Burgoon, 1996). We further explain arousal in the Research Note.

arousal
increased interest or attention when deviations from expectations occur
cognitive arousal
mental awareness of deviations from expectations
physical arousal
bodily changes as a result of deviations from expectations

A person may be both cognitively and physically aroused. **Cognitive arousal** is an alertness or an orientation to a violation. When we are cognitively aroused, our intuitive senses become heightened. **Physical arousal** includes those behaviors that a communicator employs during an interaction—such as moving out of uncomfortable speaking distances, adjusting one's stance during an interaction, and so forth. Most EVT studies have investigated cognitive arousal (via self-report inventories), yet little research has examined physiological arousal. One provocative study that examined physical arousal in conversation was undertaken by Beth LaPoire and Judee Burgoon (1996). Specifically, they asked college students to engage in a practice medical interview. During the interaction, the researchers studied heart rate, skin temperature, and pulse volume changes every five seconds while they assessed expectancy violations. Only heart rate and pulse volume demonstrated any statistical significance. Results indicated that after subjects registered cognitive arousal to a violation, they first experienced heart rate decreases and pulse volume increases. This was followed by pulse volume decreases. In sum, people notice when others are not adhering to interaction expectations. Arousal remains a complicated but important part of EVT; as you can see, arousal is more than simply recognizing when someone commits a violation.

Threat Threshold

Once arousal exists, threats may occur. A second key concept associated with EVT is **threat threshold,** which Burgoon (1978) defines as the "distance at which an interactant experiences physical and physiological discomfort by the

threat threshold
tolerance for distance violations

Research Note

Burgoon, J. K., Kelley, D. L., Newton, D. A., & Keeley-Dyreson, M. P. (1989). The nature of arousal and nonverbal indices. *Human Communication Research, 16,* 217–255.

This article focuses on a central feature of Expectancy Violations Theory: arousal. Burgoon and her colleagues begin the study by discussing the pervasiveness of arousal in research. Specifically, the authors note that arousal is a central construct in Arousal-Valence Theory, Nonverbal Expectancy Violations Theory, and Discrepancy-Arousal Theory. The authors argue that although it has enjoyed widespread attention, the construct has been integrated into research as a physiological, physical, or behavioral variable. Burgoon and her research team believe that arousal has not been explicated sufficiently, and consequently researchers employ the variable as they see fit. Therefore, the purpose of this study was to analyze the arousal variable and to discover the nonverbal behaviors associated with increased arousal.

The authors review literature associated with the way arousal has been defined in research. They then discuss the physiology as well as the causes of arousal. They conclude that from a communication vantage point, arousal is best conceived along two dimensions: arousal intensity and arousal valence. They then explore the nonverbal indicators of arousal, including emotional expression, proxemic invasions, animated facial expressions, and physical attraction.

In their study, Burgoon and associates solicited participants from newspaper advertisements, job recruitment centers, and class announcements. Fifty-two pairs conducted mock interviews for jobs. Participants were asked to submit a résumé, and for ten minutes, members of each pair took turns serving as both interviewer and interviewee. Once separated, the participants were randomly assigned

an additional interviewer-interviewee condition. Following this second interview, the participants were given a questionnaire and a videotape of their interviews.

Burgoon and colleagues note that "interviewee involvement changes should induce increased arousal for the interviewer" and set out to measure this belief. Trained coders rated the videotaped interactions using a collection of scales. Baseline arousal scores were gauged as well as observed arousal increase conditions. The researchers also tested experienced arousal in that they asked respondents to come back several months later to review their videotapes and assess their own performance. Using a high/low-involvement framework, Burgoon and her colleagues discovered that several "low-involvement participants commented on the interviewee's behavior making them uncomfortable, frustrated, and distracted, while many high-involvement participants commented on the interviewee's behavior 'putting the pressure on' or being overly aggressive and intense" (p. 238). The authors also analyzed a number of nonverbal behaviors and their relationship to positive and negative arousal. They discovered that personal space, vocal quality, and body/face/gaze orientation can be considered significant nonverbal behaviors in that they parallel arousal.

This study underscores the fact that arousal is a complex yet critical part of interactions, and it provides useful indices for measuring arousal. The work by Burgoon and her team to coherently investigate arousal effectively eliminates the various interpretations of arousal that have vexed researchers in the past.

presence of another" (p. 130). In a sense, the threshold threshold is a tolerance for distance violation. Burgoon maintains that "when distance is equated with threat, closer distances are perceived as more threatening and farther distances as less threatening" (p. 134). In this sense, distance is interpreted as a statement of threat from a communicator. People may either reward or punish a threat. Burgoon arrives at this conclusion by consulting the research on liking and attraction. This research suggests that closer distances are reserved for people

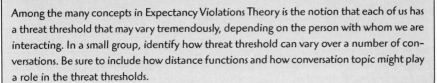
we like or to whom we are attracted. Some people don't mind when others stand close to them; their threat threshold therefore, is high. Others, however, become very uncomfortable around those who stand too close; for them, the threat threshold is low. So, for instance, if you are attracted to a person you see each morning at Starbucks, your threat threshold will likely be high as he or she talks to you and comes closer to you as your conversation progresses. During this same interaction, however, you may discover that this person is not the sort of person you want to hang out with and may find your threat threshold getting smaller, even during the conversation. Burgoon notes that the size of the threshold is based on how we view the initiator of the threat, which we discussed earlier as the communication reward valence. Once a violation occurs, however, we again interpret the violation.

Violation Valence

Throughout this chapter, we have emphasized that when people speak to others, they have expectations. Many of these expectations are based on social norms of the other person. When expectations are violated, however, many people evaluate the violation on a valence. **Violation valence** refers to the positive or negative assessment of an unexpected behavior. Violation valence differs from communicator reward valence. When we assess how valuable the person or communicator is to us, we have used the communicator reward valence. Violation valence, however, focuses on the deviation itself.

violation valence
perceived negative or positive value of a deviation from expectations

Violation valence requires making sense of a violation through interpretation and evaluation (Burgoon & Hale, 1988). Quite simply, communicators try to interpret the meaning of a violation and decide whether they like it. If, for instance, a professor is speaking very close to you, you may interpret the behavior as an expression of superiority or intimidation. Consequently, the violation valence would be negative. Or you may view the violation is something positive; you might think the professor as demonstrating a sense of connection. Your violation valence, then, would be positive.

Burgoon and her colleagues caution us, however, that not all violations are this clear, and consequently we employ communicator reward valence. If a violation is ambiguous or has multiple meanings, EVT predicts that the communicator valence will influence how the violation is to be interpreted and evaluated. Communicators interpret the violation, therefore, by using the communicator reward valence. If the person is someone we like, we will positively evaluate the violation; if it is someone we do not like, we will view the violation negatively.

To better understand the violation valence, consider two situations between co-workers Noland and Rick. Standing in the break room, Noland begins to talk about his phone call to his wife this morning. As he discusses his conversation about where they decided to go for vacation, Noland begins to close the distance between him and Rick. Rick feels very uncomfortable with the distance between him and Noland in that Rick's expectations for spatial distance between co-workers is violated. In other words, Rick is negatively aroused by Noland's distance behavior. A different situation, however, might prompt a different reaction. Imagine that Noland corners Rick to tell him that he heard that the company was laying off 20 percent of its workers within two months. Because Rick was recently hired by the company, he might be positively aroused and allow Noland to violate his personal space. In this case, Rick may use the communication reward valence to interpret the violation. Most likely, he will positively evaluate Noland and allow the violation to take place.

It may be perplexing to think that violations can be viewed positively. Yet, there are many examples. For instance, in a job interview, the candidate who is able to convince the interviewer that he or she is the most qualified is usually the person who gets the job. Most job interviews are very structured and have an agreed-on informal process. Most job candidates follow the interview script and do not violate anyone's expectations. At times, though, candidates do not follow the script; they violate expectations. Although some interviewers may think these candidates are too independent, others may see them as creative, bold, and original. These may be the qualities that ultimately get the person the job. Thus, violations may yield positive effects.

Critique and Closing

Judee Burgoon's Expectancy Violations Theory is one of the few theories specifically focusing on nonverbal communication. The theory's assumptions and its core concepts clearly demonstrate the importance of nonverbal messages and information processing. EVT also enhances our understanding of

The Theory Connection

Expectancy Violations Theory is primarily concerned with our expectations for other people's behavior, whereas Cognitive Dissonance Theory is concerned with our desire for consistency in attitudes and behavior. Show the relationship between the two theories using expectations, attitudes, and behavior as your overarching principles.

Theory * Into * Practice

In *Psychology Today,* Joann Ellison Rodgers wrote an essay regarding flirting in which she discusses how flirting is conducted in social environments. Rodgers identifies several areas of nonverbal communication in her discussion, namely the use of personal space as an important communicator of whether someone is seeking interest from another. Her work exemplifies the importance of nonverbal communication and how it can arouse others. She also presents evidence of individuals allowing others to violate their personal space even though they have just met.

Rodgers begins by noting that flirting has been trivialized and even demonized. Yet, she claims that it is still considered to be the first step in the mating process of humans. She states that "our animal and human ancestors needed a means of quickly and safely judging the value of potential mates without 'going all the way'" (p. 38). Flirting suggests attraction, and attraction is at the core of human relationship development.

A spatial framework can be applied to the flirting process. For instance, the four-stage process of flirting—attention, recognition, dancing, synchronization—includes two stages specifically dedicated to space variations. People position themselves (dancing) in such a way as to enhance their opportunities to be noticed. They then begin to synchronize their behaviors to demonstrate that two people have mutual interest.

This synchronization eventually leads people to assume intimate distances. Rodgers concludes, "All the silent swaying, leaning, smiling, bobbing and gazing eventually brought a pair into full frontal alignment. Face to face, they indulge in simultaneous touching of everything, from eyeglasses to fingertips to crossed legs" (p. 40). So, the flirting process includes all kinds of nonverbal communication.

Rodgers believes that there is a "silent language of elaborate visual and other gestures" (p. 38) in the flirting process. And this process extends across cultures—from the Far East to Africa to South America. Flirting is an ancient way of facilitating relationships that still carries significance today.

Source: Rodgers, 1999.

TIP Follow-up
Burgoon states that closer distances are reserved for people we like. How does flirting affect personal distance between people? How are violations dealt with if we don't know someone, but we seem to like him or her?

how expectations influence conversational distance. The theory uncovers what takes place in the minds of communicators and how communicators monitor nonverbal behavior during their conversations.

The theory's value may lie in its scope and boundaries. EVT is clear in that it specifically explores nonverbal communication, although later applications of the theory have centered on verbal messages. Although nonverbal communication is a very broad area, Burgoon and her colleagues have made efforts to focus many of their investigations on personal space. She has investigated other nonverbal behaviors such as eye gaze, yet her original work was clear in scope. Both strangers and familiars have been investigated in studies, thereby broadening the scope of the original model.

In addition to having scope, EVT is a theory that is very practical. Burgoon's theory presents advice on how to elicit favorable impressions and discusses the implications of space violations. Further, the theory is clear and consistent in explanation. From the early writings (Burgoon & Jones, 1976) to more recent work (Lannutti et al., 2001), research employing an EVT framework has maintained clarity.

Finally, Expectancy Violations Theory is a testable theory. In Chapter 3, we noted that testability requires that theorists be specific in their concepts. In fact, Burgoon (1978) is one of a few theorists who clearly defines her terms before embarking on a theoretical path. In doing so, she presents a clear and testable foundation from which future researchers might draw and replicate the test.

Some writers have taken issue with Burgoon's methods, and this criticism has resulted in some debate. For instance, Glenn Sparks and John Greene (1992) comment that self-perceptions of arousal are not valid measures. They specifically note that Burgoon and her associates (1989) failed to establish valid indices of observers' ratings, and to this end "we should not accept the claim about the validity of any nonverbal index until that validity has been demonstrated" (Sparks & Greene, 1992, p. 468). This intellectual debate may appear trivial to you, yet recall that arousal is a key component of EVT. Burgoon (Burgoon & LaPoire, 1992) responded to the criticism by first claiming that Sparks and Greene did not fairly reflect the objectives of Burgoon's research. Additionally, Burgoon and LaPoire contend that because arousal is such a complicated and layered concept, their approach to defining arousal remains especially valid.

EVT is an important theory because it offers a way to link behavior and cognitions. It is one of the few communication theories that offers us a better understanding of our need for both other people and personal space. For that, Burgoon's work will continue to be critical in the communication discipline.

Discussion Starters

1. In addition to distance behaviors in interviews, what other nonverbal behaviors are present in interview situations like the one between Margie and Janet?

2. Explain how EVT might inform research and thinking on touch behavior. For instance, does the theory help us to understand the difference between appropriate and inappropriate touch? Explain with examples.

3. Provide some nonverbal expectations that you have learned from your culture. Discuss what similarities and differences exist.

4. How do you suppose arousal manifests itself in conversations between supervisors and employees? Identify a few arousal mechanisms.

5. Suppose you want to study expectancy violation in school. How might you begin to investigate violations? Be as specific as possible, and identify some methods for studying expectations.

6. Employing at least two examples, differentiate between communicator reward valence and violation valence.

Terms for Review

proxemics
personal space
intimate distance
personal distance
social distance
public distance
territoriality
primary territories
secondary territories
public territories

expectations
pre-interactional expectations
interactional expectations
communicator reward valence
arousal
cognitive arousal
physical arousal
threat threshold
violation valence

 ## Online Learning Center

Visit the Online Learning Center at www.mhhe.com/west2. Use the multiple-choice and true/false quizzes to help you prepare for exams, and the glossary, crossword puzzles, and flashcards to further your knowledge of key terms.

Relationship Development

MILLIONS OF DOLLARS HAVE BEEN MADE BY AUthors of self-help books that promote ways to begin, develop, and maintain our interpersonal relationships. The sad reality is that the vast majority of these books are written by people who don't understand that there are no easy steps associated with relationship development. As we all can testify, our various relationships with friends, family, partners, co-workers, religious leaders, and others are filled with dynamics that no book writer could ever fully understand. This becomes especially important as we think about the millions of people seeking out these resources, which are pretty much void of theory.

This is precisely why the group of theories under this section called "Relationship Development" are important to consider. They represent scholarship that has examined all types of interpersonal relationships and the numerous patterns and processes involved in relationship development. In sum, the theories address how and why relationships develop and are maintained.

Five theories are discussed in this section. Uncertainty Reduction Theory suggests that when strangers meet, their focus is on reducing levels of uncertainty about each other and about their relationship. Social Penetration Theory examines how a person's decision to reveal personal information to another influences the direction of that relationship. In Social Exchange Theory, people add up their costs and benefits of being in a relationship and arrive at a net outcome. They also will compare their current relationships with others. As relationships progress, they are likely to experience conflicting pulls. Managing these tensions is the essence of Relational Dialectics Theory. Communication Privacy Management Theory states that people in relationships constantly manage boundaries between thoughts and feelings they are willing to share and those they are not.

Relational life is interesting, challenging, complex, entertaining, and exhausting. The theories we present help unravel the reasons behind why we continue to be part of other people's lives and why they stay with us. When you encounter these theories, you will also become familiar with a number of engaging topics. You will read about trust, vulnerability, intimacy, nonverbal warmth, interpersonal roles, and attraction. As you read the next five chapters, pay attention to the different ways each theory conceptualizes and explains relational life.

CHAPTER 9

Uncertainty Reduction Theory

Edie Banks and Malcolm Rogers

Edie Banks and Malcolm Rogers are in the same philosophy class at Urban University. Until today, they really had not spoken together, although they had seen each other in the class every Monday, Wednesday, and Friday for the past three months. Today, as Edie was leaving class, she noticed Malcolm staring at her from the corner of the room where he sat with his friends. Edie felt a little uncomfortable about being on the receiving end of Malcolm's gaze, and she hurried to get out of the classroom.

Unfortunately, her friend Maggie stopped her at the doorway with a question about the assignment for next week, and so Edie and Malcolm reached the hallway at the same time. There was an awkward pause as they smiled uncertainly at each other. Malcolm cleared his throat and said, "Hi. That was a pretty cool activity in class today, wasn't it?" Edie shrugged, smiled back, and replied, "I'm not sure I get what's going on in there. I'm majoring in engineering, and this is just an elective for me. Sometimes I think I should have taken bowling instead." Malcolm smiled and said, "I've been pretty happy since I decided to major in philosophy. But I guess I'd have the same reaction you're having if I got stuck in an engineering class! I probably couldn't engineer my way out of a paper bag." The two laughed for a minute. Then Edie said, "Gotta run. Catch you later," and hurried off down the hall.

Malcolm walked to his next class wondering if they would talk again, if Edie was putting down his major, if she thought he had been rude about her major, if she liked him, if he liked her, or if he cared.

Sometimes called Initial Interaction Theory, Uncertainty Reduction Theory (URT) was originated by Charles Berger and Richard Calabrese in 1975. Their goal in constructing this theory was to explain how communication is used to reduce uncertainties between strangers engaging in initial interaction. Berger and Calabrese believe that when strangers first meet, they are primarily concerned with increasing predictability in an effort to make sense out of their communication experience. As we discussed in Chapter 4, people act as naive researchers, and Berger and Calabrese think in that role we are motivated both to predict and to explain what goes on in initial encounters. **Prediction** can be defined as the ability to forecast the behavioral options likely to be chosen from

prediction
the ability to forecast one's own and others' behavioral choices

This theory is based on the research of **Charles Berger** and **Richard Calabrese.**

a range of possible options available to oneself or to a relational partner. **Explanation** refers to attempts to interpret the meaning of past actions in a relationship. These two concepts—prediction and explanation—make up the two primary subprocesses of uncertainty reduction.

Our opening example of Malcolm and Edie illustrates Berger and Calabrese's basic contentions about meeting someone for the first time. Because Malcolm does not know Edie, he is not sure how to interpret her comments to him. Nor is he certain about what will happen the next time they see each other. There are so many possible explanations for what was said that Malcolm's uncertainty level was high. This is consistent with the ideas of other theorists such as Claude E. Shannon and Warren Weaver (1949), who note in their information theory that uncertainty exists whenever the number of possible alternatives in a given situation is high and the likelihood of their occurrence is relatively equal. Conversely, they say, uncertainty is decreased when the alternatives are limited in number and/or there is an alternative that is usually chosen—for example, we are relatively certain that when we say hi to someone, that person will respond in kind. Berger and Calabrese theorize that communication is the vehicle by which people reduce their uncertainty about one another. In turn, reduced uncertainty creates conditions ripe for the development of interpersonal relationships.

After Berger and Calabrese (1975) originated their theory, it was later slightly elaborated (Berger, 1979; Berger & Bradac, 1982). The current version of the theory suggests that there are two types of uncertainty in initial encounters: cognitive and behavioral. Our cognitions refer to the beliefs and attitudes that we and others hold. **Cognitive uncertainty,** therefore, refers to the degree of uncertainty associated with those beliefs and attitudes. When Malcolm wonders whether Edie was ridiculing his major and whether he really cares, he experiences cognitive uncertainty. **Behavioral uncertainty,** on the other hand, pertains to "the extent to which behavior is predictable in a given situation" (Berger & Bradac, 1982, p. 7). Because we have cultural rituals for small talk, Edie and Malcolm probably know how to behave during their short conversation. If one of them had violated the ritual by either engaging in inappropriate **self-disclosure** (revealing pieces of information about one's self to another) or totally ignoring the other, their behavioral uncertainty would have increased. People may be cognitively uncertain, behaviorally uncertain, or both before, during, or following an interaction.

Berger (1987) speaks about the nature of behavioral uncertainty in this passage: "To interact in a relatively smooth, coordinated, and understandable manner, one must be able both to predict how one's interaction partner is likely to behave, and, based upon these predictions, to select from one's own repertoire those responses that will optimize outcomes in the encounter" (p. 41). In our opening example, if Malcolm is able to predict that Edie will be an affectionate individual who is willing to ask questions and reveal personal information to him, then he must be prepared to offer responses so that he and Edie will have a satisfying encounter or relationship.

Further, Berger and Calabrese (1975) argued that uncertainty reduction has both proactive and retroactive processes. Proactive uncertainty reduction comes into play when a person thinks about communication options before actually engaging with another person. When Edie attempted to avoid Malcolm at the classroom door, she was trying to deal with her uncertainty proactively. If Malcolm preplanned what he might say to Edie, he was also using proactive processes. Retroactive uncertainty reduction consists of attempts to explain behavior after the encounter itself. Thus, Malcolm's questions to himself about what Edie did and said and his own reactions are part of the retroactive process.

In addition to the preceding, Berger and Calabrese suggest that uncertainty is related to seven other concepts rooted in communication and relational development: verbal output, nonverbal warmth (such as pleasant vocal tone and leaning forward), information seeking (asking questions), self-disclosure, reciprocity of disclosure, similarity, and liking. Each of these works in conjunction with the others so that interactants can reduce some of their uncertainty.

Through its axioms and theorems, URT posits a dynamic movement of interpersonal relationships in their initial stages. This theory has been described as an example of original theorizing in the field of communication (Miller, 1981) because it employs concepts (such as information seeking, self-disclosure) that are specifically relevant to studying communication behavior. URT attempts to place communication as the cornerstone of human behavior, and to this end a number of assumptions about human behavior and communication underlie the theory.

Assumptions of Uncertainty Reduction Theory

As we have mentioned in earlier chapters, theories are frequently grounded in assumptions that reflect the worldview of the theorists. Uncertainty Reduction Theory is no exception. The following assumptions frame this theory:

- People experience uncertainty in interpersonal settings.
- Uncertainty is an aversive state, generating cognitive stress.
- When strangers meet, their primary concern is to reduce their uncertainty or to increase predictability.
- Interpersonal communication is a developmental process that occurs through stages.
- Interpersonal communication is the primary means of uncertainty reduction.
- The quantity and nature of information that people share change through time.
- It is possible to predict people's behavior in a lawlike fashion.

We will briefly address each assumption. First, in a number of interpersonal settings, people feel uncertainty. Because differing expectations exist for interpersonal occasions, it is reasonable to conclude that people are uncertain or even nervous about meeting others. As Berger and Calabrese (1975) state, "When persons are unable to make sense out of their environment, they usually become anxious" (p. 106). Consider the anxiety of Malcolm, for instance, as he meets Edie after class. Berger and Calabrese contend that he experiences uncertainty when meeting Edie, a classmate to whom he is attracted. Although there are a great many cues in the environment that can help Malcolm make sense out of his interaction with Edie, there are complicating factors as well. For example, Malcolm may have noticed Edie hurrying to leave the room. There are several alternative explanations for this behavior such as another class that is a distance away, a general predisposition toward hurrying, having to go to the bathroom, feeling faint and wanting fresh air, wanting to avoid meeting Malcolm at the door, and so forth. Given all these alternatives, it is likely that Malcolm (or anyone in his situation) feels uncertain and anxious.

The second assumption suggests that uncertainty is an aversive state. In other words, it takes a great deal of emotional and psychological energy to remain uncertain. People in new work environments often experience this stress. One of your authors, for instance, recalls his first teaching job. He was in a new state, knew no one, and had no previous college teaching experience. He soon realized that to understand college teaching, he needed to meet colleagues quickly. Until those initial encounters took place, he experienced a great deal of cognitive stress.

The next assumption underlying URT advances the proposition that when strangers meet, two concerns are important: reducing uncertainty and increasing predictability. At first glance, this may sound commonsensical, yet, as Berger (1995) concludes, "There is always the possibility that one's conversational partner will respond unconventionally to even the most routine message" (pp. 2–3). As we stated previously, information seeking usually takes the form of asking questions in order to gain some predictability. Politicians often ask questions when meeting their constituents. They spend time with the voters in their district and ask them questions in order to gain a sense of their needs. This process can be quite engaging, and many people do this unconsciously. To get a better sense of how questions relate to URT, consider the Research Note.

The fourth assumption of URT suggests that interpersonal communication is a process involving developmental stages. According to Berger and Calabrese, generally speaking, most people begin interaction in an **entry phase**, defined as the beginning stage of an interaction between strangers. The entry phase is guided by implicit and explicit rules and norms, such as responding in kind when someone says, "Hi! How are you doing?" Individuals then enter the second stage, called the **personal phase**, or the stage where the interactants start to communicate more spontaneously and to reveal more idiosyncratic information. The personal phase can occur during an initial encounter, but it is more likely to begin after repeated interactions. The third stage, the **exit phase**, refers to the stage during which individuals make decisions about whether they wish to continue interacting with this partner in the future. Although all people do not enter a phase in the same manner or stay in a phase for a similar amount of time, Berger and Calabrese believe that a universal framework exists that explains how interpersonal communication shapes and reflects the development of interpersonal relationships.

The fifth assumption states that interpersonal communication is the primary means of uncertainty reduction. Because we have identified interpersonal

entry phase
the beginning stage of
an interaction be-
tween strangers

personal phase
the stage in a rela-
tionship when people
begin to communi-
cate more sponta-
neously and person-
ally
exit phase
the stage in a rela-
tionship when people
decide whether to
continue or leave

Research Note

Douglas, W. (1990). Uncertainty, information-seeking, and liking during initial interaction. *Western Journal of Speech Communication, 54,* 66–81.

This research measures the uncertainty, information seeking, and liking involved when people have face-to-face interactions. The study is framed by Uncertainty Reduction Theory. In setting up the research, William Douglas incorporates a number of the conclusions espoused by Berger and Calabrese (1975). Further, he defines information seeking as self-disclosure and question asking. Liking was measured using the Interpersonal Attraction scale (McCroskey & McCain, 1974).

Participants were college students at a southwestern university. The participants were asked to sign up with someone of the same sex whom they had not previously met. Through random assignments, the dyads (two-person teams) were allowed to interact in three conditions: two-, four-, and six-minute time allotments. In addition to interacting in one of these conditions, the dyads were also told that if the partners wished to, they could have another conversation or be reassigned to other partners later. After the time elapsed in each condition, the participants were taken to a room where they completed a questionnaire. The tape-recorded conversations were transcribed and coded by trained coders.

Results indicated that uncertainty was reduced as more time was available. That is, people who interacted for six minutes were significantly less uncertain than those who interacted for shorter time periods. In addition, uncertainty reduction was associated with a decrease in question asking but with an increase in self-disclosure. During initial interactions, then, asking questions helped reduce uncertainty. Self-disclosures seemed to be reserved for after question asking had already reduced some uncertainty. Finally, liking for a partner did not change significantly across time periods.

This study adds further validity to Uncertainty Reduction Theory. Specifically, the research underscores the fact that information seeking is a function of URT. According to Douglas, future research should focus on cognitive and behavioral uncertainty.

---

communication as the focus of URT, this assumption should come as no surprise. URT draws on the interpersonal context that we discussed in Chapter 2; there we noted that interpersonal communication requires a host of preconditions—among them listening skills, nonverbal response cues, and a shared language. Most of us presume that these and other conditions are present in our conversations, yet Berger (1995) warns that there are a number of situations where "these preconditions for carrying out face-to-face encounters may not be met" (p. 4). For instance, he notes the inherent challenges in communicating with hearing-impaired or visually impaired interactants who do not have full sensory capabilities. Or you may have had some experience communicating with someone who does not speak your language. Challenges will affect these relationships. In sum, then, interpersonal communication—with all of its behaviors and nuances—is crucial in the uncertainty reduction process.

The next assumption underscores the nature of time. It also focuses on the fact that interpersonal communication is developmental. Uncertainty reduction theorists believe that initial interactions are key elements in the developmental process. To illustrate this assumption, consider the experiences of Rita, who spent a few minutes by herself before entering the YWCA to attend her first meeting of Parents, Family, and Friends of Lesbians and Gays (PFLAG). She immediately felt more comfortable when Dan, another newcomer, came over to introduce himself and welcome her to the group. As the two exchanged information about their anxieties and uncertainties, they both felt more confident. As they talked, Rita and Dan reduced their uncertainties about what the other members of the support group would be like. Charles Berger and Kathy Kellermann (1994) believe that Rita and Dan are goal directed and therefore will employ a number of communication strategies to acquire social information. Reducing uncertainty is key for both Rita and Dan. A bit later in the chapter, we will discuss some of these strategies.

The final assumption indicates that people's behavior can be predicted in a lawlike fashion. Recall from Chapter 3 that theorists bring different worldviews to the job of theory construction. As we discussed, these different views of reality prompt theorists to use different ontologies, epistemologies, and axiologies to explain communication behavior. One of the ontologies we reviewed in Chapter 3 was covering law. To remind you, a covering law approach to theory construction assumes that human behavior is regulated by generalizable principles that function in a lawlike manner. Although there may be some exceptions, in general people behave in accordance with these laws. The goal of a covering law theory is to lay out the laws that will explain how we communicate. As you might imagine, covering law theories have a difficult task. Although some aspects of the natural world may operate under laws, the social world is much more variable. That is why covering laws in the social science are called "lawlike." A pattern is outlined, but the deterministic notion implied with natural laws is relaxed a bit. Still, even to approach the goal of lawlike statements is daunting. Thus, theories like URT begin with what may seem like commonsense observations in order to establish regularities that govern people's behaviors. Covering law theories are constructed to move from statements that are presumed to be true (or axioms) to statements that are derived from these truisms (or theorems).

Axioms of Uncertainty Reduction Theory

Uncertainty Reduction Theory is an axiomatic theory. This means that Berger and Calabrese began with a collection of **axioms**, or truisms drawn from past research and common sense. These axioms, or what some researchers might call propositions, require no further proof than the statement itself. Berger and Calabrese extrapolated this axiomatic thinking from earlier researchers (Blalock, 1969), who concluded that causal relationships should be stated in the form of an axiom. Axioms are the heart of the theory because they have to be accepted as valid in order for the theory to work. Each axiom presents a relationship between uncertainty (the central theoretical concept) and one other concept. URT rests on seven axioms. To understand each, we refer back to our opening example of Edie and Malcolm.

axioms
truisms drawn from
past research and
common sense

> **Axiom 1:** Given the high level of uncertainty present at the onset of the entry phase, as the amount of verbal communication between strangers increases, the level of uncertainty for each interactant in the relationship decreases. As uncertainty is further reduced, the amount of verbal communication increases.

Regarding Malcolm and Edie's situation with reference to this axiom, the theory maintains that if they talk more to each other, they will become more certain about each other. Further, as they get to know each other better, they will talk more with each other.

Axiom 2: As nonverbal affiliative expressiveness increases, uncertainty levels decrease in an initial interaction situation. In addition, decreases in uncertainty level will cause increases in nonverbal affiliative expressiveness.

If Edie and Malcolm express themselves to each other in a warm nonverbal fashion, they will grow more certain of each other, and as they do this, they will increase their nonverbal affiliation with each other: They may be more facially animated, or they may engage in more prolonged eye contact. Further, the two might even touch each other in a friendly fashion as they begin to feel more comfortable with each other. In the movie *Jerry McGuire*, Dorothy, the female lead, comments to Jerry that she does not know all "his noises" yet. She suggests her uncertainty level remains high because she does not understand his nonverbal behaviors, yet she expects to learn them as they continue to interact.

Axiom 3: High levels of uncertainty cause increases in information-seeking behavior. As uncertainty levels decline, information-seeking behavior decreases.

This axiom, which we will discuss later, is one of the more provocative conclusions associated with URT. It suggests that Edie will ask questions and otherwise engage in information seeking as long as she feels uncertain about Malcolm. The more certain she feels, the less information seeking she will do. The same would apply to Malcolm.

Axiom 4: High levels of uncertainty in a relationship cause decreases in the intimacy level of communication content. Low levels of uncertainty produce high levels of intimacy.

Because uncertainty is relatively high between Edie and Malcolm, they engage in small talk with no real self-disclosures. The intimacy of their communication content is low, and their uncertainty level remains high. This fourth axiom asserts that if they continue to reduce the uncertainty in their relationship, then their communication will consist of higher levels of intimacy. Berger (1979) notes, however, that during this self-disclosure process, the interactants must assess the integrity of the disclosure. Is it possible that the information an individual receives is biased, overly positive, or overly negative? Such an assessment may be problematic for both people in an encounter.

Axiom 5: High levels of uncertainty produce high rates of reciprocity. Low levels of uncertainty produce low levels of reciprocity.

According to URT, as long as Edie and Malcolm remain uncertain about each other, they will tend to mirror each other's behavior. **Reciprocity** suggests that if one provides a small personal detail, the other is likely to as well. After Edie shares that she is lost in the class and that she is an engineering major, Malcolm reveals his major to her and that he would probably have troubles in

reciprocity
communication that mirrors the previous communication behavior

engineering classes. Immediate reciprocation of that sort (I tell you where I am from and you tell me where you are from) is a hallmark of initial encounters. The more people talk to each other and develop their relationship, the more they trust that reciprocity will be made at some point. If I don't tell you something that mirrors your communication today, I will probably do so the next time we talk or the time after that. With this in mind, strict reciprocity is replaced by an overall sense of reciprocity in our relationship.

> **Axiom 6:** Similarities between people reduce uncertainty, whereas dissimilarities increase uncertainty.

Because Edie and Malcolm are both college students at Urban University, they may have similarities that reduce some of their uncertainties about each other immediately. Yet, they are different sexes and have different majors—dissimilarities that may contribute to their uncertainty level.

> **Axiom 7:** Increases in uncertainty level produce decreases in liking; decreases in uncertainty produce increases in liking.

As Edie and Malcolm reduce their uncertainties, they typically will increase their liking for each other. If they continue to feel highly uncertain about each other, they probably will not like each other very much. This axiom has received some indirect empirical support. In a study examining the relationship between communication satisfaction and uncertainty reduction, James Neuliep and Erica Grohskopf (2000) found that participants playing interviewers in an organizational role play were more likely to feel positively toward the participants playing the job seekers (and more likely to hire them) when their uncertainty was low. This finding prompted Neuliep and Grohskopf to posit an additional axiom stating that during initial interaction, as uncertainty decreases, communication satisfaction increases.

theorems
theoretical statements derived from axioms, positing a relationship between two concepts

As you review these seven axioms, you can sense the comprehensive nature of URT. Based on these axioms, Berger and Calabrese offered a number of **theorems,** or theoretical statements. Axiomatic theories proceed by pairing two axioms to produce a theorem. The process follows deductive logic: If $A = B$ and $B = C$, then $A = C$.

Berger and Calabrese combined all seven axioms in every possible pair combination to derive twenty-one theorems. For instance, if the amount of verbal communication decreases uncertainty and decreased uncertainty increases intimacy levels of self-disclosures, then increased verbal communication and increased intimacy levels are positively related. You can generate the other twenty theorems by combining the axioms using the deductive formula above. In addition, you need to use the rule of multiplication for multiplying positives and negatives. For example, if two variables have a positive relationship with a third, they are expected to have a positive relationship with each other. If one variable has a positive relationship with a third whereas the other has a negative relationship with the third, they should have a negative relationship with each other. Finally, if two variables each have a negative relationship with a third, they should have a positive relationship with each other. This process allows URT to be a comprehensive theory.

Expansions of Uncertainty Reduction Theory

As we discussed early in the textbook, theories are useful insofar as they generate a great deal of discussion and stimulate research. In many ways URT satisfies this criterion very well. Many researchers have tested URT and based their studies on the tenets of the theory. Further, Berger and several colleagues continue to refine and expand the theory, taking into account research findings. URT has been expanded and modified in a few areas. These areas include antecedent conditions, strategies, developed relationships, and the intercultural context.

Antecedent Conditions

Berger (1979) has suggested that three antecedent (prior) conditions exist when seeking uncertainty reduction. The first condition occurs when the other person has the *potential* to reward or punish. If Edie is a very popular, charismatic figure on campus, her attention may be seen as a reward by Malcolm. Likewise, Malcolm might experience a rejection by her as punishing. If Malcolm perceives Edie to be boring and unattractive or if she has a bad reputation on campus, he will not see her attention as rewarding or her rejection as punishing. Thus, according to Berger, Malcolm will be motivated to reduce his uncertainty if Edie is attractive to him and not so motivated if he finds her unappealing.

A second antecedent condition exists when the other person behaves contrary to expectations. In the case of Edie and Malcolm, Berger theorizes that Malcolm expects a superficial response to his comment about the class exercise. That is, his expectation may be that Edie will smile and agree with his assessment of the class activities. When Edie disagrees and comments that she might be happier in a different class, Malcolm's expectations are violated, and thus his desire to reduce his uncertainty increases.

The third and final condition exists when a person expects future interactions with another. Malcolm knows that he will continue to see Edie in class for the rest of the semester. Yet, because he has discovered that she is an engineering major, he may feel that he can avoid her in the future. In the first case, Berger would expect Malcolm's desire to increase predictability to be high—he knows he'll be seeing Edie often; in the second case, Malcolm's desire level is lower because Edie has a different major, and they can avoid each other after this class ends.

Strategies

A second area of expansion pertains to strategies. Berger (1995) suggests that people—in attempting to reduce uncertainty—use tactics from three classes of strategies: passive, active, and interactive. At the core of each is the goal of acquiring information. First, there is the **passive strategy**, whereby an individual assumes the role of unobtrusive observer of another. The **active strategy** exists when an observer engages in some type of effort other than direct contact to find out about another person. For instance, a person might ask a third party

passive strategy
reducing uncertainties by unobtrusive observation

active strategy
reducing uncertainties by means other than direct contact

The Theory Chronicles

For the next two weeks, chronicle in your journal each time you use one of the four strategies described in the chapter for reducing uncertainty. Describe specifically what you did and label the strategy, then note how well the strategy worked for you.

interactive strategy
reducing uncertainties by engaging in conversation

for information about the other. Finally, the **interactive strategy** occurs when the observer and the other person engage in direct contact or face-to-face interaction—that is, conversation that may include self-disclosures, direct questioning, and other information-seeking tactics. Although these strategies are critical to reducing uncertainty, Berger believes that certain behaviors, such as asking inappropriately sensitive questions, may increase rather than decrease uncertainty, and people may need additional reduction strategies.

To briefly illustrate these strategies, consider Malcolm and Edie. The time they spend in class covertly observing each other falls into the passive category. If either one of them engages friends to find out information about the other, he or she will be using an active strategy. When they speak after class, they use the interactive strategy to find out about each other and to reduce their uncertainties.

Tara Emmers and Dan Canary (1996) argue that in established relationships an additional strategy is employed. They call this strategy "uncertainty acceptance," and it includes responses such as simply trusting your partner. Emmers and Canary suggest that accepting or trusting your partner even when you are not completely certain about what is happening is a viable strategy for coping with uncertainty in developed relationships.

Developed Relationships: Beyond the Initial Encounter

When Berger and Calabrese conceived their theory, they were interested in describing the initial encounters between strangers. They stated a clear and narrow boundary around their theoretical insights. In the intervening years, however, the theory has been expanded to include developed relationships, as the acceptance strategy discussed above indicates. Berger (1982, 1987) has updated his theory since its inception. First, he comments that uncertainties are ongoing in relationships, and thus the process of uncertainty reduction is relevant in *developed* relationships as well as in *initial* interactions. This conclusion broadens earlier claims by Berger and Calabrese that specifically limited URT to initial encounters.

The inclusion of the three antecedent conditions that we discussed previously (potential for reward or punishment, deviation from expectations, and anticipation of future interactions) points us toward an examination of uncertainty in developed relationships. Specifically, we will expect rewards from, be surprised by, and anticipate future interactions with those with whom we have ongoing relationships.

Uncertainty in developed relationships may be different than it is in initial encounters. It may function dialectically within relationships; that is, there may be a tension between reducing and increasing uncertainty in developed relationships (Baxter & Wilmot, 1985). Berger and Calabrese (1975) observe, "While uncertainty reduction may be rewarding up to a point, the ability to completely predict another's behavior might lead to boredom. Boredom in an interpersonal relationship might well be a cost rather than a reward" (p. 101). Gerald R. Miller and Mark Steinberg (1975) mention a similar belief, noting that people have a greater desire for uncertainty when they feel secure than they do when they feel insecure. This suggests that as people begin to feel certain about their relationships and their partners, the excitement of uncertainty becomes desirable.

We return to the notion of dialectics again in Chapter 12, but let's examine this certainty-uncertainty dialectic a bit further with an example. In our opening vignette, Malcolm and Edie met for the first time after class. If their subsequent conversations evolve into a relationship, then their relationship will involve a level of predictability—that is, both will be able to predict certain things about the other because of the time they spend together. Yet, this predictability (certainty) may get tedious after a time, and they may feel their relationship is in a rut. At this point, the need for uncertainty, or novelty, will become high and the couple might try to build some variety into their routine to satisfy this need.

Uncertainty and uncertainty reduction processes operate in dating relationships in somewhat the same ways that Berger and Calabrese theorize they do in initial interactions. Research conducted by Sally Planalp and her colleagues (Planalp, 1987; Planalp & Honeycutt, 1985; Planalp, Rutherford, & Honeycutt, 1988) reflects conclusions regarding romance and uncertainty reduction. Specifically, the researchers discovered that dating couples found that at times their uncertainty increased. When it did increase, the individuals were motivated to reduce it through their communication behaviors. In a study of forty-six married couples, Lynn Turner (1990) reached similar conclusions. Therefore, according to these researchers, we must not assume that once relationships begin, uncertainty disappears.

Another example of how Uncertainty Reduction Theory has been extended into developed relationships is found in the research of Malcolm Parks and Mara Adelman (1983). Parks and Adelman studied the social networks (friends and family members) of an individual and indicate that these third-party networks can be quite important information sources about a romantic partner. They note that network "members may comment on the partner's past actions and behavioral tendencies. They may supply ready-made explanations for the partner's behavior or serve as sounding boards for the individual's own explanations" (1983, p. 57). They conclude that the more partners communicate with their social networks, the less uncertainty they will experience. Further, the researchers found that the less uncertainty people feel, the less likely they will be to dissolve a relationship with another.

Further, based on this expansion into established relationships, Berger and Gudykunst (1991) posited an eighth axiom and seven resulting new theorems to the original theory. The new axiom asserted that romantic partners who interact with their partner's social network experience less uncertainty about their partner than do those who do not have this interaction. The more interaction with the social network, the less uncertainty there will be.

Some researchers who were interested in how URT applied to established relationships suggested that people in this stage experienced a different type of uncertainty than did those in initial encounters. This uncertainty was labeled **relational uncertainty** and defined as lack of certainty about the future and the status of the relationship. Berger (1987) discussed this new uncertainty type and noted that it mars relational stability. More recent research (e.g., Ficara & Mongeau, 2000) established that relational uncertainty is distinct from the individual uncertainty that Berger and Calabrese originally theorized about.

**relational
uncertainty**
a lack of certainty
about the future and
status of a relationship

Marianne Dainton and Brooks Aylor (2001) examined how relational uncertainty operated in three different types of relationships: long-distance relationships with no face-to-face interaction, long-distance relationships with some face-to-face interaction, and geographically close relationships. The researchers were interested to see how relational uncertainty, jealousy, maintenance, and trust interacted in these three types of relationships. This is an important investigation because, as they note, between 25 to 40 percent of romantic relationships between college students are long distance.

They found overall, as URT would predict, that the more uncertainty existed in a relationship the more jealousy, the less trust, and the fewer maintenance behaviors also existed. Dainton and Aylor also found support for trust as "a potent means for reducing relational uncertainty" (p. 183). Further, the researchers also found that face-to-face contact is critical to reducing relational uncertainty. The people in long-distance relationships with no face-to-face interaction suffered from significantly more relational uncertainty. However, those who were geographically close did not differ significantly from those in long-distance relationships with some face-to-face interaction, which is not exactly what URT would predict. The researchers conclude that this is a fruitful line for further research into the utility and heurism of URT.

The Intercultural Context

Thus far, our examples clearly relate to the interpersonal context. However, Uncertainty Reduction Theory has been applied to another context, namely, the intercultural context. Berger (1987) points out that uncertainty varies across cultures, and a number of research studies illustrate the cultural applicability of URT.

William Gudykunst and his colleagues are credited with adapting URT to communication between Americans and Asians (Gudykunst, Chua, & Gray, 1987; Gudykunst & Nishida, 1984; Gudykunst, Yang, & Nishida, 1985). These researchers conclude that in Japan, Korea, and the United States, being attracted to another most likely reduces some uncertainty in acquaintance, friend, and dating relationships. However, the researchers add that reduced uncertainty may not lead to increased attraction.

**low-context
cultures**
cultures, like the
United States, where
most of the meaning
is in the code or
message

Gudykunst and Tsukasa Nishida (1986a) discovered differences in low- and high-context cultures. According to Edward T. Hall (1977), **low-context**

cultures are those in which meaning is found in the explicit code or message. Examples of low-context cultures are the United States, Germany, and Switzerland. In these cultures, plain, direct speaking is valued. Listeners are supposed to be able to understand meaning based merely on the words a speaker uses. In **high-context cultures**, nonverbal messages play a more significant role and most of the meaning of a message is internalized by listeners or resides in the context. Japan, Korea, and China are examples of high-context cultures. These cultures value indirectness in speech because listeners are expected to ignore much of the explicit code in favor of understood meanings cued by nonverbals and context.

high-context cultures
cultures, like Japan, where the meaning of a message is in the context or internalized in listeners

With respect to research on low- and high-context cultures, Gudykunst and Nishida (1986b) found that frequency of communication predicts uncertainty reduction in low-context cultures but not in high-context cultures. The researchers also discovered that people use direct communication (asking questions) to reduce their uncertainty in individualistic cultures. In collectivistic cultures, more indirect communication is used with individuals who are yet identified as members of the cultural in-group. Based on this research, then, people from different cultures engage in different kinds of communication to reduce their uncertainty.

Mitchell Hammer and Gudykunst (1987) undertook an additional study examining URT and culture. Instead of studying cultures outside the United States, however, they focused their research on African Americans. Interestingly, they found that URT did not apply to their African American respondents. Specifically, in this study, African Americans were not more confident in their impressions of others after asking them questions, and they were not attracted to people about whom they could make predictions. Consequently, uncertainty reduction may not be applicable in all cultural communities.

A concept similar to uncertainty reduction is **uncertainty avoidance**, which is an attempt to shun or avoid ambiguous situations (Hofstede, 1991). In other words, uncertainty avoidance refers to a person's tolerance for uncertainty. Geert Hofstede believes that the perspectives of people in high uncertainty avoidance cultures is "What is different is dangerous," whereas people in low uncertainty avoidance cultures subscribe to "What is different is curious" (1991, p. 119). Gudykunst and Yuko Matsumoto (1996) point out that there are a number of cultures that differ in their uncertainty avoidance (see Figure 9.1), and understanding that these differences exist can help us understand communication behaviors in other countries.

uncertainty avoidance
an attempt to avoid ambiguous situations

Theory Application in Groups (TAG)

In small groups, debate whether URT presents an accurate view of relationship development and maintenance. Some of you should defend the social scientific, objectivist epistemology of the theory, while others should question it.

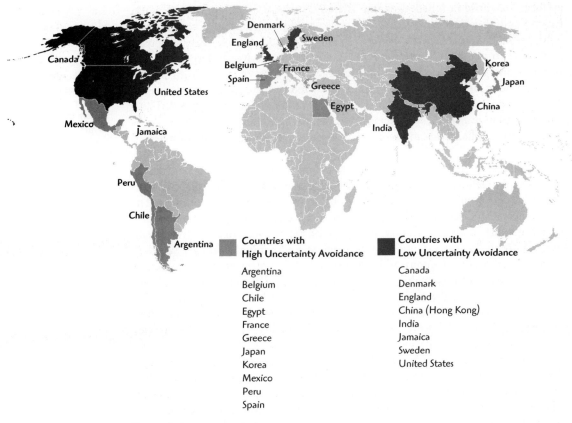

Figure 9.1
Countries and Uncertainty Avoidance

Countries with High Uncertainty Avoidance

Argentina
Belgium
Chile
Egypt
France
Greece
Japan
Korea
Mexico
Peru
Spain

Countries with Low Uncertainty Avoidance

Canada
Denmark
England
China (Hong Kong)
India
Jamaica
Sweden
United States

Critique and Closing

Over a decade after the publication of the original theory, Berger (1987) admitted that Uncertainty Reduction Theory "contains some propositions of dubious validity" (p. 40). Other writers concur. Although URT has stimulated a great deal of discussion and research, it also has been criticized. Basically, the critics find fault in two areas of the theory: the assumptions and its validity.

Some researchers believe that the major assumptions of the theory are flawed. Michael Sunnafrank (1986) argues that reducing uncertainty about the self and another in an initial encounter is not an individual's primary concern. Instead, Sunnafrank argues, "a more primary goal is the maximization of relational outcomes" (p. 9). Sunnafrank calls for a reformulation of URT that takes into account the importance of predicted outcomes during initial interactions. This has come to be known as predicted outcome value (POV). Drawing on our chapter's opening, Sunnafrank would contend that Malcolm will be more concerned with maximizing rewards in a potential relationship with Edie than in figuring out what she might do and why she is doing it. Actually, Sunnafrank

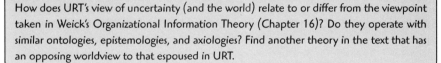

How does URT's view of uncertainty (and the world) relate to or differ from the viewpoint taken in Weick's Organizational Information Theory (Chapter 16)? Do they operate with similar ontologies, epistemologies, and axiologies? Find another theory in the text that has an opposing worldview to that espoused in URT.

suggests that URT might kick in after Malcolm decides what the predicted outcomes of talking with Edie will be.

Berger's (1986) response to Sunnafrank is that outcomes cannot be predicted without knowledge and reduced uncertainty about oneself, one's partner, and one's relationship. It is Berger's contention that uncertainty reduction is independent of as well as necessary to predicted outcome values. In fact, he believes that if one remains highly uncertain, there really are no predicted outcome values. Further, Berger responds to Sunnafrank's critique by noting that the act of predicting an outcome serves as a means to reduce uncertainty. Thus, Berger concludes that Sunnafrank has simply expanded the scope of URT rather than offering an alternative to it.

The second area of criticism of URT has to do with its validity. Recall that even Berger (1987) has admitted some validity problems. Yet, he is not willing to give up on the theory. Some of his more skeptical colleagues, however, assert that given the tight logical structure of an axiomatic theory, if one building block is wrong, then much of the resulting theory is suspect. Kathy Kellermann and Rodney Reynolds (1990) point to Axiom 3, which suggests that high uncertainty causes high levels of information-seeking behavior, as problematic.

Their study of over a thousand students failed to find support for the third axiom. Instead, they found that "*wanting* knowledge rather than *lacking* knowledge is what promotes information-seeking in initial encounters with others" (p. 71 [emphasis added]). Kellermann and Reynolds point out that many times we may be uncertain about another but because we have no interest in the other, we are not motivated to reduce our uncertainties by information-seeking behaviors. People engage in communication, therefore, not to reduce uncertainty but because they care about the other, are interested in the other, or both. In a different vein, Dale Brashers (2001) also questions the validity of Axiom 3. He notes with reference to post–September 11 anxieties that sometimes more information results in a greater sense of uncertainty. Interestingly, however, Dell McKinney and William Donaghy (1993) found some empirical support for Axiom 3, so the debate on this issue undoubtedly will continue.

Despite these shortcomings, Uncertainty Reduction Theory remains the only communication theory to specifically examine initial interactions. Incorporating our criteria for theory evaluation, this theory is, first, highly heuristic. For instance, URT has been integrated into research examining small groups (Booth-Butterfield, Booth-Butterfield, & Koester, 1988) as well as research in mass communication (Dimmick, Sikand, & Patterson, 1994) and computer-

Theory * Into * Practice

Uncertainty Reduction Theory's tenets are discussed in a 2002 *New York Times* article focusing on how roommates-to-be get acquainted with each other before the beginning of classes. The article observes that prior to the first year of college students are faced with countless unknowns. It observes that students use e-mail to reduce their uncertainties about some of these unknowns. "As incoming freshmen make their preparations this summer—a time often consumed with worry about getting a 'bad' roommate—many are minimizing fear of the unknown with a flurry of e-mail" (p. E1).

The article goes on to describe how roommates-to-be learn about one another's tastes and habits by corresponding via e-mail prior to the start of school. These e-mail messages are used by students to reduce their anxieties about who they will be living with for the next nine months. Two women who will be roommates at Kenyon College in Ohio were interviewed in the article, and both commented that e-mails had taken a lot of the pressure off them and reduced their anxiety about what their roommate would be like.

Professor Berger is interviewed in the article, and he observes that the Kenyon College students' behaviors and feelings were congruent with his theory. When people are going to an unfamiliar environment from a familiar one, uncertainty is high and information seeking is also high. Yet, Berger also notes that e-mailed information is totally different from the information that the students will gather about each other once they actually meet. Thus, they may be disappointed and confused when they live together, and they may have to reassess the impressions they formed through e-mail. A Princeton University student, Ted Lacey, is quoted in the article as saying that is exactly what happened to him. He thought that he and his roommate would be good friends from the information he gathered by e-mail prior to the start of school, but when they met, he changed his perceptions. He says that through e-mail they had agreed that they both liked to go out a lot, but in person he discovered that going out a lot meant different things to each of them. He wanted to party, whereas his roommate wanted to hang out with just one or two friends.

"The social dynamic at school was different, too. 'On e-mail you have to talk, but in person he was a real quiet guy,' Mr. Lacey said. 'Also, it was just us on e-mail, but when we got to campus all of a sudden there were all these other people'" (p. E7).

This article both confirms an axiom of URT and suggests future directions for testing the theory with reference to new media.

Source: Cohen, 2002.

TIP Follow-up

Examine the seven original axioms of URT. Do you think they are true when thinking about the contexts of new media like e-mail? Think about how to test whether any of these axioms hold true in a virtual context.

mediated communication (Walther & Burgoon, 1992). In addition, the theory is logically derived and simple in presentation—therefore passing the test of parsimony. The theorems Berger and Calabrese propose derive from the axioms, a logical progression in thinking.

Finally, URT can be considered to be tentative in that the theorists originally claimed that "there are other relevant constructs which might be explicitly incorporated into the model" (Berger & Calabrese, 1975, p. 111). Obviously, the writers were qualifying their original assumptions and conclusions, which paved the way for others to apply the theory variously.

Uncertainty Reduction Theory has made a very important contribution to the field of communication, even if it does not fully explain the communication in initial encounters between strangers. Further, although this theory may be more linear in nature (recall our discussion on communication models in Chapter 1), it has provoked a great deal of commentary and research, and it has placed communication in a central position. It marks the beginning of communication researchers focusing on their own discipline for theoretical explanations rather than borrowing theories from other disciplines. Further, it provides an ongoing dialogue as researchers continue to debate the validity of uncertainty reduction as a primary issue in relationship development.

Discussion Starters

1. Why is examining initial interactions like that of Edie and Malcolm an important undertaking for communication theorists? Provide at least one example to support your view.

2. Uncertainty reduction is the process of using communication to increase our ability to explain and predict others' behaviors. How do we use new media like e-mail, pagers, palm pilots, and so forth in this process?

3. Are there times when asking questions in initial encounters with others only results in more uncertainty? Give examples. Has reducing your uncertainty about someone ever led to you liking the person less? Describe how this occurs.

4. Do you agree with Berger and Calabrese's assumption about the developmental process of interpersonal relationships? Give examples that support or contest the notion that relationships use Communication to pass through entry, personal, and exit phases.

5. What additional factors or events exist—other than those presented in this chapter—when two people meet for the first time? Be sure to be specific and provide appropriate examples.

6. If you could talk with Berger or Calabrese, what would you say to either one of them about the utility of their theory in your life? Apply the theory to any aspect or relationship type in your life today in answering this question.

Terms for Review

prediction	self-disclosure
explanation	entry phase
cognitive uncertainty	personal phase
behavioral uncertainty	exit phase

axioms
reciprocity
theorems
passive strategy
active strategy

interactive strategy
relational uncertainty
low-context cultures
high-context cultures
uncertainty avoidance

 ## Online Learning Center

Visit the Online Learning Center at www.mhhe.com/west2. Use the multiple-choice and true/false quizzes to help you prepare for exams, and the glossary, crossword puzzles, and flashcards to further your knowledge of key terms.

CHAPTER 10

Social Penetration Theory

Jason LaSalle

About three years ago, Jason LaSalle's wife, Miranda, died in a car accident, leaving Jason a single parent of 8-year-old twins. Since his wife's death, he has struggled both financially and emotionally. He has worried about making his rent and van payments and about meeting his children's needs. For the past three years, Jason has worked odd jobs around the neighborhood to supplement his modest income as custodian for a local cinema complex. In addition, Jason has been lonely. He is shy around others, especially women. Miranda was the only woman he really felt comfortable with, and he misses her a great deal.

Jason's sister, Kayla, is always trying to get Jason out of the house. One night, she hired a baby-sitter and picked him up to go out. This evening was especially important to Kayla because she had also invited her friend Elise Porter, who was recently divorced. Kayla thought that Elise might be a good match for her brother. She was hoping that Elise's easygoing nature and her great sense of humor would appeal to Jason. Throughout the evening, Jason and Elise talked about a variety of things, including their experiences as single parents, her

divorce, and the two children they were each raising. Much of their night was spent dancing or talking to each other. The evening ended with Jason and Elise promising to get together again soon.

As Jason drove home to his apartment he couldn't help but think about Miranda. He was lonely; it had been three years since he had shared any intimacy with an adult. When he arrived home, his sadness increased as he caught sight of a family picture taken at Disney World shortly before Miranda's death. He wasn't sure if it was a good time to pursue an intimate relationship, and yet he wanted a chance to see what kind of person Elise was. He knew that future dates would inevitably require him to talk about Miranda, and he felt that such conversations would be very difficult. He would have to open up emotionally to Elise, and the thought of being placed in such a vulnerable position seemed challenging.

After he paid the baby-sitter and closed the door behind her, he walked into the twins' room and gave each a kiss on the forehead. Sitting drinking his tea in the living room, Jason felt that he was embarking upon something new, exciting, and a bit frightening.

This theory is based on the research of **Irwin Altman** and **Dalmas Taylor.**

social penetration
process of bonding
that moves a relation-
ship from superficial
to more intimate

trajectory
pathway to closeness

To understand the relational closeness between two people, Irwin Altman and Dalmas Taylor (1973) conceptualized Social Penetration Theory (SPT). The two conducted extensive study in the area of social bonding among various types of couples. Their theory illustrates a pattern of relationship development, a process that they identified as social penetration. **Social penetration** refers to a process of relationship bonding whereby individuals move from superficial communication to more intimate communication. According to Altman and Taylor, intimacy involves more than physical intimacy; other dimensions of intimacy include intellectual, emotional, and the extent to which a couple share activities (Adler & Towne, 2002). The social penetration process, therefore, necessarily includes verbal behaviors (the words we use), nonverbal behaviors (our body posture, the extent to which we smile, and so forth), and environmentally oriented behaviors (the space between communicators, the physical objects present in the environment, and so forth).

Altman and Taylor believe that people's relationships vary tremendously in their social penetration. From husband–wife to supervisor–employee to golf partners to physician–patient, the theorists conclude that relationships "involve different levels of intimacy of exchange or degree of social penetration" (1973, p. 3). The authors note that relationships follow some particular **trajectory,** or pathway to closeness. Further, they contend that relationships are somewhat organized and predictable in their development.

The opening story of Jason LaSalle and his arranged date illustrates a central feature of Social Penetration Theory. The only way for Jason and Elise to understand each other is for them to engage in personal conversations; such discussion requires each sharing personal bits of information. As the two become closer, they will move from a nonintimate relationship to an intimate one. Further, each person's personality will influence the direction of the relationship. So, Jason and Elise's relationship will be influenced by Jason's shyness and Elise's easygoing manner. The future of Jason's relationship with Elise is based on a multiplicity of factors—factors that we will explore throughout this chapter.

Early discussions of Social Penetration Theory began during the 1960s and 1970s, an era when opening up and talking candidly was highly valued as an important relational strategy. Now, however, researchers have acknowledged that cultures vary tremendously in their endorsement of openness as a relational skill. Also, today's scholars in interpersonal communication question the initial enthusiasm for relational openness in general. Therefore, as you read this chapter, keep in mind that we are discussing a theory that is rooted in a generation of which speaking freely was a highly valued characteristic. Nevertheless, much of the theory remains relevant today as we live in a society where openness is still a valued personal characteristic. Simply look at most daytime television talk shows for evidence of this.

To begin, we outline several assumptions of Social Penetration Theory. We then identify the catalyst for the theory.

Assumptions of Social Penetration Theory

Social Penetration Theory has enjoyed widespread acceptance by a number of scholars in the communication discipline. Part of the reason for the theory's appeal is its straightforward approach to relationship development. Although we alluded to some assumptions earlier, we will explore the following assumptions that guide SPT:

- Relationships progress from nonintimate to intimate.
- Relational development is generally systematic and predictable.
- Relational development includes depenetration and dissolution.
- Self-disclosure is at the core of relationship development.

First, relational communication between people begins at a rather superficial level and moves along a continuum to a more intimate level. On their date arranged by Kayla, Jason and Elise no doubt talked about trivial issues related to being single parents. They probably shared how difficult it is to have enough time in the day to do everything, but they probably did not express how desperate they feel at 3 A.M. when they awake from a nightmare, for example. These initial conversations at first may appear unimportant. Yet, as Jason discovers, such conversations allow an individual to size up the other and provide the opportunity for the early stages of relational development. There is little doubt that Jason feels awkward, but this awkwardness can pass. With time, relationships have the opportunity to become intimate.

Not all relationships fall into the extremes of nonintimate or intimate. In fact, many of our relationships are somewhere in between these two poles. Often, we may want only a moderately close relationship. For instance, we may want a relationship with a co-worker to remain sufficiently distant so that we do not know what goes on in her house each night or how much money she has in the bank. Yet, we need to know enough personal information so that we can have a sense of whether or not she can complete her part of a team project.

The second assumption of Social Penetration Theory pertains to predictability. Specifically, Social Penetration theorists argue that relationships progress fairly systematically and predictably. Some people may have difficulty with this claim. After all, relationships—like the communication process—are dynamic and ever-changing. Yet, according to Social Penetration Theory, even dynamic relationships follow some acceptable standard and pattern of development.

To better understand this assumption, again consider Jason LaSalle. Without knowing all the specifics of his situation, we could figure out that if he pursues a relationship with Elise, he will have to work through his emotions about Miranda. In addition, he must inevitably reconcile how their families might merge if the relationship progresses into more intimacy. Further, we could probably predict that the relationship will move slowly at first while both Jason and Elise work out their feelings and emotions.

These projections are grounded in the second assumption of the theory: Relationships generally move in an organized and predictable manner. Although we may not know precisely the direction of a relationship or be able to predict its exact future, social penetration processes are rather organized and predictable.

Theory Application in Groups (TAG)

This chapter attempts to demonstrate that relationships are predictable and somewhat routine in their development. There are, however, many times when relationship development is messy. In small groups, discuss those times when relationship development wasn't so predictable. Try to account for all types of relationships and include how self-disclosure functioned during those times.

We can be fairly sure, for instance, that Jason and Elise will not introduce each other to important people in their families before they date a few more times. We would also expect that neither would declare his or her love for the other before they exchanged more intimate information. Of course, a number of other events and variables (time, personality, and so forth) affect the way relationships progress and what we can predict along the way. As Altman and Taylor (1973) conclude, "People seem to possess very sensitive tuning mechanisms which enable them to program carefully their interpersonal relationships" (p. 8).

The third assumption of SPT pertains to the notion that relational development includes depenetration and dissolution. At first, this may sound a bit peculiar. Thus far, we have explored the coming together of a relationship. Yet, relationships do fall apart, or **depenetrate**. This may lead to relationship dissolution. Elise, for example, may be unprepared for Jason's disclosures and may wish to depenetrate and ultimately dissolve the relationship.

depenetrate
slow deterioration of relationship

Addressing depenetration and dissolution, Altman and Taylor liken the process to a film shown in reverse. Just as communication allows a relationship to move forward toward intimacy, communication could move a relationship back toward nonintimacy. If the communication is conflictual, for example, and this conflict continues to be destructive and unresolved, the relationship may take a step back and become less close. Social Penetration theorists think that depenetration—like the penetration process—is often systematic.

If a relationship depenetrates, it does not mean that it will inevitably dissolve. On the contrary, many individuals have either seen or been in relationships where depenetration is simply a fact of relational life. Niall Bolger and Shannon Kelleher (1993), for example, note that stress may become a precipitator to the end of a relationship, but most couples seem to manage it before the relationship dissolves. Long-lasting and stable relationships seem to be able to handle a number of different depenetrating episodes, and some partners construct strategies for reducing such depenetrating episodes as unresolved conflict. For instance, Patricia Noller and her colleagues (1994) discovered that spouses who had been married for more than two years openly let each other know about grievances throughout their marriage. Further, their conflict resolution strategies were consistently positive. Still, serious conflict that is not manageable or resolvable may lead to depenetration and dissolution.

self-disclosure
purposeful process of revealing information about one's self

The final assumption contends that self-disclosure is at the core of relationship development. **Self-disclosure** can be generally defined as the purpose-

Research Note

Gudykunst, W. B., & Nishida, T. (1986). Social penetration in close relationships in Japan and the United States. In R. Bostrom (Ed.), *Communication Yearbook 7* (pp. 592–610). Beverly Hills, CA: Sage.

The focus of this article is on how social penetration functions in the friendships of both Japanese and American college students. The authors rationalize that little research exists that compares close friendships across cultures. Employing Social Penetration Theory, William Gudykunst and Tsukasa Nishida contend that several similarities and differences may exist between the two cultures and that social penetration processes can be effectively integrated to better understand close friendships in both countries.

The authors surveyed 108 American and 118 Japanese college students; the average age of respondents was 20 years. The average length of time of the close friendship varied according to country: Americans responded that the friendships lasted an average of 57.5 months, and the Japanese sample responded 45.5 months. Integrating a Social Penetration questionnaire developed by Altman and Taylor (and translated into Japanese when needed), the researchers asked respondents to rate the intimacy of each of the items (0 = superficial; 6 = very intimate). Included among the items were topics covering religion, family, love, dating, sex, money, and politics. Based on these responses, the researchers constructed three indices: frequency, intimacy, and social penetration scales.

The results indicate that the Americans and the Japanese differ in several areas. Intimacy scores were higher for the U.S. college students than for the Japanese college students in the areas of marriage, love/dating/sex, and emotions. Japanese respondents registered higher mean scores in interest/hobbies, school/work, religion, and money/property. What these results suggest is that the Japanese and the American respondents view inti-

macy in different ways. Yet, they are similar in other ways. For example, social penetration scores were not significantly different in relationships with others, parental family, and attitudes/values. In total, Gudykunst and Nishida point out that there were significant differences in sixteen of the thirty-seven analyses and no significant differences in twenty-one of the analyses. Overall, therefore, more similarities than differences exist between the Japanese and the American college students.

The authors acknowledge a few explanations for many of the similarities between the populations. First, some of the Japanese college students may have been Westernized in their thinking—that is, they may view issues and events in an American way. Some writers have referred to this as "Caucasianization." Second, the researchers indicate that the acceptance of a group orientation in Japanese society leads individuals to overlook relational issues. Consequently, public matters may be discussed, but private matters are usually not addressed. Of course, there may be other reasons for why close friendships in Japan and the United States appear similar.

This article is a clear representation of employing Social Penetration principles in research. It focuses on self-disclosure but also examines a number of other relational issues. Further, the research is more meritorious because of its reliance on respondents both within and outside the United States. Examining friendships may appear to be abstract, but this study centers our attention on how social penetration, in particular, functions in close relationships. In doing so, the researchers add to the descriptive base of knowledge in interpersonal communication.

ful process of revealing information about yourself to others. Usually, the information that makes up self-disclosure is of a significant nature. For instance, revealing that you like to play the piano may not be all that important; revealing a more personal piece of information, such as that you are a practicing Catholic and are pro-life, may significantly influence the evolution of a relationship. The Research Note illustrates the type of scholarship undertaken by researchers interested in self-disclosure and Social Penetration Theory.

According to Altman and Taylor (1973), nonintimate relationships progress to intimate relationships because of self-disclosure. This process allows people to get to know each other in a relationship. Self-disclosure helps shape the present and future relationship between two people, and "making [the] self accessible to another person is intrinsically gratifying" (p. 50). Elise will understand the challenges that lie ahead for her in a relationship with Jason by hearing Jason reveal his feelings about his wife's death and his desire to begin dating again. In turn, because social penetration requires a "gradual overlapping and exploration of their mutual selves by parties to a relationship" (p. 15), Elise, too, would have to self-disclose her thoughts and feelings.

Finally, we should note that self-disclosure can be strategic or nonstrategic. That is, in some relationships, we tend to plan out what we will say to another person. In other situations, our self-disclosure may be spontaneous. Spontaneous self-disclosure is widespread in our society. In fact, researchers have used the phrase "**stranger-on-the-train** (or plane or bus) phenomenon" to refer to those times when people reveal information to complete strangers in public places. Think about how many times you have been seated next to a stranger on a trip, only to have that person disclose personal information throughout the journey. Interpersonal communication researchers continue to investigate why people engage in this activity.

stranger-on-the-train
revealing personal information to strangers in public places

Relationships and Onions

Earlier we discussed the importance of revealing information about one's self of which others are unaware. In their discussion of SPT, Altman and Taylor incorporate an onionskin structure (Figure 10.1). They believe that a person like Jason LaSalle can be compared to an onion, with the layers (concentric circles) of the onion representing various aspects of a person's personality. The outer layer is an individual's **public image,** or that which is available to the naked eye. Jason's public image is an African American male in his mid-forties who is slightly balding. Elise Porter is also an African American but is significantly taller than Jason and has very short hair. A layer of the public image is removed, however, when Jason discloses to his date his frustrations with being a single father.

public image
outer layer of a person; what is available to others

As the evening evolves for the two of them, Jason and Elise no doubt begin to reveal additional layers of their personalities. For instance, Elise may reveal that she, too, experiences single-parent anxieties. This **reciprocity,** or the process whereby one person's openness leads to the other's openness, is a primary component in Social Penetration Theory. Reciprocity has been shown to be significant in both established and new relationships, such as Jason and Elise's. Lawrence Rosenfeld and Gary Bowen (1991), for example, found that marital satisfaction was highest when spouses reciprocated mutual levels of self-disclosure. The researchers point out that these relationships are "probably less distressed and more stable" (p. 80). Altman and Taylor believe intimacy cannot be achieved without such reciprocity.

reciprocity
the return of openness from one person to another

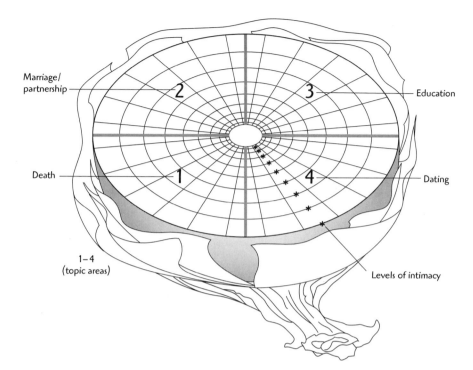

Marriage/partnership

Education

Death

Dating

1–4
(topic areas)

Levels of intimacy

Figure 10.1
The Social Penetration Process of Jason LaSalle

Breadth and Depth of Self-Disclosure

Before leaving the discussion of self-disclosure, we need to point out that penetration can be viewed along two dimensions: breadth and depth. **Breadth** refers to the number of various topics discussed in the relationship; **breadth time** pertains to the amount of time that relational partners spend communicating with each other about these various topics. **Depth** refers to the degree of intimacy that guides topic discussions. In the initial stages, relationships can be classified as having narrow breadth and shallow depth. For Jason LaSalle, it is feasible that his first date with Elise was characterized this way. Most likely, the two did not discuss many topics, and what they did discuss probably lacked intimate overtones. As relationships move toward intimacy, we can expect a wider range of topics to be discussed (more breadth), with several of those topics marked by depth.

A few conclusions are important with respect to the breadth and depth of self-disclosure. First, shifts or changes in central layers (of the onion) have more of an impact than those in outer, or peripheral, layers. Because an individual's public image, or outer layer, represents those things that others can see, or the superficial, we expect that if there are changes in the outer layer, the consequence is minimal. For example, if Elise changed her hairstyle, her relationship with Jason would be less affected than if she changed her opinion about premarital sex.

Second, the greater the depth, the more opportunity for a person to feel vulnerable. Imagine that Jason reveals some inadequacy about himself to

breadth
number of topics discussed in a relationship
breadth time
amount of time spent by relational partners discussing various topics
depth
degree of intimacy guiding topic discussion

Table 10.1 Guidelines for Self-Disclosure

ASK YOURSELF	SUGGESTION
Is the other person important to you?	Reveal significant pieces of information about yourself to those people with whom you have developed a personal relationship.
Is the risk of disclosing reasonable?	Try not to reveal significant information about yourself if there is great risk associated with it. Assess the risk potential of your disclosure.
Are the amount and type of disclosure appropriate?	Discern whether you are revealing too much or too little information. Examine the timing of the disclosure.
Is the disclosure relevant to the situation at hand?	Constant disclosure is not typically useful in a relationship. Don't share everything.
Is the disclosure reciprocated?	Unequal self-disclosure creates an imbalanced relationship. Wait for reciprocity.
Will the effect be constructive?	If not employed carefully, disclosure can be used in destructive ways. Use care in disclosing information that may be perceived as damaging.

Source: Adapted from Adler & Towne, 2002.

Elise—for instance, the fact that he was on welfare for two years after his wife's death. When he reveals this personal information to Elise, she can respond in several different ways. She can simply say, "Wow," and not venture further into the discussion. Or she can reply, "That must have been very hard for you," communicating compassion. A third possible response is "I don't see anything wrong with that. Millions of people need some help at some point in their lives." This latter response demonstrates even more compassion and an effort to diffuse the possible anxiety that Jason is feeling. How Elise responds influences how vulnerable Jason feels. As you can see, the first response may elicit a high degree of vulnerability, whereas the third response may invoke little vulnerability.

As you reflect on the topic of self-disclosure, keep in mind that an individual should be judicious in using self-disclosure. Although self-disclosure generally moves a relationship toward more closeness, if people disclose too much during the early stages of a relationship, they may actually end the relationship. Some partners may be ill equipped and underprepared to know another so intimately. Also note that trust is an inherent part of the disclosure and reciprocity processes. Mark Knapp and Anita Vangelisti (2000), for example, note that "self-disclosure of intimate information is based on trust" (p. 240). They go on to say that if we desire reciprocity in disclosure, we must try to gain the trust of the other person and, similarly, feel trustful of the other person. One goal in self-disclosure, then, is to be thoughtful and appropriate. We have included other guidelines for self-disclosure in Table 10.1.

A Social Exchange: Relational Costs and Rewards

Social Penetration Theory is grounded in several of the principles of Social Exchange Theory (Thibaut & Kelley, 1959). As we discuss in Chapter 11, this theory suggests that social exchanges "entail services that create unspecified obligations in the future and therefore exert a pervasive influence on social relations" (Blau, 1964, p. 140). Altman and Taylor based some of their work on social exchange processes, and therefore social exchange issues are relevant to our discussion.

Taylor and Altman (1987) argue that relationships can be conceptualized in terms of rewards and costs. Rewards are those relational events or behaviors that stimulate satisfaction, pleasure, and contentment in a relational partner, whereas costs are those relational events or behaviors that stimulate negative feelings. Quite simply, if a relationship provides more rewards than costs, then individuals are more likely to stay in that relationship. However, if an individual believes that there are more costs to being in a relationship, then relationship dissolution is probable. For instance, Jason LaSalle will most likely regulate the closeness of his relationship with Elise by assessing a **reward/cost ratio,** which is defined as the balance between positive and negative relationship experiences. If Jason believes that he is deriving more pleasure (nurturance, supportive teasing, and so forth) than pain (frustration, insecurity, and so forth) from being in his relationship with Elise, then it is likely that he is fairly satisfied at the moment. His own expectations and experiences must also be taken into account in the reward/cost ratio. As Taylor and Altman point out, "rewards and costs are consistently associated with mutual satisfaction of personal and social needs" (1987, p. 264).

To understand this a bit better, consider the following two conclusions observed by Taylor and Altman: (1) rewards and costs have a greater impact early on in the relationship than later in the relationship, and (2) relationships with a reservoir of positive reward/cost experiences are better equipped to handle conflict effectively. We will examine each of these briefly.

The first conclusion suggests that there are relatively few interpersonal experiences in the early stages, resulting in individuals focusing more on a single reward or a single cost. So, for instance, it is probable that Jason will be impressed with Elise if she is willing to give Jason space during the early stages of their relationship; for Jason, rushing into a relationship may be a bit overwhelming, and Elise's patience may be viewed as an important relational reward. Elise, however, may view Jason's early ambivalence as an indicator of things to come. She may, therefore, decide that his uncertainty is simply too much of a cost to endure and want to dissolve the relationship sooner than Jason does.

With respect to the second conclusion regarding costs and rewards, Taylor and Altman note that some relationships are better able to manage conflict than others. As relational partners move on in a relationship, they may experience a number of disagreements. Over the years, couples become accustomed to managing conflict in various ways, creating a unique relational culture that allows them to work through future issues. There may be more trust in handling a

reward/cost ratio
balance between positive and negative relationship experiences

conflict in established relationships. Additionally, the relationship is not likely to be threatened by a single conflict because of the couple's stockpile of experiences in dealing with conflict.

In sum, then, relationships often depend on both parties assessing the rewards and costs. If partners feel that there are more rewards than costs, chances are that the relationship will survive. If more costs are perceived than rewards, the relationship is likely to dissolve. However, keep in mind that both partners may not see an issue similarly; a cost by one person may be viewed as a reward by the other.

The Social Exchange perspective relies on both parties in a relationship to calculate the extent to which individuals view the relationship as negative (cost) or positive (reward). According to Social Exchange thinking, as relationships come together, partners ultimately assess the possibilities within a relationship as well as the perceived or real alternatives to a relationship. These evaluations are critical as communicators decide whether the process of social penetration is desirable. In the following section, we identify the stages of the social penetration process.

Stages of the Social Penetration Process

The decision about whether a potential relationship appears satisfying is not immediate. As we mentioned earlier, relationship development occurs in a rather systematic manner, and decisions about whether people want to remain in a relationship are not usually made quickly. Not all relationships go through this process, and those that do are not always romantic relationships. To demonstrate how each stage functions, we will first provide a scenario for you to think about. As we discuss each stage, we will refer back to the example. Figure 10.2 outlines the four stages of the process.

Consider the relationship between Cathy and Barbra, first-year students at Upton University, who were randomly placed as roommates in Blackstone Hall, an all-female residence on campus. The two hail from different parts of the state; Cathy is from the city, and Barbra was raised on a farm. They also differ in family makeup in that Cathy is an only child and her roommate has four siblings. Finally, both of Cathy's parents have graduate degrees, whereas Barbra is the first in her family to attend college. They have only met each other once (at new student orientation) and are now about to have their first breakfast together.

Figure 10.2
Stages of Social Penetration

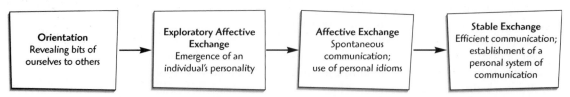

Orientation: Revealing Bit by Bit

The earliest stage of interaction, called the **orientation stage,** occurs at the public level; only bits of ourselves are revealed to others. During this stage, comments are usually on the cliché level and reflect superficial aspects of individuals. People usually act in socially desirable ways and are cautious of disturbing any societal expectations. Further, individuals smile pleasantly and react politely in the orientation stage.

Taylor and Altman (1987) note that people tend not to evaluate or criticize during the orientation stage. This behavior would be perceived as inappropriate by the other and might jeopardize future interactions. If evaluation does occur, the theorists believe that it will be couched in soft overtones. In addition, both parties actively avoid any conflict so that they have further opportunity to size up each other.

The orientation stage can be understood by examining the dialogue between Cathy and Barbra during their breakfast:

> CATHY: I must admit that I was wondering what kind of roommate I'd have. It's kind of strange; we're picked by a computer, and we have to live with each other for a year.
>
> BARBRA: I agree. [awkward silence]
>
> CATHY: But, hey, it's cool that we both love lacrosse, and maybe we'll both make the team. I think this campus . . . [Barbra interrupts]
>
> BARBRA: I love to study near . . . Sorry. You go ahead.
>
> CATHY: No, you go.
>
> BARBRA: I was going to say that I hope that we have some chances to go off campus and go to the lake. I love to study near the water. I also used to swim at a lake near my house. I haven't had time this past summer, though, because I was working too much.
>
> CATHY: Believe it or not, I don't know how to swim! I tried to learn, but I just don't seem to be coordinated.
>
> BARBRA: Hey! I'm a good swimmer. I'll teach ya when we get some time.
>
> CATHY: Great!

orientation stage
stage of social penetration that includes revealing small parts of ourselves

As you can see, both women engage in a rather superficial and sometimes awkward conversation, and neither one appears to be judging the other. In fact, Barbra has an opportunity to tell Cathy how strange it is that she doesn't know how to swim, but she chooses to stay supportive.

Exploratory Affective Exchange: The Self Emerges

exploratory affective exchange stage
stage of social penetration that results in the emergence of our personality to others

In the orientation stage, interactants are cautious about revealing too much about themselves to each other. The **exploratory affective exchange stage,** however, is an expansion of the public areas of the self and occurs when aspects of an individual's personality begin to emerge. What was once private now becomes public. The theorists note that this stage is comparable to the relationships we have with casual acquaintances and friendly neighbors. Like other stages, this stage includes both verbal and nonverbal behaviors. People might begin to use some catch phrases that are idiosyncratic to the relationship. There is a small amount of spontaneity in communication because individuals feel more relaxed with each other, and they are not as cautious about blurting out something that they may later regret. Also, more touch behavior and more affect displays (such as facial expressions) may become part of the communication repertoire with the other person. Taylor and Altman tell us that many relationships don't proceed beyond this stage.

To gain a clearer picture of the exploratory affective exchange stage, think again about Cathy and Barbra. This time, however, consider that the two have been roommates for about eight weeks, and each is getting a better idea about the personality of the other. And like many roommates, they have decided to take a class together and are preparing for their midterm history exam:

BARBRA: Hey, Cath, d'ya hear about what kind of tests Kading [the professor] gives in class?

CATHY: At my sorority rush last night, I heard that they are mostly recall, and we don't have to know dates. Ahhhh, I'm ready to scream because I can't remember all of this stuff from Chapter 3!

BARBRA: Chill. . . .

CATHY: Chill! It's easy for a straight A student to say that.

BARBRA: I *was* going to say—before I was interrupted—that I thought I'd do badly on my psych exam, and I got a B+ on it. Anyway, he may curve.

CATHY: I can't rely on a curve. I'm just too removed from this stuff to understand it. My parents will kill me if I flunk this course.

BARBRA: Well, stop talking and start studying!

Clearly, Barbra and Cathy are starting to feel more comfortable around each other. In fact, Barbra's "Chill" reflects the sort of catch phrase to which Taylor and Altman refer. Further, Cathy is slowly revealing more personal information about her parents' expectations and her ability to understand the material. Their exploratory affective exchange is relatively supportive, although their anxiety level gets the best of them at times.

Affective Exchange: Commitment and Comfortability

This stage is characterized by close friendships and intimate partners. The **affective exchange stage** includes those interactions that are more "freewheeling and casual" (Taylor & Altman, 1987, p. 259) in that communication is frequently spontaneous and individuals make quick decisions, often with little regard for the relationship as a whole. The affective exchange stage represents further commitment to the other individual; the interactants are comfortable with each other.

The stage includes those nuances of a relationship that make it unique; a smile may substitute for the words "I understand," or a penetrating gaze may translate into "We'll talk about this later." We might also find individuals using **personal idioms** (Hopper, Knapp, & Scott, 1981), which are private ways of expressing a relationship's intimacy through words, phrases, or behaviors. Idiomatic expressions—such as "sweetie" or "bubbles"—carry unique meaning for two people in a relationship. These idioms are different from the catchphrases that we discussed in the exploratory affective exchange in that idioms usually characterize more established relationships, whereas catchphrases may develop at any point in an initial interaction. We should add that this stage may also include some criticisms. As the theorists contend, these criticisms, hostilities, and disapprovals may exist "without any thought of threat to the relationship as a whole" (Altman & Taylor, 1973, p. 139). Consequently, barriers to closeness may be broken down, but many people still protect themselves from becoming too vulnerable.

Returning to our example, Cathy and Barbra have been together for a little more than twelve weeks. They have had ample opportunity to understand a number of idiosyncrasies about each other; living with someone seems to do that to people. Their conversation centers around a date that Barbra had on Saturday night:

BARBRA: He's a pig! All I could think about during the whole night is that someday, some woman will be with him! I pity her.

CATHY: He couldn't have been all that bad.

BARBRA: Oh yeah? He tried telling me that all I ever do is talk and that I don't listen enough. Give me a break!

CATHY: Well, Barb, to be truthful, you don't seem to listen as much as you talk.

BARBRA: What does that mean?

CATHY: I'm simply saying that sometimes I can't get a word in edgewise in this friendship. Every time I want to say something, all you ever do is shut me up.

BARBRA: I can't imagine that anyone can shut you up, Cathy. As a matter of fact, my business is *my* business, not *yours!*

CATHY: Then don't tell me about your pathetic dates anymore!

BARBRA: Fine.

CATHY: Fine.

affective exchange stage
stage of social penetration that is spontaneous and quite comfortable for relational partners

personal idioms
private intimate expressions stated in a relationship

As you can sense, there is noticeable tension in the relationship right now. Altman and Taylor would argue that although it appears that the two are very angry with each other at the moment, they will probably be able to move along. Many people have been in this sort of conflict before, and it seems that because a relationship carries significance and partners have emotionally invested in it, they are not prepared to end it because of a spontaneous statement. Yet, we should not forget that Cathy and Barbra are ready to offer each other criticisms, and to that extent their comments sound somewhat nasty. Nonetheless, we hope you can see that their barriers are down, and both are comfortable sharing very personal comments about each other. To review, affective exchanges may include both positive and negative exchanges.

Stable Exchange: Raw Honesty and Intimacy

**stable exchange
stage**
stage of social pene-
tration that results in
complete openness
and spontaneity for
relational partners

The fourth and final stage, stable exchange, is attained in very few relationships. The **stable exchange stage** pertains to an open expression of thoughts, feelings, and behaviors that results in a high degree of spontaneity and relational uniqueness. During this stage, partners are highly intimate and synchronized; that is, behaviors between the two sometimes recur, and partners are able to assess and predict the behavior of the other fairly accurately. At times, the partners may tease each other about topics or people. This teasing, however, is done in a friendly manner.

Social Penetration theorists believe that there are relatively few mistakes or misinterpretations in communication meaning at this stage. The reason for this is simple: Both partners have had numerous opportunities to clarify any previous ambiguities and have begun to establish their own personal system of communication. As a result, communication—according to Altman and Taylor—is efficient.

We return to our example of Cathy and Barbra. It is now final exam week, and obviously the two are very tense. Yet, they both realize that this week must not be complicated by unnecessary conflict, and each realizes that after this week, they will not see each other for a month. The stable exchange stage is very apparent when we listen to their conversation:

CATHY: I was going down the hall to Anuka's to get coffee. Want any?

BARBRA: I'm too jittery right now. Got any Sleepytime tea? [the two laugh]

CATHY: Do ya think you're ready for all the tests this week?

BARBRA: No, but that's okay. I don't have pushy parents, and they know that I'm doin' my best, and you are too.

CATHY: Yeah, I guess.

BARBRA: We've got to get good grades; otherwise we're off the team.

CATHY: I think we should just try to think positive.

BARBRA: Maybe we can call some psychic hotline and ask how we're going to do on the tests. [again, the two laugh]

CATHY: Thanks for making me laugh. I needed that.

BARBRA: We'll do fine.

The stable exchange stage suggests that meanings are clear and unambiguous. The dialogue between Cathy and Barbra is very clear, and if we read between the lines we can see that the two do care about each other. Their communication suggests support and closeness. The women appear to be willing to allow each other some breathing room, and each sounds ready to help out the other. Although our earlier example suggested a conflicted relationship, there is now what Altman and Taylor (1973) call **dyadic uniqueness,** or distinctive relationship qualities such as humor and sarcasm.

As we mentioned earlier, this stage approach to intimacy can get convoluted with periodic spurts and slowdowns along the way. In addition, the stages are not a complete picture of the intimacy process. There are a number of other influences, including a person's background and values and even the environment in which the relationship exists. The social penetration process is a give-and-take experience whereby both partners continue to work on balancing their individual needs with the needs of the relationship.

dyadic uniqueness
distinctive relationship qualities

Critique and Closing

Social Penetration Theory has been appealing since its inception nearly thirty years ago. Altman and Taylor have proposed an intriguing model by which to view relationship development. The theory is versatile, allowing students and scholars of communication to employ it in a number of ways. Researchers have integrated the simplicity of social penetration thinking into their scholarship. For instance, the effects of self-disclosure on various types of relationships has been studied and written about across a variety of populations. Families (Golish, 2000; Turner & West, 2002), teachers (Russ, Simonds, & Hunt, 2002), marriages (Dickson & Walker, 2001), and physician–patient relationships (Agne, Thompson, & Cusella, 2000) have all been studied. Therefore, the theory is heuristic as it has spawned literally hundreds of studies on self-disclosure and relationship development.

Interpersonal communication scholars, however, are not without their doubts about SPT. Specifically, some writers contend that self-disclosure in particular may be too narrowly interpreted in the theory. For instance, Valerian Derlega, Sandra Metts, Sandra Petronio, and Stephen Margulis (1993) believe that self-disclosure depends on a number of factors, not simply the need to reveal to people over time. Because people are constantly changing, the authors

The Theory Connection

Discuss how the principles of Uncertainty Reduction Theory and Social Penetration Theory overlap. How can initial interactions (as discussed in URT) be compared to developing relationships (as discussed in SPT)? Further, delineate how self-disclosure functions in both theories.

Theory ∗ Into ∗ Practice

In an essay on teasing published in the *Washington Post,* Robert Stein reports that teasing remains one of the forms of nonverbal communication that can cause a relationship either to grow or to depenetrate. Stein notes that "we tease to get closer to another person," which, according to Social Penetration Theory, prompts relational partners to self-disclose. However, Stein warns that "we also tease to keep others in their place," which can result in the depenetration of a relationship.

Stein continues by noting that teasing—in all its forms—remains a mystery in adults (much has been written about teasing with children). Yet, for the most part, teasing "can enable friends or spouses to communicate grievances in subtle, non-threatening ways. It helps newcomers learn the rules of a new environment."

Quoting a few studies conducted to better understand teasing in relationships, Stein states that "even though the nicknames and stories were often profane and clearly designed to humiliate, the members (of a fraternity house) reported [more] favorable feelings toward those who had teased them than [toward] those who had not." He quotes a researcher who states that teasing is "play," and when someone teases another, it is saying that "we're close enough to handle that."

But a fraternity house is not relational reality. Still, Stein reports research that shows that teasing may be a part of the stable exchange stage of social penetration. He notes that "couples who described themselves as more satisfied with their relationships teased each other in more positive ways than less-satisfied couples. . . . In certain types of marriages, teasing plays a pivotal role in keeping couples together."

There may be sex differences when it comes to engaging in teasing and interpreting teasing. Stein indicates that research shows that men are more likely than women to use teasing; it is a sort of playful fighting with men, whereas women are more likely to take it seriously. Much of the response to teasing depends on the relational atmosphere.

Source: Stein, 1999.

TIP Follow-up
Teasing as described above is rarely discussed in communication theory. Discuss how teasing could be considered both a reward and a cost in a relationship.

argue that what is considered to be self-disclosure often depends on the attitudes of a relational partner. Further, they indicate that self-disclosure is not always a linear relationship event. Derlega and colleagues conclude that "self-disclosure and close relationships do not necessarily develop over time in a parallel, incremental, and continuous fashion" (1993, p. 26).

Other scholars have weighed in on relational development as well. They reject the notion that relationship development is linear. Mark Knapp and Anita Vangelisti (2000), for example, believe that "relationships are nested within a network of other social relationships which affect communication patterns manifested by the partners" (p. 38). Therefore, other people may influence the direction of a relationship. In addition, the linearity of the theory suggests that the reversal of relational engagement is relational disengagement (recall that Altman and Taylor likened relationship disengagement to a film shown in reverse). Leslie Baxter (1983), however, questions whether relationship deterioration is the reversal of relationship development. In fact, Baxter (1984) discovered that several elements exist in relationship breakups. Her work suggests that relationship development is not the clean process originally reasoned by Altman and Taylor.

Finally, the model's emphasis on self-disclosure may be misguided and inappropriate. Daniel Canary, Michael Cody, and Valerie Manusov (2000), for example, conclude that once relationships are established, self-disclosure does not necessarily continue to play a pivotal role to the degree that it once did early on in the relationship. Further, Canary and his colleagues believe that intimate expressions are frequently accompanied by bouts of conflict, emotional voids, and awkwardness in communication (recall the dark side of communication presented in Chapter 1). Therefore, the theory—as Altman and Taylor conceptualize it—is somewhat limited by its linearity and its emphasis on self-disclosure.

To be fair, Altman has subsequently refined his original thinking on the social penetration processes. He now believes that being open and disclosive should be viewed in conjunction with being private and withdrawn (Altman, Vinsel, & Brown, 1981). This dialectical perspective is similar to that proposed by Baxter and Barbara Montgomery in their theory on relational dialectics (Chapter 12). To be sure, Jason LaSalle and Elise Porter will surely experience the push and pull of self-disclosure as their relationship progresses. It is likely that as both of them share pieces of information, each will also remain private about other issues. And despite the critics' charges, Taylor and Altman (1987) claim that "many researchers have been influenced by the ideas from social penetration theory, but few have directly tested propositions from the theory" (p. 272). The experiences of people like Jason LaSalle will continue to be studied by researchers. His relationship with Elise requires the sort of thinking that underscores Social Penetration Theory. Although some criticize the theory, it provides an important contribution to understanding the development of human relationships.

Discussion Starters

1. If their relationship develops further, what will Jason and Elise talk about as the two get to know each other better? Will there be any risk involved as they disclose to each other? Explain with examples.

2. When self-disclosing to another person, several things can go wrong. Explain the consequences of poorly planned or inappropriate self-disclosure. Provide examples along the way.

3. What similar patterns cut across escalating relationships? Discuss marital relationships, relationships between friends, and parent–child relationships as individuals move toward intimacy.

4. Some critics have charged that Social Penetration Theory focuses too much on self-disclosure. Others, however, contend that self-disclosure forms the basis of most intimate relationships. What do you think? Is there a compromise between the two views?

5. If you outlined the stages of a past romantic relationship of yours, would it follow the sequencing that Altman and Taylor suggest? What similarities are there to the social penetration process? What differences are there? Provide examples.

6. Apply Social Penetration Theory principles to workplace relationships you have encountered.

Terms for Review

social penetration	depth
trajectory	reward/cost ratio
depenetrate	orientation stage
self-disclosure	exploratory affective exchange stage
stranger-on-the-train	affective exchange stage
public image	personal idioms
reciprocity	stable exchange stage
breadth	dyadic uniqueness
breadth time	

Online Learning Center

Visit the Online Learning Center at www.mhhe.com/west2. Use the multiple-choice and true/false quizzes to help you prepare for exams, and the glossary, crossword puzzles, and flashcards to further your knowledge of key terms.

CHAPTER 11

Social Exchange Theory

Meredith Daniels and LaTasha Evans

Meredith Daniels and LaTasha Evans have been best friends since they served as hall monitors together in the fourth grade. After elementary school they moved on together to Collins High School. There they suffered through homework, boy problems, and other typical high school concerns. In addition, they coped with racial issues because Meredith is European American and LaTasha is African American. In their hometown of Biloxi, Mississippi, the heritage of racism formed a barrier to their friendship. Although Biloxi is now fairly progressive, Meredith's grandfather was very uncomfortable about her friendship with LaTasha. Also, LaTasha's Uncle Benjamin had participated in Freedom Marches in the 1960s and had formed some unfavorable opinions about Whites. For a short time, her uncle had been a member of a Black separatist organization. He had some difficulty with LaTasha and Meredith's friendship, too. Both of the young women had worked hard to maintain their relationship despite their family members' objections.

When LaTasha and Meredith were together, they often wondered why race was such a big deal. They seemed like sisters to each other, closer than many sisters they knew. They had the exact same sense of humor, and they could always cheer each other up with a goofy look or some silly joke about their past. They enjoyed the same movies (horror/thrillers) and the same subjects in school (English

and French) and had similar taste in clothes (baggy pants) and boyfriends (intellectual guys).

But at home, they often had to defend their friendship to their families. Meredith's parents said that they did not object to their friendship but that they were unhappy when Meredith socialized with African American boys and went to parties where she might be one of only two or three White girls in attendance. LaTasha's parents also had no problem with Meredith; they liked her and understood the friendship. But they drew the line when it came to dating White boys. LaTasha's parents were very proud of their African American heritage, and they told all their children how important it was to maintain their traditions and way of life. For them this meant that the family must stay African American: no dating or marriage with someone of another race. LaTasha's cousin had married a Japanese woman, and the whole family was having a great deal of difficulty accepting the couple.

Now that LaTasha and Meredith were entering their senior year at Collins, things had become even more difficult. LaTasha's parents were definite that she would be attending a historically Black college after graduation. Meredith's family wanted her to go to a small college in southern California because both her parents had graduated from this school, and they had many relatives living near the college. Both LaTasha and Meredith wanted to go to college together or at least be somewhat near each other. Additionally, they resented how much time and

This theory is based on the research of **John Thibaut** and **Harold Kelley.**

energy all the discussions about college seemed to take up. It was almost ruining their senior year!

When they were together, they could usually forget about all the hassle and just have fun as usual, but the pressure was taking a toll on their friendship. Although they tried not to think about it, they both were concerned about the future. It was hard not to be able to tell each other everything, as they always had in the past, but Meredith and LaTasha found that talking to each other about college was stressful, so they mainly avoided the subject. Privately, each wondered what was going to happen and how she would get along next year without her best friend.

A Social Exchange theorist examining Meredith and LaTasha's relationship would predict that it might be heading for some trouble. This prediction would be based on the fact that the relationship currently seems to be costing the two more than it is rewarding them. Social Exchange Theory (SET) is based on the notion that people think about their relationships in economic terms and that they tally up the costs and compare them to the rewards that are offered. **Costs** are the elements of relational life that have negative value to a person. For example, the stress and tension that LaTasha and Meredith feel about the issue of college are now costs of their relationship, and their relationship always had the cost of generating conflict in their respective families. **Rewards** are the elements of a relationship that have positive value. In Meredith and LaTasha's case, the fun they have together, the loyalty they show for each other, and the sense of understanding they share are all rewards.

Social Exchange theorists argue that people assess their relationships in terms of costs and rewards. All relationships require some time and effort on the part of their participants. When friends spend time with each other, which they must do in order to maintain the relationship, they are unable to do other things with that time, so in that sense the time spent is a cost. Friends may need attention at inopportune times, and then the cost is magnified. For instance, if you had to finish a term paper and your best friend just broke up with her boyfriend and needed to talk to you, you can see how the friendship would cost you something in terms of time. Yet, relationships provide us with rewards, or positives, too. Families, friends, and loved ones generally give us a sense of acceptance, support, and companionship. Some friends open doors for us and provide us with status just by being with us. Friends and families keep us from feeling lonely and isolated. Some friends teach us helpful lessons.

The Social Exchange perspective argues that people calculate the overall worth of a particular relationship by subtracting its costs from the rewards it provides:

$$worth = rewards - costs$$

Positive relationships are those whose worth is a positive number; that is, the rewards are greater than the costs. Relationships where the worth is a negative number (the costs exceed the rewards) tend to be negative for the participants. Social Exchange Theory goes even further, predicting that the worth of a relationship influences its **outcome**, or whether people will continue with a rela-

costs
elements of relational life with negative value

rewards
elements of relational life with positive value

outcome
whether people continue in a relationship or terminate it

tionship or terminate it. Positive relationships are expected to endure, whereas negative relationships will probably terminate.

Although, as we will explore in this chapter, the situation is more complex than this simple equation, it does give the essence of what exchange theorists argue. John Thibaut and Harold Kelley say, for example, that "every individual voluntarily enters and stays in any relationship only as long as it is adequately satisfactory in terms of his [sic] rewards and costs" (1959, p. 37). As Ronald Sabatelli and Constance Shehan (1993) note, the Social Exchange approach views relationships through the metaphor of the marketplace, where each person acts out of a self-oriented goal of profit taking.

We have been talking in general about exchange theories or the perspective of Social Exchange; this is because there are several theories of social exchange. Michael Roloff (1981) discusses five specific theories in his book *Interpersonal Communication: The Social Exchange Approach*. Roloff observes that these theories are tied together by a central argument that "the guiding force of interpersonal relationships is the advancement of both parties' self-interest" (p. 14). Further, Roloff notes that these theories do not assume that self-interest is a negative thing but, rather, say that when self-interest is recognized, it will actually enhance a relationship. Yet, Roloff also argues that there are significant differences among these five theories—some of which derive from the fact that they were developed by researchers in different disciplines (for example, psychology, social psychology, and sociology). It is beyond our purposes here to differentiate among all the theories of social exchange. We will concentrate on explicating what may be the most popular theory, John Thibaut and Harold Kelley's *Theory of Interdependence*. Although it is called the Theory of Interdependence, it is often referred to as Social Exchange Theory because it fits into the exchange framework. We will use the two titles interchangeably here.

Assumptions of Social Exchange Theory

All Social Exchange theories are built upon several assumptions about human nature and the nature of relationships. Some of these assumptions should be clear to you after our introductory comments. Because Social Exchange Theory is based on a metaphor of economic exchange, many of these assumptions flow from the notion that people view life as a marketplace. Additionally, Thibaut and Kelley base their theory on two conceptualizations: one that focuses on individuals and one that describes the social exchange between two people. They look to drive reduction, an internal motivator, to understand individuals and to gaming principles to understand relationships between people. Thus, the assumptions they make also fall into these two categories.

The assumptions that Social Exchange Theory makes about human nature include the following:

- Humans seek rewards and avoid punishments.
- Humans are rational beings.
- The standards that humans use to evaluate costs and rewards vary over time and from person to person.

The assumptions Social Exchange Theory makes about the nature of relationships include the following:

- Relationships are interdependent.
- Relational life is a process.

We will look at each of these assumptions in turn.

The notion that humans seek rewards and avoid punishment is consistent with the conceptualization of drive reduction (Roloff, 1981). This approach assumes that people's behaviors are motivated by some internal drive mechanism. When people feel this drive, they are motivated to reduce it, and the process of satisfying the drive is a pleasurable one. If George feels thirsty, he is driven to reduce that feeling by getting a drink. This whole process is rewarding, and, thus, "To be rewarded means that a person had undergone drive reduction or need fulfillment" (Roloff, 1981, p. 45). This assumption helps Social Exchange theorists understand why LaTasha and Meredith enjoy each other's company: They feel a need for understanding and companionship, and this need (or drive) is fulfilled (or reduced) by spending time together.

The second assumption—that humans are rational—is critical to Social Exchange Theory. The theory rests on the notion that within the limits of the information that is available to them, people will calculate the costs and rewards of a given situation and guide their behaviors accordingly. This also includes the possibility that, faced with no rewarding choice, people will choose the least costly alternative. In the case of LaTasha and Meredith, it is costly to continue their friendship in the face of all the stress and family objections. Yet, both young women may believe that it is less costly than ending their friendship and denying themselves the support and affection that they have shared for the past nine years.

The third assumption—that the standards people use to evaluate costs and rewards vary over time and from person to person—suggests that the theory must take diversity into consideration. There is no one standard that can be applied to everyone to determine what is a cost and what is a reward. Thus, LaTasha may grow to see the relationship as more costly than Meredith does (or vice versa) as their standards change over time. However, Social Exchange Theory is a lawlike theory, as we described in Chapter 3, because SET claims that although individuals may differ in their definition of rewards, the first assumption is still true for all people: We are motivated to maximize our profits and rewards while minimizing our losses and costs (Molm, 2001).

As we mentioned earlier in this chapter, Thibaut and Kelley take those three assumptions about human nature from drive reduction principles. In their approach to relationships they developed a set of principles that they call *game theory*. The classic game they developed that illustrates their first assumption about relationships is called the Prisoner's Dilemma (Figure 11.1). This game supposes that two prisoners are being questioned about a crime they deny committing. They have been separated for the questioning, and they are given two choices: They can confess to the crime, or they can persist in their denials. The situation is further complicated by the fact that the outcome for them is not completely in their own hands, individually. Instead, each prisoner's outcome is a result of the combination of their two responses. The configurations of their

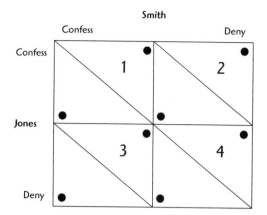

Figure 11.1
**The Prisoner's
Dilemma**

possible choices is called a 2 × 2 matrix because there are two of them and they each have two choices: confess or deny.

If we call one of the prisoners Jones and the other Smith, we can see their choices and outcomes:

Jones confesses and Smith confesses = they both receive a life sentence.

Jones confesses and Smith denies = Jones goes free and Smith is executed.

Jones denies and Smith confesses = Smith goes free and Jones is executed.

Jones denies and Smith denies = they both serve a short jail term.

It is clear from the above scenario that the outcome for Smith and Jones is interdependent. The outcome in each case depends on the relationship between Smith's and Jones's answers, not on one answer alone. This concept is so central to Thibaut and Kelley that they named their theory the Theory of Interdependence rather than Social Exchange or Game Theory. They did so because they wished to avoid the notion of win–loss in Game Theory and they wished to stress that social exchange is a function of interdependence.

When we think of LaTasha and Meredith's situation, we can see that if Meredith decides to cut back on her friendship with LaTasha, LaTasha will inevitably be affected. Her own decisions about the costs and rewards of the relationship are contingent on Meredith's decision. Thus, whenever any one member of a relationship acts, both the other and the relationship as a whole are influenced.

The second assumption that Thibaut and Kelley make is that relational life is a process. In stating this, the researchers are acknowledging the importance of time and change in relational life. Specifically, time affects exchanges because past experiences guide judgments about rewards and costs, and these judgments impact subsequent exchanges. For example, if Kathy dislikes school and has a very low opinion of teachers and then takes a class that exceeds her expectations, and she finds that she really likes this particular teacher, their relationship and Kathy's expectations about future relationships with teachers will

The Theory Chronicles

In your journal, chronicle what you see as the ontological assumptions of Social Exchange Theory. Explain your choices. Find a published study using SET and analyze whether the researcher(s) maintained consistency with the assumptions of the theory.

be shaped by the process. Further, the notion of process allows us to see that relationships constantly change and evolve.

Given these assumptions about humans and relationships, we are ready to examine two of the major parts of the theory: evaluation of a relationship and exchange patterns.

Evaluation of a Relationship: Why We Stay or Go

As we mentioned earlier, SET is more complex than the simple equation of worth that we initially presented. When people calculate the worth of their relationships and make decisions about staying in them, a few other considerations surface. One of the most interesting parts of Thibaut and Kelley's theory is their explanation of how people evaluate their relationships with reference to whether they will stay in them or leave them. Thibaut and Kelley claim that this evaluation rests on two types of comparisons: comparison level and comparison level for alternatives. The **comparison level** (CL) is a standard representing what people feel they should receive in the way of rewards and costs from a particular relationship. Thus, Meredith has a subjective feeling about what she should give and what she should get, in return, from a friendship. Her CL has been shaped by all her past friendships, by family members' advice, and by popular culture such as TV and film representations of friendships that give her an idea of what is expected from this relationship.

Comparison levels vary among individuals because they are subjective. Individuals base their CL, in large part, on past experiences with a specific type of relationship. Because individuals have very different past experiences with similar types of relationships, they develop different comparison levels. For example, if Suzanne has had many friendships that required her to do a great deal of listening and empathizing, her CL will include this. If Andrew has not experienced friends requiring this listening behavior from him, he will not expect to encounter this cost in friendship. Yet, because we often interact with people from our own culture, we share many relational expectations due to messages we have received from popular culture (Rawlins, 1992). Thus, we overlap somewhat in our expectations for relationships, and our CLs may not be totally different from one another's.

Thibaut and Kelley argue that our satisfaction with a current relationship derives from comparing the rewards and costs it involves to our CL. If our current relationship meets or exceeds our CL, the theory predicts we will be satisfied with the relationship. Yet, people sometimes leave satisfactory rela-

comparison level (CL)
a standard for what a person thinks he or she should get in a relationship

194

Table 11.1 How Outcome, CL, and CLalt Affect the State of a Relationship

RELATIVE VALUE OF OUTCOME, CL, CLalt	STATE OF THE RELATIONSHIP
Outcome > CL > Clalt	Satisfying and stable
Outcome > CLalt > CL	Satisfying and stable
CLalt > CL > Outcome	Unsatisfying and unstable
CLalt > Outcome > CL	Satisfying and unstable
CL > CLalt > Outcome	Unsatisfying and unstable
CL > Outcome > Clalt	Unsatisfying and unstable

Source: Adapted from Roloff, 1981, p. 48. Reprinted by permission of Sage Publications, Inc.

tionships and stay in ones that are not so satisfying. Thibaut and Kelley explain this seeming inconsistency with their second standard of comparison, the **comparison level for alternatives (CLalt).** This refers to "the lowest level of relational rewards a person is willing to accept given available rewards from alternative relationships or being alone" (Roloff, 1981, p. 48). In other words, the CLalt measures how people evaluate a relationship compared to the realistic alternatives to that relationship. CLalt provides a measure of stability rather than satisfaction—that is, the CLalt suggests how likely it is that Meredith would leave her relationship with LaTasha, even though it is a satisfying one, for something she thinks would be better.

> **comparison level for alternatives (CLalt)**
> how people evaluate a relationship based on what their alternatives to the relationship are

If we further examine LaTasha and Meredith's relationship using CL and CLalt, we might speculate that Meredith finds her friendship with LaTasha very satisfying in general. She might give it an 8 out of a 10-point ranking where 1 is horrible and 10 is perfect. The 8 would be Meredith's outcome score for her relationship with LaTasha. If Meredith's expectations of friendship, or her CL, is only a 6, then Meredith should be satisfied with her friendship with LaTasha. Further, if Meredith thinks that by being alone now as she decides about college she would rate herself at a 3, and she has few other friends that could even come close to her relationship with LaTasha, then her CLalt will be low, her 8 outcome with LaTasha will exceed it, and Social Exchange Theory predicts that the two will remain friends despite their problems. For example, we can plug the numbers just mentioned for Meredith's calculation of her relationship with LaTasha into the format specified in Table 11.1. In this case, Meredith's outcome, 8, is greater than her CL (6), and her CL is greater than her CLalt, which is 3. Thus, her pattern fits the first example in the table and the theory predicts that the state of her relationship is satisfying and stable.

This kind of calculation—although perhaps a little unrealistic in turning a relationship into a single number—suggests why people remain in relationships that are abusive and violent. If people see no alternative and fear being alone more than being in the relationship, Social Exchange Theory predicts they will stay. Some have written about women in abusive relationships, using this theoretical reasoning to explain why women stay with violent men (Walker, 1984). Table 11.1 summarizes six possible combinations among the outcome, the CL, and the CLalt and the resulting state of the relationship predicted by the theory. See the Research Note for an analysis of these calculations in an organizational setting.

Research Note

Cox., S. A., & Kramer, M. W. (1995). Communication during employee dismissals: Social Exchange principles and group influences on employee exit. *Management Communication Quarterly, 9*, 156–190.

In this study, Social Exchange Theory is used as a basis for examining the process of employee dismissal from organizations. The authors note that Social Exchange Theory suggests that the job of managers is to calculate the cost-benefit ratio of an employee for the organization. In this process, the managers operate with a comparison level (CL) derived from past relationships with subordinates. Additionally, managers have a comparison level for alternatives (CLalt) based on potential alternative employees who could do the job, which affects the managers' evaluation of the cost-benefit ratio of any given employee. Guided by these theoretical principles, as well as some derived from other models, the authors posed three general research questions: (1) What prompts supervisors to dismiss employees? (2) What workgroup communication influences supervisors' dismissal decisions? (3) What supervisor communication occurs during the dismissal process?

The authors interviewed twenty-four managers at their workplace. The sample represented seventeen different retail outlets including those that sell groceries (29%), hardware and building supplies (21%), apparel (21%), sporting goods (8%), and a variety of other specialty outlets (such as crafts and computers, 21%). Of the total sample of managers, 26 percent were women and 74 percent were men. Twenty-five percent had high school diplomas only, 25 percent had attended some college, and 50 percent had a B.A. or B.S. degree. The average age of the respondents was 39 years, and they had been with their company an average of 11.2 years. The researchers asked the managers a series of open-ended questions in an effort to answer the three research questions. They interviewed the managers face-to-face, recorded the interviews, gathered extensive field notes, and then content-analyzed the data to formulate answers to the research questions.

In reporting their findings, the authors note the following points that have implications for the Social Exchange Theory that framed their study: (1) Managers calculate cost-benefit ratios in making dismissal decisions, and (2) the individual exchange is embedded within a larger system of exchanges. First, the authors observe that their respondents suggested that they do monitor the employee–employer relationship rationally, continuously calculating the costs and benefits exchanged. Further, the authors note the fact that dismissed employees had an average of sixteen months on the job. They argue that this supports the notion that managers use a series of evaluations over time to make the cost-benefit analysis on any given employee. Extended time frames such as this are most likely to provide the setting for rational calculations. Additionally, the interviews indicated that managers consider past, present, and future exchanges in making their calculations.

Second, the authors find that the managers they interviewed acknowledged that they were not making these cost-benefit ratios in isolation. The respondents were aware of the influence of the group on their decision-making processes. The authors conclude that this influence indicates that the individual exchange is embedded in a larger system of social exchange. Managers reported that they considered the impact that firing one employee would have on the other employees, as well as the impact of retaining a problem employee. They also considered the cost of training a replacement employee.

The authors conclude, "A manager's dismissal decision, then, appears to be a rational, cost-benefit-based decision calculated over an extended time frame accounting for resources exchanged between supervisor, the larger workgroup, and the problematic employee, although taking into account costs for alternatives" (p. 183). In sum, the authors found support for a social exchange explanation for employee dismissals.

Exchange Patterns: SET in Action

As well as studying how people calculate their relational outcomes, Thibaut and Kelley were interested in how people adjust their behaviors in interaction with their relational partners. Thibaut and Kelley suggest that when people interact, they are goal directed. This is congruent with their assumption that human beings are rational. People, according to Thibaut and Kelley, engage in **behavioral sequences,** or a series of actions designed to achieve their goal. These sequences are the heart of what Thibaut and Kelley conceptualize as social exchange. As Thibaut and Kelley note in Game Theory, when people engage in these behavioral sequences they are dependent to some extent on their relational partner. For instance, if one person wishes to play gin rummy, cooperation from a partner is required. This interdependence brings up the concept of **power**—the dependence a person has on another for outcomes. If LaTasha depends more on Meredith for rewards than vice versa, then Meredith has greater power than LaTasha in their relationship.

There are two types of power in Thibaut and Kelley's theory: fate control and behavior control. **Fate control** is the ability to affect a partner's outcomes. For example, if Meredith withholds her friendship from LaTasha, she affects LaTasha's outcome. If LaTasha cannot replace Meredith as a friend, Meredith's behavior gives her fate control over LaTasha. This presumes that Meredith does not care about the relationship. If she does, then withholding her friendship is a punishment for her as well, which gives LaTasha a certain amount of fate control in the relationship too.

Behavior control is the power to cause another's behavior to change by changing one's own behavior. If Meredith calls LaTasha on the phone, it is likely that LaTasha will stop whatever else she is doing and talk to Meredith. If LaTasha is with Meredith and falls silent, Meredith will probably change her behavior in response. She might stop talking too, or she might question LaTasha to find out if something is wrong.

Thibaut and Kelley state that people develop patterns of exchange to cope with power differentials and to deal with the costs associated with exercising power. These patterns describe behavioral rules or norms that indicate how people trade resources in an attempt to maximize rewards and minimize costs. Thibaut and Kelley describe three different matrices in social exchange to illustrate the patterns people develop. These matrices include the given matrix, the effective matrix, and the dispositional matrix.

The **given matrix** represents the behavioral choices and outcomes that are determined by a combination of external factors (the environment) and internal factors (the specific skills each interactant possesses). When two people engage in an exchange, the environment may make some options more difficult than others. LaTasha's and Meredith's families, for instance, are part of the environment that is making their friendship more difficult. A scarcity of money would be another aspect of the given matrix that would make some alternatives less likely for some relationships. Further, the given matrix depends on the skills people bring to the social exchange. If people lack skills for ballroom dancing, for example, it is unlikely that they will spend time dancing together. To a certain degree, the given matrix represents "the hand you are dealt."

behavioral sequences
a series of actions designed to achieve a goal

power
the degree of dependence a person has on another for outcomes

fate control
the ability to affect a partner's outcomes

behavior control
the power to change another's behavior

given matrix
the constraints on your choices due to the environment and/or your own skill levels

People may be restricted by the given matrix, but they are not trapped by it. They can transform it into the **effective matrix**, "which represents an expansion of alternative behaviors and/or outcomes which ultimately determines the behavioral choices in social exchange" (Roloff, 1981, p. 51). If a man does not know how to tango, he can take lessons in this dance and learn it, transforming the given matrix into the effective matrix. If Meredith and LaTasha think their families are bothering their friendship too much, they can engage in conflict with them until they change their families' minds. Or they can stop talking about each other at home and keep their friendship secret so that they can avoid their families' negative sanctions.

The final matrix, the **dispositional matrix**, represents the way two people believe that rewards ought to be exchanged between them. If Meredith and LaTasha think that friends ought to stick together no matter how much outside interference they receive from family members, that will affect their dispositional matrix. Some people view exchanges as competition, and this belief will be reflected in their dispositional matrix.

Thibaut and Kelley assert that if we know the kinds of dispositions a person has (the dispositional matrix) and the nature of the situation in which they are operating (the given matrix), then we will know how to predict the transformations they will make (the effective matrix) to ultimately impact the social exchange. Thus, if we understand LaTasha to expect great loyalty from her friends, and from herself as a friend, and we know that her family's opposition to her friendship to Meredith is not too strong, we might predict that LaTasha will defend Meredith to her family and attempt to change their beliefs. If her family has a stronger opposition, we might predict that LaTasha will simply remain friends with Meredith without trying to change her family's beliefs. The dispositional matrix guides the transformations people make to their given matrix; these transformations lead to the effective matrix, which determines the social exchange.

In their theory, Thibaut and Kelley do not explicitly deal with communication behaviors, such as self-disclosure, a topic we explained in Chapter 10 in conjunction with Social Penetration Theory. Yet, some of their discussion about the three matrices implies that self-disclosure does play an important role in social exchange. As Roloff (1981) observes,

> Self-disclosure would seem to imply the communication of two things:
> (1) the dispositions one has, and (2) the transformations (strategy) one
> is going to employ in this exchange. Since dispositions affect a person's
> strategy, we might assume that knowledge of dispositions might well
> allow us to predict the transformations. (p. 77)

Further, this self-disclosure, like all disclosures about the self, contains risks. It could provide the relational partner with information that could be used against the discloser. If people know how another transforms the given matrix, they can have an edge in social exchanges. For example, if LaTasha knows that Meredith tries to resolve problems in a cooperative fashion, she can use Meredith's cooperative nature against her to get what she wants in an exchange. An understanding of how the matrices affect communication behavior is a large reason why communication researchers are interested in Social Exchange Theory.

Exchange Structures

Exchanges may take several forms within these matrices. These include direct exchange, generalized exchange, and productive exchange (see Figure 11.2). In a **direct exchange,** reciprocation is confined to the two actors. For instance, when Brad washes his father's car and then his dad lets him use the car on Saturday night, the exchange is direct. One social actor provides value to another and the other reciprocates. In a longtime friendship like Meredith and LaTasha have, they consistently participate in direct exchanges. It isn't necessary to reciprocate immediately, but when LaTasha does a favor for Meredith, she knows that Meredith will eventually respond in kind.

A **generalized exchange** involves indirect reciprocity. One person gives to another and the recipient responds but not to the first person. Generalized exchanges occur, for example, when someone moves away from the neighborhood and friends and neighbors help pack up the moving van. Because the person has moved away, he or she won't help any of those neighbors move when they are ready to relocate. The favor is reciprocated by helping someone else, in the new neighborhood. Generalized exchanges involve the community or social network rather than simply two specific people as in the examples we have discussed with LaTasha and Meredith.

Finally, exchanges may be productive, meaning that both actors have to contribute in order for either one of them to benefit. In a direct or generalized exchange one person is the beneficiary of another's provision of value. One receives a reward and the other incurs a cost. In a **productive exchange,** both people incur benefits and costs simultaneously. If LaTasha and Meredith do a project together for their senior English class, they engage in productive exchange. Both of them have to do the work, and they both share equally in the grade they receive.

direct exchange
an exchange where two people reciprocate costs and rewards

generalized exchange
an exchange where reciprocation involves the social network and isn't confined to two individuals

productive exchange
an exchange where both partners incur costs and benefits simultaneously

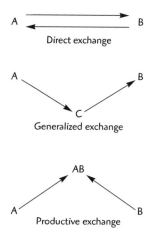

**Figure 11.2
Exchange
Structures**

Critique and Closing

Although Social Exchange Theory has generated a great deal of research, it does have its detractors and has received some serious criticisms. We will review four major critiques of the theory and its assumptions.

The first criticism is that Social Exchange Theory is not testable. As we discussed in Chapter 3, one important criterion of a theory is that it is testable and capable of being proven false. The difficulty with social exchange is that its central concepts—costs and rewards—are not clearly defined. As Sabatelli and Shehan (1993) note,

> It becomes impossible to make an operational distinction between what people value, what they perceive as rewarding, and how they behave. Rewards, values, and actions appear to be defined in terms of each other (Turner, 1978). Thus, it is impossible to find an instance when a person does not act in ways so as to obtain rewards. (p. 396)

When the theory argues that people do what they can to maximize rewards and then also argues that what people do is rewarding behavior, it is difficult, if not impossible, to disentangle the two concepts. As long as Social Exchange Theory operates with these types of circular definitions, it will be untestable and, thus, unsatisfactory in terms of that criterion. However, Roloff (1981) observes that some work has been done to create lists of rewards in advance of simply observing what people do and labeling that as rewarding because people are doing it. Edna Foa and Uriel Foa (1974, 1976) began this work of clearly defining rewards. Further, Roloff argues that despite this problem, there has been a great deal of empirical work using Social Exchange theories.

A second problem area has to do with the conceptualization of human beings painted by Social Exchange Theory. In this theoretical framework, humans are seen as rational calculators, coming up with numerical equations to represent their relational life. Many people object to this understanding of humans, asking whether people really rationally calculate the costs and rewards to be realized when engaging in a behavior or pursuing a relationship. Social Exchange, like many theories, assumes a great deal of cognitive awareness and activity, which several researchers have questioned (Berger & Roloff, 1980). Researchers have not come to a definitive answer about how much people calculate their relational life, but this calculation probably ebbs and flows according to many factors. First, some contexts may make people more self-aware than others. As LaTasha and Meredith receive more pressure to decide about college, they may think about their relationship more than they did when

Theory * Into * Practice

In an article published in the *Milwaukee Journal Sentinel* in 1999, local volunteers discussed their participation in a variety of activities that help Milwaukee's hungry and homeless. In their discussion, the volunteers invoked the central tenet of Social Exchange Theory: People's behavior is motivated by self-interest. The woman quoted in the article states that even altruistic behavior has a reward. This is exactly the point that Social Exchange Theory makes:

> One Saturday morning a month, Marian Byers fires up the commercial range in the basement kitchen of a south side church. Leading a small platoon of volunteers, she churns out several hundred servings of turkey parmigiana or salmon loaf drizzled with cream sauce, earning smiles from frayed or homeless men and women, some with babies on their hips.
>
> They come to St. John's Episcopal Church for nourishment from The Gathering interfaith meal ministry. There, Byers, a quality assurance technician in Northwestern Mutual Life's restaurant division, finds plenty of sustenance, too—of an intangible sort.
>
> Helping out "is not a selfless thing for me because I get so much out of it," she said. "I'm the needy one." (p. G1)
>
> At soup kitchens, community centers, restaurants and charity events, countless food professionals like Byers donate their kitchen expertise to improve the lot of others. Their motivations may be as numerous as peppercorns in a grinder, but personal satisfaction is the common ingredient.

Source: Guensburg, 1999.

TIP Follow-up
If altruistic behavior is done for a reward as SET argues, how useful is that insight? How can we predict anything using SET if we don't know in advance what a person will find rewarding?

they were younger. Second, some individual differences might affect how people process information. Some people are more self-aware than others (Snyder, 1979). As researchers continue to work with this theory, they must account for these and other factors relative to the calculating nature of humans.

A third problem area is related to the second. Critics wonder if people are really as self-interested as Social Exchange Theory assumes. Steve Duck (1994) argues that applying a marketplace mentality to the understanding of relational life vastly misrepresents what goes on in relationships. He suggests that it is wrong to think about personal relationships in the same way that we think about business transactions, like buying a house or a car. This suggestion relates to the ontological assumptions one brings to the theory, as we discussed in Chapters 3 and 4. For some people, the analogy of the marketplace is appropriate, but for others it is not and may be highly offensive. How people evaluate the analogy depends on the ontological framework they bring to the theory.

The final critique also focuses on ontological assumptions. This complaint suggests that Social Exchange Theory fails to explain the importance of group

The Theory Connection

Compare Social Exchange Theory to Social Penetration Theory. Explain how (or if) you see them having separate theoretical domains.

solidarity in its emphasis on individual need fulfillment (England, 1989). This critique combines some of the issues raised above and argues that "the exchange framework can be viewed as valuing the separative self to the extent that rationality and self-interest are emphasized" (Sabatelli & Shehan, 1993, p. 397). By prioritizing this value, the connected self is overlooked and undervalued.

In sum, the Social Exchange perspective provides us with a framework that many researchers have used profitably. Yet, it does not offer a clear definition of its central concepts, which leads to difficulty in actually testing the theory. Further, it presumes several things about humans that some find difficult to accept. The notion of people calculating their self-interest apart from a group's is offensive to some researchers. Yet, the emphasis that Thibaut and Kelley place on interdependence is congruent with many researchers' notions of interpersonal relationships, and Social Exchange Theory continues to generate research findings of interest to students of communication.

Discussion Starters

1. How compatible are the assumptions of Social Exchange Theory with the experiences of LaTasha and Meredith and their outlooks on the future? Do you believe people usually act based only on self-interest? When might they not do so?

2. Explain the problem with Social Exchange Theory regarding testability. Is there anything that Social Exchange theorists could do to make the theory more testable? Is it possible to quantify rewards and costs in a precise and observable manner? Explain your answer.

3. Choose a current relationship of yours and perform a cost-benefit analysis on it. Assess whether the relationship meets, fails to meet, or exceeds your comparison level. Do the same for your comparison level for alternatives. Does applying this theory help you understand the relationship? Explain your answer.

4. How does Social Exchange Theory explain the unselfish things that people do that do not seem calculated to gain rewards for themselves?

5. Have you ever stayed in a relationship because you thought you did not have any other alternatives? How does Social Exchange Theory help explain this type of behavior?

6. How realistic do you think gaming principles like those used to develop the Prisoner's Dilemma are? Give examples that support or contest the use of a 2×2 matrix to model human choices.

Terms for Review

costs

rewards

outcome

comparison level (CL)

comparison level for
   alternatives (CLalt)

behavioral sequences

power

fate control

behavior control

given matrix

effective matrix

dispositional matrix

direct exchange

generalized exchange

productive exchange

Online Learning Center

Visit the Online Learning Center at www.mhhe.com/west2. Use the multiple-choice and true/false quizzes to help you prepare for exams, and the glossary, crossword puzzles, and flashcards to further your knowledge of key terms.

CHAPTER 12

Relational Dialectics Theory

Eleanor Robertson and Jeff Meadows

Eleanor Robertson and Jeff Meadows worked swiftly to clean up the mess left from the dinner party they had just given for their friend Mary Beth's thirty-fifth birthday. They both agreed that the party had been a great success and that everyone had had a wonderful time. They were having fun talking about their friends—who was breaking up and who was getting together.

Eleanor smiled as she thought about how much she and Jeff had learned about each other and their relationship in the two years they had lived together. Eleanor used to get upset when Jeff wanted to be with friends and not spend all his time with her alone. Now she thought she understood Jeff's desire for others in their lives. She also found that the more she was able to let go of her possessive feelings and behaviors, the more Jeff wanted to be close.

Jeff came over and hugged Eleanor. He said, "Honey, that was a great party. The food was perfect—I'm glad we decided to do a Japanese theme. Thanks for all your help to make everything go so well. Mary Beth really appreciated it, I know. And since she and I have been friends forever, it really means a lot to me."

Eleanor pulled away and laughed at Jeff. "I didn't do too much, sweetheart," she said to Jeff. "You were the one who was busy in the kitchen. But I am glad Mary Beth had fun. I really like her a lot, too."

Jeff and Eleanor finished cleaning up and started talking about what they would do tomorrow. They decided they would take a picnic to Golden Gate Park and then maybe go to a movie. It sounded like a fun Sunday—they had a plan, but they could change their minds and skip the movie if picnicking in the park was too inviting.

Eleanor was very happy and thought about telling Jeff how much she loved and needed him, but she decided to keep quiet about the depth of her feelings for now. Jeff probably knew how she felt, and she was a little afraid of revealing all her feelings to him right now. It had been a perfect day, and she didn't want to spoil it by making herself completely open to him. She wasn't sure she wanted to be so vulnerable to Jeff at this point in their relationship, even though when they first started going out together, she had told him she loved him repeatedly. Now she found herself being a bit more guarded and self-protective.

This theory is based on the research of **Leslie Baxter** and **Barbara Montgomery.**

When researchers examine the story of Eleanor and Jeff, they might speculate that their relationship is moving through stages. Researchers who work within the framework of Social Penetration Theory (see Chapter 10), for example, would point to the fact that Jeff and Eleanor have worked through some of their earlier issues and now interact with each other at a deeper level of intimacy than they once did. These researchers might point to the fact that the relationship between Eleanor and Jeff is more coordinated and less conflictual than it once was as an indication that they have moved to a more intimate stage of relational development. Yet, other researchers would look at Jeff and Eleanor and see their story as best explained by a different theoretical position, called Relational Dialectics Theory.

Relational Dialectics Theory (RDT) maintains that relational life is characterized by ongoing tensions between contradictory impulses. Although that may sound confusing and messy, researchers who assert the dialectical position believe it accurately depicts the way that life is for people. People are not always able to resolve the contradictory elements of their beliefs, and they hold inconsistent beliefs about relationships. For example, the adage "absence makes the heart grow fonder" seems to coexist easily with its opposite, "out of sight, out of mind."

In Communication, Leslie Baxter and Barbara Montgomery (1996) formulate the most complete statement of the theory in their book *Relating: Dialogues and Dialectics,* although both of them had been writing about dialectical thinking for several years prior to that book's publication. Also, other researchers, notably William Rawlins (1992) and Sandra Petronio (2000), were influential in bringing the framework of dialectics to the study of communication in relationships. Baxter and Montgomery's work was directly influenced by Mikhail Bakhtin, a Russian philosopher who developed a theory of personal dialogue. Social life for Bakhtin was an open dialogue among many voices, and its essence was the "simultaneous differentiation from yet fusion with another" (Baxter & Montgomery, 1996, p. 24). According to Bakhtin, the self is only possible in context with another. Bakhtin notes that human experience is constituted through communication with others. In some ways, Bakhtin's notions relate to Mead's theory of Symbolic Interactionism (see Chapter 5) because he focuses on the importance of interaction with others for meaning making.

From Bakhtin's thinking, Baxter and Montgomery also shaped the notion of the dialectical vision. We can best explain this vision of human behavior by contrasting it to two other common approaches: the monologic view and the dualistic approach. The **monologic approach** pictures contradictions as either/or relationships. For instance, monologic thinking would lead to the belief that Jeff and Eleanor's relationship was either close or distant. In other words, the two parts of a contradiction are mutually exclusive in monologic thinking, and as you move toward one extreme, you retreat from the other. See Figure 12.1 for a visual representation of this notion.

In contrast, the **dualistic approach** sees the two parts of a contradiction as two separate entities, somewhat unrelated to each other. In our example of Eleanor and Jeff, dualistic thinkers might choose to evaluate them separately,

monologic approach
an approach framing contradiction as either/or

dualistic approach
an approach framing contradiction as two separate entities

Theory Application in Groups (TAG)

In small groups, discuss the differences among the monologic, dualistic, and dialectic approaches to relational life. Try to come to a consensus about what the dialectic approach offers that the other two do not.

dialectic approach
an approach framing contradiction as both/and

rating how close each one feels compared to the other. Further, dualism allows for the idea that relationships may be evaluated differently on these scales at different times (see Figure 12.1).

Thinkers with a **dialectic approach** maintain that multiple points of view play off one another in every contradiction. Although a contradiction involves two opposing poles, the resulting situation expands beyond these two poles. As Baxter and Montgomery (1996) observe, "Dialectical thinking is not directed toward a search for the 'happy mediums' of compromise and balance, but instead focuses on the messier, less logical, and more inconsistent unfolding practices of the moment" (p. 46).

As Eleanor and Jeff interact, many voices contribute to their sense of their relationship. Dialectic theory holds that it is not accurate to say that only one or two positions exist in relational contradictions.

As we discuss the three basic relational dialectics later in this chapter, we will point out how these three approaches conceptualize them differently. First, however, we discuss the assumptions underlying RDT.

Assumptions of Relational Dialectics Theory

RDT is grounded in four main assumptions that reflect its contentions about relational life:

- Relationships are not linear.
- Relational life is characterized by change.
- Contradiction is the fundamental fact of relational life.
- Communication is central to organizing and negotiating relational contradictions.

The most significant assumption that grounds this theory is the notion that relationships are not linear entities. Rather, relationships consist of oscillation between contradictory desires. In fact, Baxter and Montgomery (1996) suggest that we should rethink our language and our metaphors about relationships. They note that the phrase "relational development" connotes some linear movement or forward progress. Progress contains either/or thinking. Relationships that progress are pictured as having more of certain elements such as intimacy, self-disclosure, certainty, and so forth. Thus, relationships may be imagined as on a continuum of more or less intimate, open, and certain. The

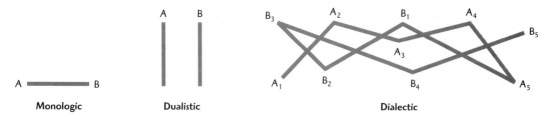

Figure 12.1
Monologic, Dualistic, and Dialectic Approaches to Relational Contradictions

either/or thinking frames the relationship as *either* intimate, open, certain *or* not. In the dialectic perspective, complexity is viewed as an *alternative* to progress. The dialectic notion of complexity introduces the concept of *both/and*.

The second assumption of RDT promotes the notion of process or change, although not necessarily framing this process as linear progress. Baxter and Montgomery observe that "relationship process or change . . . refers to quantitative and qualitative movement through time in the underlying contractions around which a relationship is organized" (1996, p. 52). Thus, Jeff and Eleanor are different now than they were a year ago. But that difference is not a linear move toward intimacy as much as it is a difference in the way they express their togetherness and their independence.

The third assumption stresses that contradictions or tensions between opposites never go away and never cease to provide tension. People manage these tensions and oppositions in different ways, but they are present continuously in relational life. The push and pull represented by the dialectics constructs relational life, and one of our main communication tasks is managing these tensions. This approach differs from other types of relational theories in that it considers homeostasis to be unnatural: Change and transformation are the hallmarks of relational interaction in this perspective (Montgomery, 1992). This represents a different ontological assumption.

The final assumption of RDT pertains to communication. Specifically, this theory gives a central position to communication. As Baxter and Montgomery (1996) observe, "From the perspective of relational dialectics, social actors give life through their communicative practices to the contradictions that organize their relationships. The social reality of contradictions is produced and reproduced by the communicative action of social actors" (p. 59). When Jeff praises Eleanor for the party, for example, he is expressing affection and negotiating closeness. When Eleanor keeps silent instead of saying, "I love you," to Jeff, she is protecting herself and keeping herself from being too open with him. As Eleanor and Jeff plan their picnic for the next day, they are discussing how much predictability and how much novelty they wish to have. Planning initially provides predictability, but the couple's stated willingness to be flexible in their plan allows for spontaneity as well. Thus, Jeff and Eleanor's communication practices organize the three central dialectics that we discuss in the chapter: autonomy and connection, openness and protection, and novelty and predictability.

Elements of Dialectics: Building the Tension

totality
acknowledges the
interdependence
of people in a
relationship

The following elements are basic to the dialectical perspective: totality, contradiction, motion, and praxis (Rawlins, 1992). **Totality** suggests that people in a relationship are interdependent. This means that when something happens to one member of a relationship, the other member(s) will be affected as well. For example, if Jeff gets a promotion at work that entails more travel than his former position, Eleanor will have to deal with his absences. She may compensate by making more friends outside their relationship, and this will affect Jeff somewhat when he is home. He will have to meet new friends and share Eleanor's time, for example.

In addition, totality means that the social and cultural context affects the process; communicating in relationships "involves the constant interconnection and reciprocal influence of multiple individual, interpersonal, and social factors" (Rawlins, 1992, p. 7). For instance, Eleanor and Jeff's relationship is affected by their social circle, by their location in San Francisco, and by the historical moment in which they live.

contradiction
the central feature
of the dialectic
approach; refers to
oppositions

Contradiction refers to oppositions—two elements that contradict each other. As such, contradiction is the central feature of the dialectic approach. Dialectics are the result of oppositions. When Eleanor desires to tell Jeff that she loves him but also wishes to withhold that information to protect herself, she is experiencing contradiction.

motion
refers to the processual
nature of relationships

Motion refers to the processual nature of relationships and their change over time. When Eleanor reflects on how different her relationship with Jeff is now compared to what they had two years ago, she is experiencing motion. Think back to one of your own relationships. Compare how you relate now to how you did when you first met. No doubt you will see motion at work also.

praxis
refers to the choice-
making capacity of
humans

Finally, **praxis** means that humans are choice makers. Although we do not have completely free choice in all instances and we are restricted by our previous choices, by the choices of others, and by cultural and social conditions, we are still conscious and active choice makers. For example, Eleanor chooses to be with Jeff, and this choice restricts other choices she might make. She must get along with Jeff's parents and siblings when they get together for the holidays. She might not ever have chosen to be with these people on her own, but because she is in love with Jeff, she must spend time with them. On a more ba-

The Theory Chronicles

In your journal, speculate about the notion of contradiction that lies at the heart of Dialectics Theory. Do you think that contradictions have to have just two polar opposites as the chapter has described? How might the theory work (or not) if there were more than two opposing tensions? How do you see the role of culture in constructing these oppositions? How likely would it be to discover the same three relational dialectics discussed in the chapter if all the research had been set in Africa or Asia?

sic level, Jeff and Eleanor did not choose the time in which they live, but the culture shapes some of their choices. If they lived in the 1950s, for instance, they would be less likely to be unmarried and living together.

Basic Relational Dialectics

Many different specific dialectics have been discussed with reference to relational life. As we mentioned earlier, the three most relevant to relationships are the dialectics of autonomy and connection, openness and protection, and novelty and predictability (Baxter, 1990). Other researchers have also found that these dialectics are common to relational life. For example, in one recent study (Erbert, 2000) marital couples were interviewed to determine how they perceived relational dialectics with reference to conflicts. Autonomy and contradiction and openness and closedness were perceived as the most important contradictions, and predictability and novelty were deemed important for some specific conflict types.

Autonomy and Connection

The dialectic between **autonomy and connection** refers to our simultaneous desires to be independent of our significant others and to find intimacy with them. As our story of Eleanor and Jeff illustrates, relational life is permeated with the conflicting desires to be both close to and separate from relational partners. Jeff appreciates Eleanor's efforts on the dinner party, which makes him feel close to her. Yet, the reason for the party in some sense celebrates his separateness from Eleanor. The fact that Jeff has a long-standing friendship with Mary Beth illustrates his autonomy. Seeing both autonomy and closeness as constants in relational life is a hallmark of RDT.

Baxter and Montgomery (1996) discuss how a dialectic of autonomy and connection differs from the two other approaches to these concepts we described previously: the monologic and dualistic approaches. As we mentioned, the monologic view conceives of connection in static terms. Partners are believed to be close if they exhibit mutual dependence, share similar values and beliefs, and have positive affection for each other. In this construction of closeness, independence, difference, and negativity are believed to be threats to connection. As Baxter and Montgomery observe, theories like Social Penetration (see Chapter 10) advance a rather static view of closeness; partners move toward closeness or away from it. From this vantage point, Eleanor and Jeff may be seen as growing closer and closer as they share more experiences and affection.

You will recall that the dualistic approach also represents closeness as static but does not value it as more important to relational development than distance. Dualistic thinking allows for the importance of distance but pictures the two as separate entities. Theories grounded in dualism reject the claim of monologic thinking that closeness increases in linear fashion as mutual dependence, similarity, and positivity increase. Instead, the dualistic view upholds the position that individuals and relationships vary in their needs for closeness. Further, dualistic thinking allows for theoretical propositions suggesting that

autonomy and connection
an important relational tension that shows our conflicting desires to be close and to be separate

people need to differentiate from others to develop healthy self-identities. For example, a dualistic approach to Jeff and Eleanor's situation might assess each of their individual needs for closeness and distance. Alternatively, a dualistic view could suggest that Eleanor and Jeff's relationship is passing through a needed stage of distance so it is not too smothering.

Neither of these two approaches satisfies the dialectic thinker, however. Dialectic theory holds that contradictions are inherent in all relating and that the dynamic interplay between autonomy and closeness is more important than their dual presence. So Jeff and Eleanor are seen by RDT as moving between closeness and distance throughout their relationship. They are not understood as moving toward or moving away from either of these two competing needs. In the movie *Three Wishes,* Patrick Swayze's character teaches a young boy how to play baseball. He suggests to the boy that he is thinking too hard about hitting a home run. Swayze counsels that he should think about striking out instead. This is good advice, Swayze contends, because every action contains its opposite. It is this simultaneous presence of oppositions that the dialectic theory seeks to capture.

Communication researchers are interested in dialectic thinking because of the communication implications of the theory. Baxter and Montgomery (1996) discuss how couples' private communication codes illustrate the presence of both connection and autonomy in relationships. For instance, nicknames celebrate something inherently individual in that they are usually highlighting an individual trait (such as Shorty, Chief, or Sweetness). Yet, they also indicate a relational closeness in that distant friends do not invoke pet names for one another. In the simple practice of calling someone by a nickname, we are coding individuation and closeness. Researchers have examined other communication practices as performing in a dialectic fashion. For instance, Leslie Baxter and Erin Sahlstein (2000) mention how gossiping can accomplish a balancing of both openness and privacy as gossipers simultaneously disclose about others while keeping silent about themselves.

Openness and Protection

A second critical tension permeating relational life has to do with openness and protection. The **openness and protection** dialectic focuses on our conflicting desire first to be open and vulnerable, revealing personal information to our relational partners, and second to be strategic and protective in our communication. As Eleanor mulls over how much to tell Jeff about her feelings, she is wrestling with the tension between disclosure and silence, or the openness and protection dialectic.

The same two lines of thinking we spoke about above, monologic and dualistic, can be contrasted with dialectic thinking concerning this tension. A monologic approach to Jeff and Eleanor's relationship might view her decision to withhold her feelings as troubling. The monologic view stresses the benefits of openness in an intimate relationship. A dualistic approach might advance the benefits of openness, for instance, or suggest that the two extremes should alternate with each other, or assert that some situations call for openness, whereas other situations call for protection. For example, Malcolm Parks (1982) argues for the importance of having superficial relationships in one's social network. Parks claims these nonintimate relationships serve important functions. The importance of privacy is also underscored in the dualistic notion of openness and protection.

In contrast, the dialectic position features both/and with respect to candor and concealment. With reference to disclosing highly personal information, Katherine Dindia (1994) argues for what she calls an "intrapersonal dialectic" of disclosure. This involves a gradual and incremental process of disclosure

openness and protection
an important relational tension that shows our conflicting desires to tell our secrets and to keep them hidden

ranging from concealment to full revelation. However, we do not have much research focusing on the actual communication practices that allow relational partners to simultaneously disclose to each other and protect themselves. Baxter and Montgomery comment on the research challenges of this position:

> The implications of viewing the utterance as both 'the said' and 'the unsaid' are substantial for scholars of personal relationships. Self-disclosure researchers, for instance, have tended to define disclosiveness in an a priori manner based on the verbalized topic. Thus, for example, revelations about one's dating history have been viewed by researchers as more disclosive than verbalizations about what one had for lunch that day. But from a [dialectic] perspective, what is revealed in an utterance may differ dramatically to insiders and to outsiders. (1996, p. 146)

For example, Eleanor's comment that she also likes Mary Beth may not be understood as disclosive to someone outside Jeff and Eleanor's relationship. Yet, Jeff may hear disclosure in Eleanor's statement based on their relational history. He may interpret the comment to mean that Eleanor has come to a new place in their relationship and that she is acknowledging that she was wrong to be jealous of his friends earlier. An outsider, lacking in knowledge of the relational history, would probably miss that disclosure.

Novelty and Predictability

**novelty and
predictability**
an important relational tension that shows our conflicting desires to have stability and change

The dialectic between **novelty and predictability** refers to the conflict between the comfort of stability and the excitement of change. Again, this tension may be viewed from the same three perspectives—monologic, dualistic, and dialectic. The monologic view of certainty holds that certainty and predictability are necessary for relationships to flourish (see Chapter 9 on Uncertainty Reduction Theory). Uncertainty Reduction Theory assumes that people move toward certainty and away from uncertainty as their relationships develop. Dualistic conceptualizations of certainty argue that although uncertainty and unpredictability are needed for the well-being of some personal relationships, the two extremes are completely separate from each other. The dialectic position sees the interplay of certainty and uncertainty in relationships. Jeff and Eleanor's planning behavior illustrates this interplay. When they make a plan together, they are accomplishing at least two things with reference to predictability about themselves and their relationship. First, their plan self-defines them as in a relationship, because planning is a relational activity. It also establishes a routine so they know what they will be doing in the short-term future. Yet, they leave the plan a bit open-ended in order to allow for creativity and novelty. With their plan for Sunday, Eleanor and Jeff have dealt simultaneously with their contradictory needs for routine and spontaneity.

**interactional
dialectics**
tensions resulting from and constructed by communication

Contextual Dialectics

What we have just discussed are **interactional dialectics** in that they are located within the relationship itself—they are part of the partners' interaction with each other (Rawlins, 1992). Researchers have also discussed other dialectics that affect relational life. William Rawlins calls these **contextual dialectics,** which means that they derive from the place of the relationship in the culture.

Contextual dialectics are formed from the tension between the public definitions of a given relationship—friendship, for example—and the private interactions within a specific friendship. Rawlins lists two contextual dialectics—between the public and the private and between the real and the ideal. Although perhaps a little less important to us than the interactional dialectics, these two do affect interpersonal communication in relationships. The **public and private dialectic** refers to the tension between the two domains—a private relationship and public life. Rawlins discusses the fact that in the public realm, friendship occupies a rather marginal position. Lillian Rubin (1998) makes the same observation, noting that public expectations favor kin relationships over friendships even when individuals may value their friends more highly than their kin. Rubin argues that people tend to prioritize commitments to their friends as less important than those to their family members. Rawlins notes that friendship suffers in comparison to other relationships because there is no institution to sanction it. Eleanor and Jeff's cohabiting relationship may have the same marginal status because, unlike marriage, it is not legally sanctioned.

Rawlins argues that tension arises in a close friendship between this marginal public status and the friendship's deep private character. Rawlins states that this dialectic results in friendships (and by implication, other unsanctioned relationships) acting with what he calls double agency. By this he means that these relationships fulfill both public and private functions. Rawlins observes that sometimes the public functions constrain the private ones. For instance, people who form friendships in the workplace may encounter negative feedback from their significant others who see the friendships as a threat to their relationship. When Jeff and Eleanor first became serious, Eleanor felt threatened by Jeff's female friends. The public aspects of friendships and love relationships provide tension.

The dichotomy of the public and the private is obvious when we think about political figures. Politicians live a public life but have private lives as well. Dialectical thinking shows us that private, relational life is intertwined with public life. Although the two spheres can be separated to an extent, in many meaningful ways Dialectic Theory shows us that they are interwoven.

This public and private dialectic interacts with the dialectic of the real and the ideal. The tension of the **real and ideal dialectic** is featured when we think of television shows like *Leave It to Beaver:* We receive an idealized message of what family life is like, and then when we look at the families we live in, we have to contend with the troublesome realities of family life. The tension between these two images forms this dialectic. If Eleanor reads a lot of romance novels emphasizing complete openness between romantic partners, she may feel a tension between that vision and her lived experience with Jeff, which involves some sharing but not complete openness.

Additionally, this dialectic contrasts all the expectations one has of a relationship with its lived realities. Generally, expectations about relationships are lofty and idealized. Friendships are seen as sites of affection, loyalty, and trust. Families are pictured as havens in a troubled world. Loved ones are believed to

contextual dialectics
tensions resulting from the place of the relationship within the culture

public and private dialectic
a contextual dialectic resulting from a private relationship and public life

real and ideal dialectic
a contextual dialectic resulting from the difference between idealized relationships and lived relationships

213

Table 12.1 Interactional and Contextual Dialectics

INTERACTIONAL DIALECTICS	CONTEXTUAL DIALECTICS
Autonomy–Connection	Public–Private
Openness–Protection	The Real–The Ideal
Novelty–Predictability	

provide unconditional affection and support. Yet, we know that interpersonal relationships are not always pleasant and, as we discussed in Chapter 1, can have a dark side that contrasts starkly with these ideals. Dialectic theory attempts to explain how people live with and manage this contradiction.

Finally, cultural and contextual factors influence these two dialectics. In cultures where friends are elevated to the status of family (some Middle Eastern cultures, for example), the tension will be experienced quite differently than in Rawlins's description, if it is felt at all. In addition, social mores and expectations vary over time, and the dialectics are influenced by these changes. For example, Ernest Burgess and Harvey Locke (1953) distinguish between an institutional and a companionate marriage. Prior to the 1950s, marriage was expected to be an economic institution, critical to the survival of the human race. More recently in the United States, marriage has been viewed as a love relationship where one's partner functions as one's best friend. Obviously, the tensions between the ideal and the real will shift depending on the contours of the socially prescribed ideal. See Table 12.1 for a summary of the basic relational dialectics.

Responses to Dialectics

Although the dialectic tensions are ongoing, people do make efforts to manage them. Baxter (1988) identifies four main strategies for this purpose: cyclic alternation, segmentation, selection, and integration (see Table 12.2). **Cyclic alternation** occurs when people choose one of the opposites to feature at particular times, alternating with the other. For instance, when sisters are very young they may be inseparable, highlighting the closeness pole of the dialectic. As adolescents they may favor autonomy in their relationship, seeking separate identities. As adults, when they are perhaps living in the same town, they may favor closeness again. **Segmentation** involves isolating separate arenas for emphasizing each of the opposites. For example, a husband and wife who work together in a family business might stress predictability in their working relationship and novelty for times they are at home. The third strategy, **selection**, refers to making a choice between the opposites. A couple who choose to be close at all times, ignoring their needs for autonomy, use selection.

Finally, **integration** involves some kind of synthesis of the opposites. Integration can take three forms: neutralizing, reframing, or disqualifying the polarities. **Neutralizing** involves compromising between the polarities. People who choose this strategy try to find a happy medium between the opposites. Jeff

cyclic alternation
a coping response to dialectical tensions; refers to changes over time

segmentation
a coping response to dialectical tensions; refers to changes due to context

selection
a coping response to dialectical tensions; refers to prioritizing oppositions

integration
a coping response to dialectical tensions; refers to synthesizing the opposition; composed of three substrategies

neutralizing
a substrategy of integration; refers to compromising between the oppositions

Table 12.2 Responses to Dialectic Tensions

RESPONSE	DESCRIPTION
Cyclic alternation	Choosing different poles for different times. Being close when young and more distant with age, for example.
Segmentation	Choosing different poles for different contexts. Being close at home and more distant at work, for example.
Selection	Choosing one pole and acting as though the other does not exist. Being an extremely close family, for example.
Integration	Synthesizing the oppositions in dialectic tensions; composed of three substrategies.
Neutralizing	A substrategy of integration; involves choosing a compromise between the oppositions. Being moderately close, for example.
Reframing	A substrategy of integration; involves transforming the oppositions so they no longer appear to oppose one another. Deciding that closeness can only be achieved if there's a little distance too, for example.
Disqualifying	A substrategy of integration; involves exempting certain issues from the general pattern. Deciding to be open on all topics except sex, for example.

and Eleanor may decide they cannot really be as open as Eleanor would like, yet they cannot be as closed as Jeff might want, either. Thus, they forge a moderately open relationship.

Reframing refers to transforming the dialectic in some way so that it no longer seems to contain an opposition. Julia Wood and her colleagues (1994) discuss how couples reframe by defining connection as including differences. Thus, the dialectic between autonomy and connection is redrawn as a unity rather than as an opposition. If Eleanor and Jeff begin to see their closeness as a function of their ability to also be separate from each other, they are reframing, or redefining, what it means to be close.

Disqualifying neutralizes the dialectics by exempting certain issues from the general pattern. A family might be very open in their communication in general yet have a few taboo topics that are not discussed at all, such as sex and finances. The Research Note suggests how these strategies are used by abusive and nonabusive couples.

Baxter and Montgomery (1996) review these and other techniques for dealing with dialectical tensions. They argue that any techniques that people use share three characteristics: They are improvisational, they are affected by time, and they are possibly complicated by unintended consequences. Let's look at these three characteristics in turn.

Improvisational, according to Baxter and Montgomery, means that whatever people do to deal with a particular tension of relational life, they do not alter the ongoing nature of the tension. For example, Jeff and Eleanor have

reframing
a substrategy of integration; refers to transforming the oppositions

disqualifying
a substrategy of integration; refers to exempting certain issues from the general pattern

Research Note

Sabourin, T. C., & Stamp, G. H. (1995). Communication and the experience of dialectical tensions in family life: An examination of abusive and nonabusive families. *Communication Monographs, 62,* 213–242.

This study uses a dialectical perspective to examine the communication behavior of ten couples with a history of abuse and ten couples without abuse. The researchers posed the following two questions: What interactional patterns or qualities of communication characterize the conversations of abusive and nonabusive couples? How do the two types of couples manage dialectical tensions?

Researchers visited the couples' homes and asked the couples to talk to each other about a typical day. Each conversation was analyzed, and the results were applied to answer the research questions. In examining the qualities of communication in the conversations of the two types of couples, the researchers found the following differences: abusive couples used more vague language, less collaborative talk, and more conflictual relational talk, expressed more anger and frustration, complained and voiced more disapproval, gave fewer compliments, and expressed less control over change in their lives than did the nonabusive couples.

Teresa Sabourin and Glen Stamp argue that these communication differences "provided a vehicle for understanding how the couples manage dialectical tensions" (1995, p. 213). The researchers find that abusive couples tended to choose selection as their strategy for dealing with dialectics such as stability and change. Thus, abusive couples favored one polarity (stability) consistently over the other (change). The researchers observe that selection can lead to rigidity in the couples' behavior, wherein they actively resist change. Sabourin and Stamp also note that Leslie Baxter's earlier research found that selection is a strategy used by dissatisfied couples for managing dialectical tensions. However, they argue that their research indicates that dissatisfied nonabusive couples may differ from dissatisfied abusive couples in strategy choice.

Although the researchers caution about overgeneralizing from their results, they suggest that the presence of the communication characteristics listed above and a preference for selection in the face of enduring dialectical tensions may describe an abusive couple.

come to a moderately open relationship to neutralize the dialectical tension, but they have not changed the fact that openness and protectiveness continue to be an issue in their relationship.

The aspect of time refers to the notion that, when dealing with dialectics, communication choices made by relational partners are affected by the past, enacted in the present, and filled with anticipation for the future. When Jeff praises Eleanor for the party they gave for Mary Beth, he does so knowing that they have argued about his friends in the past and hoping that these arguments will not continue in the future. In speaking about applying the dialectical approach to friendship, Rawlins (1992) comments that "configurations of contradictions compose and organize friendships throughout an ongoing process of change across the life course" (p. 8). He further observes that the way friends coordinate and manage their tensions over time is a key factor in dialectical analysis. The conclusion he draws is that "dialectical inquiries are intrinsically historical investigations" (p. 8), concerned with developmental processes over time.

Finally, Baxter and Montgomery point out that relational partners may enact a strategy for coping with a tension, yet it may not work out as they intended. For example, the husband and wife who work together and employ

The Theory Connection

How do you see the dialectic approach working with Uncertainty Reduction Theory as Berger suggested might be possible in Chapter 9? Do you think the metatheoretical assumptions of the two theories are compatible? Explain your answer.

segmentation as we described earlier may feel they are coping with the novelty and predictability tension, but they may become dissatisfied because they spend a lot of time at work and so do not get enough novelty in their relationship.

Critique and Closing

Dialectical process thinking adds a great deal to our conceptual frameworks about relational life. First, we can think specifically about issues around which relational partners construct meaning. Second, we can remove the static frame and put our emphasis on the interplay between change and stability. We do not have to choose between observing patterns and observing unpredictability because we recognize the presence of both within relationships. Likewise, dialectical thinking directs people to observe the interactions within a relationship, among its individual members, as well as outside a relationship, as its members interact with the larger social and cultural systems in which they are embedded. This approach helps us focus on power issues and multicultural diversity.

In general, scholars have been excited about the promise generated by Relational Dialectics Theory, and their responses to it have been positive. The theory seems to measure up well against the criteria we discussed in Chapter 3. It offers an expansive view of relationships and has generated several studies even in the short time that Baxter has been delineating the theory; therefore, it is a heuristic theory. These studies also point to the fact that the theory is testable. Perhaps the most positive appeal of the theory is that it seems to explain the push and pull people experience in relationships much better than some of the other, more linear, theories of relational life. Most people experience their relationships in ebb-and-flow patterns, whether the issue is intimacy, self-disclosure, or something else. That is, relationships do not simply become more or less of something in a linear, straight-line pattern. Instead, they often seem to be both/and as we live through them. Dialectics offers a compelling explanation for this both/and feeling.

A few questions have been raised about the theory, however. One concerns the number and limit of dialectical tensions that exist in relational life. Some question whether the dialectics of autonomy and connection, openness and protection, and novelty and predictability are the only dialectics of all relationships. For example, Rawlins (1992) does not see the novelty/certainty dialectic in his study of friendship. Instead, he finds a different dialectic, focusing on tensions of judgment and acceptance. This dialectic emerges in the tension between

T*I*P

Theory * Into * Practice

The dialectics in a mother–daughter relationship are discussed in a 1998 article in *McCall's* magazine. The article focuses on the figure skater Tara Lipinski and her efforts to grow up normally after winning Olympic gold at age 15. The article observes that Lipinski experiences many contradictions, because that is the nature of adolescence. The article also comments on her relationship with her mother and notes that tensions and contradictions pervade this relationship:

> Tara Lipinski is not a robot. The fact is, she's just a teenager—a kid on the brink of womanhood who loves loud music, boys-boys-boys ("I met Matt Damon at the Academy Awards—he's hot!") and trying on strapless designer evening gowns at photo shoots ("Don't I look glam?"). And like any teen, she feels the pull of the parental apron strings. Few girls, however, have to deal with such intense fame. Tara's mother, Pat, is aware of the awkward contradictions in her daughter's life. "You want to protect her, to keep her from ever being hurt," she explains. Lipinski leads a life in the limelight: Invitations to the Academy Awards, talk-show appearances, even Hollywood parties are all part of being an Olympic medalist. "I want her to become her own person, and I cheer her on," she says. "But it's hard. How do you be both a mother and a friend?"
>
> Pat Lipinski may not know the answer, but she's trying to find it: She's equal parts Mama Bear, bodyguard and gal pal. Sometimes her roles clash. (pp. 18, 20)

Source: Berk, 1998.

TIP Follow-up
What strategies do you suggest parents use to manage important contradictions in their relationship with their children?

judging a friend's behaviors and simply accepting them. In studying friendships in the workplace, Ted Zorn (1995) finds the three main dialectics, but he also finds some additional tensions that were specific to the workplace context. This does not seem to be a serious flaw in the theory, however, and more study will probably delineate a finite number of dialectics that may vary by context.

Baxter and Montgomery (1996) observe that dialectics is not a traditional theory in that it offers no axioms or propositional arguments. Instead, it describes a set of conceptual assumptions. Thus, it does not offer us good predictions about, for example, what coping strategies people might use to deal with the major dialectic tensions in their relationships. This problem may be the result of the relative youth of dialectics as a theoretical frame for relational life, or it may result from differing goals: Traditional theory seeks prediction and final statements about communication phenomena; Dialectics operates from an open-ended, ongoing viewpoint. Baxter and Montgomery end their 1996 book with a personal dialogue between themselves about the experience of writing about a theory that encourages conversation rather than providing axiomatic conclusions. They agree that in some ways it is difficult to shake the cultural need for consistency and closure. Yet, they conclude that it is heuristic and valuable to write about live, emerging ideas.

Many researchers agree that the dialectic approach is an extremely exciting way to conceive of communication in relational life. Expect to see more refinements of this theory and more studies testing its premises.

Discussion Starters

1. Can you think of other dialectic tensions that will pervade the relational life of Eleanor and Jeff besides those discussed in the chapter?

2. Do you think relationships are better explained through stage theories or dialectics? Why? Provide examples.

3. Do you believe it is possible to want two things at one time in a relationship—for example, to be close and to be distant? Why or why not? Use examples to support your views.

4. Can two contradictory things both be true? Provide at least one example.

5. Provide at least two examples of a dialectical tension that was managed in each of the ways suggested in the chapter.

6. What communication practices have you observed that perform a simultaneous honoring of the two oppositions in the dialectic tensions we have discussed.

Terms for Review

monologic approach
dualistic approach
dialectic approach
totality
contradiction
motion
praxis
autonomy and connection
openness and protection
novelty and predictability
interactional dialectics

contextual dialectics
public and private dialectic
real and ideal dialectic
cyclic alternation
segmentation
selection
integration
neutralizing
reframing
disqualifying

Online Learning Center

Visit the Online Learning Center at www.mhhe.com/west2. Use the multiple-choice and true/false quizzes to help you prepare for exams, and the glossary, crossword puzzles, and flashcards to further your knowledge of key terms.

CHAPTER 13

Communication Privacy Management Theory

Lisa Sanders

Lisa Sanders knew that she would have a tough time making it through her workday without being sidetracked by someone. She rushed around the office, keeping her eyes down, trying to avoid getting sucked into a conversation with anyone. She enjoyed her work and loved her co-workers, but the downside was that somebody always wanted to chat and she simply had no time to waste today. She had already used too much precious work time going through her e-mail. She had thrown out about sixty five pieces of SPAM, which was really getting to be a problem. The worst was that somehow she was on a porno list and she kept getting solicitations for all sorts of nasty things. Lisa couldn't figure out what site she'd visited that had given her e-mail address to these low-lifes. She just hoped that the office didn't have some type of surveillance to observe all the porn messages she got. It made her feel vaguely uneasy.

She was thinking about ways to reduce or eliminate all that spam when she went into the break room for a cup of coffee. That was a mistake. Yolanda and Michael were there, and they wanted to ask her opinion about a change the front office was making in how they did the billing. One thing led to another, and soon the three were talking about Yolanda's concerns about going on maternity leave next month. Lisa found herself enjoying the conversation even though she knew she had to get back to work.

After work, Lisa went to Central State to take a night class so that someday she could finish her B.A. She was hopeful that she'd finish within the year, and she had her eye on a management position that she expected would be vacant by then. During the break, she visited with her friend Doug Banda, who was also finishing up his degree. She confided in Doug that she didn't think she was doing very well balancing work, school, and her personal life. It was a continual challenge, and today it was getting the better of her. She almost surprised herself with how emotional she got while talking to Doug. She could feel tears welling up in her eyes, and she felt her hands tremble. Doug was a good friend, and he listened and offered a friendly hug of support. She felt better after talking with him.

Finally, class was over and Lisa went home. The phone rang and it was one of those annoying telemarketers. She got rid of him as soon as possible and then listened to the messages on her answering machine. Most weren't very important; Lisa's mother had called with the usual gossip about the family. Most of the message had to do with Lisa's sister-in-law, Margo. Lisa's mom didn't get along very well with Margo, and she often called Lisa to let off steam about something her daughter-in-law had done (or hadn't done). Today it was the fact

---

This theory is based on the research of **Sandra Petronio.**

that Ed's wife was taking the kids on a vacation and Lisa's mom wouldn't get to see them for two weeks. Of course, her mom was also interested in Lisa's life. While she was listening to her mother ask her if she had plans for the weekend, her roommate, Amanda Torelli, came home.

Lisa liked Amanda and she certainly couldn't afford the apartment without a roommate, but sometimes it felt like she didn't have a moment to herself. Amanda had an overpowering personality and she filled the apartment to the extent that Lisa often felt crowded. Amanda always had something to say, and she didn't seem very sensitive to Lisa's mood for listening.

Tonight was no exception. Amanda wanted to tell Lisa all about her most recent fight with her boyfriend, Joel. Amanda and Joel were always fighting, and Lisa privately thought Amanda should dump the guy. But then she realized that Amanda liked playing the drama queen role, so she stopped telling Amanda any of her true reactions to Amanda's sagas. Lisa grabbed a glass of wine and some crackers as she settled on the couch to listen to Amanda's latest tale of woe.

■

As Lisa encounters the various people in her life—co-workers, classmates, family members, roommates, and so forth—she engages in a complex negotiation between privacy and disclosure. This chapter presents the theory of Communication Privacy Management (CPM), which helps us sort through and explain the complexities of this process. Sandra Petronio (2002) states that CPM is a practical theory designed to explain the very "everyday" issues described in Lisa's activities. As Petronio observes, the question of whether to tell someone something we are thinking is a complicated one, yet it's one we face frequently in our daily lives.

Examining Lisa's day we can see at least five instances when Lisa is occupied with questions of disclosure: 1) She worries about someone at work finding out about the pornographic e-mails, 2) she engages in conversation with co-workers without telling them that she's feeling harried, 3) she confides in a friend about feeling unbalanced in her work and personal life, 4) she listens to her mother's voice-mail-recorded complaints, and 5) she hears her roommate's disclosures without telling her what she really thinks about her boyfriend.

All these examples illustrate Petronio's contention that deciding what to reveal and what to keep confidential is not a straightforward decision, but rather a continual balancing act. Both disclosure and privacy have potential risks and rewards for Lisa in all of the situations she encounters.

Further, Lisa has to think about the possible risks and rewards her decisions may create for those with whom she interacts. How would Amanda feel if Lisa told her that she thought her boyfriend was a loser? Further, the act of revealing or withholding personal information has effects on relationships as well as on individuals. What happens to the relationship between Lisa and Doug as she confides in him about her feeling? All these concerns, relational and individual, create the complicated process of balance that Petronio addresses with Communication Privacy Management Theory.

As Petronio (2002) observes:

We try to weigh the demands of the situation with our needs and those of others around us. Privacy has importance for us because it lets us feel separate from others. It gives us a sense that we are the rightful owners of information about us. There are risks that include making private disclosures to the wrong people, disclosing at a bad time, telling too much about ourselves, or compromising others. On the other hand, disclosure can give enormous benefits. . . . We may . . . increase social control, validate our perspectives, and become more intimate with our relational partners when we disclose. . . . The balance of privacy and disclosure has meaning because it is vital to the way we manage our relationships. (pp. 1–2)

Thus, there was a need for a theory like CPM that attempts to do what few other theories have done: explain the process that people use to manage the relationship between concealing and revealing private information.

Communication Privacy Management Theory is unlike any of the other theories presented in this text because it is so recent. Think about our discussion in Chapter 18 on Aristotle's *Rhetoric*—we discussed a theoretical approach to public address and persuasion that goes back thousands of years. Of course, not all of the theories in this text have the history of Aristotle's *Rhetoric*. But even more recent theories like Uncertainty Reduction Theory (Chapter 9), Expectancy Violation Theory (Chapter 8), and Adaptive Structuration Theory (Chapter 15) all appeared in the literature more than twenty years ago. Although Petronio and her colleagues have worked with some of the principles of CPM Theory for approximately twenty years, the first formal statement of Communication Privacy Management Theory didn't appear until Petronio published her book *Boundaries of Privacy* in 2002.

This recency is notable for three reasons. First, it is exciting because it indicates the currency of thought in the communication discipline. It indicates that fresh, new thinking continues to illuminate questions of communication behavior. Having new theories illustrates the vibrancy of communication as a field. In case you were tempted to dismiss theory as something from musty tomes about dead Greeks, Petronio's CPM Theory shows that theorizing is alive and well in our own century.

Second, and related to the excitement generated by its recency, is the fact that CPM grows specifically from a focus on communication. This also shows the maturing and growth of the field of communication. Some of the other theories in this text, you will remember, originated in other disciplines besides communication. Communication researchers found them useful for some reason and borrowed them for their own work. For example, Symbolic Interaction Theory (Chapter 5), comes from sociology. Communication researchers appreciate SI because it places a great deal of emphasis on the importance of interaction in developing a sense of self. Cognitive Dissonance Theory (Chapter 7) originated in psychology, yet communication scholars found it useful for the insights it sheds on persuasive practices. Communication researchers have found these and other theories extremely useful for framing their studies examining communication behaviors. Even so, it may be more helpful to have theories that place communication concepts centrally in the explanation process. CPM Theory does just that, allowing researchers to be more focused in their examinations of the communication process and specific communication practices.

Finally, the newness of CPM does not allow us to evaluate it using the test of time. Additionally, we really do not have a corpus of studies using CPM on

which to base evaluations of its utility for explaining disclosure and concealment. Thus, we must simply scrutinize the theory for its internal consistency and logic, examine the small number of studies that have employed it in its short history, and wait and see how useful CPM will be to the field of communication.

Evolution of Communication Privacy Management Theory

Even though the history of CPM Theory isn't long, it does reflect a certain development in Petronio's thinking as she and her colleagues and other communication researchers have worked with the central ideas of the theory and refined its concepts and relationships. Almost twenty years ago, Petronio and her colleagues published some studies outlining principles that would eventually become part of CPM (e.g., Petronio & Martin, 1986; Petronio, Martin, & Littlefield, 1984). In these studies, the researchers were interested in criteria for rule development in a rule management system for disclosure. They noted that men and women have different criteria for judging when to be open and when to stay silent. These criteria lead to differing rules for men and women on the subject of disclosure. The notion of gender differences and the concept of disclosure as rule governed are now parts of CPM Theory.

In 1991, Petronio published her first attempt to codify all the principles of the theory. Her work (Petronio, 1991) differed from her later (2002) conceptualization in two ways. First, the theory had more limited boundaries in 1991. At that time, Petronio referred to it as a **microtheory** because its boundaries were confined to the privacy management within a marital dyad. Now, as we will discuss in this chapter, the theory is less restricted and attempts to explain privacy and disclosure in many more contexts than marriage. Petronio now refers to CPM as a **macrotheory** because its boundaries include a large variety of interpersonal relationships including groups and organizations.

The second change in the theory was a name change. In 1991, Petronio called the theory Communication Boundary Management. When she published the fuller statement of the theory in her 2002 book, she renamed it Communication Privacy Management Theory. Petronio explained the new name as better "reflecting the focus on private disclosures. Though the theory uses a boundary metaphor to explain the management process, the name change underscores that the main thrust of the theory is on private disclosures" (2002,

microtheory
a theory with limited boundaries

macrotheory
a theory with extensive boundaries

Table 13.1 Assumptions of CPM

CPM THEORY	ALL DIALECTIC THEORIES
Human choice	Relational life governed by change
Human-made rules	Contradiction as the fundamental fact of relational life
Social concerns	

p. 2). Although the book represents Petronio's current thinking about CPM, she notes that she expects (and hopes) that the theory will continue to grow and evolve as it is applied to practical questions of disclosure in relationships.

Assumptions of CPM

Communication Privacy Management Theory is rooted in assumptions about how individuals think and communicate as well as assumptions about the nature of human beings. First, CPM adheres to aspects of both rules and systems metatheories (see Chapter 3). Given this metatheoretical foundation, the theory makes three assumptions about human nature:

1. Humans are choice makers.
2. Humans are rule makers and rule followers.
3. Humans' choices and rules are based on a consideration of others as well as the self.

Petronio (2002) notes that people make choices and rules about what to tell and what to withhold from others based on a "mental calculus" grounded in salient criteria such as culture, gender, and context, among other things. She argues that these criteria include considerations about the other person(s) involved as well as the self. For this reason, Petronio uses the terms *disclosure* and *private disclosure* rather than *self-disclosure* in CPM.

Additionally, CPM Theory is a dialectic theory. As a dialectic theory, CPM subscribes to assumptions similar to those that ground Relational Dialectics Theory (Chapter 12), including:

4. Relational life is characterized by change.
5. Contradiction is the fundamental fact of relational life.

The assumptions, taken together, represent an active perception of human beings and a picture of humans as engaged in relational life to the extent that self and other are intertwined (see Table 13.1).

Basic Suppositions of CPM

private information
information about things that matter deeply to a person

As we have noted, CPM is concerned with explaining people's negotiation processes around disclosing private information. Our first task, then, is defining **private information**. Some researchers have stated that "what makes things pri-

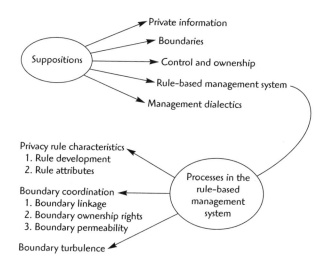

Figure 13.1
Overview of CPM
Basic Suppositions
Source: Adapted from
Petronio, 2002.

vate is in large part their importance to our conceptions of ourselves and to our relationships with others" (Schoeman, 1984, p. 406). Petronio (2000) commented that people define private information as information about things that matter deeply to them. Thus, the process of communicating private information in relationships with others becomes **private disclosures.** As we have stated previously, CPM focuses on private disclosures rather than self-disclosures.

The emphasis away from self-disclosure makes a distinction between CPM's definition of disclosure and that of traditional research on openness (e.g., Jourard, 1971). CPM views the definition differently in three ways. First, private disclosure puts more emphasis on the personal content of the disclosure than does traditional self-disclosure literature. In doing this, CPM gives more credence to the substance of disclosures, or that which is considered private. Additionally, CPM examines how people disclose through a rule-based system. Finally, CPM does not consider that disclosures are only about the self. Disclosures are a communicative process. As Petronio (2002) observes, "to fully understand the depth and breadth of a disclosure, CPM does not restrict the process to only the self, but extends it to embrace multiple levels of disclosure including self and group. Consequently, CPM theory offers a privacy management system that identifies ways privacy boundaries are coordinated between and among individuals" (p. 3).

Communication Privacy Management Theory accomplishes this goal by proposing five basic suppositions: private information, private boundaries, control and ownership, rule-based management system, and management dialectics (see Figure 13.1). We will explain each of these basic suppositions of the theory in turn.

private disclosures
the process of communicating private information to another

Private Information

The first supposition, private information, reiterates a traditional way to think about disclosure: It is the revealing of private information. However, Petronio (2002) observes that focusing on the content of disclosures allows us to disentangle the concepts of privacy and intimacy and examine how they are related. Many researchers have conflated self-disclosure with intimacy as though the two are equivalent even though they are two distinct concepts (Parks, 1982). Petronio argues that "**intimacy** is the feeling or state of knowing someone deeply in physical, psychological, emotional, and behavioral ways because that person is significant in one's life. Private disclosure, on the other hand, concerns the *process* of telling and reflects the *content* of private information about others and us" (p. 5). When Lisa tells her friend Doug about her feelings, she is engaging in private disclosure, which may be increasing the intimacy of their relationship. However, when Amanda tells Lisa about her boyfriend problems, their relationship is probably not deepening despite the disclosures.

intimacy
the feeling state of knowing someone deeply in all ways because that person is significant in one's life

private boundaries
the demarcation of private information from public information

collective boundary
a boundary around private information that includes more than one person

personal boundary
a boundary around private information that includes just one person

Private Boundaries

The second supposition is **private boundaries.** CPM relies on the boundary metaphor to make the point that there is a line between being public and being private. On one side of the boundary, people keep private information to themselves (Petronio, Giles, & Gallois, 1998); on the other side, people reveal some private information to others in social relationship with them. When private information is shared, the boundary around it is called a **collective boundary,** and the information is not only about the self; it belongs to the relationship. When private information remains with an individual and is not disclosed, the boundary is called a **personal boundary** (see Figure 13.2). When Lisa and her mother talk about Lisa's brother's wife, that information belongs to them as a dyad and

Figure 13.2
Boundary Types
Source: Reprinted by permission from *Boundaries of Privacy: Dialectics of Disclosure* by Sandra Petronio, the State University of New York Press. © 2002 State University of New York. All Rights Reserved.

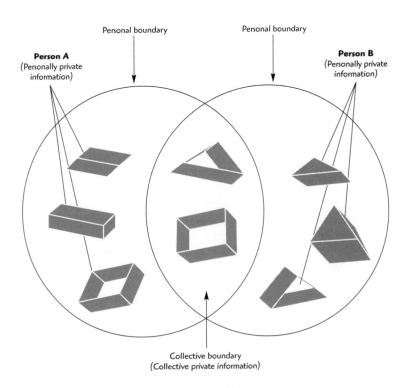

Personal boundary   Personal boundary

Person A
(Personally private information)

Person B
(Personally private information)

Collective boundary
(Collective private information)

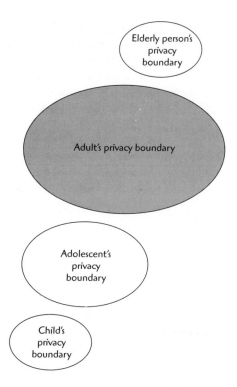

**Figure 13.3
Boundaries and the
Life Span**
Source: Reprinted
by permission from
*Boundaries of Privacy:
Dialectics of Disclosure*
by Sandra Petronio, the
State University of New
York Press. © 2002
State University of
New York. All Rights
Reserved.

neither one of them reveals it to Margo or Lisa's brother, creating a collective boundary. When Lisa privately holds her opinion of Joel, Amanda's boyfriend, that information has a personal boundary.

Boundaries can vary in other ways as well. They may be relatively permeable (easy to cross) or relatively impregnable (rigid and difficult to cross). Boundaries also may change related to life span issues. As Figure 13.3 illustrates, children in the United States maintain relatively small privacy boundaries. The boundaries increase as children grow into adolescence and adulthood and cultivate a more developed sense of privacy. As people enter old age, their boundaries begin to shrink. As Petronio and Kovach (1997) discovered, issues of caregiving for the elderly—such as their need for others to bathe them or manage their finances—causes the boundary for the elderly to diminish.

Control and Ownership

Supposition 3 relates to control and ownership. This supposition relies on the notion that people feel they own private information about themselves. As owners of this information, they believe they should be in a position to control who else (if anyone) is allowed to gain access to it. When Lisa finds herself inundated with unwanted e-mails and telephone calls, she feels she has lost control over access to her personal space. She has not told the senders of the pornographic e-mails or the telemarketers how to contact her, but they do so regardless, violating Lisa's sense of control over information she believes she owns.

Joyce Allman (1998) studied physicians utilizing a boundary management perspective that focused on the question of control. Allman explored the ethical dilemmas physicians faced when considering whether to reveal medical mistakes to patients. She discovered that physicians exercised control over this information by refusing to reveal mistakes to patients. The study found it wasn't legal or cultural factors that led doctors to exercise this control but rather the emotional issues surrounding physicians' difficulty in admitting that they made errors.

Rule-Based Management System

The fourth supposition of CPM Theory is rule-based management system. This system is the framework for understanding the decisions people make about private information. The rule-based management system allows for management on the individual and collective levels and is a complex arrangement consisting of three processes: privacy rule characteristics, boundary coordination, and boundary turbulence. Because there are many subprocesses involved in each of these three, we will describe them in a separate section below.

Management Dialectics

The fifth supposition, privacy management dialectics, focuses on the tensions between the forces advocating for revealing private information and those advocating concealing it. Petronio (2002) states that "the basic thesis of the theory is grounded in the unity of dialectics" (p. 9), which refers to the tensions people experience due to opposites and contradictions. When Lisa is drawn into the conversation with her co-workers, she experiences conflicting desires. She is enjoying the visit and wants to support Yolanda as much as she can, yet she needs to work and disclosing is taking away time from working.

These five suppositions form the heart of CPM Theory. In the section below we will detail the fourth supposition, concerning the privacy rule management system, in order to explicate the theory further.

Privacy Rule Management Processes

The fourth supposition described above depends on three privacy rule management processes: privacy rule characteristics, boundary coordination, and boundary turbulence (see Figure 13.1). The theory proposes that these regulate the process of revealing and concealing private information. See the Research Note for an example of a study examining some of the privacy rule management processes. We will discuss each of the three processes to illustrate how the theory explains the overall rule-based management system.

Privacy Rule Characteristics

Privacy rule characteristics have two main features: development and attributes. **Rule development** is guided by people's decision criteria for revealing or concealing private information. CPM Theory states that there are five decision criteria used for developing privacy rules: cultural criteria, gendered criteria, motivational criteria, contextual criteria, and risk-benefit ratio criteria. Cultural criteria depend on the norms for privacy and openness in a given culture. Individuals are guided in their own expectations for privacy by the values they obtain in their cultures. Thus, we might understand Amanda's desires to be transparent to Lisa in our opening story by noting that she is Italian American, a culture that generally values openness of expression.

Gendered criteria refer to differences that may exist between men and women in drawing their privacy boundaries (Petronio & Martin, 1986). Although these differences are not unchangeable, men and women seem to be socialized to develop different rules for how privacy and disclosure operate.

A third set of criteria revolves around motivation. People make decisions about disclosing based on their motivations. Some people may have such motives as control, manipulation, and power for disclosing or concealing private information. Others may be motivated by self-clarification or relational closeness. Additionally, there may be individual differences in people's motivations. Lisa may have a lower motivation for disclosing in general than Amanda has, for example.

In addition, contextual criteria have an influence on decisions people make about privacy. Petronio (2002) discusses two elements that make up context: social environment and physical setting. The social environment involves the special circumstances that might prompt a disclosure or a decision not to disclose. For example, Lisa's mother's disclosures might have been prompted by a recent conflict with Margo. Lisa's disclosure to Doug was stimulated by her circumstances that day, which made her feel particularly stressed and needy. The physical environment has to do with the actual location, issues of crowding, and physical space. Certain environments invite disclosures while others caution against them. When Lisa is in the break room at work, she may find the physical setting is not conducive to disclosing because it reminds her of how busy she is and because there is the constant possibility that someone else could come in during the conversation. On the other hand, in her apartment on the couch with a glass of wine might be a very inviting setting for disclosure.

Finally, rules are developed based on risk-benefit ratio criteria. This means that people evaluate the risks relative to the benefits of disclosing or keeping quiet. This is similar to the contentions of Social Exchange Theory (Chapter 11) except applied to the notion of disclosing behavior rather than relationship development.

privacy rule characteristics
one of the processes in the privacy rule management system; describes the nature of privacy rules

rule development
one of the features of privacy rule characteristics; describes how rules come to be decided

Research Note

Caughlin, J. P., Golish, T. D., Olson, L. N., Sargent, J. E., Cook, J. S., & Petronio, S. (2000). Intrafamily secrets in various family configurations: A communication boundary management perspective. *Communication Studies, 5,* 116–134.

This study begins with the observation that most research on the family suggests that family type (i.e., blended, single-parent, biological/adoptive, and so forth) makes a difference in the way family members construct boundaries. However, the authors note that even though past research acknowledges this difference, no one has systematically compared boundaries in different types of families.

This study seeks to remedy this lack in our knowledge. Based on past research and Communication Boundary Management Theory (later renamed Communication Privacy Management Theory), the authors advanced one hypothesis and generated five research questions toward their goal of investigating privacy boundaries in different types of families. These include the following:

Hypothesis 1: College students in blended families who report an intrafamily secret will be more likely to report that their original relations know the secret than they are to report that their steprelations know the secret.

Research Question 1: Will college students in blended, single-parent, and nuclear families differ in terms of their perceptions of the number of intrafamily secrets in their family?

Research Question 2: Will college students in blended, single-parent, and nuclear families report that their siblings are more likely than their parents to know the intrafamily secret that they report?

Research Question 3: Will college students in blended families, single-parent families, and nuclear families differ in terms of the topics of secrets they report?

Research Question 4: Will the perceived number of intrafamily secrets be inversely related to family satisfaction for individuals in different family types?

Research Question 5: Will college students in different family types differ in terms of the reported functions of their intrafamily secrets?

The sample for the study consisted of 615 college students from two large universities. Five hundred of the respondents were from nuclear families, 71 from blended families, and 44 from single-parent families. These students were given a questionnaire in which they were asked to do the following:

1. Identify family type.

2. Describe a secret "that some members of your family keep from other members of your family" (p. 124).

3. Estimate how many intrafamily secrets their family had and indicate whether they considered that number to be more or less than other families had.

4. Report who in the family knew and who did not know the secret they described for number 2.

5. Answer questions aimed at measuring the functions of a family secret.

6. Answer questions aimed at measuring family satisfaction.

The authors coded the answers participants' provided into three main categories for family secrets: taboo, rule violation, and conventional. Then the data were analyzed using a variety of statistical analyses to produce the following findings:

1. Hypothesis 1 was supported; participants in blended families reported that their original families were more likely to know the secret they described than their steprelations were.

2. Members of blended families, single-parent families, and nuclear families were similar in terms of the issues mentioned in the research questions: number of secrets, topics of the secrets, functions of the secrets, and relationship of secrets to family satisfaction. In all family types, the researchers found that the more family secrets the respondents reported, the more likely they were to report lower satisfaction with their family.

The authors conclude that their study shows that blended families and single-parent families are not as different from nuclear families (on the topic of family secrets) as we have previously assumed them to be. Moreover, they note that their investigation furthers an understanding of Communication Boundary Management Theory. First, their findings indicate that CBM provides a useful way to examine when boundaries will be rigid and when they will be permeable. Additionally, the theory guides us, in ways the study confirms, to examine rule management systems for disclosing secrets. Finally, the theory alerts us to the concept of co-ownership of a secret, which seemed to illuminate the findings in the study.

The five decision criteria described above help explain the process of rule development, which is one element of privacy rule characteristics. The second aspect of privacy rule characteristics concerns **privacy rule attributes.** Attributes are further divided into the ways people acquire rules and the properties of the rules. Generally, the theory suggests that people learn rules through socialization processes or by negotiation with others to create new rules.

For example, Lisa was socialized in her company through informal networks that taught her that it was important to spend time nurturing relationships with her co-workers. The organization often invoked the metaphor of a family, hosted many social events for the workers, and tried in several other ways to impress on employees that close relationships were an important part of the organizational culture. When learned rules are inadequate or need modifying, then people collaborate to forge new rules. For instance, if the company determined that its workers were disclosing to one another to the detriment of productivity, they might work to renegotiate the rules. This example also speaks to the concept of **rule properties,** which refers to the characteristics of rules. Characteristics index how stable or changeable a rule is.

Boundary Coordination

The second process under the rule-based management system is **boundary coordination,** which refers to how we manage information that is co-owned. For example, when Lisa and her mother talk about Margo, Lisa's sister-in-law, it is clear that the information is to be kept from Margo and Lisa's brother. Boundary coordination is the process through which that decision is made and through which Lisa and her mother become co-owners of private information. Petronio (2002) notes that people "regulate private information through rules that moderate boundary linkage, boundary ownership rights, and boundary permeability" (pp. 26–27).

Boundary linkage refers to the connections that form boundary alliances between people. For example, when Lisa tells private information to Doug they are linked into a privacy boundary. Physicians form linkages with their patients because the medical profession stresses patient confidentiality. If you overhear a piece of private information that wasn't intended for you, you are technically

privacy rule attributes
one of the features of privacy rule characteristics; describes how people acquire rules and the properties of rules

rule properties
the characteristics of a rule that reveal how stable or changeable it is

boundary coordination
one of the processes in the privacy rule management system; describes how we manage private information that is co-owned

boundary linkage
the connections forming boundary alliances between people

linked; however, the linkage is weak because you know you weren't the intended recipient of the information.

Boundary ownership refers to rights and privileges accruing to co-owners of private information. In order for boundary ownership to be exercised accurately, the rules need to be clear. For instance, if your friend tells you private information, are you allowed to share it with someone else? If your friend has told you explicitly not to tell anyone her secret, then the boundary is clear and unambiguous. However, if she just told you the secret without specifying whether you could tell anyone else, you might feel unsure about your co-ownership. You could suspect you aren't supposed to tell, but without instructions you feel uncertain.

Yet, boundaries are dynamic and may be redrawn over time. For example, when one of your authors was eighteen, her brother had an accident with the family car. Together, she and her brother had the car repaired and paid for the repairs without telling their parents. Now that they are both adults they have told their parents about the incident. Thus, the boundary broadened to include the whole family. Further, it may also be the case that co-owners do not agree about boundary issues. For example, Amanda might think that her tales about Joel, her boyfriend, link Lisa into a boundary that Lisa, herself, would rather not be included in.

Finally, boundary coordination is accomplished through **boundary permeability,** which refers to how much information is able to pass through the boundary. When access to private information is closed, boundaries are said to be **thick boundaries;** when access is open, people have **thin boundaries** in place. As Petronio (2002) observes:

> Although we do have secrets and people may be very open, more typically, people regulate the permeability to varying degrees through an array of access and protection rules. For example, people may completely hide health concerns from others for a period of time, cautiously expose flaws they find in themselves to certain others, use discretion in commenting on another's behavior, or be completely open with one other person. In each case, the permeability, that is how much information is allowed to pass through the boundary, varies depending on the rules for access and protection. (p. 29)

Boundary Turbulence

Boundary turbulence exists when the rules of boundary coordination are unclear or when people's expectations for privacy management come into conflict with one another. Boundary regulation is not always a smooth operating system, and the people involved can experience clashes that Petronio labels turbulence. For example, if Lisa refused to listen to Amanda's problems one evening, they might come into conflict. If you discovered that a friend told another about some private information you had shared and meant for that friend to keep private, boundary turbulence would ensue. CPM Theory asserts that when individuals experience boundary turbulence, they will try to make adjustments so that they can reduce the turbulence and achieve coordination.

boundary ownership
rights and privileges accruing to co-owners of private information

boundary permeability
how much information is able to pass through a boundary

thick boundaries
closed boundaries allowing little or no information to pass through

thin boundaries
open boundaries allowing all information to pass through

boundary turbulence
conflicts about boundary expectations and regulation

Critique and Closing

It is difficult to critique CPM Theory at this stage in its development. It hasn't been in use long enough to attract legions of adherents or detractors. Yet, it has been utilized as a framework in a variety of situations including child sexual abuse (Petronio, Reeder, Hecht, & Ros-Mendoza, 1996), disclosure of HIV or AIDS status (Cline & McKenzie, 2000), and medical mistakes (Allman, 1998).

One criticism of the theory that Petronio (2002) has discussed relates to its claim to be a dialectical theory. Petronio notes that some researchers have questioned whether CPM Theory truly is dialectical in nature. The basis for the criticism stems from Baxter and Montgomery's (1996) distinctions among monologic, dualistic, and dialectic approaches (see Chapter 12). Using these distinctions, Baxter and Montgomery have argued that CPM takes a dualistic approach, treating privacy and disclosure as independent of one another and able to coexist in tandem rather than in the dynamic interplay characteristic of dialectics.

Petronio (2002) responds to this criticism by noting that perhaps the accusation of dualistic thinking comes from the use of the terms *balance* and *equilibrium* in the early versions of CPM Theory. Petronio argues that CPM is not focused on balance in the psychological sense. "Instead, [CPM] argues for coordination with others that does not advocate an optimum balance between disclosure and privacy. As an alternative, the theory claims there are shifting forces with a range of privacy and disclosure that people handle by making judgments about the *degrees* [emphasis in original] of privacy and publicness they wish to experience in any given interaction" (pp. 12–13). Thus, Petronio argues that it is legitimate to call CPM Theory dialectical in nature.

Finally, we conclude that Communication Privacy Management Theory has an internal consistency, it is testable, and it has much promise of utility. It offers an explanation for the delicate process of coordination disclosing and concealing that people perform continually in their relationships with others. Further, CPM may provide insights as that process of coordination becomes even more complex. CPM is needed to explain those daily intrusions into our lives due to technological advances. As technology moves more and more of what we have considered private information into the public realm, we will need to understand the rule-based management system underlying this trend. All these reasons argue well for CPM Theory's future in communication studies.

T*I*P

Theory * Into * Practice

The issues surrounding privacy and disclosure are only being increased by technological advances in modern society. As Irwin Altman observed in the preface to Petronio's book about CPM (2002), the question of how "we strike a balance between the incredible positive opportunities to reach out to others made possible by modern technology, versus the dangers of losing the ability to control and regulate what others may know or have access to about us" (p. xii) is at the heart of CPM Theory. A recent book, reviewed in the *Library Journal* by Lucy Heckman (2002), also examines this question. The book, *World Without Secrets: Business, Crime, Privacy in the Age of Ubiquitous Computing*, is written by Richard Hunter, a security analyst for a technology research firm.

Heckman calls the book provocative, saying its topic is "a world 'in which very little of consequence can't and won't be known about anyone or anything'" (p. 105). Heckman observes that Hunter examines the negative impacts that technology has on personal privacy and offers some suggestions for safeguarding private information. She quotes him as saying that "by the end of the current decade, we'll be living in a man-made [sic] environment of intelligent machines that are capable of seeing, hearing, and understanding most of what we do" (p. 105).

Heckman lists some specific forms of techno-snooping discussed in the book. These include computer software linked to cameras scanning crowds, telematics allowing exchange of information between people in cars and external sources, and sophisticated methods for mining information from data collected for other purposes. Heckman notes that the book is important because of its reflections on the relationship between information gathering through technology and terrorism. She quotes the author who states that "in a globalized economy, enabled by global communications, anyone anywhere can be a terrorist, and anyone can be a victim" (p. 105).

Source: Heckman, 2002.

TIP Follow-up
How do you think the principles of Communication Privacy Management Theory work to explain technological invasions of privacy? Can the theory be applied in instances where a discloser doesn't know he or she is actually providing information to another? Explain your answer.

Discussion Starters

1. Apply CPM Theory to Lisa Sanders's case. How might it help Lisa to understand her situation?

2. Evaluate CPM Theory using three to five of the criteria listed in Chapter 3 (do not use the test-of-time criterion). What is your assessment of the theory overall? Do you think it will stand the test of time? Why or why not?

3. What metatheoretical approach does Petronio take in CPM Theory (laws, rules, systems, or some combination)? Explain your answer.

4. What other topics of interest can CPM Theory be applied to besides family secrets?

5. Can CPM Theory explain technological disclosures and privacy attempts such as those encountered in online conversations? Explain your answer.

6. Explain the concept of control with reference to communication boundaries. The chapter mentioned a study about medical mistakes that focused on control. Think of other contexts besides health care where control might be an issue. Explain your choices.

Terms for Review

microtheory
macrotheory
private information
private disclosures
intimacy
private boundaries
collective boundary
personal boundary
privacy rule characteristics
rule development

privacy rule attributes
rule properties
boundary coordination
boundary linkage
boundary ownership
boundary permeability
thick boundaries
thin boundaries
boundary turbulence

Online Learning Center

Visit the Online Learning Center at www.mhhe.com/west2. Use the multiple-choice and true/false quizzes to help you prepare for exams, and the glossary, crossword puzzles, and flashcards to further your knowledge of key terms.

Groups and Organizations

THE UNITED STATES IS A SOCIETY THAT RELIES ON groups and organizations in order to function. Small group and organizational communication has a rich tradition in communication studies. A number of articulate theoretical developments are occurring in this field. One reason we have seen such attention in this area is that most of us will work for a company or corporation at some point in our lives. Further, global, political, social, and economic changes have prompted groups and organizations to look at their roles in Western culture.

Companies and organizations are undergoing significant changes in the twenty-first century. These changes are a result of the corporate scandals of the early 2000s, the need to work together in more culturally diverse work environments, and the fact that very few jobs these days can be accomplished at work without the help of others. As Bob Dylan once sang, "The times they are a-changin'."

The four theories we present in this section of the book consider the influence that changing times have on groups and organizations. Each theory looks at the role of a group member or employee in a different way. For instance, Groupthink views group members as capable of being so connected that they fail to question the group's goals or tasks. Adaptive Structuration Theory sees individuals and teams as being both constrained and encouraged by the structure of an organization. Employees can either be bound by the rules or norms of a company or transcend these existing structures and tap into personal creativity. In Organizational Culture Theory, employees are perceived as part of a company's culture, positioned to develop and sustain a company's principles and values. Trying to make sense out of vague, misleading, or ambiguous information is at the heart of Organizational Information Theory. This theory examines how organizational members extract themselves from confusing situations while at work.

These theories view groups and organizational members as being both active and passive. Group and organizational life is precisely like that. At times, we are consumed with getting the task accomplished and may be unaware of our eagerness to get things done. At other times, though, we actively work toward clarity and toward becoming part of a company. The theories in this section help us understand a number of interesting areas, including decision making, social influence, rules, corporate climate, and employee satisfaction.

CHAPTER 14

Groupthink

Melton Publishing Board of Directors

As they sat in the seminar room at Melton Publishing, the seven men and women privately wondered whether or not they would find their next superstar author. Last week, the board heard the bad news: Their profits were down significantly, and they needed a best-seller to counter some of the company's financial loss. Elizabeth Hansen, the board's chairperson, suggested that the group review at least two books that they felt could reverse the company's losses. From early reviews of one of the books—*Red Warnings*, a science fiction novel—she felt that here was an opportunity to turn around the downward spiral and to give the small press a promising future. She knew that employee and board morale was down and felt that something had to be done quickly.

As chairperson for the past few years, Elizabeth knew that, in a way, her own credibility was on the line. She was chairing a board of literary people, for the most part; only one member previously had been on a board. She knew that the similarity among the members would likely result in them agreeing to a quick and reasonable solution to the company's financial circumstances. Although no clear solution was obvious at this difficult time in the company, Elizabeth felt that something had to be done.

The seven gathered around the table as they reviewed their financial future. Elizabeth opened the discussion with an upbeat message: "We can beat this downward spiral," she said. She reminded the group that the 9-year-old company had a history of surviving rough times. "This is just another bump in the road," she reported.

The discussion soon turned to the book *Red Warnings*, which had been reviewed favorably in a national book magazine. Since the review's publication, orders for the book had skyrocketed. Elizabeth felt that the best way to generate more money into the small company, thereby resulting in more publicity, was to market *Red Warnings* aggressively: through the media, on college campuses, and at science fiction conventions across the country. She believed that the book could bring in hundreds of thousands of dollars in profits but knew that to accomplish that would require tireless marketing. Melton Publishing is small, she thought, but not too small to promote a best-seller.

Randy Miles, another board member, disagreed with Elizabeth's plans. He thought that there was simply too much risk in concentrating so much time and money on one book. Randy's way to improve the financial situation of the company could be summed up in one word: cutbacks. After looking over the company's financial records of the past few years, he had discovered that far too many people had been hired, resulting in overspending on salary, benefits, and company discounts. He knew that cutting back on personnel was not a popular strategy but felt that this wasn't the time for being popular.

This theory is based on the research of **Irving Janis.**

The meeting dragged on, from an anticipated 2 hours to approaching 5 hours. Elizabeth and Randy continued to explain and defend their viewpoints. At times, there was heated arguing; the two would frequently raise their voices to make their points. During their arguments, the remaining board members would try to be agreeable. They knew that they weren't all that knowledgeable about how to turn the company around, and for the most part, they sat silently while the two leaders squared off against each other.

Finally, as the afternoon sun began to set, Tina, a writer from the Boston area, said, "Look, we've all been very patient while the two of you decide what's best for this company. And maybe we've learned for the future that we need to get more financial expertise on this board. But, for now, I have to speak. We need to make a decision. A hard decision. Whether a decision can be made today is iffy. I recommend that we postpone our decision until our next meeting so that we can all think about our options."

Randy interrupted, "Look, Tina, I appreciate your honesty, but this is not about whether or not we should build another bathroom! This is the company's future. I recommend that we hash this out now."

Elizabeth agreed, as did the other board members. It occurred to Tina that their "lunch meeting" was turning into a "working dinner." As the evening came, it was clear that Elizabeth and Randy were getting tired. "Listen, Randy, we're running low on energy and time. I think we should just get the two motions out and have the board vote." The other members soon agreed. It was obvious that they were all tired.

Randy reminded the group that they shouldn't rush their decision, but Tina reminded him that he was the one who hadn't wanted to postpone a decision. Although Randy tried to attack Tina's tone, the other group members began clamoring for a vote. Each member started to openly express support for Elizabeth's aggressive marketing plan. Because the group was small and he could sense the overwhelming support for Elizabeth, Randy decided to give in. He left the meeting feeling that he had been silenced by the group at the end of their discussion.

◼

Participating in small groups is a fact of life. Whether people are at school or at work, they frequently spend significant working hours in groups. To understand the nature of decision making in small groups, Irving Janis, in his book *Victims of Groupthink* (1972), explains what takes place in groups where group members are highly agreeable with one another. Studying foreign policy decision making, Janis believes that when group members share a common fate, there is great pressure toward conformity. He labels this pressure *groupthink*, a term cleverly patterned after vocabulary found in George Orwell's *1984* (for example, *doublethink*).

Groupthink is defined as a way of deliberating that group members use when their desire for unanimity overrides their motivation to assess all available plans of action. To Janis, group members frequently engage in a style of deliberating decisions where consensus seeking outweighs good sense. You may have participated in groups where the desire to achieve a goal or task was more important than developing reasonable solutions to problems. Janis believes that when highly similar and agreeable groups fail to consider fully any dissenting opinions, when they suppress conflict just so they get along, or when the group members do not fully consider all solutions, they are prone to groupthink. He argues that when groups are in groupthink, they immediately engage in a mentality to "preserve group harmony" (Janis, 1989, p. 60). To this end, making peace is more important than making clear and appropriate decisions.

Our example of the board of directors at Melton Publishing exemplifies the groupthink phenomenon. The board members are a group of people who apparently get along. The members are essentially connected by their literary backgrounds, making them more predisposed to groupthink. The group is under a deadline to come up with a thoughtful and financially prudent decision about the financial future of the company. As the chapter unfolds, we will tell you more about how this group becomes susceptible to groupthink.

Before we identify the assumptions guiding the theory, we first need to point out that Janis used government policy to exemplify his theory; therefore, many of his examples are drawn from real life. Using principles from small group research, Janis (1982) tries to explain why several foreign policy decisions are flawed or are what he considers to be fiascoes.

Janis analyzed five matters of significant national importance: (1) the preparedness policies of the U.S. Navy at Pearl Harbor in 1941, (2) the decision to pursue the North Korean Army on its own territory by President Eisenhower, (3) the decision by President Kennedy to invade Cuba at the Bay of Pigs shortly after Fidel Castro established a communist government, (4) the decision to continue the Vietnam War by President Johnson, and (5) the Watergate cover-up by President Nixon. Janis argues that each of these policy decisions was made by both the president and his team of advisors and that, because each group was under some degree of stress, they made hasty and what amounted to inaccurate decisions. He interviewed a number of people who were part of these teams and concluded that each of these policy fiascoes occurred because of groupthink. It was discovered that in each of these cases, the presidential advisors did not thoroughly test information before making their decisions.

According to Janis, the group members failed to consider forewarnings, and their biases and desire for harmony overshadowed critical assessments of their own decisions. Randy Hirokawa, Dennis Gouran, and Amy Martz (1988) came to similar conclusions when they analyzed faulty group decision making in the *Challenger* disaster. Of course, we now understand the historical significance of these faulty decisions. As Janis (1972) concludes, groupthink occurred because there was a "deterioration of mental efficiency, reality testing, and moral judgment" (p. 9) in these groups.

Assumptions of Groupthink

Groupthink is a theory associated with small group communication. In Chapter 2 we noted that small groups are a part of virtually every segment of U.S. society. In fact, emphasizing the importance of small groups, Marshall Scott Poole (1998) argues that the small group should be "THE basic unit of analysis" (p. 94). Janis focuses his work on **problem-solving groups** and **task-oriented groups,** whose main purpose is to make decisions and give policy recommendations. Decision making is a necessary part of these small groups. Among the other activities of small groups are information sharing, socializing, relating to people and groups external to the group, educating new members,

problem-solving groups
sets of individuals whose main task is to make decisions and provide policy recommendations

task-oriented groups
sets of individuals whose main goal is to work toward completing jobs assigned to them

defining roles, and reading minutes (Poole & Hirokawa, 1996). With that in mind, let's examine three critical assumptions that guide the theory:

- Conditions in groups promote high cohesiveness.
- Group problem solving is primarily a unified process.
- Groups and group decision making are frequently complex.

The first assumption of Groupthink pertains to a characteristic of group life: cohesiveness. Conditions exist in groups that promote high cohesiveness. Ernest Bormann (1996) observes that group members frequently have a common sentiment or emotional investment, and as a result they tend to maintain a group identity. This collective thinking usually guarantees that a group will be agreeable and perhaps highly cohesive.

What is cohesiveness? You may have heard of groups sticking together or having a high esprit de corps. These phrases essentially mean that the group is cohesive. **Cohesiveness** is defined as the extent to which group members are willing to work together. It is a group's sense of togetherness. Cohesion arises from a group's attitudes, values, and patterns of behavior; those members who are highly attracted to other members' attitudes, values, and behaviors are more likely to be called cohesive.

Cohesion is the glue that keeps a group intact. You may have been a member of a cohesive group, although it can be difficult to measure cohesiveness. For instance, is a group cohesive if all members attend all meetings? If all members communicate at each meeting? If everyone seems amiable and supportive? If group members usually use the word *we* instead of the word *I*? All of these? You know if you have been in a cohesive group, but you may not be able to tell others precisely why the group is cohesive.

Our second assumption examines the process of problem solving in small groups: It is usually a unified undertaking. By this, we mean that people are *not* predisposed to disrupting decision making in small groups. Members essentially strive to get along. Dennis Gouran (1998) notes that groups are susceptible to **affiliative constraints**, which means that group members hold their input rather than risk rejection. According to Gouran, when group members do participate, fearing rejection, they are likely "to attach greater importance to preservation of the group than to the issues under consideration" (p. 100). Group members, then, seem more inclined to follow the leader when decision-making time arrives. Taking these comments into consideration, then, the board

cohesiveness
the extent to which group members are willing to work together

affiliative constraints
refers to when members withhold their input rather than face rejection from the group

of directors at Melton may simply be a group who recognize the urgency associated with their financial dilemma. Listening to two board members, Elizabeth and Randy, therefore, is much easier than listening to seven. The two become leaders, and the group members allow them to set the agenda for discussion.

The third assumption underscores the nature of most problem-solving and task-oriented groups to which people belong: They are usually complex. In discussing this assumption, let's first look at the complexity of small groups and then at the decisions emerging from these groups. First, small group members must continue to understand the many alternatives available to them and be able to distinguish among these alternatives. In addition, members must not only understand the task at hand but also the people who provide input into the task. Almost forty years ago, social psychologist Robert Zajonc (1965) studied what many people have figured out for themselves: The mere presence of others has an effect on us. He offered a very simple principle regarding groups: When others are around us, we become innately aroused, which helps or hinders the performance of tasks. Nickolas Cottrell and his research team (Cottrell, Wack, Sekerak, & Rittle, 1968) later clarified the findings of Zajonc and argued that what leads people to task accomplishment is knowing that an individual will be evaluated by other individuals. Cottrell and his colleagues believe that group members may be apprehensive or anxious about the consequences that other group members bring to the group. In our opening, for instance, the board members are eager to listen to others with ideas because they do not offer ideas themselves. If any of the five nonspeakers were to openly challenge the ideas of either Elizabeth or Randy, they would be asked for their own ideas. Accordingly, they simply yield the floor to those who have a specific plan.

Marvin Shaw (1981) discusses additional issues pertaining to groups. He notes that a wide range of influences exist on a small group—namely, the age of the group members, the size of the group, the intelligence of the group members, the sex composition of the group, and the leadership styles that emerge in the group. Further, the cultural backgrounds of individual group members may influence group processes. For instance, because many cultures do not place a premium on overt and expressive communication, some group members may refrain from debate or dialogue, to the surprise of other group members. This may influence the perceptions of both participative and nonparticipative group members.

If group dynamics are both complex and challenging, why are people so frequently assigned to group work? Clearly, the answer rests in the maxim "Two heads are better than one." John Brilhart, Gloria Galanes, and Katherine Adams (2001) effectively argue this point:

> Groups are usually better problem solvers, in the long run, than solitary individuals because they have access to more information than individuals do, can spot flaws and biases in each other's thinking, and then think of things an individual may have failed to consider. Moreover, if people participate in planning the work of solving the problem, it is more likely that they will work harder and better at carrying out the plans. Thus, participation in problem solving and decision making helps guarantee continued commitment to those decisions and solution. (p. 6)

homogeneity
group similarity

Groups and group decisions, therefore, may be difficult and challenging, but through group work, people can achieve their goals more expeditiously and efficiently.

The relationship of this assumption to Groupthink should not escape you. Two issues merit attention. First, Clark McCauley (1989) indicates that those groups whose members are similar to one another are groups that are more conducive to groupthink. We term this group similarity **homogeneity**. So, as we mentioned earlier, the board of directors at Melton is homogeneous in their backgrounds—they are all part of literary inner circles. This similarity is one characteristic that can foster groupthink.

Second, group decisions that are not thoughtfully considered by everyone may facilitate groupthink. The quality of effort and the quality of thinking are essential in group decision making (Hirokawa, Erbert, & Hurst, 1996). For instance, Elizabeth and Randy clearly offer opinions on what they think is the best course of action for the company. Their charisma, their ability to communicate their vision, and their willingness to openly share their ideas with the group may be intoxicating to a board that is under pressure to resolve a financial dilemma. It's important to note that the two group leaders have clear ideas about how to proceed next, failing to identify alternative ways of looking at the problem.

What Comes Before: Antecedent Conditions of Groupthink

Janis (1982) believes that three conditions exist that promote groupthink: (1) high cohesiveness of the decision-making group, (2) specific structural characteristics of the environment in which the group functions, and (3) stressful internal and external characteristics of the situation.

Group Cohesiveness

We have already discussed cohesiveness and its effects in relation to the three assumptions that guide Groupthink. Cohesiveness is also an antecedent condition. You may be wondering how cohesiveness can lead to groupthink? One reason this may be perplexing is that cohesion differs from one group to another and different levels of cohesion produce different results. In some groups, cohesion can lead to positive feelings about the group experience and the other group members. Highly cohesive groups also may be more enthusiastic about their tasks and feel empowered to take on additional tasks. In sum, greater satisfaction is associated with increasing cohesiveness. Despite the apparent advantages, highly cohesive groups may also bring about a troubling occurrence: groupthink. Janis (1982) argues that highly cohesive groups exert great pressure on their members to conform to group standards. Janis believes that as groups reach high degrees of cohesiveness, this euphoria tends to stifle other opinions and alternatives. Group members may be unwilling to express any reservations about solutions. High-risk decisions, therefore, may be made without thinking about consequences. The risks involved in decisions pertaining to war, for instance, are high. The 2003 bombings in Iraq entailed high risks for the soldiers, for the refugees who left the country, and for those who stayed. However, the risks associated with the decision pertaining to where a homecoming committee should hold its meetings, for instance, are minimal in comparison to the bombing decision. You can see that risk varies across settings, and assessing risk is critical to the groupthink phenomenon.

Although people may feel confident that they will recognize groupthink when they see it, often they don't. Too much cohesion may be seen as a virtue, not a shortcoming. Imagine sitting around a conference table where everyone is smiling, affirming one another, and wanting to wrap things up. Would you be willing to stop the head nodding and slaps on the back and ask, "But is this the best way to approach this?" To paraphrase the words from a famous fairy tale, who wants to tell the emperor that he has no clothes? Cohesiveness, therefore, frequently leads to conformity, and conformity is a primary route to groupthink (Janis, 1982).

Structural Factors

Janis notes that there are specific structural characteristics, or faults, that cultivate groupthink. They include an insulation of the group, lack of impartial leadership, lack of clear procedures for decisions, and homogeneity of group members' backgrounds. **Group insulation** refers to a group's ability to be unaffected by the outside world. Many groups meet so frequently that they become immune from what takes place outside of their group experience. In fact, they may be discussing issues that have relevance in the outside world, and yet the members are insulated from its influence. People outside the group who could help with the decision may even be present in the organization but not asked to participate.

A **lack of impartial leadership** means that group members are led by people who have a personal interest in the outcome. An example of this point can be found in Janis's appraisal of President Kennedy's Bay of Pigs episode. When the president presided over the meetings on the Cuban invasion, Janis observes the following:

> [At] each meeting, instead of opening up the agenda to permit a full airing of the opposing considerations, he allowed the CIA representatives to dominate the entire discussion. The president permitted them to refute immediately each tentative doubt that one of the others might express, instead of asking whether anyone else had the same doubt or wanted to pursue the implications of the new worrisome issue that had been raised. (1982, p. 42)

The deference of group members to their leader can be observed in the words of Arthur Schlesinger, Jr., a member of Kennedy's policy group: "I can only explain my failure to do more than raise a few timid questions by reporting that one's impulse to blow the whistle on this nonsense was simply undone by the circumstances of the discussion" (cited in Janis, 1982, p. 39). It is apparent that Kennedy considered other opinions to be detrimental to his plan, and alternative leadership was suppressed.

group insulation
a group's ability to remain unaffected by outside influences

lack of impartial leadership
refers to when groups are led by individuals who put their personal agenda first

The final structural faults that can lead to groupthink are a **lack of decision-making procedures** and similarity of group members. First, some groups have few, if any, procedures for decision making; failing to have previously established norms for evaluation of problems can foster groupthink. In fact, Dennis Gouran and Randy Hirokawa (1996) suggest that even if groups recognize that a problem exists, they still must figure out the cause and extent of the problem. Groups, therefore, may be influenced by dominant voices and go along with those who choose to speak up. Other groups may simply follow what they have observed in previous groups, although their group may not have the same goals.

A second structural fault is the homogeneity of members' backgrounds. Janis (1982) notes that "lack of disparity in social background and ideology among the members of a cohesive group makes it easier for them to concur on whatever proposals are put forth by the leader" (p. 250). We alluded to this fault earlier in the chapter. Without diversity of background and experience, it may be difficult to debate critical issues.

Group Stress

The final antecedent condition of groupthink pertains to the stress on the group—that is, **internal and external stress** on the group may evoke groupthink. When decision makers are under great stress—whether imposed by forces outside the group or within the group—they tend to break down.

When stress is high, groups usually rally around their leaders and affirm their beliefs. Suppose you have only two weeks left before your class presentation. You and your group have been working on the project for about three months, and the project is worth about 25 percent of your final grade. The professor assigned the project during the first week of class and is expecting a top-notch presentation. Your group has a lot more work to do, however, and you know that other groups in the class seem to be much more prepared for their presentations. According to Janis, then, your group members may begin to feel the pressure to finish the project, may look to one another for moral support during this crisis time, and may be inclined to agree with ideas in order to get the project completed. Your group, we're sorry to say, is likely on its way to groupthink.

As you can see, groups frequently insulate themselves from outside criticism, form what ostensibly are close bonds, seek consensus, and ultimately develop groupthink. To get a clearer picture of what groupthink looks like, Janis (1982) identifies eight symptoms that can be assigned to three categories. We turn to these symptoms next.

Symptoms of Groupthink

Preexisting conditions lead groups to concurrence seeking. **Concurrence seeking** occurs when groups try to reach consensus in their final decision. When concurrence seeking goes too far, Janis contends, it produces symptoms of groupthink. Janis (1982) observes three categories of symptoms of groupthink:

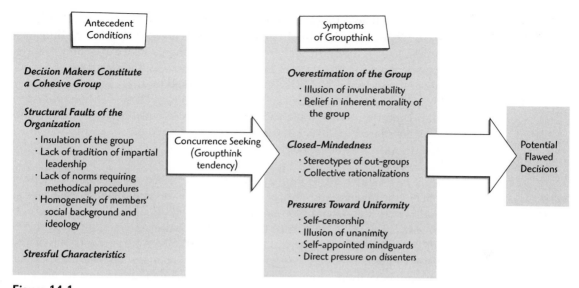

Figure 14.1
Antecedent Conditions and Symptoms of Groupthink
Source: Janis, Irving L., *Groupthink Psychological Studies of Policy Decisions and Fiascoes.* Second Edition.
Copyright © 1982 by Houghton Mifflin Company. Used with permission.

an overestimation of the group, closed-mindedness, and pressures toward uniformity. Figure 14.1 presents a model of the antecedent conditions and symptoms of groupthink.

To illustrate these symptoms, we will examine a policy decision that continues to resonate in the United States today: getting into the Vietnam war. This topic of war is especially important in a country that continues to be threatened with terrorism. Although the United States arguably had clear objectives to invade Afghanistan in 2001 in response to terrorist attacks, many people felt that the United States failed to have clear objectives for its presence in Vietnam. The U.S. involvement in the war was both supported and reviled. Protesters were prominent in the United States in the 1960s, arguing that Americans had no clear reason (that is, policy) for entering the war. We present Janis's (1982) interpretations of what took place when President Johnson's foreign policy advisors made decisions about bombing North Vietnam. Janis's comments are based on extensive discussions with individuals who were advisors or who were intimately aware of the group and its decisions, as well as on archival retrievals.

Overestimation of the Group

An **overestimation of the group** includes those behaviors that suggest that the group believes it is more than it is. Two specific symptoms exist in this category: illusion of invulnerability and a belief in the inherent morality of the group.

Illusion of Invulnerability The **illusion of invulnerability** can be defined as a group's belief that they are special enough to overcome any obstacles or setbacks. The group believes it is invincible. With respect to the Vietnam war,

overestimation of the group
erroneous belief that the group is more than it is
illusion of invulnerability
belief that the group is special enough to overcome obstacles

Janis explains that President Johnson's foreign policy group wanted to avoid peace negotiations because they did not want to be viewed as having little bargaining power. The group, therefore, was willing to take a risk and believed that selecting bombing targets in North Vietnam was a wise course of action. The group members based their decision to bomb on four issues: the military advantage, the risk to American aircraft, the potential to widen the conflict to other countries, and civilian casualties. Janis asks whether or not the group members shared the illusion that they were invulnerable when they confined their attacks to bombing targets.

Belief in the Inherent Morality of the Group   When group members have a **belief in the inherent morality of the group,** they are said to adopt the position that "we are a good and wise group" (Janis, 1982, p. 256). Because the group perceives itself to be good, they believe that their decision making must, therefore, be good. By embracing this belief, group members purge themselves of any shame or guilt, although they ignore any ethical or moral implications of their decision. Janis found it interesting that Johnson and his advisors were not concerned with bombing villages in North Vietnam; for them, the moral consequences did not outweigh the perception that the United States might be weak or fearful. In fact, the foreign policy council continued to encourage bombing of Hanoi even though peace initiatives were concurrently under way in Poland. A sense of moral certitude prevailed because the president and his advisors felt that North Vietnam would not negotiate a surrender.

Closed-Mindedness

When a group is **closed-minded,** it ignores outside influences on the group. The two symptoms discussed by Janis in this category are stereotypes of out-groups and collective rationalization.

Out-Group Stereotypes   Groups in crisis frequently engage in **out-group stereotypes,** which are stereotyped perceptions of rivals or enemies. These stereotypes underscore the fact that any adversaries are either too weak or too stupid to counter offensive tactics. For Johnson's advisors, enemy meant Communist. It was this stereotype that kept the advisors from seeing the enemy as people. Janis reasons that because the North Vietnamese were considered to be Communist enemies, this embodiment of evil justified the "destruction of countless human lives and the burning of villages" (p. 111).

Collective Rationalization   The fourth symptom of groupthink, **collective rationalization,** refers to the situation in which group members ignore warnings that might prompt them to reconsider their thoughts and actions before they reach a final decision. President Johnson and his staff were given a number of forewarnings—from intelligence agencies, among others—about the implications of bombing North Vietnam. Some in the intelligence community felt that bombing sites such as oil facilities would do nothing to erode Communist operations. Nonetheless, Johnson's group maintained its unified position on esca-

belief in the inherent morality of the group assumption that the group members are thoughtful and good, therefore the decisions they make will be good

closed-mindedness a group's willingness to ignore differences in people and warnings about poor group decisions

out-group stereotypes stereotyped perceptions of group enemies or competitors

collective rationalization situation in which group members ignore warnings about their decisions

lating the bombing. Janis (1982) observed that the men in Johnson's inner circle were very convinced of the importance of the Vietnam war to the United States. Therefore, revisiting their strategies to exit the war were out of the question.

Pressures Toward Uniformity

The **pressure toward uniformity** can be enormous for some groups. Janis believed that some groups who go along to get along may be setting themselves up for groupthink. The four symptoms in this category are self-censorship, an illusion of unanimity, the presence of self-appointed mindguards, and direct pressure on dissenters.

Self-Censorship   **Self-censorship** refers to group members' tendency to minimize their doubts and counterarguments. They begin to second-guess their own ideas. For those in President Johnson's foreign policy group, self-censorship was exhibited when group members dehumanized the war experience. These advisors would not allow themselves to think of the innocent people being killed because such thinking would only personalize the war. Janis argues that silencing one's own opposing views and using in-group rhetoric further bolster the decisions of the group.

Illusion of Unanimity   The sixth symptom of groupthink is an **illusion of unanimity,** which suggests that silence signifies consent. Although there were some advisors in Johnson's inner circle who felt differently about the Vietnam intervention, they were silent. This silence prompted others around the table to believe that there was consensus in planning and execution. For more information on the illusion of unanimity, review the Research Note, which explains a study focusing on this groupthink symptom.

Self-Appointed Mindguards   Groups in crisis may include **self-appointed mindguards**—group members who shield the group from adverse information. Mindguards believe that they act in the group's best interest. Walt Rostow, White House assistant, effectively played the role of mindguard in Johnson's group. Janis relates the following: "Rostow cleverly screened the inflow of information and used his power to keep dissident experts away from the White House. This had the intended effect of preventing the President and some of his advisers from becoming fully aware of the extent of disaffection with the war and the grounds for it" (1982, p. 119). Ironically, within the group, keeping the peace at the White House was more important than maintaining it in Vietnam.

Pressures on Dissenters   The final symptom involves pressuring any group member who expresses opinions, viewpoints, or commitments that are contrary to the majority opinion. Janis calls this **pressures on dissenters.** In his interviews with those within President Johnson's inner circle, Janis discovered that the group members formed a gentlemen's club, where mutual respect and congenial talk pervaded. Janis also later realized that these men often turned to one another for support and they were loyal to one another. Is it any wonder,

pressure toward uniformity
occurs when group members go along to get along

self-censorship
group members minimize personal doubts and counter-arguments

illusion of unanimity
belief that silence equals agreement

self-appointed mindguards
individuals who protect the group from adverse information

pressures on dissenters
direct influence on group members who provide thoughts contrary to the group's

Research Note

Cline, R. J. W. (1990). Detecting groupthink: Methods for observing the illusion of unanimity. *Communication Quarterly, 38*, 112–126.

Specifically examining the symptom of illusion of unanimity in Groupthink, Cline argues that despite the intuitive appeal of the theory, little empirical research exists that investigates Groupthink. She begins by discussing Groupthink as a theoretical model, identifying the conditions conducive to Groupthink as well as the major criticisms and revisions of the theory. Cline believes that Janis fails to define his terms clearly, and she is especially struck by the vagueness associated with the illusion of unanimity. Because she believes that this symptom can carry the most significance in group decision making, she proposes two hypotheses: (1) The deliberations of groupthink and nongroupthink groups display different distributions of agreements, disagreements, and other talk; (2) The deliberations of groupthink groups display proportionately simpler and fewer substantive agreements than the deliberations of nongroupthink groups.

Her method for investigating these hypotheses includes studying only males in the experimental groups. Cline reasons that because males dominated (almost exclusively) the case studies to which Janis refers in his research on Groupthink, studying males is appropriate. Using a measure of group cohesiveness, participants were first assigned to groups to discuss a problem, and the nongroupthink groups were compared with the groupthink groups. The problem that they were given (providing advice to their university regarding how to ensure high-quality employment for graduates) was distributed in oral and written form, and their comments were videotaped and audiotaped. Two category systems emerged from an analysis of comments. A coding reliability measure was introduced to assess the extent to which coders and the investigator agreed on placing observations into categories. High percentages of agreement (95%) were achieved.

The data were analyzed using a chi-square test, and the results indicated groupthink and nongroupthink groups differ in their use of the various types of statements (agreement, disagreement, or other). Groupthink groups expressed more agreement than nongroupthink groups. The second hypothesis was also supported in that Cline discovered that groupthink groups tended to use simpler and fewer substantiated agreements than nongroupthink groups.

Cline concludes that the results of her study are consistent with the theory of Groupthink. She states that "apparently the importance of making agreements and disagreements explicit is magnified during Groupthink" (p. 122). Cline concludes her article by identifying several directions for future research. She believes that researchers should focus on testing additional symptom-detecting coding systems to see whether they apply to Groupthink. She argues that "ultimately, researchers ought to be able to identify and validate specific communication interventions that can be employed by individuals in policy-making and decision-making groups" (p. 126).

then, that group members believed that everyone agreed to the course of action? This attitude would prevail, of course, considering that those who openly disagreed frequently resigned or were replaced (Janis, 1982). Robert McNamara, secretary of defense under President Johnson, was a dissenter who believed that bombing North Vietnam was the wrong way to get the enemy to the negotiation table. However, he was under much pressure to avoid disagreeing with the gentlemen's club.

It's All Around US

Thomas Jefferson once said that "difference of opinion leads to inquiry, and inquiry to truth." His words are still relevant, especially in foreign policy. Yet, considering that Janis studied national policy decisions, his research may leave you with the impression that groupthink cannot "hit home." As we've tried to illustrate in this chapter, however, groupthink is everywhere. In addition to the large-scale decisions we identified earlier, groupthink situations exist in decisions pertaining to Watergate, the Hubble Space Craft, the *Columbia* tragedy, and the Branch Davidian cult in Waco, Texas.

On a smaller scale, groupthink occurs all around us in "less critical" small groups. Decisions such as whether or not you will attend college, for instance, may have been prone to groupthink. If your parents went to college, your grandparents were college graduates, and you read literature stating that a college graduate will make twice as much money in a lifetime as a high school graduate, your decision to attend college may have been made without completely examining the situation. Presumably, your group is a cohesive group. Your family rationalized your attendance, the alternatives (such as going directly to work following high school) were not that appealing, and most likely, you didn't raise any objections. In other words, your small group was susceptible to groupthink.

This is but one example of the many episodes of groupthink in our daily lives. We may find conditions for groupthink with staff behind the deli counter at the grocery store, on a construction site with architects, contractors, and skilled laborers, or even at an investment club meeting where a group of people make decisions about what stocks to invest in.

Think Before You Act: Ways to Prevent Groupthink

Our discussion of Groupthink and the issues that accompany this theory may have given you the impression that all cohesive groups will indulge in groupthink. This is not true; Janis (1982) notes that cohesiveness is a necessary but not sufficient condition of groupthink. Nonetheless, frequently, when groups find themselves in highly cohesive situations and when decision makers are under great stress, groupthink may materialize. So how can group members learn to avoid groupthink? Janis (1982) offers a number of recommendations and

Table 14.1   Preventing Groupthink

RECOMMENDATION	ACTION
Require Oversight and Control	*Establish a parliamentary committee:* Develop resources to proactively monitor ongoing policy ventures; establish incentives to intervene; link personal fate to fate of group members.
Embrace Whistle-Blowing	*Voice doubts:* Avoid suppressing concerns about group processes; continue to disagree and debate when no satisfactory answers are given; question assumptions.
Allow for Objection	*Protect conscientious objectors:* Provide for group members' exits; do not play down the moral implications of a course of action; acknowledge private concerns about ethical issues in group.
Balance Consensus and Majority Rule	*Alter rules governing choice:* Relieve pressure on groups in minority positions; dissuade the development of subgroups; introduce a multiple advocacy approach to decisions.

Source: Adapted from 't Hart, 1990.

although his suggestions seem realistic, critics such as Paul 't Hart (1998) question whether Janis's recommendations inadvertently erode collegiality and foster group factionalism.

In order to avoid oversimplifying the groupthink problem, 't Hart (1990) has proposed four general recommendations for groups who may be prone to groupthink: (1) Require oversight and control, (2) embrace whistle-blowing in the group, (3) allow for objection, and (4) balance consensus and majority rule. We will look at each recommendation (Table 14.1).

First, 't Hart (1990) believes that one way to enhance group decision making is to impose some external oversight and control. He argues that groups need to hold key decision makers accountable for their actions; this should be done *before* groups begin their deliberations about issues. Accountability may take the form of a committee that serves to enforce control (vis à vis rules, governance procedures, decorum, and so forth). 't Hart theorizes that such committees prompt group members to challenge collective rationalizations and inaccurate perceptions. Reflecting on our example of President Johnson and his foreign policy group, 't Hart proposes that the inner circle of advisors was insulated from external oversight. As well, there were inadequate intragroup measures to improve the group's decisions on North Vietnam.

In addition to accountability, 't Hart (1990) proposes that **whistle-blowing** be embraced in a group's culture. That is, group members "should be encouraged to voice concerns rather than to voluntarily suppress them, to question assumptions rather than to accept them at face value, and to continue to disagree and debate when no satisfactory answers to their concerns are given by the rest of the group" (1990, p. 385). A whistle-blower in a real estate company, for in-

whistle-blowing
process in which individuals report unethical or illegal behaviors or practices to others

Groupthink is primarily concerned with how group members balance their need for cohesiveness with the need for arriving at a decision. In this chapter, we have presented symptoms of groupthink and identified some ways to prevent it. However, we have not addressed ways to help a group member out of groupthink once it's under way. As a group, identify possible remedies for assisting group members out of a groupthink situation. You may include a number of different group scenarios in your response.

stance, may be concerned with the unethical practices of a group of brokers. Perhaps the whistle-blower knows that some brokers are demanding a higher commission than what they are entitled to. The whistle-blowing may result in more ethical real estate transactions, but usually the whistle-blowers are silenced, rejected, passed over for promotion, and threatened. After all, if group members go along, they will get along. 't Hart advocates that groups protect whistle-blowers because groups frequently need dissenting voices when decisions have lasting and significant consequences.

A third suggestion by 't Hart (1990) is that groups allow **conscientious objectors,** or group members who refuse to participate in the decision-making process because it would violate their conscience. He reasons that groupthink causes groups to downplay the moral implications of their decisions, and if conscientious objectors know that they can exit a conversation based on moral or ethical grounds, then they may be more likely to speak up. Thus, these objectors may be able to raise doubts about the decision or even to protest it. President Johnson's decision to continue bombing Vietnam, therefore, may have been different if conscientious objectors had been allowed to introduce the moral implications of killing innocent people.

Finally, 't Hart (1990) advocates that groups not require consensus but work instead toward a majority of support. Because consensus demands that every group member agree on a decision, group members often feel pressured to consent (illusion of unanimity). 't Hart believes that groups should strive toward consensus but be prepared for majority support. If groups adopt this orientation, 't Hart believes, they will function more like teams. Janis (1982) discusses the fact that several members of President Johnson's inner circle of advisors (McNamara, Rusk, Bundy) wanted to temporarily halt the Hanoi bombings; we can only speculate how the passion for consensus impacted both the United States and the Vietnamese people.

conscientious objectors
group members who refuse to participate because it would violate personal conscience

Critique and Closing

Groupthink is a theory dedicated to understanding the decision-making process in small groups. Janis believes that groups frequently make decisions with profound consequences, and although he focused his efforts on foreign policy groups, the application of Groupthink terminology resonates to many other decision-making groups.

The theory of Groupthink is a heuristic undertaking; the theory and many of its elements have been employed in a number of studies and have enjoyed the attention of many communication and social psychology scholars (for example, Cline, 1990; Courtright, 1978; Hensley & Griffin, 1986; Pavitt & Johnson, 2002; Turner & Pratkanis, 1998). The theory has generated a number of different assumptions about group behavior, and Groupthink remains an important part of the literature on group decision making. Ramon Aldag and Sally Riggs Fuller (1998), for instance, state that "[groupthink] has stimulated research on group dysfunctions and encouraged viewing outcomes in problem-solving terms; shown how decision processes may be relevant to a wide range of situations; provided links to other literatures, such as stress and vigilance; and identified potentially important variables in group problem solving" (p. 57).

The scope of the theory is relatively narrow, and Janis (1972) cautions readers to keep in mind that the hypotheses he advances require more rigorous assessment before they can be fully accepted. Janis also limits his discussion to decision-making groups who are in crisis periods; he does not readily apply all of his thinking to all types of groups.

Critics, nonetheless, have been vocal in their assessments of Janis's theory. Jeanne Longley and Dean Pruitt (1980), for instance, criticize the validity of the theory. They argue that half of the symptoms of groupthink are not associated with concurrence seeking—a key feature of the theory. They charge: "A theory should be a logical progression of ideas, not a grab-bag of phenomena that were correlated with each other in a sample of six cases" (p. 80). Further, they note that Janis includes self-esteem in discussions about groupthink, yet he fails to mention self-esteem in his theory. In later writings of the theory, however, Janis (1982) addresses self-esteem as an antecedent to groupthink.

Concurrence seeking also concerns Alexander George (1993). He surmises that Janis may have unintentionally caused some to inappropriately extend his theory into other domains because Janis "did not succeed in impressing on his readers that concurrence seeking emerged under conditions of severe decisional stress" (p. 37). George remains concerned that there are no empirically observable signs of concurrence seeking in group decision making. He also wonders whether the symptoms are exclusive to concurrence seeking or whether the symptoms can occur without it.

Paul 't Hart (1991) critically observes that Janis first chose examples of foreign policy disasters and then applied Groupthink principles to see whether the decision process was affected by groupthink. 't Hart concludes that Janis consequently sacrificed objectivity in his methodology. Interestingly, however, 't Hart (1990) used similar protocol in his analyses of the 1940 Nazi invasion of Holland. For researchers, then, it appears that policy decisions are good places to find high-stress, high-risk group decision making.

Groupthink may be more intuitively appealing than empirically driven. The theory, however, continues to receive attention in research as well as in the popular press. In fact, Janis's thinking on groupthink has been quite influential in several fields of study, including communication, cognitive and social psychology, anthropology, and political science. Few would debate the failure of

Theory * Into * Practice

 T*I*P

Of the principles associated with Groupthink, the apparent presence of self-appointed mindguards was most prominent in the Salt Lake City, Utah, 2002 Winter Olympic Committee scandal. In a *New York Times* article, authors Jo Thomas and Kirk Johnson note that the committee recognized in 1991 that they would hire lobbyists and pay members of the National Bid Committee to influence the awarding of the 2002 Olympics to the Utah city. Documents from the staff of the Utah group show that there were checks paid directly to members of the International Olympic Committee and to their family members. As Thomas and Johnson state, the documents "portray an aggressive program to use money to secure votes by a city determined not to fail." Self-appointed mindguards—individuals who protect the group from any adverse or dissenting information—were apparently part of the committee. Although it was obvious to the media and the public at large that something was wrong with paying Olympic officials to influence their site selection, the committee did not find anything peculiar about it. As Thomas and Johnson note, "Senior members of Salt Lake City's bid committee have professed surprise and dismay . . . at revelations of improper payments and other inducements." In addition to the presence of self-appointed mindguards, it appears that there was also a belief in the inherent morality of the group.

The article continues by underscoring specific reasons why there was group insulation in the committee:

> The documents raise several questions that investigators say they are pursuing. Was the Salt Lake City board aware that its campaign had come to include cash payments to Olympic officials and their families? Did the board, which included experienced business executives, turn a blind eye to the activities of its staff? Or were those activities concealed by a staff that had struck out on its own?

Source: Thomas & Johnson, 1999.

TIP Follow-up

We now know that several members of the Salt Lake City committee illegally tried to bribe others to get the 2002 Olympics. We also know that the media was instrumental in bringing this to the attention of the public. Explore the role of the media in keeping groups from becoming immune to criticism.

the foreign policy fiascoes outlined by Janis: massive violence and casualties, loss of confidence in governmental decisions, and policymaking gone wrong. For these reasons alone, Janis is credited with helping us identify and examine one type of group decision-making problem.

Discussion Starters

1. What advice would you give the Melton Publishing board of directors before they meet to discuss their financial situation? Frame your advice with Groupthink in mind.

2. Janis and 't Hart have proposed a number of ways to prevent group-think. Provide at least two additional ways to avoid groupthink. Be specific and provide examples.

3. Have you ever been in a small group with too much cohesiveness? If so, did groupthink develop? If so, how did you know? If not, what prevented groupthink from occurring?

4. In his book, *Groupthink*, Janis asks if a little knowledge of groupthink is a dangerous thing. Why do you think Janis asks this question, and what are the consequences of knowing about groupthink? Incorporate examples into your response.

5. How widespread is groupthink? Do you believe that society is aware of the problem? Discuss your response using examples.

6. Apply principles of Groupthink to recent domestic and foreign policy decisions made by the United States.

Terms for Review

problem-solving groups
task-oriented groups
cohesiveness
affiliative constraints
homogeneity
group insulation
lack of impartial leadership
lack of decision-making
   procedures
internal and external stress
concurrence seeking
overestimation of the group
illusion of invulnerability

belief in the inherent morality of
   the group
closed-mindedness
out-group stereotypes
collective rationalization
pressure toward uniformity
self-censorship
illusion of unanimity
self-appointed mindguards
pressures on dissenters
whistle-blowing
conscientious objectors

Online Learning Center

Visit the Online Learning Center at www.mhhe.com/west2. Use the multiple-choice and true/false quizzes to help you prepare for exams, and the glossary, crossword puzzles, and flashcards to further your knowledge of key terms.

Adaptive Structuration Theory

Tim Vondrasek and Big City Tire Company

Big City Tire Company (BCT) is a multinational company with many employees. One of the employees, Tim Vondrasek, is a new production shift manager. Jeremy has been a production floor supervisor for twenty-five years. He has been assigned the task of showing Tim, his new boss, around for a couple of weeks.

On the first day, Jeremy takes Tim around the production floor to introduce him to the workers on his shift. When approached, all of the workers call Tim by his last name: "Good morning, Mr. Vondrasek." "It's great having you onboard, Mr. Vondrasek." Tim responds to the workers by saying, "Mr. Vondrasek is my father. Please, call me Tim."

As Tim and Jeremy walk away, Tim asks, "Why is everyone so formal?"

Jeremy responds, "That's company policy. We believe that addressing each other in this way establishes a sense of respect for our supervisors at Big City Tire."

Tim comes back with, "This is my shift, and I would really prefer if we do things my way."

Jeremy pauses, "Well, sure, this is your shift, but this is the way they have been taught to communicate with one another. After all, think of how confused they will be if they are allowed to address

you by your first name, and other managers expect to be addressed as 'Mr.' or 'Ms.'"

"You're right. I guess I'll have to get used to the workers calling me Mr. Vondrasek until I can get this straightened out. Besides, I don't want them to think that I am going against company rules or that I want to change things," Tim answers reluctantly.

Later that day, Tim talks to Angela Griffith, the human relations coordinator for BCT, about changing the policy to allow employees and staff to address one another less formally. Angela listens to Tim's ideas and agrees to call a meeting of the production shift managers to discuss the potential change.

At the meeting, the six production shift managers all voice their opinions about the change in policy. Janette, a fifteen-year veteran with BCT, points out, "Personally, I like having the workers address me more formally. It's tough enough being a female in this type of work environment, and I think this encourages respect in the workplace."

Darnell, who joined BCT only three years ago after graduating with his M.B.A. from Marden, counters by stating that he thinks the workers don't feel comfortable coming to him to discuss problems because of the formality and rules that are in place at BCT. "I think Tim's on to something here,"

This theory is based on the research of **Anthony Giddens, M. Scott Poole, David R. Seibold,** and **Robert D. McPhee.**

Darnell says. "We might be able to establish a friendlier work environment if we were less formal in how we address one another."

Wayne, who is a third-generation employee of BCT, argues, "You don't monkey with tradition. This is the way it's always been, and it's worked just fine for the past thirty years."

Angela listens to all their opinions, but the managers are split 50-50 on the policy change issue. She says, "Please, let's try to arrive at some sort of closure on this issue. Let's take a vote and see what you all think we should do." After voting numerous times, it is obvious that the issue will not be resolved. "Okay," says Angela, "I guess we'll keep the rule in place as it is for right now since you can't agree on this."

Anthony Giddens, a sociologist, first presented his Adaptive Structuration Theory in the 1970s (1979). In his research, Giddens describes how social institutions—groups and organizations, for instance—are produced, reproduced, and transformed through the use of social rules. The rules that are established by groups serve as guides for the behavior of their members. Just as blueprints are used to guide a contractor in building a structure, rules are used by members to serve as a template for the expectations of behavior and communication within the group. The influence of these rules extends beyond providing members with the expectations associated with group membership; group members maintain or alter the organization through subsequent interactions. In the opening example, those involved in the managers' meeting could potentially influence the structure of the organization through decisions made during the debate about the current rules. If they had voted to change the rule of formally addressing one another, the entire structure of the organization may have been altered.

Giddens (1979; 1993) views social structures as a double-edged sword. The structures and the rules that we create restrict our behavior. However, these same rules also enable us to understand and interact with others. We need rules to guide our decisions about how we are expected to behave. These rules may be either explicitly stated (such as grievance procedures that are outlined in an employee manual) or implicitly learned (such as respecting one another by providing each member of the group an opportunity to voice his or her opinion).

As Uncertainty Reduction Theory (Chapter 9) concludes, people tend to be uncomfortable with uncertainty. For example, students typically want to know the structure or the rules so they will understand what is expected of them in class. If a professor were to simply announce, "This semester we'll have a couple of tests, a few quizzes, and you'll need to do a project," students would likely be uncomfortable with that limited information. Students would want more specific instructions, or rules, regarding the page-length requirements of the papers, the due dates, and expectations for the exams—will they be multiple choice or essay, and will the final exam be comprehensive? Thus, the university and the instructor provide students with a blueprint of the rules for the class in the form of a course syllabus. In doing so, the structure is created and maintained. However, we also change the structure by adapting rules or creating new ones. Feedback from student evaluations may guide the instructor to alter the syllabus or the exam criteria in the future.

Groups and organizations are coordinated around various social interactions—for example, socializing new members through new employee receptions, arriving at decisions during conference calls, conducting meetings in person or via video-conference, or teaching new skills in employee training sessions. In Adaptive Structuration Theory, Giddens (1984) points out that the key to making sense of the communication that occurs in these groups and organizations is to examine the structures that serve as their foundation. He makes a distinction between the concepts of system (as we discussed in Chapter 3) and structure. The term **system**, in this sense, refers to the group or organization itself and the behaviors that the group engages in to pursue its goals. The term **structure** refers to the rules and resources that members use to create and sustain the system, as well as to guide their behaviors.

In the opening scenario, both the BCT organization and the group meeting of the shift managers can be viewed as a system. Their goal is to discuss the problem of using formal names to address one another, as well as to conduct the daily operations of the organization. To assist them in accomplishing their goals in an efficient manner, both of these systems have a formal set of rules that includes guidelines for how employees are expected to address one another at BCT as well as guidelines for allowing everyone to voice their opinion during the group meeting. These represent the structures of the group and organization. Tim Vondrasek is frustrated by the structure that restricts him from allowing his employees to communicate with him informally. The rules for interactions between supervisors and subordinates contradict what he has learned about building relationships from his past experiences as a supervisor. Angela employs rules for conducting open discussions about issues before any decisions about changes are made. Thus, BCT is created and guided by structures— rules that explain how to demonstrate respect for one another.

Marshall Scott Poole, David Seibold, and Robert McPhee (1985; 1996) extended Gidden's theory by establishing a research program that applied the theory to the processes involved in group decision making. Noting that groups were adapting certain rules to accomplish their decision making, Poole et al. expanded Giddens's work and conceptualized Adaptive Structuration Theory. "Adapting" Giddens's research was a challenging endeavor for the researchers. Issues such as the multiple steps or stages involved in group decisions and the importance of those decisions influenced Poole and his colleagues' interpretation and adaptation of this theory to group dynamics. **Structuration** in groups is described as "the process by which systems are produced and reproduced through members' use of rules and resources" (Poole, Seibold, & McPhee, 1996, p. 117). Poole et al. (1996) conclude that the key to understanding groups is through an analysis of the structures that underlie them. Rules and resources for communicating and arriving at decisions are typically learned from the organization itself and from members' past experiences and personal rules. These same rules and resources are reaffirmed as a result of their application or use; the group may decide to keep them in their existing format or alter them to meet the changing needs of the group.

In arriving at a decision on whether BCT should change its rule about having employees address one another formally, Angela enacts a rule of decision making that requires the group to discuss their viewpoints before making

system
a group or organization and the behaviors that the group engages in to pursue its goals
structure
the rules and resources used to sustain a group or organization

structuration
the production, reproduction, and transformation of social environments through rules and resources in relationships

changes. BCT may also have a rule for company meetings in which the majority vote decides the action that should be taken. If Angela fails to call a meeting of the managers to solicit their opinions, many of them might be displeased. Or, if Angela doesn't give everyone the opportunity to state an opinion on the rule while the rest of the group observes an unspoken rule to respect others' opinions (that is, challenge ideas but do not attack people), some of the group's members would be dissatisfied with the outcome of the meeting. After all, Janette depends on the rule to maintain her credibility and authority when interacting with her male employees. The fact that Angela follows the rule of calling a meeting to discuss the issue reaffirms the belief that this is a good guideline to follow in making decisions in the organization. However, some of the group's members may not be pleased with the decision to keep the rule in its current form, and they may invoke a new rule among their own teams in which they permit subordinates to address them in a less formal manner. Thus, the rule will be altered from its original state.

Structuration provides a useful foundation for examining the impact that rules and resources have on group decisions and organizational communication. In addition, it helps describe how these rules are altered or confirmed through interactions.

Assumptions of Adaptive Structuration Theory

To understand Adaptive Structuration Theory, we must first consider some of the basic assumptions that guide this theory.

- Groups and organizations are produced and reproduced through the use of rules and resources.
- Communication rules serve as both the medium for, and an outcome of, interactions.
- Power structures are present in organizations and guide the decision-making process by providing us with information on how best to accomplish our goals.

Giddens proposes that every action or behavior results in the production of something new—a fresh act. Each of the actions or behaviors in which a group or organization engages is influenced and impacted by the past. This history serves as a reference for understanding what rules and resources are required to operate within the system. When a group leader decides to conduct a vote using anonymous ballots because in the past it has been an effective way of allowing group members to privately indicate their opinion, history is influencing the rules for operation within that system.

It is important to remember that every time we communicate with someone we are establishing a new beginning by creating a new rule or expectation, by altering an existing rule, or by reaffirming rules that have been used in the past. In establishing these new beginnings, we still rely on past rules and expectations to guide our behaviors. Thus, we never escape our history—it continually influences our decisions for behavior in groups and organizations. It also influences changes that may take place in the system.

All of our communicative actions exist in relationship to the past. Giddens maintains that this structure (rules and resources) should not be viewed as a barrier to interaction but as a necessary part of the creation of the interaction. Remember: Our historical understanding of both the effective and ineffective rules may lead us to change the rules we use in future interactions with the group. Angela may have learned in past group meetings that members are not supportive of others' thoughts and opinions. She may have decided simply to state the problem and have group members vote on a potential solution without first soliciting the advice and opinions of group members. In this instance, historical rules would have been used as a reference for altering the group's rules in future interactions.

Recall the interaction between Tim and Jeremy. According to Adaptive Structuration Theory, each interaction that takes place between Tim and Jeremy is new and creates something unique in the structure of their future interactions. At the same time, Jeremy and Tim each bring to the interaction a set of rules (based on their history) and expectations that will guide and shape their communication with each other. In other words, as we observed in Chapter 1, their fields of experience become critical in their communication with one another. Jeremy addresses Tim by his last name, Mr. Vondrasek, the first time they meet. Tim responds by saying, "Please, call me Tim." Tim creates something new in the social structure by establishing a precedent (a new norm) of asking his subordinate to call him by his first name. This precedent is impacted by the past expectations that each man brings to the interaction. In other words, the experiences that Tim and Jeremy bring to the interaction influence their expectations for the structure that will guide their future communication. Tim believes that an open and relaxed communication style works, whereas Jeremy operates under a very different set of rules for interaction—formal address works best. In this case, Jeremy's rules for conversing serve the dual function of guiding his current behavior and setting expectations for future behavior.

Adaptive Structuration Theory also adopts the notion that rules simultaneously provide a guideline and constrain a group's behavior by invoking regulations based on previous expectations. The theory depicts the relationship between the regulations and expectations for communication behaviors and the structure of the group as one that is interdependent. The structure of a group includes a network of rules and resources that are used by its members in making decisions about what communication behaviors are expected. Although these rules are used to guide and encourage interaction among group members, they also serve the function of regulating interaction. As a result, the structure of the group may encourage, guide, or even restrict communication among members. Each specific communication act is not governed by one single rule but instead by a combination of rules. Some of these rules take precedence over others, and history influences the action that is enacted. The challenge lies in determining which rule will be the most efficient or productive in achieving the goals of the group or organization.

Let's take a moment to examine the previous statement a little more closely. Giddens (1979) asserts that a rule can only be truly understood "in the context of the historical development" as a whole (p. 65). So, Adaptive Structuration Theory assumes that to understand the rules of a social system, actors need to know at least some of the background resources that led to the rule. Perhaps if Tim were to investigate the origins of the rule for addressing superiors formally, he would have a better understanding of why this rule is currently enforced. There may have been a past incident when employees showed a blatant disregard for their supervisors by substituting nicknames for the informal first names that they were permitted to use in addressing their superiors. For example, Tim may discover that Wayne was called "Wayne the Pain" by his employees years earlier when the rule was not in existence. The company invoked more formal rules to help Wayne enhance his credibility and gain the respect of his employees. However, if after conducting his research Tim does not discover a satisfactory reason for the structure or rules that are in place, he may try to alter this particular rule. Not only may his refusal to attend meetings demonstrate a personal rule, but it may also be an attempt to exert his power in the group.

The third assumption guiding Adaptive Structuration Theory posits that power is an influential force in arriving at decisions in organizations. In Structuration Theory, **power** is perceived as the ability to achieve results—it enables us to accomplish our goals. Giddens (1979) believes that power is a two-way street; any time two people are engaged in communication with each other, both sources have a certain level of power that they bring to the interaction; even the subordinate has some power over the superior. Giddens adds, "subordinate positions in social systems are frequently adept at converting whatever resources they possess into some degree of control" (1979, p. 6). In other words, we all have power, but some have more than others. It is important to consider the role that rules play in this discussion of power. Based on the history of a group or organization, typically rules have been established to grant some members a particular form of power over other members. In BCT, a rule of the group is that Angela has the power to call a meeting of the members.

Tim wants his employees to call him "Tim" and not "Mr. Vondrasek." However, the structure—in this case a company norm—does not allow production floor workers to communicate informally. However, Tim's personal communication rule is that his workers should call him by his first name. His rule is based on his training, which taught him that in this situation it would be better for worker morale if subordinates were permitted to call him "Tim." Tim's decision to tell Jeremy to support keeping things the way they are for the time being is based not solely on one rule but also on Tim's power as a supervisor in this organization. In convincing Angela to call a meeting of shift managers to discuss the feasibility of adopting this rule at BCT, Tim is once again able to exert a sense of power that is granted to him as a member of the group and as a shift manager. However, we see that all of the shift managers bring power in one form or another to the group decision-making process. Darnell brings the power associated with his knowledge of managerial techniques as a result of his M.B.A. Wayne's extensive background and knowledge of the organization's history afford him a different type of power to bring to the discus-

power
imposition of personal
will on others

sion. Angela contributes the power associated with her position as human resources coordinator at BCT.

To summarize, when it comes to decision making, no one power structure in the web of organizational rules is more important than the other. Giddens views power as a two-way street, and the fact that an actor is even invited to participate in discussions and decision making indicates that he or she has a certain amount of power over others.

Elements of Adaptive Structuration Theory

To better understand Adaptive Structuration Theory, let's break it down into its component parts. We'll also look at the various elements that are central to understanding the complexity of rules and the influence they have on communication within systems. The elements we wish to discuss include agency and reflexivity, duality of structure, and social integration.

Agency and Reflexivity

Adaptive Structuration Theory is based on the simple notion that human activity is the source that creates and re-creates the social environment in which we exist. Thus, **agency** is defined as the specific behaviors or activities that humans engage in and that are guided by the rules and contexts in which interactions take place. **Agent** is a term that is used to refer to the person(s) who engage in these behaviors. For example, students serve as the agents who engage in the agency of attending classes at a university. The context of the classroom provides a blueprint of rules that the agents (students) are expected to follow. If the context of the class is a large lecture setting, the rules might dictate that the particular agency (behaviors) to be performed in asking a question be formal in nature (for example, raising one's hand to ask a question).

Poole, Seibold, and McPhee (1986; 1996) apply the notion of agency to their examination of small groups by proposing that a group's members are aware of and knowledgeable about the events and activities that take place around them. This awareness guides their decision to engage in particular behaviors (agency). Adaptive Structuration Theory states that groups and organizations engage in a process of reflexivity. Members of an organization are able to look into the future and make changes in the structure or system if it appears as though things are not going to work according to plan. **Reflexivity** essentially refers to the actors' ability to monitor their actions and behaviors. A large part of this reflexivity is based on the past rules and experiences of the agent. If a student in a large lecture class has discovered in the past that the professor does not have time to answer all the questions that are asked in a room filled with 400 classmates, reflexivity might guide a decision to visit the instructor during office hours to ask the question in a more private setting. An important element in the processes of agency and reflexivity is the ability of an actor to articulate the reasons for his or her choices of behavior. When an instructor asks a student why she didn't ask the question during class time, the student may

agency
behaviors or activities used in social environments

agent
a person engaging in behaviors or activities in social environments

reflexivity
a person's ability to monitor his or her actions or behaviors

respond that the number of questions being asked was too overwhelming for her to receive personal attention at that time. Thus, the agent has a level of consciousness about his or her behavior and can explain why a particular behavior was chosen over another.

In employing the processes of agency and reflexivity, organizations and groups reflect on the structures and systems that are in place, and members have the ability to explain the reasons for the behaviors as well as the ability to identify their goals. This awareness occurs on two levels. **Discursive consciousness** refers to the ability of a person to state his or her thoughts in a language that can be shared with other members of the organization. **Practical consciousness** refers to those actions or feelings that cannot be put into words.

For example, in the opening scenario, Tim may have been able to explain the reasons why he proposed the change in BCT's rule for supervisor–subordinate communication. It is likely that he will engage in reflexivity by describing his past supervisory experiences and the success that he had in relating to his former employees. Thus, he is using a level of discursive consciousness. What Tim may not be able to articulate is the practical consciousness, or the internal feelings, that he experiences in a formal work environment. Tim might find it difficult to explain the warm, familial feelings that emerge when his employees address him by first name. He also might not realize the fact that when they address him as "Mr. Vondrasek," he feels as though they are addressing his father or grandfather—maybe he does not perceive himself as being old enough to be addressed as "Mr." The agency, Tim's decision to address the issue, is based on his ability to reflect on previous experience.

Reflexivity also enables Tim to make a prediction about how these behaviors will impact employer–employee relationships in the future. Tim's ability to articulate his reasons for his attitudes and actions provide others with an understanding of why he pursues these goals. There are both personal rules and organizational rules that are influencing the decision of how employees should address supervisors in the organization. The task that Tim faces is in deciding whether to maintain the organizational rule or alter it to accommodate his personal rules.

Duality of Structure

Rules and resources fulfill dual functions in organizations. According to the principle of **duality of structure,** members of an organization depend on rules and resources to guide their decisions about the behaviors or actions that they will employ in their communication. However, the fact that the individual has chosen to either follow a rule or alter it will result in a change in that rule or resource in future communication interactions.

To better understand this relationship, let's explore the distinction between rules and resources. In Adaptive Structuration Theory, the term **rules** is used to refer to general routines that the organization or group has or follows in accomplishing its goals. Rather than viewing rules as strictly guidelines for *why* something must be done, it is more useful to view them as an instruction manual for *how* a goal may be accomplished. As was stated earlier in this chapter, these rules may be explicitly stated or implicitly learned.

discursive consciousness
a person's ability to articulate personal goals or behaviors

practical consciousness
a person's inability to articulate personal goals or behaviors

duality of structure
rules and resources used to guide organizational decisions about behaviors or actions

rules
general routines that the organization or group follows in accomplishing goals

Tim realizes that it would not be effective simply to change the communication expectations for his team without first consulting the other managers in the organization. He employs a personal rule that states that he should respect his colleagues and their reasons for organizational protocol. He accomplishes that goal by implementing this rule; he requests a meeting with the human resources coordinator. Next, a group meeting is called in order to give all shift managers the opportunity to express their opinions. The group's rule of giving every member equal voice in arriving at decisions is employed. Finally, a vote is taken to decide the preferred action of the majority of the group's members. Tim could initially decide to simply invoke his own rules and disregard the rules of the organization, but he decides to discuss the issue with his colleagues and supervisors in order to arrive at a decision. A vital element in understanding why some rules are enforced over others lies in understanding the power that certain agents have in the decision-making process.

Resources refers to the power that actors bring to the group or organization. This power is influential because it leads an individual to take action or initiate change. There are two types of resources that an organization can employ. **Allocative resources** refers to the material assistance generated by an organization to help the group in accomplishing its goal. Suppose a group of university students wants to have access to a facility where they can exercise during their breaks between classes or during their "off" time. Some of the group's members decide to write a proposal to the administrators of the university and to provide them with a list of activities that they are willing to undertake in order to raise some of the money if the university will match the funds that are collected. Thus, a plan for providing allocative, or material, resources has been established.

Authoritative resources refers to the interpersonal characteristics that are employed during communication interactions. Interpersonal communication is the primary means through which an organization is able to engage in the process of activity. One of the primary goals of interpersonal communication is to influence others.

John French and Bertrand Raven (1959) identify five bases of social power that can be used to describe the various types of authoritative resources employed in groups and organizations. Although power often has a negative connotation, there are positive outcomes of power that are gained from interacting with others. Each power type is explained below and in Table 15.1.

Reward Power **Reward power** is based on a person's perception that another has the ability to provide positive reinforcements. These rewards may come in the form of praise, material rewards, or simply removal of negative aspects of the system. Tim's employees may decide to accommodate his request to address him by first name because they perceive him as having power to promote them or give them raises. If this is the case, reward power is a resource that is impacting communication in the organization.

Coercive Power If Tim's employees fear that they will be demoted or fired as a result of failing to comply with his wishes to establish relationships on a first-name basis, coercive power may be influencing decisions and communication.

resources
attributes or material goods that can be used to exert power in an organization
allocative resources
material assistance used to help groups accomplish their goals

authoritative resources
interpersonal assistance used to help groups accomplish their goals

reward power
perception that another person has the ability to provide positive outcomes

Table 15.1 Power Type as a Resource in an Organization

TYPE OF POWER	DEFINITION
Reward	Chris has the ability to provide something of value to Pat.
Coercive	Chris can deliver punishment to Pat.
Referent	Chris achieves agreement or compliance because Pat respects Chris and desires to be like Chris.
Legitimate	Chris exerts control over Pat because of Chris's title or position.
Expert	Chris possesses special knowledge or expertise that Pat needs.

coercive power
perception that
another person has
the ability to enact
punishment

Coercive power is power that is based on the expectation that an individual has the ability to exact punishment. A person may comply with another's request simply to avoid negative consequences such as losing credibility in front of one's co-workers or getting a rotten work schedule.

referent power
perception that an-
other person has the
ability to achieve
compliance because
of established per-
sonal relationships

Referent Power Perhaps Tim's employees choose to address him by first name primarily because he is a friendly, likable person who demonstrates a genuine interest in his workers. Then, the resource guiding the communication decisions is due to **referent power,** or the ability of an individual to engage compliance based on the fact that personal relationships have been established between the two interactants.

legitimate power
perception that an-
other person has the
ability to exert
influence because of
title or position

Legitimate Power Recall Tim's comment to Jeremy: "This is my shift, and I would really prefer if we do things my way." When a person exerts influence on the basis of his or her position or title, **legitimate power** is being exerted. If shift managers decide to retain the current communication rules simply because they respect Wayne and his tenure with the company, legitimate power is a resource guiding their decision. This type of power is associated with one's right to exert influence.

expert power
perception that an-
other person has the
ability to exert
influence due to spe-
cial knowledge or
expertise

Expert Power **Expert power** refers to one's ability to exert influence over others based on the knowledge or expertise that one possesses. In the opening scenario we learned that Darnell holds an M.B.A. from Marden and has extensive knowledge about effective managerial communication strategies in the workplace. If the shift managers decide to base their decision to adopt a less formal environment in the workplace on Darnell's knowledge, his expert power serves as a resource in the decision.

If we were to view power as a resource, as defined in Adaptive Structuration Theory, duality of structure could be applied to explain how power was used in generating action in the group as well as in determining if power was altered or changed as a result of the action that was taken. For example, many students have assigned expert power to a teacher based on their previous experiences in classes with knowledgeable instructors. However, if an instructor enters a classroom and employs profanity or only provides examples based on

supermarket tabloids, those same students may alter their personal rule that all teachers possess expert power; they may decide to employ a rule in the future that requires them to be tentative in their decision to assign power to an instructor. In that case, duality of structure has taken place.

Social Integration

The third concept, **social integration,** refers to the reciprocity of communication behaviors among persons in interactions. It refers to an ongoing process whereby members of an organization or group become acquainted with one another and form expectations based on previous impressions or information that is learned. If group members are interacting with one another for the first time, their knowledge of one another will be quite limited, and the process of social integration will be much more extensive. However, as group members become acquainted with one another, the social integration process relies heavily on structures that are recalled from past interactions.

Each interactant brings his or her own background, experiences, and expectations to a communication event. However, as a member of an organization or group, an individual brings knowledge to the situation that is subject to change based on the influence of both internal and external sources. As we gain a sense of how we and others fit into the group, we begin to communicate and act in ways that indicate the roles we expect each member to fulfill. Expectations for patterns of behavior are established, but these expectations could potentially change as the members of the group interact and evolve. Recall the meeting of the shift managers. Because Tim is the newest member of the group, the other shift managers may be uncertain about what type of power to attribute to him as he presents his ideas. The same applies to Tim's interactions with his subordinates. As Tim and the others engage in subsequent interactions, his view of himself and others' views of Tim will evolve.

social integration
reciprocity of communication behaviors in interaction

Application of Time and Space

We now explain the impact of time and space on group decision making in our discussion of Adaptive Structuration Theory. Structures themselves are viewed as "non-temporal and non-spatial," and, as Giddens (1984) maintains, to represent action and structure as interdependent "we must grasp the time-space relations inherent in the constitution of all social interaction" (p. 3). The actual communication or interaction that takes place in the group can be examined as

Theory Application in Groups (TAG)

In small groups, talk about how you would describe Adaptive Structuration Theory to a family member. What would you tell that person to demonstrate the importance of the theory in everyday life? What is especially critical to talk about in a society plagued by ethical lapses by organizational leaders?

existing in real time and as taking place in real space. We hear the message as it occurs in a context. However, we need to look deeper in determining the factors that have motivated the message that is verbally communicated. The structures—or rules and resources—that influence these interactions are the result of an actor's memory or thoughts. One makes reference to past experiences or looks ahead to potential consequences in determining the action or communication that should occur. Thus, these reference points do not exist in the concepts of time and space.

Essentially, space is viewed as a contextual element that has meaning for the various members of a group or organization. The elements of time and space are factors that enable us to engage in communication. One's view of his or her tenure in a group spans both time and space and influences the decisions that are made. For example, it is not likely that a single event or a single location has solely influenced Tim's action to request a change in the company's policy. Rather, it is a series of experiences and references that are the result of his own managerial history—and perhaps even his own experience as an employee in an organization—that have influenced his choice of action.

In addition to understanding the influence that space and time have on the structures that are employed in an organization, one must also consider the dynamics of group interaction. How do first impressions affect the rules and resources (structures) that are implemented by members in their communication with others? The concept of social integration allows us to consider this element in comprehending yet another dimension of the complex activity of group decision making.

Adaptive Structuration and Group Decision Making

Poole, Seibold, and McPhee (1985; 1996) are credited with the movement to study structuration in the context of group communication. They identify two variables that impact the ability of a group to arrive at a decision effectively. These factors allow the group to determine whether it has the resources and rules (structures) that are essential to arriving at a decision or to accomplishing a goal.

objective factors characteristics (e.g., clarity, rules) associated with achieving a group task

Objective factors are used to describe the attributes associated with the task. Is the information easily understood? Are there any guidelines or rules that must be followed in pursuing a solution or decision? What are the value or moral implications that need to be considered in arriving at a decision? In the case of the decision before the BCT shift managers, the range of options is relatively limited: Should they revoke the rule for the use of formal address in the organization? Although their options are limited in scope, the shift managers also need to consider the long-term implications of their decision: What organizational values are at stake if this communication expectation is changed? Will employees still demonstrate respect for their supervisors? Are there implications for other divisions in BCT if the workers are allowed to make this change?

Group factors, associated with the group itself, also impact the decision-making process. These factors are broken down into two dimensions: group-task factors and group-structural factors. **Group-task factors** are those resources that the group has available for accomplishing the task or goal. Are there members of the group who have experience or expertise that will assist in predicting the potential outcomes of the decision? Does the organization or group have sufficient resources to implement the decision? When the shift managers meet to decide on communication issues at BCT, there is a variety of experience and expertise that could be offered by the group's members. Tim could share his personal experiences, Darnell could talk about academic research on the consequences and benefits of informal address, and Wayne could offer some background information on why the policy was established in the first place.

The other group aspects that should be considered are the **group-structural factors** that impact a decision. Is the structure of the group one that promotes a majority rule? What types of power are represented by the members, and how will this power influence decisions? Does the group typically arrive at consensus easily, or is this a lengthy process? Angela demonstrates the structure of BCT's decision-making procedures when she declares that the group needs to resolve the issue and achieve closure on the topic. She encourages the group to vote and states that the majority vote will decide the outcome. Thus, decisions are reached in this group structure very quickly.

In applying Adaptive Structuration Theory to research in group decision making, Poole and Jonelle Roth (1989) created a typology to describe the various paths that groups employ in arriving at decisions. These include a unitary path, a complex cyclic path, and a solution-oriented path. When applying the *unitary path,* the group follows essentially the same rules or steps to arrive at solutions for a variety of problems. A group that adopts the philosophy of "let's just vote and see what the majority of the group want" follows a unitary path. If a decision needs to be reached quickly and efficiently, the group may have to rely on a unitary path.

Groups that follow a *complex cyclic path* engage in back-and-forth interactions. The communication serves the function of comparing potential solutions for the problem as it has been defined. Often this requires that the group revisit the way in which it has operationalized the problem. If Angela were to encourage the shift managers to consider the rules that were coming into play in arriving at a decision, reevaluate how they fit with the problem, and continue a cycle of interaction to discuss the relationship between the resources and the

group factors
group-related characteristics associated with achieving a group task

group–task factors
individual group resources available to a group to achieve its task

group-structural factors
systemic resources available to a group to achieve its task

problem, a complex cyclic path would be adopted. It is up to the group to decide what resources it has available to allocate in a more complex decision-making process.

Finally, some groups focus strictly on the *solution-orientation path,* with little or no regard for engaging in problem analysis. The goal of the group is to arrive at a solution that is acceptable to the group's members and implement it. Unlike the unitary path, the solution-orientation path may employ a variety of methods to arrive at a decision, but the primary goal is not to understand the root of the problem. Rather, the goal is to arrive at a solution that will meet the needs of the group. If Angela were to simply encourage the shift managers to share their solution to the problem and ask them to decide on the most efficient solution, a solution orientation would be adopted. Various methods might be used in arriving at an agreeable solution, which distinguishes this approach from the unitary approach.

Critique and Closing

Organizations and groups are a central part of our lives. Consider the number of groups and organizations to which you currently belong. It has been estimated that those employed in organizations may spend as much as 85 percent of their time in groups or team meetings. Adaptive Structuration Theory is useful in providing an understanding of how the structures that are created in groups influence communication and decisions. Further, it is useful in examining the role that power plays in the development of groups and in the accomplishment of their goals. Scholars who have studied structuration in groups and organizations have emphasized the importance of understanding the relationship between the inputs into groups (resources and rules) and the outputs (feedback). However, it is important not only to understand the existence of resources but also to examine how these resources evolve and change as a result of the communication activity that takes place within the group in making decisions.

Adaptive Structuration Theory can be applied to virtually all social settings and virtually all communication interactions. The areas of communication that have applied the theory with the most success are organizational communication and group decision making. A vast amount of research has examined structuration's impact on the atmosphere of an organization (e.g., Scott, Corman, & Cheney, 1998; Sherblom, Keranen, & Withers, 2002; Kirby & Krone,

Research Note

Sherblom, J. C., Keranen, L., & Withers, L. A. (2002). Tradition, tension, and transformation: A structuration analysis of a game warden service in transition. *Journal of Applied Communication Research, 30,* 143–162.

Applying several of the principles of Adaptive Structuration Theory, Sherblom and his colleagues set out to discover the role of the game warden in the state of Maine. They begin by noting that the job is quite involved in that a warden is responsible for checking weapons, inspecting coolers, examining boating and hunting licenses, and other law-related activities. In all, about 50,000 checks are made on people in the state.

In order to unravel the complexities of the job and its characteristics, the research team set out to examine the job of game warden. After completing a 12-week observation program of wardens to understand the culture, the researchers developed a number of conclusions which underscore that the service must balance between tradition and transformation.

First, Sherblom and his team found the warden service to have a "highly centralized" and "military style chain of command and titles" (p. 146). Second, game wardens represent a homogenized group of individuals. There is little "visual diversity" in terms of race, ethnicity, and sex. The researchers found a tension in that there is increasing pressure from outside the service to hire people who are more diverse than the individuals currently employed. Although the application and screening process are "highly selective," a need still exists to find more diversity. A structuration analysis revealed several interesting points.

A tension in agency and reflexivity exists in the service. The tradition of being "tough and rugged" and understanding wildlife now appears to be substituted with the need to have the ability to arrest drug users (not necessarily a violation requiring rugged individualism). Wardens do work with landowners—to rid them of rabid foxes, for instance—however, wardens now report that they have become sensitive to drug use in the wild as well. This, according to the researchers, requires an expansion beyond the traditional role and requires "different interactions with the public" (p. 152).

Duality of structure also exists in the game warden service. The traditional view of the warden working for hours, sometimes days, in isolation is slowly being transformed into a game warden receiving memos from "headquarters that are not relevant to their work in the field" (p. 153). Tensions and conflicts are also created when decision makers count the number of citations, inspections, and prosecutions in performance appraisals. The tension, then, between an independent game warden and a centralized chain of command becomes apparent.

The third feature of Adaptive Structuration Theory, social integration and institutional reproduction, has also undergone transformation. The traditional view of the warden as connected to family and community is being reconfigured with a perception of the warden as a person trained in law enforcement. Recently hired wardens now have more education (some with master's degrees) and more diverse cultural backgrounds.

Finally, the time and space component of the theory has been found to exist with game wardens. For example, Sherblom and his team found that by tradition, most wardens worked more than 40 hours a week and significantly more during hunting season. The transformation in the job includes working only 40 hours as set by legislative directive; if they work longer, they may not get paid for their service. Also, when the warden takes a day off, the space obligations become blurred. Sherblom et al. write: "One warden's day off means a larger territory coverage and more driving for another warden resulting in less time in the field attending to job priorities, longer response times, and more fuel and vehicle expense" (p. 158).

Clearly, the warden has undergone transformation from a position steeped in New England tradition. Sherblom, Keranen, and Withers provide a compelling analysis using several of the elements of Adaptive Structuration Theory. Their research is instrumental in understanding the practical value of the theory.

T*I*P

Theory * Into * Practice

An article in *Fortune* describes the changes that are planned for Boeing, whose products are responsible for nearly three-fourths of all air travel. The corporate giant holds the distinction of being the largest U.S. exporter as well as the leading supplier for NASA and the U.S. government. Its total employee population exceeds 230,000 workers who are directly associated with the company, with estimates of more than 600,000 additional affiliates through other related companies.

In 1997, Boeing experienced severe financial difficulties. Production at two assembly plants was halted, and a total of $1.6 billion was charged against its earnings for 1997. Its leading competitor was steadily acquiring Boeing's clients, and the stock picture was bleak—shares were down more than 33 percent from the previous year.

By the end of the year, analysts were predicting that Boeing's chief executive, Phil Condit, a veteran with the company, would be replaced by a man who had managed McDonnell Douglas, a company that Boeing had merged with earlier in the year (Condit stayed on for several years). Condit realized at the time that some decisions needed to be made quickly, and he conducted a retreat of his senior staff members to discuss options. The group arrived at four goals: (1) Alleviate the production problems, (2) increase the higher-profit divisions of defense and space clients, (3) regain the credibility and confidence of investors on Wall Street, and (4) eliminate the paternalistic organizational culture that had dominated Boeing.

Changes that were enforced included a ban on the use of the term *heritage employees* to refer to those who had tenure with Boeing. The reasoning behind this decision to eliminate a family atmosphere was that it is difficult to fire family for poor performance; the focus of Boeing should be on performance, not seniority. The overall goal was to change Boeing's organizational atmosphere from one that is warm and fuzzy to one that is tough and conservative.

Source: Labich, 1999.

TIP Follow-up
Discuss how Condit utilized the concept of reflexivity with Boeing employees. Can reflexivity be effectively used by both supervisor and employee? Explain.

2002) and its effects on small groups (Seyfarth, 2000). The theory, therefore, has heuristic value. The Research Note features an analysis of group decision making as viewed through the lens of Adaptive Structuration Theory.

Stephen Banks and Patricia Riley (1993) point out that some communication scholars are frustrated by Adaptive Structuration Theory because it is difficult to read and understand; in addition, some claim that the theory lacks parsimony. Banks and Riley (1993) present many concepts as they examine the intricate process of how organizations and groups structure their communication and arrive at decisions. Their advice to those who are researching this theory in an attempt to understand organizations and groups is to "begin at the beginning" (p. 181). Thus, they recommend that we break down a group into its various parts in order to completely understand the dynamics that influence communication and decision making. This requires insight and understanding of the historical rules that are brought into the group by each of the members—and this is an extremely difficult task to accomplish. Further, Banks and Riley suggest that scholars resist the temptation to apply preestablished categories in explaining how organizations and groups are developed and how they experience change. The reason for this suggestion lies in the evolutionary nature of the resources and rules that guide the organization, making the system unique.

The challenge for researchers is to continue their study on the dynamics of Adaptive Structuration Theory to describe its applicability in real-life situations. Although Adaptive Structuration Theory is intimidating due to the vast number of elements that must be considered in order to understand the group or organizational communication process, it is useful in exploring the complexities involved in the evolution of groups and organizations.

Discussion Starters

1. Recall a time when you were involved in a group similar to the Big City Tire Company—a time when a decision had to be made. What were some of the rules that influenced the process of decision making? Were the rules changed as a result of the decision that was reached or the process that was followed in arriving at that decision? If so, how?

2. One of the assumptions of this theory is that power structures are present in groups and guide the decision-making process by providing us with information on how to best accomplish our goals. Discuss the potential positive and negative implications of power as an element of structuration.

3. Giddens proposes that structure (rules and resources) should not be viewed as a barrier to interaction but as a necessary part of the creation of the interaction. Do you agree or disagree with this position? Defend your answer.

4. Identify elements of other communication theories that are evident in the Adaptive Structuration approach to groups and organizations.

5. Adaptive Structuration Theory proposes that structures themselves should be viewed as being nontemporal and nonspatial. Discuss the significance of this idea. Provide an example from your own experience of the influence of time and space in a group or organization.

6. How would you explain your family using any of the principles of Adaptive Structuration Theory?

Terms for Review

system	agency
structure	agent
structuration	reflexivity
power	discursive consciousness

practical consciousness
duality of structure
rules
resources
allocative resources
authoritative resources
reward power
coercive power

referent power
legitimate power
expert power
social integration
objective factors
group factors
group-task factors
group-structural factors

Online Learning Center

Visit the Online Learning Center at www.mhhe.com/west2. Use the multiple-choice and true/false quizzes to help you prepare for exams, and the glossary, crossword puzzles, and flashcards to further your knowledge of key terms.

CHAPTER 16

Organizational Culture Theory

Fran Callahan

As an employee of Grace's Jewelers, Fran Callahan knows that her job is unlike those of her friends'. The company employs about 150 people throughout its twenty-six stores in the southeastern United States and targets primarily teenage girls who frequent malls. Its founder, Grace Talmage, makes it a point to visit employees like Fran each week, helping them to feel good about working in such a small company.

Fran's relationship with Grace has always been quite cordial. Why wouldn't it be? She receives excellent commission rates and a reasonable health-care package (including dental and vision care) and gets along superbly with her supervisor. In addition, Fran and the other employees are able to wear casual clothing to work, which makes them the envy of other workers in the mall. All of this may explain why Fran has worked for the company for almost nine years and why she had no plans to leave—until now.

After thirty-three years in the business, Grace decided it was time to sell the business and retire. Because of the profits that Grace has shown over the years, Jewelry Plus, a large retail jewelry store, decided to bid for the small chain. Although Grace did not want to sell to such a retail giant, their bid was simply too good to pass up. In the end, she decided to sell her business, much to the disappointment of her employees. Fran was especially concerned after hearing gossip about the larger company's treatment of its employees and its way of handling day-to-day operations. She privately wondered how much would change once Grace sold the stores. She needed the job, though, and decided to stay on.

Fran's instincts were right. Once the company's transition was completed, she had to undergo a "new employee" orientation, which meant standing in front of all of the new employees and explaining why she had applied to the company. Among the new company policies were new dress codes and a new policy for store exchanges. Fran could no longer wear casual clothing; instead, she had to wear a company uniform and black shoes with low heels.

With respect to store exchanges, company policy changed from "complete satisfaction or 100% money-back guarantee" to "product must be returned within 10 days with register receipt." Although Fran felt that this new policy would turn many customers away, the success of Jewelry Plus was proof enough that it had worked in the past.

Finally, with the new company, her health benefits no longer included dental or vision coverage. This lack of coverage was grist for the gossip mill. The story that Fran heard during her orientation was that an employee actually lost two back teeth because she couldn't afford the dental bills!

This theory is based on the research of **Clifford Geertz, Michael Pacanowsky,** and **Nick O'Donnell-Trujillo.**

With all the changes in store policies, dress codes, and company philosophies, Fran and a number of her co-workers felt overwhelmed. In fact, many of Fran's co-workers, with whom she had worked over the past nine years, quit their jobs. As a single parent, however, Fran felt that she couldn't resign.

On top of all that, her new boss was a disaster! Fran and her co-workers nicknamed him "The Shadow" because he was right behind them as they waited on and rang up their customers. Having her supervisor watch everything she did was annoying and seemed pointless to Fran, especially considering the fact that most of her customers were teenagers and that they were fickle in their purchasing behaviors.

Despite these concerns, Fran went to the company's first picnic. She didn't really want to, but she felt that she had to give the company a chance. As she and her old and new co-workers drank ice tea and ate hot dogs, they seemed to bond. Former employees of Grace's Jewelers told the workers of the retail giant about the way things used to be. They seemed to be genuinely interested in hearing about people like Gabby, the 70-year-old retiree who wouldn't stop talking to customers. There was a great deal of laughing about the old times.

The day ended in quite a different way than Fran had envisioned. She made a few friends, reminisced about the past, and felt a bit more comfortable with her future. Although she knew that her boss would be difficult to deal with, Fran decided that she would try to make the most out of her job. At the very least, she thought, she had some people in whom to confide.

Once you graduate from college, it's likely that many of you will work for an organization. Organizational life is characterized as much by change as it is by anything else. Change is frequently marked by excitement, anxiety, uncertainty, frustration, and disbelief. These emotions are especially acute during stressful times, for example, when companies lay off their employees.

Go to any bookstore on campus or at the mall, and you're sure to see a number of books on organizational life. This pop culture approach to the world of corporate America is everywhere. Some authors tell us that there are *10 Easy Ways to Get a Raise* or that there are *8 Safe Steps to Being Promoted*. Other authors have made millions touting the importance of *Communicating with Difficult People* and *Working to Live and Living to Work*. Most of these books center on what people can do to make their lives easier in the workplace. The problem, however, is that organizational life is very complex. It's safe to say that there are few "easy ways" to anything in organizations.

To understand organizational life beyond pop culture—including an organization's values, stories, goals, practices, and philosophies—Michael Pacanowsky and Nick O'Donnell-Trujillo (1982; 1983) conceptualized Organizational Culture Theory. Pacanowsky and O'Donnell-Trujillo feel that organizations can be best understood using a cultural lens, an idea originally proposed by anthropologist Clifford Geertz. They believe that researchers are limited in their understanding of organizations when they follow the scientific method, a process we outlined in Chapter 4. According to Pacanowsky and O'Donnell-Trujillo, the scientific method is constrained by its task of measuring, rather than discovering. Pacanowsky and O'Donnell-Trujillo (1982) argue that Organizational Culture Theory invites all researchers "to observe, record,

"I don't know how it started, either. All I know is that it's part of our corporate culture."

and make sense of the communicative behavior of organizational members" (p. 129). They embrace the "totality or lived experience within organizations" (Pacanowsky, 1989, p. 250). The theorists paint a broad stroke in their understanding of organizations by stating that "culture is not something an organization has; a culture is something an organization *is*" (Pacanowsky & O'Donnell-Trujillo, 1982, p. 146). Culture is communicatively constructed by organizational practices, and culture is distinct to an organization. For the theorists, understanding individual organizations is more important than generalizing from a set of behaviors or values across organizations. These thoughts form the backdrop of the theory.

Think about the types of organizations to which you now belong. They may vary in scope and size and may contain a number of practices that are unique to the organization. For instance, one organization that we all have in common is an academic one—a college or university. You've heard and perhaps shared stories about certain professors and classes to take or to avoid. There are various rites of passage in college, such as freshman orientation, fraternity or sorority rush, and cafeteria food. Practices such as advising and internships also characterize most institutions of higher education.

It is clear that the essence of organizational life is found in its culture. In this sense of the word, *culture* does not refer to the variety of races, ethnicities, and backgrounds of individuals, a perspective we discussed in Chapter 2. Rather, culture is interpreted to mean the essence of an organization. According to Pacanowsky and O'Donnell-Trujillo (1983), culture is a way of living in an organization. Organizational culture, therefore, includes all of the symbols (actions, routines, conversations, and so forth) and the meanings that people attach to these symbols. Cultural meaning and understanding are achieved through the interactions employees and management have with one another. We begin our discussion of Organizational Culture Theory by first interpreting culture and then presenting three assumptions of the theory.

The Cultural Metaphor:
Of Spider Webs and Organizations

organizational culture
the essence of organizational life

The origin of the word *culture* is interesting. Culture originally referred to preparing the ground for tending crops and animals. It was interpreted as fostering growth. Pacanowsky and O'Donnell-Trujillo (1982) believe that organizational culture "indicates what constitutes the legitimate realm of inquiry" (p. 122). In other words, **organizational culture** is the essence of organizational life. As we mentioned earlier, they apply anthropological principles to construct their theory. Specifically, they adopt the Symbolic-Interpretive approach articulated by Clifford Geertz (1973) into their theoretical model. Geertz remarks that people are animals "suspended in webs of significance" (p. 5). He adds that people spin webs themselves. A primary goal of researchers, then, should be to think about all possible weblike configurations (features) in organizations.

Geertz invokes the image of a spider web deliberately. He believes that culture is like the webs spun by a spider. That is, webs are intricate designs, and each web is different from all others. For Geertz, cultures are like this as well. Basing his conclusions on various cultures around the world, Geertz argues that cultures are all different and that their uniqueness should be celebrated. To understand a culture, Geertz believes that researchers should begin to focus on the meaning shared within it. We examine more of Geertz's beliefs later.

Pacanowsky and O'Donnell-Trujillo (1983) apply these basic principles to organizations. Employees and managers alike spin their webs. People are critical in the organization, and therefore it is important to study their behaviors in conjunction with the overall organization. Pacanowsky and O'Donnell-Trujillo claim that members of organizations engage in a number of communication behaviors that contribute to the culture of the company. They may do this through gossiping, joking, backstabbing, or becoming romantically involved with others.

So, the organizational culture at Jewelry Plus will be revealed in a number of ways. You will recall that Fran learned of the new owner through gossip and that the company picnic was a way for her to learn more about the new company culture. No doubt she will experience an organizational culture with her new job very different from what she experienced with Grace's Jewelers. The company has changed, the faces are new, and the rules reflect new ownership. Fran also contributes to the spinning of the organizational web by both responding to company stories and passing them on to others. In sum, the web of organizational culture has been spun. This broad perspective underscores why Pacanowsky and O'Donnell-Trujillo (1983) argue that organizational culture "is not just another piece of the puzzle; it is the puzzle" (p. 146).

At the heart of Organizational Culture Theory is the belief that organizations have various symbols, rituals, and values that make them unique. In small groups, discuss whether or not an organization could have symbols, rituals, and values that could serve to damage the culture of the organization. Be sure to provide specific examples of your thinking and what the potential consequence would be to an organization's culture.

Assumptions of the Cultural Approach

Three assumptions guide Organizational Culture Theory. As you work through these assumptions, keep in mind the diversity and complexity of organizational life. Also, understand that these assumptions emphasize the process view of organizations that Pacanowsky and O'Donnell-Trujillo advocate:

- Organizational members create and maintain a shared sense of organizational reality, resulting in a better understanding of the values of an organization.

- The use and interpretation of symbols are critical to an organization's culture.

- Cultures vary across organizations, and the interpretations of actions within these cultures are diverse.

The first assumption pertains to the importance of people in organizational life. Specifically, individuals share in creating and maintaining their reality. These individuals include employees, supervisors, and employers. At the core of this assumption is an organization's values. **Values** are the standards and principles within a culture that have intrinsic worth to a culture. Values inform organizational members about what is important. Pacanowsky (1989) notes that values derive from "moral knowledge" (p. 254) and that people display their moral knowledge through narratives, or stories. The stories that Fran hears and shares, for example, will result in her understanding the organization's values.

People share in the process of discovering an organization's values. Being a member of an organization requires active participation in that organization. The meanings of particular symbols—for instance, why a company continues to interview prospective employees when massive layoffs are under way—are communicated by both employees and management. The symbolic meaning of hiring new people when others are being fired will not escape savvy workers; why dedicate money to new personnel when others are losing their jobs? Pacanowsky and O'Donnell-Trujillo (1982) believe that employees contribute to the shaping of organizational culture. Their behaviors are instrumental in creating and ultimately maintaining organizational reality.

values
standards and principles in a culture

279

Table 16.1   Symbols of an Organizational Culture

GENERAL CATEGORY	SPECIFIC TYPES/EXAMPLES
Physical Manifestations	art/design/logo buildings/decor dress/appearance material objects physical layout
Behavioral Manifestations	ceremonies/rituals communication patterns traditions/customs rewards/punishments
Verbal Manifestations	anecdotes/jokes jargon/names/nicknames explanations stories/myths/history heroes/villains metaphors

Source: Adapted from Hatch, 1997.

The reality (and culture) of an organization is also determined in part by the symbols, the second assumption of the theory. Earlier we noted that Pacanowsky and O'Donnell-Trujillo adopted the Symbolic-Interpretive perspective of Geertz. This perspective underscores the use of symbols in organizations, and as we mentioned in Chapter 1, symbols are representations for meaning. Organizational members create, use, and interpret symbols every day. These symbols, therefore, are important to the company's culture. Mary Jo Hatch (1997) extends the notion of symbols in her discussion of the categories of symbolic meaning (Table 16.1).

Symbols include the verbal and nonverbal communication in an organization. Frequently, these symbols communicate an organization's values. Symbols may take the form of slogans that carry meaning. For example, several companies have slogans—past and present—that symbolize their values, including Motorola ("Intelligence Everywhere"), the *New York Times* ("All the News That's Fit to Print"), and Disneyland ("The Happiest Place on Earth"). The extent to which these symbols are effective relies not only on the media but also on how the company's employees enact them. For example, Disneyland's belief that it is the happiest place on earth would be quite ineffective if their employees didn't smile or if they were rude.

For further evidence of verbal symbols in an organization, consider this story. A supervisor named Derrick communicates a great deal about values in casual conversation with his employees. Derrick frequently tells long stories about how he handled a particular issue at a previous workplace. He often launches into detailed accounts of how, for instance, he managed to get his employees a bonus at the end of the year. His stories inevitably begin with a short vignette about his upbringing in Arkansas and end with a moral. At first, employees were unsure how to handle this type of communication. As time went on, however, they soon realized that Derrick was trying to demonstrate a connection with his employees and to indicate that although problems may seem insurmountable, he knows ways to handle them. Through many of his stories, he communicates that he cares about the issues of the company and the workers; he also communicates a new view of what he thinks the organizational culture should be. To review the importance of spoken symbols, see the Research Note on the next page.

Our third assumption of Organizational Culture Theory pertains to the variety of organizational cultures. Simply put, organizational cultures vary tremendously. The perceptions of the actions and activities within these cultures are just as diverse as the cultures themselves. Consider what it is like for Fran as she moves from Grace's Jewelers to Jewelry Plus. We have already provided a number of examples that underscore the various cultural issues within each company. Her perceptions, however, and her participation in the culture may differ from those of others. Some people might appreciate a cultural change after working nine years for the same small company.

As an employee in a small jewelry store, Fran knew that a store's problems could readily be resolved and that any suggestions for changes were welcomed and enacted. The culture was such that employees were empowered to make quick decisions, often without supervisor approval. Exceptions to the store return policy, for instance, were handled by all employees. The store's founder felt that employees were in the best position to deal with difficult problems needing quick resolutions. In addition, employee rewards for customer service were routine, and conflict mediation and anger management programs were available for both employees and management. These organizational practices communicate the importance of a shared sense of organizational reality among employees. Employees at Grace's Jewelers got together regularly for F.A.C.— Friday Afternoon Club—at a local restaurant. These activities communicate the esprit de corps in the company. The employees of Grace's were members of an organizational culture who "constitute and reveal their culture to themselves and to others" (Pacanowsky & O'Donnell-Trujillo, 1982, p. 131).

The organizational culture of Jewelry Plus is very different from that of Grace's, and Fran's experiences with Jewelry Plus are very different from hers with Grace's Jewelers. The corporate giant has no exception to its policy on store returns, and any suggestions for store improvement must be placed in the employee suggestion box or e-mailed to the national headquarters. A sense of community is not encouraged at Jewelry Plus because tasks clearly promote autonomy. There are some efforts to ensure that employees have time together— either through breaks, lunch, or holiday gatherings—but these opportunities are too limited to foster collegiality. Without collegiality, stories, rituals, and rites of passage are restricted. Obviously, significant differences exist in the organizational cultures of Grace's and Jewelry Plus.

We have presented three assumptions of Organizational Culture Theory. Each is grounded in the belief that when researchers study organizational cultures, they will uncover a complex and intricate web. Pacanowsky and O'Donnell-Trujillo believe that the symbolic-interpretive perspective provides a

Research Note

Rudd, G. (1995). The symbolic construction of organizational identities and community in a regional symphony. *Communication Studies, 46,* 201–221.

Basing his research on ethnography, a central feature of the Organizational Culture Theory, Gary Rudd examined the workings of a regional symphony. Through a specific examination of spoken symbols, Rudd documented the manner in which "the Symphony members symbolically construct a sense of personal and social identity" (1995, p. 201). Three cultural categories were presented: the musicians, the board of directors, and the administration. Rudd extrapolated cultural terms or themes in an effort to identify significant meaning for the symphony members.

Several themes emerged in each category. First, within the musicians category, references to "professionals" occurred. For instance, members of the orchestra felt that despite the impasse in contract negotiations taking place, the orchestra members communicated to the community that their professional credentials required them to be paid higher wages. They felt that the professional training along with their professional experience warranted professional compensation. Rudd discovered that the musicians aligned themselves with other professionals such as physicians and attorneys, further invoking the need to be treated in a certain way.

The musicians also noted that they were "stressed" and considered themselves "activists." As a theme, stress related to orchestra members working in a demanding profession with so little reward. Stories about auditioning and the stress associated with that process were common. Rudd noted that activism could be understood by listening to the need to be unionized and by observing their involvement on several committees with the board of directors. Activism was also demonstrated by distributing flyers to the public announcing "Musicians Need to Eat Too."

Finally, the musicians believed that playing music allows them to feel "fulfilled." Their desire to continue despite what they viewed as irreverent conditions highlighted their commitment to playing. Rudd noted that several musicians expressed a passion for playing.

The board of directors category contained three primary self-referents: raising money, serving as resources for business expertise, and acting as advocates. Board members frequently noted the important role that they played in securing funding for the symphony. In fact, donating money to the symphony was noted as a criterion for serving as a board member. Increasing corporate donations and holding special events were specifically identified by the members.

Board members also felt that they were there as business consultants. That is, they felt that if the symphony encountered any financial or legal difficulties, their business savvy would come in handy. Several commented that the symphony was a business, and to that end, should be run as a business. Finally, board members felt that they were advocates of the symphony. They felt that they were ambassadors for the arts in their community and had to communicate their advocacy boldly. Appealing to all constituents—even City Hall—was a necessary part of their responsibilities.

The final category of analysis identified by Rudd was the administration. The management communicated three themes: They were mediators, they were caught in the middle, and they were devoted to the music profession. As mediators, the administrators felt that they had to weigh the business end of the symphony with the artistic end. These two sides often collided, and several commented that it was their role to mediate any clashes. In addition, administrators felt that they were frequently caught in the middle of the three-unit system: the orchestra, the board, and the community. Not only did some feel that some of their relationships were tenuous, but some also felt that they were the target of abuse from all sides. Finally, administrators noted that they were devoted to the symphony and felt that despite the stress, it filled a necessary void in their lives.

Rudd continued the article by discussing four themes associated with the musicians, the board of directors, and the administrators. These four themes included realistic/unrealistic, informed/ uninformed, creative/uncreative, and passionless/ passionate. Rudd noted that each cultural category was represented in conversations using these four themes.

Rudd's study is clearly an important and unique contribution to the research on organizational cul-

ture. His findings demonstrate the interconnection among various units in an organization. Specifically, his findings suggest "that the expression of personal and collective identities was a powerful force in redefining the cultural boundaries of the Symphony" (1995, p. 220).

realistic picture of the culture of a company. To gain a better sense of how they went about studying organizations, we turn our attention to the primary methodology employed in their work and the work of their predecessor, Clifford Geertz: ethnography.

Ethnographic Understanding

Communication and performance studies researcher Dwight Conquergood (1992; 1994) studied one of the most provocative of all research topics in communication: gang communication. In an effort to understand gang communication, Conquergood moved into a run-down building in Chicago known at the time as "Big Red." He lived in the building for nearly two years, observing and participating in virtually all parts of life occupied by gang members. Through observing, participating, and taking notes, Conquergood's research offered a view of gang communication virtually ignored in the media. He uncovered many private rituals and symbols and his work enabled the gang population to have a "voice" never written about in the communication discipline. His efforts in revealing gang-related stories to others is part of ethnography, the underlying methodology of Organizational Culture Theory.

You will recall that Pacanowsky and O'Donnell-Trujillo based much of their work on Geertz's. Because Geertz's work was ethnographic in nature, let's briefly discuss the ethnographic orientation of Geertz and explain its relationship to the theory.

Geertz (1973) argues that in order to understand a culture, one must see it from the members' points of view. In order to do this, Geertz believes researchers should become ethnographers. In Chapter 4 we identified ethnography as a qualitative methodology that uncovers and interprets artifacts, stories, rituals, and practices in order to reveal meaning in a culture. Ethnographers frequently refer to their study as naturalistic research in that they believe that the manner in which they study cultures is much more natural than, say, that of quantitative researchers. In this spirit, Geertz remarked that ethnography is

field journal
personal log to record
feelings about com-
municating with
people in a different
culture from one's
own
thick description
explanation of the
layers of meaning in
a culture

not an experimental science but rather a methodology that uncovers meaning. Discovering meaning, then, is paramount to ethnographers. Geertz, and later Pacanowsky and O'Donnell-Trujillo, primarily subscribes to direct observation, interviews, and participant observation in finding meaning in culture.

As an ethnographer, Geertz spent many years studying various cultures. His writings have addressed a number of diverse subjects, from Zen Buddhism to island life in Indonesia. During his stay in some of these places, he relied heavily on field notes and kept a **field journal,** recording his feelings and ideas about his interactions with members of a specific culture. In his writings, Geertz (1973) concludes that ethnography is a kind of **thick description,** or an explanation of the intricate layers of meaning underlying a culture. Ethnographers, therefore, strive to understand the thick description of a culture and "to ferret out the unapparent import of things" (p. 26). Interestingly, Geertz believes that any cultural analysis is incomplete because the deeper one goes, the more complex the culture becomes. Therefore, it is not possible to be completely certain of a culture and its norms or values.

Geertz (1983) points out that this qualitative methodology is not equivalent to walking a mile in the shoes of those studied. This thinking only perpetuates "the myth of the chameleon fieldworker, perfectly self-tuned to his [her] exotic surroundings, a walking miracle of empathy, tact, patience, and cosmopolitanism" (p. 56). Geertz suggests that a balance must be struck between naturally observing and recording behavior and integrating a researcher's values into the process. He states that "the trick is to figure out what the devil they think they are up to" (p. 58). This, as you might imagine, can be quite difficult for ethnographers.

Pacanowsky and O'Donnell-Trujillo were drawn to Geertz's ethnographic experiences and his articulation of the importance of observation, analysis, and interpretation. Their own research experiences with different co-cultures within a larger culture proved invaluable. For instance, Pacanowsky (1983) observed police in the Salt Lake [Utah] valley, and Trujillo (1983) studied a new and used car dealership. The diversity of their experiences in these smaller cultures in the United States prompted them to acknowledge that cultural performances, or what we call storytelling, are instrumental in communicating about an organization's culture. We return to the topic of performance a bit later in this chapter.

Organizational Culture Theory is rooted in ethnography, and organizational culture can only be viewed by adopting ethnographic principles. Let's explore ethnography by using our example of Fran Callahan. If ethnographers were interested in studying the culture of her new job at Jewelry Plus, they might begin by examining several areas: For instance, what sort of new corporate rules are in place? What do new employees like Fran think about them? What types of strategies are used to ease the transition for employees like Fran? Are there any corporate philosophies or ideologies? Are there morale problems? How are they resolved? Has the company responded to employee complaints? If so, how? If not, why not? These and a host of other questions would begin the ethnographic process of understanding the organizational culture of Jewelry Plus.

We could never fully capture the excitement of ethnography in this limited space. Yet, we hope that you have grounding in the basic processes associated

with ethnography and an understanding of why Pacanowsky and O'Donnell-Trujillo embraced such a methodology in their work on organizational culture. We now wish to expand on the topic of performance, a key component in Organizational Culture Theory.

The Communicative Performance

Pacanowsky and O'Donnell-Trujillo contend that organizational members act out certain communication performances, which result in a unique organizational culture. **Performance** is a metaphor that suggests a symbolic process of understanding human behavior in an organization. Organizational performances frequently take on a theatrical flavor, whereby both supervisor and employees choose to take on various roles, or parts, in their organization.

performance
metaphor suggesting that organizational life is like a theatrical presentation

Although the category system is not necessarily exclusive, you will get an idea about the extent to which organizations vary in terms of how human behavior can be understood. The theorists outline five cultural performances: ritual, passion, social, political, and enculturation. In Table 16.2, we identify these performances. As you read this material, keep in mind that these performances may be enacted by any member of the organization.

Ritual Performances

Those communication performances that occur on a regular and recurring basis are termed **ritual performances**. Rituals include four types: personal, task, social, and organizational. **Personal rituals** include those things that you routinely do each day at the workplace. For instance, many organizational members regularly check their voicemail or e-mail when they get to work each day. **Task rituals** are those routinized behaviors associated with a person's job. Task rituals get the job done. For instance, task rituals of employees of the Department of Motor Vehicles include issuing eye and written examinations, taking pictures of prospective drivers, administrating driving tests, verifying car insurance, and collecting fees. **Social rituals** are the verbal and nonverbal routines that normally take into consideration the interactions with others. For instance, some organizational members get together for a happy hour in bars on Fridays, celebrating the week's end. With respect to your own social rituals, consider the social routines you experience in your classes. Many of you arrive early to catch

ritual performances
regular and recurring presentations in the workplace
personal rituals
routines done at the workplace each day
task rituals
routines associated with a particular job in the workplace
social rituals
routines that involve relationships with others in the workplace

Table 16.2   Cultural Performances in Organizations

Ritual Performances	personal rituals—checking voicemail and e-mail, task rituals—issuing tickets, collecting fees, social rituals—happy-hour gatherings, organizational rituals—department meetings, company picnics
Passion Performances	storytelling, metaphors, and exaggerated speech—"this is the most unappreciative company," "follow the chain of command or it'll get wrapped around your neck"
Social Performances	acts of civility and politeness; extensions of etiquette—customer thank-yous, water cooler chat, supporting another's "face"
Political Performances	exercising control, power, and influence—"barking" bosses, intimidation rituals, use of informants, bargaining
Enculturation Performances	acquired competencies over organizational career—learning/teaching roles, orientations, interviews

up with your classmates on what has happened since the last time you spoke and continue the social ritual either during a class break or after class. Social rituals may also include nonverbal behaviors in an organization, including casual Fridays and employee-of-the-month awards. Finally, **organizational rituals** include frequently occurring company events such as division meetings, faculty meetings, and even company picnics like the one Fran Callahan attended.

organizational rituals
routines that pertain to the organization overall

Passion Performances

The organizational stories that members enthusiastically relate to others are termed **passion performances.** Many times, people in organizations become fervent in their storytelling. Consider, for instance, the experience of Adam, who works at a national retail store. Adam and his co-workers hear and retell stories about their department supervisor. The story goes that the boss walks the perimeter of their department every thirty minutes to get an expanded view of the workers and customers. If the supervisor sees something that he feels is peculiar, he calls the employee into the back room, reviews a videotape of the event, and asks the employee what he or she will do to improve any future problems. Adam relates that all of his co-workers passionately tell this story over and over to both new and seasoned employees. In fact, even after six years, Adam's passion for sharing the story is the same as when he told it for the first time.

passion performances
organizational stories that employees share with one another

Social Performances

Whereas passionate performances, like Adam's, appear to have little regard for the butt of the story, **social performances** are the common extensions of civility, politeness, and courtesy in order to encourage cooperation among organizational members. The adage that "a little goes a long way" relates directly to

social performances
organizational behaviors intended to demonstrate cooperation and politeness with others

this performance. Whether with a smile or a "good morning" greeting, establishing some sense of collegiality is frequently part of an organization's culture.

Yet, it is often difficult to be polite. When the mood is tense, it is both trying and somewhat insincere to smile or to wish another a "good morning." Most organizations wish to maintain a professional decorum, even in difficult times, and these social performances help to accomplish this.

Political Performances

When organizational cultures communicate **political performances**, they are exercising power or control. Acquiring and maintaining power and control is a hallmark of U.S. corporate life. In fact, some might argue that power and control pervade organizational life. Nonetheless, because by their nature most organizations are hierarchical, there must be someone with the power to accomplish things and with enough control to maintain the bottom line.

When organizational members engage in political performances, they essentially communicate a desire to influence others. That is not necessarily a bad thing. Consider the experiences of a group of nurses, for instance, at Spring Valley Hospital. For years, the nurses were content with their second-class status relative to the hospital's physicians. Recently, however, the nurses decided to speak out about their treatment. They talked to physicians, to other medical staff, and to patients. In this instance, they were exercising more control over their jobs. Their cultural political performances centered on being recognized for their competency as medical professionals and for their commitment to the mission of the hospital. Their goal was to be legitimized in the hospital by the physicians, their co-workers, and the patients. Their performances, no doubt, were critical in establishing a modified organizational culture.

Enculturation Performances

The fifth type of performance identified by Pacanowsky and O'Donnell-Trujillo is termed enculturation performance. **Enculturation performances** refer to how members obtain the knowledge and skills to be contributing members of the organization. These performances may be bold or subtle, and they demonstrate a member's competency within an organization. For instance, a number of performances will be enacted to enculturate Fran into her new position. She will

political performances
organizational behaviors that demonstrate power or control

enculturation performances
organizational behaviors that assist employees in discovering what it means to be a member of an organization

watch and listen to her colleagues "perform" their thoughts and feelings on a number of issues, namely work hours, employee discounts, and the company newsletter, among others. In sum, Fran will begin to know the organization's culture.

As we mentioned earlier, these performances may overlap. It is possible, therefore, to have social performances considered ritual performances. Think about, for instance, greeting one co-worker with "Good morning" or fetching coffee for another each day. In this example, the acts of politeness are considered to be a personal (and even task) ritual. Therefore, the performance may be both a social and a ritual performance.

Further, performances may arise from a conscious decision to act out thoughts and feelings about an issue, as in our example of the nurses at Spring Valley Hospital. Or the performances may be more intuitive, as in our example of Fran Callahan. It is clear that Pacanowsky and O'Donnell-Trujillo believe that communicative performances are critical to an organization's culture.

Critique and Closing

Organizational Culture Theory "has become a major theoretical rallying point" (Mumby, 1988, p. 4). Pacanowsky and O'Donnell-Trujillo were instrumental in directing researchers' attention toward an expansive understanding of organizations. The theoretical principles of the theory emphasize that organizational life is complex and that researchers must take into consideration not only the members of the organization but their behaviors, activities, and stories.

The appeal of Organizational Culture Theory has been far and wide, resulting in a heuristic theory. For instance, it has framed research examining Muslim employees (Alkhazraji, 1997), law enforcement officers (Frewin & Tuffin, 1998), and pregnant employees (Halpert & Burg, 1997). Even more relevant to us in higher education, the theory has been used to study the stories of undergraduate students and their perceptions of "fitting in" at a college or university (Kramer & Berman, 2001). The approach is also useful because much of the information from the theory (e.g., symbols, stories, rituals) has direct relevance to many different types of organizations and their employees. Because the theorists' work is based on real organizations with real employees, the researchers have made the theory more useful and practical.

Finally, the logical consistency of the model should not go unnoticed. Recall that logical consistency refers to the notion that theories should follow a logical arrangement and remain consistent. From the outset, Pacanowsky and O'Donnell-Trujillo did not stray from their belief that the organization's culture is rich and diverse; listening to the communicative performances of organizational members is where we must begin in understanding corporate culture. This is the basis from which much of the theory gained momentum.

The appeal of the theory is tempered by its criticisms. First, Eric Eisenberg and H. L. Goodall (1993) observe that Organizational Culture Theory relies heavily on the shared meaning among organizational members. They comment that "most cultures show considerably more alignment in practice than they do

Theory * Into * Practice

In an article in the *New York Times,* Jeffrey Seglin highlights the importance of corporate values to an organization's culture. His essay is presented in a unique form: He writes a memo to Microsoft chief executive Steven Ballmer. Seglin creatively questions Ballmer's open letter to the 50,000 employees of Microsoft that contained Ballmer's belief that corporate values "must shine through in all our interactions—in our work groups, across teams, with partners, within our industry, and most of all, with our customers" (p. C4).

Seglin applauds Ballmer for using words like "integrity, trust, accountability, and honesty" in his memo. Yet he questions the ultimate success of Ballmer's method for getting at achieving his corporate goals. Ballmer will require formal discussions of corporate values with yearly reviews. Seglin believes that simply saying a company stands for honesty and excellence doesn't go far enough. For instance, how will Microsoft balance profitability with the need to be trustful and honest? Seglin quotes ethics experts who note that Microsoft will have to have reward systems in place for those who live by the company's values.

Seglin continues by stating that Microsoft's leaders will have to be the first to demonstrate the same corporate values they expect of their employees. For instance, Microsoft has suffered several ethical dilemmas over the years. Actually practicing the values Ballmer expects of others, Seglin writes, requires Microsoft to take "bold steps" (p. C4). The company must set up clear financial statements, avoid corporate conflicts of interest, and rotate financial auditors. Seglin concludes: "You want people to know about Microsoft's values and what the company stands for? Show us" (p. C4).

Source: Seglin, 2002.

TIP Follow-up

Discuss how large corporations like Microsoft should develop corporate values. Should values emanate from employees, employers, and/or society? Should they reflect contemporary times, or should they be timeless?

in the attitudes, opinions, or beliefs of individual members" (p. 152). Second, Organizational Culture Theory suffers from expansive boundaries. For instance, cultural performances constitute a critical part of an organization's culture, and when you consider that performances may address almost any topic, the vastness (and potential vagueness) of the theory becomes apparent.

Finally, Organizational Culture Theory may view organizational life as too unique. Pacanowsky and O'Donnell-Trujillo argue that organizational cultures differ because the interactions within those cultures differ, so generalizing about life in organizations is nearly impossible. Consider Fran Callahan, for instance. Researchers using a symbolic-interpretive perspective in studying the organizational culture of Grace's Jewelers may also be interested in studying the corporate culture of Jewelry Plus. As our examples have shown, each is a unique organization with unique organizational environments. Because ethnography requires thick description of each, it may be difficult—if not impossible—to point out the similarities for generalization purposes. As Stephen

Littlejohn (2002) argues, the theory presupposes that organizations must be studied independently, and in doing so, generalizing across organizations is difficult.

Pacanowsky (1989) responds to his critics by noting that the theory is more concerned with the unique values of an organization and not the "reproducibility of representation" (p. 253). In fact, early writings by Pacanowsky and O'Donnell-Trujillo were clear in noting that although there may be shortcomings in the perspective, the authors believe that the time is ripe to forge a new path in asking questions about organizations. They recognize that critics may be quick to judge the feasibility and effectiveness of their approach; yet the theory's value outweighs the criticisms.

Organizational Culture Theory, articulated by Pacanowsky and O'Donnell-Trujillo, will continue to elicit opinion in the communication discipline. It is a way of "rethinking communication" (Dervin, Grossberg, O'Keefe, & Wartella, 1989), and its value will continue to be realized by scholars of all methodological stripes. Perhaps looking at organizational culture in this way will enable researchers to appreciate the importance of connecting with the people and their performances in an organization.

Discussion Starters

1. How can employees like Fran Callahan ease into a new and different organizational culture? What advice would you give her as she begins her new job with Jewelry Plus?

2. Consider some of the organizations to which you belong. Identify the cultural performances that you have either observed or shared. How could you use these performances in your work?

3. Geertz has compared culture to a spider web. What other metaphors can you think of that could represent organizational cultures?

4. Explain how organizational culture can vary within a large organization. Use examples in your response.

5. Imagine that you're an ethnographer who has been assigned to study your school's culture. How might you go about studying it? What sort of cultural artifacts or rituals would you find?

6. Based on your job experiences, explain the frequency of the various cultural performances identified by Pacanowsky and O'Donnell-Trujillo.

Terms for Review

organizational culture	performance
values	ritual performances
field journal	personal rituals
thick description	task rituals

social rituals
organizational rituals
passion performances

social performances
political performances
enculturation performances

Online Learning Center

Visit the Online Learning Center at www.mhhe.com/west2. Use
the multiple-choice and true/false quizzes to help you prepare for
exams, and the glossary, crossword puzzles, and flashcards to further
your knowledge of key terms.

CHAPTER 17

Organizational Information Theory

Dominique Martin

The year was 1999 and Dominique Martin could feel the stress build as the year progressed. She was an expert on computer conversion to Y2K (year 2000) and was very busy as companies continued to call her for her assistance in converting their systems. In fact, she became even busier as media coverage caused many people to question the ability of companies to adapt their systems to the year 2000. The task was not an easy one, and many organizations developed special project teams to deal with the challenge of bringing their systems up-to-date.

As she approached the door of the conference room, Dominique thought about how happy and relieved she would be once the year was over. But, for now, she had to deal with NowBank's Year 2000 Conversion Team. She had been appointed project manager, and today she would meet for the first time with members of various teams via a video-conference. Employees from Dallas, Denver, and Phoenix offices would take part. The Y2K project goal involved the conversion of all NowBank computer systems so that they would be compatible for the changes that would take place in the new millennium. The Y2K project team consisted of approximately eighty people who would be responsible for various aspects of the conversion. Dominique was used to managing a team of twelve employees who were all located in the same city, so this was a new challenge.

As Dominique began the meeting, she asked each team leader in the various cities to introduce their team members and to share their overall goals for the project. As they went around to the various locations, Dominique became overwhelmed. There were so many different areas to manage in this project: maintaining communication with the computer technicians, coordinating information with the federal regulatory agencies regarding their rules for computer configurations, providing updates to and obtaining feedback from the bank's customers to monitor their awareness and concerns about NowBank's readiness for Y2K, keeping the other divisions within the bank informed of changes that were being made to the computer systems and how those changes would affect their departments . . . and that was only the beginning! Each of the teams needed to be kept informed about the others' progress in order to meet their deadlines.

As the meeting progressed, Dominique realized that the success of this project would depend on effective communication. The team from Phoenix insisted that they needed more support staff to collect information from NowBank customers in a timely manner. The Dallas team leader pointed out that her team needed this customer information in order to develop a promotion strategy to gain public confidence. Denver's team argued that they would need to provide federal regulatory information to the computer technicians to ensure that their changes met the government's standards.

This theory is based on the research of **Karl Weick.**

After the meeting, Dominique consulted with her team leaders via a telephone conference call. They developed a communication strategy to help keep the teams in the different offices across the country informed of the events associated with the project. The plan included hiring an internal communication coordinator to manage all the messages that would be sent about Y2K computer conversions. Next, they decided that a company electronic chat area would be established so that all project members could communicate about the information needed to complete the project. Also, an electronic newsletter would be distributed weekly to update all members of NowBank about the progress that was being made. In addition, survey questionnaires were included in the monthly statements sent to all NowBank customers to gain insight about their attitudes and concerns regarding Y2K. Finally, they decided that they would use computer software to record the goals, resources, deadlines, and accomplishments associated with the project.

Although several years have passed since that time, Dominique continues to wonder whether or not she facilitated the Y2K project effectively. She knew that she was a good team leader, but even today, she thinks about whether her thoughts, actions, and activities were the most appropriate at the time. She felt confident that everyone had a voice in the matter and that their conversations helped move the project along. Still, she couldn't rid herself of a nagging doubt about whether she managed the events to the best of her ability. ∎

The task of managing vast amounts of information is a typical challenge for many organizations. As our options for new communication channels increase, the number of messages that we send and receive, as well as the speed at which we send them, increases as well. Not only are organizations faced with the task of decoding the messages that are received, but they are also challenged with determining the people who need to receive the information in order to help achieve the organization's goals. As we noted in Chapter 1, new media are enabling companies to accomplish their goals in ways never before seen. Video-conferencing, teleconferencing, e-mail chat areas, and interactive television allow people like Dominique to provide teams with the opportunity to simultaneously share and react to great amounts of information. Each of the teams was given the opportunity to decide what information was essential to its tasks or to request additional information that would be needed in the future.

Sometimes, the information that an organization receives may be ambiguous. In the case of the Y2K project, each of the teams depends on the others to provide information so that it can complete its portion of the project. Teams need the information to be presented in a way that they can understand. After all, the customer service team has little knowledge of computer jargon, so they depend on the technicians to clarify the information and present it to them in a way that they can then communicate to their customers. Without this exchange and management of information, several gaps would exist and Now-Bank's computer conversion would probably fail.

Some organizational communication theorists have used the metaphor of a living system to describe organizations. Just as living systems engage in a process of activities in order to maintain their functioning and existence, an organization must have a procedure for dealing with all the information it needs

Theory Application in Groups

Discuss further the metaphor of Organizational Information Theory which suggests that organizations are living organisms. What does this mean to you? What examples can you point to in our society that illustrate this metaphor?

to send and receive in order to accomplish its goals. Much like systems, organizations are made up of persons and teams that are interrelated. They depend on one another to complete their goals.

Consider the process that colleges and universities go through to recruit new students. The publications office conducts research to find out what criteria are attractive to potential students. Are graduation rates and job placement something that high school students are looking for in deciding where to pursue their education? Is the diversity of the student body an important factor in making a decision? Will the recent rating by *Money* magazine have an impact on student decisions? Or are students attracted to a campus that has superior computer facilities? After collecting these data, the publications office will use this information to develop publicity materials that appeal to potential students. Recruitment fairs may be held in major cities to provide parents and students with the opportunity to ask admissions counselors about the school. While this process is taking place, the school collects feedback and monitors the reactions of potential students and their parents in order to make changes in their current recruitment strategies. The admissions office reduces uncertainty about what qualities are attractive to students while at the same time assisting students in making their decision by providing information about the school.

Karl Weick developed an approach to describe the process by which organizations collect, manage, and use the information that they receive. Rather than focusing his attention on the *structure* of the organization in terms of the roles and rules that guide its members, Weick emphasizes the *process* of organizing. In doing so, the primary focus is on the exchange of information that takes place within the organization and how members take steps to understand this material. Weick (1995) believes that "organizations talk to themselves" (p. 281). To this end, organizational members are instrumental in the creation and maintenance of message meaning. Weick sees the organization as a system taking in confusing or ambiguous information from its environment and making sense out of it. Therefore, according to Organizational Information Theory, organizations will evolve as they try to make sense out of themselves and their environment. Rather than focusing on Dominique's role as project manager or on the specific communication rules for sending messages between superiors and subordinates, Weick's Organizational Information Theory directs our attention to the steps that are necessary to manage and use the information for the NowBank project. As it becomes more difficult to interpret the information that is received, an organization needs to solicit input from others (often multiple sources) in order to make sense of the information and to provide a response to the appropriate people or departments.

The Only Constant Is Change (in Organizations)

Weick first presented his theoretical approach explaining how organizations make sense of and use information in his book *The Social Psychology of Organizing* (1969). He later updated his theory to clarify potential confusion (1995). The theory focuses on the process that organizations undergo in their attempt to make sense out of all the information that bombards them on a daily basis. Often the process results in changes in the organization and its members. In fact, Weick states, "Organizations and their environments change so rapidly that it is unrealistic to show what they are like now, because that's not the way they're going to be later" (1969, p. 1). According to this approach, it would be unrealistic to try to depict what the university and its surrounding environment look like today, because it is likely that they will change. The major fields of study chosen by students may change as organizations' needs for employees change. Consider, for instance, the end of the 1990s. Many organizations were seeking graduates in the fields of computer technology and management information systems to assist them in making changes in their computer systems. (Today, some of these graduates are returning to the problems of the 1990s.) Once a problem is solved, the hiring needs of these organizations may change, and students may become interested in other majors that are attractive to employers. As you can see in this example, a lot of information has been collected and shared among employers, students, and school officials.

The focus of Organizational Information Theory is on the communication of information that is vital in determining the success of an organization. It is quite rare that one person or one department in an organization has all the information necessary to complete a project. This knowledge typically comes from a variety of sources. However, the task of information processing is not completed simply by attaining information; the difficult part is in deciphering and distributing the information that is gained. To better understand this process, we will discuss how two major theoretical perspectives influenced Organizational Information Theory. We first examine General Systems Theory and then the Theory of Sociocultural Evolution.

General Systems Theory

To explain the influence of information from an organization's external environments and to understand the influence that an organization has on its external environments, Weick applied General Systems Theory in the development of his approach to studying how organizations manage information. As you may recall from Chapter 3 in our discussion on General Systems Theory, Ludwig von Bertalanffy (1968) is the researcher most frequently associated with the systems approach. von Bertalanffy believed that patterns and wholes exist across different types of phenomena. To this end, he proposed that when there is a disruption in one part of a system, it affects the entire system. In sum, systems theorists argue that there are complex patterns of interaction among the parts of a system and understanding these interactions will help us understand the entire system.

General Systems Theory is especially useful in understanding the interrelationships that exist among various organizational units. Organizations are often made up of different departments, teams, or groups. Although these units are often focused on independent tasks, the goals of the organization as a whole typically require sharing and integrating the information that each of the teams has in order to arrive at a solution or conclusion. Organizations depend on combined information so that they can make any necessary adjustments in order to reach their goal. They may need additional information, they may need to send information to other departments or people within the organization, or they may need outside consultants to make sense of the information. If one team fails to address the information needed to fulfill its obligation in the completion of the project, achieving the final goal will probably be delayed for the entire organization.

In the opening scenario, we learned that the Phoenix team was responsible for collecting information from NowBank customers in order to identify their level of knowledge about the Y2K conversion. The team from Dallas was responsible for developing a publicity plan to gain public confidence that Now-Bank's computers would be compatible for the year 2000. However, the Dallas team could not begin to develop their campaign until they received information about the issues that concerned the customers. If the Phoenix team was not efficient in providing this information, the entire process would be delayed.

feedback
information received by an organization and its members

An important component of General Systems Theory, and one that is essential to making sense of information in an organization, is feedback. **Feedback** can be defined as information that is received by an organization and its members. It's important to remember that this information can be either positive or negative. The organization and its members can then choose to use the information to maintain the current state of the organization or can decide to initiate some changes in accordance with the goals that the system is trying to accomplish. It is through feedback that units are able to determine if the information that is being transmitted is clear and is sufficient to achieve the desired goals.

In the NowBank example, the Dallas team needs to provide feedback to Phoenix that the Dallas team needs the customer information by a specific deadline. If the deadline is not possible, Phoenix will provide feedback to request a later date. This process is likely to continue until a deadline is agreed on that is feasible for both teams. The interrelatedness of these teams results in a cycle of communication that is designed to reduce the ambiguity or confusion of the information being requested. No one unit is more important in the organization; each depends on the other to achieve the final goal. It is apparent that both teams are interdependent on each other for feedback that is essential to meeting their project deadlines.

The decision of the organization to request or provide feedback reflects a selective choice made by the group in an effort to accomplish its goals. If an organization hopes to survive and accomplish its goals, it will continue to engage in cycles of feedback in order to obtain necessary information and reduce its uncertainty about the best way to accomplish its goals. This process reflects a Darwinian approach to how organizations manage information, as we discuss next.

Darwin's Theory of Sociocultural Evolution

Another theory that has been used to describe the process by which organizations collect and make sense out of information is the **theory of sociocultural evolution.** Although this approach is used to describe the social interactions that take place in an organization with regard to making sense out of information, its origins are in the field of biology. The theory of evolution was originally developed to describe the adaptation processes that living organisms undergo in order to thrive in a challenging ecological environment. Charles Darwin (1948) explained these adaptations in terms of mutations that allow organisms to cope with their various surroundings. Some organisms could not adapt and died, whereas others made changes and prospered. Taking the example of Dominique Martin and the Y2K computer challenge, it has been suggested that those companies who took steps to manage the information and convert their systems to accommodate the new millennium have a greater chance to prosper and thrive. Those who did not make the attempt to adapt to the changing environment may be faced with severe consequences.

Campbell (1965) extends this theory to explain the processes by which organizations and their members adapt to their social surroundings. The sociocultural theory of evolution examines the changes that people make in their social behaviors and expectations in order to adapt to changes in their social surroundings. Three stages are involved in this process: People notice that there are differences, or *variations*, in the norms for behaviors that they expect and the expectations that others have for their performance. As a result of the variations in norms, they look at the possible options and *select* the behaviors that are the most socially acceptable in the group. Once the accepted behaviors have been identified, people will likely *retain* these behaviors and apply them in future interactions.

Consider the scenario at the beginning of this chapter. Suppose that Dominique had a team of representatives from NowBank's offices in Japan involved in this project. If she wanted to make a quick decision on how to address the Y2K changes in the Japanese offices, her first tendency would likely be to employ a communication style that U.S. employees would perceive as efficient. However, she would soon realize that the Japanese approach to business is quite different from that practiced in the United States. Instead of quickly presenting the facts and signing on the dotted line, Japanese bank employees prefer an approach that emphasizes the development of rapport. Only after the relationship has been developed would the issue of signing an agreement have been presented. Dominique must engage in the process of sociocultural evolution to adapt to the norms and expectations of her overseas team.

**theory of
sociocultural
evolution**
Darwin's belief that
only the fittest can
survive challenging
surroundings

Weick adapts the theory of sociocultural evolution to explain the process that organizations undergo in adjusting to various information pressures. These pressures may be the result of information overload or ambiguity. Although the evolutionary approach is useful in describing the adaptations that are necessary to process information, systems theory is also an essential piece in this puzzle because it highlights the interrelatedness among organizational teams, departments, and employees in the processing of information. We now continue our discussion of Organizational Information Theory and identify its underlying assumptions.

Assumptions of Organizational Information Theory

Organizational Information Theory is one way of explaining how organizations make sense out of information that is confusing or ambiguous. It focuses on the process of organizing members of an organization to manage information rather than on the structure of the organization itself. There are a number of assumptions that underlie this theory:

- Human organizations exist in an information environment.
- The information an organization receives differs in terms of equivocality.
- Human organizations engage in information processing to reduce equivocality of information.

The first assumption states that organizations depend on information in order to function effectively and accomplish their goals. Weick (1979) views the concept of information environment as distinct from the physical surroundings in which an organization is housed. He proposes that these information environments are created by the members of the organization. They establish goals that require them to obtain information from both internal and external sources. However, these inputs differ in terms of their level of understandability.

Consider the university admissions office example previously in this chapter. There are numerous channels that a school can use to gain information about student needs: It may develop a website to answer prospective students' questions and to solicit student feedback; it may conduct surveys at high school academic fairs to gain more information about student desires; it may host focus group interviews with current students to find out their needs and concerns; or it may ask alumni to provide examples from their educational experiences to use in attracting future students. Once it has received messages from all of these external sources, the university must decide how to communicate messages internally in order to establish and accomplish its goals for current and future students. The possibilities for information are endless, and so the university must decide how to manage all the potential messages that are available in its information environment.

One additional point merits attention. Although Weick made little mention of information environments as mediated, some scholars are beginning to view the information environment as a media environment. Of course, no discussion of information theory can be complete without an acknowledgment of new media. Broadly defined, then, the information environment includes those surroundings that are affected by new technologies. We return to information environment a bit later.

The second assumption proposed by Weick focuses on the ambiguity that exists in information. Messages differ in terms of their understandability. An organization needs to determine which of its members are most knowledgeable or experienced in dealing with particular information that is obtained. A plan to make sense of the information needs to be established.

At NowBank, it is likely that the publicity team will be able to comprehend and make sense out of the information that is provided by the customer survey team. However, when they receive messages from the computer technician team, the publicity team may not understand the content of the messages and how it applies or relates to their portion of the project. Messages, according to Weick's theory, are frequently equivocal. **Equivocality** refers to messages that are complicated, uncertain, and unpredictable. Equivocal messages are often sent in organizations. Because these messages are not clearly understood, people need to develop a framework or plan for reducing their ambiguity about the message. When people in an organization reduce equivocality, then, they engage in a process to make sense out of excessive information that is received by the organization.

equivocality
the extent to which organizational messages are uncertain, ambiguous, and/or unpredictable

In an attempt to reduce the ambiguity of information, the third assumption of the theory proposes that organizations engage in joint activity to make information that is received more understandable. Weick (1979) sees the process of reducing equivocality as a joint activity among members of an organization. It is not the sole responsibility of one person to reduce equivocality. Rather, this is a process that may involve several members of the organization. Consider the NowBank example. Each department needs to use information from other departments, but they also need to provide information to these same departments in order to accomplish the tasks necessary to meet the organization's Y2K goal. This illustrates the extent to which departments in an organization may depend on one another to reduce their ambiguity. An ongoing cycle of communicating feedback takes place in which there is a mutual give-and-take of information.

Concepts of Organizational Information Theory

Weick's theory of Organizational Information contains a number of key concepts that are critical to an understanding of the theory. They include information environment, information equivocality, rules, and cycles. We now explore each in detail.

Information Environment: The Sum Total

Earlier we noted information environment as an integral part of Weick's theory. Information environment is a core concept in understanding how organizations are formed as well as how they process information. Every day, we are faced

**information
environment**
the availability of
all stimuli in an
organization

with literally thousands of stimuli that we could potentially process and interpret. However, it is unrealistic to think that an organization or its members could possibly be able to process all the information that is available. Thus, we are faced with the tasks of selecting information that is meaningful or important and focusing our senses on processing those cues. The availability of all stimuli is considered to be the **information environment.** Organizations are composed of information that is vital to their formation and continues to be essential to their existence. For example, the Y2K project team was formed as a result of information about concerns over the capacity of computers to deal with the date change at the start of the new millennium. There was enough information received by the NowBank organization that a smaller organization (the project team) was formed to manage this knowledge. Now the Y2K organization depends on additional information in order to be able to solve the problem and reach its goal.

Essentially, organizations have two primary tasks to perform in order to successfully manage these multiple sources of information: (1) They must interpret the external information that exists in their information environment, and (2) they must coordinate that information to make it meaningful for the members of the organization and its goals. These interpretation processes require the organization to reduce the equivocality or ambiguity of the information in order to make it meaningful.

Information Equivocality: Are You Sure About This?

As stated earlier, organizations depend on and receive vast amounts of information. The challenge lies in the ability of organizations to make sense of the information that is received. Organizations receive information from multiple sources; they must decode the information and determine whether it is comprehensible, which person or department is most qualified to deal with the information, and whether multiple departments require this information to accomplish their tasks. Without clarity in these areas, there is information equivocality.

The fact that much of the information that organizations receive is ambiguous is central to Organizational Information Theory. *Equivocality* is the term used to describe this ambiguity. Weick posits that an organization's challenges stem not from the fact that it has too little information but from the fact that it receives mass amounts of information that lead to the potential for multiple interpretations (Weick, 1995). A primary goal for the organization is to assign meaning to an otherwise ill-defined information environment and to develop a plan of action so that its members can achieve its goals.

Within an organization, a multitude of tasks must be accomplished on any given day. Information is essential for accomplishing these goals. However, the organization has the potential to receive vast amounts of information through a variety of channels. Much of the information that is received requires that members of the organization engage in information processing to reduce the equivocality to the point where members have a clear understanding of how and why the information is meaningful. Richard Daft and Robert Lengel (1984) introduce the concept of "information richness" to describe the abun-

The Theory Chronicles

Weick contends that organizing is a primary organizational behavior and all employees engage in the organizing process. Comment on how various organizational levels might organize in their jobs. For instance, how might employees in the mail room, human resources, and payroll engage in the organizing process?

dant inputs with which organizations are faced. They point out that new media has afforded organizations access to a vast amount of information, but then the members of those organizations are faced with the task of reducing the messages to a form that will assist them in achieving their goals.

Recall the multiple sources for information that Dominique utilizes in the Y2K example. She has the ability to meet with all her teams from various parts of the country. Additionally, the teams have the opportunity to engage in discussions online and to send one another messages very rapidly. Thus, the amount of information that potentially could be received and interpreted could be overwhelming. Rather than having an opportunity to process information one piece at a time, Dominique and the team members are faced with the daunting task of rapidly making sense of this information in order to apply it to their goal.

In order to successfully process information, organizations must engage in a series of behaviors in which the complexity of the communication effort is equal to the equivocality of the message. Simply stated, organizations are often unable to understand information or events that are more complicated than they are. Imagine a prospective student trying to understand complex information regarding financial aid. This student may only be able to grasp the information after engaging in extensive communication with people who comprehend the terminology and steps involved in the financial aid process. In the same way, organizations must engage in various forms of communication to comprehend information that is complex or ambiguous.

This is referred to as **requisite variety**, which is the process of engaging in communication behaviors that are as complex as the messages themselves. To interpret highly ambiguous information, highly complex communication is required. If the information is easily understood by some members in the organization, less complex communication is required. Weick explains this principle with the example of a man with a cold who is seeking treatment from his doctor. The doctor instructs the patient to come back when he has pneumonia, because the doctor knows how to treat pneumonia. The information on cures for the common cold is highly equivocal, thus it requires much more extensive communication. Doctors have little understanding of how to cure the cold; rather, they know how to relieve some of the symptoms and often advise patients to let the cold run its course. Weick summarizes the notion of requisite variety by stating, "It takes equivocality to remove equivocality" (1969, p. 40). The Research Note presents a study that further explores information equivocality.

requisite variety engaging in communication that is as complex as the messages received

301

Research Note

Kreps, G. (1980). A field experimental test and revaluation of Weick's model of organizing. In D. Nimmo (Ed.) *Communication Yearbook 4* (pp. 389–398). New Brunswick, NJ: Transaction Books.

This study applies Organizational Information Theory in a field experimental test of an organization's response to informational equivocality. Kreps points out that Weick's theory of information systems in organizations proposes a direct relationship between the level of equivocality of information and the amounts and types of communication behaviors that an organization employs in an attempt to reduce the equivocality.

The faculty senate at the University of California served as the population for this study. Faculty senate groups are formed in order to represent faculty voices in university governance. Many of its goals are accomplished via meetings in which motions are presented, discussed, and decided. Thus, the focus of this study was to examine the relationship between the level of equivocality of the motions that were presented to the faculty senate and the communication responses that were used as a means of reducing ambiguity.

Over a nine-month period, twenty-four motions were examined for their level of equivocality, and faculty discussion on each motion was examined to determine the frequency of communication cycles that were employed in order to clarify information. To determine the perceived level of equivocality of the motions, printouts of the motions were distributed to a sample of 42 percent of the faculty senate members, and they were asked to rate the information based on the three dimensions of equivocality as proposed by Weick: ambiguous-unambiguous, predictable-unpredictable, and complicated-uncomplicated. Content analysis procedures were used to operationalize the verbal feedback provided by the faculty senate members with regard to each motion.

Results supported Weick's theory that as equivocality of messages increases, so do the cycles of communication we employ to reduce the equivocality. In the study, as the level of equivocality of the motions increased, so did the number of communication cycles that the senate members used to reduce their ambiguity.

Rules: Guidelines to Analyze

Weick (1979) proposes two communication strategies that are essential if the organization hopes to reduce message equivocality. The first strategy requires that organizations determine the rules for reducing the level of equivocality of the message inputs as well as for choosing the appropriate response to the information that is received. In Organizational Information Theory, **rules** refer to the guidelines that an organization has established for analyzing the equivocality of a message as well as for guiding responses to information. For example, if any of the Y2K team leaders experience ambiguity over the information that is provided to them from the computer technicians, they are instructed to contact the technician team leader for clarification. If they were to contact Dominique first, an additional step would be added to the process of reducing equivocality because she would have to contact the technicians and then report back to the team leaders. Recall the example of the university admissions office, which conducted research in order to design materials that appeal to students. As a result, when it receives information from students inquiring about the university, the rule that it applies in dealing with the information environment is that it responds to that message by sending out their informational brochure.

rules
guidelines in organizations as they review responses to equivocal information

Both organizations have rules for determining the equivocality of the information and for identifying the appropriate way in which they should respond to the messages.

Weick (1979) provides examples of rules that might cause an organization to choose one cycle of information or feedback over another for reducing the equivocality of messages. These rules include duration, personnel, success, and effort. Examples of duration and personnel rules guiding communication can be seen in the Y2K example. **Duration** refers to a choice made by an organization to engage in communication that can be completed in the least amount of time. For example, NowBank has rules that state who should be contacted in order to clarify technical information. These rules prevent people from asking those who are not knowledgeable on the topic. In establishing these rules, NowBank increases its efficiency by having employees go directly to the person who can provide the necessary information, thus eliminating delays that might result from having to channel questions through several different people. In doing so, NowBank is also guided by the rule of **personnel.** This rule states that people who are the most knowledgeable should emerge as key resources to reduce equivocality. Computer technicians, not human resources personnel, are consulted to reduce equivocality of technical information associated with the Y2K project.

When an organization chooses to employ a plan of communication that has been proved effective in the past at reducing equivocality of information, **success** is the influential rule that is being applied. A university knows that many of its potential students' questions and concerns can be answered via a well-researched brochure. It has proved to be a successful recruiting tool in the past, as the enrollment figures of the school have increased by 4 percent per year over the past five years. Thus, the university knows that this is a successful way of reducing information ambiguity for students.

Effort is also a rule that influences the choice to use a brochure to promote the university. This rule guides organizations in choosing an information strategy that requires the least amount of effort to reduce equivocality. Rather than fielding numerous phone calls from potential students asking the same questions about the school, the university's decision to print a brochure that answers frequently asked questions is the most efficient means of communicating all the university has to offer. The decision made by many companies to implement automated telephone customer service is another example of how organizations reduce equivocality of information. Rather than requiring a customer to explain the reason for the call multiple times, as the customer is connected to various employees, the customer chooses a number that best matches the problem or concern. This directs the customer directly to the appropriate department.

Cycles: Act, Respond, Adjust

If the information that is received is highly equivocal, the organization may engage in a series of communication behaviors in an attempt to decrease the level of ambiguity. Weick labels these systems of behavior **cycles.** The cycle of communication behaviors used to reduce equivocality includes three stages: an act,

duration
organizational rule stating that decisions regarding equivocality should be made in the least amount of time

personnel
organizational rule stating that the most knowledgeable workers should resolve equivocality

success
organizational rule stating that a successful plan of the past will be used to reduce current equivocality

effort
organizational rule stating that decisions regarding equivocality should be made with the least amount of work

cycles
series of communication behaviors that serve to reduce equivocality

act
communication be-
haviors indicating a
person's ambiguity in
receiving a message

a response, and an adjustment. An **act** refers to the communication statements and behaviors used to indicate one's ambiguity. For example, Dominique may say to the computer technician, "The customer research team wants to know if the compatibility of customers' personal computers could potentially impact their ability to effectively conduct transactions online." In deciding to share her ambiguity with the computer technician directly, Dominique is employing the rule of personnel.

A second step in the communication cycle is response. **Response** is defined as a reaction to the act. That is, a response that seeks clarification in the equivocal message is provided as a result of the act. The technician might reply, "It is essential that customers contact their computer manufacturer to see if their machines are Y2K compatible. If they're not, they may experience difficulty in using our online banking services even though our computers are compatible."

As a result of the response, the organization formulates a response in return as a result of any **adjustment** that has been made to the information that was originally received. If the response to the act has reduced the equivocality of the message, an adjustment is made to indicate that the information is now understood. If the information is still equivocal, the adjustment might come in the form of additional questions that are designed to further clarify the information. Dominique's response to the technician—"I'll contact the publicity department immediately so they can inform our customers of this new information"—indicates that the equivocality of the original message has been decreased.

**double interact
loops**
cycles of an organiza-
tion (e.g., interviews,
meetings) to reduce
equivocality

Feedback is an essential step in the process of making sense of the information that is received. Weick uses the term double interact loops to describe the cycles of act, response, and adjustment in information exchanges. **Double interact loops** refer to multiple communication cycles that are used to assist the organization's members in reducing the equivocality of information. These communication cycles are essential for reducing the equivocality of information so that organizational members can make sense of and apply the information to attain their goals. Because these cycles require members in the organization to communicate with one another to reduce the level of ambiguity, Weick suggests that the relationships among individuals in the organization are more important to the process of organizing than the talent or knowledge that any one individual brings to the team. Hence, the system theory philosophy—"the whole is greater than the sum of its parts"—is apparent.

The Principles of Equivocality

There are three principles that organizations use when dealing with equivocality. First, an organization must analyze the relationship among the equivocality of information, the rules the organization has for removing the equivocality, and the cycles of communication that should be used. When analyzing the relationship among these three variables, a few conclusions are possible. If a message is highly equivocal, chances are that the organization has few rules for dealing with the ambiguity. As a result, the organization has to employ a greater number of cycles of communication in order to reduce the level of equivocality of the information. The organization will examine the degree of equivocality of the information (inputs) it receives and determine if it has sufficient rules that will be of assistance in guiding the cycle of communication that should be employed to reduce the ambiguity.

To exemplify, a technical question is one that is highly equivocal to those who are not trained in the field of expertise. Thus, the organization may not have a set of rules to guide communication responses and may rely solely on one rule (that is, personnel) to guide the cycles of communication. If inputs are easily understood by many members of the organization (for example, a customer may ask, "Is NowBank doing anything to prepare for the Y2K computer problems?"), there will be more rules (that is, success, effort, duration) that can be employed in reducing the equivocality. The more equivocal the message, the fewer rules that are available to guide cycles of communication; the less equivocal the message, the more rules that are available to assist the organization in reducing equivocality, thus reducing the number of cycles that are needed to interpret the information.

A second principle proposed by Weick (1979) deals with the association between the number of rules that are needed and the number of cycles that can be used to reduce the equivocality. If the organization has only a few rules that are available to assist it in reducing equivocality, a greater number of cycles will be needed to filter out the ambiguity. In the example above, a majority of the members in the organization view technical information as highly equivocal. The only rule that many of them have for dealing with this equivocality is to communicate with a person who is knowledgeable in the area of technology (personnel). Thus, there will be more cycles of information exchange that are employed between the technician and the organization's employees to reduce the ambiguity of the information. If a large number of rules are available for an organization's members to choose from in reducing equivocality, there is less need for using communication cycles to reduce the ambiguity of an input that is already understood. When there are fewer rules for an organization to use, it must increase the number of cycles it uses to reduce equivocality of information.

The third principle proposed by Weick regards a direct relationship between the number of cycles used and the amount of equivocality that remains. The more cycles that are used to obtain additional information and make adjustments, the more equivocality is removed. Weick proposes that if a larger number of cycles are used, it is more likely that equivocality can be decreased than if only a few cycles are employed.

Although NowBank has increased the potential for equivocality of information by providing its employees with multiple resources for obtaining information about the project's status (videoconferences, telephone conferences, chat areas), it has also provided its employees with a larger number of potential cycles that can be employed to reduce this equivocality. Employees can engage in online dialogues in an attempt to answer their questions and concerns about the project. They can download database files that track the progress of the project and inquire if other teams will be meeting various deadlines that are crucial to their success in the project's completion. And they have the benefit of having an internal communication team to manage all the messages they receive from various sources. Thus, there is the potential for a greater number of cycles that can be used to reduce the equivocality of information.

Reducing Equivocality: Trying to Use the Information

The process of reducing equivocality can be complex; organizations evolve through three stages in an attempt to integrate the rules and cycles so that information will be meaningful and easily understood. The three stages in this process are enactment, selection, and retention (Weick, 1995).

Enactment: Inventing Your Environment

enactment
interpretation of the information received by the organization

Enactment refers to how information will be received and interpreted by the organization. During this stage, the organization must analyze the inputs it receives to determine the amount of equivocality that is present and to assign meaning to the information. Existing rules are reviewed in making decisions about how the organization will deal with the ambiguity. If the organization determines that it does not have a sufficient number of rules for reducing the equivocality, various cycles of communication must be analyzed to determine their effectiveness in assisting the organization in understanding the information. Weick posits that this action stage is vital to the success of an organization. If a university made no effort to interpret information from potential students, it would not be able to effectively address their concerns and desires in choosing a college to attend.

Selection: Interpreting the Inputs

selection
choosing the best method for obtaining information

Once the organization has employed various rules and cycles to interpret the new inputs in its information environment, it must analyze what it knows and choose the best method for obtaining additional information to further reduce the level of equivocality. This stage is referred to as **selection** or "retrospective sensemaking." In this stage of organizing, the group is required to make a decision about the rules and cycles that will be used. If the information is still ambiguous, the organization has to look into the resources that it has available and determine if it has any additional rules that could help in reducing the ambiguity or if additional cycles of communication are necessary to enable the organization to better understand the inputs. Dominique was overwhelmed with all the inputs that would require her attention on the Y2K project (equivocality). She organized a videoconference with team members throughout the nation to gain some insight as to the various tasks they would be required to complete in order for the organization to meet its goal (enactment). However, she was even more overwhelmed by the vast amounts of information that she received as a result of the videoconference. So Dominique reviewed the existing communication plan for sharing information among the various teams (selection). She reviewed the rules that the organization originally had in place for

Organizational Information Theory and Adaptive Structuration Theory each deal with the role of communication activities in an organization. Differentiate between the two theories by discussing how communication functions in both theories. Be sure to interpret what is meant by communication activities in each theory and how the theorists might interpret the information and relationships inherent in an organization.

recording information about the status of the project (all projects would be tracked by the individual team leaders), as well as the rules for channels of communication that could be used (all questions should be addressed to the project manager, Dominique). She also reviewed the potential cycles for communication in reducing equivocality about the project (videoconference, e-mail, newsletter, chat area).

Retention: Remember the Small Stuff

Once the organization has reviewed its ability to deal with ambiguity, it analyzes the effectiveness of the rules and cycles of communication and engages in **retention.** In the retention stage, the organization saves information for later use. This stage requires organizations to look at what to deal with and what to ignore or leave alone. If a particular rule or cycle was beneficial in assisting the organization in reducing the equivocality of information, it's likely that it will be used to guide the organization in future decisions of a similar nature. Suppose that Dominique found the videoconferences to result in even more confusion among the team members because they were bombarded with more information than was either desired or required to complete various tasks in the project. She will retain that valuable insight and likely refrain from using the technology as a means of sharing project information in the future. Instead, she may choose to use online discussions to allow team members to choose the information essential to their portion of the task and skip over that information that is of little relevance to them. If strategies for dealing with equivocality are deemed to be useful, they will be retained for future use.

retention
collective memory allowing people to accomplish goals

Critique and Closing

Weick's Organizational Information Theory has been identified as a powerful theoretical framework for explaining how organizations make sense of the information that is essential for their existence. Organizational Information Theory draws from other theoretical perspectives that explain the processes that organizations undergo to receive input from others. Specifically, Weick emphasizes the importance of human interaction as central to processing information;

Theory * Into * Practice

An article by S. L. Smith in *Occupational Hazards* discusses the rebirth of the National Institute for Occupational Safety and Health (NIOSH). For several years, public critics and even members of Congress have accused NIOSH of conducting research without first examining its applicability or validity in the real world. In fact, there was a threat that NIOSH would be eliminated as a federal organization.

In 1995, officials at NIOSH realized that they could not ignore these criticisms any longer if they wished to remain in existence. They asked their critics in the public and in Congress for advice on how to address their concerns. Some of the feedback provided to NIOSH included recommendations that it should take the lead in providing a rationale for research funding by government agencies, increase potential funding partnerships with the private sector, and develop a more user-friendly approach. NIOSH officials were overwhelmed. In fact, one member stated, "Some people at NIOSH had the attitude of 'We're scientists. We don't have to explain ourselves.'" He went on to explain that the organization had a serious challenge ahead of them because very few people in the public sector knew about NIOSH and the work it did.

The first step that was taken in the rebirth of NIOSH was to include its end users in the decisions that it made about funding and research. Several projects were implemented in an attempt to raise awareness and understanding about NIOSH research—in fact, some research activities were taken to real-life workplaces instead of simply conducting studies in laboratories. Also, a telephone information line was created to publicize the agency's research efforts.

Next, a NIOSH website was created to provide the public with information about the organization, its standards, any alerts that needed to be publicized, as well as the plans for investigating health hazards and the outcome reports of these investigations. NIOSH reviewed its publications and determined that it needed to rewrite some in lay terms for readability.

Reducing ambiguity about NIOSH as an organization has been extremely beneficial to the organization. In fact, NIOSH's National Occupational Research Agenda has been used as a model by other organizations and was selected as a semifinalist for the Innovations in American Government Award.

Source: Smith, 1998.

TIP Follow-up
Examine how organizations with a history similar to that of NIOSH might try to reduce ambiguity. How would companies that have been in existence for decades work toward "rebirth" as NIOSH did?

---

thus, communication is the central focus of his theory. The primary idea is that organizations are not simply structures but are instead continually transforming and changing entities, created by their members. By making the process of reducing equivocality central to his theory, Weick emphasizes the importance of communication to the ability of organizations and their members to achieve goals.

The theory's utility is underscored by its focus on the communication process, a topic that we explored in Chapter 1. Organizational Information

Theory focuses on the *process* of communication rather than on the role of communicators themselves. This is of great benefit to understanding how members of an organization engage in collaborative efforts with both internal and external environments to understand the information that they receive. The theory has inspired thinking and research in negotiation (Putnam, 1989), public discourse (Robichaud, 1999), and organizational learning (Weick & Westley, 1996). Charles Bantz (1989) observed that in terms of Weick's influence on research overall, "it is not surprising that a variety of scholars picked up the organizing concept directly from Weick or integrated into their on-going research" (p. 233). Weick was clearly influential, thereby making Organizational Information Theory a heuristic theory.

The prevailing criticism of Organizational Information Theory pertains to Weick's belief that people are guided by rules in an organization. Yet, Tom Daniels, Barry Spiker, and Michael Papa (1997) note that "we puzzle and mull over, fret and stew over, and generally select, manipulate, and transform meanings to come up with an interpretation of a situation" (p. 52). In other words, people may have little concern with the communication rules in their work environments. Individuals are not always so conscious or precise in their selection procedures, and their actions may have more to do with their intuition than with organizational rules.

An additional criticism of Organizational Information Theory is that it looks at organizations as static units in society (Taylor & Van Every, 2000). These researchers challenge Weick's view by noting that "at no point are inherent contradictions in organizational structure and process even remotely evoked" (p. 275) in his research. Taylor and Van Every believe that organizations have ongoing tensions and these need to be examined in light of Weick's theory.

Weick's work has inspired other scholars to apply his theory in examining various aspects of how organizations communicate in an attempt to make sense of the information they receive. He has provided researchers and practitioners with an excellent beginning in understanding the importance of communication in organizational activities. Organizational Information Theory will remain an influential theory in organizational behavior.

Discussion Starters

1. Based on your understanding of the concepts of Organizational Information Theory, what additional avenues could Dominique engage in to facilitate a solution to the Y2K problem in NowBank? Respond using at least two concepts discussed in the chapter.

2. Recall an organization in which you are or were a member. Can you remember an incident when you or the organization received ambiguous information? If so, what rules did you or the organization use in dealing with this equivocality?

3. Weick describes the process of enactment, selection, and retention to understand how organizations deal with information inputs. Provide an

example of how your school has employed these strategies in making sense of information on your campus.

4. Discuss the importance of the principle of requisite variety in dealing with ambiguity. Do you think that highly equivocal information requires more complex communication processes in order to make sense of the input? Defend your answer.

5. Does your college or university solicit feedback from students regarding its promotion of the organization? Discuss the methods that your school uses.

6. Discuss how organizational rules function in Organizational Information Theory.

Terms for Review

feedback	effort
theory of sociocultural evolution	cycles
equivocality	act
information environment	response
requisite variety	adjustment
rules	double interact loops
duration	enactment
personnel	selection
success	retention

 ## Online Learning Center

Visit the Online Learning Center at www.mhhe.com/west2. Use the multiple-choice and true/false quizzes to help you prepare for exams, and the glossary, crossword puzzles, and flashcards to further your knowledge of key terms.

The Public

WHEN WE LISTEN TO A SPEECH, WATCH A PLAY, participate in a conversation, or consume media, we are members of an audience. We are the public. As audience members, we act out the transactional nature of communication discussed in Chapter 1. We simultaneously serve as both sender and receiver of messages. Both verbal and nonverbal communication, therefore, are important in audience-centered messages.

The public is at the core of the four theories we selected for this section of the book. As one of the classic works of the Western world, the *Rhetoric* is an attempt to show speakers that to be persuasive with their audiences, they should follow some suggestions. This advice includes looking at the speech, considering the speaker, and analyzing the audience. Dramatism pertains to the important role that the public plays in speech making. Dramatists believe that unless the audience identifies with the speaker, persuasion is not possible. The Narrative Paradigm proposes to look at the audience as participants in a storytelling experience. Narrative theorists contend that a person's stories are effective because they appeal to a listener's values. Finally, Cultural Studies holds that audience members are part of a cultural hierarchy. At times, audiences have little control over their future; at other times, they exercise control.

The public in communication theory refers to how we—as listeners, consumers, and audiences—play a role in deciding the extent to which others will affect us. Reading about the theories in this section will introduce you to several noteworthy topics related to the audience, including audience analysis, speech effectiveness, speaker integrity, credibility, and character.

CHAPTER 18

The *Rhetoric*

Camille Ramirez | Camille Ramirez knew that she would have to take a public speaking course for her major. Although she had been active in high school—serving as treasurer for the student council and playing on the lacrosse team—she had never done any public speaking. Now that she was in her second semester at the university, she wanted to get the required course out of the way, so she had enrolled in Public Speaking 101.

The class seemed to be going quite well. She felt fairly confident about her speaking abilities; she had received two As and one B on her speeches so far. The final speech, however, would be her most challenging. It was a persuasive speech, and she decided that she would speak on the dangers of drinking and driving. The topic was a personal one for Camille because she would talk about her Uncle Jake, a wonderful man who had died last year in an accident with a drunk driver. As she prepared for the speech, she thought that she would blend both emotion and logic into her presentation. Camille also thought that she would have to identify both sides of the drinking issue—the desire to let loose and the need to be responsible.

On the day of her speech, Camille took several deep breaths before the class started; it was a strategy that worked before her previous speeches. As she approached the lectern, she could feel the but-

terflies well up in her stomach. Yet, she reminded herself about the topic and its personal meaning. So, as planned, she began with a short story about her favorite time with Uncle Jake—the time they went to Philadelphia to see the Liberty Bell. Camille then talked about the night—two weeks after her trip—that her uncle died; he was driving home from his daughter's soccer game, and a drunk driver slammed his car from behind, forcing Jake to the embankment. His car eventually slid into a pond where he drowned.

The room was silent as Camille finished the story. She proceeded to identify why she was speaking on the topic. She told the group that considering their classroom was filled with people under the age of 25, it was important that they understand how fragile life is. Her words resonated with the group. For the next five minutes, Camille mentioned her Uncle Jake several times as she repeated the importance of not drinking and getting behind the wheel of a car.

Camille felt relieved as she finished her speech. She thought that she had done a decent job with her assignment, and she also felt that it helped her to be able to talk about her uncle again. After class, several of Camille's classmates came up and congratulated her. They thought that it took a lot of guts to talk about such a personal subject in front of so many people. A few of them also com-

---

This theory is based on the writing of **Aristotle.**

mented that they felt her topic was perfect for the audience; in fact, one of her classmates said that he wanted Camille to give the same speech to his fraternity brothers. As Camille walked to her dorm, she couldn't help but think that she had made a difference and that the speech was both a personal and professional success.

Modern life is filled with opportunities to speak in front of others. Politics and education, in particular, are areas where people spend much of their time speaking to others. Studying public speaking is important in U.S. society for several reasons. First, surveys reveal that among the communication skills employers need from their employees is effective public speaking (Curtis, Winsor, & Stephens, 1989; Winsor, Curtis, & Stephens, 1996). Second, public speaking, by definition, suggests that as a society we are receptive to listening to views that may conflict with our own. Third, when one speaks before a group, the information resonates beyond that group of people. For instance, when a politician speaks to a small group of constituents in southwest Missouri, what he says frequently gets told and retold to others. When a minister consoles her congregation after a fatal shooting at a local middle school, the words reverberate even into the living rooms of those who were not present at the service. At times, the politician becomes the consoler. Consider, for instance, the number of times that then-mayor Rudy Giuliani of New York City presented speeches of comfort to groups of people after the bombing of the World Trade Center in 2001. Clearly, public speaking has the ability to affect individuals beyond the listening audience, and it is a critical skill in a democratic society.

Despite the importance of public speaking in our lives, it remains a dreaded activity. In fact, some opinion polls state that people fear public speaking more than they fear death! Comedian Jerry Seinfeld reflects on this dilemma: "According to most studies, people's number one fear is public speaking. Number two is death. Death is number two. Does that seem right? This means to the average person, if you have to go to a funeral, you're better off in the casket than doing the eulogy" (Seinfeld, 1993, p. 120). However, public speaking is not so funny to people like Camille Ramirez. She must work through not only her anxiety about speaking before a group but also her anxiety about discussing a very personal topic. For Camille, having a sense of what to speak about and what strategies to adopt are foremost in her mind. Based on her classmates' reactions, her speech was quite effective. Camille may not know that the reasons for her success may lie in the writings of Aristotle, published more than twenty-five centuries ago.

Aristotle is generally credited with explaining the dynamics of public speaking. The *Rhetoric* consists of three books—one primarily concerned with public speakers, the second focusing on the audience, and the third attending to the speech itself. His *Rhetoric* is considered by historians, philosophers, and communication experts to be one of the most influential pieces of writing in the Western world. In addition, many still consider Aristotle's works to be the most significant writing on speech preparation and speech making. In a sense, Aristotle was the first to provide the "how to" for public speaking. Lane Cooper (1932) agrees. More than seventy years ago, Cooper observed that "the rhetoric of Aristotle is a practical psychology, and the most helpful book extant for writers of prose and for speakers of every sort" (p. vi). According to Cooper, people in all walks of life—attorneys, legislators, clergy, teachers, and media writers—will all benefit in some way when they read Aristotle's writings. That is some accolade for a man who has been dead for over 2,500 years!

To understand the power behind Aristotle's words, it's important to first understand the nature of the *Rhetoric*. In doing so, we will be able to present the simple eloquence of rhetorical theory. First, we present a brief history of life in Aristotle's day followed by a discussion of his definition of rhetoric.

The Rhetorical Tradition

The son of a physician, Aristotle was encouraged to be a thinker about the world around him. He went to study with his mentor, Plato, at the age of 17. Aristotle and Plato had conflicting worldviews; therefore, their philosophies differed as well. Plato was always in search of absolute truths about the world. He didn't care much whether these truths had practical value. Plato felt that as long as people could agree on matters of importance, society would survive. Aristotle, however, was more interested in dealing with the here and now. He wasn't so much interested in achieving absolute truth as he was in attaining a logical, realistic, and rational view of society. In other words, we could argue that Aristotle was much more grounded than Plato, trying to understand the various types of people in Athenian society.

Because he taught diverse groups of people in Greek society, Aristotle became known as a man committed to helping the ordinary citizen—at the time, a land-owning male. During the day, common citizens (men) were asked to judge murder trials, oversee city boundaries, travel as emissaries, and defend their property against would-be land collectors (Golden, Berquist, & Coleman, 2001). Because there were no professional attorneys at that time, many citizens hired **Sophists**, teachers of public speaking, to instruct them in basic principles of persuasion. These teachers established small schools where they taught students about the public speaking process and where they produced public speaking handbooks discussing practical ways to become more effective public speakers. Aristotle, however, believed that many of these handbooks were problematic in that they focused on the judicial system to the neglect of other contexts. Also, he thought that authors spent too much time on ways to arouse judges and juries: "It is not right to pervert the judge by moving him to anger or envy or pity—one might as well warp a carpenter's rule before using it," Aristotle observes (cited in Rhys & Bywater, 1954, p. 20). Aristotle reminds speakers not to forget the importance of logic in their presentations.

The *Rhetoric* could be considered Aristotle's way of responding to the problems he saw in these handbooks. Although he challenges a number of prevailing assumptions about what constitutes an effective presentation, what remains especially important is Aristotle's definition of **rhetoric:** the available

Sophists
teachers of public speaking (rhetoric) in ancient Greece

rhetoric
the available means of persuasion

means of persuasion. For Aristotle, however, availing oneself of all means of persuasion does not translate into bribery or torture, common practices in ancient Greece, where slavery was institutionalized. What Aristotle envisions and recommends is for speakers to work beyond their first instincts when they want to persuade others. They need to consider all aspects of speech making, including their audience members. When Camille prepared for her speech by assessing both her words and her audience's needs, she was adhering to Aristotle's suggestions for successful speaking.

For some of you, interpreting rhetoric in this way may be unfamiliar. After all, the word has been tossed around by so many different types of people that it may have lost Aristotle's original intent. For instance, Jasper Neel (1994) comments that "the term *rhetoric* has taken on such warm and cuddly connotations in the postmodern era" (p. 15), that we tend to forget that its meaning is very specific. For people like Neel, we must return to Aristotle's interpretation of rhetoric or we will miss the essence of his theory. Politicians often indict their opponents by stating that their "rhetoric is empty" or that they're all "rhetoric, with little action." These sorts of criticisms only trivialize the active and dynamic process of rhetoric and its role in the public speaking process.

Assumptions of the *Rhetoric*

To this end, let's examine two primary assumptions of rhetorical theory as proposed by Aristotle. You should be aware that rhetorical theory covers a wide range of thinking in the communication field, and so it is nearly impossible to capture all of the beliefs associated with the theory. Nonetheless, Aristotelian theory is guided by the following two assumptions:

- Effective public speakers must consider their audience.
- Effective public speakers utilize a number of proofs in their presentations.

The first assumption underscores the definition of communication that we presented in Chapter 1: Communication is a transactional process. Within a public speaking context, Aristotle suggests that the speaker–audience relationship must be acknowledged. Speakers should not construct or deliver their speeches without considering their audiences. Speakers should, in a sense, become audience-centered. They should think about the audience as a group of individuals with motivations, decisions, and choices and not as some undifferentiated mass of homogeneous people. The effectiveness of Camille's speech on drinking and driving derives from her ability to understand her audience. She knows that students, primarily under the age of 25, rarely think about death, and, therefore, her speech prompts them to think about something that they normally would not consider. Camille, like many other public speakers, engaged in **audience analysis**, which is the process of evaluating an audience and its background (such as age, sex, educational level, and so forth) and tailoring one's speech so that listeners respond as the speaker hopes they will.

Aristotle felt that audiences are crucial to a speaker's ultimate effectiveness. He observes, "Of the three elements in speech-making—speaker, subject, and person addressed—it is the last one, the hearer, that determines the speech's

audience analysis
an assessment and
evaluation of listeners

The Theory Connection

Discuss the role of the audience in the *Rhetoric* and the role of the audience in Cultural Studies. How does Aristotle and Stuart Hall differ in their interpretation of the audience? How are they similar?

end and object" (cited in Roberts, 1984, p. 2159). Each listener, however, is unique, and what works with one listener may fail with another. Expanding on this notion, Carnes Lord (1994) observes that audiences are not always open to rational argument. Consider Camille's speech on drinking and driving. Her speech may have worked wonderfully in the public speaking classroom, but she may have different results with a group of alcohol distributors. As you can see, understanding the audience is critical before a speaker begins constructing his or her speech.

The second assumption underlying Aristotle's theory pertains to what speakers do in their speech preparation and their speech making. Aristotle's proofs refer to the means of persuasion, and, for Aristotle, three proofs exist: ethos, pathos, and logos. **Ethos** refers to the perceived character, intelligence, and goodwill of a speaker as they become revealed through his or her speech. Eugene Ryan (1984) notes that ethos is a broad term that refers to the mutual influence that speakers and listeners have on each other. Ryan contends that Aristotle believed that the speaker can be influenced by the audience in much the same way that audiences can be influenced by the speaker. Aristotle felt that a speech by a trustworthy individual was more persuasive than a speech by an individual whose trust was in question. **Logos** is the logical proof that speakers employ—their arguments, rationalizations, and discourse. For Aristotle, logos involves using a number of practices, including using logical claims and clear language. To speak in poetic phrases results in a lack of clarity and naturalness. **Pathos** pertains to the emotions that are drawn out of listeners. Aristotle argued that listeners become the instruments of proof when emotion is stirred in them; listeners judge differently when they are influenced by joy, pain, hatred, or fear. Let's return to our example of Camille to illustrate these three Aristotelian proofs.

The ethos that Camille evokes during her presentation is important. Relating a personal account of her relationship with her Uncle Jake and describing his subsequent death at the hands of a drunk driver bolster perceptions of her credibility. Undoubtedly, her audience feels that she is a credible speaker by virtue of her relationship with Jake and her knowledge of the consequences of drinking and driving. Logos is evident in Camille's speech when she decides to logically argue that although drinking is a part of recreation, it can also be a deadly mix. Using examples to support her claims underscores Camille's use of logical proof. The pathos inherent in the speech should be apparent from the subject matter. She chooses a topic that appeals to her college listeners. They

ethos
the perceived character, intelligence, and goodwill of a speaker

logos
logical proof; the use of arguments and evidence in a speech

pathos
emotional proof; emotions drawn from audience members

most likely will feel for Camille and reflect on how many times they or their friends have gotten behind the wheel after having a few drinks. The Aristotelian theory, therefore, guides Camille's effectiveness.

Although ethos, logos, and pathos may seem very straightforward, Aristotle delineates logos much further. In his discussion, he notes that speakers who consider logos must necessarily consider syllogisms and enthymemes. We now turn our attention to these Aristotelian principles.

Syllogisms and Enthymemes: A Three-Tiered Argument

We noted that logos is one of the three proofs that, according to Aristotle, create a more effective message. Nestled in these logical proofs is something called syllogisms. The term requires clarification because there is some debate among scholars on its precise meaning.

Communication scholars have studied the *Rhetoric* and its meaning for years and have attempted to untangle some of Aristotle's words. Two of the most discussed terms are *syllogism* and *enthymeme*. Let's clarify both of these terms because Aristotle's original thinking associated with these concepts was a bit unclear. The first word, syllogism, has evoked some scholarly concern among rhetorical theorists (e.g., Bitzer, 1959). For our purposes, we define **syllogism** as a set of propositions that are related to one another and draw a conclusion from the major and minor premises. Typically, syllogisms contain two premises and a conclusion. A syllogism is nothing more than a deductive argument, which, as you may recall from Chapter 4, is a group of statements (premises) that lead to another group of statements (conclusions). In other words, premises are starting points or beginners used by speakers. They establish justification for a conclusion. In a syllogism, both major and minor premises exist. Syllogistic reasoning in Camille's speech might look something like this:

> *Major Premise:* A high percentage of alcohol-related fatalities involve college-age drinkers.

> *Minor Premise:* College students have the wisdom and education to not drink and drive.

> *Conclusion:* Therefore, you (Camille's audience) can use your experience and wisdom to take the lead and drive sober.

Lloyd Bitzer (1959) defined an **enthymeme** as a "syllogism based on probabilities, signs, and examples, [and] whose function is rhetorical persuasion." Let's explore the three elements of his definition: probabilities, signs, and examples.

Probabilities are statements that are generally true. According to Aristotle, enthymemes rest on probabilities and not on absolute truth. For speakers, probabilities are suggested in their speeches. For instance, "People want to behave responsibly" could be a statement of probability in Camille's presentation. **Signs** are statements that identify reasons for a fact. Aristotle believes that some signs are established with certainty, whereas others warrant scientific proof. For instance, an irrefutable sign may take the following form: "Drinking too

syllogism
a set of propositions that are related to one another and draw a conclusion from the major and minor premises

enthymeme
a syllogism based on probabilities, signs, and examples

probabilities
statements that are generally true, but still require conjecture

signs
statements that identify reasons for a fact

much and getting behind the wheel of a car can jeopardize lives." This is a sign that has been validated by research. However, "She is drinking and will get into a car accident" needs further scientific validation because not everyone who drinks gets into an accident. Finally, **examples** pertain to those statements that are either actual or invented by the speaker. Aristotle maintains that examples are inductively derived—that is, from a specific claim, audiences develop general beliefs about the topic. For instance, Camille's specific example of drinking and driving will lead audience members to the general proposition: "Drinking and driving produces irresponsible behavior."

How does the enthymeme relate to persuasive speaking? Omar Swartz (1998) comments that audiences favor messages whereby they can supply a premise or deduce a conclusion for themselves rather than being told what to do or think. Formal syllogisms can offend an audience if they are too obvious in structure. For a persuasive speech, then, speakers should afford the audience some opportunity to fill in the blanks. For example, there is no need for Camille Ramirez to relate all of the horrors of her uncle's tragedy. Audiences probably already have information about the topic from the media or from their own experiences. Again, as with other aspects of Aristotelian theory, the audience remains a critical part of the enthymeme.

Aristotle confuses many readers of the *Rhetoric* by noting that the enthymeme is both similar to and different from the syllogism. Some scholars (Golden et al., 2000) have attempted to clear up the confusion. They observe that Aristotle regarded the enthymeme as a method of persuasion "which has the same relationship to rhetoric that the syllogism has to logic" (p. 28). The authors note that both are forms of reasoning, both are types of knowledge, and both are essentially the same in structure. The primary difference between the two is that while syllogisms deal with certainties, enthymemes deal with probabilities. To distinguish between a syllogism and an enthymeme, consider the following example:

SYLLOGISM

Some politicians are crooked and deceitful. (Major Premise)

Sara Collier is a politician. (Minor Premise)

Therefore, Sara Collier is a crooked and deceitful politician. (Conclusion)

ENTHYMEME

Some politicians are crooked and deceitful. (Premise)

Therefore, Senator Sara Collier may be crooked or deceitful. (Conclusion)

As you can see, syllogisms lead to a conclusion supported by what could be called universal truths. For instance, there are some politicans who are crooked and who deceive. It can also be proved that Sara Collier is a politician. The enthymeme, however, leads to a conclusion drawn from an incomplete premise. In other words, the enthymeme leaves off a critical premise that the syllogism contains.

Our discussion of the enthymeme and its relationship to other Aristotelian proofs merits a brief comment. First, it is important to understand that although Aristotle believes that the enthymeme is directly related to logos, some rhetorical scholars wish to link enthymemes with other proofs, as the preceding example does. James McBurney (1994), for instance, reminds us that the enthymeme is the foundation of all persuasive discourse. It, therefore, is necessarily linked with ethos and pathos. Larry Arnhart (1981) effectively argues the interrelationship between the enthymeme and the forms of proof when he concludes that an enthymeme's persuasive power lies in its ability to be logical, ethical, and pathetical. He contends that "enthymemes may be used not only to establish a conclusion as a probable truth but also to alter the emotions of the listeners or to develop their confidence in the character of the speaker" (p. 10). An audience member may accept the logic of an argument, for example, because the argument elicits some emotion from the audience (pathos) and the speaker is seen as credible (ethos). Hence, enthymemes should be viewed expansively.

Enthymemes are a critical part of the speaking process for Aristotle. Speakers use them to enhance effectiveness in their speeches. In addition to enthymemes, speakers also incorporate other techniques. We now examine five different strategies for speakers that Aristotle labeled canons.

Canons of Rhetoric

Aristotle was convinced that, for a persuasive speech to be effective, speakers must follow certain guidelines or principles, which he called canons. These are recommendations for making a speech more compelling. Classical rhetoricians have maintained Aristotle's observations, and to this day, most writers of public speaking texts in communication follow Aristotelian canons for effective speaking.

Although his writings in the *Rhetoric* focused on persuasion, these canons have been applied in a number of speaking situations. Aristotle points to five prescriptions for effective oratory: invention, arrangement, style, delivery, and memory. We discuss these five canons below and highlight them in Table 18.1.

Invention

The first canon is invention. This term can be confusing because invention of a speech does not mean invention in a scientific sense. **Invention** is defined as the construction or development of an argument that is relevant to the purpose of a speech. Invention is closely connected to logos, which we explored earlier. Invention, therefore, can include the use of enthymematic reasoning in one's speech. In addition, invention is broadly interpreted as the body of information and knowledge that a speaker brings to the speaking situation. This stockpile of information can help a speaker in his or her persuasive approaches. Suppose, for instance, you are presenting a speech on the benefits of exercise. The invention associated with this speech would include both the logical appeals presented in your speech ("You will live longer" or "Your health insurance premiums will be lower") and the body of knowledge you have about health in general. In constructing your arguments, you will draw on all of this.

invention
a canon of rhetoric that pertains to the construction or development of an argument related to a particular speech.

Table 18.1   Aristotle's Canons of Rhetoric

CANON	DEFINITION	DESCRIPTION
Invention	Integration of reasoning and arguments in speech	Using logic and evidence in speech makes a speech more powerful and more persuasive.
Arrangement	Organization of speech	Maintaining a speech structure—Introduction, Body, Conclusion—bolsters speaker credibility, enhances persuasiveness, and reduces listener frustration.
Style	Use of language in speech	Incorporating style ensures that a speech is memorable and that a speaker's ideas are clarified.
Delivery	Presentation of speech	Effective delivery complements a speaker's words and helps to reduce speaker anxiety.
Memory	Storing information in speaker's mind	Knowing what to say and when to say it eases speaker anxiety and allows a speaker to respond to unanticipated events.

topics
an aid to invention that refers to the arguments a speaker uses

civic spaces
a metaphor suggesting that speakers have "locations" where the opportunity to persuade others exists

Aids to invention are identified as topics. Topics, in this sense, refer to the lines of argument or modes of reasoning a speaker uses in a speech. Speakers may draw on these invention aids as they decide which speaking strategy will persuade their audiences. Topics, therefore, help speakers enhance their persuasiveness. Speakers look to what are called civic spaces, or the metaphorical locations where rhetoric has the opportunity to effect change, "where a speaker can look for 'available means of persuasion'" (Kennedy, 1991, p. 45). Recall, for instance, Camille's decision to talk about drinking and driving in her public speaking class. As she speaks, she defines her terms, looks at opposing arguments, and considers ideas similar to her own. That is, she identifies a "location" in her speech where she is able to adapt to an audience that may be losing attention. Camille does whatever it takes to ensure that she has the chance to persuade her audience.

Arrangement

arrangement
a canon of rhetoric that pertains to a speaker's ability to organize a speech

A second canon identified by Aristotle is called arrangement. Arrangement pertains to a speaker's ability to organize a speech. Aristotle felt that speakers should seek out organizational patterns for their speeches to enhance the speech's effectiveness. Artistic unity among different thoughts should be foremost in a speaker's mind. Simplicity should also be a priority because Aristotle believed that there are essentially two parts to a speech: stating the subject and finding the proof, or what he calls "demonstrating it" (Kennedy, 1991, p. 258).

At the time, he felt that speakers were organizing their speeches haphazardly, making them less effective speakers.

Aristotle, however, is very clear in his organizational strategy. Speeches should generally follow a threefold approach: introduction, body, and conclusion. The **introduction** should first gain the audience's attention, then suggest a connection with the audience, and finally provide an overview of the speech's purpose. George Kennedy (1991) relates Aristotle's words regarding introductions:

> All sorts of things will lead the audience to receptivity if the speaker wants, including his [her] seeming to be a reasonable person. They pay more attention to these people. And they are attentive to great things, things that concern themselves, marvels, and pleasures. As a result, one should imply that the speech is concerned with such things. (p. 263)

Introductions can be quite effective in speeches that are intended to emotionally arouse. Gaining attention by incorporating emotional wording is an effective persuasive technique. Consider Camille's introductory words. She obviously captures the audience's attention by personalizing a very difficult subject. She then suggests her relationship with the topic, followed by an overview of her speaking purpose:

> Jake McCain was killed by someone he didn't know. Jake was a wonderful man and the person who killed him never knew that. Yet, Jake's death could have been prevented. You see, he was killed by someone who was drunk. The driver may have a future, but Jake will never have a chance to see his grandchild grow up or see his sister get married. I know about Jake McCain: He's my uncle. Today, I wish to discuss the dangers of drunk driving and identify how you can avoid becoming one of the many thousands who get behind a wheel after drinking too much.

Arrangement also includes the body and conclusion of the speech. The **body** includes all of the arguments, supporting details, and necessary examples to make a point. In addition to the entire speech being organized, the body of the speech also follows some sort of organizational structure. Aristotle felt that audiences need to be led from one point to another.

Finally, the **conclusion** or epilogue of a speech is aimed at summarizing the speaker's points and arousing emotions in the audience. Conclusions should be arrived at logically and should also attempt to reconnect with listeners. Camille's conclusion clearly demonstrates her desire to leave her listeners with a message:

> So I leave you today after examining the prevalence of drunk driving, the current laws associated with this behavior, and what you and I can personally do to help rid our society of this terrible and overlooked part of being a college student. The next time you go and have a drink, don't forget to give your keys to a friend. Or get a cab. I'm sure your family will thank you. Do it for me. Do it for my Uncle Jake.

We can feel Camille's passion for a topic that is both personal and personally difficult.

introduction
part of an organizational strategy in a speech that includes gaining the audience's attention, connecting with the audience, and providing an overview of the speaker's purpose

body
part of an organizational strategy in a speech that includes arguments, examples, and important details to make a point

conclusion
part of an organizational strategy in a speech that is aimed at summarizing a speaker's main points and arousing emotions in an audience

321

Theory Application in Groups (TAG)

Considering the canon of arrangement, construct a speech on why your school should keep tuition as it is and not raise it. Develop the structure of the speech and specify why you chose your particular arrangement.

Style

style
a canon of rhetoric that includes the use of language to express ideas in a speech

glosses
outdated words in a speech

metaphor
a figure of speech that helps to make the unclear more understandable

The use of language to express ideas in a certain manner is called **style.** In his discussion of style, Aristotle includes word choice, word imagery, and word appropriateness. He believes that each type of rhetoric has its own style, and, yet, style is often overlooked. He notes that strange words or **glosses** (outdated words) should be avoided. Yet, speaking in terms that are too simplistic will also turn off an audience. To bridge this gap between the unfamiliar and the too familiar, Aristotle introduces the notion of **metaphor,** or a figure of speech that helps to make the unclear more understandable. Metaphors are critical devices to employ in speeches, according to Aristotle, because they have the capacity to "alter the content and activities of one's mind" (Moran, 1996, p. 391). The Research Note on the following page highlights the use of metaphor.

Style can be better understood through an example from Camille's speech on drunk driving. If Camille were concentrating on style, her speech would have the following passage:

> Drinking is often looked at as a means to release. After a very long day at work or at school, there is nothing so soothing as a cold beer. So they say. Yet, too often one beer turns into two, which by the end of a few hours, has turned into a six-pack. And the result can be tragic: How many times have you watched your friend or family member get into a car after a six-pack? It's as if this person is a bullet, unleashed from a gun that is randomly pointed at someone. If you must drink, it's not only your business; but, now, it's our business, too.

Camille's words evoke some strong imagery; mentally, we can re-create the scene that she has laid out. Her word choice is unmistakable in that she does not use unfamiliar words. Finally, she uses a compelling metaphor of a bullet.

Delivery

delivery
a canon of rhetoric that refers to the nonverbal presentation of a speaker's ideas

Thus far we have concentrated on how a speech is constructed. Aristotle, however, was also interested in how a speech is delivered. In this case, **delivery** refers to the nonverbal presentation of a speaker's ideas. Delivery normally includes a host of behaviors, including eye contact, vocal cues, pronunciation, enunciation, dialect, body movement, and physical appearance. For Aristotle, delivery specifically pertains to the manipulation of the voice. He especially encouraged speakers to use appropriate levels of pitch, rhythm, volume, and emotion. He believed that the way in which something is said affects its intelligibility.

Research Note

Aden, R. C. (1989). Entrapment and escape: Inventional metaphors in Ronald Reagan's economic rhetoric. *The Southern Communication Journal, 54,* 384–400.

Focusing on the metaphor, one of Aristotle's central principles in the *Rhetoric,* Roger Aden engages in an analysis of President Reagan's economic rhetoric. Aden begins by noting that Reagan's rhetoric was crucial to his success as a president but is not the sole reason why Reagan was so effective. Aden contends that voters frequently voted according to the current U.S. economic conditions, and Reagan was instrumental in tapping into voter sentiment. Using the metaphors of entrapment and escape, Reagan helped define himself and led voters to his way of thinking.

Aden takes the reader on a historical journey of life in the United States in 1980, the year Reagan defeated President Carter. At that time the country was in an economic spiral, fueled by the Iranian hostage situation (U.S. business investment in Iran was at a standstill) and the worsening energy crisis. As governor of California, Reagan capitalized on the nation's economic insecurity by employing specific language in a number of his speeches, both during his campaign and during his presidency.

Aden focuses on four speeches by Reagan. He finds that Reagan frequently invoked images of entrapment, a metaphor that "produces an image of big government that builds up walls around the American people" (p. 389). According to Aden, Reagan repeatedly stated that the United States is "trapped" in a deep recession, leading to both eco-nomic and psychological depression. Reagan, how-ever, felt that there was an escape from big government, a second metaphor frequently used in his speeches. Aden suggests that Reagan built up the public's confidence in their own abilities to overcome big government, to rise above the walls that encroach them. Aden also states that Reagan enticed the public by noting that their genius and energy would help them escape one of the country's most difficult economic times.

Aden argues that Reagan's rhetoric suited the times. Reagan helped the public blame the government for their problems, not themselves. In four years and presumably better times, Reagan could then tell the public that they were responsible for the economic surge, not big government. Aden believes, however, that Reagan began to rely too heavily on the entrapment and escape metaphors. In fact, although Reagan supported an economic bill of rights, the public preferred to increase spending in a number of areas that Reagan could never support. His belief that Americans were "trapped" and needed an "escape" was no longer effective. Reagan's words, in a sense, became out of step with the voters.

Aden concludes his article by comparing Reagan to Shakespearean verse. If "all the world's a stage," then Reagan was an actor who repeated the same lines over and over. Consequently, Reagan moved from center stage to stage right exit.

Aristotle felt that delivery could not be easily taught, yet it is crucial for a speaker to consider. He also believed that speakers should strive to be natural in their delivery. Speakers should not use any vocal techniques that may detract from the words and should strive to capture a comfortable presence in front of an audience.

Memory

Storing invention, arrangement, and style in a speaker's mind is **memory.** Unlike the previous four canons, Aristotle does not spend significant time delineating the importance of memory in speech presentation. Rather, he alludes to memory in his writings. Throughout the *Rhetoric,* for instance, Aristotle

memory
a canon of rhetoric that refers to a speaker's effort in storing information for a speech

reminds us to consider a number of issues prior to the presentation (such as examples, enthymemes, signs, metaphors, delivery techniques, and so forth). He further notes that to speak persuasively a speaker would have to have a basic understanding of many of these devices when constructing and presenting a speech. In other words, speakers would need to have memorized a great deal before getting up to speak.

Today, people interpret memory in speech making differently from Aristotle. Memorizing a speech often means having a basic understanding of material and techniques. Although other rhetoricians like Quintilian made specific recommendations on memorizing, Aristotle felt that familiarizing oneself with the speech's content was understood. When Camille presents her speech on drinking and driving, for example, she has some parts of her speech committed to memory and other parts overviewed on notes.

The canons of rhetoric are incorporated into a number of different persuasive speeches. Our exploration of Aristotle's rhetorical theory concludes with a discussion of the three types of rhetoric.

Types of Rhetoric

You will recall that during Aristotle's time citizens were asked to take part in a number of speaking activities—from judge to attorney to legislator. It was in this spirit that Aristotle identified different speaking situations for citizens to consider when conversing on trade, finance, national defense, and war. He denoted three types of rhetoric, or what he called three types of oratory: forensic, epideictic, and deliberative. **Forensic rhetoric** pertains to speakers eliciting feelings of guilt or innocence. **Epideictic rhetoric** is discourse related to praise or blame. **Deliberative rhetoric** concerns speakers who must determine a course of action—something should or should not be done. The three types refer to three different time periods: forensic to the past, epideictic to the present, and deliberative to the future. We discuss these three rhetorical types below and illustrate them in Figure 18.1.

Forensic oratory, or judicial rhetoric, specifically refers to speaking in courtrooms. Its intent is to establish guilt or innocence; in Aristotle's day, forensic speakers directed their presentation to courtroom judges. Aristotle examined forensic rhetoric within a legal framework, and thus many of his beliefs on the law are found in the *Rhetoric*. Amelie Rorty (1996) notes that forensic

forensic rhetoric
a type of rhetoric that pertains to speakers prompting feelings of guilt or innocence from an audience
epideictic rhetoric
a type of rhetoric that pertains to praising or blaming
deliberative rhetoric
a type of rhetoric that determines an audience's course of action

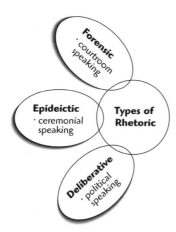

Figure 18.1
Types of Rhetoric

speaking requires focusing on arguments that tap into judges' psyches, including their beliefs about why certain criminals act the way they do and which types of occasions tempt people to break the law. Because past actions are frequently indicative of a person's current behavior, forensics orators rely upon previous behaviors.

Aristotle recognized that a person's character is critical in forensic rhetoric. He interprets character as both status (that is, whether a person is young or old, rich or poor, fortunate or unfortunate) and morality (whether a person is just or unjust, reasonable or unreasonable). If people act voluntarily, Aristotle argued, the choices they make have consequences. To establish guilt, the forensic speaker needs to establish motivation for doing wrong. In speaking before an audience, then, speakers will invoke what Aristotle called the "moral habits" of a person.

Examples of forensic rhetoric abound in our society. Forensic rhetors have played prominent roles in U.S. courtrooms. Attorneys, in particular, have effectively and persuasively used their forensic rhetoric over the years. One of the most memorable forensic presentations took place in the closely watched trial of O. J. Simpson. Prosecutors tried to implicate Simpson's morals by playing a tape recording of a 911 call in which Simpson could be heard yelling at his wife and by showing pictures of her beaten body to the jury. More recent forensic efforts by prosecutors include the legal proceedings of corporate executives accused of stealing hundreds of millions of dollars from company profits. In all these cases, forensic speaking was used to undercut the moral integrity of the defendant and to establish guilt.

The second type of rhetoric, epideictic, is also called ceremonial speaking. Speeches during Aristotle's time were given in public arenas with the goal of praising, honoring, blaming, or shaming. Epideictic rhetors include people, events, organizations, or nations in their speeches. These speeches usually focus on social issues because—according to Aristotle—people are interested in the here and now. Epideictic speaking cannot be separated from ethos, Aristotle stated. He believed that by understanding the need to praise or blame, epideictic speakers understand the importance of their own character. For instance, a speech criticizing prison conditions may not resonate deeply with an audience if the speaker is on death row for rape and murder.

Epideictic speaking is greatly informed by the study of virtues or values—a theme that Aristotle borrowed from Plato. The epideictic speaker must be able to relate the virtues of the topic to a diverse audience. Aristotle felt that courage and justice ranked above all virtues, but virtue is defined according to the law of the land.

Epideictic rhetoric is exemplified in funeral practices in our country. Eulogies, which are commonplace at many funerals, usually laud the life of the deceased. Commenting on contemporary values, the epideictic speaker at a funeral frequently compares the virtues of the dead person with those of society. For instance, after the death of his grandmother, one of the authors was asked to give the eulogy at the funeral. During his speech, he talked about his grandmother's uplifting spirit and how she rarely complained about her ailments or about her financial situation. He evoked images of contemporary society in his speech, noting how unusual it is today for someone to refrain from self-centered complaining. His speech centered on a prevailing virtue of his grandmother—her selflessness—and also commented on society as a whole.

The third type is deliberative rhetoric, also called political rhetoric, and was the focus of much of Aristotle's comments on rhetorical discourse. Aristotle believed that although many writers failed to discuss this rhetorical form, it deserves attention because it has the potential to elicit the most change in an audience. As we mentioned earlier, deliberative rhetoric is associated with the future—what an audience will do or think as a result of a speaker's efforts. Deliberative speaking, then, requires the speaker to be adept at understanding how his or her thoughts are aligned with those of the audience. The deliberative speaker should be prepared to consider subjects that are relevant to the audience and to which the speaker can personally relate. Aristotle believed that there are five subjects on which people deliberate: revenue, war and peace, the defense of the country, commerce, and legislation (Arnhart, 1981). Today's list of deliberative topics might include health insurance, taxes, relationships, education, and personal wellness. Deliberative speakers might try to raise interest in these topics, and once interest is peaked, they might find that listeners are more prone to being persuaded.

Larry Arnhart (1981) comments that the deliberative rhetorician needs to know not only the actual subject of deliberation but also the elements of human nature that influence deliberation. There are a number of topics, therefore, that are suited for deliberation and others that are not. Aristotle focused on what deliberative speakers can say to an assembly (a body of legislators, for example), and, today, this deliberative oratory continues. Consider the following example. When asked to give a short presentation to her state's legislative committee on health insurance, Beverly, a 64-year-old mother of four, spoke about the health insurance of elderly people. As the caretaker of her 90-year-old mother-in-law, a patient in a local nursing home, Beverly knew precisely the kinds of persuasive strategies to use with the group of politicians. Her speech focused on the difficulties of being old and how these problems are amplified by not having enough insurance. She asked the legislators to consider their own aging parents in their discussions. She outlined five "points of action" for the committee to follow. Three of the points could be undertaken immediately: establishing a task force, interviewing elderly citizens, and setting up a toll-free number to solicit citizen concerns and complaints. The remaining two required funding from the legislature. At the conclusion of her brief speech, Beverly was satisfied that her suggestions would not be ignored.

Aristotle would have been proud of Beverly's rhetoric. Her recommendations were doable (the committee enacted three of the five), and she made her experiences relevant to her audience by asking the group to think about their own parents. This approach elicits personal identification, which is an important tactic in deliberative speaking. By eliciting these feelings, Beverly knew that she would be able to get her audience to agree with her thinking.

Critique and Closing

Aristotle's *Rhetoric* remains an influential foundation in communication. You can pick up any public speaking text and find discussions on delivery, organization, and style. Students of public speaking have benefited greatly from the words of Aristotle, and for this reason, the theory is useful. The theory's value, however, transcends the communication discipline. Scholars in political science, medicine, English composition, and philosophy have studied rhetorical theory, incorporating several Aristotelian principles in their scholarship. The theory, therefore, is heuristic. In addition, it is apparent that this theory—more than any other in the discipline—has withstood the test of time.

Critics of Aristotle's theory are not so quick to endorse the entire theory, however. For instance, Aristotle has been criticized for contradiction and incoherence (Lord, 1994). Lord contends that in developing his theory, Aristotle blasts his contemporary rhetorical writers for focusing too much on the audience's emotions. Although Aristotle encourages speakers to avoid focusing on emotions when making their point, he proceeds to do just that when he stresses the importance of presenting emotions and invoking audience passions (pathos) during a speech.

John Cooper (1996) challenges Lord's critique. He argues that Aristotle was simply responding to the Sophists' messages of the day. Because most of the speeches in ancient Greece were directed to judges and rulers, Aristotle felt that speakers should try to elicit feelings of pity in the courtroom. To do that, Aristotle felt that speakers should try to view judges in congenial ways.

Another critique of Aristotle's work centers on its apparent incoherence. For instance, scholars agree that the *Rhetoric* is a rather unorganized undertaking; in fact, the theory is assembled from Aristotle's lecture notes (Kennedy, 1991; Lord, 1994). It is not surprising, then, that Aristotle seems to discuss topics in a random and arbitrary manner. At times, Aristotle introduces a topic and then drops it, only to return to it later. His terminology is especially unclear. For example, he advocates the use of enthymemes in public speaking and yet fails to clearly define the term. Scholars continue to differ about whether an enthymeme *is* a syllogism or whether it is *like* a syllogism. Much of this

Theory * Into * Practice

In an article in *USA Today,* Deborah Mathis presents evidence that rhetorical skills are still in fashion. During former President Clinton's impeachment trial in the Senate, former Democratic Senator Dale Bumpers of Arkansas was asked by the Clinton defense team to present closing arguments. The choice of Bumpers as a speaker was obvious from the start. First, Mathis observes that he and the president bring "almost a brotherly empathy" to the fight for Clinton's acquittal. Second, Mathis notes that the attorneys were aware that the Democratic constituency (the president's audience) needed to be solidified during this difficult time. Finally, the perception of Bumpers as "an old country lawyer from Charleston" was instrumental in communicating his credibility with former Senate colleagues. Bumpers's ability to wow his Senate friends rests in his ability to connect with them. Mathis writes that he has several Republican friends who have a pretty close relationship with the Arkansan. She continues, "Some consider him one of the most stirring and sharp-witted orators the chamber has produced."

Dale Bumpers's rhetorical skills are apparent when considering the reactions of both his Democratic and Republican colleagues. His credibility, therefore, is without question. He knows his audience, has valuable speaking experience, and can engender emotions. These qualities highlight the suggestions advanced by Aristotle.

Source: Mathis, 1999.

TIP Follow-up

Explain the difference between audiences in the U.S. Senate and those in your classrooms. What kind of reaction would Senator Bumpers have received at your house? Discuss how the audiences that U.S. presidents face in Congress differ from those surrounding you.

confusion is rooted in Aristotle's definitions, or lack of definitions. Arnhart (1981) concludes that Aristotle defined his terms in less than precise ways so that audiences (readers) would have a broader understanding of his words and ideas. Arnhart believes that this conscious decision to remain equivocal does not mean that Aristotle's thoughts should be discarded.

Finally, the *Rhetoric* tends to view the audience in a passive way. Critics charge Aristotle with ignoring the critical nature of many listeners. For instance, Jasper Neel (1994) states, "Aristotle makes clear that the introduction [of a speech] has nothing to do with the 'speech itself.' It exists only because of the hearer's weak-minded tendency to listen to what is beside the point" (p. 156). Eugene Ryan (1984) is more blunt: "Aristotle is thinking of listeners who have some difficulty keeping their minds on the speaker's business, are easily distracted, tend to forget what has gone on before, [and] are not absorbed with abstract ideas" (p. 47). From these writers, we get the impression that Aristotle perceived audiences to be incapable of being discriminating listeners or critical thinkers. It's important to note, though, that Aristotle was writing at a time when people were rather passive listeners; they did not watch the evening news and did not have access to information about world events. Further, when one considers that the *Rhetoric* is based on lecture notes and that students back then were not accustomed to openly challenging their mentors, Aristotle's view of the audience is not so implausible.

With over twenty centuries behind us, we are in a position to reflect on some of the greatest written works of all time. The *Rhetoric* is clearly such a work. Aristotle's words continue to resonate in a society that is far different from his day. Some people may reject his thoughts as outdated in an age where multiple ways of knowing are embraced. Nonetheless, a theory focusing on how speakers use and engender emotions, logic, and trustworthiness cannot be ignored.

Discussion Starters

1. Camille Ramirez relied on Aristotle's view of public speaking. Do you believe that she could have been more effective? In what way? Use examples in your response.

2. Aristotle's critics have focused on the fact that his theory is simply a collection of lecture notes that are contradictory, vague, and often narrow. Do you agree or disagree, based on the information in this chapter? What examples can you point to for support?

3. Employ enthymematic reasoning for and against each of the following topics: physician-assisted suicide, abortion, and medicinal marijuana use.

4. Discuss what canon of rhetoric is most important when politicians speak to their constituents. Use examples to defend your view.

5. If Aristotle were alive today and you were his student, what additional suggestions would you offer him for a new edition of the *Rhetoric*? Why do you believe that your suggestions are important to address in public speaking? Incorporate examples in your response.

6. Aristotle spent a great deal of time discussing the role of the audience. If you were giving a speech on safety to a group of convenience store employees, what sort of audience analysis would you undertake?

Terms for Review

Sophists	examples
rhetoric	invention
audience analysis	topics
ethos	civic spaces
logos	arrangement
pathos	introduction
syllogism	body
enthymeme	conclusion
probabilities	style
signs	glosses

metaphor
delivery
memory

forensic rhetoric
epideictic rhetoric
deliberative rhetoric

 Online Learning Center

Visit the Online Learning Center at www.mhhe.com/west2. Use the multiple-choice and true/false quizzes to help you prepare for exams, and the glossary, crossword puzzles, and flashcards to further your knowledge of key terms.

CHAPTER 19

Dramatism

Karl Elliott

Karl Elliott really looked forward to this part of his morning routine. He settled down with his first cup of coffee and the morning paper. He allowed himself an hour to read all the news of the day and savor his caffeine fix. In many ways this was his favorite part of the day, and he got up extra early to make sure he would have enough time after his workout and before he left for the office. But today he was not happy. He looked at the headlines with disgust. He was so sick of reading about fat cats who had no common sense. Today he was reading about the case of Martha Stewart's sale of her ImClone stock. The congressional committee was turning the case over to the Justice Department, and Stewart seemed to be in trouble.

Karl looked up from his paper just as his partner Max came into the breakfast room. Karl asked, "Max, have you been reading about Martha Stewart? She makes something like a billion dollars a year, and she's a greedy liar who used insider trading to make more money!"

Max just shrugged and laughed. He was used to Karl getting worked up over current events. It didn't seem that important to him. He grabbed a cup of coffee and left to go to work. Karl went back to reading the paper.

Stewart's defense seemed to be that she had a long-standing agreement with her broker to sell her shares of ImClone stock any time the price fell be-low $60 a share. She said she spoke to her broker on the afternoon of December 27, 2001, and he sold the stock for her shortly thereafter. Stewart claimed she had no inside information about ImClone, which was founded and run by her good friend Samuel Waksal. It was just a coincidence that she was able to unload close to 4,000 shares before the company crashed and the stock became worthless.

Karl fumed to himself that this story seemed pretty far-fetched. He didn't believe that Stewart could have talked to her good friend, Samuel Waksal, and not gotten some hint that it would be in her financial best interest to sell her shares. "That's just how the rich get richer," Karl thought. He had also read that even her broker had said that the "sell if the price fell below $60" story had been concocted after the fact. Karl thought it was pathetic that all the little stockholders of ImClone had to lose money while Stewart might get away with a crime just because she had connections.

Karl noticed that it was getting late so he put the rest of the newspaper in his briefcase and left for work. When he got to the office, a couple of people were talking about Martha Stewart. His colleague, Diane, agreed with him and commented that she couldn't believe that she had seen her own retirement nest egg take a big hit in the stock market. Karl looked at Diane and smiled. "You're right," he said. "People all over the country suffered with this market downturn. Stewart should have too." Another colleague, Randy, disagreed, saying that

---

This theory is based on the research of **Kenneth Burke.**

we are always forgiving people for mistakes of this nature. He thought that Stewart was telling the truth anyway.

As Karl drove home from work that night, he heard the news commentator on the radio say that Martha Stewart was the icon that America loved to hate. She was now reaping public hatred that had been brewing against her for being such a symbol of perfection. The radio story went on to say that the United States loved to build up public figures and loved even more to see them fall. Martha Stewart was just the latest example. Karl disagreed. He thought Martha Stewart deserved disapproval because of her illegal actions, not because Americans loved to see the powerful brought to their knees on the public stage. Plus Karl couldn't respect Stewart's behavior during the investigations of her stock trading. She had simply remained silent, and her lawyers were quoted as saying she'd take the Fifth Amendment if she were subpoenaed. Karl figured if you did something wrong, you ought to be big enough to admit it and take your punishment.

■

Some rhetoricians might analyze Martha Stewart's problems and Karl's responses to them using Dramatism, a theoretical position seeking to understand the actions of human life as drama. Kenneth Burke is known as the originator of Dramatism, although he did not initially use that term himself. Burke, who died in 1993 at the age of 96, was a fascinating person, and he was unlike many of the other theorists in this book. Burke never earned an undergraduate degree, much less a Ph.D. Yet he was self-taught in the areas of literary criticism, philosophy, communication, sociology, economics, theology, and linguistics. He taught for almost twenty years at several universities, including Harvard, Princeton, and the University of Chicago. His breadth of interests and perhaps his lack of formal training in any one discipline made him one of the most interdisciplinary theorists we will study. His ideas have been applied widely in various areas including literature, theater, communication, history, and sociology. No doubt one reason why Burke is so widely read and applied has to do with his focus on *symbol systems*—the primary means of intellectual exchange and scholarly effort for most researchers working in the humanities. Dramatism provides researchers with the flexibility to penetrate an object of study from a variety of angles.

Dramatism, as its name implies, sees life as a drama, placing a critical focus on the acts performed by various players. Just as in a play, the acts in life are central to revealing human motives. Dramatism provides us with a method that is well suited to address the act of communication between the text (how Karl perceives and relates to what he learns about Stewart) and the audience for that text (Karl), as well as the inner action of the text (Stewart's motives and choices). As C. Ronald Kimberling (1982) notes, "Dramatism assuredly provides critical insights that cannot be generated by any other method" (p. 13). When Karl reads about Stewart's case and her claims, it is as if he sees her as an actor. In Burke's terms, Karl could better understand Stewart as an actor in a scene, trying to accomplish purposes because of certain motives. Thus, he comments on her motives as he evaluates her act of selling her shares of Im-Clone just before the stock crashed. Burke's theory of Dramatism allows us to analyze both Stewart's rhetorical choices in this situation (how she framed her case as within the letter of the law) and Karl's responses to her choices (his rejection of her explanations).

Drama is a useful metaphor for Burke's ideas for three reasons: (1) Drama indicates a grand sweep, and Burke does not make limited claims; his goal is to theorize about the whole range of human experience. The dramatic metaphor is particularly useful in describing human relationships because it is grounded in interaction or dialogue. In its dialogue, drama both models relationships and illuminates relationships. (2) Drama tends to follow recognizable types or genres: comedy, musical, melodrama, and so forth. Burke feels that the very way we structure and use language may be related to the way these human dramas are played out. As Barry Brummett (1993) observes, "Words string out into patterned discourses at the macroscopic level of whole texts or discourses. Burke argues that recurring patterns underlying texts partially account for how those texts move us" (p. xiv). (3) Drama is always addressed to an audience. In this sense, drama is rhetorical. Burke views literature as "equipment for living," which means that literature or texts speak to people's lived experiences and problems and provide people with responses for dealing with these experiences. In this way, Dramatism studies the ways in which language and its usage relates to audiences.

Assumptions of Dramatism

Assumptions provide a sense of a theorist's ontology. As we discussed in Chapters 3 and 4, ontologies consist of views of human nature. Recall that some ontological issues concern how much choice and free will humans possess. The assumptions we make about human nature are articles of faith about basic reality. Kenneth Burke's thinking is so complex that it is difficult to reduce it to one set of assumptions or to a specific ontology. Some of the assumptions that follow illustrate the difficulty of labeling Burke's ontology. Researchers such as Brummett (1993) have called Burke's assumptions a symbolic ontology because of his emphasis on language. Yet, as Brummett cautions, "The best one can do, in searching for the heart of Burke's thought, is to find a partial ontology, a grounding-for-the-most-part. For Burke, people *mainly* do what they do, and the world is *largely* the way it is, because of the nature of *symbol systems themselves*" (p. xii; emphasis in original). Brummett's comment prefigures the following three assumptions of Burke's Dramatism theory:

- Humans are animals who use symbols.
- Language and symbols form a critically important system for humans.
- Humans are choice makers.

The first assumption speaks to Burke's realization that some of what we do is motivated by our animal nature, and some of what we do is motivated by symbols. For example, when Karl drinks his morning coffee, he is satisfying his thirst, an animal concern. When he reads the morning paper and thinks about the ideas he encounters there, he is being influenced by symbols. The idea that humans are animals who use symbols represents a tension in Burke's thought.

As Brummett (1993) observes, this assumption "teeters between the realizations that some of what we do is motivated by animality and some of it by symbolicity" (p. xii). Of all the symbols that humans use, language is the most important for Burke, and this leads to the second assumption.

In the second assumption (the critical importance of language), Burke's position is somewhat similar to the concept of linguistic relativity known as the Sapir-Whorf hypothesis (Sapir, 1921; Whorf, 1956). Sapir and Whorf noted that it is difficult to think about concepts or objects without words for them. Thus, people are restricted (to an extent) in what they can conceive by the limits of their language. For Burke, as well as Edward Sapir and Benjamin Whorf, when people use their language, they are used by it as well. When Karl tells Max that Stewart is a greedy liar, he is choosing the symbols he wishes to use, but at the same time his opinions and thoughts are shaped by hearing himself use these symbols. Further, when a culture's language does not have symbols for a given motive, then speakers of that language are unlikely to have that motive. Thus, because English does not have many symbols that express much nuance of opinion about Stewart's behavior and motivations, our discussions are often polarized. When Karl talks with his colleagues Diane and Randy, the discussion is focused on whether Stewart was right or wrong. There is not much choice in between, and Burke would argue that this is a direct result of our symbol system. Think back to other controversies you have talked about (such as President Clinton's affair with Monica Lewinsky, the World Trade Center tragedy, bombing Iraq, the possible baseball strike, and so forth). You may remember the discussions as either/or propositions—She said/He said. Burke's response is that symbols shape our thoughts and motivations.

Burke asserts that words, thoughts, and actions have extremely close connections with one another. Burke's expression for this is that words act as "terministic screens" leading to "trained incapacities," meaning that people cannot see beyond what their words lead them to believe (Burke, 1965). For example, despite educational efforts, U.S. public health officials still have difficulty persuading people to think of the misuse of alcohol and tranquilizers when they hear the words "drug abuse." Most people in the United States respond to "drug abuse" as the misuse of illegal drugs, such as heroin and cocaine (Brummett, 1993). The words "drug abuse" are "terministic screens," screening out some meanings and including others. For Burke, language has a life of its own, and "anything we can see or feel is already *in* language, given to us *by* language, and even produced *as us* by language" (Nelson, 1989, p. 169; emphasis in original). This explanation is somewhat at odds with the final assumption of Dramatism.

The second assumption suggests that language exerts a deterministic influence over people (Melia, 1989), but the third assumption states that human beings are choice makers. Burke persistently suggests that the deterministic ontology of behaviorism has to be rejected because it conflicts with what he views as a cornerstone of Dramatism: human choice. Thus, as Karl reads about Martha Stewart, he forms his opinions about her behavior through his own free will. Much of what we discuss in the rest of the chapter rests on the conceptualization of agency, or the ability of a social actor to act out of choice. As Charles Conrad and Elizabeth Macom (1995) observe, "The essence of agency is choice" (p. 11). Yet, as Conrad and Macom go on to discuss, Burke grappled with the concept of agency throughout his career, largely because of the difficult task of negotiating a space between complete free will and complete determinism. Burke's thinking continued to evolve on this point, but he always kept agency in the forefront of his theorizing. In order to understand Burke's scope in this theory, we need to discuss how he framed his thinking relative to Aristotelian rhetoric.

Dramatism as New Rhetoric

In his book *A Rhetoric of Motives* (1950), Burke was concerned with persuasion, and he provides an ample discussion of the traditional principles of rhetoric articulated by Aristotle (see Chapter 18). Burke maintains that the definition of rhetoric is, in essence, persuasion, and his writings explore the ways in which persuasion takes place. In so doing, Burke proposes a new rhetoric (Nichols, 1952) that focuses on several key issues, chief among them being the notion of identification. In 1952, Marie Nichols said the following about the difference between Burke's approach and Aristotle's: "The difference between the 'old' rhetoric and the 'new' rhetoric may be summed up in this manner: whereas the key term for the 'old' rhetoric was *persuasion* and its stress was upon deliberate design, the key term for the 'new' rhetoric is *identification* and this may include partially 'unconscious' factors in its appeal" (p. 323; emphasis in original). Yet, Burke's purpose was not to displace Aristotle's conceptualizations but rather to supplement the traditional approach.

Identification and Substance

Burke asserts that all things have **substance**, which he defines as the general nature of something. Substance can be described in a person by listing demographic characteristics as well as background information and facts about present situation, such as talents and occupation. Thus, we understand Karl's substance by noting he is a 38-year-old European American male, high school math teacher, collector of rare coins, tennis player, and crossword puzzle enthusiast. In addition Karl has been in a relationship with Max for seven years and lives in Hartford, Connecticut. Of course, there are many other pieces of information that make up Karl's substance, but these facts give us a starting point.

> **substance**
> the general nature of something

Burke argues that when there is overlap between two people in terms of their substance, they have **identification.** The more overlap that exists, the greater the identification. The opposite is also true, so the less overlap between individuals, the greater the **division** that exists between them. For instance, the fact that Martha Stewart is a wealthy divorced female who owns multiple homes and appears in the media frequently provides little in terms of identification between her and Karl. They are both European American professionals who live in the United States, but they overlap on little else.

> **identification**
> when two people have overlap in their substances
> **division**
> when two people fail to have overlap in their substances

However, it is also the case that two people can never completely overlap with each other. Burke recognizes this and notes that the "ambiguities of substance" dictate that identification will always rest on both unity and division.

Individuals will unite on certain matters of substance but at the same time remain unique, being "both joined and separated" (Burke, 1950, pp. 20–21). Further, Burke indicates that rhetoric is needed to bridge divisions and establish unity. Thus, potentially, Martha Stewart could have made some rhetorical appeals that may have convinced Karl that the divisions between them could be bridged. Burke refers to this process as **consubstantiation,** or increasing their identification with each other.

The Process of Guilt and Redemption

Consubstantiality, or issues of identification and substance, are related to the guilt/redemption cycle because guilt can be assuaged as a result of identification and divisions. Patricia Sullivan and Lynn Turner (1993) argued that the case of Zoe Baird, President Clinton's first, unsuccessful, nominee for U.S. Attorney General, acted as a sacrificial vessel for the country to expiate our feelings of guilt about inadequate child care. Using Burke, Sullivan and Turner argue that Baird was consubstantial with many Americans because the problems of adequate child care are widespread. Yet, her uncommon wealth separated her from most, allowing people to blame her without condemning themselves. Martha Stewart as an icon we love to hate might be a similar phenomenon. Stewart could be seen as consubstantial with many people because she devotes herself to homemaking. Yet her perfection and wealth separate her from most people who are responsible for their homes.

For Burke, the process of guilt and redemption undergirds the entire concept of symbolizing. **Guilt** is the central motive for all symbolic activities, and Burke defines guilt broadly to include any type of tension, embarrassment, shame, disgust, or other unpleasant feeling. Central to Burke's theory is the notion that guilt is intrinsic to the human condition. Because we are continuously feeling guilt, we are also continuously engaging in attempts to purge ourselves of guilt's discomfort.

This process of feeling guilt and attempting to assuage it finds its expression in Burke's cycle, which follows a predictable pattern: order, or hierarchy, the negative, victimage (scapegoat or mortification), and redemption.

Order or Hierarchy   Burke suggests that society exists in the form of an **order,** or **hierarchy,** that is created through our ability to use language. Language enables us to create categories like richer and more powerful—the haves and

consubstantiation
when appeals are made to increase overlap between people

guilt
tension, embarrassment, shame, disgust, or other unpleasant feeling

order or hierarchy
a ranking that exists in society primarily because of our ability to use language

the have-nots. These categories form social hierarchies. Often we feel guilt as a result of our place in the hierarchy. If we are privileged, we may feel we have power at the expense of those with less. This feeling prompts guilt.

The Negative   **The negative** comes into play when people see their place in the social order and seek to reject it. Saying no to the existing order is both a function of our language abilities and evidence of humans as choice makers. When Burke penned his often-quoted definition of Man, he emphasized the negative:

> Man is
> the symbol-using inventor of the negative
> separated from his natural condition by instruments
> of his own making
> goaded by the spirit of hierarchy
> and rotten with perfection. (1966, p. 16)

When Burke coined the phrase "rotten with perfection," he meant that because our symbols allow us to imagine perfection, we always feel guilty about the difference between the real state of affairs and the perfection that we can imagine.

the negative
rejecting one's place
in the social order;
exhibiting resistence

Victimage   **Victimage** is the way in which we attempt to purge the guilt that we feel as part of the human condition. There are two basic types of victimage, or two methods to purge our guilt. Burke calls victimage that we turn in on ourselves **mortification.** When we apologize for wrongdoing and blame ourselves, we engage in mortification. Had Martha Stewart said she did the wrong thing with her stocks, she would have attempted mortification. In 1998, Republican leaders said they would have felt more sympathetic about President Clinton's sex scandal if he had admitted he was wrong and had not perjured himself. Clinton refused to engage in mortification. Instead he turned to another purging technique called scapegoating.

In **scapegoating,** blame is placed on some sacrificial vessel. By sacrificing the scapegoat, the actor is purged of sin. Clinton attempted to scapegoat the Republicans and Kenneth Starr as deserving the real blame for the country's problems after confessing to an inappropriate relationship with Monica Lewinsky. When the news of the sex scandal first broke in 1998, before Clinton admitted his relationship with Lewinsky, Hillary Rodham Clinton appeared on television suggesting that the rumors about her husband were the result of a complex "right-wing conspiracy" that was out to get her and her husband. This type of rhetoric illustrates Burke's concept of scapegoating. In the aftermath of the World Trade Center tragedy, President Bush also engaged in scapegoating. When Bush spoke of the "Axis of Evil" and used stark contrasts between good and evil, he operated within Burke's concept of scapegoating. People who objected to this rhetoric pointed out that the United States itself had some responsibility for the fact that people from developing countries harbored resentments against the United States.

victimage
the way we attempt
to purge the guilt we
feel as part of being
human
mortification
one method of purging
guilt, by blaming
ourselves

scapegoating
one method of purging
guilt, by blaming
others

Redemption   The final step in the process is **redemption,** which involves a rejection of the unclean and a return to a new order after guilt has been temporarily purged. Inherent in the term *redemption* is the notion of a Redeemer. The

redemption
A rejection of the unclean and a return to
a new order after guilt
has been temporarily
purged

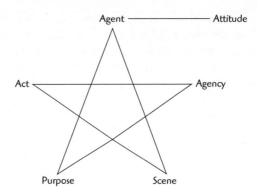

Agent ——————— Attitude

Act ——————— Agency

Purpose   Scene

Figure 19.1
Burke's Pentad

Redeemer in the Judeo-Christian tradition is the Savior (Christ) or God. When politicians blame problems on the media or on the opposing party, they offer themselves as potential Redeemers—those who can lead the people out of their troubles. A key in the redemption phase is the fact that guilt is only temporarily relieved, through the Redeemer or any other method. As any order or hierarchy becomes established, guilt returns to plague the human condition.

The Pentad

In addition to devising the theory of Dramatism, Burke (1945) created a method for applying his theory toward an understanding of symbolic activities. He called his method the **pentad** because it consists of five points for analyzing a symbolic text like a speech or a series of articles about Martha Stewart, for instance. The pentad may help determine why a speaker selects a particular rhetorical strategy for identifying with an audience. The five points that make up the pentad include the act, the scene, the agent, agency, and purpose. The Research Note shows an application of Burke's method to a medical crisis. Almost twenty years after creating this research tool, Burke (1968) added a sixth point, attitude, to the pentad, making it a hexad, although most people still refer to it as the pentad. (See Figure 19.1.) We will examine each of the points in turn.

pentad
Burke's method for applying Dramatism

The Act   Burke considered the **act** to be what is done by a person. In the case of Martha Stewart, the act might be selling her ImClone stock.

act
one prong of the pentad; that which is done by a person

The Scene   The **scene** provides the context surrounding the act. In Stewart's case, the scene would include a time period in which corporate America is under fire for corruption. Accounting firms like Arthur Anderson and corporations like Enron have caused people to be suspicious of the business world. We don't have much information about the way Martha Stewart would contextualize the scene because she has provided very limited information publicly about any contributing factors to the act.

scene
one prong of the pentad; the context surrounding the act

The Agent   The **agent** is the person or persons performing the act. In the case of Martha Stewart, she is the agent. However, if a researcher wished to analyze Karl's act of deciding he did not support Stewart, then Karl would be the agent.

agent
one prong of the pentad; the person performing the act

Research Note

Kenny, R. W. (2001). Toward a better death: Applying Burkean principles of symbolic action to interpret family adaptation to Karen Ann Quinlan's coma. *Health Communication, 13,* 363–385.

In this study, Kenny considers how families come to accept the "collapse of identity" (p. 363) of a family member after a medical crisis. Further, Kenny is interested in exploring how health-care providers can balance the needs of families in this dire circumstance with the needs of the medical institutions they serve. Kenny uses Dramatism as a template for examining the 1975 case of Karen Ann Quinlan, a young woman who mysteriously fell into a coma, was admitted to the hospital in an unconscious state, and never recovered. The study "examines the function of symbolic activity in the midst of a family health tragedy to illustrate how people whose sense of meaning has been disrupted and scattered by an unexpected event come to a consensus of meaning. . ." (p. 363).

Kenny tells the story of Karen Quinlan through the perspective of her parents, Joe and Julia Quinlan. The Quinlan's received word that their daughter was admitted to a hospital in serious condition. They rushed to her side and stayed with her for several days while she remained unconscious. She recovered consciousness but was never able to recognize her family, her surroundings, or speak again. The Quinlans moved from disbelief to denial to becoming leaders in the right-to-die movement.

Kenny's purpose in the study is to illustrate how the family initially resists Karen's transformation from family member to body and how they are eventually guided toward accepting this transformation. To explicate this movement, Kenny uses Burke's pentad. He states that Karen is moved from "her primary pentadic identity as actor to a new dominant identity as agency" (p. 375). Kenny notes that this is accomplished through symbolic actions such as when the nurses tie Karen to the bed so she won't hurt herself by thrashing around and when Julia allows the nurses to cut Karen's prized long hair because it is too difficult to care for in the hospital. Through these symbolic actions, Karen is constituted as "agency (a thing to be handled) rather than agent (a person with rights). At the same time, the purpose of the action shows how Karen herself is still being considered" (p. 375).

Kenny's analysis shows that these and other actions set the stage for terminating Karen's life support and transforming the family's image of Karen. Further, the analysis shows the utility of Burke's principles. As Kenny notes, "others will change in their actions toward Karen. Her body will be placed in new scenes. New people (agents) will be involved with her. The equipment (agency) that is used in her life will change. These are the primary elements of the dramatistic model. As practical shifts are made in them, there will be an implicit transformation in the identity of Karen. Eventually, it will be understood that she is no longer living" (p. 375).

Agency   **Agency** refers to the means used by the agent to accomplish the act. Possible forms of agency include message strategies, storytelling, apologies, speech making, and so forth. In Stewart's case, the agency included the justification Stewart made concerning her long-standing sell agreement with her broker.

Purpose   The **purpose** refers to the goal that the agent had in mind for the act—that is, why the act was done. In Stewart's case, the purpose was contested. She argued that she did it routinely. Karl believed she did it to capitalize on inside information and save herself a big loss.

Attitude   **Attitude** refers to the manner in which an actor positions him- or herself relative to others. Again, in Stewart's case, this is a contested point. Karl might say that she acted from an attitude of superiority. Many of the articles he

agency
one prong of the pentad; the means used to perform the act

purpose
one prong of the pentad; the goal the agent had for the act

attitude
a later addition to the pentad; the manner in which the agent positions himself or herself relative to others

read commented that Stewart believed herself to be above the law. Karl felt that Stewart's attitude derived from her money and status, leading her to see herself as better than others who have to live by laws and regulations. Stewart would no doubt characterize her attitude differently.

When using the pentad to analyze a symbolic interaction, the analyst first determines all the elements of the pentad and identifies what occurred in a particular act. After labeling the points of the pentad and fully explicating each, the analyst then examines the **dramatistic ratios**, or the proportions of one element relative to another. By isolating any two parts of the pentad and examining their relationship to each other, we determine a ratio. An agent: act ratio, for instance, is at issue when we attempt to understand how a good person might do a bad thing. In analyzing the ratios in this manner, the researcher is able to discover a dominant element. Is the agent emphasized more than the situation or vice versa? An examination of the dramatistic ratio suggests something about point of view and rhetorical strategies.

dramatistic ratios
the proportions of one element of the pentad relative to another element

Critique and Closing

There is no question that Kenneth Burke has made an immeasurable contribution to the field of communication with his theory of Dramatism. Various researchers have praised Burke in the following terms: "He has become the most profound student of rhetoric now writing in America" (Nichols, 1952, p. 331); "Kenneth Burke is more than a single intellectual worker; he is the ore for a scholarly industry" (Brummett, 1993, p. xi); "Few critics have revealed the scope, imagination, insights, and dazzling concern for symbol using which Kenneth Burke possesses" (Chesebro, 1993, p. xii); and in 1981, the *New York Times* recognized Burke as a leading American critic, saying he was "the strongest living representative of the American critical tradition, and perhaps the largest single source of that tradition since its founder, Ralph Waldo Emerson" (cited in Chesebro, 1993, p. xi). Burke's work is widely praised and frequently cited. In fact, the National Communication Association, one of the main organizations for communication teachers, researchers, and professionals, has an entire division devoted to Burkean criticism. Several of the regional associations also have interest groups that focus on Burkean analysis. No other single theorist is similarly represented in our associations.

Yet, a few criticisms of Burke's theory have appeared and warrant our attention here. Some critics complain that Burke is too unclear and obtuse. Dramatism is seen by some as overly complex and confusing (Foss, Foss, &

The Theory Connection

Compare Burke's concept of the dramatic structure of life with Fisher's Narrative Paradigm. In what ways do they differ and how are they similar? Would it be possible for a researcher to work comfortably with both theories without having ontological or epistemological conflicts? What other theory in the text would be impossible to combine with Dramatism? What are the reasons for your choice?

Trapp, 1991). Even proponents of Burke acknowledge that he is difficult to read. Marie Hochmuth Nichols concluded her 1952 essay on Burke's Dramatistic Theory of Rhetoric by saying,

> Burke is difficult and often confusing. He cannot be understood by casual reading of his various volumes. In part the difficulty arises from the numerous vocabularies he employs. His words in isolation are usually simple enough, but he often uses them in new contexts. To read one of his volumes independently, without regard to the chronology of publication, makes the problem of comprehension even more difficult because of the specialized meaning attached to various words and phrases. (p. 330)

However, Nichols also provides a rebuttal to some of these criticisms by concluding that some of the difficulty arises from "the compactness of his writing, the uniqueness of his organizational patterns, the penetration of his thought, and the breadth of his endeavor" (p. 330). In other words, Burke is a genius and worth the effort it requires to understand his original thinking. When a student is diligent, Burke's theory repays the hard work with many rewards.

Somewhat related to the above criticism is the idea that Dramatism is too wide in scope. Burke's goal is no less than to explain the whole of human experience with symbolic interaction. This is an extremely broad and ambitious goal, and some critics believe it renders the theory too broad to be meaningful. When you contrast Dramatism with a theory like Uncertainty Reduction Theory, which we discussed in Chapter 9, you can see the two extremes of theoretical scope. URT seeks to explain the first few minutes of an initial encounter between strangers. Dramatism encompasses all human symbolic interaction. Some critics might suggest that when a theory attempts such a lofty goal it is doomed to be overly complex and obtuse. Whether or not you see the range of Dramatism's goal as a weakness is somewhat subjective. Obviously, for Burke and many who followed him, the wide scope of Dramatism is part of its appeal.

A final critique, advanced by Celeste Condit (1992) in her essay titled "Post-Burke: Transcending the Sub-Stance of Dramatism," involves several considerations of what is omitted in Dramatism. In this essay, Condit does not so much criticize Dramatism as suggest areas that Burke left undeveloped and that should be used as starting points for moving post-Burke. She highlights at least two contexts that require extension and modification in the theory:

gender and culture. Condit observes that although Burke was supportive of feminism, his support came mainly in the form of including women under the sign of "man." She notes that given the historical context in which Burke wrote, his support for women was not inconsequential. Many writers in Burke's generation completely ignored women, so Burke was making a contribution by including women at all. Condit maintains, however, that today the scene has altered, and it is inappropriate to subsume women under the word *man*. Here Condit is talking both about the use of the generic "man" to represent all people and about our ability as a society to begin to think in new ways about sex and gender.

As Condit notes, "We must extend our language beyond duality to a broad 'humanity' and to 'human beings,' discovering ways to speak that emphasize human plurality" (1992, p. 351). Condit says the definition of Man that Burke provides, which we discussed earlier in the chapter, is not adequate to include Woman. She recasts the definition from the perspective of a radical feminist who would see the following as descriptive of Man's woman:

Woman is
the symbol-receiving (hearing, passive) animal
inventor of nothing (moralized by priests and saints)
submerged in her natural conditions by instruments of man's making
goaded at the bottom of hierarchy (moved to a sense of orderliness)
and rotted by perfection. (p. 351)

Then she recasts the definition to move beyond an essentialism defining men and women as opposite to each other and essentially the same as others of the same sex:

People are
players with symbols
inventors of the negative and the possibility of morality
grown from their natural condition by tools of their collective making
trapped between hierarchy and equality (moved constantly to reorder)
neither rotten nor perfect, but now and again lunging down both paths.
(p. 352)

Condit's argument is simply that Burke's approach needs to be broadened to include women and to move past a focus on one sex or the other to be truly inclusive of both. But she feels that merely broadening the language of "man/his" to include "people/their" will not in itself be sufficient to challenge the hold that language exerts as a terministic screen against women in the United States. We need to change both our language and our thinking about women, men, gender, and inclusivity for significant progress to occur.

Condit also suggests that Burke emphasizes universality among cultures at the expense of particularity. For Condit, this is especially the case in the matter of Burke's contention that victimage is a transcultural experience—a method for purging guilt in all cultures. She argues that cultures other than Western Christian ones (from which Burke draws almost exclusively) might not see victimage as the dominant motive for human conduct. For example, Buddhism might provide different motives than Christianity does. Further, if we examine trickster tales from the Native American culture or African American versions

In January 1999, *Time* magazine used a Burkean approach as it framed Hillary Rodham Clinton's public pronouncements about "a vast right-wing conspiracy" as a dramatistic strategy to recast the elements in the story of President Clinton and Ken Starr's investigation of his presidency. In a long, complimentary article about Hillary Rodham Clinton entitled "The Better Half," *Time* quoted one of Hillary's friends as saying, "Her natural reaction is to remain clear-headed and not let the emotional part guide her thinking. If there is an emotional part, it is something for her to take home."

Time noted that Rodham Clinton has the ability to focus on one thing and exclude all else from her thinking. This ability stood her in good stead during the Starr investigations. Rodham Clinton was able to focus on her hatred of Ken Starr and thus cast President Clinton more as a victim than as a villain. She saw Starr as the enemy who was placing her and her husband under siege. The prosecutor had "questioned her integrity, made her run the gauntlet of cameras to testify before a Washington grand jury, implicated her in every alleged White House misdeed" (p. 117). Thus, Rodham Clinton saw the situation as a fight between her family and Ken Starr and she prepared to do battle.

The article states that Hillary's feelings about Starr were useful both as a private motivation for her and as a public defense. When Rodham Clinton appeared on the *Today* show shortly after the scandal broke, she was confronting a public and a media that spoke almost exclusively about what Clinton had done and whether he could survive as president after this. "Then Hillary sat down across from co-host Matt Lauer and challenged the press to pay attention to a different story: 'this vast right-wing conspiracy that has been conspiring against my husband since the day he announced for President.' She shone the light on Starr—his agenda, his henchmen, his ideological gene pool—and suggested that this was the real story, the real danger, rather than anything her husband might have done" (pp. 117–118).

Initially, Rodham Clinton's story was mocked, and Hillary was seen as a woman desperate to say anything to make the scandal disappear. Yet, the perception changed over time, and *Time* notes that by the end of the year most of the public had come to agree with her about Ken Starr. Hillary Rodham Clinton's story, casting Starr as the villain, was generally accepted.

Source: Tulmulty & Gibbs, 1999.

TIP Follow-up
Use the pentad to analyze the episode described above.

---

we might see victimage characterized in a strikingly different fashion from what Burke describes. The trickster is in a low power position, relative to the rest of the society, but is able to triumph through wits and cleverness. The trickster is not a victim in the Christian sense that we see in Dramatism; rather, the trickster emerges victorious by turning the rules of the system against those in power.

In sum, Condit's critique does not deny the enormous contribution made by Burke's theory. Instead, she simply suggests some extensions and modifications for improving the theory. Thus, there is general consensus that Burke's theory provides us with imaginative and innovative insights into human motives and interaction. Dramatism provides us with a theory that works with the big picture. It allows an analysis of human motivations and behavior, and its focus on language as the critical symbol system makes it especially attractive to communication researchers.

Discussion Starters

1. How could Karl talk about Martha Stewart's situation in a less polarized fashion? What are the linguistic barriers to such a discussion? Does a feminist critique of Burke's theory enable you to think of less polarized language? Explain your answer.

2. Use the pentad to analyze Stewart's situation described in the chapter opener. Or choose another public figure and apply the pentad to that discourse.

3. How do you understand the use of the pentad as a method relative to Dramatism as a theory? Do all theories have specific methods that are used only with them? Why or why not?

4. Do you agree with Burke that guilt is the primary human motive? If not, what do you think is the primary human motive?

5. Burke believes that symbols, and language, in particular, are critical in life. When he says that symbolic action is more than mere physical or material reality, what do you think he means?

6. Do you agree with Condit that Burke's theory is culture specific rather than universal? Explain your answer.

Terms for Review

substance
identification
division
consubstantiation
guilt
order or hierarchy
the negative
victimage
mortification
scapegoating

redemption
pentad
act
scene
agent
agency
purpose
attitude
dramatistic ratios

 Online Learning Center

Visit the Online Learning Center at www.mhhe.com/west2. Use the multiple-choice and true/false quizzes to help you prepare for exams, and the glossary, crossword puzzles, and flashcards to further your knowledge of key terms.

CHAPTER 20

The Narrative Paradigm

Miles Campbell

Miles Campbell rolled over in bed and turned off his screaming alarm. He burrowed under the covers for a minute before he realized he'd better get up or he would miss his chem lab. He was tempted to sleep in, but a vision of his mother's face flashed before him, and he thought about how hard she had worked to help him get to college. He didn't want to disappoint her by not doing his very best now that he was here. So Miles sighed and shrugged off the covers. He slipped out of bed and splashed cold water on his face. By the time he was dressed and headed for the kitchen, he felt better about his day and his life in general.

In the kitchen he heard his housemates, Robert and Carlos, arguing about something. Seems like a normal morning, Miles thought. Those two can never get along. "What has got you guys up and yelling so early in the morning?" Miles asked as he pulled his breakfast together from the pantry. Both Robert and Carlos looked up and grinned at Miles. "You won't think it's a big deal, Miles," Carlos said, "but we are discussing the candidates who are running for president of the Student Multicultural Association." "Yeah, you're right, Carlos," Miles laughed. "That doesn't seem like something worth arguing about to me!"

Robert handed Miles a copy of two campaign flyers. "Well, you might not think it's all that big a deal, but look at the difference between these two

and tell me that Laura Huyge doesn't make more sense than Jorge Vega." Miles glanced at the two flyers that Robert had given him. Huyge was an Asian American graduate student, and she had presented a list of ten points that represented her platform. She claimed to be interested in promoting cultural sensitivity and appreciation for diversity within the student body. Her flyer also listed a few ways that she planned to accomplish her goals. Her first big initiative, if she were elected, would be to sponsor a workshop with outside speakers and several hands-on activities to get students of different races and ethnicities talking to one another about difference and respect.

Miles looked up at Robert and Carlos and said, "Well, Laura sounds reasonable enough." Robert clapped Miles on the back, smiling broadly. Carlos interrupted, saying, "Hey, man, you haven't even looked at what Jorge has to say. Keep reading, man."

Miles put Laura's flyer aside and took up Jorge's. Jorge had chosen a completely different presentation style for his campaign flyer. Instead of laying out a specific platform point by point as Laura had, Jorge's flyer told a series of short stories. In the first one, Jorge related an incident in class when an African American woman could not get the professor's attention for anything she had to say. Every time she tried to contribute in class, the professor ignored her and asked a European American's opinion. Because she was the only person of color in the class,

---

This theory is based on the research of **Walter Fisher.**

this woman believed the professor was prejudiced, but she wasn't sure what she could do about it. Another story in the flyer described a classroom situation where the two Hispanic students enrolled believed that they were called on to give the "Latin perspective" on every issue the professor raised. They were both really tired of being tokens. A third story talked about how certain bars on campus were considered "Black" and others were "Latino" and others were "White." This story told of two African American students who went to a White bar and felt really isolated.

As Miles read these stories, he thought that Jorge had it down cold. His description of life at the university was totally accurate. He himself had been ignored in classes and wondered if it had been because of his race. He'd also experienced being asked for the "Black" opinion, and he really resented that. Also, his social life rarely included people outside his own race, except for Carlos and a couple of Carlos's friends who were Hispanic. He never socialized with the Whites on campus. Jorge had given Miles a lot to think about, and, if he voted, he would vote for Jorge.

∎

Throughout this book we have begun each chapter with a story about a person or several people who experience something through which we can illustrate the chapter's theory. The reason we have made this editorial choice may be found within the theory of narration that Walter Fisher calls the Narrative Paradigm. The Narrative Paradigm promotes the belief that humans are storytellers and that values, emotions, and aesthetic considerations ground our beliefs and behaviors. In other words, we are more persuaded by a good story than a good argument. Thus, Fisher would explain Miles's decision to vote for Jorge on the basis of the stories Jorge presented in his campaign flyer. Fisher asserts that the essence of human nature is storytelling.

Fisher is not alone in this belief. Robert Rowland (1989) comments that the idea that people are essentially storytellers has been adopted by many different disciplines including history, biology, anthropology, sociology, philosophy, psychology, and theology. Communication studies has also been influenced by the interest in narration. John Lucaites and Celeste Condit (1985) note "the growing belief that narrative represents a universal medium of human consciousness" (p. 90). Thus, Fisher's perspective is widely shared.

It is notable that Fisher calls his approach a paradigm rather than simply a theory. As we mentioned in Chapter 3, a paradigm is a broader concept than a theory. Fisher uses the term to signal the breadth of his vision. Fisher states that "there is no genre, including technical communication, that is not an episode in the story of life" (1985, p. 347). Thus, Fisher has constructed an approach to theoretical thinking that is more encompassing than any one specific theory. Fisher states that his use of the term *paradigm* refers to an effort to formalize and direct our understanding of the experience of all human communication.

Further, the use of the term *paradigm* indicates that Fisher's thinking represents a major shift from the thinking that had supported most previous theories of communication. Fisher believes that he is capturing the fundamental nature of human beings with the insight that we are storytellers and that we experience our lives in narrative form. He contrasts his approach with what he calls the rational paradigm that characterizes previous Western thinking. In this way, Fisher presents what can be called a **paradigm shift,** or a significant change in the way people think about the world and its meanings.

Fisher (1987) explains the paradigm shift by recounting a brief history of paradigms that have guided Western thinking. He notes that originally logos meant a combination of concepts including story, rationale, discourse, and thought. Fisher explains that this meaning held until the time of Plato and Aristotle, who distinguished between logos as reason and mythos as story and emotion. In this split, mythos, representing poetical discourse, was assigned a negative status relative to logos, or reason. The concept of rhetoric fell somewhere between the lofty logic of logos and the inferior status of poetics or mythos. This structure of Aristotle's reinforced the concept that not all discourse is equal. In fact, according to Aristotle (Chapter 18), some discourse is superior to others by virtue of its relationship to true knowledge. Only logos, found in the discourse of philosophy, leads to true knowledge because it provides a system of logic that can be proved valid. Other forms of discourse lead to knowledge, but the knowledge they produce is probabilistic, not *true* in an absolute, invariable sense.

This Aristotelian distinction did not prevent Aristotle himself from valuing different forms of communication, but it did provide a rationale for later theorists in preferring logic and reason over mythos, or story, and rhetoric. Much subsequent scholarship has focused on a struggle over these major forms of discourse. The scientific revolution dethroned philosophy as the source of logic, placing logic instead within science and technology. But Fisher contends that this change was not a far-reaching one because both philosophy and science privilege a formal system of logic that continues to leave poetics or rhetoric in a devalued position. The mind-set of logic as primary that scholars employ is what Fisher calls the **rational world paradigm.**

Struggles among these different branches of knowledge continue today, but Fisher asserts that the Narrative Paradigm finds a way to transcend these struggles. Fisher argues that "acceptance of the narrative paradigm shifts the controversy from a focus on who 'owns' logos to a focus on what specific instances of discourse, regardless of form, provide the most trustworthy, reliable, and desirable guides to belief and to behavior, and under what conditions" (1987, p. 6). Thus, the Narrative Paradigm represents a different way of thinking about the world than that posited by the rational world paradigm. With narrative, Fisher suggests, we move away from an either/or dualism toward a more unified sense that embodies science, philosophy, story, myth, and logic. The Narrative Paradigm presents an alternative to the rational world paradigm without negating traditional rationality.

Fisher argues that the Narrative Paradigm accomplishes this shift through recognizing that "some discourse is more veracious, reliable, and trustworthy in respect to knowledge, truth, and reality than some other discourse, but no *form* or *genre* has final claim to these virtues" (1987, p. 19; emphasis in original). In asserting this, Fisher lays the groundwork for reclaiming the importance of the narrative, or story, without denigrating logic and reason, and he establishes a new way of conceptualizing rhetoric. Further, Fisher asserts that story, or mythos, is imbued in all human communication endeavors (even those

paradigm shift
a significant change in the way most people see the world and its meanings

rational world paradigm
a system of logic employed by many researchers and professionals

The Theory Connection

Compare the process of persuasion as it is explained through the Narrative Paradigm with how Aristotle explains it in the *Rhetoric*.

involving logic) because all arguments include "ideas that cannot be verified or proved in any absolute way. Such ideas arise in metaphor, values, gestures, and so on" (1987, p. 19). Fisher thus attempts to bridge the divide between logos (rational argument) and mythos (story, or narrative).

Assumptions of the Narrative Paradigm

Despite Fisher's attempt to show the Narrative Paradigm as a fusion of logic and aesthetic, he does point out that narrative logic is different from traditional logic and reasoning. We will discuss how these two differ throughout the chapter because this is an important distinction for Fisher and one that he continually refined as his thinking about the Narrative Paradigm evolved. An important aspect of the assumptions of the Narrative Paradigm is that they contrast with those of the rational world paradigm, just as the two logics differ. Fisher (1987) stipulates five "essential postulates of the paradigm" (p. 5); we can see how these clearly contrast to the parallel assumptions Fisher sees in the rational world paradigm. This contrast is revealed in Table 20.1. We will briefly discuss each of the assumptions of the Narrative Paradigm, comparing them with their opposites in the rational world paradigm.

First, the Narrative Paradigm assumes that the essential nature of humans is rooted in story and storytelling. As our example with Miles illustrates, stories persuade us, move us, and form the basis for our beliefs and actions. Miles had not heard much about the election for the president of the Multicultural Student Association on campus. In fact, Miles was rather apathetic about the election and had no real interest or opinions about either candidate. Yet, after reading the compelling stories that Jorge included in his campaign literature, Miles had decided to vote for Jorge. Miles had found Laura's campaign material interesting but not nearly as involving as Jorge's. If the assumption of the rational world paradigm held true, we would expect the more rational argument to hold sway over Miles, and he should have decided to vote for Laura. The Narrative Paradigm explains his preference for Jorge.

Fisher also believes in this first assumption because he observes that narrative is universal—found in all cultures and time periods. Fisher asserts that "Any ethic, whether social, political, legal, or otherwise, involves narrative" (1984, p. 3). This universality of narrative prompts Fisher to suggest the term *Homo narrans* as the overarching metaphor for defining humanity. Fisher was influenced in his approach by reading moral theory espoused by Alasdair MacIntyre (1981). MacIntyre observes that "man [sic] is in his actions and practice,

Table 20.1   Contrast Between Narrative and Rational World Paradigms

NARRATIVE PARADIGM	RATIONAL WORLD PARADIGM
1. Humans are storytellers.	1. Humans are rational beings.
2. Decision making and communication are based on "good reasons."	2. Decision making is based on arguments.
3. Good reasons are determined by matters of history, biography, culture, and character.	3. Arguments adhere to specific criteria for soundness and logic.
4. Rationality is based in people's awareness of how internally consistent and truthful to lived experience stories appear.	4. Rationality is based in the quality of knowledge and formal reasoning processes.
5. The world is experienced by people as a set of stories from which to choose among. As we choose, we live life in a process of continual re-creation.	5. The world can be reduced to a series of logical relationships that are uncovered through reasoning.

as well as in his fictions, essentially a story-telling animal" (p. 201). Fisher used MacIntyre's ideas as the foundation for the Narrative Paradigm. James Elkins (2001) agrees with Fisher's assumption about the centrality of stories for humans. Elkins observes that

> we use stories in virtually every aspect of our everyday lives—to pass the time, convey information, to let someone know who we are (or at least who we want to be), to locate ourselves in a place, family, and community. We turn to stories to both survive and to imagine, as well as for a host of instrumental purposes, for pleasure, and because we must. Stories are part of our human inheritance. (p. 1)

The second assumption of the Narrative Paradigm asserts that people make decisions about which stories to accept and which to reject on the basis of what makes sense to them, or good reasons. We will discuss what Fisher means by good reasons later in the chapter, but he does not mean strict logic or argument. This assumption recognizes that not all stories are equally effective; instead, the deciding factor in choosing among stories is personal rather than an abstract code of argument, or what we traditionally call reason. From Fisher's point of view, in our beginning vignette, Laura has told a story in her campaign flyer, too. Miles simply chooses to reject her story and accept Jorge's because it is more personally involving to him. Recent events—ranging from NATO's mistaken bombing of the Chinese embassy in Belgrade in 1999, to the House managers' impeachment case against President Clinton and Clinton's lawyers' rebuttal in 1999, to the media frenzy surrounding Gary Condit after Chandra Levy's 2001 disappearance, to the tragic events of September 11, 2001—show us the reality of competing stories.

As people listen to these conflicting stories, they choose among them. Their choices do not stem from traditional logic but from narrative logic. As people

THE DYING ART OF STORYTELLING

shift from traditional logic to narrative logic, Fisher believes that people's lives will be based on values, as narrative logic is more democratic than formal logic. As Fisher (1984) asserts, "All persons have the capacity to be rational in the narrative paradigm" (p. 10). Whereas formal logic calls for an elite trained in the complexities of the logical system, the Narrative Paradigm calls on the practical wisdom that everyone possesses.

The third assumption deals with what specifically influences people's choices and provides good reasons for them. The rational world paradigm assumes that argument is ruled by the dictates of soundness (Toulmin, 1958). For Stephen Toulmin, the anatomy of an argument is a movement from data to a conclusion. This movement needs to be judged by soundness, or an examination of the formal logic that guides the conclusion. In contrast, the Narrative Paradigm suggests that soundness is not the only way to evaluate good reasons. In fact, soundness may not even be an accurate way of describing how people make this judgment. The Narrative Paradigm assumes that narrative rationality is affected by history, biography, culture, and character. Thus, Fisher introduces the notion of context into the Narrative Paradigm. People are influenced by the context in which they are embedded; they do not simply make judgments based on the criteria implied by the situation. Therefore, the material that appears persuasive to Miles is the material that is specifically relevant to him personally. It is not material that adheres to a code of formal logic and persuasion.

Theory Application in Groups (TAG)

In small groups, debate the following proposition: Managers who are able to use narratives as a rhetorical method with their employees will have greater success in communication at work than managers who cannot use narratives. Narrative allows managers to develop relationships with diverse audiences to a much greater degree than technical arguments will.

The fourth assumption forms a core issue of the narrative approach. It asserts that people believe stories insofar as the stories seem internally consistent and truthful. We will discuss this further in the next section when we describe the concept of narrative rationality.

Finally, Fisher's perspective is based on the assumption that the world is a set of stories, and as we choose among them, we experience life differently, allowing us to re-create our lives. Miles's choice to support Jorge may cause him to cast his own life story differently. He may no longer see himself as a loner. He may change his sense of political action based on his choice of Jorge's story. You can see how the narrative paradigm contrasts with the rational world paradigm, which tends to see the world as less transient and shifting and which discovers truth through rational analysis, not through narrative logic's emotional responses to compelling stories.

A recent study illustrates these assumptions in an interesting context: the courtroom. In their study examining the Narrative Paradigm's utility for professional communication, Christine Kelly and Michele Zak (1999) assert that O. J. Simpson's acquittal was due to the triumph of narrative argument over rational argument. Kelly and Zak observe that the defense was victorious because they framed Simpson's story in a manner that resonated with the jury while the prosecution relied on the rational world paradigm, directed more toward the judge and the opposing lawyers. Kelly and Zak note that the prosecutors "drew on the language of technical expertise and took responsibility for presenting a careful case in a court of law without reference to the lives of the jury" (p. 301).

Key Concepts in the Narrative Approach

Tracing the assumptions of the Narrative Paradigm leads us to a consideration of some of the key concepts that form the core of the theoretical framework: narration, narrative rationality, coherence or probability, fidelity, and the logic of good reasons.

Narration

Narration is often thought of as simply a story. But for Fisher, narration is much more than a plotted story with a beginning, middle, and end. In Fisher's perspective, **narration** includes any verbal or nonverbal account with a sequence of events to which listeners assign a meaning. Specifically, Fisher states,

narration
an account to which listeners assign meaning

"When I use the term 'narration,' I do not mean a fictive composition whose propositions may be true or false and have no necessary relationship to the message of that composition. By 'narration,' I mean symbolic actions—words and/or deeds—that have sequence and meaning for those who live, create, or interpret them" (1987, p. 58). This definition implies the need for a storyteller and a listener.

Fisher's definition is extremely broad and parallels what many people think of as communication itself. This, of course, is Fisher's point: All communication is narrative. He argues that narrative is not a specific genre (stories as opposed to poems, for example), but rather it is a mode of social influence. Further, it is his contention that all life is composed of stories or narratives. When you listen to a class lecture, when you give an excuse to a professor for not turning in a paper on time, when you read the newspaper, watch television, talk to your friends, you are hearing and shaping narratives.

Narrative Rationality

Given that our lives are experienced in narratives, we need some type of method for judging which stories to believe and which to disregard. This standard can be found in **narrative rationality,** which provides us with a means for judging narratives that is quite different from the traditional methods found in the rational world paradigm. As we mentioned previously, traditional tests of rationality include whether claims correspond to actual facts, whether all relevant facts have been considered, whether arguments are internally consistent, and whether the reasoning used conforms to standards of formal and informal logic (Fisher, 1978). The Research Note illustrates an application of the test of narrative rationality to President Ronald Reagan's speeches. Narrative rationality, in contrast to traditional logic, operates on the basis of two different principles: coherence and fidelity.

narrative rationality
a standard for judging which stories to believe and which to disregard

Coherence

The principle of coherence is an important standard for assessing narrative rationality, which will ultimately determine whether or not a person accepts a particular narrative or rejects it. **Coherence** refers to the internal consistency of a narrative. When judging a story's coherence, the listener would ask whether the narrative seemed to hang together in a consistent manner. Narratives possess coherence when all the pieces of the story are present; we do not feel that the storyteller has left out important details or contradicted elements of the story in any way. When many in the United States heard Kenneth Starr's narrative accusing President Clinton of perjury and obstruction of justice, they responded to a lack of coherence. Some people protested that the story did not seem to make sense when considering the amount of money that was spent on Starr's investigation, for example. Coherence is the standard of sense making applied to a given narrative. This sense making is usually obtained when the characters in a story behave in relatively consistent ways.

When Miles read the narratives contained in Jorge's campaign literature, he saw a consistent thread running through them: His university has racial prob-

coherence
a principle of narrative rationality judging the internal consistency of a story

Research Note

Lewis, W. F. (1987). Telling America's story: Narrative form and the Reagan presidency. *Quarterly Journal of Speech, 73,* 280–302.

Lewis uses Fisher's Narrative Paradigm to analyze former President Ronald Reagan's rhetoric. Lewis observes that the narrative framework explains Reagan's success at "re-invigorating" the country and the seeming contradiction between the strength of Reagan's personal popularity and the relatively weak support for his policies. Lewis notes that when Reagan became president, the United States had lost its sense of direction due to economic problems and several foreign policy failures. Reagan was able to bring back national pride. Further, Lewis observes, Reagan accomplished this through his powers as a communicator. Lewis thus applies the Narrative Paradigm to many of Reagan's speeches to analyze how he was able to achieve this. Lewis concludes that "When Reagan is seen as a storyteller and his message is seen as a story, it becomes evident why he was so successful in 're-invigorating' the country—his story gave a clear, powerful, reassuring, and self-justifying meaning to America's public life" (p. 295).

Lewis notes that Reagan's stories fit well with commonly held myths about America, what it means to be an American, and myths about the American president as a hero. Due to this fit, Lewis argues, the narrative is able to overcome even Reagan's occasional factual inaccuracies. The meaning of the general story is more important than the accuracy of any one specific detail. The narrative rationality is strong enough to override any flaws in the traditional, rational world paradigm evaluation of Reagan's speeches.

Lewis asserts that Reagan's success is predicated on coherence and consistency, as the Narrative Paradigm suggests. Reagan's consistency provides the American public with a simple framework for processing complicated problems. Lewis comments that although this was a successful formula for Reagan's presidency, it offers dangers by making good judgment and active challenges more difficult for the public. Lewis concludes that these dangers and the lack of a moral argument in Reagan's storytelling suggest that Fisher's belief that people have a natural tendency to prefer that which is true and just may be erroneous and may require more careful consideration.

lems. If Jorge had presented some problems based on race and then shaped the narrative to conclude that all was well with race relations at the university, Miles would have rejected the story for being inconsistent.

Coherence is often measured by the organization and structural elements of a narrative. When a storyteller skips around and leaves out important information, interrupts the flow of the story to add elements forgotten earlier, and generally is not smooth in the structuring of the narrative, the listener may reject the narrative for not possessing coherence. Coherence is based on three specific types of consistency: structural coherence, material coherence, and characterological coherence.

Structural Coherence   The type of consistency Fisher calls **structural coherence** rests on the degree to which the elements of the story flow smoothly. When stories are confusing, when one part does not seem to lead to the next, or when the plot is unclear, then they lack structural coherence.

Material Coherence   **Material coherence** refers to the degree of congruence between one story and other stories that seem related to it. When you hear

structural coherence
a type of coherence referring to the flow of the story

material coherence
a type of coherence referring to the congruence between one story and other related stories

some gossip about a good friend of yours indicating that she is not as honest as you thought her to be, you might react by challenging the material coherence of the narrative.

Characterological Coherence   **Characterological coherence** refers to the believability of the characters in the story. In 1998 and 1999, most people who read about Linda Tripp's taping of personal conversations between herself and Monica Lewinsky, concerning Lewinsky's sexual relationship with President Clinton, could not accept a story where Tripp appeared heroic. Her character was established as a faithless friend, a backstabber, and a villain. Her attempts to repair her image and retell her story after President Clinton was acquitted were generally rejected as not possessing characterological coherence.

Fidelity

The other critical standard for assessing narrative rationality is **fidelity,** or the truthfulness or reliability of the story. Stories with fidelity ring true to a listener. When Miles reads the stories that Jorge has in his campaign literature, he thinks to himself that those events have happened to him at the university. Miles wonders if Jorge has been following him around campus, watching what goes on in his life. This makes the stories powerful to Miles. They possess a great deal of fidelity for him. Fisher (1987) notes that when the elements of a story "represent accurate assertions about social reality" (p. 105), they have fidelity.

The Logic of Good Reasons

Related to Fisher's notion of fidelity is the primary method that he proposes for assessing narrative fidelity: the logic of good reasons. Fisher asserts that when narratives possess fidelity, they constitute good reasons for a person to hold a particular belief or take an action. For example, Miles sees Jorge's stories as possessing fidelity, which makes the stories persuasive; the stories form good reasons for Miles to vote for Jorge.

Fisher (1987) explains his concept of logic by saying that it means "a systematic set of procedures that will aid in the analysis and assessment of elements of reasoning in rhetorical interactions" (p. 106). Thus, logic for the narrative paradigm enables a person to judge the worth of stories. The logic of **good reasons** presents a listener with a set of values that appeal to her or him and form warrants for accepting or rejecting the advice advanced by any form of narrative. This does not mean that any good reason is equal to any other; it simply means that whatever prompts a person to believe a narrative is bound to a value or a conception of what is good.

As Fisher describes it, this logic is a process consisting of two series of five questions that the listener asks about the narrative. The first five questions are the following:

1. Are the statements that claim to be factual in the narrative really factual?

2. Have any relevant facts been omitted from the narrative or distorted in its telling?

---

characterological coherence
a type of coherence referring to the believability of the characters in the story

fidelity
a principle of narrative rationality judging the credibility of a story

good reasons
a set of values for accepting a story as true and worthy of acceptance; provides a method for assessing fidelity

3. What are the patterns of reasoning that exist in the narrative?

4. How relevant are the arguments in the story to any decision the listener may make?

5. How well does the narrative address the important and significant issues of this case?

These questions constitute a logic of reasons. To transform this into a logic of *good* reasons, there are five more questions that introduce the concept of values into the process of assessing practical knowledge. These questions are as follows:

1. What are the implicit and explicit values contained in the narrative?

2. Are the values appropriate to the decision that is relevant to the narrative?

3. What would be the effects of adhering to the values embedded in the narrative?

4. Are the values confirmed or validated in lived experience?

5. Are the values of the narrative the basis for ideal human conduct?

Fisher illustrates the logic of good reasons with a book written by Jonathan Schell (1982). This book, which was very popular in the 1980s, argues that the nuclear weapons race must cease. Fisher asserts that even though experts found the book inaccurate on technical grounds, the narrative it espouses was extremely popular with the general public. Fisher argues that this was because the book tells a story that meets the criteria of coherence and fidelity. It focuses on a set of values that many people found relevant at that point in history. As the Narrative Paradigm predicts, the well-told story—complete with narrative rationality and the logic of good reasons—was more compelling to readers than the expert testimony that refuted the factual accuracy of the narrative. The relationship among these elements is illustrated by Figure 20.1.

Critique and Closing

Fisher's Narrative Paradigm offers new insights into communication behavior and directs our attention to democratic processes in the area of rhetorical criticism. Fisher contributes the sense that people's lived experiences make them capable of analyzing rhetoric. Further, the Narrative Paradigm helps us to see the nature of multiple logics at work in our communication encounters. Thus,

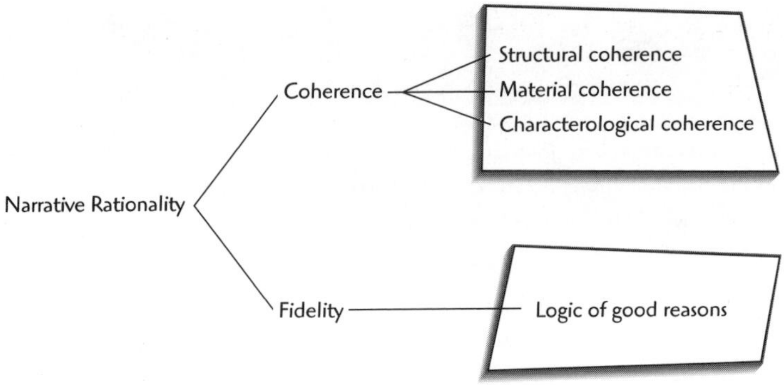

Figure 20.1
Elements of Narra-
tive Rationality

the Narrative Paradigm has made a substantial contribution to our understanding of human communication and human nature in general.

Yet, it also has attracted a great deal of criticism and revision. Given that it
is a relatively recent theoretical framework (Fisher's first conceptualization of
the theory appeared in 1978), this is to be expected. In fact, the dialogue stimulated by the claims of the Narrative Paradigm may be seen as healthy growing
pains for the discipline. The critique of the Narrative Paradigm falls into four
major categories: (1) the breadth of the theory's coverage, (2) the conservative
nature of the framework, (3) its failure to remain consistent to its claims of democracy, and (4) its failure to actually provide an alternative to the rational
world paradigm. We will briefly discuss each of these criticisms.

The critique that the Narrative Paradigm is too broad mainly focuses on
Fisher's claim that all communication is narrative. Researchers object to that
claim for two reasons: First, some have questioned the utility of a definition that
includes everything. How meaningful is the definition of narrative if it means
all communication behavior? Further, how testable is a theory that is so broad
and inclusive? Second, some researchers, notably Robert Rowland (1987;
1989), suggest that some forms of communication are not narrative in the way
that Fisher maintains. According to Rowland, science fiction and fantasy do
not conform to most people's values. Rather, these genres often challenge existing values. Further, Rowland questions the utility of considering a novel
(such as Arthur Koestler's *Darkness at Noon*) and a political pamphlet (such as
one produced by the Committee on the Present Danger) both as narratives. Although both tell stories about the repressive character of the Soviet system, they
do so in such different ways that Rowland believes it does a disservice to both
writings to place them in the same category. Further, it complicates our understanding of the definition of narrative when two such disparate examples can
both be labeled as narrative.

The second critique deals with the conservative bias inherent in the narrative approach. William Kirkwood (1992) observes that Fisher's logic of good
reasons focuses on prevailing values and fails to account for the ways in which
stories can promote social change. In some ways, both Kirkwood and Fisher
agree that this observation is more of an extension to the theory than a punishing critique. Fisher (1987) claims that humans are inventive and that we can
accept new stories when they appeal to us. In this process we can change our

Theory * Into * Practice

T*I*P

An article in the Milwaukee *Journal Sentinel* illustrates some of the tenets of the Narrative Paradigm. The article discusses how parents can talk to their adopted children about the adoption, suggesting that parents need to help develop a good story around the adoption rather than creating a lengthy rational explanation for their children. The notion of the centrality of story for people is emphasized in the article. The author describes a conversation he had with a colleague about her discussions with her 6-year-old adopted daughter, Lilly.

The friend told him that her daughter had come to her looking somber and asked her the following questions: "Why did we get adopted? Where did we go? What's adopted?" (p. L6).

When the author asked his colleague what she wanted to tell her daughter in response, she replied, "That she is so so special. She really is. I obviously don't want her to feel that she was rejected by her natural parents.

"I'm going to tell her that she was adopted because she is so so special. That she was chosen. That she was so special that we chose her and wanted her and loved her. I thought I would explain to her that every day of her 6 years, she has been precious and that we are so lucky" (p. L6).

The author advised his colleague that although her ideas were great, Lilly didn't need so much justification. Instead the author suggested that Lilly would probably benefit more by hearing a story about the adoption. He asked his colleague if she could remember an important or funny narrative from the time she spent in China when she adopted Lilly.

His colleague responded with the following story:

Well, when we went to the birthing building, where Lilly had been for several days, we were tense and cautious. People were walking around, carrying babies. Then we saw this pretty young woman walking toward us with a New York Yankees baseball hat on and a T-shirt that read: "Just Do It." Everything else was very foreign, very Chinese for us. Well, she was the mom. She just said, in English, "Hi." That's the only English she spoke. Then we all started laughing. And she let me hold her. It should have been a very serious moment, but it was all just funny. It was fun. (p. L6)

The author told his friend that that was a wonderful story, and it was what she should tell her daughter. He observed that, in his experience with adopted children,

they need a few narratives rather than long complicated explanations about their adoption. It helps to have a narrative that's happy and upbeat. . . . Finally, remember that parents cannot achieve the full story for their child. The goal is, instead, to provide some of the ingredients that will enable the child to construct her historical continuity. Parents can give their child true and fun vignettes, when the child asks for them. These vignettes will become the building blocks that the youngster will use to construct her personal life story. (p. L6)

The article concludes with the author noting that his colleague told him later that her daughter loved the story about the New York Yankees hat and wanted it repeated about once a week. For each repetition, Lilly wanted to hear it word for word just as her adoptive parents had told it to her the first time.

Source: Schwarzbeck, 1999.

TIP Follow-up
How does Lilly's adoption story illustrate Fisher's concept of narration? His concept of coherence? And fidelity?

values rather than demand that stories simply confirm our existing values. To a degree, Miles changed his values regarding the importance of voting and involvement in student life as a result of Jorge's narratives.

The last two criticisms of the Narrative Paradigm take it to task for failing to live up to its claims. Rowland (1987) finds that the narrative approach does not actually provide a more democratic structure compared to the hierarchical system espoused by the rational world paradigm, nor does it completely offer an alternative to that paradigm. Rowland says that Fisher overstates the problem of domination of the public by the elite, or by the expert, in the rational world paradigm. Additionally, Rowland argues that "there is nothing inherent in storytelling that guarantees that the elites will not control a society" (p. 272).

Despite criticisms, which primarily urge refinements of the theory, not its abandonment, Fisher's Narrative Paradigm has contributed a great deal to the study of human communication. Fisher has provided a new paradigm for understanding human nature, squarely located in the symbolic realm of communication. The idea that humans are essentially storytellers is a captivating one. Storytelling seems an apt metaphor for understanding how humans use communication to make sense of the world (Opt, 1988). Future scholarship will extend the framework of the Narrative Paradigm to remediate its shortcomings and capitalize on its strengths. In constructing the Narrative Paradigm, Fisher has provided a rich framework for such scholarship to take place.

Discussion Starters

1. Can you think of any other explanations besides the Narrative Paradigm for Miles's preference for Jorge's candidacy after he read the campaign flyers?

2. Do you agree with Fisher that humans are storytellers? What does that mean to you in a practical sense? If we are not storytellers, what metaphor could you use to describe us?

3. When you listen to others' stories, do you evaluate them based on coherence and fidelity? Can you think of any other criteria that you use to evaluate the stories that you hear?

4. What support does Fisher have for his contention that all communication is narration? Can you think of some communication that is not narrative in nature? If all communication is narration, can the theory be tested in a meaningful way? Explain your response.

5. The Narrative Paradigm suggests that when an expert argument is compared to a good story, the expert argument will fail because it will lack the coherence and the fidelity that a narrative possesses. Do you agree or disagree with this claim? Give an example where expert testimony failed to persuade you. Give an example where a good story failed to persuade you.

6. Choose a story that has been in the news recently and analyze it for narrative rationality.

Terms for Review

paradigm shift
rational world paradigm
narration
narrative rationality
coherence

structural coherence
material coherence
characterological coherence
fidelity
good reasons

Online Learning Center

Visit the Online Learning Center at www.mhhe.com/west2. Use the multiple-choice and true/false quizzes to help you prepare for exams, and the glossary, crossword puzzles, and flashcards to further your knowledge of key terms.

CHAPTER 21

Cultural Studies

Lisa and John Petrillo

Lisa and John Petrillo have lived in the same trailer park for four years, and with two young children, they realize that the wages they earn as migrant workers will probably never permit them to own their own home. They appreciate that Mr. DeMoss, the owner of the egg farm where they work, has provided housing for them, but they wish that they could have more privacy so that their neighbors would not be able to hear every word they say in the evening. The Petrillos do not have any desire to leave their tiny city because they realize that jobs are not that plentiful in New England. So they get by in the trailer park, and they dream about a big backyard where their two kids and their dog, Scooter, can play.

The Petrillos' dream often unfolds on the television shows that they watch at night. Even though cable TV is expensive and not a necessity, they both love to watch shows that help them escape their daily routines. Watching TV, Lisa and John are bombarded with messages about how easy it is to get a home mortgage. These commercials imply that without having a home, you cannot claim to have achieved the American dream. They watch the many infomercials that promote "Easy Home Ownership" or "Ten Ways to Get Your American Dream." They look at each other, wondering why they continue to live the way they do—two children, two bedrooms, and a common bathing area in the migrant camp. They both know that they don't have the money to purchase a home, but they also know that they aren't happy with the way things are.

Recently, Mr. DeMoss's farm was investigated by the government for unsanitary living and working conditions. DeMoss was told to clean up the place and was threatened with stiff fines unless he improved the situation. As a result, he had authorized spending thousands of dollars for individual lavatory facilities and was talking to the local grocery chain to ask for their help in granting discounts to employees at the egg farm. As a gesture of goodwill, DeMoss was also prepared to increase each worker's paycheck by 10 percent by the end of the month. He also promised to help relocate families with children to more suitable accommodations.

The Petrillos were ecstatic. They dreaded the communal bathing area and welcomed more privacy for their children and themselves. They were very excited about the opportunity to save money at the grocery store, and of course they were thrilled that their paychecks would increase almost immediately. This, they thought, was the beginning of saving for their American dream. They knew that they made just enough money to pay all of their bills, and now with the raise, the extra money would go into a rainy day fund that could eventually be used to purchase a home.

Lisa wrote to her brother in South America to tell him the good news. She wrote about how relatively easy it is to get a home in the United States.

This theory is based on the research of **Stuart Hall.**

She quoted the commercials she saw so frequently on television: "Good sense, good money, and a good deal," she related. She had watched the evening news reports about the low interest rates and had even gone to the library to read up on mortgages. She thought that if they saved their extra money, within a year, she and her family could be living in a new home. For now, though, Lisa was excited about the chance to move to what DeMoss called "suitable" housing. "It has to be better than this," she thought. Lisa was starting to think that her luck was beginning to change.

■

We cannot overstate how much the U.S. culture relies on the media. Each day, for instance, millions of homes tune in to dozens of different "news" programs on television. In fact, Stanley Baran and Dennis Davis (2003) conclude that "the media have become a primary means by which many of us experience or learn about many aspects of the world around us" (p. 215). However, the manner in which the media report events can vary significantly. Some journalists take pride in their fact finding. Others rely on personal testimony. Still others seek out experts to comment on events as they unfold. For instance, the coverage of the school shootings in 1999 in Littleton, Colorado, in 2000 in Mount Morris, Michigan, in 2001 in Gary, Indiana, and in 2002 in New York City underscore the various ways the media report an event. The tragedy was first reported live. Reporters then interviewed witnesses to get a firsthand account of the shootings. Finally, journalists gathered experts on both sides of the gun control issue to assess whether gun control laws are sufficiently tough. This last activity involving experts seems to beg other questions about the media's role in such events: Are they trying to convey a larger message about society in general? Is the reporting of images and stories done thoughtfully and conscientiously? Do the media have hidden agendas?

Reporting events with a hidden agenda has several implications. When the media fail to report all aspects of a story, someone or some group is inevitably affected. Nowhere is this more apparent than in the early coverage of AIDS, which was first diagnosed in the gay community. Edward Alwood (1997) notes that because most news editors did not consider gay deaths to be newsworthy, major news outlets such as the *New York Times* failed to provide coverage of the disease. In fact, the disease was killing far more people than the thirty-four who died from Legionnaires' disease in 1976 and the eighty-four women who died of toxic shock syndrome in 1980. Yet, it wasn't until the death of actor Rock Hudson in 1985 that major news stories were devoted to the subject of AIDS. By that time, however, more than 6,000 people had died from the disease. Again, the media's message is implied but significant: The deaths of gay men are not newsworthy.

Stuart Hall is a theorist who questions the role of elite institutions such as the media and their frequently false and misleading images. Unlike other communication theorists, however, Hall has focused on the role of the media and their ability to shape public opinions of marginalized populations, including people of color, the poor, and others who do not reflect a White, male, heterosexual (and wealthy) point of view. For Hall, the personal is the political; as a

Jamaican, he speaks "of being the 'blackest' in his family, the 'one from the outside,' who didn't fit and who found that experience of marginality both replicated and amplified" (cited in Morley & Chen, 1997, p. 13).

This orientation underscores his work in Cultural Studies. Before we continue, we define Cultural Studies as a theoretical perspective that focuses on how culture is influenced by powerful, dominant groups. Unlike several other theoretical traditions in this book, Cultural Studies does not refer to a single doctrine of human behavior. In fact, Stuart Hall (1992) persuasively argues that "Cultural Studies has multiple discourses; it has a number of different histories. It is a whole set of formations; it has its own different conjunctures and moments in the past. . . . I want to insist on that!" (p. 278). Although Hall and other theorists in Cultural Studies have applied many of the theory's concepts to the media, Cultural Studies extends beyond the media (Downing, 1996) and has often been referred to as "audience studies" (Angus, Jhally, Lewis, & Schwichtenberg, 1989). Cultural Studies concerns the attitudes, approaches, and criticisms of a culture since culture is the principle feature of the theory. It is an intellectual framework that addresses the public and its position as an adjunct class in society.

Cultural Studies has its background and its beginnings in Britain, although the United States has also taken a lead in understanding Cultural Studies (e.g., Grossberg, 1984). As a cultural theorist and the former director of the Center for Contemporary Cultural Studies (CCCS) at the University of Birmingham in England, Stuart Hall (1981; 1989) contends that the media are powerful tools of the elite. Media serve to communicate dominant ways of thinking, regardless of the efficacy of such thinking. Cultural Studies emphasizes that the media keep the powerful people in control while the less powerful absorb what is presented to them. Lisa and John Petrillo, for instance, exemplify a marginalized group (the poor) who have been taken in by the American dream of owning a home. Of course, cultural theorists would argue that the media—in this case, the infomercial sponsors—are taking advantage of a couple who will probably never have enough money to own a home. And yet, the message from the popular media is that it is possible. All that is needed, according to the message, is good sense and good money.

Cultural Studies is a tradition rooted in the writings of German philosopher Karl Marx. Because Marxist principles form the foundation of the theory, let's look further into this theoretical backdrop. We then examine the two assumptions of Cultural Studies.

The Marxist Legacy: Power to the People

Philosopher Karl Marx (1963) is generally credited with identifying how the powerful (the elite) exploit the powerless (the working class). He believed that being powerless can lead to **alienation,** or the psychological condition whereby people begin to feel that they have little control over their future. For Marx, though, alienation is most destructive under capitalism. Specifically, when people lose control over their own means of production (as happens in capital-

alienation
perception that one
has little control over
his or her future

ism) and must sell their time to some employer, they become alienated. Capitalism results in a profit-driven society, and workers in a capitalistic society are measured by their labor potential.

Marx believed that the class system—a monolithic system that pervades all society—must be unearthed by the collective working class, or *proletariat*. He felt that laborers were often subjected to poor working and living conditions because the elite were unwilling to yield their control. As with Lisa and John Petrillo, laborers across society are constantly relegated to secondary status. The elite, or ruling, class's interests become socially ingrained, and therefore people become enslaved in society. One of Marx's principal concerns was ensuring that some revolutionary action of the proletariat be undertaken to break the chains of slavery and ultimately to subvert alienation under a capitalistic society.

Marxist thinkers who believed the working class was oppressed because of corporate-owned media have been called the **Frankfurt School theorists.** These thinkers and writers believed that the media's messages were constructed and delivered with one goal in mind: capitalism. That is, although the media might claim that they are delivering information for the "common good," the bottom line (money) frames each message. Those affiliated with the Frankfurt School felt that the media could be considered an "authoritarian personality," which meant that they were opposed to the male-centered/male-owned media. In fact, Herbert Marcuse, a Frankfurt thinker, was the leader of a group of social revolutionaries whose goal was to break down this patriarchal system.

Frankfurt School theorists
a group of scholars who believed that the media were more concerned with making money than with presenting news

The application of Marxist principles to Cultural Studies is more subtle than direct. This has prompted some scholars to consider the theory to be more **neo-Marxist,** which means Cultural Studies diverges from classical Marxism to some extent. First, unlike Marx, those in Cultural Studies have integrated a variety of perspectives into their thinking, including those from the arts, the humanities, and the social sciences. Second, theorists in Cultural Studies expand the subordinate group to include additional powerless and marginalized people, not just laborers. These groups include homosexuals, ethnic minorities, women, the mentally ill, and even children. Third, everyday life for Marx was centered on work and the family. Writers in Cultural Studies have also studied recreational activities, hobbies, and sporting events in seeking to understand how individuals function in society. In sum, Marx's original thinking may have been appropriate for post–World War II populations, but his ideas now require clarification, elaboration, and application to a diverse society. Cultural Studies

neo-Marxist
limited embracement of Marxism

moves beyond a strict, limited interpretation of society toward a broader conception of culture.

Now that you have a brief understanding of how theorists in Cultural Studies were influenced by the writings of Marx, we examine the two primary assumptions of Cultural Studies.

Assumptions of Cultural Studies

Cultural Studies is essentially concerned with how elite groups such as the media exercise their power over subordinate groups. The theory is rooted in a few fundamental claims about culture and power:

- Culture pervades and invades all facets of human behavior.
- People are part of a hierarchical structure of power.

Our first assumption pertains to the notion of culture, a concept we addressed in Chapter 2. To review, we identified culture as a community of meaning. In Cultural Studies, we need a different interpretation of the word, one that underscores the nature of the theory. The various norms, ideas, values, and forms of understanding in a society that help people interpret their reality are part of a culture's ideology. According to Hall (1981), **ideology** refers to "those images, concepts and premises which provide the frameworks through which we represent, interpret, understand, and 'make sense' of some aspect of social existence" (p. 31). Hall believes that ideologies include the languages, the concepts, and the categories that different social groups collect in order to make sense of their environments.

ideology
framework used to
make sense of our
existence

To a great extent, cultural practices and institutions permeate our ideologies. We cannot escape the cultural reality that as a global community, actions are not in a vacuum. Graham Murdock (1989) emphasizes the pervasiveness of culture by noting that "All groups are constantly engaged in creating and remaking meaning systems and embodying these meanings in expressive forms, social practices, and institutions" (p. 436). Interestingly and predictably, however, Murdock notes, being part of a diverse cultural community often results in struggles over meaning, interpretation, identity, and control. These struggles, or **culture wars,** suggest that there are frequently deep divisions in the perception of the significance of a cultural issue or event. Individuals often compete to help shape a nation's identity. For example, both pro-life and pro-choice groups want to define the "product" of conception. One wants to define it as a "fetus" and the other as a "baby." Both groups strive to make their meanings dominant. The struggle takes place not only in the courts but in the media and in the classroom.

culture wars
cultural struggles over
meaning, identity,
and influence

In addition to the various ideologies, Judith Martin and Tom Nakayama (2000) note that culture includes a number of diverse activities of a population. In the United States, there are many behaviors, some done daily and others less frequently. For instance, it is common for people to date within their race, for families to visit one another during holidays, and for people to attend religious services at least once a week. There are also more mundane behaviors, such as getting your driver's license renewed, running on the treadmill, pulling weeds from your garden, or listening to public radio while driving home from work. For those interested in Cultural Studies, it is crucial to examine these activities in order to understand how the ideology of a population is maintained. Paul du Gay, Stuart Hall, Linda Janes, Hugh Mackay, and Keith Negus (1997) explain that these practices intersect to help us understand the production and dissemination of meaning in a culture. At the same time, the meaning of a culture is reflected by such practices. Culture, then, cannot be separated from meaning in society. In fact, uncovering prevailing cultural meanings is one important aim of researchers in Cultural Studies.

Meaning in our culture is profoundly sculpted by the media. The media could simply be considered the technological carrier of culture, but as this chapter will point out, the media are so much more. Consider the words of Michael Real (1996) regarding the media's role in the U.S. culture: "Media invade our living space, shape the taste of those around us, inform and persuade us on products and policies, intrude into our private dreams and public fears, and in turn, invite us to inhabit them" (pp. xiii–xiv). No doubt, for example, that the media contain messages—intentional or unintentional—that get the Petrillos to accept the goals, dreams, and standards of success portrayed in the media.

A second assumption of cultural theory pertains to people as an important part of a powerful social hierarchy. Power operates at all levels of humanity (Grossberg, 1989). However, power in this sense is not role based, as we considered it in our discussion of Adaptive Structuration Theory in Chapter 15. Rather, Hall is interested in the power held by social groups or the power between groups. Meaning and power are intricately related, for as Hall (1989) contends, "Meaning cannot be conceptualized outside the field of play of power relations" (p. 48). In keeping with the Marxist tradition, power is something that subordinate groups desire but cannot achieve. Often there is a struggle for power, and the victor is usually the person at the top of the social hierarchy. An example of what we are discussing here can be observed in the U.S. culture's preoccupation with beauty. Theorists in Cultural Studies contend that because beauty is often defined as thin and good-looking, anyone not matching these qualities would be considered unattractive. Hall believes that the slender people—at the top of the social hierarchy—are able to wield more power than those at the bottom of the hierarchy (the unattractive).

Perhaps the ultimate source of power in our society, however, is the media. Hall (1989) maintains that the media are simply too powerful. He is not shy in his indictment of the media's character by calling it dishonest and "fundamentally dirty" (p. 48). In a diverse culture, Hall argues, no institution should have the power to decide what the public hears. Gary Woodward (1997) draws a similar conclusion when he states that there is a tradition whereby journalists serve as guardians of the nation's cultural activities: If the media deem something to have importance, then something has importance; an otherwise unimportant event suddenly carries importance.

Let's revisit our story of Lisa and John Petrillo. Theorists in Cultural Studies would argue that as members of a minority population, the Petrillos have been inherently relegated to a subordinate position in society. Their work environment—as migrant workers on a large egg farm—is the product of a capitalistic society, one in which laborers work under difficult conditions. Although they will inevitably have difficulty owning their own home because of their low wages, writers in Cultural Studies would point to the media's barrage of images and stories touting the American dream. Although the message may convey hope for the Petrillos, their dream of owning their own home might better be called a fantasy because the elite power structure (the media) does not honestly convey the reality of their circumstances. Perhaps unknown to the Petrillos, the media are a tool of the dominant class. The future of Lisa and John Petrillo, then, will overtly and covertly be influenced by the ruling class.

Hegemony: The Influence on the Masses

The concept of hegemony is an important feature of Cultural Studies, and much of the theory rests on an understanding of this term. **Hegemony** can be generally defined as the influence, power, or dominance of one social group over another. The idea is a complex one that can be traced back to the work of Antonio Gramsci, one of the founders of the Italian Communist Party who was later imprisoned by the Italian fascists. Writers in Cultural Studies have called Gramsci a "second progenitor Marxist" (Inglis, 1993, p. 74) because he openly questioned why the masses never revolted against the privileged class:

> The study of hegemony was for him [Gramsci], and is for us, the study of the question why so many people assent to and vote for political arrangements which palpably work against their own happiness and sense of justice. What on earth is it, in schools or on the telly, which makes rational people accept unemployment, killing queues [wards] in hospitals, ludicrous waste on needless weaponry, and all the other awful details of life under modern capitalism? (Inglis, 1993, p. 76)

hegemony
the domination of one group over another, usually weaker, group

false consciousness
Gramsci's belief that people are unaware of the domination in their lives

Gramsci's notion of hegemony was based on Marx's idea of **false consciousness,** a state in which individuals become unaware of the domination in their lives. Gramsci contended that audiences can be exploited by the same social system they support (financially). From popular culture to religion, Gramsci felt the dominant groups in society manage to direct people into complacency. Consent is a principle component of hegemony. Consent is given by populations if they are given enough "stuff" (e.g., freedoms, material goods, and so forth). Ultimately, people will prefer to live in a society with these "rights" and consent to the dominant culture's ideologies.

The application of Gramsci's thinking on hegemony is quite applicable to today's society. Under a hegemonic culture, some profit (literally) while others lose out. What happens in hegemonic societies is that people become influenced by consent rather than coercion (Real, 1996). The public is susceptible to a frequently subtle imbalance in power. That is, people are likely to support tacitly the dominant ideology of a culture. The complexity of the concept is further discussed by Hall (1989). He notes that hegemony can be multifaceted in that the dominant, or ruling, class is frequently divided in its ideologies. That means that during the subtle course of being influenced, the public may find itself pushed and pulled in several directions. Unraveling such complexity is one goal of researchers in Cultural Studies.

Research Note

Fiske, J., & Dawson, P. (1996). Audience violence: Watching homeless men watch *Die Hard*. In J. Hay, L. Grossberg, & E. Wartella (Eds.), *The audience and its landscape* (pp. 297–316). Boulder, Co: Westview.

This study demonstrates a number of themes associated with Cultural Studies, namely oppressed populations, the media, and hegemony. The researchers conducted an ethnographic study of homeless men watching a violent movie *(Die Hard)* in a church shelter. They were interested in understanding how the movie elicited comments pertaining to violence and how violent themes were transported from the media—in this case, the film industry.

The researchers begin with an overall discussion of the pervasiveness of homelessness in the United States. They present a range of logical and emotional reasons why homelessness exists in contemporary U.S. society: job loss, family breakups, ill health, and so forth. The writers also capture the look of the shelter in their description of the furniture as well as the shelter's policies (for example, men must be out of the shelter between 8 A.M. and 5 P.M.).

Fiske and Dawson then comment on the men's decision to check out films in the shelter's library. Among the most frequently checked-out films were *Sudden Impact, Robocop,* and *Die Hard,* three movies renowned for their violence. The viewing of *Die Hard* became the point of analysis for this research.

According to the research team, the men were selective viewers of the movie. They paid attention to some violent episodes but ignored others. What was especially striking was the attention paid to violence against what Fiske and Dawson call the social order (or what Hall would call the elite). The men seemed to side with the terrorists who were against the corporation, and they were also empathetic toward the hero who was fighting the terrorists. As the movie continued, the support of the hero diminished because he began to side with the establishment: the police force.

At this point, the researchers take the reader on a cultural trip, observing the fact that the homeless men were themselves victims of a Reagan–Bush aristocracy. They believe that "when homelessness is a structural and systematic deprivation of the weak by a society which is also theirs, and whose material security they feel ought to be one of their rights,

then the conditions are ripe for the taste of violence to develop" (1996, pp. 302–303). What they are saying here is that the men in this study may be prone to viewing the violent episodes and identifying with the violent individuals because they are a cultural product of a violent society. As the authors conclude, "The taste for violence is a discriminating one" (p. 304).

Fiske and Dawson imply that power—a key concept in Cultural Studies—plays an integral role in the movie and in their analysis. Power is evident in the masculinity of the lead character, and it is no coincidence that many homeless wanted to define themselves as similar to their hero—that is, however, until he becomes closely associated with law enforcement. Interestingly, the homeless men also identified with the less powerful forces in the movie. The powerless endure great pains, an apt metaphor for the homeless in our society.

The authors conclude their research by discussing issues pertaining to censorship and control in the shelter. The shelter's librarian confirmed that homeless men are enthusiastic about checking out violent films, and he expressed concern that this violence may elicit violence in the homeless men. The researchers report that the librarian was disturbed over some obsessive behavior in the men, such as one man viewing the shower scene from *Psycho* over and over for many hours. In all, the discussion on censorship and control focuses on the fact that if the librarian censored what could be checked out, this was simply another example of the dominant forces (that is, the ruling class) taking control of the marginalized.

This study is an attempt to examine an oppressed population and its interpretation of violence through film. The authors comment that the men seemed to enjoy scenes where the dominant forces were wiped out (for instance, the men cheered the death of a CEO). Fiske and Dawson believe that the "audience is a cultural site" (p. 311) and that researchers should continue to study groups such as the homeless in this bottom-up manner.

Hegemony can be further understood by looking at today's corporate culture, where—using Marx's thinking—ruling ideas are ideas of the ruling class. In most corporate cultures, where decision making is predominantly made by White, heterosexual males, we expect certain ideologies to be present that support this class of people. Hall questions whether this dominant way of thinking and relating is legitimate or whether it simply perpetuates the subordination of the masses. How is consciousness raised and how is new consciousness presented? Perhaps it is the language used in an organization, for as Hall (1997) states, "Language in its widest sense is the vehicle of practical reasoning, calculation and consciousness, because of the ways by which certain meanings and references have been historically secured" (p. 40). People must share the same way of interpreting language, however, to achieve meaning in a context, and Hall notes that meanings change from one culture or era to another. So what exists in one organizational setting may not exist in another. To better understand hegemony and how the media influence the oppressed, review the Research Note on violence in homeless men.

theatre of struggle
competition of various cultural ideologies

What all this means is that there are multiple ideologies in a society as complex as the United States. This translates into what Hall calls a **theatre of struggle**, which means that various ideologies in society compete and are in temporary states of conflict. Thus, as attitudes and values on different topics shift in society, so do the various ideologies associated with these topics. For example, think about what it meant to be a woman before 1920 and what it means to be a woman today. Before 1920, women were unable to vote and were generally dismissed as subordinate and subservient to men. Then in August 1920, the amendment giving women the right to vote was ratified. Today, of course, women not only vote but hold high political office. Although U.S. society still does not provide entirely equal opportunity for women and they continue to be targets of discrimination, the culture and ideology pertaining to women's rights have changed with the times.

Hegemony is but one component of the intellectual currents associated with Cultural Studies. Although people (audiences) are frequently influenced by dominant societal forces, at times, people will demonstrate their own hegemonic tendencies. We explore this notion further.

Counter-Hegemony:
The Masses Start to Influence the Dominant Forces

We have noted that hegemony is one of the core concepts associated with Cultural Studies. Yet audiences are not always duped into accepting and believing everything presented by the dominant forces. At times, audiences will use the same resources and strategies of dominant social groups. To some extent, individuals will use the same practices of hegemonic domination to challenge that domination. This is what Gramsci called **counter-hegemony**.

counter-hegemony
when at times, people will use hegemonic behaviors to challenge the domination in their lives

Counter-hegemony becomes a critical part of Cultural Studies thinking because it suggests that audiences are not necessarily willing and compliant. In other words, we—as audience members—are not dumb and submissive! Danny Lesh in *Counter Heg* (a newsletter dedicated to the counter-hegemonic movement; www.lesstreet/com/dan/counterheg) observes that part of the goal of counter-hegemony "is to understand history from other lenses, particularly from women's, workers', and racial minorities' perspectives." That is, in counter-hegemony, researchers try to raise the volume on muted voices. Think of counter-hegemony as a point where individuals recognize their consent and try to do something about it.

Counter-hegemonic messages, ironically enough, occur in television programming. In particular, two shows—*The Cosby Show* and *The Simpsons*—exemplify counter-hegemony. Both shows are effective examples of how television content challenges the priorities established by the dominant forces. With respect to *The Cosby Show,* Bishetta Merrit (1991) notes that, in an effort to defy social stereotypes, this television family featured two working parents, one a gynecologist and the other an attorney. Further, instead of having five children who argued all the time, Herman Gray (1989) claimed that in almost every episode, the children were taught the values of honesty, respect, and responsibility. Finally, the show was an educational tool as well, referencing many historically Black colleges, playing music by Black artists (e.g., jazz and rap), and depicting symbols of African American heritage. To this end, the show was an effort to dispel the messages that the media elite were presenting on nightly news: the absent father, the uneducated family members, and the poverty-ridden living environment. Counter-hegemony, then, takes shape with the presentation of the Cosbys as Black America.

Like *The Cosby Show, The Simpsons* contains satiric counter-hegemonic messages aimed at showing that individuals who are dominated use the same symbolic resources to challenge that domination. One of the longest-running shows in television history, *The Simpsons* has included references to the Beatles, Kafka, *The Adventures of Ozzie and Harriet,* Tennessee Williams, talk shows, and *Citizen Kane* (Campbell, 1998).

The core cast of characters—Marge (the mother), Homer (the father), Bart (son), Lisa (daughter), and Maggie, (the infant daughter)—each present different counter-hegemonic messages. For Marge, although cultural representations of a homemaker/housewife suggest a doting and supportive wife and mother, she is arguably the most independent of all the characters. She has tried a number of other professions, from police officer to a protester against handgun violence. Homer, an employee at a local nuclear power plant, shows that despite what the government may tell us about the safety of these facilities, bumbling, inept people like Homer continue to stay employed. Lisa, contesting societal expectations that a "child should be seen and not heard," shows that she is intellectually curious, artistically savvy, and environmentally aware.

One of the more central characters of the show is Bart Simpson. Interestingly, although society tends to shut down boys of Bart's age (and girls to some extent), Bart manages to shut down the same society that tries to subdue him. His pranks range from harassing a local bar with sophomoric phone calls to disrespecting his grade school principal to calling his father by his first name. In the end, however, despite the 21 minutes of chaos, the family members show that they have high regard for each other in personal ways. As Carl Matheson (2001) notes, the show advocates "a moral position of caring at the level of the individual, one which favors the family over the institution" (p. 4). *The*

Simpsons, therefore, continues to challenge prevailing religious, political, and cultural notions that the family is dismantling.

Audience Decoding

decoding
receiving and comparing messages

No hegemonic or counter-hegemonic message can exist without an audience's ability to receive the message and compare it with meanings already stored in their minds. This is called **decoding,** the final topic of Cultural Studies we wish to address. When we receive messages from others, we decode them based on our perceptions, thoughts, and past experiences. So, for instance, when Lisa Petrillo from our opening story interprets information on purchasing a home, she is relying on several mental behaviors, including her desire to have a home, her conversations with people who have already purchased a home, her library visits, and the fact that she and her family have never owned a home. Lisa will store the information she receives pertaining to a new home and retrieve it when someone engages her in a conversation on the topic. All of this is done instantaneously; that is, she will make immediate decisions about how to interpret a message once she receives it.

Decoding is central to Cultural Studies. But before we delve further into this, let's review the gist of Cultural Studies up to this point. You will recall that the public receives a great deal of information from the elite and that people unconsciously consent to what dominant ideologies suggest. Theorists reason that the public should be envisioned as part of a larger cultural context, one in which those struggling for a voice are oppressed (Budd & Steinman, 1992). As in our previous discussion, hierarchical social relations (between the elite bosses and the subordinate workers, for example) exist in an uneven society. This results in subordinate cultures decoding the messages of the ruling class. Usually, according to Hall, the media connote the ruling class in Western society.

Hall (1980a) elaborates on how decoding works in the media. He recognizes that an audience decodes a message from three vantage points, or positions: dominant-hegemonic, negotiated, and oppositional. We explore each of these below.

dominant-hegemonic position
operating within a code that allows a person to have control over another

Hall claims that individuals operate within a code that dominates and exercises more power than other codes. He terms this the **dominant-hegemonic position.** The professional code of television broadcasters, for instance, will always operate within the hegemony of the dominant code. Hall relates that professional codes reproduce hegemonic interpretations of reality. This is done with subtle persuasion. Consider John and Lisa Petrillo. The television images

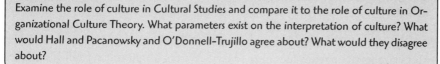

Examine the role of culture in Cultural Studies and compare it to the role of culture in Organizational Culture Theory. What parameters exist on the interpretation of culture? What would Hall and Pacanowsky and O'Donnell-Trujillo agree about? What would they disagree about?

of owning a home prompt the Petrillos to believe that owning a home is within their reach. The selection of words, the presentation of pictures, and the choice of spokespeople in infomercials are all part of the staging in the professional code. Audiences, like the Petrillos, are prone to either misunderstanding a message or selectively perceiving only certain parts of a message. Why? Hall writes, "The viewer does not know the terms employed, cannot follow the complex logic of argument or exposition, is unfamiliar with the language, finds the concepts too alien or difficult or is foxed by the expository narrative" (1980a, p. 135). Television producers are worried that people like the Petrillos will not accept the intended and preferred media message of owning a home. They (the media) therefore ensure that their professional code is placed in the larger, dominant cultural code of meaning. This ensures that John and Lisa Petrillo will work toward buying a home.

The second position is a **negotiated position**; audience members are able to accept dominant ideologies but will operate with some exceptions to the cultural rule. Hall holds that audience members always reserve the right to apply local conditions to large-scale events. This happens frequently when the media report on laws that are enacted at the national level and interpreted at the state or community level. For example, Hall might argue that although audiences may accept the elite's interpretation of a welfare reform bill in Washington, D.C. ("All people should work if they are able to"), they may have to negotiate when it does not coincide with a local or personal principle ("Children need parents at home"). Hall notes that due to the difficulty of negotiations, people are prone to communication failures.

The final way in which audiences decode messages is by engaging in an oppositional position. An **oppositional position** occurs when audience members substitute an alternative code for the code supplied by the media. Critical consumers reject the media's intended and preferred meaning of the message and instead replace it with their own way of thinking about a subject. Consider, for instance, the manner in which the media communicate feminine images of beauty. To many, the media present feminine beauty as a way to serve the sexual desire of men (Schwichtenberg, 1987). Some consumers, however, reject this capitalistic message and substitute more realistic portrayals.

Hall accepts the fact that the media frame messages with the covert intent to persuade. Audience members have the capacity to avoid being swallowed up in the dominant ideology, yet, as with the Petrillo family, the messages the audience receives are often part of a more subtle campaign. Theorists in Cultural

negotiated position
accepting dominant ideologies, but allowing for cultural exceptions

oppositional position
substituting alternative messages presented by the media

371

Studies do not suggest that people are gullible but rather that they often un-knowingly become a part of the agenda of others (Hall, 1980b).

Critique and Closing

Although Cultural Studies began at the CCCS in England, its influence on writers, researchers, and theorists in the United States has been profound. The theory has attracted the attention of critical theorists in particular, because it is founded on principles of criticism. Its Marxist influence has also drawn in scholars from philosophy, economics, and social psychology (Surber, 1998), and its emphasis on underrepresented groups in society has enticed writers in sociology and women's studies to take notice (Long, 1989).

In addition, many of the principles and features of Cultural Studies have been investigated. Ideology has been examined (Lewis & Morgan, 2001; Soar, 2000), and the concept of hegemony has been applied to episodes of *The Mary Tyler Moore Show* (Dow, 1990). Research by Janice Radway (1984, 1986) focused on romance novels and the women who read them. She discovered that many women read these books to silently protest male domination in society. Lawrence Grossberg (1986) and Linda Steiner (1988) found oppositional coding with audiences in their research. Grossberg found that punk music was an oppositional response to rock and roll music because rock and roll allowed for "new possibilities" (1986, p. 57) in the music industries. Steiner looked at a decade of the "No Comment" section of *Ms.* magazine, which is devoted to covert and overt male domination in society. Steiner claimed that the manner in which women read these sections was tantamount to oppositional decoding; they read the comments in a way that suited their own interests and not the superiority of males.

Clearly, the above examples illustrate the heuristic nature of Cultural Studies. In addition, the theory can be considered to be highly useful. James Carey (1989) writes that Cultural Studies "make up a vehicle that can alter our self-image" (p. 94); therefore, it's possible to translate some of the theory into daily life. Its utility can also be found in its dedication to studying the cultural struggles of the underprivileged. According to Hall (1997), these populations have remained subordinate for too long. By concentrating on these marginalized social groups, a number of subfields have emerged, namely ethnic studies and gay/lesbian/bisexual/transgendered studies (Surber, 1998). Hall and his work in Cultural Studies prompted Carey to conclude that Hall's work is "theoretically, historically, and often, empirically elegant and very much deserves the influence it has acquired" (1989, p. 31).

Despite what appear to be glowing endorsements, Cultural Studies has evoked quite a bit of criticism, even among its own group of advocates. Some of the criticism seems to be more "turf wars" than anything else. For example, we noted that the theory has its beginnings in Britain but has been embraced by researchers in the United States. To this, Stuart Hall (1996) provocatively states, "I don't know what to say about American cultural studies. I am completely dumbfounded by it" (p. 273). He believes comparisons between the two camps can be dangerous because the theory was conceptualized in a British context.

Theory * Into * Practice

In a *Boston Globe* article, Derrick Jackson comments on the digital divide that exists in the United States and how our elected leaders like President Bush shrug off the differences. Jackson's thoughts reflect a central feature of Culture Studies: the oppressed and marginalized must have a voice in a hegemonic society. Jackson notes that the budget of the Bush administration calls for an end to low-income communities' opportunities to build computer labs for children's education, adult literacy, and job training. Jackson notes that the Clinton administration began programs to help "Indian tribes communicate across miles of desert and plain, helped elders learn to use computers, and helped teenagers do research after school" (p. A23).

Jackson presents statistics to support his thinking that the Internet, for instance, continues to separate the "haves" from the "have-nots." For instance, although over half the country has a personal computer and Internet access, there are racial gaps. While over 70 percent of Asian Americans and White Americans use computers, only 56 percent of African Americans and Latinos use computers. And although 60 percent of Asian Americans and White Americans have Internet access, over 40 percent of African Americans and 32 percent of Latinos use the Internet.

Jackson contends that the availability of computers and Internet access has helped low-income districts. He is clear in stating that "without further federal and state investments, any information and education gaps related to the Internet will not improve" (p. A23). Jackson encourages the Bush administration to avoid scaling back the programs that assist all racial communities equally.

Source: Jackson, 2002.

TIP Follow-up
How might Stuart Hall and other Cultural Studies theorists respond to the inequities in a technological society such as the United States? What remedies to the inequities would be proposed by the theorists?

U.S. researcher Lawrence Grossberg (1996) responds by noting that as Cultural Studies gains more attention by communication researchers, "its relationship to a specific British body of work disappears" (p. 178). So for Grossberg and others, Cultural Studies belongs to no one, yet Grossberg (who studied in Birmingham, England) has lamented that the theory may have lost some original value due to the haphazard application of its concepts in a diverse array of disciplines, including English, philosophy, and linguistics.

A second criticism of Cultural Studies relates to the audience. Even though some audiences resist the role of dupe, are they able to become interpretive and active resisters? In other words, to what extent can audiences be counter-hegemonic? In fact, Mike Budd, Robert Entman, and Clay Steinman (1990) suggest that some cultural theorists overestimate the ability of the oppressed and marginalized populations to escape their culture. They lack the skills, insight, and networks to be so political in their resistance.

Cultural Studies remains one of the few theoretical traditions that has attracted the attention of scholars from a variety of disciplines outside communication. Researchers interested in understanding the thinking, experiences, and activities of historically oppressed populations usually endorse Cultural Studies. Although some critics have faulted the theory for a number of reasons, Stuart Hall is credited with criticizing the elite and with drawing attention to oppressed voices in society. Hall's commitment to understanding the everyday acts and commonly accepted events is admirable.

Discussion Starters

1. Should the Petrillo family be blamed for not trying to leave their current situation? If they are not able to achieve the American dream of owning a home, should the media be blamed? Include examples when expressing your opinion.

2. Discuss how hegemony functions in world events. Now apply the concept to your campus. Identify any similarities and differences between the two applications. Use examples in your response.

3. What other cultural artifacts exist in our society that could be studied within a Cultural Studies framework? Integrate the circuit of culture to explain their influence in society.

4. British Cultural Studies is strongly focused on class differences. What do you think about applying the thinking of British Cultural Studies to Cultural Studies in North America? Are the concepts and principles relevant to all countries? Why or why not?

5. Do you agree or disagree with the belief that oppressed populations have little voice in the United States? How does this view relate to how you feel about the theory?

6. How might Cultural Studies theorists view poverty in the United States?

Terms for Review

alienation	theatre of struggle
Frankfurt School theorists	counter-hegemony
neo-Marxist	decoding
ideology	dominant-hegemonic position
culture wars	negotiated position
hegemony	oppositional position
false consciousness	

Online Learning Center

Visit the Online Learning Center at www.mhhe.com/west2. Use the multiple-choice and true/false quizzes to help you prepare for exams, and the glossary, crossword puzzles, and flashcards to further your knowledge of key terms.

The Media

ARGUABLY, VERY FEW INSTITUTIONS IN OUR LIVES affect us more than the media. Their presence almost invades us. Radio, television, film, DVDs, VCRs, cell phones, answering machines, and fax machines seem to be our technological friends. And we're all "virtually" followed by the Internet. Media have become part of our lives, and it's apparent we'll never be able to reverse this fact.

It is in this spirit that we offer the four theories in this section called "The Media." Each theory places various media as central to our lives, and these respective media theorists believe that we respond in different ways to the barrage of electronic technology. Cultivation Analysis focuses on the role of television in our lives. This theory is concerned with the effects of long-term exposure on people's perceptions of the world. Uses and Gratifications Theory, however, suggests that the viewer/listener is able to discriminate in media consumption. It concerns itself with what people do with particular media. The central feature of the Spiral of Silence Theory pertains to the influence of media on whether or not people will speak out about an issue. Examining how technology has ruled our lives, Medium Theory argues that the primary media of the age (currently the Internet, for instance) usually takes precedence over the content of the message.

We will continue to be affected by media throughout our lives. Technology continues to develop, and even as we write these words, new ways of bringing messages to people are being conceptualized. While learning about the theories in this section, you will encounter a number of timely topics pertaining to the media: dominance, patriarchy, personal needs and values, and the ethics associated with media reporting.

CHAPTER 22

Cultivation Analysis

Joyce Jensen

Joyce Jensen was preparing to vote for the very first time. She had been looking forward to this privilege since she was 12 years old. She considers herself a news junkie, and she's always devoured the morning newspaper, the local TV news, CNN, the national network news, and *Time* and *Newsweek*. She made it a point to watch C-SPAN, a cable station dedicated to the world of politics. She knew that she was one of only a handful in her class who could identify all of the U.S. Supreme Court justices. She was ready to take some flak as a news nerd, but the world fascinated her. She knew that when she turned 18, she'd be prepared for the right and responsibility of voting.

Now she was faced with a decision as she voted for her state's governor. Although undecided, she was leaning toward Roberta Johndrew, the tough-on-crime candidate. Johndrew favored greater use of the death penalty, limits on appeals by people convicted of crimes, and putting more police on the street. Yet, Joyce thought that the other candidate, Frank Milnes, the education candidate, had some good ideas as well. Crime—in Joyce's state and in the country as a whole—was down for the sixth consecutive year. The statistics were most impressive, Milnes said, when considering violent crime. All types of violent crime had been in decline for nearly a decade. Milnes argued that money being spent for more police, more prisons, and more executions would be better spent on improving schools. After all, Milnes asserted, more dollars in the state were being spent on incarceration than on educating young people. Better schools, he argued, would mean even less crime in the future. "What kind of state do we live in," he demanded in his campaign literature, "when we refuse to give raises to our teachers and pay our prison guards more than our elementary or high school teachers?"

Those were powerful arguments, thought Joyce. She regretted that teachers were not getting paid commensurate with their expertise and responsibilities. She knew that she wanted to have children eventually, and she wanted them to get the best education possible. She could see how paying teachers more might help achieve that.

But as a young, single woman, these arguments were secondary to safety considerations. There seemed to be so much crime in the city. Every night when she watched the news on television, there seemed to be more crimes to report. She was often uncomfortable when she was out at night. At times, she even felt uneasy being at home alone. Maybe it is an irrational fear, she thought to herself, but it's there, and for her it is real.

As Joyce pondered her vote in the booth, so much was going through her mind. She considered her present situation as a single woman as well as her future as a mother. She reflected on both Ro-

---

This theory is based on the research of **George Gerbner**.

berta Johndrew and Frank Milnes and their comments over the past several months. She even thought about the historical moment of her first vote. As she contemplated her options for another moment or two, she felt she would be able to make a good decision. So much depended on citizens making informed choices. Joyce was thrilled to exercise her right as a U.S. citizen.

■

Television is as much a part of the human experience in the United States as family. All across our country, people tune in to a variety of television programs, from soap operas to C-SPAN. We are a society that has become increasingly reliant on TV and what it has to offer each day. Television has found its way into our living rooms, our conversations, and even our psyches. This invention of the 1940s has not only sustained itself into the new millennium but has become the dominant force of a changing society.

Responding to the pervasiveness of television in society thirty years ago, George Gerbner and his colleague Lawrence Gross (1972) commented that people watch television as though they were attending church, except that they typically watch television more religiously. Focusing their work on the effects of television (a topic we return to later), Gerbner and his colleagues embarked on the Cultural Indicators Project, conducting regular, periodic examinations of television programming and the "conceptions of social reality that viewing cultivates in child and adult audiences" (Gerbner & Gross, 1972, p. 174). In initiating what would become known as Cultivation Analysis, they were making a **causal argument** (television cultivates—causes—conceptions of social reality). Cultivation Analysis is a theory that predicts and explains the long-term formation and shaping of perceptions, understandings, and beliefs about the world as a result of consumption of media messages. Gerbner's line of thinking in Cultivation Analysis suggests that mass communication, especially television, cultivates certain beliefs about reality that are held in common by mass communication consumers. As Gerbner observes, "most of what we know, or think we know, we have never personally experienced" (Gerbner, 1999, p. ix). We "know" these things because of the stories we see and hear in the media.

> **causal argument**
> an assertion of cause and effect, including the direction of the causality

Cultivation researchers can easily explain Joyce Jensen's voting quandary. Official statistics that indicate that violent crime is in steady decline are certainly real enough. But so, too, is Joyce's feeling of unease and insecurity when she is alone. Cultivation Analysis would refer to these feelings of insecurity as her social reality. Moreover, that reality is as real as any other for Joyce, and it is media fueled, if not media created and maintained.

Iver Peterson (2002) made a similar observation about the anthrax scares in the United States post–September 11, 2001. He notes that although the (media-fueled) fears about anthrax are very pervasive and real, the actual cases of anthrax contamination are rare. Peterson quotes Clifton R. Lacy, commissioner of the New Jersey Department of Health and Senior Services, as saying that the risks to the citizens of New Jersey by anthrax spores are "vanishingly small" (p. A21). Dr. Lacy also urges people to take to heart the message that there have been no new cases in the state since October 2001.

Calvin and Hobbes   by Bill Watterson

Gerbner's view that media messages alter traditional notions of time, space, and social groupings was a direct challenge to the prevailing thought that media had little, if any, effect on individuals and on the culture. Like Uses and Gratifications Theory, which we discuss in Chapter 23, Cultivation Analysis was developed in response to the limited effects paradigm that was dominant at the time. More important, however, it reflects media theory's slow transformation from reliance on the transmissional perspective to greater acceptance of the ritual perspective of mass communication.

transmissional perspective
a position depicting the media as senders of messages across space

ritual perspective
a position depicting the media as representers of shared beliefs

The **transmissional perspective** sees media as senders of messages—discrete bits of information—across space. This perspective and limited effects theories are comfortable partners. If all media do is transmit bits of information, people can choose to use or not use that information as they wish. In the **ritual perspective**, however, media are conceptualized not as a means of transmitting "messages in space" but as central to "the maintenance of society in time" (Carey, 1975). Mass communication is "not the act of imparting information but the representation of shared beliefs" (Carey, 1975, p. 6).

Developing Cultivation Analysis

Gerbner first used the term *cultivation* in 1969; however, Cultivation Analysis, as a discrete and powerful theory, did not emerge for a number of years. It evolved over time through a series of methodological and theoretical steps by Gerbner and his colleagues and, as such, reflects that development.

During the 1960s, interest in media effects, particularly effects of television, ran very high. The federal government was concerned about media's influence on society, especially media's possible contribution to rising levels of violence among young people. In 1967, President Lyndon Johnson ordered the creation of the National Commission on the Causes and Prevention of Violence. It was followed in 1972 by the surgeon general's Scientific Advisory Committee on Television and Social Behavior. Both groups examined media (especially television) and their impact (especially the effects of aggression and violence). Gerbner, a respected social scientist, was involved in both efforts.

Gerbner's task was to produce an annual **Violence Index,** a yearly content analysis of a sample week of network television prime-time content that would show, from season to season, how much violence was actually present on television. Its value to those interested in the media violence issue was obvious: If the link between television fare and subsequent viewer aggression was to be made, the presence of violence on television needed to be demonstrated. Moreover, observers would be able to correlate annual increases in the amount of violent television content with annual increases in the amount of real-world violent crime. But the index was immediately challenged by both media industry and limited effects researchers. How was violence defined? Was verbal aggression violence? Was obviously fake violence on a comedy counted the same as more realistically portrayed violence on a drama? Why examine only prime-time network television, because children's heaviest viewing occurs at other times of the day? Why focus on violence? Why not examine other social ills, such as racism and sexism?

Gerbner and his associates continuously refined the Index to meet the complaints of its critics, and what their annual counting demonstrated was that violence appeared on prime-time television at levels unmatched in the real world, and it was violence unlike that found in the real world. The 1982 Index, for example, showed that "crime in prime time is at least 10 times as rampant as in the real world (and) an average of five to six acts of overt physical violence per hour involves over half of all major characters" (Gerbner, Gross, Morgan, & Signorielli, 1982, p. 106). The Research Note provides an example of an updated methodology used to test the basic premises of Cultivation Analysis.

Assumptions of Cultivation Analysis

In advancing the position that mediated reality causes consumers to develop their social reality, Cultivation Analysis makes a number of assumptions. Because it was and remains primarily a television-based theory, these three assumptions speak to the relationship between that medium and the culture:

- Television is essentially and fundamentally different from other forms of mass media.
- Television shapes our society's way of thinking and relating.
- The influence of television is limited.

The first assumption of Cultivation Analysis underscores the uniqueness of television. Television is in more than 98 percent of all U.S. homes. It requires no literacy, as do the print media. Unlike the movies, it is free (beyond the initial cost of the set and the cost of advertising added to the products we buy). Unlike radio, it combines pictures and sound. It requires no mobility, as do church attendance and going to the movies or the theater. Television is the only medium ever invented that is ageless—that is, people can use it at the earliest and latest years of life, as well as all those years in between.

Because of this accessibility and availability to everyone, television is the "central cultural arm" of our society (Gerbner, Gross, Jackson-Beeck,

Violence Index
a yearly content analysis of prime-time network programming to assess the amount of violence represented

Research Note

Diefenbach, D. L., & West, M. D. (2001). Violent crime and poison regression: A measure and a method for cultivation analysis. *Journal of Broadcasting & Electronic Media, 45,* 432–445.

This study performed a content analysis of network prime-time television to discover the rate of violent crime for television characters. Further, the researchers surveyed people to determine their beliefs about the prevalence of violent crime relative to their TV viewing habits. The researchers hypothesized that the rate of violence for television characters would be higher than the rate of violent crime in the United States. They also hypothesized that respondents who watched more television would estimate higher rates of violent crime in their community.

This study basically tested the classic tenets of Cultivation Analysis, but it also served as a refinement of other studies posing similar questions. First, it used a more limited definition of violence, and second, it employed a more sophisticated method of statistical analysis, allowing it to detect relationships when variables are distributed in a nonnormal fashion.

The study used the U.S. Department of Justice's definition of violent crimes, which includes murder, rape, robbery, and aggravated assault. The authors advance that using this definition provides at least two advantages over previous Cultivation Analysis research. First, it eliminates "the potential ambiguity of measures of televised violence cited by some critics of media violence research" (p. 433). Second, using a U.S. Department of Justice definition allows a clear comparison between televised violence and violence in the "real world." This also counters a persistent criticism of Cultivation Analysis, namely, that there is no standard of comparison to use with reference to the televised violence. Diefenbach and West observe that "the inclusion of classes of violent crimes in the operationalization of television vi-

olence will allow television rates to be compared to national crime rates or to other geographic regions for which crime data are available" (p. 433).

They tested the first hypothesis by analyzing the content of one week of prime-time television (8 P.M to 11 P.M.) and found that 2,960 victimizations occurred per 100,000 characters in the prime-time shows. Overall, this rate of violent crime is significantly higher than the rate in the United States, providing support for the hypothesis and Cultivation Analysis. Murder was especially overrepresented on television. Forty-five percent of the televised violent crimes were murders, resulting in a murder rate of 932 per 100,000. According to Department of Justice statistics cited in the study, the murder rate in the United States is 9.4 per 100,000 per year. The authors also noted that the murder rate in the county where they circulated the survey was even lower at 4.8 per 100,000 per year.

The second hypothesis was tested by analyzing the results of the survey. The researchers found that their respondents were, on the whole, likely to overestimate murders in the community. Utilizing their statistical analysis, they found that higher levels of television viewing resulted in higher estimates of murder in the community, even controlling for age, gender, and education.

They conclude that their study tends to confirm and extend the claims of Cultivation Analysis. They suggest that future research use their readily quantifiable definition of violence as violent crime and utilize their statistical method to continue exploring the effects of Cultivation Analysis in other areas to examine how television shapes our worldview.

Jeffries-Fox, & Signorielli, 1978, p. 178). Television draws together dissimilar groups and can show their similarities. For instance, during the 2003 war in the Persian Gulf, television was able to transmit live signals from Baghdad. Those in support of the bombings pointed to the importance of hitting key military targets, whereas those opposed to the war noted the number of civilian casualties. It was television that allowed both sides to invoke disparate images of the

war. In other words, television is the culture's primary storyteller and has the ability to gather together different groups. Additionally, who can doubt the role that television has played in working through the nation's story about the tragedy of September 11?

The second assumption pertains to the influence of television. Gerbner and Gross (1972) comment that "the substance of the consciousness cultivated by TV is not so much specific attitudes and opinions as more basic assumptions about the 'facts' of life and standards of judgment on which conclusions are based" (p. 175). That is, television doesn't so much persuade us (it didn't try to convince Joyce Jensen that the streets are unsafe) as paint a more or less convincing picture of what the world is like. Gerbner (1998) cogently observed that television reaches people, on average, more than seven hours each day. During this time, television offers "a centralized system of story-telling" (p. 177). Gerbner agrees with Walter Fisher, whom we discussed in Chapter 20, that people live in stories. Gerbner, however, asserts that most of the stories in modern society now come from television.

Television's major cultural function is to stabilize social patterns, to cultivate resistance to change. Television is a medium of socialization and enculturation. Gerbner and his cohorts eloquently state that

> the repetitive pattern of television's mass-produced messages and images forms the mainstream of the common symbolic environment that cultivates the most widely shared conceptions of reality. We live in terms of the stories we tell—stories about what things exist, stories about how things work, and stories about what to do—and television tells them all through news, drama, and advertising to almost everybody most of the time. (Gerbner et al., 1978, p. 178)

Where did Joyce Jensen's—and other voters'—shared conceptions of reality about crime and personal safety come from? Cultivation researchers would immediately point to television, where, despite a nationwide 20 percent drop in the homicide rate between 1993 and 1996, the number of murder stories on the network evening news soared 721 percent (Kurtz, 1998).

Based on this assumption, Cultivation Analysis supplies an alternative way of thinking about TV violence. Some theories, like Social Learning Theory (Bandura, 1977) assume that we become more violent after being exposed to violence. Other approaches, like the notion of catharsis, would suggest that watching violence purges us of our own violent impulses and we actually become less violent. Cultivation Analysis does not speak to what we will do based on watching violent television; instead, it assumes that watching violent TV makes us feel afraid because it cultivates within us the image of a mean and dangerous world.

The third assumption of Cultivation Analysis states that television's effects are limited. This may sound peculiar, given the fact that television is so pervasive. Yet the observable, measurable, independent contributions of television to the culture are relatively small. This may sound like a restatement of minimal effects thinking, but Gerbner uses an ice age analogy to distance Cultivation Analysis from limited effects. The **ice age analogy** states that "just as an average temperature shift of a few degrees can lead to an ice age or the outcomes of elections can be determined by slight margins, so too can a relatively small but pervasive influence make a crucial difference. The 'size' of an 'effect' is far less critical than the direction of its steady contribution" (Gerbner, Gross, Morgan, & Signorielli, 1980, p. 14). The argument is not that television's impact is inconsequential. Rather, although television's measurable, observable, independent effect on the culture at any point in time might be small, that impact is nonetheless present and significant.

ice age analogy
a position stating that television doesn't have to have a single major impact, but influences viewers through steady limited effects

Processes and Products of Cultivation Analysis

Cultivation Analysis has been applied to a wide variety of effects issues, as well as to different situations in which television viewers find themselves. In doing so, researchers have developed specific processes and products related to the theory.

The Four-Step Process

To empirically demonstrate their belief that television has an important causal effect on the culture, Cultivation researchers developed a four-step process. The first step, *message system analysis*, consists of detailed content analyses of television programming in order to demonstrate its most recurring and consistent presentations of images, themes, values, and portrayals. For example, it is possible to conduct a message system analysis of the number of episodes of bodily harm on such shows as *Law and Order* and *CSI*.

The second step, *formulation of questions about viewers' social realities*, involves developing questions about people's understandings of their everyday lives. For example, a typical Cultivation Analysis question is, "In any given week, what are the chances that you will be involved in some kind of violence? About 1 in 10 or about 1 in 100?" Another is, "Of all the crime that occurs in the United States in any year, what proportion is violent crime like rape, murder, assault, and robbery?"

The third step, *surveying the audience*, requires that the questions from step two be posed to audience members *and* that researchers ask these viewers about their levels of television consumption.

Finally, step four entails *comparing the social realities of light and heavy viewers*. For Gerbner, a "cultivation differential" exists between light and heavy viewers and perceptions of violence. **Cultivation differential** can be defined as the percentage of difference in response between light and heavy television viewers. Gerbner (1998) explains that amount of viewing is used in relative terms. Thus, heavy viewers are those who watch the most in any sample of people that are measured, whereas light viewers are those who watch the least.

cultivation differential
the percentage of difference in response between light and heavy television viewers

Mainstreaming and Resonance

How does television contribute to viewers' conceptions of social reality? The process of cultivation occurs in two ways. One is mainstreaming. **Mainstreaming** occurs when, especially for heavier viewers, television's symbols dominate other sources of information and ideas about the world. As a result of heavy viewing, people's constructed social realities move toward the mainstream—not a mainstream in any political sense, but a culturally dominant reality that is more similar to television's reality than to any measurable, objective external reality. Heavy viewers tend to believe the mainstreamed realities that the world is a more dangerous place than it really is—that all politicians are corrupt, that teen crime is at record high levels, that African American families are all on welfare, and so forth.

mainstreaming
the tendency for heavy viewers to perceive a similar culturally dominant reality to that pictured on the media although this differs from actual reality

Mainstreaming means that heavy television viewers of different co-cultures are more similar in their beliefs about the world than their varying group membership might suggest. Thus, African Americans and European Americans who are heavy television viewers would perceive the world more similarly than might be expected. As Gerbner (1998) states, "Differences that usually are associated with the varied cultural, social, and political characteristics of these groups are diminished in the responses of heavy viewers in these same groups" (p. 183).

The second way cultivation operates is through resonance. **Resonance** occurs when things on television are, in fact, congruent with viewers' actual everyday realities. In other words, people's objective external reality resonates with that of television. Some urban dwellers, for example, may see the violent world of television resonated in their deteriorating neighborhoods. As Gerbner (1998) notes, this provides "a 'double dose' of messages that 'resonate' and amplify cultivation" (p. 182). The social reality that is cultivated for these people may in fact match their objective reality, but its possible effect is to preclude the formation of a more optimistic social reality; it denies them hope that they can build a better life. See Figure 22.1 for a representation of mainstreaming and resonance.

resonance
occurs when a viewer's lived reality coincides with the reality pictured in the media

Cultivation, either as mainstreaming or as resonance, produces effects on two levels. **First order effects** refer to the learning of facts—how many employed males are involved in law enforcement, what proportion of marriages end in divorce. For example, Joyce Jensen knew from candidate Milnes's television spots that the amount of crime in her state was in decline. **Second order effects** involve "hypotheses about more general issues and assumptions" that people make about their environments (Gerbner, Gross, Morgan, & Signorielli, 1986, p. 28). Questions like "Do you think people are basically

first order effects
a method for cultivation to occur; refers to learning facts from the media
second order effects
a method for cultivation to occur; refers to learning values and assumptions from the media

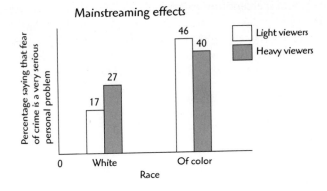

Mainstreaming effects

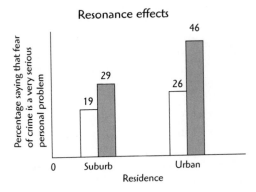

Resonance effects

Figure 22.1
Effects of
Mainstreaming
and Resonance
Source: Adapted from
Gerbner el al., 1980.
Reprinted by per-
mission of Oxford
University Press.

honest?" and "Do you think police should be allowed to use greater force to subdue criminals?" are aimed at these second order effects.

The Mean World Index

A product of Cultivation Analysis is the Mean World Index (Gerbner, Gross, Morgan, & Signorielli, 1980), which consists of a series of three statements:

- Most people are just looking out for themselves.
- You can't be too careful in dealing with people.
- Most people would take advantage of you if they got the chance.

Cultivation Analysis predicts that agreement with these statements from heavy and light viewers will differ, with heavy viewers seeing the world as a meaner place than light viewers. It also predicts that the amount of television viewing is the best predictor of people's answers, overwhelming other kinds of distinctions among different people—for example, income and education.

Gerbner and his colleagues (1980) demonstrated the efficacy of their Mean World Index in a study that showed heavy viewers as much more likely to see the world as a mean place than were light viewers. Better-educated, financially better-off viewers in general saw the world as less mean than did those with less

The Theory Connection

Different media theories examine different aspects of the media. Cultivation Analysis concentrates on media effects that also involve an investigation of media messages (primarily messages representing violence). How does this compare with the focus in McLuhan's theory about the media? Is McLuhan interested in effects and media content? Can these two theories inform one another?

education and income. But, in testing the power of television, the researchers demonstrated that heavy viewers from the better-educated, better-off groups saw the world as being as dangerous as did low-income and less-educated people. In other words, heavy viewers held a mainstreamed perception of the world as a mean place, regardless of factors such as education and income. Cultivation researchers see this as evidence that television content is a factor in the construction of social realities for heavy viewers, regardless of individual or social differences.

Gerbner and his associates identify a number of other areas where the two types of viewers might differ. They include their beliefs about the likelihood of involvement with a violent crime, their fear of walking at night, and their perceptions of law enforcement. The findings are intriguing. First, they found that those people with light viewing habits believed that about 1 in 100 will be a victim of violence; heavy viewers of television predicted that about 1 in 10 will be involved in violence. Second, they found that more women than men were fearful of walking alone at night and that heavy viewers overestimated the amount of violent crime. Third, heavy viewers felt that 5 percent of the culture is involved in law enforcement, whereas light viewers felt that 1 percent is involved. Important to the logic of Cultivation Analysis is that the responses of the heavy viewers mirror quite accurately the results of content analyses of television, where violence is usually recorded in heavy doses: Because violence is so common on television, heavy viewers are more likely to be fearful or mistrustful of the real world. Given what we've presented here, Joyce Jensen's viewing habits may be influencing her thinking about her choice between Milnes and Johndrew.

Cultivation Analysis as Critical Theory

Cultivation Analysis has made an important contribution to contemporary thinking about mass communication. Horace Newcomb (1978), an early critic of Cultivation Analysis, wrote of Gerbner and his colleagues: "Their foresight to collect data on a systematic, long-term basis, to move out of the laboratory and away from the closed experimental model, will enable other researchers to avoid costly mistakes. Their material holds a wealth of information" (p. 281).

But just what is the role of television in our culture uncovered by the Cultivation Analysis researchers? Cultivation theorists would argue that Joyce

Jensen's apprehension—and the vote for the tough-on-crime candidate it might produce—is based on a view of the world that is cultivated by television. Federal crime statistics indicate that violent and property crime is at a 23-year low in the United States, but content analyses of television news and fiction content (Cultivation Analysis's message system analysis) indicate that the amount of on-screen mayhem has increased steadily over that same period (Kurtz, 1998).

People must learn about their world from somewhere, and the influence of television on that learning cannot be dismissed. Learning from television produces not only perceptions of a mean world (which researchers in Cultivation Analysis argue become a self-fulfilling prophecy as people's distrust of others breeds an atmosphere of further distrust) but also a warping of political, social, and cultural discourse. How many political candidates, they ask, have the courage to argue against the building of more prisons or against the death penalty? The issue is not the validity of these positions but the absence of meaningful, objective debate on them. The argument here is similar to that offered by Elizabeth Noelle-Neumann's Spiral of Silence Theory, which we discuss in Chapter 24: People may be less willing to speak out about alternative approaches to crime and crime prevention because the media, especially television, cultivate a dominant social reality that renders these possible conversations out of step with the voters.

How can television be so powerful a force that even if its influence occurs as slowly as the coming of the ice age? Gerbner answers this question with his **3 Bs of television**. Television, he wrote, blurs traditional distinctions of people's views of their world, blends people's realities into television's cultural mainstream, and bends that mainstream to the institutional interests of television and its sponsors. Television's power rests in its utilization by powerful industries and elites to meet their, rather than the culture's, interests. Cultivation Analysis is a critical theory, as we described it in Chapter 3, because it is concerned with the way that communication perpetuates the dominance of one group over another (Littlejohn, 2002). As James Shanahan and Victoria Jones (1999) argue,

3 Bs of television
blurring of distinctions among worldviews, blending of realities into the cultural mainstream, and bending of the mainstream to institutional and corporate interests

> Cultivation is sometimes taken as a return to a strong "powerful effects" view of mass media. This view isn't completely incorrect, but it misses the point that cultivation was originally conceived as a *critical* theory, which happens to address media issues precisely and only because the mass media (especially television) serve the function of storytelling. (p. 32)

Cultivation Analysis, as a critical theory, does examine an important social institution (television) in terms of how it uses its storytelling function to serve ends other than the benefit of the larger society. But it shares another characteristic with other critical theories: It is political; that is, in accepting its assumptions, its proponents must commit to doing something about the situation.

Cultivation researchers point to television's stories about crime, the issue so perplexing as Joyce Jensen prepares to cast her vote. Why does violent crime dominate television news? Because it is visual, is easy to edit, requires little writing to provide context, and attracts audiences. But if the vast majority of crime in this country is nonviolent, why does television news ignore that non-violent crime? Because coverage of nonviolent crime is not as easy and in-expensive to produce. For instance, reports on consumer fraud, abuses in the banking system, and other white-collar crime are not visual and require a much larger expenditure of resources than does pointing a camera at a pool of blood on a city sidewalk. Violent crime dominates dramatic television for almost the same reasons: It is visual, requires little writing or contextualization, fits the small screen quite well, and is an audience builder. Critical researchers, including those in Cultivation Analysis, ask if the benefits of certain kinds of content and production (in this case, violence) do a disservice to the larger culture, even as they serve the interests of a few—in this case, broadcasters and advertisers.

George Gerbner has taken to heart the critical researcher's call to action. In the mid-1990s, he developed the PROD (Proportional Representation of Diversity) index. The goal of the index was to examine the distortion in representation of various co-cultures "across the demography of the media landscape" (Shanahan & Morgan, 1999, p. 223). The index determined how well or poorly groups were represented on television relative to their numbers in the population. The first index Gerbner produced surveyed broadcast network programming and major Hollywood films for 1995–1996. Almost every group (women, African Americans, Latinos, Asians, Native Americans, under age 18, over age 65, gays and lesbians, disabled, and the poor or lower class) listed in the diversity index was grossly underrepresented in the media. The only group that was not was Native Americans, and this is probably explained by their relatively low population proportionally.

Gerbner took his critical role seriously and stated in a press release associated with the presentation of the index, "Far from being 'quotas' to be imposed on creative people, the Index reflects the limitations on creative freedom in the television and motion picture industries. This is a 'report card' of industry performance. We look forward to steady improvement in the diversity and equity of the cultural environment into which our children are born and in which they come to define themselves and others" (Gerbner, 1997, cited in Shanahan & Morgan, 1999, p. 223). Gerbner believes it is important to highlight how the media industries reflect the needs and perspectives of dominant groups. A more recent report analyzing the 2001 fall session of network programing came to similar conclusions (UCLA Center for African American Studies, 2002).

In 1996, Gerbner helped found the worldwide Cultural Environment Movement to assist people in their struggle against powerful media industries. Its *Viewers' Declaration of Independence* reads, in part, "Let the world hear the reasons that compel us to assert our rights and take an active role in the shaping of our common cultural environment. . . . Humans live and learn by stories. Today they are no longer hand-crafted, home-made, community-inspired. They are no longer told by families, schools, or churches but are the products of a complex mass-production and marketing process" (Cultural Environment Movement, 1996, p. 1). Gerbner (1998) continues to be concerned with the effects created by stories told by agencies that do not aim to teach but rather aim to sell.

Critique and Closing

Gerbner and his colleagues have been influential in identifying television as a shaping force in society. Cultivation Analysis helps explain the implications of viewing habits. The theory's heuristic qualities are especially noteworthy. For example, Cultivation Analysis has been applied to crime (Signorielli, 1990), fear of victimization (Sparks & Ogles, 1990), attitudes toward racism (Allen & Hatchett, 1986), feelings of alienation (Morgan, 1986), anxiety (Zillman & Wakshlag, 1985), gender stereotyping (Carveth & Alexander, 1985; Preston, 1990), affluence (Potter, 1991), the aged (Gerbner et al., 1980), American stereotypes (Tan, 1982), civil liberties (Carlson, 1983), divorce (Potter, 1991), materialism (Reimer & Rosengren, 1990), values (Potter, 1993), and health issues (Molitor, 1994; Potter, 1991).

Cultivation Analysis has generated not only much interesting research and some social activism but heavy criticism as well. Some of the complaints are territorial, but many are methodologically and theoretically based. First, the research supporting Cultivation Analysis employs social scientific methods typically identified with the transmissional perspective and limited effects findings. Yet Cultivation Analysis examines larger cultural questions most often raised by humanists. Horace Newcomb (1978) writes, "More than any other research effort in the area of television studies the work of Gerbner and Gross and their associates sits squarely at the juncture of the social sciences and the humanities" (p. 265). By asserting cultural effects, Cultivation Analysis offends many humanists, who feel that their turf has been improperly appropriated and misinterpreted. "The question," writes Newcomb, "'What does it all mean?' is, essentially, a humanistic question" (p. 266). Many humanists, quite at ease when discussing the relationship between literature (novels, art, music, theater) and culture, have great difficulty accepting television as the culture's new, dominant "literature."

According to Newcomb, three problems exist with Cultivation Analysis. First, television's ideas and the symbols that express them on that medium are not created there. Television's representations of things in the culture have history and meaning in the culture that have existed long before their appearance on television. Violence, for example, has always had many meanings for people. Second, Cultivation Analysis ignores the wide variety of "organization and expression of these ideas in the world of television" (Newcomb, 1978, p. 281). In other words, violence, for example, is not presented as uniformly on television as Cultivation Analysis assumes. Third, Cultivation Analysis does not permit the possibility that individual members of the television audience can apply different, individual meanings to what they see on television. As Newcomb argues, "It may be that all the messages of television speak with a single intent and are ruled by a single dominant symbol whose meaning is clear to a mass audience, or to that part of the audience heavily involved with those messages. But I have yet to see evidence sufficient to warrant such a reductive view of human experience in America" (1978, p. 271).

Cultivation Analysis assumes that television's portrayals of such things as crime, violence, divorce, and so on are uniform—an especially weak assumption in the modern era of scores of channels. Cultivation offers two related responses to this criticism. First, although there may be many more channels and people may have greater control over selectivity than they once had, television's dramatic and aesthetic conventions produce remarkably uniform content within as well as across genres. Second, because most television watching is ritual—that is, selected more by time of day than by specific program or the availability of multiple channels—heavy viewers will be exposed *overall* to more of television's dominant images.

Additionally, Cultivation Analysis assumes that people view television nonselectively; that is, they watch what's on television rather than making personally relevant selections. Critics regard this as a negative view of people and argue that even if this was true when Cultivation Analysis was first developed, cable television's numerous channels and technologies like the VCR, the remote control, and TiVo give viewers significant power to select. The counterargument is that most viewers, even with dozens of channels available to them, primarily select from only five or six, evidencing a very limited range of selection.

Another concern regarding Cultivation Analysis is that it has done a poor job of clarifying the concept of television's dominance in people's lives. Heavy viewers, for example, may watch very little content that speaks to the issues being examined by a cultivation researcher. Conversely, as W. James Potter (1993) writes, "It is possible for a person to watch very little television and still be influenced by television's messages by picking up those perceptions and attitudes in interpersonal conversations and observing institutions that themselves have been influenced more directly through television" (p. 577). Cultivation Analysis, however, only measures the relationship between level of viewing and perceptions.

Cultivation researchers respond to this critique by arguing that the issue of television's dominance in people's lives is a transmissional argument. Whether people's perceptions are developed directly from television or from contact with the culture and others in it, it is still a television-dominated environment within which most people exist.

As Gerbner and his colleagues respond to the humanists' complaints about the source of people's views of violence, they remind us that perceptions have to come from *somewhere*, and television has become our "chief creator of synthetic cultural patterns" (Gerbner et al., 1978, p. 178). Cultivation theorists ask if viewers do believe that the world is a dangerous place and therefore stay home and watch television, where did that fear come from in the first place?

Criticism aside, Cultivation Analysis has been and remains one of the most influential mass communication theories of the last two decades. It is the

T*I*P

*Theory * Into * Practice*

A recent *New York Times* article addresses the role the media play in cultivating the public's worldview. The article observes that people fear natural disasters like hurricanes, tornadoes, and forest fires. These, and other similar types of disasters, are highly publicized in the media because they "make for good headlines and even better visuals" (Bahrampour, 2002, p. D5). Yet these disasters kill relatively few people in the United States compared to heat waves, which receive relatively little media attention and few people really fear.

"It would be hard to make a blockbuster movie about a heat wave. Heat waves come on subtly, raising summer temperatures just a little higher than normal and then receding. But they kill more people in the United States than all other natural disasters combined" (p. D5). The article notes that a deadly heat wave occurred most recently in Chicago in 1995 where over 700 people died in a week of 100-degree temperatures. The author provides the following context for that number: The Chicago fire of 1871 killed half that many, 62 people died in the San Francisco earthquake of 1989, and 26 people perished in 1992 in Hurricane Andrew.

Yet few people remember the 1995 Chicago heat wave, and even those who lived through it fail to think of it as so deadly. The *Times* article quotes Dr. Eric Klinenberg, a sociologist from New York University, who interviewed Chicago residents who lived through the 1995 heat wave. Dr. Klinenberg states that his respondents thought that about 100 people had died and were very surprised when he told them that over 700 people had died.

Source: Bahrampour, 2002.

TIP Follow-up

Cultivation Analysis focuses mainly on violence and the media. This example illustrates a different arena where people's perceptions and fears are affected by media representations. What other areas do you think may be distorted by media images that are not commensurate with real-world occurrences?

foundation of much contemporary research and, as we've seen, has even become an international social movement. Another source of its influence is that it can be applied by anyone. It asks people to assess their own media use alongside their socially constructed reality of the world they inhabit. Imagine yourself as Joyce Jensen preparing to cast an important vote. You may well undergo the same mental debate as she. Yet, think of how even a passing understanding of Cultivation Analysis might help you arrive at your decision and understand your motivations.

Discussion Starters

1. Are you like Joyce Jensen in that you do not feel safe walking in your neighborhood at night? How much television do you watch? Do you fit the profile offered by Cultivation Analysis? Why or why not?

2. Cultivation Analysis is a critical theory and demands action from its adherents. Do you believe researchers and theorists should become politically active in the fields they study? Why or why not?

3. Do you agree with the hypothesis concerning the Mean World Index? Why or why not?

4. How do you define violence on television? Do you think it is possible to calculate violent acts as Gerbner and his colleagues have done? Why or why not?

5. Do you believe that the world is a mean place? What real-world evidence do you have that it is? What television evidence do you have that it is?

6. How do you respond to the criticism that more television channels and more divisions among viewers mean that Cultivation Analysis's assumptions are no longer valid?

Terms for Review

causal argument
transmissional perspective
ritual perspective
Violence Index
ice age analogy
cultivation differential

mainstreaming
resonance
first order effects
second order effects
3 Bs of television

Online Learning Center

Visit the Online Learning Center at www.mhhe.com/west2. Use the multiple-choice and true/false quizzes to help you prepare for exams, and the glossary, crossword puzzles, and flashcards to further your knowledge of key terms.

CHAPTER 23

Uses and Gratifications Theory

Ryan Grant

It's a dreary Friday night and 16-year-old Ryan Grant is trying to figure out what he wants to do. He works for his father in a local hardware store, and without question, this was a rough week. He had to put in a lot of extra hours because it was inventory week and his dad needed an extra set of hands to catalogue the merchandise. In addition, this morning he had taken an exam in his social studies class. Because he hadn't studied last week, Ryan had crammed until 2 A.M. It was the end of the work week, he thought, and time to escape both work and school.

Ryan felt exhausted and burned out. He wanted to be with others, but he knew he wouldn't be the best company. He considered two choices for the evening: He could stay at home and watch television, either with friends or alone, or he could try to get a group of friends together to go to the movies. He could see the value of going out with people who would help him loosen up. He could also appreciate being at home without having to exert any energy.

Ryan was faced with two opposing arguments. Here was an argument for watching television: First, he wouldn't have to spend a dime. He could dress and look how he wanted, and he could watch what he wanted when he wanted. And because it was Friday night, there were a couple of shows on that Ryan liked. At home, he could also command the best seat in the house. If he wanted to, he could also invite over as many friends as he wished, making the night more social.

The arguments for going out to the movies seemed just as strong. First, he could see that new action/adventure movie he'd been waiting to see. Also, because Ryan was a "techie" who appreciated all technology, the movie theater's excellent fidelity THX system appealed to him. Finally, he could easily have fun in an evening out. Although he had never really thought about it too seriously, he enjoyed sitting with his friends in the dark, sharing the same experience. And Ryan loved movie popcorn!

Still, he was torn, so Ryan weighed the positives and negatives of each medium. If he chose television, he would have to deal with watching on a small screen. Second, if he did have friends over, he might have to endure fighting over what to watch. On the other hand, he could turn off the television if nothing good was on and simply hang out with his friends. The arguments for and against going to the movies seemed equivalent. He knew that first he'd have to drive to the cineplex and try to find a parking space. He also might have to stand in a long line, which he hated. To top it off, he would have to pay close to $15 for the movie ticket and popcorn. Yet he knew that watching a movie was a great escape from the real world, and he would be able to talk about the movie on Monday.

Ryan's decision about what to do came down to a simple question: What does a movie offer and what does television offer? As Ryan considered this question, a third alternative occurred to him: going to bed early.

This theory is based on the research of **Elihu Katz, Jay G. Blumler,** and **Michael Gurevitch.**

yan is doing what we all do when dealing with the mass media: He is making choices. Most of us actively engage the media when making choices about what to do at different times in our lives. Consider how many times you have found yourself in a situation similar to Ryan's. You may have decided that you needed some relaxation and thought about all the options before making up your mind. The process may not have taken very long, but it was a process that required thinking about what was available.

In the early days of mass media (the era of the penny newspaper, radio, movies, and talkies), **Mass Society Theory**—the idea that average people are helpless victims of powerful mass media—defined the relationship between audiences and the media they consumed (see our discussion of the Spiral of Silence Theory in Chapter 24). This notion was eventually discredited, in large part because social science—and simple observation—could not confirm the operation of all-powerful media and media messages. Obviously, not only were most people not directly affected by media messages, but when they were influenced, they were not all influenced similarly.

In time, Mass Society Theory was replaced by what we now call **limited effects** theories, conceptions of media influence that view it as minimized or limited by certain aspects of individual audience members' personal and social lives. Two approaches to the limited effects orientation have been identified. First, the **Individual Differences Perspective** sees media's power as shaped by such personal factors as intelligence and self-esteem. For example, smart people and more secure people are better able to defend themselves against unwanted media impact. A second limited effects approach, the **Social Categories Model,** views media's power as limited by audience members' associations and group affiliations. For example, Republicans tend to spend time with other Republicans, who help them interpret media messages in a consistent, Republican-friendly manner. This effectively limits any influence media messages they themselves might have.

A close reading of these few paragraphs illustrates that these views afford audience members little credibility. The former suggests that people simply are not smart or strong enough to protect themselves against unwanted media effects. The latter suggests that people have relatively little personal choice in interpreting the meaning of the messages they consume and in determining the level of impact those messages will have on them. Eventually, in response to these unflattering views of typical audience members, theorists Elihu Katz, Jay G. Blumler, and Michael Gurevitch (1974) presented a systematic and comprehensive articulation of audience members' role in the mass communication process. They formalized their thinking and identified Uses and Gratifications Theory. The theory holds that people actively seek out specific media and specific content to generate specific gratifications (or results). Theorists in Uses and Gratifications view people as active because they are able to examine and evaluate various types of media to accomplish communication goals. As we saw in our opening, Ryan not only identified the specific media that he was willing to consider, but was also able to determine for himself the uses he could and would make of each and the personal values of those uses. Researchers in Uses and Gratifications Theory ask the question, What do consumers do with the media?

**Mass Society
Theory**
the idea that average
people are the victims
of the powerful forces
of mass media

limited effects
the perspective replacing Mass Society
Theory; holds that
media effects are limited by aspects of the
audience's personal
and social lives
**Individual
Differences
Perspective**
a specific approach
to the idea of Limited Effects; concentrates on the limits
posed by personal
characteristics
**Social Categories
Model**
a specific approach to
the idea of limited
effects; concentrates
on the limits posed by
group membership

Figure 23.1
Maslow's Hierarchy
of Needs
Source: Adapted from
MOTIVATION AND
PERSONALITY 2/E by
Maslow © 1970. Re-
printed by permission
of Pearson Education,
Inc. Upper Saddle
River, N.J.

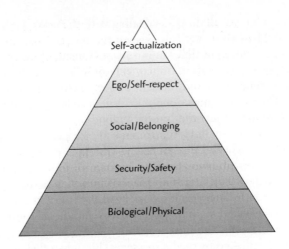

So this audience-centered media theory underscores an active media consumer. Considering that this overarching principle contradicts the views offered
by other media theorists and other theoretical perspectives, it is important to
briefly trace the theory's development. We present the beginnings of Uses and
Gratifications Theory in the next section followed by the assumptions of the
theory.

Stages in Uses and Gratifications Research

Uses and Gratifications Theory is an extension of needs and motivation theory
(Maslow, 1970). In needs and motivation theory, Abraham Maslow posited
that people actively seek to satisfy a hierarchy of needs. Once they have achieved
the goals they seek on one level of the hierarchy, they are able to move to the
next level (see Figure 23.1). This picture of humans as active seekers, out to satisfy specific needs, fit well with the conceptions that Katz, Blumler, and Gurevitch brought to their studies of how people consume mass communication.

People can and do actively participate in the mass communication process,
as researchers had acknowledged before Katz, Blumler, and Gurevitch. Wilbur
Schramm (1954), for example, developed a means of determining "which of-
ferings of mass communication will be selected by a given individual" (p. 19).
His **fraction of selection** visually represents precisely the process that Ryan goes
through when he makes his choice of a movie or a television show:

fraction of
selection
Schramm's idea of
how media choices
are made: the expec-
tation of reward
divided by the effort
required

$$\frac{\text{Expectation of Reward}}{\text{Effort Required}}$$

Schramm sought to make clear that audience members judge the level of reward
(gratification) they expect from a given medium or message against how much
effort they must make to secure that reward—an important component of what
would later become known as the Uses and Gratifications perspective.

Even earlier, the classic and pioneering work of Herta Herzog (1944) began the first stage of Uses and Gratifications research. She sought to classify reasons why people engage in different forms of media behavior, such as newspaper reading and radio listening. Herzog studied the role of the audience's wants and needs, and she is sometimes credited with having originated Uses and Gratifications Theory (although its label was to come much later).

Wanting to understand why so many women were attracted to radio soap operas, Herzog interviewed dozens of soap opera fans and identified three major types of gratification. First, some people enjoyed the dramas because they allowed them emotional release in listening to the problems of others. Second, listeners seemed to engage in wishful thinking—that is, they gained a vicarious satisfaction from listening to the experiences of others. Finally, some people felt that they could learn from these programs because "if you listen to these programs and something turns up in your life, you would know what to do about it" (Herzog, 1944, p. 25). Herzog's work was instrumental in the development of Uses and Gratifications because she was the first published researcher to provide an in-depth examination of media gratifications.

The second stage of Uses and Gratifications research began when researchers created typologies representing all the reasons people had for media use. For example, Alan Rubin (1981) found that motivations for television use clustered into the following categories: to pass time, for companionship, excitement, escape, enjoyment, social interaction, relaxation, information, and to learn about a specific content. Other researchers (McQuail, Blumler, & Brown, 1972) asserted that media use could be categorized with only four basic divisions: diversion, personal relationships, personal identity, and surveillance.

Jay Blumler and another colleague, Denis McQuail (1969), began untangling reasons why people watch political programs. They found a number of motives for watching political broadcasts. This work formed an important foundation for researchers in Uses and Gratifications. Later work by McQuail, Blumler, and Joseph Brown (1972) and Katz, Gurevitch, and Hadassah Haas (1973) would begin to specifically point out how people see mass media. These teams of researchers found that there was a need either to connect with or to disconnect from others. Among the categories identified by individuals are needs associated with acquiring information or knowledge, pleasure, status, strengthening relationships, and escape. As you will recall, Ryan Grant was trying to work through two simultaneous needs: the need for strengthening friendships and the need to escape.

In the third and most recent stage, Uses and Gratifications researchers are interested in linking specific reasons for media use with variables such as needs, goals, benefits, and the consequences of media use (Faber, 2000; Rubin, 1994). In this effort, researchers are working to make the theory more explanatory and predictive. Alan Rubin and Mary Step (2000) conducted a study that exemplifies this stage of Uses and Gratifications research. Rubin and Step examined the relationship of motivation, interpersonal attraction, and **parasocial interaction** (the relationship we feel we have with people we know only through the media) to listening to public affairs talk radio. They found that a motivation for exciting entertainment and information acquisition interacted with perceptions

**parasocial
interaction**
the relationship we
feel we have with
people we know only
through the media

of the parasocial relationship to explain why listeners tuned in to talk radio and why they found a host credible.

The gap between research such as Herzog's on audience use of media and the firm establishment of the perspective as an important and valuable theory some thirty years later was due to the dominance of the limited effects paradigm. A paradigm, you will recall from Chapter 3, is an encompassing, organizing theoretical perspective, and because it was limited effects that defined most mass communication theory and research at the time, attention was focused on what it was about media, messages, and audiences that limited media's influence. Little attention was paid to *how* audiences use media. The pioneering work of Katz, Blumler, and Gurevitch would change this state of affairs.

Uses and Gratifications Theory and its assumptions gained acceptance for a number of reasons. First, the limited effects researchers began to run out of things to study. Once all the variables that limited media influence were chronicled, what was left to say about the process of mass communication? Second, the limited effects perspective failed to explain why advertisers spend billions of dollars a year to place their ads in the media or why so many people spend so much time consuming the media. Third, some observers speculate that people often decide whether specific media effects are desirable and intentionally set out to achieve those effects. If this is so, researchers ask, what does this say about *limited* effects? Finally, those who do not live under the rules of the dominant paradigm were being neglected in the research. That is, psychologists—who were demonstrating on a regular basis the causal relationship between viewing mediated violence and subsequent aggressive behavior—were focusing too much attention on unintended negative effects. In the meantime, positive uses of media were left unexamined.

These factors produced a subtle shift in the focus of those researchers working within the limited effects paradigm. Their attention moved from the things media do *to* people to the things people do *with* media. If effects occur at all, either positive or negative, it is because audience members want them to happen, or at least let them happen.

Assumptions of Uses and Gratifications Theory

Uses and Gratifications provides a framework for understanding when and how individual media consumers become more or less active and the consequences of that increased or decreased involvement.

Many of the assumptions of Uses and Gratifications were clearly articulated by the founders of the approach (Katz, Blumler, & Gurevitch, 1974). They contend that there are five basic assumptions of Uses and Gratifications Theory:

- The audience is active and its media use is goal oriented.
- The initiative in linking need gratification to a specific medium choice rests with the audience member.
- The media compete with other sources for need satisfaction.

Table 23.1 Needs Gratified by the Media

NEED TYPE	DESCRIPTION	MEDIA EXAMPLES
Cognitive	Acquiring information, knowledge, comprehension	Television (news), video ("How to Install Ceramic Tile"), movies (*The Pianist*)
Affective	Emotional, pleasant, or aesthetic experience	Movies (*Star Wars, Episode 1: The Phantom Menace*), television (sitcoms, soap operas)
Personal integrative	Enhancing credibility, confidence, and status	Video ("Speaking with Conviction")
Social integrative	Enhancing connections with family, friends, and so forth	Internet (e-mail, chat rooms, listservs)
Tension release	Escape and diversion	Television, movies, video, radio, Internet

Source: Adapted from Katz, Gurevitch, & Haas, 1973.

- People have enough self-awareness of their media use, interests, and motives to be able to provide researchers with an accurate picture of that use.
- Value judgments of media content can only be assessed by the audience.

The theory's assumption about an active audience and goal-oriented media use is fairly straightforward. Individual audience members can bring different levels of activity to their use of media. Audience members are also driven to accomplish goals via the media. As we mentioned previously, McQuail and colleagues (1972) identify several ways of classifying audience needs and gratifications. They include **diversion,** which is defined as escaping from routines or daily problems; **personal relationships,** which occurs when people substitute the media for companionship; **personal identity,** or ways to reinforce an individual's values; and **surveillance,** or information about how media will help an individual accomplish something. In Table 23.1, we present additional categories of needs that are fulfilled by the media.

In our opening, we saw Ryan choosing between two competing media—television and film. All of us have our favorite content within a given medium, and we all have reasons for selecting a particular medium. At the movies, for instance, many of us like love stories rather than historical war films; some of us prefer to be entertained at the end of a long day rather than be educated about a historical event (diversion). Some drivers prefer to talk on their cellular phones over long trips; it not only passes the time, but also allows people to stay connected with their family and friends (personal relationships). Truck drivers in particular may prefer to listen to call-in radio talk shows rather than spend their long nights driving in silence (personal identity). Finally, there are people who enjoy watching home improvement shows on cable so that they can

diversion
a category of gratifications coming from media use; involves escaping from routines and problems

personal relationships
a category of gratifications coming from media use; involves substituting media for companionship

personal identity
a category of gratifications coming from media use; involves ways to reinforce individual values

surveillance
a category of gratifications coming from media use; involves collecting needed information

learn how to do projects around the house (surveillance). Audience members choose among various media, then, for different gratifications.

Uses and Gratifications' second assumption links need gratification to a specific medium choice that rests with the audience member. Because people are active agents, they take initiative. We choose shows like *Friends* when we want to laugh and *CNN World News Tonight* when we want to be informed, but no one decides for us what we *want* from a given medium or piece of content. We may well choose CNN because we want to be entertained. The implication here is that audience members have a great deal of autonomy in the mass communication process.

The third assumption—that media compete with other sources for need satisfaction—means that the media and their audiences do not exist in a vacuum. Both are part of the larger society, and the relationship between media and audiences is influenced by that society. On a first date, for example, going out to the movies is a more likely use of media than is renting a video and watching it at home. Someone who is an infrequent consumer of media—who, for example, finds more gratification in conversations with friends and family—may turn to the media with greater frequency when seeking information during a national political election.

Uses and Gratifications' fourth assumption is a methodological issue that has to do with researchers' ability to collect reliable and accurate information from media consumers. To argue that people are self-aware enough of their own media use, interests, and motives to be able to provide researchers with an accurate picture of that use not only reaffirms the belief in an active audience; it also implies that people are cognizant of that activity. In fact, the early research in Uses and Gratifications included questioning respondents about why they consumed particular media. This qualitative approach, which we explained in Chapter 4, included interviewing respondents and directly observing their reactions during conversations about media. The thinking surrounding this data collection technique was that people are in the best position to explain what they do and why they do it. Interestingly, as the theory evolved, the methodology also evolved. Researchers began to abandon their qualitative analysis in favor of more experimental procedures. Yet, the questionnaires employed in these procedures emanated from many of the interviews and observations.

The fifth assumption is also less about the audience than it is about those who study it. In asserting that researchers should suspend value judgments linking the audience's needs to specific media or content, theorists in Uses and Gratifications argue that because it is individual audience members who decide to use certain content for certain ends, the value of media content can be assessed only by the audience. According to theorists in Uses and Gratifications, even tacky content found in such talk shows as *Jerry Springer* may be functional if it provides gratifications for the audience. People are critical consumers. According to researchers J. D. Rayburn and Philip Palmgreen (1984), "[A] person may read a particular newspaper because it is the only one available, but this does not imply that she is perfectly satisfied with that newspaper. Indeed, she may be dissatisfied enough to drop her subscription if an alternative paper becomes available" (p. 542).

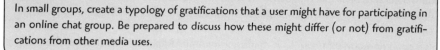

Theory Application in Groups (TAG)

In small groups, create a typology of gratifications that a user might have for participating in an online chat group. Be prepared to discuss how these might differ (or not) from gratifications from other media uses.

Some contemporary mass communication researchers (such as Turow, 2003) lament what they see as the negative, debasing influence of consumer product advertising on U.S. culture. The United States is fast becoming a nation of consumers: Love has been reduced to giving someone flowers; freedom now means the ability to buy a Big Gulp rather than a canned soda at 7-Eleven; a "good" mother is one who packs Lunchables in her child's lunchbox. Here we illustrate the influence of the limited effects paradigm. In the absence of hard evidence of the large-scale effect some critics fear, it's easier to assume that watching ads for these products—and the subsequent purchase of flowers, a Big Gulp, and Lunchables—is not only an individual choice, but a harmless one. (We discussed the intersection of media, culture, and individuals in Chapter 21 on cultural studies.)

The Active Audience

A theory that is based on the assumption that media consumers are active must delineate what it means by "the active audience." Mark Levy and Sven Windahl (1985) deal with the issue this way:

> As commonly understood by gratifications researchers, the term "audience activity" postulates a voluntaristic and selective orientation by audiences toward the communication process. In brief, it suggests that media use is motivated by needs and goals that are defined by audience members themselves, and that active participation in the communication process may facilitate, limit, or otherwise influence the gratifications and effects associated with exposure. Current thinking also suggests that audience activity is best conceptualized as a variable construct, with audiences exhibiting varying *kinds* and *degrees* of activity. (p. 110)

Jay G. Blumler (1979) offers several suggestions as to the kinds of audience activity in which media consumers could engage. They include utility, intentionality, selectivity, and imperviousness to influence. We explain each below.

First, the media have uses for people, and people can put media to those uses. This is termed **utility**. People listen to the car radio to find out about traffic. They go online to buy CDs. They read fashion magazines to keep abreast of styles. **Intentionality** occurs when people's prior motivations determine their consumption of media content. When people want to be entertained, they tune in to an HBO comedy. When they want greater detail about a breaking news story, it's Ted Koppel and *Nightline*. The third type of audience activity is

utility
using the media to accomplish specific tasks
intentionality
occurs when people's prior motives determine use of media

Research Note

Massey, K. B. (1995). Analyzing the uses and gratifications concept of audience activity with a qualitative approach: Media encounters during the 1989 Loma Prieta earthquake disaster. *Journal of Broadcasting and Electronic Media, 39,* 328–349.

In this study, Massey uses a detailed analysis of media consumption diaries to test the Levy and Windahl Typology of Audience Activity, a commonly accepted model of audience activity. Levy and Windahl argue that audience activity is composed of two dimensions: audience members' *orientation* (what they are doing with media content) and their temporal location in the *communication sequence*. Orientation consists of *selectivity* (making choices), *involvement* (determining and granting different levels of involvement to content), and *utility* (the use of content). The communication sequence consists of the time before exposure, during exposure, and after exposure. For example, selectivity before exposure might entail searching for a satisfactory television show; selectivity during exposure might involve selectively interpreting the content that is aired; selectivity after exposure could entail remembering only selected portions of the program.

Massey identifies a problem in the Levy and Windahl model: its reliance on discrete communication episodes with a beginning, middle, and end. She points to selectivity. Quite possibly, she argues, selectivity before exposure may in fact be selectivity after exposure, for example, if having seen a particularly good episode of a television show is what leads a viewer to select it again. In other words, selectivity before exposure to the second episode is actually selectivity after exposure to the first episode. She notes that the two theorists themselves have been battling with similar difficulties in their own application of their model. Her idea, then, was to test what she saw as a valuable Uses and Gratifications scheme in an ongoing media consumption situation to explore the *process* of audience activity.

As sometimes happens in science, fate presented her with this opportunity. As part of a university course she was teaching, Massey had asked her students to maintain a diary of all their media consumption for one week, complete with their comments and their reactions to what they were writing down. As the students began the exercise, the San Francisco Bay Area was rocked by the 1989 Loma Prieta earthquake. School was closed for ten days, but twenty-nine students maintained their diaries for the required week. What Massey had, then, was a rich accounting of people's media activity before, during, and after a natural disaster. She justifies her study of this "abnormal" period with the idea that "abrupt dislocations of (media consumption) pattern are likely to heighten people's awareness of what they take for granted and thus enhance the accuracy of people's perceptions of their media-related needs" (p. 333).

Upon completion of her analysis, she offers three conclusions. She confirms the Levy and Windahl notion that activity must be conceptualized as multifaceted and changing over time. She offers strong support for Katz, Blumler, and Gurevitch's emphasis on the power of social situations to shape uses of media and the gratifications sought from that use. As you can imagine, with roads unpassable, buildings closed, essential services disrupted, unreliable electrical power, and reports of death and destruction on a large scale, people were making heavy use of media, seeking very specific gratifications, all shaped by this dramatic social situation. Finally, Massey is able to highlight the difficulties in assessing audience activity. Almost all of her diary keepers, at one time or another, actively decided to select no media, to simply avoid altogether television, radio, and newspapers (when they were available). These active media consumers were consuming no media; they were engaging in activity that, from the outside, appeared to demonstrate no activity.

termed **selectivity**, which means that audience members' use of media may reflect their existing interests and preferences. If you like jazz, you might listen to the jazz program on the local NPR radio station. If you regularly surf the Web, you are a likely reader of *Wired*. If you're interested in local politics, you probably subscribe to the local paper. Ryan Grant was selecting his medium based on the fact that he wanted to escape from the week at school and work. Finally, an **imperviousness to influence** suggests that audience members construct their own meaning from content and that meaning influences what they think and do. They often actively avoid certain types of media influence. For example, some people buy products on the basis of quality and value, rather than in response to advertising campaigns. Or they exhibit no aggression against others, no matter how much they enjoy action/adventure films and television shows.

Uses and Gratifications also distinguishes between activity and activeness to better understand the degrees of audience activity. Although the terms are related, **activity** refers more to what the media consumer does (for example, she chooses to go online for news rather than read it in the newspaper). **Activeness** is closer to what really interests researchers in Uses and Gratifications: the audience's freedom and autonomy in the mass communication situation. Examine the Research Note to gain a better sense of audience activity.

Activeness is relative. Some people are active participants in the mass communication process; others are more passive. We all know people who live their lives through talk shows or who follow every fad and fashion presented in the mass media. Terms like *couch potato* and *boob tube* developed from the idea that many folks simply sit back and suck up whatever is presented. On the other hand, we also know people who are quite adroit at consuming media. Your friend may listen to gangsta rap because of the beat. You may listen to rap not only for its rhythms, but for its social commentary. For you, *Titanic* may have been a warm love story with great special effects. Your brother may have interpreted it as an allegory of class struggle.

Activeness is also individually variable. A person can be inactive at times ("I'll just turn on the television for background noise") and then become quite active ("The news is on! I'd better watch"). Our level of activeness often varies by time of day and type of content. We can be active users of the Internet by day and passive consumers of late-night talk shows on television.

Media Effects

We saw earlier that Uses and Gratifications Theory was developed in part to help solve a fairly important problem for mass communication theorists: How could they hold to notions of limited effects when there is so much evidence of media influence all around? Some researchers working in Uses and Gratifications believe its value lies in its ability to clarify how effects can and do happen.

Sven Windahl (1981) calls for the combination of the Uses and Gratifications Theory and the effects traditions into what he labels the "uses and effects" model. Similarly, Philip Palmgreen, Lawrence Wenner, and Karl Rosengren (1985) write that "a variety of audience gratifications [both sought and

selectivity
audience members' use of media reflects their existing interests

imperviousness to influence
refers to audience members' constructing their own meaning from media content

activity
refers to what the media consumer does
activeness
refers to how much freedom the audience really has in the face of mass media

401

obtained] are related to a wide spectrum of media effects, including knowledge, dependency, attitudes, perceptions of social reality, agenda-setting, discussion, and various political effects variables" (p. 31). Blumler (1979) offers his suggestions on using Uses and Gratifications to predict and explain media effects:

> How might propositions about media effects be generated from . . . gratifications? First, we may postulate that cognitive motivation will facilitate information gain. . . . Second, media consumption for purposes of diversion and escape will favour audience acceptance of perceptions of social situations in line with portrayals frequently found in entertainment materials. . . . Third, involvement in media materials for personal identity reasons is likely to promote reinforcement effects. (pp. 18–19)

In other words, even when audience members are active—even when they determine for themselves the uses they wish to make of mass media and the gratifications they seek from those uses—effects can and do occur. The failure of researchers in traditional Uses and Gratifications to consider the possibility of important media effects led the authors of the original work to chastise their colleagues eleven years later by noting that a "vulgar gratificationism" (Blumler, 1985, p. 259) should be purged from the theory. It was not their intention to imply that audience members are always totally free in either the uses they make of media or the gratifications they seek from them; the world in which media consumers live shapes them just as surely as they shape it, and content does have intended meaning.

These Uses and Gratifications theorists point to a second set of premises that make clear their belief that people's use of media and the gratifications they seek from it are inextricably intertwined with the world in which they live. Katz and his colleagues (1974) originally wrote that "social situations" in which people find themselves can be "involved in the generation of media-related needs" (p. 27) in five ways. First, social situations can produce tensions and conflicts, leading to pressure for their easement through the consumption of media. That is, we live in the world, and events in it can compel us to specific media and content. In 1999, nearly everyone was talking about President Clinton's legal and political problems in the wake of the special prosecutor's report to Congress. It was a notable time in our country's history. For many of you, it was difficult to make sense of the mess simply because you believe in the rule of law, the dignity of the presidency, and fairness. This was a social situation wrought with tension and conflict. Where did you go to ease the pressure?

Second, social situations can create an awareness of problems that demand attention, information about which may be sought in the media. Simply stated, the world in which we live contains information that makes us aware of things that are of interest to us, and we can find out more about those interests through the media. Everyone everywhere—work, school, virtually every social situation you entered—was talking about the president's difficulties. This problem demanded your attention. You probably turned to the media—for information, perspective, and analysis.

Third, social situations can impoverish real-life opportunities to satisfy certain needs, and the media can serve as substitutes or supplements. In other words, sometimes the situations in which you find yourself make the media the

The Theory Chronicles

For the next week, chronicle in your journal all of your media choices. List what need each choice fulfilled. Compare your list to one of the typologies in the chapter.

best, if not the only, source possible. Your social situation—college student—made it impossible for you to go to Washington to hear the debate in Congress. You could not call President Clinton on the phone for his perspective. You needed to know what was going on in this historic crisis, but the reality of your position in the society meant that you had little choice but to rely on the media to meet that need.

Fourth, social situations often elicit specific values, and their affirmation and reinforcement can be facilitated by the consumption of related media materials. Again, you are a college student. You are an educated person. You value knowledge and awareness. The media offer an appropriate location for their affirmation and reinforcement.

Finally, social situations demand familiarity with media; these demands must be met to sustain membership in specific social groups. As a college student, you are viewed as the future of our country. Not only should you have had an opinion about Clinton's situation, but you should have had something to say about the media's performance throughout that crisis. Lacking those opinions, you may have been regarded as out of it or uninformed.

In rejecting "vulgar gratificationism," Katz and his colleagues (1974) note that we should ask three things. First, are the mass media instrumental in creating this social situation? How, for instance, did we find out about the president's problems? What role did various media outlets play in bringing about the crisis in the first place? On what information did we form our opinions? Second, are the mass media instrumental in making the satisfaction of this situation's related needs so crucial? Why, for instance, was it important to have an opinion at all? Who put this issue on the public's agenda? Who determined that it was more important than any of the myriad events that happen in the world every day?

Finally, we should ask if the mass media might not have been instrumental in making themselves, the media, the most convenient and effective means of gratifying our needs in this situation. Was the media projecting the view "All the news, all the time. You can trust us"?

Uses and Gratifications and New Media

Many researchers (and mass media consumers) believe the future will change the way we watch television and use media in general. For example, Gilder (1994) talks about the way a hybrid of the television and the computer would affect our culture:

Rather than exalting mass culture, the teleputer will enhance individualism. Rather than cultivating passivity, the teleputer will promote
creativity. Instead of a master-slave architecture, the teleputer will have
an interactive architecture in which every receiver can function as a
processor and transmitter of video images and other information. The
teleputer will usher in a culture compatible with the immense powers
of today's ascendant technology. Perhaps most important, the teleputer
will enrich and strengthen democracy and capitalism around the world.
(p. 46)

In the decade since Gilder's predictions, some of what he suggests has come to
pass, but although television viewing has changed somewhat and now must
compete with multiple media, much of what Gilder spoke of remains unrealized.

Although Gilder's predictions are not (yet) reality, almost everyone expects
that new media will continue to change our future. In a study investigating that
premise, Louis Leung and Ran Wei (2000) examined the uses and gratifications
of the cellular phone. Leung and Wei were interested in why people use cell
phones and whether their reasons differed from why they used the old wired and
"land-based" telephones. Additionally, Leung and Wei observed, similar to
Gilder's assertions, that "the new cellular phone represents a converged new
technology hybrid as it dissolves boundaries between telecommunications and
broadcast industries" (p. 318). However, unlike Gilder's conclusions, Leung and
Wei's study indicated that Uses and Gratifications Theory, especially when combined with another theory, Diffusion of Innovations, can explain cell phone use.

Leung and Wei's ability to apply Uses and Gratifications Theory to a new
technology is explained by Shanahan and Morgan's (1999) observation that
there is an "underlying consistency of the content of the messages we consume
and the nature of the symbolic environment in which we live" (p. 199) even if
the delivery technology changes. Shanahan and Morgan assert that new technologies have always developed by adopting the message content from the technology that was previously dominant. Films, for example, they argue, took
their content from serialized literature; radio did the same, and television simply repackaged radio programming. Marshall McLuhan (see Chapter 25)
noted that new media merely provide new bottles for old wine.

The question for Uses and Gratifications researchers is whether the motivations people brought to their use of "old" media will apply to new media.
Theorists are interested in finding out whether new media so alter the message
and the experience that Uses and Gratifications Theory no longer applies or has
to be radically modified. Access to new technologies has changed and extended
our abilities for entertainment and information gathering, and media researchers require greater understanding of the personal and social reasons
people have for using new media.

In a paper investigating computerized video game playing, John Sherry and
his colleagues (Sherry, Lucas, Rechtsteiner, Brooks, & Wilson, 2001) noted
that video game playing is overwhelmingly popular among young people. The
average number of hours that their female participants played per week was 9,
whereas males played 14 hours a week on average. Sherry et al. took a Uses and
Gratifications approach to this activity and found that video game playing

The Theory Connection

Do you see a relationship between an interpersonal theory like Uncertainty Reduction Theory (especially axiom 4, which posits a positive relationship between intimacy and degree of certainty) and Uses and Gratifications Theory? Explain your opinion.

satisfied the following motivations for their respondents: challenge, arousal, diversion, fantasy, competition, and social interaction.

The finding of social interaction was especially interesting because these types of games have often been assumed to be isolating and lacking in social presence (Perse & Courtright, 1993; Straus, 1997). Sherry and his co-researchers found that adolescents played video games with friends and saw game playing as a time to gather and make connections with others. In addition to this interesting finding, the researchers conclude that although the medium is different, the Uses and Gratifications framework still helps explain its appeal.

Likewise, Zizi Papacharissi and Alan Rubin's (2000) work predicting Internet use found a Uses and Gratifications perspective explanatory. Papacharissi and Rubin found that people had five primary motives for Internet use, and the most important was information seeking. They also found that people who felt valued interpersonally used the Internet primarily for information gathering and those who felt less secure in their face-to-face interactions turned to the Internet for social motives. Overall, they concluded that Uses and Gratifications Theory provided an important framework for studying new media.

Critique and Closing

Uses and Gratifications, as a recognizable, discrete theory, had its greatest influence in the 1970s and 1980s. The limited effects paradigm held sway at the time, and media theorists needed a framework within which they could discuss the obvious presence of media effects without straying too far from disciplinary orthodoxy. This is not the reason that Katz, Blumler, and Gurevitch formalized the approach, but it is why the approach took on its particular character.

Two other factors shaped how it would be and is now used. The first is the simple nature of its development. Its founders were interested in how people use media in quite specific situations. They were political scientists and sociologists, so their focus was on political and informational campaigns. Therefore, researchers in traditional Uses and Gratifications Theory studied how people used the *information* provided by media. They approached media as outlets of information rather than of symbols. It is only logical, then, that they envisioned the possibility—even the probability—of discerning, reflective audience members selecting the information they wanted and needed. Uses and Gratifications,

Theory * Into * Practice

Jennifer Lee, in the *New York Times,* describes how new electronic media are serving a variety of uses for students and their parents while posing some challenges for the schools. Lee observes that electronic "gadgets" in the school building can often be unwanted disturbances for faculty and administrators. "Cellphones go off in class, disrupting lessons. Students leave classrooms to make calls in the hallways. Others play video games or watch movies that they have downloaded onto their laptops. Some students even use hand-held organizers and cellphone messaging to exchange answers and cheat during tests" (p. E1). Despite the problems the schools may have, you can see the variety of uses students have for these new media.

The article goes on to state further uses: storing information such as locker combinations, relieving boredom, and staying in touch. Many parents are interested in having the schools allow cell phones so they can keep in contact with their children. Because many families do not have a parent at home during the school day, cell phones can be very helpful. Since Columbine and September 11, parents and students both appreciate the connection provided by electronic gadgets.

The article concludes with a potential problem for Uses and Gratifications research. Many of these electronic devices are blurring the line between entertainment and education. "Hand-held organizers are merging with cellphones (like the Handspring Treo), cellphones are mixing with downloadable music (Motorola V2282), organizers become game machines—with the right software—and many laptop computers come with DVD players for watching movies" (p. E7). One school administrator questions what he will do when everything is wrapped into one electronic device. Uses and Gratifications Theory might ask the same question.

Source: Lee, 2002.

TIP Follow-up
What elements of Uses and Gratifications Theory help to explain media use when the medium is multifunctional? How is the theory able to predict which function a user might choose at a given time?

therefore, is quite straightforward when discussing how people use newspapers (newspapers are made up of discrete sections, each aimed at a specific type of reader seeking specific types of information) or magazines (publications with very specific, demographically targeted readers) to come to some specific decision or judgment.

Finally, the heuristic nature of the theory is without question. The research has spanned several decades, and the theory has framed a number of research studies. In addition to the early pioneers Katz, Blumler, and Gurevitch and their colleagues, others have employed the theory and its thinking into their research on home computer use (Perse & Courtright, 1993; Perse & Greenberg-Dunn, 1998), the remote control (Bellamy & Walker, 1996; Ferguson, 1992), and the Internet (Morris & Ogan, 1996).

Uses and Gratifications Theory is not without its critics. First, the notion of the active audience has been questioned. Some researchers (Kubey & Csikszentmihalyi, 1990) note that people report that their television watching in particular is passive and requires little concentration. Further, the theory seems to highlight a reasoned media consumer, one who does not accept everything the media present. The theory does not take into consideration the fact that individuals may not have considered all available choices in media consumption. For instance, Ryan Grant has considered two choices: stay at home or go out to the movies. What other options could he consider? Uses and Gratifications does not pay attention to the myriad unconscious decisions made by individuals.

Denis McQuail (1984) believes that the theory suffers from a lack of theoretical coherence. He thinks that some of the theory's terminology needs to be further defined. He also notes that the theory relies too heavily on the functional use of media, because there are times when the media can be reckless. For example, there have been instances of sloppy, inaccurate, or unethical journalism: In 1999, a Kentucky journalist was fired after falsely reporting that she had AIDS; in the late 1990s there was an erroneous CNN report about the U.S. government's knowledge of its military's use of poisonous gas in Vietnam. What if the active consumer sought out these media for information about AIDS or the U.S. involvement in Vietnam? This irresponsibility of the media is not addressed in the theory.

The value of Uses and Gratifications Theory today is in its ability to provide a framework for the consideration of the audience and individual media consumers in contemporary mass communication research and theory. Uses and Gratifications may not be the defining theory in the field of mass communication, but it serves the discipline well as a "perspective through which a number of ideas and theories about media choice, consumption, and even impact can be viewed" (Baran & Davis, 2003, p. 241).

Discussion Starters

1. Are there choices other than those identified, for Ryan Grant to consider in his decision to do something on Friday night? How do these alternatives relate to Uses and Gratifications Theory? Use examples in your response.

2. How active a media consumer are you? Are you always thoughtful in your choice of media content? Do you bring different levels of activeness to different media—newspapers versus radio, for example?

3. Uses and Gratifications Theory has been criticized for being too apologetic of the media industries and overly supportive of the status quo. Can you explain why this is so? Do you agree with these criticisms? Does such criticism have any place in scientific theory?

4. Uses and Gratifications Theory assumes that media present content and consumers consume it. How does the Internet threaten to disrupt this model? How might Uses and Gratifications adapt to allow for this transformation of traditional media consumers into online media users?

5. What feature of Uses and Gratifications Theory is most appealing or most applicable to you? Why? Incorporate examples into your response.

6. What difference would it make, according to the theory, if Ryan's movie choice was an action/adventure film and the main choices on TV were romantic comedies? How does Uses and Gratifications Theory account for media content?

Terms for Review

Mass Society Theory
limited effects
Individual Differences Perspective
Social Categories Model
fraction of selection
parasocial interaction
diversion
personal relationships

personal identity
surveillance
utility
intentionality
selectivity
imperviousness to influence
activity
activeness

 ## Online Learning Center

Visit the Online Learning Center at www.mhhe.com/west2. Use the multiple-choice and true/false quizzes to help you prepare for exams, and the glossary, crossword puzzles, and flashcards to further your knowledge of key terms.

CHAPTER 24

Spiral of Silence Theory

Carol Johansen

Each morning, Carol Johansen attends the seniors' breakfast at the local senior center. She can afford to go out to a restaurant for breakfast, but she goes to the center because she enjoys the company. She encounters a rambunctious cast of characters including Earl, a World War I veteran who sings Broadway songs; Nancy, a former nurse who tells lively stories about former patients; and Nick, a New England lobsterman who is an avid newspaper reader. This morning's breakfast was especially interesting because the conversation quickly turned to a newspaper article on spanking children.

Nick read the article to the group, and after he was done, he offered his opinion on the topic: "I agree with this writer. I don't see anything wrong with spanking a kid. Look at this survey in the paper. Over 60 percent of the state believe it's okay to spank, but only 40 percent of the country do. Nowadays, though, you can't lay a hand on a kid. They're ready to sue you, or you'll get some state worker to come in your own house and take your kid away. It's not right."

"I agree," said Nancy. "I can tell you that my neighbor's daughter is almost 8 and a holy terror. But her mother won't touch her! I don't get it. If that was my child, I wouldn't mind putting her over my knee and giving her a good wallop! The girl's mom and dad don't want to send 'the wrong message' to her so she gets away with a lot."

Earl became more interested in the subject as Nancy spoke. Like the others, Earl had a strong opinion on the subject: "Look. How many people at this table were spanked when they were little?" All seven raised their hands. "And how many of you think that you're violent people?" None showed any response. "There. That's my point. Today, they tell you that if you spank your own kid, then that kid is going to end up violent. But look at us. We aren't violent. We don't hurt anyone. There's just too much of this political correctness out there, and too many parents simply have no rights anymore."

Carol continued glancing at one of Nick's newspapers. She, like the others, had an opinion on the subject. But her thoughts differed from those of the others. She did not believe in spanking a child at all. She had been spanked like the rest of her friends, but her dad had not known when to stop. Carol had often been physically abused. She thought about the number of parents who are not able to stop at just one slap on the behind. She also thought about what hitting accomplished. Children can be taught right and wrong, she felt, without being hit.

"Hey, Carol," Nick interrupted, "you're pretty quiet. What's your take on all this?"

Carol thought for a quick moment. Should she disagree with the rest of them? What about all the people in her community who also agree with spanking? Carol recalled seeing a news program on the topic about a week ago, and the reporter had interviewed several adult children who had been

This theory is based on the research of **Elisabeth Noelle-Neumann.**

spanked and who felt that spanking was the only discipline to use on them during their childhood. She knew that she disagreed with her breakfast colleagues, but how could she begin to explain all of her thoughts? They wouldn't understand. It's probably better to simply go with the flow, she surmised.

"Oh, I don't know. I can see how some kids need 'special attention.' But sometimes, parents get too angry."

"C'mon Carol," Nancy interrupted. "You can't have it both ways. There are a lot of . . ."

"Well, I guess I agree with it. I hope that it's not done that often, though."

As the volunteer arrived at the table to pour more coffee, the conversation quickly turned to other news. Privately, Carol thought about why she had deferred to the group's will. She didn't want to be alone in her viewpoint, nor did she want to explain the personal and sordid details of her past. As Nick began to talk about last night's city council meeting, Carol wondered whether she would ever speak up on the subject again.

■

The opinions that we have of events, people, and topics change periodically in our lives. Consider, for example, your opinions about dating when you were a 10-year-old and your opinions about dating now. Or consider the opinions you held of your parents during your adolescence and those you hold today. Even your opinions on various topics—including premarital sex and raising children—may have evolved over the years. Our opinions are not static and frequently change over the years.

One important influence on our opinions is the media. Media have helped to shape who we are today. Often, this influence is subtle; at other times it is more direct. The media's influence on public opinion is what Elisabeth Noelle-Neumann studied, dating back to the 1930s and 1940s. It was in the early 1970s, however, that she conceptualized the Spiral of Silence Theory.

Noelle-Neumann focuses on what happens when people provide their opinions on a variety of issues that the media have defined for the public. The Spiral of Silence Theory suggests that people who believe that they hold a minority viewpoint on a public issue will remain in the background where their communication will be constrained; those who believe that they hold a majority viewpoint will be more encouraged to speak. Noelle-Neumann (1983) contends that the media will focus more on the majority views, underestimating the minority views. Those in the minority will be less assertive in communicating their opinions, thereby leading to a downward spiral of communication. Interestingly, those in the majority will overestimate their influence and may become emboldened in their communication. Subsequently, the media will report on their opinions and activities.

The minority views of Carol Johansen and the behavior of her breakfast friends underscore the gist of the Spiral of Silence Theory. Listening to her colleagues' opinions on spanking, Carol feels that she is alone in thinking that spanking is wrong. The theory suggests that Carol is influenced by media reports of over 60 percent of the state supporting spanking for discipline and also by her own recollection of a television news show that lauded the benefits of spanking by adult children who had been spanked themselves. Carol perceives her opinion to be a minority view, and consequently she speaks less. Conversely, those who agree with spanking as discipline (Nick, Nancy, and Earl) are no doubt inspired by the state survey responses; this prompts even more assertive communication on their part.

The difference between this majority and minority view at the senior center is further clarified by Noelle-Neumann (1991). She believes that those in the majority have the confidence to speak out. They may display their convictions by wearing buttons, brandishing bumper stickers, and emblazoning their opinions on the clothes they wear. Holders of minority views are usually cautious and silent, which reinforces the public's perceptions of their weakness. Nick, Nancy, and Earl are clearly confident in their opinions, whereas Carol fosters a sense of weakness by her lack of assertiveness in expressing her opinion.

The Spiral of Silence Theory uniquely focuses on public opinion. To better understand public opinion, an integral component of the theory, we first discuss its meaning in the theory. We then examine three assumptions fundamental to the theory.

The Court of Public Opinion

As a researcher, Noelle-Neumann was interested in clarifying terms that may have multiple meanings. At the core of the Spiral of Silence Theory is a term that is commonly accepted but one that she felt was misconstrued: public opinion. As a founder and director of the Allensbach Institute, a polling agency in Germany, Noelle-Neumann contended that interpretations of *public opinion* have been misguided. In fact, although she identified more than fifty definitions of the term since the theory's inception, none satisfied her.

In her provocatively titled book, *The Spiral of Silence: Public Opinion— Our Social Skin,* Noelle-Neumann (1984; 1993) separates *public opinion* into two discrete terms: *public* and *opinion.* She notes that three meanings of **public** exist. First, there is a legal association with the term. Public suggests that it is open to everyone, as in "public lands" or "public place." Second, public pertains to the concerns or issues of people, as in "the public responsibility of journalists." Finally, public represents the social-psychological side of people. That is, people not only think inwardly but also think about their relationships to others. The phrase "public eye" is relevant here. Noelle-Neumann concludes that individuals know whether they are exposed to or sheltered from public view, and they adjust themselves accordingly. She claims that the social-psychological side of public has been neglected in previous interpretations of public opinion, and yet, "this is the meaning felt by people in their sensitive social skin" (1993, p. 62).

An **opinion** is an expression of an attitude. Opinions may vary in both intensity and stability. Invoking the early French and English interpretation of opinions, Noelle-Neumann notes that opinion is a level of agreement of a particular population. In the spiral of silence process, opinion is synonymous with something regarded as acceptable.

Putting all of this together, Noelle-Neumann defines **public opinion** as the "attitudes or behaviors one must express in public if one is not to isolate

public
legal, social, and social-psychological concerns of people

opinion
expression of attitude

public opinion
attitudes and behaviors expressed in public in order to avoid isolation

oneself; in areas of controversy or change, public opinions are those attitudes one *can* express without running the danger of isolating oneself" (Noelle-Neumann, 1993, p. 178). So, for Carol Johansen, her opinion on spanking would not be regarded as acceptable by her breakfast club. Because she fears being isolated from her particular early-morning community, she silences her opinions.

Essentially, public opinion refers to the collective sentiments of a population on a particular subject. Most often, the media determine what subjects will be of interest to people, and the media often make a subject controversial. For example, the drug Viagra, used to treat impotence, was considered a medical marvel until the media discovered that many health plans covered this drug but did not cover female contraceptives. Many media outlets subsequently reported that this practice was overt sexism. Noelle-Neumann (1991) notes that public opinion may be influenced by who approves or disapproves of our views. Your opinion on whether or not Viagra should be covered by health plans may be influenced by others, including spokespersons for both sides of the issue as well as your friends and family members. The spiral of silence is the response to these shifting opinions of others.

Assumptions of Spiral of Silence Theory

With public opinion as our backdrop to the theory, we now explore three assumptions of the Spiral of Silence Theory. Noelle-Neumann (1991; 1993) has previously addressed these assertions:

- Society threatens deviant individuals with isolation; fear of isolation is pervasive.
- This fear of isolation causes individuals to try to assess the climate of opinion at all times.
- Public behavior is affected by public opinion assessment.

The first assumption asserts that society holds power over those who do not conform through threat of isolation. Noelle-Neumann believes that the very fabric of our society depends on people commonly recognizing and endorsing a set of values. And it is public opinion that determines whether these values have equal conviction across the populations. When people agree on a common set of values, then fear of isolation decreases. When there is a difference in values, fear of isolation sets in.

Like many theorists, Noelle-Neumann is concerned with the testability of this assumption. After all, she notes, are members of a society really threatened with isolation? How could this be? She believes that simple polling could not tap this area (for instance, How much do you fear isolation?). Questions such as these ask respondents to think too abstractly, because it's likely that few respondents have ever thought about isolation.

Noelle-Neumann employs the research values of Solomon Asch, a social psychologist in the 1950s. Asch conducted the following laboratory experiment more than fifty times with eight to ten research subjects:

Which of the following lines on the right is equal to the line on the left?

_____

1. _____

2. _____

3. _____

You are probably quick to say that line 3 is equal to the line on the left. The group of research subjects, however, disagreed. After going around the room, the experimenter's assistants (who were in on the experiment) all named line 1 as the one that was equal to the line on the left. The unsuspecting subjects began to name line 1 as the correct response. In fact, Asch discovered that several times around, the unsuspecting subjects named the incorrect response. Asch believed that individuals frequently feel great pressure to agree with others, even though the others are incorrect. Borrowing from the theory, there is a very real fear of isolation.

Responding to primary criticisms of the Asch studies—that people did not have a real fear of isolation but rather a lack of confidence in their own judgment—Noelle-Neumann engaged in a more realistic threat-of-isolation test. She believed that requiring subjects to assess a moral or aesthetic conviction was more realistic than any laboratory experiments conducted by Asch. During interviews with smokers, she showed them a picture with a person angrily saying, "It seems to me that smokers are terribly inconsiderate. They force others to inhale their health-endangering smoke." Respondents were asked to phrase responses to the statement. The results indicated that in the presence of non-smokers, many smokers were less willing to overtly support smokers' rights.

The second assumption of the theory identifies people as constant assessors of the climate of public opinion. Noelle-Neumann contends that individuals receive information about public opinion from two sources: personal observation and the media. First, let's discuss how people are able to personally observe public opinion and then examine the role of the media.

Noelle-Neumann (1991) states that people engage in a quasi-statistical ability to appraise public opinion. A **quasi-statistical sense** means that people are able to estimate the strength of opposing sides in a public debate. They are able to do this by listening to the views of others and incorporating that knowledge into their own viewpoints. For instance, Carol Johansen's quasi-statistical sense makes her believe that she is the only person at her breakfast table who opposes spanking. She can see that she is vastly outnumbered on the topic and therefore is able to assess the local public opinion on the subject. Noelle-Neumann calls this a quasi-statistical frequency organ in that she believes that people like Carol are able to numerically estimate where others fall on the topic. The theorist states that this organ is on "high alert" during periods of instability. So our quasi-statistical sense works overtime when we see that our opinions on a subject are different from those of the majority around us.

Personal observations of public opinion can often be distorted and inaccurate. Noelle-Neumann (1993) calls the mistaken observations about how most people feel **pluralistic ignorance**. She notes that people "mix their own direct perceptions and the perceptions filtered through the eyes of the media into an

quasi-statistical sense
personal estimation of the strength of opposing sides on a public issue

pluralistic ignorance
mistaken observation of how most people feel

indivisible whole that seems to derive from their own thoughts and experiences" (p. 169). Consider Carol's assessment of the opinions on spanking. With the vast majority of people around her supporting this type of discipline, she may believe that she is clearly in the minority. One or both sides in the debate, however, can overestimate their ability to estimate opinion. Especially with such lopsided support on a topic (as with the group at the senior center), Noelle-Neumann believes that people can become disillusioned.

People not only employ their personal observations of public opinion, but also rely on the media. Yet, Noelle-Neumann insists that the media's effects are frequently indirect. Because people are inherently social in nature, they talk about their observations to others. People seek out the media to confirm or disconfirm their observations and then interpret their own observations through the media. This can be illustrated through Carol's future behaviors. First, if she returns home from the senior center and reveals her beliefs on spanking to others, she may encounter several neighbors who share her opinion. Next, if she watches the evening news and learns that the majority of the country oppose spanking, this will resonate deeply with her. She will also be affected by any media reports that disproportionately publicize opposition to spanking. Finally, later discussions that Carol might have on the subject may invoke the media. She may tell others that even the media reports underscore her point of view. We will return to the powerful role of the media in the Spiral of Silence Theory a bit later in the chapter.

The final assumption of the theory is that the public's behavior is influenced by evaluations of public opinion. Noelle-Neumann (1991) proposes that public behavior takes the form of either speaking out on a subject or keeping silent. If individuals sense support for a topic, then they are likely to communicate about it; if they feel that others do not support a topic, then silence is maintained. She continues, "The strength of one camp's signals, or the weakness of the other's, is the driving force setting the spiral in motion" (p. 271). In sum, people seem to act according to how other people feel.

Noelle-Neumann believes that human beings have an aversion to discussing topics that do not have the support of the majority. To test this assumption, consider interviewing people on your campus about a controversial issue such as physician-assisted suicide. If straw polls in your campus newspaper show that almost 70 percent of the campus oppose this, then according to the theory, students, faculty, and staff are probably going to be less inclined to speak out in favor of the practice. A willingness to speak out may have more to do with one's convictions and an assessment of overall trends in society. That is, if there is a liberal climate on your campus, there may be more willingness to speak out; if a conservative climate exists, people may feel less inclined to offer their opposition.

These three assumptions are important to consider as we further delineate Noelle-Neumann's theory. In Figure 24.1, we illustrate several concepts and themes emerging from the theory's assumptions.

Personal opinions, a fear of being alone in those opinions, and public sentiment lay the groundwork for discussing the remainder of the theory. Each of these areas is influenced by a powerful part of U.S. society: the media. Let's now overview the powerful influence of the media in the Spiral of Silence Theory.

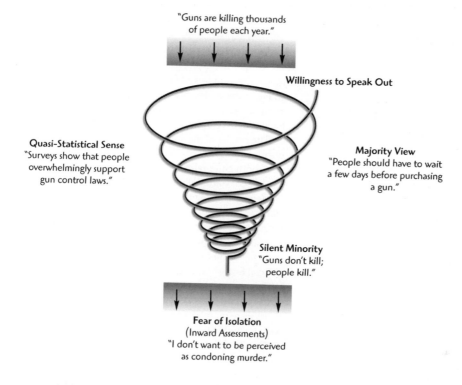

PUBLIC OPINION AS COMMUNICATED BY THE MEDIA

"Guns are killing thousands of people each year."

Willingness to Speak Out

Quasi-Statistical Sense
"Surveys show that people overwhelmingly support gun control laws."

Majority View
"People should have to wait a few days before purchasing a gun."

Silent Minority
"Guns don't kill; people kill."

Fear of Isolation
(Inward Assessments)
"I don't want to be perceived as condoning murder."

Figure 24.1
The Spiral of Silence: Gun Control

The Media's Influence

As we have discussed, the Spiral of Silence Theory rests on public opinion. Noelle-Neumann cautions, however, that "much of the population adjusts its attitudes to the tenor of the media" (Noelle-Neumann, 1993, p. 272). A willingness to speak out depends greatly on the media. Without support from others for divergent views, people will remain consonant with the views offered in the media. In fact, Noelle-Neumann believes that the media even provide words and phrases so people can confidently speak about a subject. If no repeated words or expressions are used, then people fall silent. The extent to which Carol Johansen will offer her views about spanking, then, will rest on what position the various media have taken on the subject. Yet, as George Gerbner (Cultivation Analysis, Chapter 22) says, television is the most influential of all media forms, although the Internet is fast becoming highly influential.

In explaining why the media have such influence, Noelle-Neumann believes that the public is not offered a broad and balanced interpretation of news events. Consequently, the public is given a limited view of reality. This restrictive approach to covering news narrows an individual's perception. Examine the influence of media in public perception in the Research Note.

Consider the theorist's three characteristics of the news media: ubiquity, cumulativeness, and consonance. **Ubiquity** refers to the fact that the media are pervasive sources of information. Because media are everywhere, they are relied

ubiquity
the belief that media are everywhere

Research Note

Lin, C. A., & Salwen, M. B. (1997). Predicting the Spiral of Silence on a controversial public issue. *Howard Journal of Communications, 8,* 129–141.

This study incorporates the Spiral of Silence hypothesis—namely, that public opinion expression is related to the media's presentation of a topic. The subject under study is the public debate over whether English should be adopted as the official language of the United States. The article begins by examining research related to the media and an audience's ability to examine public opinion. The investigators explored research related to same- and cross-cultural perceptions of media coverage. Lin and Salwen hypothesized several claims about opinion expression on the Official English issue.

They studied two very different cities to test their hypotheses: Carbondale, Illinois, and Miami, Florida. The researchers felt that Carbondale residents—as members of a small town in the country's heartland—may "identify their community culture as close to any small American town's culture" (p. 132). Miami residents were considered to regard themselves as unlike other cities across the United States. Therefore, the two cities were believed to be different—not only in population and demographics, but also in values.

Telephone surveys were conducted in the two cities. Trained phone interviewers made several attempts to contact those who could not be initially reached. To obtain the final sample for analysis, a screening question was asked that pertained to the Official English question. The final sample consisted of 546 residents from Carbondale and 437 residents from Miami. A combined 983 residents, therefore, participated in the research.

Several measures were incorporated in the study. To assess public opinion, respondents were asked to indicate how willing or unwilling they were to express an opinion on the Official English topic. To understand respondents' sense of community, they were asked to report the perceived degree of similarity between their community and the nation's communities. A simple yes or no response was recorded when respondents were asked to indicate whether or not they supported English as the official language of the United States. Perceptions of the local and the national media climates were also assessed. Finally, demographic information was solicited.

The results of the study showed significant support for the Spiral of Silence Theory. Respondents from both cities reported similar perceptions regarding the national media climates. Carbondale residents perceived that their local public and media climates were more in favor of English as the official language than Miami residents. Supporters and opponents of the issue were found to be "equally likely to engage in public expression" (p. 139). That is, Official English was equally relevant to both groups. Willingness to publicly discuss the issue came from both supporters and opponents. In Miami, residents were more inclined to speak out if the media were favorable toward the subject.

Finally, the ethnic background of respondents was analyzed in relationship to the hypotheses posed. Generally, Hispanics and non-Hispanics did not differ in their views of media climates and in their perceptions of community identification. Hispanics were as willing to speak out on the issue as were non-Hispanics. The researchers caution, however, that the Cuban Hispanics of Miami may not be representative of other Hispanic groups (for example, Puerto Ricans, Mexicans, and others).

The study is important for various reasons. First, it examines the cultural implications of the Spiral of Silence Theory. Second, the study provides support for the influence of positive media coverage on controversial issues such as the Official English debate. Finally, the research demonstrates that people are capable of discerning the tone of the media's coverage on an issue. "Media coverage does not always reveal a clear direction or pattern of public opinion" (p. 140), and this study assists in uncovering perceptions of respondents who can identify the tenor of the media.

on when people seek out information. For instance, Nick, a member of Carol Johansen's morning group, is quick to point out the recent surveys done in the state about perceptions of spanking. He has the source immediately at hand. And as the media strive for agreement from the majority of the public, they will be everywhere.

The **cumulativeness** of the media refers to the process of the media repeating themselves across programs and across time. Frequently, you will read a story in the morning newspaper, listen to the same story on the radio as you drive to work, and then watch the story on the evening news. Noelle-Neumann calls this a "reciprocal influence in building up frames of reference" (1993, p. 71). What becomes problematic is that the original source may be left unquestioned, and yet four media (newspaper, radio, television, and the Internet) rely on that source. The theory suggests that conformity of voice influences what information gets released to the public to help them develop an opinion.

> **cumulativeness**
> the belief that media repeat themselves

Finally, **consonance** pertains to the similarities of beliefs, attitudes, and values held by the media. Noelle-Neumann states that consonance is produced from a tendency for newspeople to confirm their own thoughts and opinions, making it look as if those opinions were emanating from the public. Each of these three qualities—ubiquity, cumulativeness, consonance—allows for majority opinions to be heard. Those wishing to avoid isolation remain silent.

> **consonance**
> the belief that all media are similar in attitudes, beliefs, and values

It is not surprising that the media are influential in public opinion. Many surveys have demonstrated that people consider the media to have too much power in U.S. society. Consider also that, as we discussed in Chapter 22, information is frequently filtered through news reporters and their agencies. As a result, what is presented—or in the case of this theory, what is perceived—may not be an accurate picture of reality. For instance, most people can attest to the diversity found in the United States, and yet most media do not report with this diversity in mind. Imagine, for instance, the anxiety and frustration of many disabled individuals as they read or listen to media reports about the success of the Americans with Disabilities Act passed in the early 1990s. What is not often reported, however, is the high percentage of disabled people who remain unemployed or who continue to experience discrimination in the workplace. Or perhaps you have read or heard about the success of affirmative action policies, neglecting the fact that much of today's discrimination is often covert and subtle (Jandt, 2000). Maybe you have read about the many people who have been forced off of welfare, but you probably haven't seen many stories describing the dire circumstances of many families due to this decreased funding. If the media report these "success" stories often enough, Noelle-Neumann says, they are setting the news agenda—identifying what should be noticed, deciding what questions should be asked, and determining whether various social policies and programs are effective. In other words, people experience the climate of public opinion through the mass media.

As you can see, then, when people look to media for a glimpse into the perceptions and beliefs of the population, they are likely to receive anything but an impartial representation. **Dual climates of opinion** often exist—that is, a climate that the population perceives directly and the climate the media report. For instance, Carol Johansen may compare her personal perceptions of

> **dual climates of opinion**
> difference between the population's perception of a public issue and the way the media report on the issue

spanking to those surveyed perceptions published in the newspaper. What is remarkable is that despite the differences in opinion, many people decide to remain silent. To understand what motivates people to speak out, Noelle-Neumann developed the train test.

The Train Test

Examining whether or not people will speak out requires a methodology that is clear, testable, representative, and replicable. To prove this, Noelle-Neumann conceptualized the train test (Today, the test can be applied to a plane or bus as well.) The **train test** is an assessment of the extent to which people will speak out with their own opinion. According to the Spiral of Silence Theory, people on two different sides of an issue will vary in their willingness to express views in public. To study this, the researchers gave respondents sketches showing two people in conversation. The researcher asked a respondent, "Which of the two would you agree with, Person A or Person B?" This question would then be followed up with a more pivotal question, for example, one that might test the waters on opinions pertaining to food safety. Essentially, the train (or plane or bus) test asks people a question such as the following:

> Suppose that you have a five-hour train ride ahead of you, and a person sits next to you and starts to discuss the problems of food safety. Would you talk or not talk about the topic to the person?

This question was repeated several times with various subjects. It focused on a number of topics, ranging from nuclear power plants to abortion to racial segregation. The test revealed a number of factors that help determine whether a person will voice an opinion. They include the following:

- Supporters of a dominant opinion are more willing to voice an opinion than those in the minority opinion.
- People from large cities who are male and between the ages of 45 and 59 are more willing to speak out.
- There are various ways of speaking out—for example, hanging posters, displaying bumper stickers, and distributing flyers.
- People are more likely to voice an opinion if it agrees with their own convictions as well as fits within current trends and the spirit of the age. People will voice an opinion if it aligns with societal views.
- People tend to share their opinions with those who agree with them more than with those who disagree.
- People draw the strength of their convictions from a variety of sources, including family, friends, and acquaintances.
- People may engage in **last-minute swing**, or jumping on the bandwagon of the popular opinion during the final moments of conversation.

The train test has proved to be an interesting approach to studying public opinion. The method simulates public behavior when two schools of thought

train test
assessment of the extent to which people will speak out

last-minute swing
jumping on the bandwagon of popular opinion after opinions have been expressed

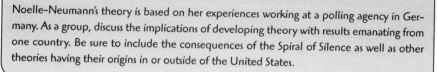

Theory Application in Groups (TAG)

Noelle-Neumann's theory is based on her experiences working at a polling agency in Germany. As a group, discuss the implications of developing theory with results emanating from one country. Be sure to include the consequences of the Spiral of Silence as well as other theories having their origins in or outside of the United States.

exist on a subject. For those who are willing to speak out, there are opportunities to sway others. And there are times when the minority opinion speaks out loudly. We now examine this group.

The Hard Core

Every now and then, the silent minority rises up. This group, called the **hard core**, "remains at the end of a spiral of silence process in defiance of the threats of isolation" (Noelle-Neumann, 1993, p. 170). Noelle-Neumann recognizes that like most things in life, there is an exception to every rule or theory. The hard core represent a group of individuals who know that there is a price to pay for their assertiveness. These deviants try to buck the dominant way of thinking and are prepared to directly confront anyone who gets in their way (see Figure 24.2).

Noelle-Neumann invokes the work of social psychologist Gary Shulman in attempting to better understand the hard core. Shulman argues that if the majority opinion becomes large enough, the majority voice becomes less powerful

hard core
group(s) at the end of the spiral willing to speak out at any cost

Figure 24.2
Examples of the "Hard Core" in the United States

Abortion protesters
• National Abortion Rights Action League
• Focus on the Family

Antiwar coalition
• *Paux Christi*
• Win Without War

THE HARD CORE
"Individuals Willing to Buck the Trend"

Animal rights groups
• Animal Liberation Front
• People for the Ethical Treatment of Animals (PETA)

Environmental advocates
• Greenpeace
• Sierra Club

because no alternative opinions exist. A few years back, for instance, it was not uncommon for people to believe that those with AIDS should be quarantined (majority opinion). It didn't take long, however, for people's opinions to reject this narrow-minded view, primarily due to the hard core's efforts to educate the public. In fact, ironically, the media were pressed into educating the public about AIDS. It was not long before this silent hard core discovered that others had adopted their view. In this situation, the hard core was instrumental in changing public opinion.

For further evidence of the hard core, let's discuss an example pertaining to religion and religious opinion. Although we realize that not all people believe in God, God pervades our intellectual, political, and popular culture. For instance, people often say "God bless you" when others sneeze. In the political environment, each session of the U.S. Congress begins with some sort of prayer (there's even a U.S. House of Representatives chaplain), and many politicians conclude their speeches with "God bless America." "In God We Trust" appears on paper money, and the Pledge of Allegiance contains clear references to God ("one nation under God").

Despite pervasive references to God, many people in the United States do not believe in God. Some of these individuals contend that the country's Constitution requires a separation between church and state, and therefore any religious references in tax-supported venues should be eliminated. However, this opinion may not be shared by the majority of the United States because over half of the country affiliate with an organized religion (Lindner, 2001). Whether the media report on visits by the pope, present video clips of politicians leaving religious services each week, or solicit quotes for news stories from the clergy, they continue to imply that religion is an integral part of people's lives.

The minority—those civil libertarians who advocate extracting religion from public-supported activities—have been vocal regarding their opinions; these hard-core dissenters have not blended into the background. Some of the effects of this hard core can be seen in that the Pledge of Allegiance is no longer required in every school district. In fact, in 2002, a federal appeals court in San Francisco ruled that the Pledge was unconstitutional in that it referenced God and violated the separation of church and state clause (Nieves, 2002). Although the ruling was challenged, it prompted considerable discussion on the references to God in state-sponsored efforts. The hard core might also claim victory as they see villages and cities remove religious icons (nativity sets, crucifixes, and so forth) from city parks during holidays. And with media outlets covering such legal victories, the hard core may be reconfiguring majority opinion.

Noelle-Neumann (1993) indicates that the hard core consists of people like Don Quixote, a literary figure who, because of his outdated clothing and weaponry, found himself ridiculed, defeated, and isolated. This tragic hero, according to Noelle-Neumann, had a desire to engender the respect of the world; his endless and futile combats were testimony to his undying commitment to chivalry. She concludes, "The 'hard core' [like Quixote] remains committed to the past, retaining the old values while suffering the isolation of the present" (p. 218). She adds that the hard core are the minority at the end of the spiral of silence who defy any threats of isolation.

Critique and Closing

The Spiral of Silence Theory is one of the few theories in communication that focuses on public opinion. Indeed, the theory has been identified as an important foundation for examining the human condition (Csikszentmihalyi, 1991). The consequence of studying public opinion as Elisabeth Noelle-Neumann proposes is identified by Mihaly Csikszentmihalyi: "In an electoral democracy, but indeed even in the most tyrannical forms of government . . . the right to lead and to decide must eventually rest on the agreement of a significant segment of the population" (1991, p. 288). The theory has been called "extraordinarily influential" (Kennamer, 1990, p. 395), and others have labeled it "dynamic" (Merten, 1985), meaning that it underscores the process nature of communication that we discussed in Chapter 1. The theory has attracted scholars, making it heuristic. Researchers have employed the theory in their studies on a number of topics, including whether the United States should declare English as its official language (Lin & Salwen, 1997), the Persian Gulf war (Signorielli, Eveland, & McLeod, 1995), the O. J. Simpson criminal trial (Jeffres, Neuendorf, & Atkin, 1999), the popularity of radio stations (Wedel, 1994), affirmative action (Moy, Domke, & Stamm, 2001), and abortion (Salmon & Neuwirth, 1990).

Noelle-Neumann's theory has not avoided substantial criticism. Criticism has focused on the theory's principles and concepts. Charles Salmon and F. Gerald Kline (1985) feel that the Spiral of Silence fails to acknowledge a person's ego involvement in an issue. At times, people may be willing to speak because their ego is involved in the topic (for example, if a promotion at work depends on assertiveness). Carroll Glynn, Andrew Hayes, and James Shanahan (1997) raise the issue of various selectivity processes, such as cognitive dissonance, which we explored in Chapter 7. Individuals will avoid a topic that conflicts with their own views. Glynn and colleagues also note that there is little empirical support for the claim that people speak out only because they perceive support for their views. J. David Kennamer (1990) supports this criticism: "[I]t is hard to imagine either the pro-life or the pro-choice sides of the abortion issue giving up the fight because they perceive themselves to be in the minority" (p. 396).

Carroll Glynn and Jack McLeod (1985) note two additional shortcomings about the theory. First, they believe that the fear of isolation may not motivate people to express their opinions. They claim that Noelle-Neumann did not

The Theory Chronicles

Noelle-Neumann observes that with respect to social issues such as cigarette smoking, abortion rights, or nuclear power, people will either speak out or remain silent. Are there topics that people may not be so clear about? That is, are there times when people may have a more moderate position on a topic? Explain what types of topics and when those topics would not elicit such a binary response as speaking out or remaining silent.

empirically test her assumption that fear of isolation prompts people to speak out. Second, they argue that Noelle-Neumann does not acknowledge the influence that people's communities and reference groups have on their opinions. They believe that she focuses too much on the media. Along with that concern, the fact that the development of the Spiral of Silence relies on the media in 1985 West Germany troubles Glynn and McLeod. They doubt whether the characteristics of the media then and there (ubiquitous, cumulative, and consonant) apply to the media in the United States today. During their examination of a U.S. presidential election, Glynn and McLeod discovered little support for media bias. They do not question the relatively intimate bond among media in Germany, but they do wonder whether the theory has limited cultural application in the United States.

Noelle-Neumann has responded to several of her critics, notably in defending her emphasis on the media. She remains convinced that the media is instrumental in public opinion. She writes that "by using words and arguments taken from the media to discuss a topic, people cause the point of view to be heard in public and give it visibility, thus creating a situation in which the danger of isolation is reduced" (Noelle-Neumann, 1985, p. 80). She continues by noting that not once did the spiral of silence process contradict the media's position on a topic (Noelle-Neumann, 1993). In terms of application across cultures, Noelle-Neumann (1993) agrees that any theory of public opinion must have cross-cultural applicability. However, she posits, it is important to note that most U.S. researchers desire a rational explanation for human behavior, but not all behavior can be explained sensibly. Yet, she does accept that the train test may be limited in cross-cultural adaptation. As a result, Noelle-Neumann (1993) updated the version to read:

> Assume you are on a five-hour bus trip, and the bus makes a rest stop and everyone gets out for a long break. In a group of passengers, someone starts talking about whether we should support [insert topic] or not. Would you like to talk to this person, to get to know his or her point of view better, or would you prefer not to? (p. 217)

Of course, you may doubt whether simply changing a train test to a bus test broadens the cross-cultural application of the theory.

The Spiral of Silence will continue to generate discussion among media scholars. The theory has sustained considerable criticism, and with a central emphasis on political discussion, researchers will continue to assess the theory's

Theory * Into * Practice

The influence of the media on public opinion is suggested by John Leo in *U.S. News & World Report*. Using the 2000 U.S. Census as a backdrop, Leo notes that the media has presented census figures in various ways. In doing so, they shape public opinion differently. For instance, in reporting the numbers of same-sex households, one newspaper reported that there were "huge increases" in the number of gay and lesbian households. An activist told the newspaper that the numbers evidence a "political weapon" for gays and lesbians. The reality of the numbers, according to Leo, is that these households represent one-half of 1 percent of all households, numbering almost 250,000 households.

Leo laments the culture of the newsroom, which he believes is "sympathetic to the gay cause" (p. 17). In fact, he believes that the news culture is homogenized in its perception of such diverse topics as welfare reform, the death penalty, abortion, the environment, and school choice. He indicts his colleagues for lacking objectivity when reporting about child care as well. Leo states: "If any study shows that day care tends to have some bad effects on some children, the newsroom will erupt with articles proving the study untrue" (p. 17).

Leo specifically addresses the manner in which newspapers engage in silencing opposing opinions, a central feature of Noelle-Neumann's theory. He identifies the *Boston Globe* and *Washington Post* as examples of manipulating news to readers. The *Globe*, according to Leo, inappropriately labeled the head of Massachusetts Planned Parenthood as a woman who risks her life every day. Leo argues that "in the newsroom culture, 'pro-choicers' are allies; 'pro-lifers' are dangerous zealots" (p. 17). The problem with the *Post,* Leo believes, is that it reports surveys of race activists who want to bring racial inequality to the foreground of news. Leo is puzzled by the *Post's* depiction of bias and disparity in the African American community, and he believes the newspaper wrongly castigated White Americans in its analysis of the data. He concludes his essay by noting that a "newsroom monoculture" exists in the United States.

Source: Leo, 2001.

TIP Follow-up

Based on your reading of news, does Leo illustrate a concern expressed by Noelle-Neumann and other Spiral of Silence theorists? Explain, using examples from print media.

vitality. We live in a political world, dominated by a bold Western media. Whether people openly express majority or minority viewpoints on an issue may not be directly proportional to the media's involvement on the issue, but it is clear that the public will come to rely on the media in the global society. The theory, therefore, may have lasting effects that have not been imagined.

Discussion Starters

1. Carol Johansen feels embarrassed about offering her opinions to a group that does not share her beliefs. Consider a similar time in your life. Did you speak out or did you decide to remain quiet? What motivated your decision?

2. Discuss the times that you have been part of the hard-core minority. How did you behave? How did your confidence and self-esteem influence your behavior?

3. As students of communication theory, should you pay attention to the personal views of a theorist? Why or why not? Use examples.

4. Do you believe that the U.S. media is ubiquitous, consonant, and/or cumulative? Justify your answer.

5. Noelle-Neumann believes that the media help to influence minority views. Based on your observations of the media over the past several years, do you agree or disagree with this claim? What examples can you provide to defend your position?

6. Comment on the influence of the Internet in public opinion.

Terms for Review

public
opinion
public opinion
quasi-statistical sense
pluralistic ignorance
ubiquity

cumulativeness
consonance
dual climates of opinion
train test
last-minute swing
hard core

Online Learning Center

Visit the Online Learning Center at www.mhhe.com/west2. Use the multiple-choice and true/false quizzes to help you prepare for exams, and the glossary, crossword puzzles, and flashcards to further your knowledge of key terms.

CHAPTER 25

Medium Theory

Tiera Abrams

Tiera Abrams was bored. She was studying for her midterm in statistics and needed a break. She felt as though she would freak out if she continued to look at and memorize any more calculations. As she got up to get a drink, she thought about going online to a chat room she found while surfing the Internet. Tiera figured a 5-minute break from studying wouldn't hurt too much. As she sat and chatted with e-mail colleagues, she became particularly interested in a man from Canada. As a New Yorker, Tiera was accustomed to meeting interesting people every day. Today, though, she soon found herself in private e-mail discussions with Marcus. Marcus seemed very different from any other person she had "chatted" with over the Internet—so much so that the two exchanged e-mail addresses.

Over the course of a month, Tiera and Marcus continued to e-mail each other. They were amazed how much they had in common. They both loved country music and had dozens of country music CDs. They also were amazed to find out that they were both "tech junkies" in that they both were interested in the latest palm organizers and personal video recorders, and they couldn't imagine what life would be like without digital cable (Tiera's local cable company offered 800 channels!). They also talked about each other's family and each other's views of relationships. Neither of them was especially excited about being married, and neither one

wanted children. Tiera thought that Marcus was simply too good to be true. And Marcus was quite enamored with Tiera. All of this, and they had never even met in person!

Eventually, they decided to talk over the phone. Tiera was quite nervous; she wasn't sure whether she and Marcus would make as good a "connection" talking to each other as they had through e-mail. The conversation went great! They talked nonstop and covered a range of topics. Of course, they couldn't talk that long because of the long distance. Yet the half-hour phone call would be the beginning of something more significant.

In fact, after the phone call, Tiera called her best friend to tell her about it. The two talked for hours. Tiera was seriously thinking of trying to hook up with her newfound friend, but she still felt a bit afraid of the entire thing. She had heard horror stories about these sorts of Internet connections and wasn't sure if she should meet Marcus in Albany, a city in upstate New York. Tiera had relatives in Albany whom she could stay with, and she thought it would be a good central location for the two to meet. She decided that during spring break, she would meet Marcus and would make sure that her friends and mother knew where she was all the time.

As she drove, Tiera talked to her friends and family on her cell phone. She assured them that she would be careful and had thought about the trip a lot before she made her decision. Despite their urging her to stay at home, Tiera wanted to meet

---

This theory is based on the research of **Marshall McLuhan.**

the man who she thought would be part of her future.

The two met at a parking lot in a strip mall outside of Albany. When Tiera saw Marcus's car, she dialed her cell phone to her mother and got out of the car to meet him. (Even though she was confident that everything would go okay, she didn't want to take any chances.) Marcus was a complete gentlemen. They took separate cars to a restaurant, had dinner, went to the bar to have a drink, and talked all the while they were together. As they stood outside the restaurant, Tiera and Marcus spoke of getting together the next day for breakfast. She said that she could be reached at her uncle's house and gave Marcus the phone number. The two embraced and went to their respective cars.

As she pulled out of the parking lot of the restaurant, Tiera was a bit surprised to hear her cell phone ring. It was Marcus. He called to thank her again and to tell her to have a great night's sleep. When she hung up the phone, Tiera's head was spinning. She still couldn't believe that all of this happened because she went online during a night of studying!

Technology is often described as the most important influence on society. Few can challenge this claim. The Western world is filled with examples of how technology influences life. For instance, no doubt many of you begin your day by turning off your alarm clock, waiting for the coffeemaker to finish, turning on morning television, and going to work or school, immediately booting up the computer once you start the workday. Maybe you rely on instant messenger. Perhaps you use a handheld electronic organizer for your appointments or respond to voice mail by using your cell phone. When you return home, you probably turn on the television or radio to listen to the day's events. And it's fair to say, you begin and end each weekday in pretty much the same manner, probably unaware of your reliance on communication technology.

Like a lot of people today, Tiera Abrams finds herself in the middle of what could be called tech-dating. Although she is a self-described "tech junkie," very few could have predicted—even twenty years ago—that our society would find itself where Tiera Abrams is. There was a time when seeing a person up close was a primary prerequisite to communication with that person (your authors remember it well). Yet the technological times we live in have been expanded to the extent that "up close" simply means up close to one's computer monitor!

One theorist who could understand and interpret Tiera's relational circumstance is Marshall McLuhan. In his book *Understanding Media* (1964; 1994), McLuhan wrote about the influence of technologies such as clocks, televisions, radios, movies, telephones, and even roads and games. Although today we would not classify some of these as technologies, at the time, McLuhan was interested in the social impact of these primary mediated forms of communication. In other words, what is the relationship between technology and members of a culture? It's fair to say that McLuhan himself was part of the culture's media. He appeared regularly on television talk shows, had a cameo role in the Woody Allen film *Annie Hall*, and even was interviewed by *Playboy!*

McLuhan was a Canadian scholar of literary criticism who used poetry, fiction, politics, musical theatre, and history to suggest that mediated technology shapes people's feelings, thoughts, and actions. McLuhan suggests that we

The Theory Connection

Compare McLuhan's view of the audience in Medium Theory with Katz, Blumler, and Gure-vitch's view of the audience in Uses and Gratifications Theory. What conclusions can you draw regarding how active or passive the audience is in each theory?

have a symbiotic relationship with mediated technology; we create technology, and technology in turn re-creates who we are.

Electr(on)ic media has revolutionized society, according to McLuhan. In essence, McLuhan feels that societies are highly dependent on mediated technology and that a society's social order is based on its ability to deal with that technology. Media, in general, act directly to mold and organize a culture. This is McLuhan's Medium Theory. Although some scholars have referred to the theory as Technological Determinism, the growing consensus among scholars is that the phrase is an overstatement of McLuhan's theory (Cohen, 2000; Grosswiler, 1997; Levinson, 2001) and that it renders an audience passive and detached. In fact, audiences in McLuhan's writings are capable of being active: "Today, electronics and automation make mandatory that everybody adjust to the vast global environment as if it were his [sic] little home town" (McLuhan & Fiore, 1968, p. 11). Because it centralizes the many types of media, scholars aptly term McLuhan's work *Medium Theory* (e.g., Littlejohn, 2002).

McLuhan (1964) based much of his thinking on his mentor, Canadian political economist Harold Adams Innis (1951). Innis felt that major empires in history (e.g., Rome, Greece, Egypt) were built by those in control of the written word. Innis argued that Canadian elites used a number of communication technologies to build their "empires." Those in power were given more power because of the development of technology. Innis referred to the shaping power of technology on a society as the **bias of communication**. For Innis, people use media to gain political and economic power and, therefore, change the social order of a society. Innis claimed that communication media have a built-in bias to control the flow of ideas in a society.

McLuhan extended the work of Innis. Philip Marchand (1989) observes that "not long after Innis's death, McLuhan found an opportunity to explore the new intellectual landscape opened up by his [Innis] work" (p. 115). McLuhan, like Innis, felt that it's nearly impossible to find a society that is unaffected by electronic media. Our perceptions of the media and how we interpret those perceptions are the core issues associated with Medium Theory. We now discuss these themes in the three main assumptions of the theory.

bias of communication Harold Innis's contention that technology has a shaping power on society

Assumptions of Medium Theory

We have noted from the above discussion that the influence of media technology on society is the main idea behind Medium Theory. Let's examine this notion a bit further in the three assumptions framing the theory:

427

- Media infuse every act and action in society.

- Media fix our perceptions and organize our experiences.

- Media tie the world together.

Our first assumption underscores the notion that we cannot escape media in our lives: Media permeate our very existence. We cannot avoid nor evade media, particularly if we subscribe to McLuhan's broad interpretation of what constitutes media. You will recall that many Medium theorists interpret media in far-reaching terms. For instance, in addition to looking at more traditional forms of media (e.g., radios, movies, television), McLuhan also looked at the influence that numbers, games, and even money can have on society. We explore these three in more detail in order for you to understand the breadth of McLuhan's definition of media.

McLuhan (1964) looked at numbers as mediated. He explains: "In the theater, at a ball, at a ball game, in church, every individual enjoys all those others present. The pleasure of being among the masses is the sense of the joy in the multiplication of numbers, which has long been suspect among the literate members of Western society" (p. 107). McLuhan felt that in numbers, a "mass mind" (p. 107) was constructed by the elites in society to establish a "profile of the crowd" (p. 106). Therefore, it may be possible to create a homogenized population, capable of being influenced.

In addition to numbers, McLuhan (1964) looks at games in society as mediated. He observes that "games are popular art, collective, social reactions to the main drive or action of any culture" (p. 235). Games are ways to cope with everyday stresses and, McLuhan notes, they are models of our psychological lives. He further argues that "all games are media of interpersonal communication" (p. 237), which are extensions of our social selves. Games become mass media because they allow for people to simultaneously participate in an activity that is fun and that reflects who they are.

An additional mediated form is money (McLuhan, 1964). McLuhan concludes that "like any other medium, it is a staple, a natural resource" (p. 133). The theorist also calls money a "corporate image" that relies on society for its status and sustenance. Money has some sort of magical power that allows people access. Money allows people to travel the globe, serving as transmitters of knowledge, information, and culture. McLuhan notes that money is really a language that communicates to a diverse group, including farmers, engineers, plumbers, and physicians.

McLuhan, then, contends that media—interpreted in the broadest sense—are ever-present in our lives. These media transform our society, whether through the games we play, the radios we listen to, or the televisions we watch. At the same time, media depend on society for "interplay and evolution" (McLuhan, 1964, p. 49).

A second assumption of Medium Theory relates to our discussion above: We are directly influenced by media. Although we alluded to this influence earlier, let's be more specific about how McLuhan views the influence of media in our lives.

Medium theorists believe that media fix perceptions and organize our lives. McLuhan suggests here that media are quite powerful in our views of the world. Consider, for instance, what occurs when we watch television. If television news reports that the United States is experiencing a "moral meltdown," we may be watching stories on child abductions, illegal drug use, or teenage pregnancies. In our private conversations, we may begin to talk about the lack of morals in society. In fact, we may begin to live our lives according to the types of stories we watch. We may be more suspicious of even friendly strangers, fearing they may try to kidnap our child. We may be unwilling to support laws legalizing medicinal marijuana, regardless of their merits, because we are concerned about possible increases in drug activity. We may also aggressively advocate an "abstinence-only" sex education program in schools, fearing that any other model would cause more unwanted pregnancies.

What occurs with each of these examples is what McLuhan asserts happens all the time: We become (sometimes unwittingly) manipulated by television. Our attitudes and experiences are directly influenced by what we watch on television.

A third assumption of Medium Theory has elicited quite a bit of popular conversation: Media connect the world. McLuhan used the phrase **global village** to describe how media tie the world into one great political, economical, social, and cultural system. Recall that although the phrase is almost a cliche these days, it was McLuhan—over forty years ago—who felt that the media can organize societies socially. Electronic media in particular have the ability to bridge cultures that would not have communicated prior to this connection.

global village
the notion that humans can no longer live in isolation, but rather will always be connected by continuous and instantaneous electronic media

The effect of this global village, according to McLuhan, is the ability to receive information instantaneously (an issue we return to later in the chapter). As a result, we should be concerned with global events, rather than remaining focused on our own communities. He observes that "the globe is no more than a village" (p. 5) and that we should feel responsible for others. Others "are now involved in our lives, as we in theirs, thanks to the electric media" (p. 5).

Let's revisit our opening example of Tiera Abrams to illustrate this assumption further. As a consumer of the Internet, Tiera frequently visits "chat rooms," which allow her to communicate with a number of different people at once. During this time, she encountered Marcus, whom she decided to meet. As a Canadian, Marcus would not normally visit the same social places as Tiera. It was electronic media that allowed this international relationship to get off the ground. If the two continue to see each other, they will naturally find out more about the other's family, community, and culture.

The global village of Marshall McLuhan follows the systems perspective we outlined in Chapter 3. You will recall that systems theorists believe that one part of a system will affect the entire system. Medium theorists believe that the action of one society will necessarily affect the entire global village. Therefore, floods in Europe, famine in Africa, and war in the Middle East affect the United States, Australia, and China. According to McLuhan, we can no longer live in isolation.

You have now been introduced to the primary assumptions of Medium Theory. McLuhan's theory relies heavily on a historical understanding of

Table 25.1   McLuhan's Media History

HISTORICAL EPOCH	PROMINENT TECHNOLOGY/ DOMINANT SENSE	McLUHAN'S COMMENTS
Tribal Era	Face-to-Face Contact/Hearing	"An oral or tribal society has the means of stability far beyond anything possible to a visual or civilized and fragmented world" (McLuhan & Fiore, 1968, p. 23).
Literate Era	Phonetic Alphabet/Seeing	"Western man [woman] has done little to study or to understand the effects of the phonetic alphabet in creating many of his [her] basic patterns of culture" (McLuhan, 1964, p. 82).
Print Era	Printing Press/Seeing	"Perhaps the most significant of the gifts of typography to man [woman] is that of detachment and noninvolvement—the power to act without reacting" (McLuhan, 1964, p. 173).
Electronic Era	Computer/Seeing, Hearing, Touching	"The computer is by all odds the most extraordinary of all the technological clothing ever devised . . . since it is the extension of our central nervous system" (McLuhan & Fiore, 1968, p. 35).

epoch
era or historical age

media. He felt that the media of a particular time period were instrumental in organizing societies. He identified four distinct time periods, or **epochs**, in history (see Table 25.1). We address each below.

Making Media History and Making "Sense"

McLuhan (1962; 1964) and Quentin Fiore (McLuhan & Fiore, 1967) claim that the media of an era define the essence of a society. They present four eras, or epochs, in media history (Table 25.1), each of which correspond to the dominant mode of communication of the time. Further, McLuhan contends that media act as extensions of the human senses. We explain each era below.

The Tribal Era

tribal era
age when oral tradition was embraced and hearing was the paramount sense

According to McLuhan, during the **tribal era**, hearing, smell, and taste were the dominant senses. During this time, McLuhan argues, cultures were "ear-centered" in that people heard with no real ability to censor messages. This era was characterized by the oral tradition of storytelling whereby people revealed their traditions, rituals, and values through the spoken word. In this era, the ear became the sensory "tribal chief" and for people, hearing was believing.

The Literate Era

This epoch, emphasized by the visual sense, was marked by the introduction of the alphabet. The eye became the dominant sensory organ. McLuhan and Fiore (1967) stated that the alphabet caused people to look at their environment in visual and spatial terms. McLuhan (1964) also felt that the alphabet made knowledge more accessible and "shattered the bonds of tribal man" (p. 173). Whereas the tribal era was characterized by people speaking, the **literate era** was a time when written communication flourished. People's messages became centered on linear and rational thinking. Out was storytelling; in was mathematics and other forms of analytic logic. This "scribal world" had the unintended consequence of forcing communities to become more individualistic rather than collectivistic (McLuhan & Fiore, 1967). People were able to get their information without help from their communities. This was the beginning of people communicating without the need to be face-to-face.

literate era
age when written communication flourished and the eye became the dominant sense organ

The Print Era

The invention of the printing press heralded the **print era** in civilization and the beginning of the industrial revolution. Although it was possible to do a great deal of printing by woodcut prior to this era, the printing press made it possible to make copies of essays, books, and announcements. This provided for even more permanency of record than in the literate age. The printing press also allowed people other than the elite to gain access to information. Further, people didn't have to rely on their memories for information as they had to do in the past.

print era
age when gaining information through the printed word was customary and seeing continued as the dominant sense

McLuhan (1964) observes that the book was "the first teaching machine" (p. 174). Consider his words today. Very few courses in college exist without a textbook. Even with technological teaching approaches such as distance learning or interactive television, the majority of courses still require textbooks. Books remain indispensable in the teaching–learning process.

Exemplifying the print era more specifically, McLuhan (1964) writes:

> Margaret Mead has reported that when she brought several copies of the same book to a Pacific island there was great excitement. The natives had seen books, but only one copy of each, which they had assumed to be unique. Their astonishment at the identical character of several books was a natural response to what is after all the most magical and potent aspect of print and mass production. It involves a principle of extension by homogenization that is the key to understanding Western power (p. 174).

What McLuhan notes here is that mass production produces citizens who are similar to each other. The same content is delivered over and over again by the same means. This visual-dependent era, however, produced a fragmented population because people could remain in isolation reading their mass-produced media.

The Electronic Era

Few can argue with the fact that the age we live in now is electronic. Interestingly, McLuhan (1964) and his colleague (McLuhan & Fiore, 1967) note that this epoch, characterized by the telegraph, telephone, typewriter, radio, and television, has brought us back to tribalization and the art of oral communication. Instead of books being the central repository of information, electronic media decentralized information to the extent that individuals are now one of several primary sources of information. This era has returned us to a primitive-like reliance on "talking" to each other. Today, though, we define "talking" differently than the way it occurred in the tribal era. We talk through television, radio, records/tapes/CDs, photographs, answering machines, cell phones, and e-mail. The **electronic era** allows different communities in different parts of the world to remain connected, a concept we discussed earlier as the global village.

McLuhan (1964) provocatively relates a description of various technologies in the electronic age:

electronic era
age in which electronic media pervades our senses, allowing for people across the world to be connected

> The telephone: speech without walls.
>
> The phonograph: music hall without walls.
>
> The photograph: museum without walls.
>
> The electric light: space without walls.
>
> The movie, radio, and TV: classroom without walls (p. 283).

The electronic era presents unique opportunities to reevaluate how media influence the people they serve. This age allows for ear and eye and voice to work together. See the Research Note for an illustration of this connection.

This historical presentation of media by McLuhan suggests that the primary media of an age prompts a certain sensory reaction in people. McLuhan and Fiore (1968) theorize that a **ratio of the senses** is required by people, which is a conversation of sorts between and among the senses. That is, a balance of the senses is required, regardless of the time in history. For instance, with the Internet, we reconcile a variety of senses, including visual stimulation of website pictures and the auditory arousal of downloaded music.

ratio of the senses
phrase referring to the way people adapt to their environment (through a balance of the senses)

The Medium Is the Message

Medium Theory is perhaps best known for the catchphrase **the medium is the message** (McLuhan 1964). Although followers of McLuhan continue to debate the precise meaning of this equation, it appears to represent McLuhan's scholarly values: The content of a mediated message is secondary to the medium (or communication channel). The medium has the ability to change how we think about others, ourselves, and the world around us. So, for instance, in our opening example of Tiera Abrams, what she and Marcus communicated is less important than that they communicated via a computer, the Internet, and e-mail.

the medium is the message
phrase referring to the power and influence of the medium—not the content—on a society

McLuhan did not dismiss the importance of content altogether. Rather, as Paul Levinson (2001) points out, McLuhan felt that content gets our attention more than the medium does. McLuhan thinks that although a message affects

Research Note

Haynes, W. L. (1990). Public speaking pedagogy in the media age. *Communication Education, 39,* 89–102.

This essay articulates the need to look at how public speaking is taught in the United States. Haynes comments that because students are living in an electronic age (epoch), courses in public speaking should begin to draw from the electronic media surrounding today's society. Relying on the traditional print media only will do a disservice to students. Haynes (1990) noted that "we must move beyond literate analytical scholarship to electronic synthetic means of seeking not literate knowledge but its electronic counterpart, *whatever that may be*" (p. 90).

Haynes invokes the writings of McLuhan in outlining the case for public speaking courses to be revamped. He states that our oral culture is now a culture "bombarded with 'vid-oral' communication" (p. 91). The author points to public speaking textbooks that fail to take into consideration the new media age in which we live. He envisions a vid-oral classroom where students are encouraged to rely more on interaction. Haynes believes that since television allows its viewers to be part of the world of the characters, "should we not expect media-conditioned audiences to demand at least as much from their speakers?" (p. 93). This vid-oral environment will help audience and speaker become the responsible conversationalists they should be.

The vid-oral public speaking classroom identified by Haynes is the O-I-C approach to learning. For instance, *orientation* requires the student to clarify intentions, then explain what he or she desires from the audience. Limited notes are fine; however, they should not interfere with the opportunity to interact with the audience.

The second step in preparing for public speaking is called *incubation.* This step stresses an "out of awareness processing" (p. 101), which essentially means that speakers should allow the mind time to process the material gathered during the orientation step.

Composition, the third step, is oral, not written. Haynes states that speakers should practice over and over again and imagine themselves in front of an audience. Each time the speech is practiced, the words and phrases may change, which has the benefit of making the final speech appear less rigid and more spontaneous. As composition proceeds, Haynes notes, the mind will edit, adapt, and change as it constructs new ways of preparing a speech.

Haynes is concerned with how conscious the speech-making process has become. He urges teachers of public speaking to engage in efforts that tap into the media age in which Western culture exists. He argues his point in the spirit of McLuhan: "we must seek ways to study the electronic media on their own terms" (p. 90).

our conscious state, it is the medium that largely affects our unconscious state (Soules, 2001). So, for example, we unconsciously embrace television as a medium while receiving a message broadcast around the world. Consider September 11, 2001, when the World Trade Center was hit by terrorists in planes. Many of us went to CNN immediately and instinctively, captivated by the horror and the images as they occurred. We were pretty much unconscious of the medium, but rather consumed with the message. Nonetheless, we turned to television again and again for updates as the days and months progressed, rather unaware of its importance in our lives. This represents McLuhan's hypothesis that the medium shapes the message and it is, ironically enough, our unawareness of the medium that makes a message all the more important.

McLuhan and Fiore (1967) claim that in addition to the medium being the message, the medium is the "massage." By changing one letter, they creatively presented readers with another view of media. It's not clear whether or not the authors were making a pun on the "mass-age" or whether they were reinforcing McLuhan's earlier writings on the power of the media. McLuhan and Fiore argue that not only are we influenced by the media, but we can become seduced by it. As a population, we are entranced with new technologies. For instance, it is now customary for national media such as the *New York Times* and *USA Today* to feature special sections on technology and culture. New gadgets, gizmos, and technological inventions (and their prices) are featured for those desiring the latest. Indeed, the medium massages the masses, is part of the "mess-age" (McLuhan & Parker, 1969), and can be understood in a "mass-age" (McLuhan & Nevitt, 1972).

We have presented several key assumptions and issues associated with Medium Theory. We have also discussed media in very broad terms. McLuhan felt that some unifying and systematic way of differentiating media was necessary. The result was an interesting analysis of hot and cool media.

Gauging the Temperature: Hot and Cool Media

In order to understand the "large structural changes in human outlook" (McLuhan, 1964, p. vi) of the 1960s, McLuhan set out to classify media. He explains that media can be classified as either hot or cool, language he borrowed from jazz slang. This classification system remains confounding to many scholars, and yet it is a pivotal aspect of Medium Theory. We distinguish between the two media below and provide examples of each in Figure 25.1.

hot media
high-definition communication that demands little involvement from a viewer, listener, or reader

Hot media is described as media that demand very little from a listener, reader, or viewer. Hot media is high-definition communication that has relatively complete sensory data; very little is left to the audience's imagination. Hot media, therefore, are low in audience participation. Meaning is essentially provided. An example of a hot medium is a movie, because it requires very little of us. We sit down, watch the film, react, maybe eat some popcorn, and then watch the credits. Hot media give the audience what they need—in this case, entertainment.

We should add that McLuhan believes that radio is a hot medium. He acknowledges that radio can serve as background sound, as noise-level control, or for listening pleasure. No involvement is needed with radio. However, McLuhan wrote before the proliferation of radio talk shows. Would he consider radio to be low involvement today?

cool media
low-definition communication that demands active involvement from a viewer, listener, or reader

Unlike hot media, **cool media** require a high degree of participation; they are low definition. Little is provided by the medium, so much has to be filled in by the listener, reader, or viewer. Cool media require audiences to create meaning through high sensory involvement. Consider, for instance, cartoons. Generally, we get a few frames of illustrations and perhaps some words of phrases. Cartoons are low definition and provide very little visual information. We need to determine the meaning of the words and the pictures, and even supply missing words or ideas that are not provided in the cartoon.

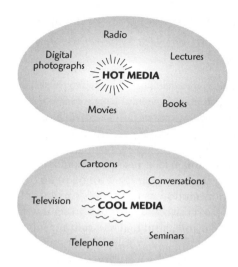

**Figure 25.1
Examples of Hot
and Cool Media**

Let's make one more point about cool media. Interestingly, McLuhan (1964) contends that television can be considered a cool medium. He argues that TV is a medium that requires viewers to be actively involved. In fact, he notes that television "engages you. You have to be *with* it" (p. 312). Yet, with the digital age upon us, television has taken on new meaning that perhaps even McLuhan could never have imagined. Would he still consider television a cool medium today?

To illustrate the hot and cool media, McLuhan analyzed the 1960 presidential debates between John F. Kennedy and Richard Nixon. McLuhan discovered that for those who watched the debate on television, Kennedy had won because he exuded an objective, cool persona, perfect for the cool medium. For those who listened to the debates on the radio (a hot medium), Nixon was the winner. He was considered hot (which, in fact, his sweating showed he was!). So, the medium influences others' perceptions.

The Circle Is Complete: The Tetrad

We continue our discussion of Medium Theory by examining the most recent expansion of McLuhan's thinking about the media. With his son, Eric (McLuhan & McLuhan, 1988), and to respond to those who believed that there was no scientific grounding in his work, McLuhan developed a way to look further into the effects of technology on society. His expansion of Medium Theory included a thorough discussion of the **laws of media**.

Although McLuhan's earlier work identified in this chapter did not fully take into account the advent of the computer, his posthumous work with his son took into consideration the influence of the Internet. Their work was an effort to bring Medium Theory full circle: Technology affects communication through new technology, the impact of the new technology affects society, and the changes in society cause further changes in technology. McLuhan and

laws of media
further expansion
of Medium Theory
with focus on the im-
pact of technology
on society

tetrad
organizing concept to understand the laws of media

McLuhan (1988) offer the **tetrad** as an organizing concept that allows scholars to understand the past, present, and current effects of media.

To give us a new way of looking at the role of technology in our culture, McLuhan and McLuhan (1988) offer four laws of media, phrased as questions: (1) What does media *enhance?* (2) What does media make *obsolete?* (3) What does media *retrieve?* (4) What does media *reverse?* (See Table 25.2). Let's examine each and identify examples of their role in culture. We pay particular attention to the role of the Internet in our discussion.

Enhancement

enhancement
law that states media amplifies or strengthens society

The first law of media is **enhancement**; that is, media enhance or amplify society. The telephone enhanced the spoken word found in face-to-face conversations. Radio, of course, amplified the voice across distance. Television amplified the word and the visual across continents.

The Internet has enhanced society in different ways. First, it has the potential to enhance a number of senses, including sight and sound. Second, the existence of the Internet has enhanced the accessibility of information. For instance, we can now obtain birth records, credit card balances, and missing person information over the Internet. Third, the Internet can enhance class division. The "haves and the have-nots" exist along this information superhighway. Finally, decentralization of authority is enhanced by the Internet. No longer do our political leaders solely possess information; that information becomes available online.

Table 25.2 Laws of Media

LAWS OF MEDIA	DESCRIPTION
Enhancement	What does the medium enhance or amplify?
Obsolescence	What does the medium push aside or make obsolete?
Retrieval	What does the medium retrieve from the past?
Reversal	When pushed to its limits, what does the medium reverse or flip into?

Obsolescence

McLuhan and McLuhan (1988) note that the second law of media is that media eventually render something obsolete or out-of-date. Television made radio obsolete, although many of us continue to turn to radio each day while we drive. Levinson (2001) notes that radio rendered motion pictures obsolete, which in turn resulted in fewer movies to watch. The VCR may have also attempted to make movies obsolete, but we know that its efforts have been only somewhat successful.

The Internet, too, has brought about **obsolescence**. For example, as we learned earlier, the global village now exists, thanks largely to the Internet. The geographical splits are pretty hard to find; even the remote villages of Africa are becoming accessible by the Internet. Second, the Internet is slowly targeting micromedia (specific audiences) rather than macromedia (large masses), thereby making traditional media outlets such as CBS, NBC, and ABC change their news reporting. Finally, face-to-face dialogues are becoming outdated with the Internet. Former "tribal" conversations are now electronically derived.

obsolescence
law that states media eventually renders something out-of-date

Retrieval

The third law is **retrieval**, meaning that media recover or restore something that was once lost. What older, previously obsolesced media is brought back? Television, for instance, restored the importance of the visual that radio did not achieve, but that was once in face-to-face conversations. Radio retrieved the town crier, the prominent voice of newsworthy events over 200 years ago in the United States. Print retrieved the tribe's universality of knowledge. And the Internet recovers a community that was once lost to other media. For instance, chat rooms where people like Tiera Abrams from our opening vignette visit have electronically rekindled conversations that flourished before radio and television.

retrieval
law that states media restores something that was once lost

Reversal

When "pushed to the limit of its potential" (McLuhan & McLuhan, 1988, p. 99), what do media produce or become? What do media reverse into? When too many constraints exist on a medium, it will "overheat" and become ineffective. **Reversal** contains characteristics of the system from which it arose. For instance, the public's desire to have access to entertainment in a relatively cheap medium led to the creation of radio dramas and comedy programs. The need to "see" what was heard led to the creation of these programs on television. Yet we can videotape television programs and what was once seen by millions of people at the same time is reversed into private videotaped "performances." Television, then, reversed into the early days of the print era when people could consume media privately.

The Internet—as a medium pushed to its potential—reverses society into a new and unique place. The Internet has the potential to bring tribal people together when they discuss websites or chat room conversations with each other. Looking at the number of people who "surf the net" each day, we can

reversal
law that states media will—when pushed to their limit—produce or become something

T*I*P

Theory * Into * Practice

The theme of technological obsolescence is depicted in an essay by Rick Lyman in the *New York Times*. Lyman notes that the videocassette recorder is now being replaced by digital videodiscs in the United States. He notes that about a third of households now have DVD players. Many film companies are making more money from DVD releases than from a first-run in movie theatres. Lyman compares this conversion to the time when people began to replace their vinyl records with discs.

Lyman quotes the president of Warner Home Video to demonstrate the technological phenomenon under way: "In five years, it has gone from zero to 30 million households, and a quarter of those have more than one DVD player. Nothing else has come close to doing that in such a short time, not CDs, not VCRs, not personal computers, not even television itself" (pp. A1, A15). Lyman notes that the surge in interest in DVDs can be attributed to their relatively low cost, their quality compared to videocassettes, and the fact that many games and CDs can be played on DVDs. Therefore, switching to digital videodiscs serves more than a single purpose. Currently, over $5 billion is spent on DVDs in the United States.

Is the videocassette recorder now obsolete? Lyman presents some evidence that the DVD may be eclipsing the VCR. For instance, the average household used to purchase five videocassettes per year; currently, the average consumer is now buying 15 DVDs per year. Lyman also observes that personal computers have DVD drives, enabling a "cross pollenization" of media. Finally, large electronic chain stores like Circuit City have stopped selling videotapes altogether with Wal-Mart soon to follow.

Future projections of the DVD indicate that the VCR may become a technological relic. The "bells and whistles" (p. A13) associated with a DVD cannot be ignored. Interviews with filmmakers, extra scenes not found in the original release, and even film gaffes and bloopers are found on DVDs. The audience has become interactive, then, with the DVD and therefore has become charmed by its presence.

Source: Lyman, 2002.

TIP Follow-up

Discuss whether or not you believe that the DVD is consistent with McLuhan's belief that the "medium is the message." Why do you suppose Western society is supportive of the DVD when the VCR has not been in existence very long?

confidently state that the Internet can isolate people just as television can. With the ability to download music, television shows, and short films, the Internet has reversed itself into a medium with significant visual and auditory appeal. Finally, the Internet is a medium that "flips" on its user. That is, although it can serve to erode power, it can also perpetuate power differences among people. As a result, the Internet provides opportunities for both.

Carrying the McLuhan Banner: Postman and Meyrowitz

Two influential contemporary scholars have worked to integrate McLuhan's thinking into their own scholarship. Neil Postman (1992), in *Technopoly: The*

Surrender of Culture to Technology, and Joshua Meyrowitz (1985), in *No Sense of Place,* remain influential students and thinkers associated with McLuhan and Medium Theory. We close our discussion with an overview of this scholarly expansion of Medium Theory.

Postman's work has "mined the dark side of McLuhan" (Levinson, 2001). That is, Postman hypothesized that technology negatively changes the fabric of society. He coined the term **technopoly**, which means that we live in a culture in which technology dominates our thinking and behaviors. In a technopoly, Postman argues, technological tools serve to take over the culture in which they thrive. We live in a society where being technologically driven may result in being driven mad! We trust that our technology will bring us safety and salvation and seem to lose any sense of humility, discipline, and rationality regarding our reliance on and trust in current media. As a result, Postman laments that "tradition, social mores, myth, politics, ritual, and religion have to fight for their lives" (p. 28). Postman, like McLuhan, asks whether or not we want to live in a culture with such unwavering dependence on technology.

In addition to Postman, Joshua Meyrowitz's research interconnects with McLuhan's work. Meyrowitz agrees with McLuhan that electronic media have social consequences. Meyrowitz expands the notion that power relations and social class can be traced to electronic media. He draws on sociology research to conclude that media have brought about a blurring of formerly distinct roles or places. He states that "many Americans may no longer seem to 'know their place' because the traditionally interlocking components of 'place' have been split apart by electronic media. Wherever one is now—at home, at work, or in the car—one may be in touch and tuned in" (p. 308). Meyrowitz points to television. For instance, examine talk shows and you can get a sense of how the blurring of places occurs. What was once private (for instance, discussing your mother's alcoholism) is now public on Jerry Springer. Masculine and feminine roles now blur. Even our political leaders are now at the level of everyone else. In fact, in small states such as Maine, the governor can be contacted directly by phone, e-mail, or fax!

Both Postman and Meyrowitz remain thoughtful, articulate, and effective stewards of Marshall McLuhan. They carry the banner which boldly proclaims that electronic media have unraveled Western society's foundation. To be sure, the two scholars prompt us to consider McLuhan's work in more contemporary ways. As Gary Wolf (1996) noted in *Wired* magazine: "McLuhan is relevant again" (p. 124).

technopoly
a term coined by Postman that means we live in a society dominated by technology

Critique and Closing

You probably have already figured out that Marshall McLuhan has caused quite a reaction in both academic and public circles. His ideas are provocative, and at times, have been unilaterally dismissed by many. In fact, if you reviewed his original work, you may be challenged by the frequent eccentricity of his writing style. Some have labeled his thinking "McLuhanacy" (Gordon, 1982), while others feel his writing is equivalent to "genre bending" (Carey, 1998).

McLuhan's work and reputation, however, have been invoked with considerable regard. *Wired* magazine named him their "Patron Saint," and *Life* magazine called him the "Oracle of the Electronic Age." There exists a concentration in McLuhan Studies at the University of Toronto, a McLuhan newsletter, symposia on McLuhan's research, a McLuhan festival, and even a secondary high school in Canada named the Marshall McLuhan Catholic School. It's hard to escape his influence both in research and in societies across the world.

Medium Theory has been met with some enthusiasm. James Carey (1998) observes that McLuhan's work "represented a genuine and multifaceted intellectual advance that has become part of our inheritance . . . and [he] was a critical figure in our understanding of culture, media, and communication" (pp. 294, 306). Researchers continue to embrace several components of his theory (e.g., Gow, 2001; Rogers, 2000), thereby making Medium Theory a heuristic theory. Further, the fact that the theory remains a comment on the role of technology in our culture reflects the utility of the theory. Sue Barnes (2003), for example, has explored the timely role of online relationships in our society (like that of Tiera Abrams), embracing the technology-reliant society on which McLuhan commented.

Despite these rather glowing assessments, Medium Theory has come under attack for a variety of reasons. Media scholars Stanley Baran and Dennis Davis (2003) note that the theory is "overly optimistic" about the role of technology in society. That is, McLuhan may have put too much emphasis on how much technology influences society. George Gordon (1982) is more direct: "Not one bit of sustained and replicated scientific evidence, inductive or deductive, has to date justified any one of McLuhan's most famous slogans, metaphors, or dicta" (p. 42). Dwight Macdonald (1967) also attacked his writing by noting that "he has looted all culture from cave painting to *Mad* magazine for fragments to shore up his system against ruin" (p. 203).

A great deal of criticism has been directed at McLuhan's use of words and his clarity. To some, his ideas make little sense. Some writers believe that McLuhan failed to define his words carefully and used too much exaggeration. In the *Chronicle of Higher Education*, Paul Levinson (1999) concludes that his work "was not your professor's writing—no long paragraphs of logically developed argument" (p. B10). He writes in a zigzag fashion, weaving in one point after another with no apparent topic sentence or sustained idea. Although some writers indict this process, McLuhan (1967) offers no apology: "I don't explain—I explore" (p. i).

Marshall McLuhan and Medium Theory will continue to resonate for years to come. Perhaps one day we will revisit McLuhan's original thinking on historical epochs in media history! New media will continue to evolve in our society and so will the application of McLuhan's thinking. Was McLuhan an absurd reactionary? Or was McLuhan a cultural prophet? On his gravestone are the words "The Truth Will Set You Free." Did McLuhan think he discovered Truth? Or, even in his death, does he continue to play with our imaginations? Perhaps McLuhan's biographer, Philip Marchand (1989), best illustrates McLuhan's contribution to the study of media: "McLuhan's comments had at

least one virtue: they seemed to suggest that the world was more interesting than any of us had previously thought it to be" (p. xiii).

Discussion Starters

1. Discuss whether Tiera Abrams's experience with an online relationship is representative of the future of relationships or if similar experiences will eventually fade away.

2. How might Medium theorists like Marshall McLuhan react to the current news on television today? What would be his major criticisms and his major objections? What would he be particularly interested in?

3. Do you agree or disagree with McLuhan regarding television being a cool medium? Use examples to defend your view.

4. Suppose you were asked to have dinner with scholars Neil Postman and Joshua Meyrowitz. What types of questions would you ask them? How would the conversation proceed?

5. Interpret and comment on the following statement: "Technology is the end of our beginning." Use examples to defend your view.

6. What is your impression of theorists who do not explain their concepts in detail or fully interpret their ideas? Does this provide an opportunity for multiple interpretations of the theory? Does it cause more frustration for researchers trying to understand the theory? Does it matter? Use examples.

Terms for Review

bias of communication	electronic era
global village	ratio of the senses
epoch	the medium is the message
tribal era	hot media
literate era	cool media
print era	laws of media

tetrad
enhancement
obsolescence

retrieval
reversal
technopoly

Online Learning Center

Visit the Online Learning Center at www.mhhe.com/west2. Use the multiple-choice and true/false quizzes to help you prepare for exams, and the glossary, crossword puzzles, and flashcards to further your knowledge of key terms.

Culture and Diversity

WE ALL BELONG TO A CULTURAL COMMUNITY. SOME of us are members of a culture that has a long history in the United States. Others of us belong to cultures that have recently found prominence in this country. As you learned in Chapter 1, the term *culture* has many different meanings. The theories presented in this section underscore the various interpretations of culture.

We have selected four communication theories that fall under "Culture and Diversity": Face-Negotiation Theory, Standpoint Theory, Muted Group Theory, and Communication Accommodation Theory. We chose these theories because they represent a cross-section of what it means to be a member of a cultural community.

To this end, each of these theories takes into consideration what happens when we communicate with people who come from different cultural backgrounds with different cultural expectations. For example, Face-Negotiation Theory points to the cultural effects of conflict. The theory answers the question "How do members from two different types of cultures manage their interpersonal conflict?" Standpoint Theory states that people view the world according to their position in life. So the theory necessarily takes into consideration socioeconomic class and its application to a variety of marginalized populations, including women, the poor, gay men and lesbians, and many racial and ethnic groups. In Muted Group Theory, women are viewed as less powerful and less eloquent because their words have been provided by men to suit men's experiences. Finally, focusing on the role of both verbal and nonverbal communication in conversations, Communication Accommodation Theory rests on the belief that people from various cultural communities will adjust their communication to accommodate others.

Each theory in this section centers on the role that society plays in the communication between and among cultural groups. Reading and learning about the theories will expose you to a variety of important themes: dominance, control, oppression, power, and cultural identity.

CHAPTER 26

Face-Negotiation Theory

Professor Jie Yang and Kevin Johnston

The first ten weeks of her academic term in the United States had gone quite well. As a faculty member from China, Jie Yang felt that the communication courses that she taught were well attended by students who were eager to participate. Students frequently asked her questions about what Chinese life was like, often concentrating on college life in particular. Jie was more than willing to answer their questions. She, too, had asked students about life in the United States and about what students thought of Chinese–U.S. relations. Although there were a few intercultural difficulties in translation, overall she felt that excellent relationships had been cultivated in such a short period of time. She had no reason to think that things wouldn't continue to unfold comfortably.

Her instincts, however, were incorrect. As her intercultural communication class began to prepare for their individual presentations, class members were showing signs of tension. In addition to a written final project on a research topic of their choice, Professor Yang had asked that each student provide a brief oral presentation of what they had studied. Throughout the term, she had listened to student complaints about the library staff, about how difficult it was to do research in their small college library, and about the time crunch. Still, she believed in her assignments and didn't back down despite the complaining.

One evening after class, Kevin Johnston, a graduating senior, challenged Professor Yang directly. He complained that there simply wasn't going to be enough time to complete his final presentation. He believed that Professor Yang was asking too much of him, considering that he had missed two weeks of class early in the term because of pneumonia. "It's not fair," Kevin lamented. "This is too much for me right now."

Professor Yang was sympathetic to Kevin's concerns. She agreed that he was under some pressure and reassured him that he was capable of finishing his project despite his past attendance record. "You're an excellent student, Kevin," the professor related. "And based on what I see, I know that you're very upset. But you're a hard worker and I know you want to do your best. You surely don't want me to treat you any differently than the others. Everyone is under pressure here."

Kevin wouldn't hear of it. "This is too much! I refuse to believe that you won't let a good student have some extra time. It's not like I'm not going to do it." Kevin continued by outlining his plan. If she would give him an "incomplete," then he would turn in the final paper two weeks after the class ended. "I'll try to give my presentation on what I've written," he continued, "but I'm not sure it's going to be that good."

Professor Yang was growing weary of the discussion. "Kevin, you underestimate yourself. You have a few weeks left. I trust you'll be able to finish it thoroughly."

This theory is based on the research of **Stella Ting-Toomey.**

The tone of the conversation quickly changed. "Look," Kevin interrupted, "I don't think you know the American system yet. I'm being up front and honest about the fact that I won't be able to finish the project. You keep telling me that I will. I know that you've only been in the States a short time, but you've got to give students a chance. Right now, I feel like I'm talking to a brick wall." His voice now matched the passion of his words.

Professor Yang wouldn't concede. "Kevin, in this class, we all have time constraints and outside responsibilities. I, like others, have a great deal to accomplish before the end of the term. But we can't simply abandon our responsibilities. You're a reasonable student. I'll make you a deal. How about if you turn in a detailed outline of your paper,

I'll approve it; you write about two-thirds of the paper and then see if you have time to finish the rest."

Kevin followed her lead. "I can't promise you that my paper is gonna be the best. But if you'll look it over before I turn it in, that will help a lot."

"All any professor can ask is for students to do their best," Professor Yang replied. "And you should know that I do expect you to do your best. I'm sure you will get everything done on time."

As Kevin walked away from his conversation, he couldn't help but think that a different approach to his conflict might have had a different result. He knew that he had a great deal of work to do and knew that the boundaries were clearly set for him by Professor Yang.

Working out conflicts like Kevin's is not easy. In the United States particularly, individuals try to manage their conflicts in a solution-oriented manner, frequently disregarding the other's cultural values or norms. Although people from a number of different cultures share Kevin's approach, some cultures would not endorse his strategies for conflict resolution.

Kevin finds himself in a situation common to many students. Yet, unlike many students, Kevin overtly confronts Professor Yang about her expectations. Although he was given the assignment in the early part of the term, he knows that the remaining time will not be sufficient to complete the task. He then tries to negotiate a different result with his professor. His dominating approach does little to rattle Professor Yang; she calmly works toward closure on this conflict.

Kevin's conflict with Professor Yang underscores the thinking behind Face-Negotiation Theory by Stella Ting-Toomey. The theory is multifaceted, incorporating research from intercultural communication, conflict, politeness, and "facework." Face-Negotiation Theory has cross-cultural appeal and application because Ting-Toomey has focused on a number of different cultural populations, including those in Japan, South Korea, Taiwan, China, and the United States. This is underscored by Ting-Toomey's (1988) comments: "Culture provides the larger interpretive frame in which 'face' and 'conflict style' can be meaningfully expressed and maintained" (p. 213). Face-Negotiation Theory is one of the few theories that explicitly acknowledge that people from different cultures perceive and manage conflict differently. Ting-Toomey asserts that members from different cultural backgrounds have various concerns for the "face" of others. This concern leads them to handle conflict in different ways. These comments form the backdrop to Face-Negotiation Theory.

Our opening example of Kevin Johnston and Professor Yang represents the heart of Face-Negotiation Theory. Representing two different cultural backgrounds, Kevin and his professor seem to have two different interpretations of how to manage the difficulty that Kevin is having with his final project. Kevin clearly desires to turn his work in late, whereas Professor Yang wants him to turn it in with the rest of the class. She tries to ease the conflict between the two by highlighting Kevin's qualities, and clearly she does not want to embarrass Kevin. Rather, she encourages him to work out this conflict by focusing on his ability to get things done, not the remaining time left in the term.

Professor Yang and Kevin Johnston engage in behavior that researchers have termed *face*. Because face is an extension of one's self-concept, it has become the focus of much research in a number of fields of study. In fact, Face-Negotiation Theory rests primarily on this concept. Let's first interpret the meaning behind the term and then examine the central assumptions of the theory.

About Face

Ting-Toomey bases much of her theory on face and facework. Face is clearly an important feature of life, a metaphor for self-image that David Ho (1976) believes pervades all aspects of social life. The concept of face has evolved in interpretation over the years. It originates with the Chinese, who, as Ho argues, have two conceptualizations of face: *lien* and *mien-tzu,* two terms describing identity and ego.

According to Ho, "face can be more important than life itself" (p. 867). Erving Goffman (1967) is generally credited with situating face in contemporary Western research. He noted that **face** is the image of the self that people display in their conversations with others. Ting-Toomey and her colleagues (Oetzel, Ting-Toomey, Yokochi, Masumoto, & Takai, 2000) observe that face pertains to a favorable self-worth and/or projected other worth in interpersonal situations. People do not "see" another's face; rather, face is a metaphor for the boundaries that people have in their relationships with others. Goffman described face as something that is maintained, lost, or strengthened. At the time of his writing, Goffman did not envision that the term would be applied to close relationships. As a sociologist, he believed that face and all that it entailed was more applicable to the study of social groups. Over time, however, the study of face has been applied to a number of contexts, including close relationships and small groups.

face
a metaphor for the public image people display

Ting-Toomey incorporates some of the thinking from research on politeness that concludes that the desire for face is a universal concern (Brown & Levinson, 1978). Ting-Toomey (1988; 1991) expands on Goffman's thinking and argues that face is a projected image of one's self and the claim of self-respect in a relationship. She believes that face "entails the presentation of a civilized front to another individual" (Ting-Toomey, 1994a, p. 1) and that face is an identity that two people conjointly define in a relational episode. Ting-Toomey and her colleague Beth Ann Cocroft (1994) succinctly identify face as a "pancultural phenomenon" (p. 310), meaning that individuals in all cultures share and manage face; face cuts across all cultures.

Regarding our opening story, Ting-Toomey and other Face-Negotiation theorists would be interested in knowing that Professor Yang is from China and Kevin Johnston is American. Their cultural variability influences the way that they relate to each other and the way face is enacted. That is, Ting-Toomey believes that although face is a universal concept, there are various representations of it in various cultures. Face needs exist in all cultures, but all cultures do not manage the needs similarly. Ting-Toomey contends that face can be interpreted in two primary ways: face concern and face need. **Face concern** may relate to either one's own face or the face of another. In other words, there is a self-concern and an other-concern. Face concern answers the question, Do I want attention drawn toward myself or toward another? **Face need** refers to an inclusion–autonomy dichotomy. That is, Do I want to be associated with others (inclusion) or do I want dissociation (autonomy)?

face concern
interest in maintaining one's face or the face of others
face need
desire to be associated or disassociated with others

Face and Politeness Theory

As we noted earlier, Ting-Toomey was influenced by research on politeness. Penelope Brown and Stephen Levinson's (1978) politeness theory contends that people will use a politeness strategy based on the perception of face threat. The researchers drew from over a dozen different cultures around the world and discovered that two types of universal needs exist: positive face needs and negative face needs. **Positive face** is the desire to be liked and admired by significant others in our lives; **negative face** refers to the desire to be autonomous and unconstrained. Karen Tracy and Sheryl Baratz (1994) note that these "face wants" are part and parcel of relationships. They support their claim as follows:

positive face
desire to be liked and admired by others
negative face
desire to be autonomous and free from others

> Recognition of existing face wants explains why a college student who wanted to borrow a classmate's notes typically would not ask for them boldly ("Lend me your notes, would you?"), but more frequently would ask in a manner that paid attention to a person's negative face wants ("Would it be at all possible for me to borrow your notes for just an hour? I'll xerox them and get them back to you right away.") (p. 288)

Brown and Levinson's research illustrates a dilemma for individuals who try to meet both types of face needs in a conversation. Trying to satisfy one face need usually affects the other face need. For instance, our opening example shows that Professor Yang wants to have Kevin work at achieving his full potential. Her positive face needs, however, are met with the challenges of putting in more time with Kevin, thereby costing her negative face needs.

Facework

When communicators' positive or negative face is threatened, they tend to seek some recourse or way to restore their or their partner's face. Ting-Toomey (1994a), following Brown and Levinson, defines this as **facework,** or the "actions taken to deal with the face wants of one and/or the other" (p. 8). In other words, facework pertains to how people make whatever they're doing consistent with their face. Ting-Toomey equates facework with a "communication dance that tiptoes" between respect for one's face and the face of another. So

facework
actions used to deal with face needs/wants of self and others

Professor Yang's comments to Kevin about his ability to complete the project and presentation illustrate how the professor simultaneously saves her face (not reneging on the assignment) and also Kevin's face (providing him praise).

Te-Stop Lim and John Bowers (1991) extend the discussion by identifying three types of facework: tact, solidarity, and approbation. First, **tact facework** refers to the extent that one respects another's autonomy. This allows a person freedom to act as he or she pleases while minimizing any impositions that may restrict this freedom. For instance, Professor Yang engages in tact facework with Kevin while he relates his problems with the course assignments. She could, of course, respond to him by stating that he should just keep quiet and work, but instead she uses tact facework strategies—she asks him for suggestions while avoiding directives.

The second type of facework, **solidarity facework,** pertains to a person accepting the other as a member of an in-group. Solidarity enhances the connection between two speakers. That is, differences are minimized and commonalities are highlighted through informal language and shared experiences. For instance, Professor Yang notes that, like Kevin, she, too, has responsibilities, and people cannot simply go back on their duties because of a time crunch. Her conversational style reflects an approachable professor, not one who uses language reflecting a status difference.

The final type of facework is **approbation facework,** which involves minimizing blame and maximizing praise of another. Approbation facework exists when an individual focuses less on the negative aspects of another and more on the positive aspects. It is clear that despite her real feelings about Kevin's experiences, Professor Yang employs approbation facework by noting that he is a hard worker and an excellent student. She also explains that he has the ability to get everything accomplished. In other words, she recognizes Kevin's positive attributes while avoiding blame.

Our introductory comments on face and facework form an important backdrop to the understanding of Face-Negotiation Theory. The theory proposed by Ting-Toomey also rests on a number of other issues needing attention and clarification. We begin to unravel the theory in more detail by presenting three key assumptions of the theory.

Assumptions of Face-Negotiation Theory

A number of assumptions of Face-Negotiation Theory take into consideration the key components of the theory: face, conflict, and culture. With that in mind, the following guide the thinking of Ting-Toomey's theory:

- Self-identity is important in interpersonal interactions, with individuals negotiating their identities differently across cultures.
- The management of conflict is mediated by face and culture.
- Certain acts threaten one's projected self-image (face).

The first assumption highlights **self-identity,** or the personal features or character attributes of an individual. In their discussion of face, William

tact facework
extent to which a person respects another's autonomy

solidarity facework
accepting another as a member of an in-group

approbation facework
focusing less on the negative aspects of another and more on the positive aspects

self-identity
personal attributes of another

The Theory Connection

How does Ting-Toomey's conceptualization of the "self" relate to the conceptualization of "self" in the Coordinated Management of Meaning? Interpret the term *self* from each theoretical position and provide examples.

Cupach and Sandra Metts (1994) observe that when people meet, they present an image of who they are in the interaction. This image is "an identity that he or she wants to assume and wants others to accept" (p. 3). Self-identity includes a person's collective experiences, thoughts, ideas, memories, and plans. People's self-identities do not remain stagnant but rather are negotiated in their interactions with others. People have a concern with both their own identity or face (self-face) and the identity or face of another (other-face).

Just as culture influences self-identity, the manner in which individuals project their self-identities varies across cultures. Mary Jane Collier (1998) relates that cultural identity is enacted and "contested in particular historical, political, economic, and social contexts" (p. 132). Delores Tanno and Alberto Gonzalez (1998) note that there are "sites of identity," which they define as "the physical, intellectual, social, and political locations where identity develops its dimensions" (p. 4). Self-identity, therefore, is influenced by time and experience. Consider, for example, the self-identity of a politician as she begins her new term in office. She is certainly going to be overwhelmed and perhaps frustrated by her new position and the responsibilities that go along with it. Yet, over time and with experience, that frustration will be replaced with confidence and a new perspective on her identity as a representative of others.

Inherent in this first assumption is the belief that individuals in all cultures hold a number of different self-images and that they negotiate these images continuously. Ting-Toomey (1993) states that a person's sense of self is both conscious and unconscious. That is, in scores of different cultures, people carry images that they habitually or strategically present to others. Ting-Toomey believes that how we perceive our sense of self and how we wish others to perceive us are paramount to our communication experiences.

The second assumption of Face-Negotiation Theory relates to conflict, which is a central component of the theory. Conflict in this theory, however, works in tandem with face and culture. For Ting-Toomey (1994b), conflict can damage the social face of individuals and can serve to reduce the relational closeness between two people. As she relates, conflict is a "forum" for face loss and face humiliation. Conflict threatens both partners' face, and when there is an incompatible negotiation over how to resolve the conflict (such as insulting the other, imposing one's will, and so forth), the conflict can exacerbate the situation. Ting-Toomey states that the way humans are socialized into their culture influences how they will manage conflict. That is, some cultures, like the United States, value the open airing of differences between two people; other

cultures believe conflict should be handled discreetly. We return to these cultural orientations a bit later in the chapter.

This confluence of conflict, face, and culture can be exemplified in our story of Professor Yang and Kevin Johnston. It is apparent that Kevin's conflict with Professor Yang centers on his desire to receive an "incomplete" and her determination to have him complete the project. Because Professor Yang does not acquiesce to his wishes, Kevin tries to maintain his face by agreeing to his professor's compromise. In other words, he expresses a need to preserve his face with his professor. And, as we mentioned earlier, Professor Yang saves Kevin's face by lauding his abilities. This face-saving seems to prevent an escalation of conflict between the student and his professor. Finally, we note that Professor Yang is from China, a culture that Ting-Toomey (1988) identifies as being more concerned with creating positive face than the United States.

A third assumption of Face-Negotiation Theory pertains to the effects that various acts have on one's face. Incorporating politeness research, Ting-Toomey (1988) asserts that face-threatening acts (FTAs) threaten either the positive or the negative face of the interactants. FTAs can be either direct or indirect and occur when people's desired identity is challenged (Tracy, 1990). Direct FTAs are more threatening to the face of others, whereas indirect FTAs are less so.

Ting-Toomey and Mark Cole (1990) note that two actions make up the face-threatening process: face-saving and face restoration. **Face-saving** involves efforts to prevent events that either elicit vulnerability or impair one's image. Face-saving often prevents embarrassment. For instance, one of your author's best friend's primary language is French. Although he does speak fluent English, he periodically uses French phrases in his conversations with others. Because others are usually not prepared for this, your author introduces him as someone whose primary language is French. In this example, your author is using a face-saving technique.

face-saving
efforts to avoid embarrassment or vulnerability

Face restoration occurs after the loss of face has happened. Ting-Toomey and Cole observe that people attempt to restore face in response to the events. For instance, people's excuses are face-restoration techniques when embarrassing events occur (Cupach & Metts, 1994). Excuses ("I thought it was her job") and justifications ("I'm not a morning person") are commonplace in face restoration. These face-maintenance strategies and their relationship to each other are represented in Figure 26.1.

face restoration
strategy used to preserve autonomy and avoid loss of face

451

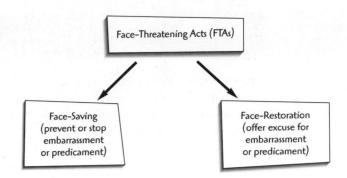

Figure 26.1
Face-Maintenance
Framework
Source: Adapted
from Ting-Toomey
& Cole, 1990.

So far, we have detailed face and facework as well as three primary assumptions of Face-Negotiation Theory. We now turn our attention to a discussion of additional dimensions of the theory. First, we explore individualism and collectivism, and then we examine how conflict functions in the theory.

Individualistic and Collectivistic Cultures

Culture, according to Ting-Toomey (1988), is not a static variable. It is interpreted along many dimensions. To this end, she examines culture and how it interrelates with face and conflict by employing thinking derived from both Harry Triandis (1972; 1988) and Geert Hofstede (1980). Both were instrumental in identifying the cultural variability used to explain cultural differences in behavior. Culture can be organized around two ends of a continuum: individualism and collectivism. At one end is a culture that places a premium on the value of individual identity; at the other end is a culture that values group identity. Individualistic cultures are "independent self" cultures, and collectivistic cultures are "interdependent self" cultures. Cultures across the world vary in individualism and collectivism (Table 26.1). These two dimensions play a prominent role in the way that facework and conflict are managed.

Ting-Toomey and her colleagues Ge Gao, Paula Trubisky, Shizhong Yang, Hak Soo Kim, Sung-Ling Lin, and Tsukasa Nishida (1991) clarify that individualism and collectivism apply not only to national cultures but also to co-cultures within national cultures. That is, different racial and ethnic groups within the United States may vary in their individualism and collectivism. For example, Ting-Toomey and her colleagues (1991) observe that whereas many European Americans in the United States identify with individualistic values and beliefs, when first-generation immigrant groups from Mexico or Japan arrive, they tend to retain their collectivistic orientation. Let's explore these two concepts further.

Individualism and Collectivism

individualism
a cultural value that
places emphasis on
the individual over
the group

In chapter 6, we briefly discussed these terms. You may recall that when people emphasize the individual over the group, they are articulating an individualistic perspective. **Individualism** refers to the tendency of people to highlight indi-

Table 26.1

Rankings of Individualism and Collectivism Around the World*

COUNTRY	RANKING	COUNTRY	RANKING
USA	1	India	21
Australia	2	Japan	22
Great Britain	3	Argentina	23
Canada	4	Iran	24
Netherlands	5	Brazil	25
New Zealand	6	Turkey	26
Italy	7	Greece	27
Belgium	8	Philippines	28
Denmark	9	Mexico	29
Sweden	10	Portugal	30
France	11	Yugoslavia	31
Ireland	12	Hong Kong	32
Norway	13	Chile	33
Switzerland	14	Singapore	34
Germany	15	Thailand	35
South Africa	16	Taiwan	36
Finland	17	Peru	37
Austria	18	Pakistan	38
Israel	19	Colombia	39
Spain	20	Venezuela	40

*The lower the score, the more individualistic the country is rated; the higher the score, the more collectivistic the country is rated.
Source: Hofstede, 1980.

vidual identity over group identity, individual rights over group rights, and individual needs over group needs (Ting-Toomey, 1994b). Individualism is the "I" identity (I want, I need, and so forth). Larry Samovar and Richard Porter (1995) believe that individualism is the "single most important pattern" found in the United States. They continue, "Individualism emphasizes individual initiative ('Pull yourself up by your own boot straps'), independence ('Do your own thing'), individual expression ('The squeaky wheel gets the grease'), and even privacy ('A man's [woman's] home is his [her] castle')" (p. 85).

As you see, individualism involves self-motivation, autonomy, and independent thinking. Individualism suggests direct communication with another. Think about Kevin Johnston's comments expressing his desire to complete his project on his own time. He is projecting individualism to Professor Yang.

According to intercultural communication scholars, individualism is esteemed in the United States (Chen & Starosta, 2000). In addition to the United States, a number of other cultures are viewed as individualistic. Australia, Great Britain, Canada, the Netherlands, and New Zealand are examples of individualistic cultures. Italy, Belgium, and Denmark are considered individualistic. These cultures stress individual achievement and value independence (see Table 26.1).

Whereas individualism focuses on one's personal identity, collectivism looks outside the self. Ting-Toomey (1994b) comments that **collectivism** is the

collectivism
a cultural value that places emphasis on the group over the individual

emphasis of group goals over individual goals, group obligations over individual rights, and in-group needs over individual wants. Collectivism is the "we" identity (we can do this, we are a team, and so forth). People in a collectivistic culture value working together and viewing themselves as part of a larger group. Collectivistic societies, consequently, value inclusion.

Examples of collectivistic cultures include Indonesia, Colombia, Venezuela, Panama, Mexico, Equador, and Guatemala. In these countries, we should point out, the general population is poor; in fact, some of the most severe poverty in the world is found in these countries. Therefore, it's fair to say that people in some of these cultures are guided less by rules and function as a group more out of physical and economic necessity. See our Research Note for more information on collectivism and facework.

Face Management and Culture

So, how do individualism and collectivism relate to Ting-Toomey's theory? Ting-Toomey (1988) observes that "individualistic cultures are concerned with the authenticity of their self-presentation (face) image, [whereas] collectivist cultures are concerned with the adaptability of their self-presentation (face) image" (p. 224). In this spirit, authenticity refers to the ability to be one's self and preserve autonomy (negative face). If you are a citizen of an individualistic society, you are more likely to be concerned with controlling your own autonomy and boundaries for behavior. You would also want choices to satisfy self-face needs. Dissatisfied with the assignment and its deadline, Kevin Johnston is seeking autonomy and wants another choice from his professor. Ting-Toomey believes that in individualistic cultures, **face management** is overt in that it involves protecting one's face, even if it comes to bargaining. Kevin Johnston engages in face negotiation that promotes confrontation, and as Ting-Toomey notes, members of individualistic cultures like Kevin will tend to use more autonomy-preserving face strategies in managing their conflict than will members of collectivistic societies.

face management
the protection of
one's face

Collectivistic cultures "are concerned with the adaptability of self-presentation image" (Ting-Toomey, 1988, p. 224). Adaptability, then, allows for interdependent bonds with others (positive face). What this means is that members of collectivistic communities consider their relationship to others when discussing matters and feel that a conversation requires ongoing maintenance by both communicators. For instance, Professor Yang makes efforts to demonstrate her connection to Kevin by empathizing with his conflict. She also demonstrates a collectivistic orientation by asking whether it would be fair to grant Kevin an extension and not offer the same alternative to other students. Professor Yang, then, as a member of a collectivistic culture, seeks both self-face and other-face needs. For more information on collectivistic and individualistic cultures, see the Research Note.

Ting-Toomey believes that conflict is often present when members from two different cultures—individualistic and collectivistic—come together and that individuals will use a number of different conflict styles. Face-Negotiation Theory takes into consideration the influence that culture has on the way that conflict is managed.

Research Note

Morisaki, S., & Gudykunst, W. B. (1994). Face in Japan and the United States. In S. Ting-Toomey (Ed.), *The challenge of facework* (pp. 47–94). Albany, NY: SUNY.

This scholarship focuses on the cultural differences in face and facework in Japan and the United States. Morisaki and Gudykunst first present a historical overview of face, noting that it has its beginning in Chinese culture. They then note that social psychologist Erving Goffman, influenced by the Chinese concept of face, applied it to Western society. The authors trace Goffman's work and how it influenced current interpretations of face in research.

In a thorough review of past research, Morisaki and Gudykunst delineate several cross-cultural comparisons of face in Japan and the United States. Drawing on Ting-Toomey's work on individualistic and collectivistic cultures, the writers note that the "concept of face and facework appear to be affected by the individualism-collectivism dimension" (p. 57), and they discuss a number of differences between the two cultures. Among the conclusions drawn from past research are several important claims about face and facework: Members of individualistic cultures use more self-face maintenance than members of collectivistic cultures; members of collectivistic cultures use approval-seeking strategies more than members of individualistic cultures; and in-groups are more important in collectivistic cultures than in individualistic cultures.

Additional conclusions identified by Morisaki and Gudykunst pertain to the independent and interdependent nature of face in the two countries. For Western societies such as the United States, "a person's face is independent of any other person's face" (independent face), and face negotiation occurs when only two people are in a conversation (p. 57). In societies such as Japan, "one person's face is interdependent with the face of others in his/her group" (interdependent face) (p. 58). Face negotiation, therefore, exists only when a person is interdependent with another. Expanding on this thinking, Morisaki and Gudykunst contend that an independent sense of self dominates in individualistic cultures, whereas an interdependent sense of self dominates in collectivistic cultures.

The chapter concludes with a summary of propositions on face in Japan and the United States. The authors encourage future research to examine the independent-interdependent dimension of face. Further, they call for researchers to study other cultural groups such as Asian Americans and Native Americans to ascertain whether they use an interdependent or an independent self. Embarking on this research will help lay important groundwork for future discussions of face in Japan and the United States.

Managing Conflict Across Cultures

The individualistic-collectivistic cultural dimension influences the selection of conflict styles. These styles refer to patterned responses, or typical ways of handling conflict across a variety of communication encounters (Ting-Toomey et al., 1991). The styles include avoiding (AV), obliging (OB), compromising (CO), dominating (DO), and integrating (IN). In **avoiding**, people will try to stay away from disagreements and avoid unpleasant exchanges with others ("I'm busy" or "I don't want to talk about that"). The **obliging** style includes a passive accommodation that tries to satisfy the needs of others or goes along with the suggestions of others ("Whatever you want to do is okay with me"). In **compromising**, individuals try to find a middle road to resolve impasses and use give-and-take so that a compromise can be reached ("I'll give up the first week of my vacation; you give up one week of yours"). The **dominating** style

avoiding
staying away from disagreements

obliging
satisfying the needs of others

compromising
using give-and-take to achieve a middle-road resolution

dominating
using influence or authority to make decisions

Figure 26.2
Cultural Variability and Conflict

integrating
collaborating
with others to
find solutions

includes those behaviors that involve using influence, authority, or expertise to get ideas across or to make decisions ("I'm in the best position to talk about this issue"). Finally, the **integrating** style is used by people to find a solution to a problem ("I think we need to work this out together"). As opposed to compromising, integrating requires a high degree of concern for yourself and for others. In compromising, a moderate degree exists.

Ting-Toomey believes that the decision to use one or more of these styles will depend on the cultural variability of communicators. Yet, conflict management necessarily takes into consideration the concern for self-face and other-face. We illustrate this relationship in Figure 26.2. Kevin Johnston, using a dominating style of conflict management, apparently has little concern for the face of his professor (self-face). Professor Yang, however, is more compromising in the way that she handles the conflict with her student (other-face).

Let's continue to clarify Ting-Toomey's discussion of conflict management by identifying the relationship of conflict style to facework. Ting-Toomey notes several relationships among conflict styles and face concern/face need. First, both AV and OB styles of conflict management reflect a passive approach to handling conflicts. A CO style represents a mutual-face need by finding middle-ground solutions to a conflict. Finally, a DO style reflects a high self-face need and a need for control of the conflict, whereas the IN conflict style indicates a high self-face/other-face need for conflict resolution.

With respect to comparisons across five cultures (Japan, China, South Korea, Taiwan, and the United States), Ting-Toomey and her research colleagues (1991) made a number of discoveries:

- Members of the U.S. culture use significantly more dominating styles of conflict management.
- The Taiwanese report using significantly more integrating styles of conflict management.
- The Chinese and Taiwanese use significantly more obliging conflict styles.
- The Chinese use higher degrees of avoidance as a conflict style than other cultural groups.
- The Chinese use a higher degree of compromising than other cultures.

Their research also showed that collectivistic cultures (China, Korea, and Taiwan) had a higher degree of other-face concern.

It is clear from the research on face and conflict that cultural variability influences the way that conflict is managed. Let's reflect back on our discussion of Kevin Johnston and Professor Yang. According to Face-Negotiation Theory,

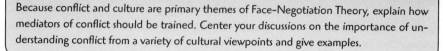

Theory Application in Groups (TAG)

Because conflict and culture are primary themes of Face-Negotiation Theory, explain how mediators of conflict should be trained. Center your discussions on the importance of understanding conflict from a variety of cultural viewpoints and give examples.

because Professor Yang is a member of the Chinese culture—defined as a collectivistic society—she is likely to compromise with Kevin in their conflict. As you saw in our opening, she does try to compromise by asking him to write up a detailed outline and then write about two-thirds of the paper (not the entire paper). She also has a high degree of other-face concern. Kevin, on the other hand, is very dominating in his conflict style and possesses a great deal of self-face concern.

Critique and Closing

Face-Negotiation Theory assumes that people of every culture are concerned with the presentation of their face. It is a theory that infuses conflict into its framework, trying to explain why members of two different cultures manage conflict differently. Ting-Toomey asserts that different cultural values exist in dealing with conflict, and these conflictual episodes, in turn, are influenced by the face concerns and face needs of communicators.

The theory has sparked some interest among intercultural researchers. Several of the key features of the theory have been studied. Ting-Toomey's interfacing of conflict and face has prompted researchers to investigate differences between the Japanese and the Americans (Morisaki & Gudykunst, 1994). Ringo Ma (1992) studied the effects of face maintenance by mediators in conflict episodes, and Mark Cole (1989) looked at self-face and face threats in formal, public, and nonintimate settings. Yuling Pan (2000) employed facework in research on face-to-face interactions of the Chinese. Finally, face and facework in conflict have been studied analyzing cultures of China, Germany, Japan, and the United States (Oetzel, Ting-Toomey, Masumoto, Yokochi, Pan, Takai, & Wilcox, 2001). The theory, then, is heuristic. The way in which Ting-Toomey presents her theory—effectively intersecting face, culture, and conflict—also makes this theory's scope and boundaries clear.

There are a few concerns with the theory, however. For instance, you will recall that the theory rests on the differing experiences and perceptions of individualistic and collectivist cultures. Ting-Toomey uses this foundation to lay out the core of her theory. At times, however, this cultural dimension may not fully explain cultural differences. For instance, in her own research, Ting-Toomey and colleagues (1991) discovered some discrepancies. She found that Japanese respondents showed more concern for self-face than U.S. respondents.

T*I*P

Theory * Into * Practice

In a *New York Times* article, John Broder discusses the effect that losing face has on the U.S. presidency. He writes that an offhand remark by President Clinton at a fundraising dinner resulted in a "major diplomatic incident" between two countries. The president told his audience that he was "eager as a kid with a new toy" to relate his enthusiasm about meeting the newly elected prime minister of Israel, Ehud Barak.

The Israeli community was quick to jump on his remark, Broder indicates. Some took offense at the president's comment and felt it was disrespectful; an Israeli journalist felt that it was patronizing. President Clinton was uncertain why there was such a flap over what he felt was an innocuous statement. He tried to explain to the media, "In English, what that means is that you are very excited. It has no reference to the Prime Minister. I would never do that."

To clear the air, even Mr. Barak joined in. Broder reports that Barak was insistent: "I believe we are all under urgent need to deal very seriously, not with tricky interpretation of innocent favorable statements, but by looking into the real problems and focus on solving them."

Even the CNN news anchor Wolf Blitzer tried to explain why the Israeli journalist felt that the remark was patronizing. Mr. Clinton reiterated his intent by claiming that he would never be patronizing to such a dignitary.

Source: Broder, 1999.

TIP Follow-up
Cultural faux pas surround U.S. presidents with almost every new administration. Discuss why such communication problems occur, resulting in face loss of the host and/or the guest.

In addition, although Ting-Toomey proposes that individualistic cultures are not usually compromising in their conflict styles, the highly individualistic U.S. respondents used a significantly high degree of compromising when faced with a conflict. In this study, then, the I identity of the U.S. respondents was displaced.

Ting-Toomey and Cocroft (1994) respond to these differences in expectations by noting that looking at facework from the individualistic and collectivistic orientation "is a necessary starting point for facework behavior research" (p. 314). The researchers also state that many of the facework category systems in research reflect individualism–collectivism thinking, and therefore, Face-Negotiation Theory must necessarily begin from this vantage point.

Finally, as we have mentioned, Ting-Toomey (1988) has positioned Face-Negotiation Theory within the politeness perspective of Brown and Levinson (1978). She incorporates a number of the components of their thinking, including positive face and negative face. Yet, Tracy and Baratz (1994) believe that such labeling in Brown and Levinson's framework "may be too general to capture the face-concern most central to an interactant" (p. 290). That is, other issues pertaining to face concern exist that are not identified by the researchers.

Ting-Toomey's endorsement and application of politeness research, then, may be questionable. Interestingly, Ting-Toomey and Cocroft (1994) agree with the fact that Brown and Levinson have presented an original template from which to draw but report data that demonstrates several problems with their research.

Face-Negotiation Theory will continue to intrigue communication researchers. Particularly at a time when culture pervades nearly all aspects of life and the global village is becoming smaller, the theory will have lasting appeal. When two people from two different cultures have a conflict, understanding how they maintain and negotiate face will have implications beyond the encounter. Ting-Toomey has given us an opportunity to think about how we can mediate the potential difficulties in communication among cultures, and she elegantly presents important information on a world dependent on communication.

Discussion Starters

1. If he had to do it over again, what communication strategies would you recommend for Kevin Johnston in his conflict with Professor Yang? How might he save his own face and the face of his professor?

2. Have you been to one of the countries categorized here as collectivistic? If so, what communication differences did you notice between that culture and U.S. culture?

3. Do you believe that Face-Negotiation Theory relies on people being reasonable agents who are capable of handling conflict? Can conflict become unreasonable? Explain with examples.

4. Interpret the following statement by Ting-Toomey through description and example: "Collectivists need to work on their ethnocentric biases as much as the individualists need to work out their sense of egocentric superiority." Do you agree or disagree with her view?

5. What evidence do you have that face maintenance is a critical part of U.S. society? Use examples in your response.

6. Discuss the role of power in facework. How can it both help and hinder face-saving in your interactions with others?

Terms for Review

face	solidarity facework
face concern	approbation facework
face need	self-identity
positive face	face-saving
negative face	face restoration
facework	individualism
tact facework	collectivism

face management
avoiding
obliging

compromising
dominating
integrating

Online Learning Center

Visit the Online Learning Center at www.mhhe.com/west2. Use the multiple-choice and true/false quizzes to help you prepare for exams, and the glossary, crossword puzzles, and flashcards to further your knowledge of key terms.

CHAPTER 27

Standpoint Theory

Angela Coburn and Latria Harris

Angela Coburn banged her books together and left class with a frown. She was really steaming. Usually she enjoyed her linguistics class and she liked Professor Townsend. But today she was upset and offended. Professor Townsend had explained the concepts of denotation and connotation by discussing a case that she had read about in the newspaper. The case concerned a European American aide to the mayor of Washington, D.C., who had lost his job for using the word *niggardly* in a meeting with two others, one European American and one African American. The aide had been explaining that he had very little money in the budget and so had to spend it sparingly. When Angela had read the report of this event, she had gasped out loud. As an African American, the sound of that word was extremely offensive to her. No matter that the aide said it meant miserly; she knew a racial slur when she heard one. She was older than most of the students at Mead University, and she remembered the civil rights struggles of the 1960s. Further, she knew that there was a lot of racism in the United States, even today. So Angela couldn't believe it when she heard Professor Townsend begin to tell the story of the aide in Washington to illustrate the lesson. There were racist students at Mead—even in class with her—and Angela felt that using that example sent the wrong message.

She was still fuming later that evening when she met Latria Harris at the coffee shop for their study group. Latria was also in Professor Townsend's linguistics class, and she and Angela studied together every Wednesday. Angela enjoyed their meetings; they helped her keep on top of the assignments for a challenging class, and it was nice to socialize with another African American woman at the university. Angela and Latria got along well despite the difference in their ages and circumstances. Angela was a 48-year-old mother of three grown children; her husband had left her many years ago, and she had raised the kids alone. She had begun her studies toward a B.A. six years ago, and she was hoping to finish this year. Latria was a 20-year-old single woman who had come to college straight from a college-prep high school.

As soon as Angela sat down, she burst out with her displeasure at Professor Townsend and the linguistics class. She spoke about how upset she was for some time until she noticed a blank look on Latria's face. "Don't you agree with me, Latria?" Angela asked.

"Well," Latria responded, "I saw how upset it made you, but I can't say that I felt the same. My family doesn't use that word, but it doesn't really bother me to hear it. I know a lot of people who use it. Also, I understood Townsend's point. The words sound alike but are defined completely differently. I guess Townsend was trying to say

This theory is based on the research of **Nancy C. M. Hartsock.**

that people's connotations about the meaning of one word may poison their responses to the other word."

Angela looked at Latria in silence for a while. Finally, she spoke: "Latria, I understand the point too. I just think a different example should have been used to illustrate it. Those words sound too much alike for me. And that's all some of the racists around here need to hear—a professor speaking a word like that. They will start to think it's okay to say such a thing. And it is not okay. No way. People have died because of that word."

Latria looked at Angela in some disbelief. "I know you're upset, but I think you are carrying this too far. I want to stand by you in this, but I just can't see it as such a big deal."

Angela and Latria fell silent, each pursuing her own thoughts. Finally, Angela said, "Girl, I guess we aren't going to agree about this. Maybe we should just get to studying this week's assignments." Angela smiled as she spoke and looked warmly at her friend, so Latria opened her book with relief. The last thing she wanted to do was to offend or disrespect Angela. Latria gave Angela a lot of credit for everything she had gone through and for how hard she worked at all her classes. Really, Angela was an inspiration to Latria. She grinned back at Angela as they began their work.

Standpoint Theory provides an entry point for understanding some of the dynamics that Angela and Latria experience as they talk about their linguistics course. Standpoint Theory (ST) provides a framework for understanding systems of power. This framework is built on knowledge generated from the everyday lives of people—acknowledging that individuals are active consumers of their own reality and that individuals' own perspectives are the most important sources of information about their experiences (Riger, 1992). Standpoint Theory gives authority to people's own voices.

The theory claims that people's experiences, knowledge, and communication behaviors are shaped in large part by the social groups to which they belong. Thus, insofar as Angela and Latria share membership in social groups, they may share a standpoint. The fact that they are both African American women makes their standpoints similar, yet their generational differences cause their standpoints to diverge. Additionally, Standpoint Theory argues that there is no objective standard for measuring standpoints. Essentially, all statements, assertions, and theories must be understood as simply representing a subjective social location. Thus, Latria's position is valid in regard to her standpoint, whereas Angela's position is true to hers.

Everyday people provide the framework for Standpoint Theory because of the belief that they possess knowledge different from that of those in power. From this difference comes the basis for the critique of the structures of power that form the status quo. Standpoint Theory advocates criticizing the status quo because it is a power structure of dominance and oppression. Further, in this critique are possibilities for "envisioning more just social practices" (Hartsock, 1997, p. 373). Thus, Standpoint Theory points to the problems in the social order as well as suggesting new ways of organizing social life so that it will be more equitable and just. In this regard, ST belongs to the class of theories we called critical theories (see Chapter 3).

Historical Foundations of Standpoint Theory

Although communication researchers have only recently begun to apply Standpoint Theory to studies of communication behavior (see, for example, Buzzanell, 1994), it is a theoretical framework with a long history. In fact, although we are profiling the theory as conceptualized by Nancy Hartsock, she is only one of many researchers who have contributed to developing this theory.

Standpoint Theory's rich history begins in 1807, when the German philosopher Georg Wilhelm Friedrich Hegel discussed how the master–slave relationship engendered different standpoints in its participants. Hegel wrote that although slaves and masters live in a common society, their knowledge of the society is vastly different. These differences stem from the very different positions they occupy within the society. Hegel argued that there can be no single vision concerning social life. Each social group perceives a partial view of society. Karl Marx also claimed that the position of the worker (vis à vis class) shapes the worker's access to knowledge.

Nancy Hartsock drew on Hegel's ideas and Marxist theory to begin to adapt Standpoint Theory for use in examining relations between women and men. From her work with these ideas, in 1983, Hartsock published "The Feminist Standpoint: Developing the Ground for a Specifically Feminist Historical Materialism." Hartsock was concerned with the debates regarding feminism and Marxism that occurred in the 1970s and early 1980s, focusing on the absence of women's issues in Marxist theory. Hartsock's interest was to "make women present" in Marx's theory and in so doing, to forge a feminist-Marxist theory (Hartsock, 1997).

Hartsock is interested in expanding Marx's account to include all human activity rather than simply focusing on what was primarily male activity within capitalism. She focuses on Marx's claim that "a correct vision of class society is available from only one of the two major class positions in capitalist society" (Hartsock, 1983, p. 106). On the basis of this proposal, Hartsock observes, Marx developed a powerful critique of class structure. Hartsock suggests that it is Marx's critique of class relationships rather than his critique of capitalism that is most helpful to feminists.

Hartsock applies Hegel's concepts about masters and slaves and Marx's notions of class and capitalism to issues of sex (the biological categories of male and female) and gender (the behavioral categories of masculinity and femininity). This is a common adaptation of ST, and consequently people sometimes refer to Standpoint Theory as Feminist Standpoint Theory, as Nancy Hartsock labeled it in 1983. In some ways this complicates matters, because there is no consensus on the exact meaning of feminist. Many authors have noted that there are different kinds of feminism (Cirksena & Cuklanz, 1992). For our purposes, we need to acknowledge this diversity yet stipulate that the defining characteristic that unites all types of **feminism** is a focus on women's particular social position and a desire to end any subjugation based on sex or gender.

feminism
focusing on women's social position and desiring to end oppression based on sex

This brings us to an interesting difference between this theory and many others in this book. In many ways, Standpoint Theory expresses and embodies a critique of other mainstream theories and approaches to research. The critique lodged by Standpoint theorists begins with the observation that most

The Theory Connection

Both Feminist Standpoint Theory and Muted Group Theory deal with groups on the margins that are silenced. How do the two theories differ in their conceptualizations of marginalized groups and in what ways are they similar?

research in the past has flowed from one common standpoint: that of the White, middle-class male. Some feminist researchers argue that traditional approaches to research inquiry (see Chapter 4) are male defined and block women's unique perspectives. Thus, the critique continues, this White, middle-class male standpoint has served to silence any other perspective as a valued contributor to scientific knowledge (Chafetz, 1997).

This critique acknowledges that Feminist Standpoint Theory must begin by highlighting the relationship between power and knowledge. In doing so, "feminist standpoint theory tries to hold together two tensions: the search for better knowledge and the commitment to the idea that knowledge is always intertwined with issues of power and politics. As a consequence, the foundational tenet of feminist standpoint theory is that knowledge always arises in social locations and is structured by power relations" (O'Brien Hallstein, 2000, p. 3). This points out that ST begins with an imperfect epistemology, one devised by men in power, and seeks to develop a better epistemology, while recognizing that knowledge is not separable from politics.

It is important to keep in mind that although the feminist version of Standpoint Theory is the one that is commonly conceptualized, Standpoint Theory can be used to analyze a variety of standpoints, such as, for example, those that Angela and Latria bring to their conversation, based on age, race, and class. In this chapter, we are explaining ST as Nancy Hartsock details it, applying its principles to women's particular standpoint. Yet it is wise to remember that a variety of standpoints, such as those provided by status, race, and so on, can be explained by ST. The theory lends itself well to application in other co-cultural groups: "Standpoint focuses on perspectives of women, but could also take the perspectives of African American women, poor white women/men, nonwhite women and men and individuals belonging to minority ethnic and religious groups outside modern Western society" (Wallace & Wolf, 1995, p. 270). Other theorists, such as Mark Orbe (1998), use Standpoint Theory to examine race and culture.

Assumptions of Standpoint Theory

Feminist Standpoint Theory rests first on the four characteristics that Janet Saltzman Chafetz (1997) discusses as descriptive of any feminist theory: (1) Sex or gender is a central focus for the theory; (2) sex or gender relations are viewed as problematic, and the theory seeks to understand how sex or gender is related to inequities and contradictions; (3) sex or gender relations are viewed as changeable; and (4) feminist theory can be used to challenge the status quo when the status quo debases or devalues women. As applied to women, the theory assumes that women are devalued in our culture, but that is a changeable situation. Using women's unique standpoint will bring out information that can challenge this situation.

In addition, Standpoint Theory, as Hartsock conceptualizes it, rests on five specific assumptions about the nature of social life:

- Material life (or class position) structures and limits understandings of social relations.

- When material life is structured in two opposing ways for two different groups, the understanding of each will be an inversion of the other. When there is a dominant and a subordinate group, the understanding of the dominant group will be both partial and harmful.

- The vision of the ruling group structures the material relations in which all groups are forced to participate.

- The vision available to an oppressed group represents struggle and an achievement.

- The potential understanding of the oppressed (the standpoint) makes visible the inhumanity of the existing relations among groups and moves us toward a better and more just world.

We will discuss each of these assumptions briefly. They are framed in the modified Marxist perspective that Hartsock favors.

The first assumption sets forth the notion that individuals' location in the class structure shapes and limits their understandings of social relations. Although not completely rooted in the class structure, our story of Angela and Latria illustrates the power of one's location in society for shaping understanding. Because of Angela's standpoint, based on her difficult circumstances raising her children alone and struggling to finish her degree, her response to the class discussion differs sharply from Latria's, whose experience and age have somewhat shielded her from the bitterness that influences Angela's viewpoint. In a simple example, a rich person's understanding of poverty is severely limited.

Second, Feminist Standpoint Theory assumes that all standpoints are partial, but those of the ruling class can actually harm those of the subordinate group. This point leads naturally to the third assumption, which asserts that the ruling group structures life in such a way as to remove some choices from the subordinate group. Hartsock comments that in the United States people have very little choice about participating in a market economy, which is the preferred mode for the ruling class. As Hartsock (1997) comments, the vision of the rulers structures social life and forces all parties to participate in this structure. "Truth is, to a large extent, what the dominant groups can make true; history is always written by the winners" (1997, p. 96). Further, the ruling class promotes propaganda that describes the market as beneficial and virtuous.

The fourth assumption asserts that the subordinate group has to struggle for their vision of social life. This leads to the final assumption, which claims that this struggle results in a clearer, more accurate vision for the subordinate group than that possessed by the ruling class. With this clear vision, the

The Theory Chronicles

Conduct an interview with someone who occupies a different social location than you do. In your journal, record their answers to your questions about their standpoint. Compare their standpoint to yours.

subordinate group can see the inherent inhumanity in the social order and can thus attempt to change the world for the better. This set of assumptions leads to the conclusion that although all groups possess a standpoint, the standpoint of the oppressed group is clearer and more developed than that of the ruling, or dominant, group. This is true because the oppressed group needs to pay careful attention to the dominant group. Their welfare in many cases is dependent on their knowledge of the dominant group. The reverse does not usually hold true. Further, the dominant group does not wish to scrutinize the social hierarchy closely because it is to their advantage to maintain the status quo. Scrutiny usually leads to desires for changing the status quo.

Added to these assumptions that characterize Hartsock's Marxist view of Standpoint Theory, most conceptions of ST also embody an epistemology, or a way of knowing, and an ontology, or a belief in what is worth knowing (see Chapter 4). The Standpoint epistemology and ontology are also grounded in another set of assumptions, as follows:

- All knowledge is a product of social activity, and thus no knowledge can be truly objective.
- Cultural conditions "typically surrounding women's lives produce experiences and understandings that routinely differ from those produced by the conditions framing men's lives" (Wood, 1992, p. 14). These different understandings often produce distinct communication patterns.
- It is a worthwhile endeavor to understand the distinctive features of women's experience.
- We can only know women's experience by attending to women's interpretations of this experience.

The epistemological and ontological assumptions of the standpoint approach suggest both what is worth studying and how to go about studying it. First, the assertion is made that knowledge is not an objective concept but rather is shaped subjectively by knowers. This suggests an approach to knowing that is much different from that suggested by a belief in objective truth. This assumption opens the door for the concept of multiple (though partial) truths that is central to Standpoint Theory.

The second assumption points to the different social locations that men and women inhabit in the United States even when they work and live in what seem to be similar situations. In a study examining sexual harassment in the workplace, Debbie Dougherty (2001) begins with a notion derived from ST that while sexual harassment may be dysfunctional for women, it may serve some functions for men. She used discussion groups and interviews with the employees of a large health-care organization and discovered that what women saw as dysfunctional and distressful behaviors, men interpreted as a form of coping behavior for work-related stressors, a mode of therapy, and a means for demonstrating camaraderie. Dougherty concludes that her findings indicate how different standpoints have shaped men's and women's viewpoints on sexual harassment. Dougherty also discusses how managers can use this information to develop workshops that address how the functions can be satisfied for men without providing distress for women in the organization.

The third assumption deals with ontology, or what is worth knowing. This assumption places marginalized people (women) at the starting place for theorizing and research. This makes Standpoint Theory feminist and somewhat revolutionary by replacing the dominant standpoint outside the cultural mainstream. Sandra Harding (1991) comments on this by saying, "What 'grounds' feminist standpoint theory is not women's experiences but the view from women's lives . . . we start our thought from the perspective of lives at the margins" (p. 269).

Finally, Standpoint Theory operates from an epistemology positing that the only way to achieve Harding's sentiment above is by having women talk about their experiences and interpret them. As we discussed in Chapter 4, this approach to research takes much of the power and control out of the hands of the researcher and makes research more of a collaborative process. The research participant is an active partner in the endeavor. It is a continuing goal for feminist standpoint theorists to develop new methodologies that give voice to those who have been silenced previously (Ford & Crabtree, 2002).

Through these assumptions we get a picture of Standpoint Theory as an evolving framework, grounded in Marxism, but rejecting some of the central tenets of that perspective in favor of a feminist approach. Standpoint Theory seeks to understand the influence that a particular location exerts on people's views of the world and on their communication. In this quest, researchers in Standpoint Theory wish to begin with the marginalized and focus on their stories and interpretations. As Standpoint theorists work with research participants, they recognize the limited view of their own vision and they acknowledge the subjective nature of truth(s). The Research Note provides an example of a researcher working with these concepts.

Key Concepts of Standpoint Theory

The theory rests on several key concepts: standpoint, situated knowledges, and sexual division of labor. We will discuss each concept briefly.

Standpoint

The central concept of the theory, **standpoint,** is a location, shared by a group, within the social structure that lends a particular kind of sense making to a person's lived experience. Further, from Hartsock's perspective, "A standpoint is

standpoint
an achieved position based on a social location that lends an interpretative aspect to a person's life

Research Note

Allen, B. J. (1996). Feminist Standpoint Theory: A black woman's (re)view of organizational socialization. *Communication Studies, 47,* 257–271.

This essay embodies some of the tenets of Standpoint Theory by examining organizational socialization from the author's vantage point as an African American faculty member at a predominantly White university. The author uses her own experiences to demonstrate the value of the outsider within perspective. The essay focuses on the utility of this perspective, derived from Standpoint Theory, to analyze the process of integrating a new employee into an organizational setting.

Allen first briefly reviews Standpoint Theory and the concept of organizational socialization. Then she delineates her own standpoint by recounting autobiographical data obtained through a self-interview. Allen recorded her own responses to interview questions that she plans later to pose to research participants. She weaves her own answers into an analysis of the stages of organizational socialization presented by Frank Jablin (1985, 1987) and Jablin and Kathleen Krone (1987). For example, Allen begins by noting that Jablin's model of organizational socialization contends that the process begins before a newcomer actually assumes a specific role within the organization. The process begins in what Jablin labels "anticipatory socialization," which "occurs as individuals receive information about work and work-related communication from family, part-time job experiences, education institutions, peers and friends, and the media" (Allen, 1996, p. 262). After recounting this segment of Jablin's model, Allen interposes her autobiographical information as follows:

I always wanted to be a teacher. Black folks in the lower classed community where I lived [in the 1950s] placed a high value on education, and they expected smart little girls like me to become teachers or nurses when they grew up. They were proud of my scholastic accomplishments, and they always encouraged me to succeed. In school, I was always the [White] teacher's pet, so this gave me a good feeling about educational settings. Since we didn't have a TV then, I wasn't exposed to much else. (p. 262)

In this manner, Allen incorporates her own voice in much the same way that Standpoint Theory advises. Allen ends her essay by discussing the implications it has for research and practice. She first affirms that Feminist Standpoint Theory can provide a viable method for understanding organizational socialization in a new light. She asserts that her experiences as an African American woman reveal aspects of organizational socialization that previously have not been exposed. For example, her research indicates that "socialization does not occur in the clear-cut stages that models imply. Moreover, the process is neither completely rational nor always one way (i.e. organization to newcomer)" (p. 267). Additionally, Allen concludes that her research efforts have been geared toward social change and emancipation. She notes that she herself has felt empowered through this research endeavor, and she believes that other women of color will feel similarly when she interviews them for future projects.

not simply an interested position (interpreted as bias) but is interested in the sense of being engaged" (1998, p. 107). The concept of engagement is amplified by researchers who distinguish between a standpoint and a perspective (Hirschmann, 1997; O'Brien Hallstein, 2000). As O'Brien Hallstein observes, it is easy to confuse the two, but there is a critical difference. A perspective is shaped by experiences that are structured by a person's place in the social hierarchy. A perspective may lead to the achievement of a standpoint but only through effort. As O'Brien Hallstein argues, standpoints are only achieved after thought, interaction, and struggle. Standpoints must be actively sought;

they are not possessed by all people who have experienced oppression. Standpoints are achieved through experiences of oppression added to active engagement, reflection, and recognition of the political implications of these experiences.

Further, standpoints are not free of their social and political contexts. As Sandra Harding (1991) notes, "standpoints are socially mediated" (p. 276). Because standpoints are defined by specific social locations, they are by necessity **partial,** or incomplete. The location allows only a portion of social life to be viewed by any particular group. In addition, the political aspect of standpoints stresses that individuals go through a developmental process in acquiring them. As Welton (1997) states, developing a standpoint requires "active, political resistance to work against the material embodiment of the perspective and experience of the dominant group. It is the act of having to push against the experience-made-reality of the hegemonic group, that makes it a political standpoint and potentially liberating" (p. 11). Moreover, as O'Brien Hallstein (1999; 2000) argues, standpoints are political because they are achieved in collaboration and dialogue with others rather than in isolation.

A specific type of standpoint is described by Patricia Hill Collins (1986; 1989; 1991) when she describes herself as an African American woman academic. This social position places her as an **outsider within,** or a person who normally would be marginalized but has somehow gained access to the inside. In the case of outsiders moving into a social location that historically excluded them, Collins suggests that a particular clarity of vision occurs. Ruth Frankenberg (1993) concurs, saying that "the oppressed can see with the greatest clarity, not only their own position but . . . indeed the shape of social systems as a whole" (p. 8). This clarity of vision suggests, as Standpoint Theory argues, that the lower positions on the hierarchy possess the greatest accuracy in their standpoints, where **accuracy** refers to the ability to transcend the limits of partial vision and see beyond one's own specific social location.

Situated Knowledges

Donna Haraway (1988) contributes the term **situated knowledges,** meaning that any person's knowledge is grounded in context and circumstances. Haraway's concept suggests that knowledges are multiple and are situated in experience. Thus, what one person learns from her position as a caregiver for her ailing parents is different from the knowledge that another person develops from her position as an electrical engineer. Situated knowledges reminds us that what we

partial
a recognition that no one has a complete view of the social hierarchy

outsider within
a person in a normally marginalized social position who has gained access to a more privileged location

accuracy
the ability to see more than what's available to one's own specific social location

situated knowledges
what anyone knows is grounded in context and circumstance

469

learn is not innate but the result of our experiences. So if the engineer cared for elderly family members, she also would learn the caregiving knowledge.

Sexual Division of Labor

sexual division of labor
allocation of work on the basis of sex

Hartsock's Marxist-inspired Feminist Standpoint Theory rests on the notion that men and women engage in different occupations based on their sex, which results in a **sexual division of labor.** Not only does this division simply assign people to different tasks based on sex, but it also exploits women by demanding work without providing wages while making "women responsible for the unwaged maintenance and reproduction of the current and future labor force" (Chafetz, 1997, p. 104). Further, the inequities that women suffer in the workplace when involved in labor for wages are linked to their responsibility for unwaged domestic work. Additionally, as Nancy Hirschmann (1997) points out, a feminist standpoint "enables women to identify the activities they perform in the home as 'work' and 'labor,' productive of 'value,' rather than simply the necessary and essential byproducts of 'nature' or the function of biology which women 'passively' experience" (p. 81). Thus, Standpoint Theory highlights the exploitation and distortion that result when labor is divided by sex.

Relationship to Communication

Standpoint Theory has become popular with communication researchers because it advances a reciprocal relationship with communication behavior and standpoints. Communication is responsible for shaping our standpoints to the extent that we learn our place in society through interaction with others. Thus, when Angela's mother told her stories about her African American heritage and about her ancestors who were slaves, Angela learned much about her standpoint. Every time a teacher told Angela that she probably could not go to college and receive a B.A. degree, communication shaped her standpoint. By the same token, Latria's standpoint was also shaped by communication, although the content may have been very different. Latria probably did not hear stories of slavery and may have been encouraged to go to college by her teachers. Thus, communication from others shaped different standpoints for the two women.

Similarly, one of the assumptions of the theory is that those who share a standpoint will share certain communication styles and practices. Thus, we expect that women who take care of children communicate in a maternal fashion, whereas men who are not responsible for such caregiving do not (Ruddick, 1989). Further, Marsha Houston (1992) has pointed out that some communication behaviors among African American women—like loud talking and interrupting—are shaped by their standpoints and are misunderstood by those outside the group. Houston points out that some European American researchers interpret these communication behaviors differently (and usually more negatively) than do members of the group themselves.

Standpoint Theory, thus, illustrates the centrality of communication in both shaping and transmitting standpoints. Further, the theory points to the use of communication as a tool for changing the status quo and producing change. By giving voice to those whose standpoints are infrequently heard, the methods associated with the theory focus on communication practices. As Julia Wood (1992) notes, "Whether women's own voices are granted legitimacy seems especially pertinent to communication scholars' assessments of the value of alternative theoretical positions" (p. 13). The concepts of voice, speaking out, and speaking for others are important to Standpoint Theory and Standpoint epistemology, and they are all concepts rooted in communication.

Critique and Closing

Standpoint Theory, or Feminist Standpoint Theory, has generated a great deal of research, interest, and spirited controversy, so it appears to be heuristic. Yet some of the issues that scholars have raised concerning the theory warrant discussion here. We will explore two areas of critique: the charge that Standpoint Theory relies on essentialism and the complaint that it focuses on the dualisms of subjectivity and objectivity.

The complaint most commonly leveled against Standpoint Theory revolves around essentialism, and a great deal has been written on this topic. As we will discuss again in Chapter 28 with reference to Muted Group Theory, **essentialism** refers to the practice of generalizing about all women (or any group) as though they were essentially the same. Essentialism obscures the diversity that exists among women. The story of Angela and Latria illustrates the mistake we make if we engage in essentialism. Although they are both African American women attending the same university, the differences between them cause them to interpret the classroom discussion differently. Because Standpoint Theory focuses on the location of social groups, many researchers have argued that it is essentialist. For example, Catherine O'Leary (1997) argues that although Standpoint Theory has been helpful in reclaiming women's experiences as suitable research topics, it contains a problematic emphasis on the universality of this experience, at the expense of differences among women's experiences.

Implicit in this critique (and often explicit) are the ways that many White women researchers have excluded the standpoints and voices of women of color, women who are disabled, lesbians, poor women, and women from Third World nations (Collins, 1990). Yet this criticism may be unfair to Hartsock's conceptualization of the theory. Hartsock (1981) has stated that although there are many differences among women, she is pointing to specific aspects of women's experience that are shared by many: unpaid household labor and provision of caregiving and nurturance. Hirschmann (1997) argues that Feminist Standpoint Theory really does accommodate difference by allowing for a multiplicity of feminist standpoints. Hirschmann suggests that standpoints can be developed from Hartsock's framework that will bring a useful approach to the tension between shared identity and difference. Wood (1992) concurs with this rebuttal, and she suggests that Standpoint Theory is different from essentialist views of women in one important way: The theory does not suggest that men and women are fundamentally different (or have different essences); rather, ST begins with the assumption that social and cultural conditions that typically surround women's lives produce different experiences and understandings from

essentialism
the belief that all women are essentially the same, all men are essentially the same, and the two differ from each other

the social and cultural conditions typically surrounding men's lives. Wood concludes, "There is nothing in the logic of standpoint epistemology that precludes analysis of the intersections among conditions that structure race, class, and gender relations in any given culture" (p. 14). Thus, Angela and Latria's conversation could be understood as a constellation of standpoints—some of which shape their experiences in a similar fashion and some of which cause them to diverge significantly.

Further, some more current research conducted under the ST framework has made the tension between difference and commonality central to its focus. For example, Katrina Bell, Mark Orbe, Darlene Drummond, and Sakile Camara (2000) used Black Feminist Standpoint Theory to examine African American women's communication practices. Bell and her colleagues purposely collected information from very diverse women in an effort to capture different lived experiences. This resulted in a sample of women who shared a racial identity but differed in terms of many of their other social locations including age, religion, sexual orientation, professional and economic status, and so forth.

The researchers found that despite their diversity, the participants in their study did share a multiple consciousness of oppression as a result of racism, sexism, classism, and heterosexism. Yet the participants also voiced ways in which the issue of diversity existed among African American women. Throughout their data, the participants described other aspects of their identity that became salient in their interactions with others and in many instances impeded their sense of connection with African American women. As such, the researchers saw multiple consciousness as a "dynamic process of constant negotiation" (p. 50). Thus, the researchers conclude that Black Feminist Standpoint Theory allows for the assumption of commonality of oppression while acknowledging various expressions of this common experience.

In a study of academic women, Debbie Dougherty and Kathleen Krone (2000) also sought to apply ST to a group of diverse women to capitalize on the creative tensions between similarity and difference. They interviewed four women in the same department in an academic institution and from the interviews they created a narrative that, although fictional, attempted to capture the standpoints voiced in the interviews. Then they had the participants comment on the narrative and identify areas for change and develop action plans. In this process, the researchers found both commonality and difference among the standpoints of the participants.

The women agreed that their standpoints were shaped by a sense of isolation, a strong desire for community, and the feeling of invisibility. Yet they differed in their consciousness of their own oppression. However, rather than ignoring these differences or using them to divide themselves from one another, the women used differences to strengthen their relationship. The researchers note that the critique focused on essentialism may miss the point. Dougherty and Krone observe that "differences and similarities create and recreate each other, becoming so intertwined that they are difficult to separate" (p. 26).

A second area of criticism concerns the notion of dualisms, or dualistic thinking. Feminists (Cirksena & Cuklanz, 1992) note that much of Western thought is organized around a set of oppositions, or **dualisms.** Reason and emotion, public and private, nature and culture, and subject and object are

dualisms
organizing things
around pairs of
opposites

Theory * Into * Practice

Standpoint Theory suggests that people sharing the same group characteristics will have experiences in common that will shape their understanding of the world. At the same time, the theory points out that those who differ on certain characteristics will have different experiences and view the world from a different standpoint. An article in the *Johns Hopkins Magazine* points out that class can be a large factor in shaping a standpoint. The article focuses on a Hopkins's professor's research about kinship support in African American families. The research was an investigation of the claim that family support could be marshaled in place of welfare when teenagers became pregnant. The professor, Katrina Bell McDonald, found that the traditional support system in African American families may be fraying:

> She has also found frustration among traditional "othermothers," black women (neighbors, aunts, friends, cousins) who in the past had stepped in with money, housing or guidance (most are biological mothers too). Today, some of these women are overwhelmed, [McDonald] says; they struggle daily with the issue of just how much to give young women in their community.
>
> There's conflict especially among some middle class black women who have earned college degrees or established careers to reach a higher standard of living. Some feel distanced from the experiences of urban, poor black women. "It shows up in a lot of the language people are using to express themselves, buzz words like low class and ghetto-type behavior," says McDonald. "They wrestle with the question: What do we have in common?" (p. 36)

Source: Cavanaugh, 1999.

TIP Follow-up
Discuss the situation described above with reference to the difference between the terms standpoint *and* perspective. *Do these women have standpoints or perspectives? Explain your answer.*

---

just a few of the pairs of opposites that are common organizing principles in Western thinking. Feminists have been concerned with these dualisms for two related reasons: First, dualisms usually imply a hierarchical relationship between the terms, elevating one and devaluing the other. When we suggest that decisions should be made rationally, not emotionally, for example, we are showing that reason holds a higher value in our culture than does emotion. Related to this issue is the concern that these dualisms often become gendered in our culture. In this process, men are associated with one extreme and women with the other. In the case of reason and emotion, women are identified with emotion. Because our culture values emotion less than reason, women suffer from this association. Feminist critics are usually concerned with the fact that dualisms force false dichotomies onto women and men, failing to see that life is less either/or than both/and, as Relational Dialectics Theory (Chapter 12) holds.

O'Leary (1997) argues that Standpoint Theory does not present us with a sufficiently complex understanding of experience, and as a result, it still rests on a dualism between subjective experience and objective truth. O'Leary suggests that Hartsock's framework cannot accommodate the complexities of multiple knowledges. Yet, Hartsock specifically allows for this very thing within her original theory, arguing for clusters of standpoints. Overall, as Hartsock (1997) notes, the controversies engendered by Standpoint Theory indicate a "fertile terrain" for debate and open the possibilities for expanding and refining the theory so that it is more responsive to diversity and clearer about the distinctions between subjectivity and objectivity.

In sum, Standpoint Theory presents us with another way of viewing the relative positions, experiences, and communication of various social groups. It has a clear political, critical bent, and it locates the place of power in social life. It has generated much controversy as people find it either offensive or compatible with their own views of social life. Certainly, ST is heuristic and provocative. The theory may be compatible with other theories, enabling us to combine them to get richer explanations for human communication behaviors. For example, ST may need support from a version of Dialectics Theory to explain the tension between commonality of social groups and uniqueness of individuals within the groups. Scholars need to continue refining Standpoint Theory, applying it to other co-cultural groups and resolving some of the issues of essentialism and dualism that critics have uncovered. Yet, Standpoint Theory holds much promise for illuminating differences in the communication behaviors of different social groups. It remains to be seen whether ST will generate findings that help us to understand our world and our communication behaviors.

Discussion Starters

1. Do you accept the argument of Standpoint Theory that all standpoints are partial? Explain your answer. How does the case of Angela and Latria, from the beginning of the chapter, illustrate this claim?

2. Give an example of situated knowledges.

3. The chapter identifies Standpoint Theory as a feminist theory. Does it make sense to you that a theory can be identified with a political ideology? Explain your answer.

4. If all truths are understood as coming from some subjective standpoint, how is it possible for people to communicate? If there is no objective truth, how do we reach agreement among people with different standpoints?

5. What are the limits of difference that ground a standpoint? Might we eventually end up with standpoints that are so particular that only relatively few people share them? How would this help us to understand communication between and among people?

6. How well do you think more recent scholarship has done in incorporating the tension between sharing a common standpoint and recognizing differences? Give some examples.

Terms for Review

feminism

standpoint

partial

outsider within

accuracy

situated knowledges

sexual division of labor

essentialism

dualisms

Online Learning Center

Visit the Online Learning Center at www.mhhe.com/west2. Use the multiple-choice and true/false quizzes to help you prepare for exams, and the glossary, crossword puzzles, and flashcards to further your knowledge of key terms.

CHAPTER 28

Muted Group Theory

**Patricia
Fitzpatrick**

Patricia Fitzpatrick sat in the back row in her Political Science 100 lecture; she closed her eyes, letting the professor's words wash over her. She was wondering what in the world had possessed her to go back to college at the age of 40. It had seemed like a good idea when she first thought about finishing the B.A. she had begun over twenty years ago, but now she thought she must have been out of her mind to try this. She felt like she was not understanding a word her professors said, and she was having an extremely difficult time keeping current with her assignments. Most of the other students were much younger than she, as well as seeming to have a lot more disposable income. She really hadn't spoken to many of them beyond a quick hello. All in all, this college idea was turning into a big hassle, making Patricia feel really negative.

It wasn't supposed to be this way. Initially, she had thought it would improve her self-esteem if she could finish her degree. She was also hoping it might get her out of the dead-end job she had with Hudson's Department Store. She worked nights as a shipping clerk for the store, sending out orders for their mail-order business. She had been working for Hudson's for the past seven years, and it did not seem as if there were much possibility for advancement there. It was a pretty boring job with low pay, and Patricia was hopeful that a degree might give her more opportunities. As a single mom with three kids, she really needed a better job.

But Patricia was starting to feel despair about her prospects. One of the most disturbing things so far had been how tongue-tied she felt in class. She had so much trouble articulating what she wanted to say about the material that she ended up not saying anything in most of her classes. Patricia worried that this would count against her, especially in her smaller classes, where the professors really seemed to encourage class participation. She had expected that she would have a lot to say as she learned new things, but she was finding it difficult to express her opinions. So, instead of increasing her self-esteem, college was making her feel worse about herself.

Actually, this wasn't the first time that Patricia had felt inarticulate. She admitted to herself that she had had a hard time speaking up long before she returned to college. At work, she was the only woman on her shift, and the men didn't seem to pay attention to her when she spoke. Once she had tried to compare something at work to an experience she had had teaching her son to read, and the other workers had looked at her like she was nuts. Then they all had started laughing and calling her "Mom." Another time she had been the chair of a committee at her daughter's school. The committee was supposed to research ways the school could

---

This theory is based on the research of **Cheris Kramarae.**

raise money for more computer equipment. Patricia had to get up in front of representatives from the parents' group, teachers, and administrators and report on the committee's findings. Although the report had been okay, Patricia thought she had paused too much while she spoke. Even though she had spent a great deal of time preparing for the speech, she had still found herself groping for words occasionally.

She had hoped that college would help her become more articulate. It would be wonderful to be able to speak up and say what was on her mind. Patricia wasn't ready to give up, but things certainly weren't going as planned.

S ome researchers analyzing Patricia's situation might be tempted to examine her individual traits, noting that she might have problems with reticence or communication apprehension. However, the theory that we discuss in this chapter offers a different approach to explaining Patricia's problems. Muted Group Theory (MGT) asserts that, as a female, as a single mom, and as a person of low income, Patricia is a member of several groups whose experiences are not well served by her language system—a language system that was devised primarily by men to represent their own experiences. Thus, Patricia and others are muted because their native language often does not provide a good fit with their life experiences. Muted Group Theory explains that women trying to use man-made language to describe their experiences is somewhat like native English speakers learning to converse in Spanish. To do so, they have to go through an internal translation process, scanning the foreign vocabulary for the best word to express their thoughts. This process makes them hesitant and often inarticulate as they are unable to use the language fluently for their purposes.

As Cheris Kramarae (1981) observes,

> The language of a particular culture does not serve all its speakers equally, for not all speakers contribute in an equal fashion to its formulation. Women (and members of other subordinate groups) are not as free or as able as men are to say what they wish, when and where they wish, because the words and the norms for their use have been formulated by the dominant group, men. (p. 1)

As you can probably guess from our discussion thus far, MGT is a critical theory as we defined it in Chapter 3. That is, MGT points out problems with the status quo and suggests ways to remediate these problems. Later in this chapter, we will describe some of the action steps advocated by Muted Group Theory.

Origins of Muted Group Theory

Muted Group Theory originated with the work of Edwin and Shirley Ardener, social anthropologists who were concerned with social structure and hierarchy. In 1975, Edwin Ardener noted that groups making up the top end of the social hierarchy determine the communication system for the culture. Lower-power groups in the society, such as women, the poor, and people of color, have to learn to work within the communication system that the dominant group has

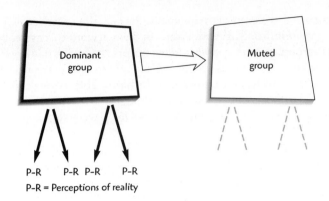

**Figure 28.1
Muted Group
Theory**
Source: Adapted from
Ardener, 1975.

established. Turning this generalization to the specific case of women in a culture, Edwin Ardener observed that social anthropologists study women's experiences by talking almost exclusively to men. Thus, not only do women have to contend with the difficulties of a language that does not completely give voice to their thoughts, but their experiences are represented through a male perspective.

In 1975, Edwin Ardener commented on why ethnographers (who at the time were mainly men) tended to speak and listen to men in the cultures they studied. Ardener noted, "Those trained in ethnography evidently have a bias towards the kinds of model that men are ready to provide (or to concur in) rather than towards any that women might provide. If the men appear 'articulate' compared with the women, it is a case of like speaking like" (1975, p. 2). Further, Shirley Ardener (1978) observed that women's mutedness is the counterpart to men's deafness. Thus, she explains that women (or members of any subordinate group) do speak, but their words fall on deaf ears, and when this happens over time, they tend to stop trying to articulate their thoughts, and they may even stop thinking them. In Ardener's words, "Words which continually fall upon deaf ears may, of course, in the end become unspoken, or even unthought" (1978, p. 20).

The Ardeners might argue that Patricia Fitzpatrick is twice muted: once by the failure of her language to act as an accurate tool for her use and once by observers who label her as inarticulate rather than poorly served by language. For Edwin Ardener, muted groups are rendered inarticulate by the dominant group's language system, which grows directly out of their worldview and experience. For the muted group, what they say first has to shift out of their own worldview and be compared to the experiences of the dominant group. Thus, articulations for the muted group are indirect and broken. See Figure 28.1.

This line of thinking is especially true for the English language because it was developed and formalized by male clerics and academics. Because women were not instrumental in formalizing the English language, and were dominated in the culture that created it, Kramarae theorized that women would be a muted group. As Anita Taylor and M. J. Hardman (2000) observe,

> English does not name concepts important to women but to men (e.g., one can have a "seminal" idea; but was one ever described as "ovular"?).

English also devalues concepts important to women but not to men (again, the "seminal" idea is an example; if one nurtured or incubated an idea it would have quite a different feeling, as would ovulating it). English uses male referents and terms (e.g., the "generic" he and the conclusion that number is more important than gender for the third-person indefinite pronoun). (p. 8)

For these reasons, among others, MGT concludes that women are silenced by their language.

Two examples should clarify this line of thinking. One example comes from the work of Hilary Callan (1978), who suggests that many female nurses have difficulties with assuming authority. Callan argues that this difficulty is not because they are unable to take orders or to give them but rather because they experience a tension between elements of their self-definition. Nurses have been defined by others as either battle-axes who have renounced femininity or superfeminine angels of mercy. These two extremes pose problems for nurses themselves, who struggle to reconcile the complexities of their situations and self-perceptions with the two labels. Further, as Callan concludes,

> The nurses' problem—and mine as ethnographer—is that the capacities and handicaps they may have [as] biological females are manifested and mapped on to a terrain of experience which includes (among many other things) the existence of traditional male authority patterns (which may or may not be an authentic model for women) as well as the relevant parts of the profession's own encapsulated history. (p. 212)

Thus, language constrains these nurses as they struggle to define themselves and their own profession. Language fails to serve their needs.

A second example comes from the work of Helen Sterk (1999), who has spent several years gathering birth stories from mothers in an effort to understand the experience of birth from the mothers' point of view. A central issue that Sterk identifies is that although birth seems to be the quintessential female experience, for many women birth is medically managed in such a way that they feel somewhat removed from it. If a woman gives birth in a hospital, the language of the process is mainly the doctor's. The progress of the birth experience is noted in the observing doctor's language as to how many centimeters a woman's cervix has dilated, for example. As Sterk explains, this language is completely insufficient for women, and they are frequently reduced to repeating, "I simply cannot explain how I felt."

Makeup of Muted Groups

Much of the theorizing and application of Muted Group Theory has focused on women as a muted group. Yet, as researchers such as Mark Orbe (1998) note, the theory can be validly applied to any nondominant group. Orbe suggests that in the United States and several other cultures, the society privileges specific characteristics and perspectives: European American, male, heterosexual, able bodied, youthful, middle and upper class, and Christian. People with these perspectives form the **dominant group,** or the group that holds the power in the culture. Other groups that coexist with the dominant

dominant group
the group that holds the power in a given culture

group are generally subordinate to it in that they do not have access to as much power as do members of the dominant group. Thus, African Americans, gays and lesbians, the elderly, the lower class, disabled people, and non-Christians all can be members of muted groups, in the same way that women are.

In fact, some researchers have suggested that men might be part of a muted group as well. Radhika Chopra (2001) examines the issue of muting for nurturing fathers. Chopra argues that the discourse of mothering represented by Nancy Chodorow's (1978) book, *The Reproduction of Mothering,* reduced the father to a "depersonalized cipher" whose presence is "posited as an absence, in contrast with the hands-on vital involvement of the mother" (p. 447). Chopra notes that this discourse not only silences the father but also fails to account for fathering in other societies or periods of history where the distant, silent father did not exist.

Chopra points to fathers in the early American colonial period who were very involved in teaching their children both reading and writing skills as well as moral and religious teachings. Further, Chopra notes that ethnographies of societies like the Trobriand islanders (Weiner, 1976) allow a glimpse at fathers who maintained lifelong relationships with their children that are "characterized by love, protection, and nurture" (p. 448).

Although some Muted Group theorists might disagree that fathers are ever in a low-power position, Chopra concludes that giving voice to "father-care" is a critical process that will remove the category of caregiving from female ownership and in so doing transform the concept of gender identity completely. Yet, because most of the research in the area of Muted Group Theory has focused on men as the dominant group and women as the muted group, we shall pay most attention to that relationship in this chapter.

In training our focus on men and women, we need to clarify two terms: *sex* and *gender.* Generally, researchers use **sex** to mean biological categories, male and female, determined by the presence of XX chromosomes for females and XY chromosomes for males. Philip Smith (1985) observes that most people believe that sex is "an inherent and/or God-given attribute of individuality, an inalienable, incontrovertible fact of human existence" (p. 20). In contrast, **gender** is defined as the learned behaviors that constitute femininity and masculinity in a given culture. Thus, gender is changeable and reflects whatever the culture accepts at a given time for these roles. Currently, it is within the definition of masculinity to have pierced ears, and it is within the definition of femininity to have tattoos. At an earlier time, these attributes would not have been deemed appropriate. However, it is also the case that the terms *sex* and *gender* are often blurred because women are socialized to be feminine and men are encouraged to be masculine. Therefore, we will use the terms interchangeably in this chapter.

sex
biological category divided into male and female

gender
social category consisting of the learned behaviors that constitute masculinity and femininity for a given culture

Assumptions of Muted Group Theory

After the Ardeners' groundwork in developing the concepts of Muted Group Theory, Cheris Kramarae (1981) built on the theory to focus it more specifically on communication. Additionally, as Kramarae comments, her aims are somewhat more limited than those of the Ardeners, who were concerned with

"Talk to me, Alice. I speak woman."

applying Muted Group Theory across many cultures. Kramarae's interest is in the "questions the theory raises and [the] explanations it . . . provide[s] for the communication patterns among and between women and men in Great Britain and the United States" (1981, p. 4). Toward this end, Kramarae first isolates three assumptions she believes are central to Muted Group Theory:

- Women perceive the world differently than men because of women's and men's different experiences and activities rooted in the division of labor.

- Because of their political dominance, men's system of perception is dominant, impeding the free expression of women's alternative models of the world.

- In order to participate in society, women must transform their own models in terms of the received male system of expression. (1981, p. 3)

We will review each of these assumptions in turn.

Gender-Based Differences in Perception

This assumption begins with the premise that the world is a different place for women and men and that their experiences differ. Further, the assumption posits an explanation for these differences. The explanation lies in the division of labor that allocates work on the basis of sex, such that women are responsible for tasks in the home and men are responsible for work outside the home. The division of labor began in Western countries in the eighteenth and nineteenth centuries as a result of social transformations, in large part related to the industrial revolution (Coontz, 1988). The industrial revolution took work out of the home and made it a paid activity. Prior to that, work had been intertwined with home life because all members of the family contributed to the family's survival, usually on subsistence farms. No one was literally paid for their specific labor; the money the family realized came from selling their produce or livestock, the result of collective work by the entire family.

**gender
polarization**
viewing men and
women as polar
opposites

The separation of the workplace from the home led to a recognition of the two as separate spheres; the conceptualization of public and private came about, and the family was classed as private life (Tronto, 1993). The result of this division was to cast women's role in the home, or private life, and men's role in the workplace, or public life. This had the effect of clearly delineating women's tasks in the home and sharply dividing what women's responsibilities were in contrast to men's. Stephanie Coontz (1988) notes that this trend occurred in all classes and ethnic groups in the United States except African Americans.

You can see the logic of blaming the division of labor for men's and women's differing worldviews. When people's occupations differ greatly, they tend to see the world in different ways. If your day is spent caring for children and the home, your experiences will vary a great deal from those of someone whose day is spent selling merchandise to others. Further, Sandra Bem (1993) argues that this initial division also created what she labels a **gender polarization** lens that caused people to see women and men as very different from each other. In 1909, Clara E. Hasse, a student at Milwaukee Downer Women's College, wrote a senior essay revealing how she looked through the lens of gender polarization. She wrote about the topic of single-sex schooling, saying, "It were far better not to class girls with boys while receiving their education, the most important reason being that they are so entirely different and therefore should be taught diversely" (1909, p. 10). To the extent that we in the United States have subscribed to the notion that women and men are radically different from each other, we might expect that they have been treated differently. Different treatment should certainly result in different experiences.

As we have written elsewhere with Judy Pearson (Pearson, West, & Turner, 1995), "From birth it is clear that male and female babies are treated differently. . . . Male [infants] are more likely than female infants to be described as 'strong,' 'solid,' or 'independent.' Female infants, on the other hand, are often described as 'loving,' 'cute,' and 'sweet'" (p. 49). In Chapter 5, when we discussed Symbolic Interaction Theory, we commented on the power of other people's predictions on self-concept formation. We can see how males and females are treated differently and expected to do different activities. Even when women work outside the home, they are often still expected to take primary responsibility for the home and care for children or elderly parents as the need arises (Wood, 1994). Arlie Hochschild (1989) talks about the phenomenon of the **second shift**, where working mothers put in eight hours at their paid job and then come home to do a second shift there.

second shift
the phenomenon of
working women put-
ting in eight hours on
the job and another
day's work at home

One of your authors asked her class to describe situations that they believe are uniquely experienced by their own sex and for which, currently, no word exists and then to give those experiences a name (Turner, 1992). This was patterned after an activity Judy Pearson (1985) calls creating "genlets" or "sexlets." The results were not completely supportive of Muted Group Theory because men generated essentially the same number of "genlets" as women, indicating that language fails men as well as women.

However, the types of words created did differ between men and women. Men coined words concerned with drinking and competition, whereas women created words focusing on relationships and personal issues such as appearance. Women also noted experiences where they felt fearful or uncertain, and this concern was not included in the men's words. For instance, women coined the word *herdastudaphobia*, which meant feeling fear when passing a group of strange men on the street, and they created the word *piglabelphobia*, to designate a woman's tendency to limit what she eats in front of a date for fear of being labeled a pig. Women also coined the term *Brinkley-mirror*, to refer to the insecurity women feel at being compared to glamour models. Men created words such as *scarfaholic*, an eating contest among men; *gearheaditis*, an obsession with fixing up your car to have it be the best on the road; and *Schwarzenegger-syndrome*, working out overtime to build muscles bigger than the other guys'. Interestingly, when men focused on issues of eating and body building, their concern was competitive. When women addressed these same issues, their concern was on their own insecurities and their desire to please others. Thus, the assumption that men and women have different experiences was supported by these results.

All of these instances support the first assumption of Muted Group Theory: that women perceive the world differently than men because of women's and men's different experiences and activities rooted in the division of labor.

Male Dominance

The second assumption of Muted Group Theory goes beyond simply noting that women and men have different experiences. This assumption states that men are the dominant group, and their experiences are given preference over women's. Specifically, men are in charge of naming and labeling social life, and women's experiences are often unnamed as a result. Women then have difficulties talking about their experiences. For example, Kramarae (1981) tells the following story about a woman who attended a workshop on the topic of women as a muted group and spoke about a common problem she experienced with her husband:

> She and her husband, both working full-time outside the home, usually arrive home at about the same time. She would like him to share the dinner-making responsibilities but the job always falls upon her. Occasionally, he says, "I would be glad to make dinner. But you do it so much better than I." She was pleased to receive this compliment but as she found herself in the kitchen each time she realized that he was using a verbal strategy for which she had no word and thus had more difficulty identifying and bringing to his awareness. She told the people at the seminar, "I had to tell you the whole story to explain to you how he was using flattery to keep me in my female place." She said she needed a word to define the strategy, or a word to define the person who uses the strategy, a word which would be commonly understood by both women and men. (p. 7)

In this example, the woman had difficulty naming her experience although she knew something was occurring that she wished to talk about. In a similar fashion, Patricia Fitzpatrick from our opening vignette is experiencing problems speaking out in class, talking to the other students, speaking to her co-workers, and generally articulating her ideas. She is uncomfortable about her difficulties, and she is blaming herself because things are not working out as she planned.

Muted Group Theory takes a different perspective, however, noting that these problems are not the result of women's inadequacies but rather are caused by the unresponsiveness of the language women have to express themselves. Muted Group Theory argues that any speaker would be inarticulate if there were no words to describe her or his thoughts.

The second assumption of Muted Group Theory asserts that men's political dominance allows their perceptions to be dominant. This forces alternative perceptions—those that women hold as a result of their different experiences—into a subordinate position. Women's communication is constrained because of this subordinate position. Dale Spender (1984) suggests that when people talk about sex and use the word *foreplay,* men's perspective is privileged. Most women would say that one of the things they like best about intimate contact is cuddling. Calling it "foreplay" relegates the activity to something of lesser importance than the "main event" of sexual intercourse. Spender argues that when women talk about sexual activity using language like "foreplay," they are not able to give full expression to their experience, and many times they do not even realize that language is separating them from their own sense of the experience.

Cindy Reuther and Gail Fairhurst (2000) discuss the "glass ceiling" for women in organizational hierarchies and comment on how (White) men's experiences dominate the world of work. They observe that patriarchal values tend to reproduce themselves in organizations to men's advantage. They note:

> The practices leading to the replication of white males in senior levels are based in ideology. In often subtle and unconscious ways (e.g., in language, dress, and work rituals), white women and men and women of color are pressured to commit to patriarchal and white interests and value systems. The upshot is that replication promotes conformity rather than a pluralistic system in which individuals can interact and work according to personal principles. (p. 242)

Overall, then, MGT assumes that men's, especially White men's, experiences are dominant and women and people of color need to subordinate their own experiences to the extent that they can in order to partake in social and organizational success.

Women's Translation Processes

The final assumption of Muted Group Theory speaks to the process of translation that women must go through in order to participate in social life. Women's task is to conceptualize a thought and then scan the vocabulary, which is really better suited to men's thinking, for the best words for encoding that thought. You can see how this renders women less fluent speakers than men. Tillie Olsen (1978), the author of *Silences,* says that although men are supposed to tell it straight, women have to "tell it slant" (p. 23).

The pauses that worry Patricia Fitzpatrick in our opening scenario are attributable, according to Muted Group Theory, to this cumbersome process of

In small groups, create a role play that illustrates the three central assumptions of Muted Group Theory. Be prepared to explain how your role play relates to each of the assumptions.

translation that women have to engage in when speaking. Some researchers (Hayden, 1994) suggest that women's groups engage in a great deal of overlaps and simultaneous speaking because they are helping one another cope with a language system that is not well suited to their tasks. Thus, when women speak with one another, they collaborate on storytelling—not so much because women are collaborative by nature but rather because they need to help one another find the right words to encode their thoughts.

Some of the problems inherent in the translation process are highlighted by examining instances of women's words for experiences becoming part of the general vocabulary. Before the 1970s, the term *sexual harassment* did not exist. Women who experienced what we now call sexual harassment had nothing to use for labeling their experiences. As Gloria Steinem has said, before the term was accepted into the vocabulary, women simply accepted harassment as part of life. Years ago, one of your authors had a job in a library, and her boss was a male who liked to comment on her figure and compare it to his wife's. At the time, your author could only say that she had a bad job with a weird boss. This lack of terminology makes the experience individual and minimizes the inappropriateness of the behavior in the workplace. Labeling it sexual harassment places it in a category, suggests some coping strategies, and points to its seriousness. Further, giving the experience a term, *sexual harassment,* allows us to see that it exists broadly and is supported at many levels of society. Social change is possible when we recognize the phenomenon with a label. Similarly, the terms *date rape, marital rape,* and *stalking* all name crimes that without the labels might simply be seen as individual problems and not be recognized as serious offenses. Without these words, women faced silence when they wanted to talk about their experiences, and they were at a loss for instituting social change.

Marsha Houston (Houston & Kramarae, 1991) points out that silencing can be accomplished *by* women as well, as can be seen by examining some talk between African American and European American women. Houston's observation is that silencing occurs not only through preventing talk but also by shaping and controlling the talk of others. When White women criticize African American women's talk as "confrontational," "the message to black women in white women's pejorative use of this term is, 'Talk like me, or I won't listen'" (p. 389). If subordinate group members hear this message and try to conform to it, their talk is slowed and disempowered. When Patricia Fitzpatrick thinks about how her contributions sound and attempts to speak like the other students, she is hampered in her fluency.

The Process of Silencing

The central assertion of Muted Group Theory is that women are silenced and rendered inarticulate as speakers. This silencing does not rely on explicit enforcement or coercion. As Robin Sheriff (2000) observes, silencing of muted groups is a socially shared phenomenon. "Unlike the activity of speech, which does not require more than a single actor, silence demands collaboration and the tacit communal understandings that such collaboration presupposes. Although it is contractual in nature, a critical feature of this type of silence is that it is both a consequence and an index of an unequal distribution of power" (p. 114). Thus, silence is accomplished through a social understanding of who holds the power and who does not. In this section we will briefly review a few of the methods used to accomplish this power distribution and resulting silencing. This is not an exhaustive list of methods of silencing. Perhaps you can think of other ways you have experienced or observed.

Ridicule

Houston and Kramarae (1991) point out that women's speech is trivialized. "Men label women's talk chattering, gossiping, nagging, whining, bitching (Cut the cackle!)" (p. 390). Men often tell women that they talk about meaningless things and that they cannot understand how women spend so much time on the phone talking to their girlfriends. Women themselves often refer to their own talk as gabbing or gossiping. Women are also told that they have no sense of humor, and this is an opportunity for ridicule (see the Research Note). Also, women's concerns are often trivialized by men as not being important enough to listen to, yet women are expected to be supportive listeners for men.

Ritual

Some people have pointed out that many social rituals have the effect of silencing women or advocating that women are subordinate to men. One such ritual is the wedding ceremony. There are a number of aspects in the traditional ceremony that silence the bride. First, the groom stands at the front while the bride is "delivered" to him on the arm of her father. The father then "gives her away" to the groom. Further, the groom stands at the right hand of the minister (or whoever officiates), and this is traditionally a place of higher status than the bride's position, to the left. The groom says all of the vows first. The bride wears a veil and a white gown to indicate that she has been "preserved" for the groom. The groom is told at the end that he may kiss the bride. The couple is pronounced "man" and "wife," and traditionally, the bride changes her name to the groom's. In many services, the couple is introduced immediately after the vows as Mr. and Mrs. John Smith. Although many couples work to individualize the ceremony and have changed some of these aspects, the traditional ritual points to subordination for the bride.

Research Note

Neuliep, J. W. (1987). Gender differences in the perception of sexual and nonsexual humor. *Journal of Social Behavior and Personality, 2,* 345–351.

This article examines the influence of a person's gender on the perception of sexist and nonsexist jokes. The study was framed by Muted Group Theory. Specifically, James Neuliep argues that the issue of women's mutedness is especially acute in the area of humor because one of the most consistent beliefs that men share about women's speech behavior is that they lack a sense of humor. MGT suggests that this male assumption—that women have no sense of humor because they do not find men's jokes to be funny—is a result of differing concerns and experiences and unequal access to language.

Neuliep surveyed 120 undergraduates (60 female and 60 male) at a midwestern college to test the following three hypotheses derived from Muted Group Theory: (1) Perceived humor is a function of joke type—either sexist or nonsexist; (2) perceived humor is a function of the joke teller's gender—either male or female; and (3) perceived humor is a function of the joke receiver's gender—either male or female. These hypotheses follow the logic set out by MGT. Kramarae (1981) asserts, and Neuliep concurs, that humor is largely culture specific. Thus, from the perspective of MGT, we would expect that women would tend to find men's jokes (sexist humor) less funny than men do because the people who are in power (men) overlook women's concerns because they differ from their own.

The 120 respondents heard jokes that Neuliep classified as either sexist or nonsexist and evaluated their level of humor. Neuliep found support for hypotheses 1 and 3. His results indicated that men perceive sexist humor as funnier than women do, women perceive nonsexist humor as funnier than sexist humor, and the gender of the joker had no significant impact on perceived humor of either sexist or nonsexist jokes.

Neuliep discusses these results in the context of Muted Group Theory. He concludes that they provide tentative support for the theory. Although societal sexism was observed by the fact that men found sexist jokes funnier than women did, men did not rate jokes told by women to be less funny than those told by men. Neuliep suggests that perhaps the emergence of successful female comics on television, comedy albums, and movies might have changed perceptions about women's sense of humor.

Finally, Neuliep notes that his study had a few limitations. First, his use of college students as respondents might have biased the results because college students may be more sensitive to women's issues than the general public. Second, his method involved giving the participants jokes in written form with a description of the joke teller as either a male or female friend who tells great jokes. Had the participants actually heard real people telling these jokes, the results might have been different.

Men as Gatekeepers

Researchers have noted that men decide what goes into history books, leaving women's history untapped (Smith, 1979). Additionally, the media are controlled by men; women's talk and contributions get relatively little coverage in mainstream media. Further, many communication practices place men as central and women as eclipsed. For instance, the practice of women taking men's family names when they marry exemplifies men's control of the public record and the silencing of women's voice and identity. In her (1981) book, Kramarae talks about the process she went through concerning her name changes. When she married, her husband's name was Kramer and her name upon marriage became Cheris Rae Kramer. At the time of her marriage, it was not legal for a wife

to keep her own name. Later the laws changed, and Kramarae combined her husband's last name with her middle name and created her own name. This change was accomplished with a great deal of discussion and controversy, and many people questioned her judgment. Kramarae points out that no one questioned her husband throughout the entire process, and his name remained unchanged.

A communication behavior that keeps men in control is interruptions. When men interrupt women, the women often switch to talk about whatever topic the men raise. When women interrupt men, this is usually not the case. Men frequently go back to what they originally were talking about (DeFrancisco, 1991). Additionally, men often fail to attend to their partners' talk; they refuse to consider what the women are speaking about and shift the topic to one of their preference (DeFrancisco, 1991).

Harassment

Elizabeth Kissling (1991) writes about street harassment, noting that women do not have free access to public streets. Men control public spaces in that women walking there may receive verbal threats (sometimes couched as compliments). Sexual harassment in the workplace is another method of telling women that they do not belong out of the domestic sphere. Mary Strine (1992) shows how some talk in universities naturalizes harassment, making it seem like an acceptable practice. When women who have experienced sexual harassment are labeled as hysterical, overly sensitive, or troublemakers, their concerns are dismissed and defined as unimportant (Clair, 1993).

Strategies of Resistance

As we mentioned at the beginning of this chapter, Muted Group Theory is a critical theory; as such, it goes beyond explaining a phenomenon—such as women's muting—to advocating change in the status quo. Houston and Kramarae (1991) offer several strategies for this purpose. One strategy of resistance consists of naming the strategies of silencing as we have suggested above. Through this process, the silencing is made accessible and a topic for discussion. A second approach advocated by Houston and Kramarae is to reclaim, elevate, and celebrate "trivial" discourse. Houston and Kramarae mention that

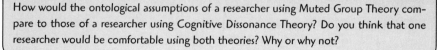

women are beginning to celebrate and study oral histories, diaries and journals, and the so-called alternative means of expression like sewing, weaving, and other handwork that is often done by women. Through examining these forums for expression, women are recognizing the "effectiveness, impact, and eloquence of women's communicative experiences as well as men's" (Foss & Foss, 1991, p. 21).

Women also are creating a new and more representative language to capture their experiences. Although changing the language is an ambitious task, language is malleable, and as new concepts enter our culture, new words are created to describe them. Think of all the words we now have to talk about computers and computer-mediated communication (itself a new term!). Suzette Elgin (1988) invented a whole language, which she calls Laadan, focusing on women's experiences. Kramarae and Paula Treichler (1985) compiled a feminist dictionary to give woman-centered definitions to words of importance in women's experiences.

Through naming strategies of silencing, reclaiming, elevating, and celebrating women's discourse, and creating new language for uniquely gendered experiences, muting can be resisted. In short, there are many approaches to changing the situation that Muted Group Theory delineates and explains.

Critique and Closing

Muted Group Theory has many adherents, but as you would expect with such a politically charged theory, it also has detractors. The critique of the theory revolves around three main points: The theory overly essentializes men and women; the theory exaggerates women's mutedness; and the theory has not received much empirical support. We will briefly discuss each in turn.

First, like Standpoint Theory, Muted Group Theory has been criticized for essentialism, or the belief that all men are essentially the same and all women are essentially the same and the two differ from each other. These critics note that there is great difference within groups; sometimes the difference within a group (such as women) can be greater than the difference between groups (women and men). Some approach this from the standpoint of other influences on communication besides gender, such as status, age, ethnicity, or upbringing. Others disavow the notion of influences altogether, claiming that both individuals and groups are constantly changing through communication. Therefore,

T*I*P

Theory * Into * Practice

Some see computers as posing a new language system—a system that also may pose some problems for women in terms of articulation. As computers are often seen as men's domain, women have not had as much exposure or experience with them and thus can feel less competent about using them and expressing themselves electronically. An article in *USA Today* from 1998 speaks to this issue:

> Frustrations with her computer literally drove Anne Cortina underneath her desk at Hunterdon Central Regional High School in Flemington, N.J.
>
> "The computer wasn't working the way I wanted it to," explains the 17-year-old senior, who last year joined an after-school pilot technology program that produces the on-line magazine *Electric Soup*. She was tackling her first issue as editor.
>
> "I just hid under the desk and called a friend over and said, please do this for me."
>
> Now laughing at the memory, Cortina says the friend, a boy, worked out the problems. "It was just a little glitch, but it was very frustrating when I had no idea why it was doing that."
>
> Cortina's experiences underscore findings in a report released Tuesday by the American Association of University Women (AAUW) Educational Foundation that points to a major new gender gap in technology. Boys clearly outnumber girls in higher-skill computer courses, says the report. . . .
>
> "A competitive nation cannot allow girls to write off technology as an exclusively male domain. Teachers will need to be prepared to deal with this issue," says the report, researched by the Washington-based American Institutes for Research.
>
> Cortina believes a lot of girls suffer similar anxieties when first confronted with the complexities of computers and other technology. "It's been touted primarily as a man's field. It's the whole math, science, technology thing goes together with the left brain and that's for men. Women can sit and write the poetry and men can put it on the computer. I think that's the general stereotype."
>
> AAUW director Janice Weinman says there are subtle messages for girls interested in computers, such as video games with violent and sports themes aimed at boys. The study said boys tend to take more challenging roles, such as computer programming and problem solving. (p. 4D)

Source: Henry, 1998.

TIP Follow-up
Do you agree that women are a muted group when it comes to technology use? How might technology resolve some of the problems that MGT points out?

any attempt to state what women or men are like falsely "freezes" those groups in time, as if they have a natural, unchangeable essence.

This argument was discussed in Chapter 27 in our consideration of Standpoint Theory. Like proponents of Standpoint Theory, supporters of Muted Group Theory agree that there are many groups that are muted and many standpoints. However, being female is a central grouping in our culture, and thus, even though women are not all alike and there is no essential womanness that all women possess, women in the United States are often treated alike. This treatment forms a common set of experiences that allows Muted Group Theory to make generalizations about men and women.

The second criticism is related to the first. Some critics maintain that women do speak out in public forums, and they point to women like Hillary Rodham Clinton, Christine Todd Whitman, Condoleeza Rice, and Elizabeth Dole as examples of women who are not muted at all. Muted Group theorists would agree that some women have gained a public forum, but they would also point out that they may have done so by becoming extremely adept at translation. Women who bring a uniquely female perspective to the table have not fared as well, according to these theorists. Further, until we are able to hear from a wide diversity of voices rather than forcing all who wish to speak out to conform to a narrow range of options defined by the dominant group, we will still need the critical commentary of Muted Group Theory.

Finally, some critics would note that not too much empirical evidence supports this theory, and related to this is the notion that the theory was derived over twenty years ago. Thus, critics claim the theory should be discarded because its dated assumptions are not empirically validated. Proponents would respond to this in two ways: First, more testing needs to be done, and second, a critical theory like Muted Group is not as conducive to hypothesis testing as an axiomatic theory like Uncertainty Reduction Theory (Chapter 9), for example.

Certainly Muted Group Theory is provocative and causes us to think about biases in language. It also trains a light on what we accept and what we reject from public speakers. Further, MGT explains some problems women experience in speaking out in many settings. It is up to us to decide if these issues form a systematic bias against subordinate groups and in favor of the dominant group, as Muted Group Theory asserts.

Discussion Starters

1. Do you think Muted Group Theory provides a good explanation for Patricia Fitzpatrick's difficulties in her classes and elsewhere? Why or why not? What other explanations might you offer to more satisfactorily understand her situation?

2. Have you had the experience of fumbling for words to describe something that you were feeling or something that happened to you? Do you think Muted Group Theory explains that experience for you? Why or why not? Do you consider yourself part of a group that is muted? Why or why not? Does being a member of a muted group affect one's perception of social reality? How?

3. Can you coin terms for experiences that women have and men do not? What about the reverse? Do you agree with Muted Group Theory that the English language fits the male experience of the world better than the female experience? Explain your answer.

4. We mentioned that one criticism of Muted Group Theory is that it overstates the problem that women have with language. Do you agree or disagree with this criticism? What specific evidence do you have for your position?

5. Have any of the reforms that are suggested by Muted Group Theory taken hold in our language? Give examples of changes in the language that have made it more responsive to women's experiences.

6. What other social groups might be muted in the United States? Does MGT provide a good explanation for groups, other than women, who are silenced? Why or why not?

Terms for Review

dominant group	gender polarization
sex	second shift
gender	

Online Learning Center

Visit the Online Learning Center at www.mhhe.com/west2. Use the multiple-choice and true/false quizzes to help you prepare for exams, and the glossary, crossword puzzles, and flashcards to further your knowledge of key terms.

CHAPTER 29

Communication Accommodation Theory

Luke Tomsha and Roberto Hernandez

As an upcoming spring graduate, 22-year-old Luke Tomsha was already preparing for the onslaught of interviews he would face graduating with a 3.86 grade point average. Luke knew that his grades were excellent, and as a double major (Spanish and communication), he felt that his chances of landing a good job were pretty good.

Luke's day to shine was upon him. He got an interview with a large accounting firm looking to hire someone in their human resources (HR) department. The position required proficiency in two languages. He flew to Denver for his first face-to-face interview with Roberto Hernandez, the HR director. The interview would be one that both men would remember for quite some time.

"Buenos dias, Luke," Roberto said.

"Good morn . . . I mean, buenos dias to you, Mr. Hernandez," Luke replied. Already, the initial tension eased. Luke immediately felt comfortable with his future boss.

Roberto continued, "Please, have a seat. I hope your flight last night was fine. I know that this time of the year can get a little bumpy, especially over the Rockies."

"Oh, it was great. I like to fly. This time, I got a chance to watch a movie that I hadn't seen yet. Personally, I love movies while I fly. It distracts me from the other noise and loud talking," Luke responded.

Their conversation continued. Luke was certainly a bit on edge but noticed that his accelerated speech rate slowed to match that of his interviewer. Yet, Luke still felt awkward because he did not know exactly when Mr. Hernandez would change the subject from flying to the job.

Roberto began to talk further about his two sons, both of whom love to fly. "Like you, I love to fly," Roberto related. "My wife, though, is a different story. I wish she had the same attitude as you."

Luke replied, "Hey, maybe it's simply *machismo*, but I'm never afraid to fly."

Roberto was struck by Luke's use of the term *machismo*. Was he adjusting his speech to Spanish simply because Roberto was Mexican? As an interviewer, he knew that job candidates get nervous, and maybe this was simply a nervous habit of his. Of course, it didn't escape Roberto's notice that Luke was speaking Spanish to a Mexican American man who happened to have a strong accent. Yet he didn't want to make anything out of it. "I trust you've come here with a lot of questions, Luke. Let me begin by answering one that we haven't really addressed over the phone—your salary."

"Está bien—that's okay. I just need to know more about the job and what it involves. We can get to the salary a bit later if you'd like," Luke answered.

"Ahem . . . no," said Roberto. "I can tell you that based on your application you are an excellent candidate, and we are willing to pay you 27.5. We're all happy to see your interest."

This theory is based on the research of **Howard Giles.**

"Thanks," Luke remarked. "I have to say that I wasn't ready to immediately discuss salary, but, hey, I appreciate it. Muchas gracias," he said with a slight smile.

Roberto was now agitated by Luke's frequent insertion of Spanish words into the conversation. He could handle the initial greeting; after all, he had initiated it. But Luke's continuing in this manner only made Roberto more uneasy. He didn't know whether to ask Luke to leave or simply to say how confused he was over Luke's persistent behavior. Of course, he could always remain silent and simply send Luke a rejection letter. Roberto decided to confront the young college student.

"Luke, I'm a bit taken aback by your Spanish. I realize that you are interviewing with a Chicano, I recognize your bilingual abilities, and I know I began with a friendly welcome in Spanish. But, frankly, it's a bit much, don't you think? Maybe I'm reaching here, but it's pretty patronizing." Roberto stared at the young job candidate.

"Mr. Hernandez," Luke explained, "I apologize if I've offended you. I realize that sometimes I was breaking into Spanish, and to be honest with you, yes, I guess I was a bit inappropriate. I was using Spanish to show you some respect, to ah . . . to show that I can weave Spanish into our conversation. . . . I really am sorry if I was out of place."

Luke was extremely nervous. He wasn't sure what Mr. Hernandez would say next. He was mad at himself for sounding like an idiot and assumed that he had lost the job. Maybe he tried too hard to adapt to his interviewer. Maybe an interview was the worst place for him to demonstrate his fluency in Spanish. Maybe he misread the situation.

"Listen, Luke," Roberto advised. "I've been around this firm for almost fifteen years. I've seen people come and go. I want you to be one of those who come and stay. I hope you don't get too upset by this. I know that I should've started out with a traditional Denver greeting and . . ."

". . . and I think," Luke interrupted, "that I should keep my mouth shut and not pretend I'm some expert in a foreign language! Really, I'm sorry about this."

Roberto smiled. "Now, let's get on with the rest of this interview."

When two people speak, they frequently mimic each other's speech and behavior. Often, we will talk to another who uses the same language we do, gestures similarly, and even speaks at a similar rate. We, in turn, may respond in kind to the other communicator. Imagine, for instance, situations where you have spoken to someone who has not gone to college. Chances are that you avoided using jargon that is unique to high school or college life—for example, talking about midterms or finals ("bombed the exam"), studying ("hit the books"), cafeteria food ("where's the beef?"), and so forth.

Although we all have these types of experiences at the interpersonal level, sometimes there are group- or culture-based differences, such as perceived differences in age group, in accent or ethnicity, or in the pace and rate of speech. Whether in an interpersonal relationship, in a small group, or across co-cultures, people adjust their communication to others. This adaptation is at the core of Communication Accommodation Theory, developed by Howard Giles. Formerly known as Speech Accommodation Theory (but later conceptualized more broadly to include nonverbal behaviors), Communication Accommodation Theory rests on the premise that when speakers interact, they adjust their speech, their vocal patterns, and/or their gestures to accommodate others. Giles and his colleagues believe that speakers have various reasons for being accommodative to others. Some people wish to evoke a listener's approval, others want to achieve communication efficiency, and still others want to maintain a positive social identity (Giles, Mulac, Bradac, & Johnson, 1987). As you can see in our opening story, however, we do not always achieve what we aim for. Clearly, accommodation involves some consequences. We address this topic a bit later in the chapter.

Communication Accommodation Theory had its beginnings in 1973, when Giles first introduced the notion of an "accent mobility" model, which is based on various accents heard in interview situations (similar to the situation with Luke and Roberto). Much of the subsequent theory and research has remained sensitive to the various communication accommodations undertaken in conversations among diverse cultural groups, including the elderly, people of color, and the visually impaired (for example, Gallois, Callan, & Johnstone, 1984; Gallois, Franklyn-Stokes, Giles, & Coupland, 1988; Klemz, 1977). We discuss this theory with this cultural diversity in mind.

To get a sense of the central characteristic of Communication Accommodation Theory, we first delineate what is meant by the word *accommodation*. For our purposes, **accommodation** is defined as the ability to adjust, modify, or regulate one's behavior in response to another. Accommodation is usually done unconsciously. We tend to have internal cognitive scripts that we draw on when we find ourselves in conversations with others. Think of accommodation as a kind of Rolodex where each conversation we have requires a particular card for response. We instinctively pull the conversational card out of a file stored in our head. In a conversation with a 15-year-old girl, you might find yourself using teen vocabulary; with an 85-year-old, you might slow your speech and use more facial animation. This is all done without much thought.

accommodation
adjusting, modifying, or regulating behavior in response to others

Like several other theories in this book, Communication Accommodation Theory is derived from research first conducted in another field, in this case, social psychology. To this end, it's important to address the theoretical vehicle that launched Giles's thinking: Social Identity Theory.

Social Psychology and Social Identity

Much of the research and theory in the field of social psychology pertain directly to how people search for meaning in the behaviors of others and how this meaning influences future interactions with others. Stephen Worchel (1998) summarizes the field this way: "Typically, social psychology searches for effects [of behaviors] and the causes of these effects" (p. 53). One of the central concepts discussed in the research of social psychology is identity. Recognizing the importance of the self and its relationship to group identity, Henri Tajfel (1982) and his colleague John Turner (Tajfel & Turner, 1986) articulated **Social Identity Theory,** which argues that a person's social identity is primarily determined by the groups to which he or she belongs. Researchers and theorists in Social Identity suggest that people are "motivated to join the most attractive groups and/or give an advantage to the groups to which one belongs (in-group)"

Social Identity Theory
a theory that proposes a person's identity is shaped by the groups to which he or she belongs

in-groups
groups in which a
person feels he or she
belongs
out-groups
groups in which a
person feels he or she
does not belong

(Worchel, Rothgerber, Day, Hart, & Butemeyer, 1998, p. 390). When people are given an opportunity, Worchel and colleagues contend, they will provide more resources to their own groups, rather than to out-groups. And when in-groups are identified, an individual decides the extent to which the group is central to his or her identity. Social identity, then, is primarily based on the comparisons that people make between **in-groups** (groups to which a person feels he or she belongs) and **out-groups** (groups to which a person feels he or she does not belong).

Tajfel and Turner (1986) note that people strive to acquire or maintain positive social identity, and when social identity is perceived as unsatisfactory, they will either join a group they feel more at home in or make the existing group a more positive experience. Summing up the Social Identity perspective, Tajfel and Turner observe that "the basic hypothesis, then, is that pressures to evaluate one's own group positively through in-group/out-group comparisons lead social groups to attempt to differentiate themselves from each other" (p. 16). Tajfel and Turner note that communication exists on a continuum from "interindividual" to "intergroup." So, according to the theory, the more that Luke perceives Roberto to be either a "Chicano" or a "boss" rather than simply "Mr. Hernandez," the more Luke will rely on stereotypes or group-level impressions to understand Roberto's behavior.

Giles was influenced by the thinking of Social Identity Theory. He felt that we accommodate not only to *specific* others but also to those we perceive as members of other groups. Thus, intergroup variables and goals influence the communication process. Giles, like many social psychologists, believes that people are influenced by a number of behaviors. Specifically, he argues that an individual's speech style (accent, pitch, rate, interruption patterns) can affect the impressions that others have of the individual. Giles and Smith (1979) also comment that the nature of the setting, the conversation topic, and the type of person with whom one communicates will all intersect to determine the speech manner one adopts in a given situation. If an individual is viewed favorably, communicator A will shift his or her speech style to become more like that of communicator B; that is, communicator A has *accommodated* communicator B. Giles and Smith maintain that people accommodate their speech style to how they believe others in the conversation will best receive it. In our opening, you can see how Luke shifts his speech to accommodate what he believes (incorrectly) Mr. Hernandez will appreciate.

Communication Accommodation Theory is based on many of the same principles and concepts as Social Identity Theory. Giles was influenced by the belief that when members of different groups come together, they compare themselves. If their comparisons are favorable, a positive social identity will result. Giles expands on this notion by claiming that the same can be said when speech style is considered.

With this theoretical footing in place, we now turn our attention to the assumptions guiding the development of Communication Accommodation Theory. As we discuss these, you will be able to sense the influence of social psychology, and Social Identity Theory in particular.

Assumptions of Communication Accommodation Theory

Giles and other Accommodation Theory proponents would be interested in the accommodation taking place between Luke Tomsha and Roberto Hernandez. Their conversation exemplifies a number of issues that underlie the basic assumptions of the theory. Recalling that accommodation is influenced by a number of personal, situational, and cultural circumstances, we identify these below:

- Speech and behavioral similarities and dissimilarities exist in all conversations.

- The manner in which we perceive the speech and behaviors of another will determine how we evaluate a conversation.

- Language and behaviors impart information about social status and group belonging.

- Accommodation varies in its degree of appropriateness, and norms guide the accommodation process.

First, many principles of Communication Accommodation Theory rest on the belief that there are similarities and dissimilarities between communicators in a conversation. Past experiences, you may recall, form a person's field of experience, a concept we discussed in Chapter 1. Whether in speech or behaviors, people bring their various fields of experiences into a conversation. These varied experiences and backgrounds will determine the extent to which one person will accommodate another. The more similar our attitudes and beliefs are to those of others, the more we will be attracted to, and accommodate those others.

Let's look at a few examples to illustrate this assumption. Consider our opening scenario with Luke and Roberto. They are clearly from different professional backgrounds with different levels of work experience. Presumably, they are products of different family backgrounds with different beliefs and values. The two are clearly dissimilar in some ways, yet they are similar in others—for example, they both like to fly, and they both have an interest in working at the accounting firm.

To illustrate this assumption further, consider the following dialogue between a grandparent and a teenage granddaughter:

GRANDMOTHER: I don't know why you're wearing all black. You'll have people talking.

GRANDDAUGHTER: So? People talked about your generation wearing weird stuff, too. It's the style now.

GRANDMOTHER: But we only wore black for funerals.

GRANDDAUGHTER: Yeah, and that's because back then, that's the most excitement you had! You people never had any fun.

GRANDMOTHER: You would be surprised how much fun we had. It was different from what you think now. We did a lot when I was younger.

In this conversation, the granddaughter draws conclusions about the grandparent using group-based expectations: Older people don't understand

perception
process of attending to and interpreting a message
evaluation
process of judging a conversation

teenagers. This expectation influences the teenager's communication with her grandmother.

The second assumption rests on both perception and evaluation. Communication Accommodation is a theory concerned with how people both perceive and evaluate what takes place in a conversation. **Perception** is the process of attending to and interpreting a message, whereas **evaluation** is the process of judging a conversation. People first perceive what takes place in a conversation (for instance, the other person's speaking abilities) before they decide how to behave in a conversation. Consider, for example, Luke's response to Roberto. The interviewer's informality at the beginning of the interview is perceived by Luke as a good way to break the ice and eliminate some of his tension. Luke's subsequent behavior reflects a relaxed style. Luke is like most people in their first interview: He gets a sense of the interview atmosphere (perception) and then reacts accordingly (evaluation).

Motivation is a key part of the perception and evaluation process in Communication Accommodation Theory. That is, we may perceive another person's speech and behaviors, but we may not always evaluate them. This often happens, for instance, when we greet another person, engage in small talk, and simply walk on. We normally don't take the time to evaluate such a conversational encounter.

Yet there are times when perceiving the words and behaviors of another leads to our evaluation of the other person. We may greet someone, for instance, and engage in small talk, but then be surprised when we hear that the other person recently got divorced. According to Giles and colleagues (1987), it is then that we decide our evaluative and communicative responses. We may express our happiness, our sorrow, or our support. We do this by engaging in an accommodating communication style.

The third assumption of Communication Accommodation Theory pertains to the effects that language has on others. Specifically, language has the ability to communicate status and group belonging between communicators in a conversation. Consider what occurs when two people who speak different languages try to communicate with each other. Giles and John Wiemann (1987) discuss this situation:

> In bilingual, or even bidialectal, situations, where ethnic majority and minority peoples coexist, second language learning is dramatically unidirectional: that is, it is very common for the dominant group to acquire the linguistic habits of the subordinate collectivity. . . . Indeed, it is no accident that cross-culturally what is "standard," "correct," and "cultivated" language behavior is that of the aristocracy, the upper or ruling classes and their institutions. (p. 361)

The language used in a conversation, then, will likely reflect the individual with the higher social status. In addition, group belonging comes into play because inferred in this quotation is a desire to be part of the "dominant" group.

To better understand this assumption, let's return to our opening. In the interview situation with Mr. Hernandez, Luke's language and behaviors are guided by the interviewer. This is what normally occurs in interviews: The individual with the higher social status sets the tone through his or her language

and behaviors. Although Roberto is a member of a co-culture that has been historically oppressed, he nonetheless has the power to establish the interview's direction. Those wishing to identify with or to become part of another's group—for example, Luke wishing to be offered a job by Mr. Hernandez—will usually accommodate.

Finally, the fourth assumption focuses on norms and issues of social appropriateness. We note that accommodation can vary in social appropriateness and that accommodation is rooted in norm usage. It's important to understand that accommodation may not always be worthwhile and beneficial. Certainly, there are times when accommodating another is important, yet there are also times when accommodation is inappropriate. For instance, Melanie Booth-Butterfield and Felicia Jordan (1989) found that people from marginalized cultures are usually expected to adapt (accommodate) to others.

Norms have been shown to play some role in Giles's theory (Gallois & Callan, 1991). **Norms** are expectations of behaviors that individuals feel should or should not occur in a conversation. The varied backgrounds of communicators like Luke and Roberto, for instance, or those of a grandparent and grandchild will influence what they expect in their conversations. The relationship between norms and accommodation is made clear by Cynthia Gallois and Victor Callan (1991): "Norms put constraints of varying degree . . . on the accommodative moves that are perceived as desirable in an interaction" (p. 253). Therefore, the general norm that a younger person is obedient to an older person suggests that Luke will be more accommodative in his communication to Mr. Hernandez. Of course, the interview context itself entails special expectations for behavior.

These four assumptions form the foundation for the remainder of our discussion of the theory. We now examine the ways that people adapt in conversations.

norms
expectations of behavior in conversations

Ways to Adapt

Communication Accommodation Theory suggests that in conversations, people have options. They may create a conversational community that entails using the same or similar language or nonverbal system, they may distinguish themselves from others, or they may try too hard to adapt. These choices are labeled convergence, divergence, and overaccommodation. We examine each below and illustrate them in Figure 29.1.

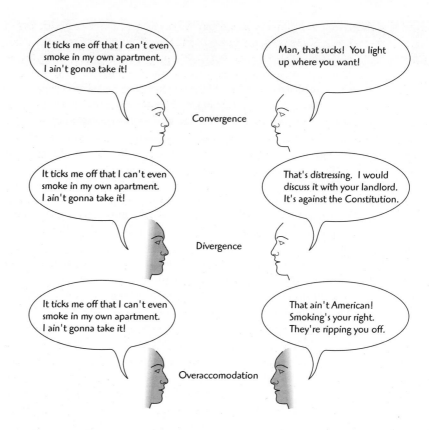

It ticks me off that I can't even smoke in my own apartment. I ain't gonna take it!

Man, that sucks! You light up where you want!

Convergence

It ticks me off that I can't even smoke in my own apartment. I ain't gonna take it!

That's distressing. I would discuss it with your landlord. It's against the Constitution.

Divergence

It ticks me off that I can't even smoke in my own apartment. I ain't gonna take it!

That ain't American! Smoking's your right. They're ripping you off.

Overaccomodation

Figure 29.1
Ways to Adapt or Accommodate in Conversation

Convergence: Merging Thoughts Ahead

The first process associated with Communication Accommodation Theory is termed *convergence*. Giles, Nikolas Coupland, and Justine Coupland (1991) define **convergence** as "a strategy whereby individuals adapt to each other's communicative behaviors" (p. 7). People may adapt to speech rate, pause, smiling, eye gaze, and other verbal and nonverbal behaviors. Convergence is a selective process; we do not always choose to enact a convergent strategy with people. When people do converge, they rely on their perceptions of the other person's speech or behaviors. What this means is that Luke Tomsha's decision to use Spanish in his interview with Roberto Hernandez is partially based on his knowledge that Mr. Hernandez began the interview with a greeting in Spanish; Luke attempts to converge with the opening tone set by his interviewer.

In addition to the perception of the other's communication, convergence is also based on attraction (Giles et al., 1987). Usually, when communicators are attracted to others, they will converge in their conversations. Attraction is a broad term that encompasses a number of other characteristics, such as liking, charisma, and credibility. Giles and Smith (1979) believe that there are a number of factors that affect our attraction for others—for example, the possibility of future interactions with the listener, the speaker's ability to communicate, and status differential between communicators. Having similar beliefs, having

convergence
strategy used to adapt to another's behavior

a similar personality, or behaving in similar ways causes people to be attracted to each other and is likely to prompt convergence. Remember, however, that uncovering similarities occurs over time. People may not instantly know whether they are attracted to each other and whether this will lead to identifying their similarities. And the relational history between communicators may be a critical issue in convergence. For instance, Richard Street's (1991) research indicates that physicians differ in their convergence patterns with first-time patients and with repeat patients. He cautions, however, that differences in convergence may be explained by looking at the traditional roles of doctor and patient as well as the time lag between visits.

At first view, convergence may appear to be a positive accommodating strategy, and it usually is. Our discussion so far implies that the other person is viewed as similar to the individual or that at least one is attracted to the other in a conversation. Yet, as we explained above, convergence may be based on stereotypical perceptions. As Giles and colleagues (1987) conclude, "Convergence is often cognitively mediated by our stereotypes of how socially categorized others will speak" (p. 18). What this means is that people will converge toward stereotypes, rather than toward real speech and behaviors.

There are obvious implications of stereotypical convergence. For example, gay fathers and lesbian mothers report that too many people—including educators—rely on outdated stereotypes of homosexuals when they communicate with them (West & Turner, 1995). Examining the cultural experiences of African Americans, Mark Orbe (1998) notes that African Americans are often identified in stereotypical ways. He points out that **indirect stereotyping** exists, that is, stereotyping when European Americans talk to their African American friends about what they believe to be African American "subjects" (sports, music, and so forth). Some African Americans report that if they speak nonstandard dialect, they are especially prone to stereotypical reactions. Marsha Houston (2000) agrees. Her research shows that when describing themselves, White women in particular identify their speech as appropriate and standard and describe African American female speech as nonstandard, incorrect, or deviant.

indirect stereotyping imposing outdated and rigid assumptions of a cultural group upon that group

Other cultural groups have also been the target of stereotyping. Edwin Vaughan (1998), for example, contends that blind people are repeatedly addressed as if they are deaf. Shobha Pais (1997) maintains that Asian Indian women in the United States are often perceived as strange because of their sari (fabric draped over the shoulder and head) or *salwar kameez* (pantsuit). And Charmaine Shutiva (2000) bemoans the fact that the Native American culture is erroneously viewed as stoic and unemotional, when in reality, it involves a great deal of humor and joy. These examples demonstrate that a number of cultural groups continue to be stereotyped. Stereotyped perceptions may influence the extent to which an individual will converge.

Before we leave our discussion of convergence, we need to briefly discuss the evaluation of convergence. Specifically, what occurs when people attempt to converge in their conversations? How do people respond? We have already illustrated a number of examples that demonstrate both positive and negative consequences of convergence. But how do we know how our convergence will be met?

Theory Application in Groups (TAG)

An essential feature of Communication Accommodation Theory is the notion of convergence. In small groups, discuss the possible range of reactions to and evaluations of the issue of convergence in intercultural encounters. Be sure to discuss the ways people converge and how others might react to that convergence.

First, we need to consider that an evaluation of convergence usually depends on whether the convergence is thoughtful. When convergence is perceived as good, it can enhance the dialogue; when it is perceived as bad, it can break down the communication process. If a communicator speaks or behaves in a style similar to a listener's, the convergence will probably be favorably perceived. But converging to ridicule, tease, or patronize will most likely be perceived negatively. There is a fine line between whether or not convergence will be perceived in the intended way. Consider, for instance, what happens when a nurse speaks to a patient in a nursing home about eating lunch (Ryan, Maclean, & Orange, 1994):

NURSE: It's time for lunch, Mrs. James.

RESIDENT: But I'm not hungry. And I don't particularly like this kind of soup.

NURSE: Everyone has to eat now, Mary. We have to get on with our day's work. Besides that, we can't suit everyone's tastes all of the time. We don't make the soup just for you, you know.

RESIDENT: I'd really rather just rest in my room and have a cup of tea later.

NURSE: Look, dearie, if you don't eat now, you won't get anything later. Let's stop being so fussy, all right?

RESIDENT: Fine.

In this conversation, you can see how convergence by the nurse might be construed as condescending by Mrs. James. In fact, Ryan and colleagues found that this style of communicating was rated as less respectful, less nurturing, and more frustrating for the resident. There are other standards of evaluating convergence, including the norms of the situation (Did the speaker converge in an offensive way?), the ability to pull it off effectively (How does a 50-year-old use the "cool" talk of a high school student?), and the value of a language to a community (Should European Americans employ Black English vernacular in their interactions with African Americans?).

Divergence: Vive la Différence

Accommodation can be two-way, where both communicators accommodate, one-way, or no way! Giles (1980) believes speakers sometimes accentuate the verbal and nonverbal differences between themselves and others. He terms this

divergence. Divergence differs greatly from convergence in that it is a dissociation process. Instead of showing how two speakers are alike in speech rate, gestures, or posture, divergence is when there are no attempts to demonstrate similarities between speakers. In other words, two people speak to each other with no concern about accommodating each other. Divergence has not received as much research attention as convergence, and so our knowledge about the process is limited to a few claims about its function in Communication Accommodation Theory.

First, divergence should not be misconstrued as an effort to disagree or to not respond to another communicator. Divergence is not the same as inattentiveness. When people diverge, they have simply chosen to dissociate themselves from the communicator and the conversation. Because the reasons for divergence vary, we discuss them below.

Divergence is a way for members of various cultural communities to maintain social identity. Giles and his colleagues (1987) observe that there are occasions when people—namely, racial and ethnic groups—"deliberately use their language or speech style as a symbolic tactic for maintaining their identity, cultural pride, and distinctiveness" (p. 28). Individuals may not wish to converge in order to preserve their cultural heritage. Imagine, for example, that you are traveling in France; everywhere you go the French people you encounter encourage you to speak French. You are surprised at that until you realize that you, as a visitor, should not expect the French to converge to your language.

We've already learned that some cultural groups are immediately stereotyped and that people communicate with this categorization in mind. It's no wonder, then, that some cultural groups remain committed to divergence in their conversations with others. To illustrate this point, consider the conclusions of Richard Bourhis and Giles (1977). In this classic study, the research team studied Welsh people who were very proud of their ethnic identity but who did not know the Welsh language. As they learned the language, the researchers asked several questions in a standard English format. During the question-and-answer period, the researchers asked the group why they wanted to learn Welsh since it is "a dying language with a dismal future." The Welsh sample rebutted with not only a strong Welsh dialect but also Welsh words and phrases. Remarkably, the group could link together difficult Welsh words! The group, then, began to diverge from the English that was spoken to them, ostensibly out of ethnic pride.

A second reason why people diverge pertains to power and role differences in conversations. Divergence frequently occurs in conversations when there is a power difference between the communicators and when there are distinct role differences in the conversation (physician–patient, parent–child, interviewer–interviewee, and so forth) (Street, 1991; Street & Giles, 1982). Street (1991), for instance, comments that "interactants having greater status may speak for longer periods, initiate most of the conversational topics, speak more slowly, and maintain a more relaxed body posture than does the less powerful" (p. 135). Divergence, then, occurs when someone wishes to render another less powerful. Consider, for instance, the interview situation of Luke and Roberto.

divergence
strategy used to accentuate the verbal and nonverbal differences between communicators

Because Roberto is in the more powerful position as the person conducting the interview and the one who will ultimately decide whether Luke will be offered the position, he exercises considerable influence on the content and structure of the interview. As an interviewer who holds more status than Luke, Roberto could engage in language and stories that are unique to the company (and unknown by Luke), ask questions about Luke's qualifications (which Luke cannot ask of Roberto), talk for a greater proportion of the interview time, and effectively use silence as an interview strategy. In other words, Communication Accommodation Theory maintains that because Roberto and Luke hold different roles in the conversation, one is able to freely diverge from the conversation of the other.

Finally, although not as often as for the reasons cited above, divergence is likely to occur because the other in the conversation is viewed to be a "member of undesirable groups, considered to hold noxious attitudes, or display a deplorable appearance" (Street & Giles, 1982). To this end, Giles and his colleagues (1987) contend that divergence is used to contrast self-images in a conversation. To understand this point, consider the number of so-called undesirable groups in society today. Christopher Jencks (1994), for instance, notes that homeless people are historically part of what society labels as unappealing or vulgar. Employing the accommodation principle of divergence, then, a homeless man asking for money outside a movie theater may find himself in a conversation with a communicator (we'll call this person Pat) who wishes to diverge to demonstrate differences between the two. Pat's divergence may take the form of an increased rate of speech or a more clipped manner. Pat may also use vocabulary and pronunciation that clearly mark him as a member of the upper-middle class. In each case, the divergence is carried out by the individual who wishes to imply a status difference between the two.

Giles and colleagues (1987) conclude that such divergence enacted by Pat may have the goal of bringing another's behavior (and appearance) "to an acceptable level" (p. 32) and that Pat's divergence is a type of self-disclosure that illustrates that certain kinds of speech and behavior are not shared between two people. As is often the case, the homeless person's situation is viewed as his problem. Divergence is simply a way of further communicating this value. As our third assumption points out, language and behaviors frequently communicate status.

Overaccommodation: Miscommunicating with a Purpose

over-accommodation
attempt to overdo efforts in regulating, modifying, or responding to others

Jane Zuengler (1991) observes that **overaccommodation** is "a label given to a speaker whom the addressee considers is overdoing it" (p. 239). The term is attributed to people who, although acting from good intentions, are perceived instead as patronizing. Consider, for example, the overaccommodation taking place in Luke Tomsha's interview. Luke's efforts in speaking Spanish are undermined by Roberto's perception that Luke is patronizing him. In this case, and as some researchers (Coupland, Coupland, Giles, & Henwood, 1988) argue, the overaccommodation yields miscommunication. Luke is not trying to patronize Roberto Hernandez. Although the speaker apparently has the intention of showing respect, the listener perceives it as distracting and disrespectful.

Overaccommodation can exist in three forms: sensory overaccommodation, dependency overaccommodation, and intergroup overaccommodation (Zuengler, 1991). Let's define these and present an example of each.

Sensory overaccommodation occurs when a speaker overly adapts to another who is perceived as limited in some way. Limitation, in this sense, refers to either a linguistic or a physical limitation. That is, a speaker may believe that he or she is sensitive to another's language disability or physical disability but overdoes the accommodation.

Nikolas Coupland and colleagues (1988) believe that sensory overaccommodation occurs frequently in conversations between the elderly and others. For example, in her study on patients with Alzheimer's disease, Heidi Hamilton (1991) felt that she had underestimated the level of competence of an Alzheimer's patient and found herself overaccommodating. Because Hamilton believed that Alzheimer's patients typically respond better to questions about the here and now rather than about past times or places, she framed her conversations with patients with this in mind. It turned out, however, that she underestimated the mental capabilities of her interviewees. Hamilton believed that she spent much more interview time on the environment surrounding the Alzheimer's patient than was necessary. This resulted in making patients seem more incompetent than they actually were.

The second type of overaccommodation is **dependency overaccommodation,** which occurs when a speaker consciously or unconsciously places the listener in a lower-status role, and the listener is made to appear dependent on the speaker. In dependency overaccommodation, the listener also believes that the speaker controls the conversation to demonstrate higher status. This can be seen by examining the treatment of a number of immigrant populations in the United States.

Many cultural groups are marginalized in the United States, and dependency overaccommodation, it appears, may be one reason for this ostracizing. For instance, during assimilation into their new communities, many refugees are made to feel subordinate when conversing with others. Although government workers may believe that during their conversations with refugees they are doing what is right (helping refugees understand various procedures and rules associated with documentation), refugees may feel quite dependent on the speaker (immigration official). Given that many newly arrived strangers do not know the English language, do not have a basic understanding of cultural values or norms, and do not have a clear sense of their job skills (Gudykunst & Kim, 1992; Kim, 1989), their perceptions of dependency are warranted.

In addition to sensory and dependency overaccommodation, there is a third type of overaccommodation called **intergroup overaccommodation.** This involves speakers lumping listeners into a particular group, failing to treat each person as an individual. At the heart of this overaccommodation is stereotyping, and there can be far-reaching consequences. Although maintaining racial and ethnic identity is critical, individual identity is equally important.

Consider when a speaker uses language that assigns a listener to a particular cultural group. The speaker may feel comfortable suggesting, for instance, that Mexican Americans have never been given a chance to succeed in the United States because they have been busy raising their families. To a Mexican

sensory over-accommodation overly adapting to others who are perceived as limited in their abilities (physical, linguistic, or other)

dependency over-accommodation occurs when speakers place listeners in a lower-status role

intergroup over-accommodation occurs when speakers place listeners in cultural groups without acknowledging individual uniqueness

American, this generalization may be perceived negatively. Communicating with this perception in mind may cause some Mexican Americans to accommodate negatively.

Overaccommodation usually results in listeners perceiving that they are less than equal. There are serious implications to overaccommodation, including losing motivation for further language acquisition, avoiding conversations, and forming negative attitudes toward speakers and society (Zuengler, 1991). If one goal of communication is achieving intended meaning, overaccommodation is a significant roadblock to that goal.

Critique and Closing

Communication Accommodation Theory focuses on the role of conversations in our lives. The theory has been incorporated in a number of different studies. For instance, accommodation has been studied in the mass media (Bell, 1991), with families (Fox, 1999), with Chinese students (Hornsey & Gallois, 1998), with the elderly (Harwood, 2002), on the job (McCroskey & Richmond, 2000), in interviews (Willemyns, Gallois, Callan, & Pittam, 1997), and even with messages left on telephone answering machines (Buzzanell, Burrell, Stafford, & Berkowitz, 1996) (see our Research Note).

There is no doubt that the theory is heuristic. The theory is expansive enough to be very complete, and it has been supported by research from diverse authors. In addition, the theory's core processes of convergence and divergence make it relatively easy to understand, underscoring the simplicity of the theory.

The strengths of the theory may be quite significant because the theory has elicited little scholarly criticism. Still, a few shortcomings of the theory merit attention. Judee Burgoon, Leesa Dillman, and Lesa Stern (1993), for example, question the convergence-divergence frame advanced by Giles. They believe that conversations are too complex to be reduced simply to these processes. They also challenge the notion that people's accommodation can be explained by just these two practices. For instance, what occurs if people both converge *and* diverge in conversations? Are there consequences for the speaker? The listener? What influence—if any—does race or ethnicity play in this simultaneous process? One might also question whether the theory relies too heavily on a rational way of communicating. That is, although the theory acknowledges conflict between communicators, it also rests on a reasonable standard of conflict. Perhaps you have been in conflicts that are downright nasty and with

Research Note

Buzzanell, P. M., Burrell, N. A., Stafford, R. S., & Berkowitz, S. (1996). When I call you up and you're not there: Application of Communication Accommodation Theory to telephone answering machine messages. *Western Journal of Communication, 60,* 310–336.

This study applied principles of Communication Accommodation Theory to telephone answering machine messages. The authors devised an innovative study that examined whether callers converged to the script of a message or to the relational aspects found in the recorded messages. The researchers offered several research questions that asked the extent to which callers accommodated the messages left on answering machines.

Buzzanell and colleagues recruited 129 participants to take part in the study. They first gave the group a pretest that focused on perceptions and feelings about new forms of technology. They were interested in discovering the overall sentiments of the population prior to the actual research analyses. In addition, the researchers constructed the recorded answering machine messages from the responses in the pretest. From the pretests, Buzzanell and her colleagues examined the "most bizarre" recorded messages identified, including those with music, humor, comedy routines, and in-group phrasing. Three general types of messages were devised: a humorous message in the form of a limerick, a jargon-filled message, and a message requesting a large amount of information. They also developed a "routine" message.

To get their data, the team of investigators instructed the 129 participants to phone their professor and schedule an appointment. Participating professors recorded each of the message types using a conversational style. The researchers developed a coding scheme that assessed levels of similarity and convergence, message length, and the extent to which the message was considered novel or "script-like." Messages were also assessed for immediacy, or the relative closeness a communicator expresses to another.

Several results were reported in the study. There was moderate convergence on the immediacy aspects as well as on message length used in the machine message. The researchers note that the callers made no effort to accommodate limerick or jargon-like messages, but callers did seem to appreciate message novelty. The high-demand messages were accommodated significantly. Callers were found to be no more likely to hang up on the novel messages than on the routine message.

The study concluded by identifying limitations of this type of research. First, among the limitations identified, the results may have been influenced by the fact that callers had not received their grades yet. This may have affected their reactions to the messages. A second limitation was the age of the sample (18 to 22 years), and the authors note that this age group has grown up with technology, possibly resulting in more convergence than with older populations.

This study concludes with a call for future research on the practical applications of Communication Accommodation Theory. The authors observe that future research might explore the degree to which workers respond to memos, voicemail, and e-mail messages. Looking at the goals of callers was also identified as a future research avenue. Investigations might focus on whether the caller intended to get a return call, and this information may be framed within the convergence literature. Calls for "theoretical extensions" of Communication Accommodation Theory are noted.

people who have no sense of reason. It appears that the theory ignores this possible dark side of communication (see Chapter 1).

In his earlier writings on the theory, Giles challenged researchers to apply Communication Accommodation Theory across the life span and in different cultural settings. For the most part, his suggestions have been heeded. His research has broadened our understanding of why conversations are so complex. Through convergence, Giles sheds light on why people adapt to others in

Theory * Into * Practice

In a *New York Times Magazine* article, Michael Lowenthal writes of his experiences as a Jewish traveler to another country. His sojourn underscores the importance of perception on the evaluation process. Lowenthal traveled to Djerba, a tiny island off the Tunisian coast. Feeling disconnected from his religion and his Jewish ancestors, he traveled to this distant place with one goal: "Could the stalwart Djerbans make me feel truly Jewish?" Knowing that only 2,000 Jews were living in an area that is 99 percent Muslim, he knew that his pilgrimage would be challenging yet very worthwhile, because the synagogue he was to visit was proclaimed to possess a holy stone that was dropped from heaven.

Most challenging was the difficulty he faced in achieving accommodation. He headed into the Jewish quarter—Hara Sghira—hoping to find the local people in prayer. Lowenthal noted that there were only two men present; one nonverbally communicated that he should remove his shoes and handed him a yarmulke. Then Lowenthal saw the second man extend his arm as if to welcome him. Believing that the message was, "Come, cousin, we've been expecting you," Lowenthal experienced further nonverbal divergence as he saw that the man had coins in his palm, suggesting that he was collecting admission!

As Lowenthal noticed a third local, he tried to converge in what he thought would demonstrate his kinship to his Jewish "cousins." In a mix of pidgin French and Hebrew, Lowenthal tried to elicit some affirming reaction from the man, but to no avail. This third man "grew more perturbed, and finally pointed angrily to the wall" (p. 84). There was a message in a variety of languages that indicated that Lowenthal should be paying yet another donation for the privilege of speaking to this man. Lowenthal tried yet again to converge with the gentleman: "But I'm not a tourist. . . . I'm like you. I'm Jewish, too," he related.

As he walked away feeling disappointed with his experience, Lowenthal lamented that perhaps his Jewish heritage was not precisely Jewish but rather that of an "alienated Jew." He concludes his personal experiences by noting that upon his departure from the synagogue, he was once again reminded that he was not at home: He had to return his yarmulke.

Source: Lowenthal, 1998.

TIP Follow-up
Why is there such a difficult cultural challenge when using the language of a country you are visiting? Discuss the role of the host, your role, and the values of a particular culture.

their interactions. Through divergence, we can understand why people choose to ignore adapting strategies. He has pioneered a theory that has helped us better understand the culture and diversity around us.

Discussion Starters

1. What divergent strategies can you develop to rewrite our opening example of Luke Tomsha and Roberto Hernandez? Incorporate real dialogue in your response.

2. Explain how convergence might function in the following relationships: teacher–student, therapist–client, and supervisor–subordinate. In your response, choose a conversational topic that might be unique to the relationship and integrate convergence accordingly.

3. We have noted that overaccommodation results in miscommunication. Some research in Communication Accommodation Theory has also examined underaccommodation, or the process of not adapting sufficiently to another communicator. What do you believe are some examples of underaccommodation?

4. Giles contends that self-perception can influence the accommodation process. How does a person's self-perception affect accommodation? Provide examples to illustrate your thoughts.

5. Giles's theory has been framed in the intercultural communication context. Based on your understanding of the theory, under what additional context(s) can the theory be understood?

6. How does accommodation lead to social identity? Explain using examples from your life.

Terms for Review

accommodation	convergence
Social Identity Theory	indirect stereotyping
in-groups	divergence
out-groups	overaccommodation
perception	sensory overaccommodation
evaluation	dependency overaccommodation
norms	intergroup overaccommodation

Online Learning Center

Visit the Online Learning Center at www.mhhe.com/west2. Use the multiple-choice and true/false quizzes to help you prepare for exams, and the glossary, crossword puzzles, and flashcards to further your knowledge of key terms.

PART Three

Casting New Directions

Chapter 30
Moving in New
Directions 512

WE CONCLUDE OUR BOOK WITH AN EXAMINA-
tion of how communication theory functions in our professional and personal lives. We hope that as you read this material, you continue to realize that communication theory is
not esoteric nor unfamiliar. We hope that taking this course
and reading this text helps you understand the links between being an everyday theorist and a professional scholar.

As we wrote this book, we imagined relating communication theory in an inviting
and practical way. We continue this goal in this final chapter by presenting some future
uses and applications of communication theory. We illustrate the usefulness of having
a background in communication in a number of different career paths. While reflecting on this material, keep in mind that we live in a world that requires theoretical thinking. You now have the basic tools needed to work toward understanding your self, your
relationships, and the society in which you live.

Moving in New Directions

Laura Niles and Mike Salinsky

Laura Niles and Mike Salinsky hurried across campus to the Brew Bayou. They ordered lattes, sat down at their favorite table, and smiled at each other. They had been going for coffee together every Tuesday and Thursday after their Intro to Communication class, and this morning they had just finished the final exam.

"This is the mother of all coffee breaks today," Mike laughed. "I am so psyched to be finished with our first year! There were some days when I thought we'd never make it."

Laura laughed quietly, thinking of all she and Mike had been through since they started their freshman year at Milton College. It was hard to believe how much had happened in less than a year. Last summer, she and Mike hadn't even known each other and now they were so close. He was her best friend at school, and she really valued their friendship.

She looked over at Mike and asked, "How do you think you did on the Comm final?"

Mike put down his coffee and seemed to think seriously about the question. Then he smiled broadly and said, "I really think I did well . . . no, I *know* that I did well. But I'll be honest. A lot had to do with studying with you. You helped me focus on the important concepts and organize the material. It made a big difference. That question on the relationship of the self and communication was really a breeze after we covered Symbolic Interac-

tionism, Uncertainty Reduction Theory and Standpoint Theory last week. I think I nailed that answer, thanks, of course, to our study session. How did you do?"

"I felt the same way," Laura said. "Studying with you always helps me, and this time we really focused on the right stuff. Because we went over that material on Expectancy Violations Theory, I think I really gave a good answer on that question about nonverbal communication."

Laura and Mike smiled at each other. "It feels great, doesn't it?" Mike asked.

"I agree," Laura nodded as she spoke. "Plus, I really think I learned a lot this term. Just look at us. I think that I understand a lot more about us because of this theory class."

Mike put down his coffee and leaned over to Laura, saying, "Yeah, it sounds a little dumb, but when we talked about men and women's friendships, it did help me understand us . . . just a bit better. I have really never had a close female friend before you. And you already know that our friendship means a lot to me."

"I feel the same way. There were so many things we talked about in that class that applied to my life," Laura observed. "Remember that section on dialectics? That told me a lot about what I'm going through with my mother—that stuff on separation and closeness pretty much describes us to a T."

Laura and Mike grinned at each other, feeling pretty satisfied with themselves. "Now," Mike said, "the only problem will be getting some type of a job where we can use this stuff. My dad is still asking me what jobs I can get after graduation with a communication major."

"Yeah," Laura agreed. "We ought to go to the internship meeting at the beginning of next semester; I bet we can find some good job possibilities there."

"Great idea. Let's plan to do that. Meanwhile, we better finish this coffee and get to studying for our philosophy exam!"

As the two finished drinking their coffees and pulled their books together to leave, they both thought about how much fun this year had been. Time had flown by while they were learning so much and making such great friends. Who would have thought that theory would apply to them?

■

Mike and Laura have taken a course like the one you are now finishing. Their comments reveal that they found the material involving and relevant. Hopefully, you too have observed that communication is important. As a college student, it is estimated that you spend 75 percent of your day communicating, and this is expected to continue throughout your life (Morreale & Vogl, 1998). Further, communication skills are increasingly important in today's information age. New information technology continues to revolutionize the process of communication and affects how we engage in that process. You don't have to be a communication professional to know how important communication is to people's lives. An economics professor notes, "We are living in a communications revolution comparable to the invention of printing. . . . In an age of increasing talk, it's wiser talk we need most. Communication studies might well be central to colleges and universities in the 21st century (McCloskey, 1993, p. 12). Laura and Mike conclude that wiser talk is informed by theories about communication. We hope you agree.

We also hope that after reading this book you feel, like Mike and Laura, that you have gained an understanding of your own communication behaviors and how they affect important relationships in your life, as well as how the media influence us all. It is true that communication theory pervades our daily activities, and its application to everyday life and our careers cannot be overstated.

Still, like Mike and Laura, you might be wondering how a knowledge of communication theory and a major in communication might help you in securing a job. Although we, and other liberal arts experts, recognize that attaining a job is not the only goal of your college experience, we also know that it is necessary to consider future employment prospects to help you pay the bills! If you are a communication major, you may already be aware of the employment opportunities awaiting you. If you are not a communication major, you should know that a communication degree provides an excellent background for a wide variety of jobs.

The theories covered in this text offer rich possibilities for application in both work and leisure activities. We should try to engage in "practicing theory." Sandra Petronio (1999) agrees, observing that we need to seize the opportunity to "translate our scholarship into practice."

To conclude our text on communication theory, we wish to do the following: (1) identify some prominent areas that are on the theoretical horizon;

Calvin and Hobbes   by Bill Watterson

(2) suggest career paths for those with a communication degree; and (3) propose tips for seeking that career using your degree. In short, we want to study for your final exam with you—both the actual final you may take in this class and the lifelong final you take when you apply what you learned in a meaningful way outside the classroom. We expect that the issues you have learned in this class will continue to apply to your daily lives long after you take the final exam at the end of the term. U.S. Congressman Richard Gephardt said the following about the utility of his communication major: "Hardly a day passes in the halls of Congress that I don't draw on the lessons I learned as an undergraduate major in communication—not so much the substance of a specific course but the ability to think analytically and to view the world with a critical and constructive eye" (cited in Morreale & Vogl, 1998, p. 12).

Thinking About the Future

Throughout this book, we have introduced you to theoretical thinking and the application of this thinking to research questions investigating the communication process. We have profiled many specific theories about communication and illustrated how they affect our understanding of communication processes. And although it is our contention that these theories help you to achieve "wiser talk," no one theory we have discussed reveals everything there is to know about communication in all its complexities. As we pointed out in Chapter 3, theory is like a lens that focuses your attention on some areas of communication. Yet, in so doing, it also blinds you to other areas that are outside the parameters of the lens. Further, this lens of theory points to what we value as researchers and as a society—for example, open and disclosive communication, developing relationships, disseminating information, and individual effects on communication behaviors. In concentrating on these values, we often ignore other communication practices that are not valued by us, even though they may occur frequently in our interactions—for example, deception, short-term relationships, computer-mediated communication, and destructive communication.

Focusing is inevitable, and in many ways it is a useful process. Without focus, we cannot understand the nuances of a particular phenomenon. Putting some aspects of the communication process under the microscope, so to speak, allows for a fine-grained picture of those aspects. If we try to see everything at once, our vision is too cluttered, and we cannot concentrate sufficiently on the details.

It is also the case, however, that blocking out some things so that we can concentrate on others may lead to bias and inaccurate or oversimplified thinking. We may be overlooking extremely important parts of the process that would change our perspective completely if we only moved or widened our lens slightly. Recall the old story of the blind men examining an elephant. Each man only examines one small part of the elephant and thus gets a distorted impression of what an elephant is like. The man who feels the tail, for instance, says an elephant is like a rope, whereas the man who feels the tusk thinks an elephant is like a sword. It is our argument that several trends in modern life compel us to examine communication in somewhat different ways than theorists have done in the past.

It is clear how important and relevant communication is in our lives. Thus, it is critical that we continue to think in meaningful ways about the communication process. We must continue to widen and change our lenses to understand what we focus on and what we leave out. When researchers study areas that we once took for granted, new insights are gained. For instance, researchers have already begun to study the effects of new technology on the teaching–learning process (Shedletsky & Aitken, 2001). One result of this sort of research is the ability for colleges and universities to determine whether teaching online courses is in the best interests of the school, teacher, and student. This information is an important beginning in unraveling the complexities of electronic teaching. Thus, when we observe that technology is changing interpersonal relationships (such as online personal ads), we necessarily expand that discussion to include looking at the role of technology in the classroom.

We believe that four themes suggest important trends for the future of our culture and will affect our future and help us refocus: technology, work and family life, aging and health, and culture and identity. As we reviewed the theories in this book, we discovered areas where cultural change and development have left gaps. There are issues that our theories do not explain. We suggest that these changes call for new theoretical thinking. When issues of equality between women and men became critical in our culture, feminists promoted theoretical thinking like Standpoint Theory and Muted Group Theory to help us explain these issues. In the same way, now that we have entered the twenty-first century, we need to move in new directions theoretically. Although the theories we have reviewed in this book explain a great deal about communication, some developments in our social life cry out for new thinking to aid our understanding. The four themes we have listed above provide a starting place for this new thinking. We will review each of the themes briefly, suggesting how they may impact our daily lives and our theoretical thinking.

Technology

The theme of technology is inescapable for anyone living today. Every day we are bombarded with messages from various technological innovations ranging from our telephones (cell or standard) to our computers, televisions, and fax machines. The use of technology is not limited to the young, who are growing up in a world pervaded by technological innovations. The Pew Research Center (www.pewinternet.org), for instance, found in their 2001 survey of computer use that four million seniors 65 and over are online, sending e-mail to family members and surfing the Web. The AARP (Association for the Advancement of Retired Persons) notes that about 400,000 members go online each month.

The boundaries between interpersonal communication and computers are not clear-cut. The two may often overlap, as the subfield computer-mediated communication (CMC) demonstrates. The fact that interpersonal communication and mass communication cannot always be viewed as separate contexts has implications for our theorizing. For example, when we think about a theory like Relational Dialectics Theory (Chapter 12), we are directed to think about people in face-to-face relationships. The salience of closeness and distance as a pervasive tension seems most applicable when you think of dating partners, spouses, or parents and children. That dialectic may not be as relevant in a relationship that is conducted online. The mediated nature of the relationship may necessitate a new theory to describe it (Walther, 1992).

When we consider a theory like Social Penetration Theory (Chapter 10), we are reminded of one of the biases that Martin Lea and Russell Spears (1995) point out: the idea that relationships move from one point to another. As Lea and Spears note, the metaphor of movement is pervasive in our theories about relationship development. The very name Social Penetration connotes the move from a surface level to deeper and deeper levels of intimacy. Yet, as the writers suggest, this metaphor may preclude our study of computer-mediated communication, which occurs outside the realm of movement as described by Social Penetration Theory. We need other theories to help us understand what happens in online relationships.

Some researchers (such as Elliott, 1999) note that we are no longer a nation of readers. Instead, people get most of their information from interactive media or from television. This has had serious implications for newspapers as well as for interpersonal communication patterns. Further, news outlets have the capacity to create electronic newspapers specifically tailored to individual needs and interests. Marketers are already capable of targeting specific individuals and of sending ads that deal with products they are likely to buy. If you use Amazon.com, for example, the company probably knows more about your reading habits than you do yourself.

With all these individualized, targeted media abounding, what will hold us together as a community? Years ago, the television set served as a focal point for families to gather around and come together. Further, once a television episode of *All in the Family, The Cosby Show, The Golden Girls,* or *Seinfeld* was aired, the episode was talked about the next morning at breakfast, at the office, or even at the gym. Today, however, we have different technologies that have caused our society to redefine what it means to be a community. Many of our theories of mass communication presume that the same messages are reaching the masses. In today's and tomorrow's technological world, that may not be the case. Technological changes and innovations change our communication behaviors and may even change the process of communication. New theoretical developments in computer-mediated communication have been enlightening. For instance, Joseph Walther (1992; 1993; 1994) has been instrumental in advancing our knowledge of how computer-mediated communication influences interpersonal relationships. This line of research continues and will be informative as our culture continues to grapple with the role of technology in our personal and professional lives.

Work and Family Life

A second trend in our society involves increased pressures to balance work and home, or family, life. Many companies are seeking ways to assist employees with the difficult task of juggling a lot of different stressors. Consequently, you may have read about companies that are instituting perks for their employees, such as personal shoppers and in-house services like laundries and child-care centers. These are steps to help employees manage the ever-increasing demands of home and work. As Christena E. Nippert-Eng (1996) points out, the way we divide life and erect boundaries is socially constructed. Boundaries are arbitrary, cultural distinctions. One of the important boundaries constructed in Western culture has been that between home and work. Yet we see in today's culture more interplay between these two categories. Consider, for instance, how many people are working from their homes or how many families now homeschool their children.

Although in many ways the blurring of these boundaries may be helpful, it is confusing as well. In times of confusion, we can turn to theory for guidance. As we noted in this book, communication theories on organizational life are quite separate from those that explain relational life. Yet, as people spend more and more time on the job, many important relationships contain elements of both work life and social life. As Theodore Zorn (1995) observes, we know very little about the dynamics of friendship at work. This is especially the case, Zorn notes, when the personal relationship involves people at different hierarchical work levels. When a boss is an employee's friend or is romantically linked with a subordinate, what theories explain the development of their relationship? Although romantic ties between a supervisor and a subordinate have been broadly discussed, these relationships can vary tremendously from one organization to another and from one individual to another. Again, we need theories to begin to explain the experiences in these situations.

Further, people's experience of work has changed over time. It is now rare for people to stay with one organization for their entire work life. Thus, the number of workplace relationships has increased tremendously, and we need to pay attention to this phenomenon to help us understand our interactions. As people move to different workplaces, they experience different organizational climates and cultures. Some companies may consider themselves a "family" and thus foster interpersonal ties among their employees. Other companies may have a more formal approach and may discourage personal relationships among employees. Theoretical thinking can be helpful in sorting out these differences.

Communication is a process that both maintains and integrates the boundary between work and family. For example, when we speak differently at work and at home, we use talk to maintain a distance between the two realms. Think about the vocabulary you use with your family and with your co-workers. Often we may be more formal at work, or we may use work-related jargon on the job. Yet this is not always the case. Nippert-Eng (1996) writes about a son who took a summer job working for his father. The son, Kim, saw and heard a different side of his father while at work: "his father's style of talk was not only chock full of expletives at work but . . . these were often hurled in red-faced, yelling fits at his subordinates" (p. 77). The all-male, blue collar industrial environment promoted a side of his dad that Kim never fathomed. Theories are needed to explain the processes of separating and integrating work and family.

Additionally, Nippert-Eng comments that "cross-realm talk," or talk that functions to integrate the two areas of life, is important. As we spend more and more time working, we deprive our families of a communication resource if we do not engage in cross-realm talk. The same is true, to a lesser extent perhaps, in the workplace. Nippert-Eng points out that our personal lives and problems do not disappear when we go to work. Co-workers who are also personal friends can provide needed support. Communication scholars including Erika Kirby and Kathleen Krone (2002), Annis Golden (2000), and Bonnie Farley–Lucas (2000) have begun examining the work–family relationship and the communication surrounding this delicate balance in life. We can expect to read about theoretical developments in this area over the next few years.

Aging and Health

As medical advances help our population live longer, we are confronting more issues of aging. According to the U.S. Census Bureau (www.census.gov), the population of those 65 and older will grow from 34 million to 82 million in 2050, a 135 percent increase. In 2030, the number of seniors over the age of 65 will comprise nearly 20 percent of the entire population of the United States. This brings to the forefront issues of coping with age and diseases of the elderly. Further, general health-care concerns and life-threatening diseases have created new communication challenges.

Many theories in communication tend to center on youthful relationships: dating, early marriage, and parenting of young and adolescent children. The discipline does not have many theories that address marriages that have lasted for fifty years, parents communicating with adult children, or older family members who require at-home care. What occurs, for instance, when an elderly parent is taken into an adult child's home? What effects are there on the family? On the senior? What support systems will help offset communication difficulties?

Communication professionals have applied existing theoretical thinking to problems of aging and health care. For example, some research has examined physician–patient communication, specifically medical interviews, through the prism of the Narrative Paradigm (Chapter 20). In these studies (Sharf, 1990; Sharf & Poirier, 1988), researchers found that doctors and patients did not believe each other's stories fulfilled the criteria for a good story. The authors conclude that a narrative-based training program for health-care professionals would improve the quality and the experience of medical interviews for both patients and physicians. To further demonstrate the need to understand health-related issues in our society, consider the words of Barron Lerner, a physician who worked with Catherine, a colleague/patient with a highly aggressive form of cancer. Lerner (2002) thoughtfully relates a story that showed Catherine's health slowly deteriorating:

> Catherine soon announced that she was tired. We hugged and I said goodbye. She died the the next day. I will always remember my last encounter with Catherine as one of the greatest privileges I have had as a doctor, and as a friend. Displaying unbelievable dignity and grace, Catherine taught us how patients cope with severe illness. And she taught us how we should care for patients. We should be frank, attentive, and patient. Most important, we should not emotionally distance ourselves from the sick (p. D4).

This example illustrates the importance of applying theoretical thinking to practical problems. Ethical questions abound when we have the medical technology to prolong life, clone life, and create life. In fact, Matthew Kreuter, David Farrell, Laura Olevitch, and Laura Brennan (2000) explore the confluence of health, humans, and technology. They found that health communication experts now have a number of nonprint technologies (e.g., interactive computer kiosks, video games, Internet sites) at their disposal to get health-oriented messages across the various populations (seniors, infants, caretakers, and so forth).

Aging and health issues will preoccupy communication researchers for some time to come. Scholars such as Dawn Braithwaite and Teresa Thompson (2000) have begun an ambitious undertaking to better understand one area related to health communication: disability. They have called for more theoretical thinking in the area of communication and disability, from perceptions of people with disabilities in the media to how disability issues are dealt with in the classroom. Their work has inspired other scholars to work toward developing a conceptual framework related to a pressing health-related topic in the twenty-first century.

Culture and Identity

As our society becomes increasingly diverse in terms of race and ethnicity, issues of culture and identity become important. Researchers have called for inclusion of diversity in definitions of family (Turner & West, 2002), in dating relationships (Huston & Schwartz, 1995), and in politics (Sullivan & Turner,

1996). Yet, so much more attention is needed on the issues of cultural diversity. How do we need to change our current institutional structures to embrace a more diverse society? How do we address issues of language and cultural values as the workforce becomes increasingly diverse? New theories such as Co-Cultural Communication Theory (Orbe, 1998) are being tested and are beginning to be embraced by scholars to understand culture, identity, and community.

Further, as Tsukasa Nishida (1996) points out, "In order to understand the communication behaviors of any culture, it is important to examine them in light of communication theories that have developed within the culture itself" (pp. 102–103). Nishida's point rests on the problems of cultural ethnocentrism that arise when theory proponents do not have the same values as the culture to which they are applying a given theory. Thus, cultural sensitivity and awareness are critically important considerations for future theorizing about communication in various cultures.

Stella Ting-Toomey and Leeva Chung (1996) point out that identity is a meaningful issue for future theorizing in communication. They note that given the large number of marriages across cultures in the United States, several questions become salient. They ask, "How do members from two contrastive groups negotiate their identity differences? How do the offspring of intergroup marriages conceptualize their cultural identities? How do these identities affect their interpersonal relationship development patterns?" (p. 255). Further, they observe that gender and ethnic identity issues need more conceptual frameworks. They ask, How do we know when gender and/or ethnicity will be salient when a person constructs his or her identity? What are the conditions that prompt someone to identify himself as a 35-year-old European American male college professor rather than an adventurous, fun-loving, risk-taking man, for example? Theoretical thinking will help us find answers to these important questions about culture and identity.

Thinking About Career Opportunities

As we think about these issues, we can apply our theoretical knowledge to career options. The field of communication offers many career opportunities. We wish to clarify that our emphasis on applying theoretical thinking to the world of work does not indicate that we believe that education is the same as vocational training. Far from it. A college education is much more than training for one specific job, as we hope you agree. Instead, understanding the process of communication and the ability to think critically about the process enables you to live a fuller life as well as to be better at whatever you eventually decide to do for your career. We certainly believe, however, that many careers await people who have the skills and critical tools that you are acquiring. For an example of various careers related to communication, see Table 30.1.

We have identified several important areas that you should consider in your career opportunities. Remember, however, that this list should not be viewed as a substitute for your own efforts; planning and strategizing a career in communication should begin as you enter college. You can learn the "rules of the

Table 30.1   Careers Related to Communication

FIELDS	CAREERS	RELATED COURSES
Advertising	Copy writer, media planner, advertising specialist, media sales representative	Persuasion, advertising and society, mass media, media production, small group communication, communication theory, ethics, listening
Communication Education	High school speech teacher, debate coach, college or university professor, language arts coordinator, communication curriculum specialist	Oral interpretation, public speaking, interpersonal communication, research methods in communication, cross-cultural communication, communication theory, ethics, listening
Electronic and New Media	Broadcasting station manager, director of broadcasting, film editor, news director, technical director, actor, news anchor, announcer, researcher	Public speaking, interpersonal communication, mass communication, media research, media theory, media criticism, studio and field production, media ethics, visual communication, listening, organizational communication
Journalism	Reporter, editor, copy writer, script writer, news service researcher, technical writer	Public speaking, media theory, media research, print journalism, media ethics, visual communication, listening
Public Relations	Publicity manager, press agent, corporate public affairs specialist, fund raiser, media analyst, researcher	Business and professional communication, public speaking, interpersonal communication, media theory, media research, ethics, listening
Business	Sales representative, manager, negotiator, customer service representative, communication trainer, human resources manager	Public speaking, business and professional communication, interpersonal communication, organizational communication, managerial communication, small group communication, interviewing, ethics, listening
Health Care	Health educator, medical grants writer, hospital director of communication, hospice manager, health-care counselor, medical training supervisor	Health communication, interpersonal communication, ethics, public relations, conflict and communication, family communication, communication theory, research methods, listening
International Relations	Corporate representative, translator, student tour coordinator, diplomat, foreign relations officer, foreign correspondent	Intercultural communication, international communication, nonverbal communication, communication theory, research methods, ethics, conflict and communication, political communication, persuasion, listening
Law	Public defender, corporate attorney, public interest attorney, legal secretary, paralegal, legal reporter, law professor, arbitrator	Public speaking, interpersonal communication, media law, legal communication, argumentation and debate, persuasion, listening, small group communication, conflict and communication, ethics, communication theory
Social and Human Services	Public administrator, social worker, recreational supervisor, human rights officer, counselor, religious leader	Public speaking, interpersonal communication, family communication, listening, small group communication, ethics, communication theory, conflict and communication

Table 30.2

Principles of Ethical Communication

- We advocate truthfulness, accuracy, honesty, and reason as essential to the integrity of communication.
- We endorse freedom of expression, diversity of perspective, and tolerance of dissent to achieve the informed and responsible decision making fundamental to a civil society.
- We strive to understand and respect other communicators before evaluating and responding to their messages.
- We promote access to communication resources and opportunities as necessary to fulfill human potential and contribute to the well-being of families, communities, and society.
- We promote communication climates of caring and mutual understanding that respect the unique needs and characteristics of individual communicators.
- We condemn communication that degrades individuals and humanity through distortion, intimidation, coercion, and violence and through the expression of intolerance and hatred.
- We are committed to the courageous expression of personal convictions in pursuit of fairness and justice.
- We advocate sharing information, opinions, and feelings when facing significant choices while also respecting privacy and confidentiality.
- We accept responsibility for the short- and long-term consequences of our own communication and expect the same of others.

Source: National Communication Association (www.natcom.org).

job game" throughout your academic career. Although these suggestions are aimed at those who are communication majors, they are also applicable for nearly every other major on your campus.

Remain Ethical

Without doubt, your ethics will always be challenged at work. In fact, in 2002, the large number of corporate scandals challenged the bedrock of ethical principles in the United States. As we mentioned in Chapter 1, stay focused on what is right and wrong while at work. Be honest with yourself. Work toward producing the best product, whether you are by yourself, with a supervisor, or with a team of colleagues. Perhaps ethics is best summed up with the following question: Are you doing your very best? We have provided a doctrine of ethical beliefs articulated by the National Communication Association (Table 30.2). Examine these and construct your own ethical principles. Remember, ethics surrounds us each day. Being ethical is the most important characteristic of being human.

Be Flexible

As you enter the workforce, you will need to be flexible about working either independently or with a team. You will also be required to work in various office environments, which means that you will have to adjust to the people and the context. Being flexible does not mean being uncommitted. Flexibility suggests that to be successful at work, you should be willing to take on new jobs, work with difficult people, hone new skills, and respond to seemingly ridiculous circumstances. The workplace, like the college classroom, can be quite unpredictable, and being flexible in response to this unpredictability will give you an edge over others.

Embrace Diversity

We have already mentioned that the United States is becoming more culturally diverse than it was just ten years ago. This fact should not only be acknowledged but dealt with directly. As consumers in and of the global village, we have no choice but to work toward understanding people who are different from us. We must welcome the diversity that is currently part of the fabric of the United States and of the world. Simply admitting that the world is diverse, however, is insufficient. We must work toward understanding that diversity. We might do this by reading, volunteering in agencies that assist diverse populations, or cultivating respect for the language, customs, and traditions of various racial, ethnic, and religious groups. We might also review the history of the United States to understand those groups who have been disparaged, marginalized, oppressed, and overlooked. As you can see, embracing diversity involves more than realizing that the world is filled with different kinds of people.

Cultivate New Technologies

Like diversity, new technologies will remain part of the U.S. landscape forever. Years ago, merely being able to type sixty words per minute was sufficient for job security. Now, of course, the technological vista is vastly different. Most jobs require some sort of technological know-how. Computer-aided design and computer-assisted systems tie all work environments together. Whether you find yourself gathering, creating, sorting, storing, or distributing information, technology will be present. Being able to work with new technologies, even some you are presently unfamiliar with, will be the hallmark of a lasting employee.

Yet, as we mention technological prowess, we are sadly aware of the disparity in technological availability. Not all people have access to computers and other technologies. Susan Barnes (2003), for example, clearly points out the discrepancy among different parts of the world. In the United States and Canada, over 167 million people are online. In Europe, that number drops to 113 million. Latin Americans number 16 million, and Africa is the lowest at a little over 3 million people online. As you can see, despite the population variations, there is a great deal of variability in Internet use around the world. This unequal access must be considered as we work toward a global understanding with others.

Maintain Creativity

There is a saying in the corporate world that too often, people can't "think out of the box." At the core of this saying is the inability to think creatively. Too often, we are unable or refuse to color outside the lines. Alexander Hiam in *The*

Futurist (1998) reports that "visual thinking" can be a valuable way of looking at a problem. He continues:

> Draw a diagram or picture of the problem you're working on, or think up visual analogies by asking yourself to name 10 things that the problem looks like. Then seek ways of generating fresh perspectives by analyzing these images: Ask yourself why the problem looks like that thing. (p. 33)

Try using visual thinking in your college life as well. You will be surprised to discover what Hiam concludes: "It pays to discuss not just *what* you think but *how* you think" (p. 33).

Don't Forget Basic Skills

There is no doubt that although society continues to evolve, the need to sharpen basic skills in reading, writing, listening, and speaking will never go out of style. Too often as career opportunities unfold, we tend to neglect one or several of these basic life skills. Yet what career is absolved from knowing how to locate, understand, and interpret information? Can you name a career that does not rely in some way on memos, letters, manuals, reports, or graphs? Is there a career that doesn't require workers to receive and to send verbal and nonverbal messages? And, important to this course you are now concluding, there are virtually no careers that do not ask people to organize their ideas and to communicate them orally. Clearly, reading, writing, listening, and speaking are central to all careers, and you should continue building these skills both inside and outside the college classroom.

Keep a Sense of Humor

We don't have to discuss this recommendation in too much detail. We're sure you understand what it means to have a sense of humor. As you experienced in college, at home, or in your workplace, things can and do go wrong. Sometimes it may seem that splashing hot coffee on your face would be less painful than continuing your day! Well, before you start brewing (and stewing), make a genuine effort to see the funny side of life. We're not suggesting that you laugh at everything that goes wrong (although there might be some value to that suggestion!). Rather, we encourage you to not take your job nor your work too seriously.

Conclusion

We hope you agree with us that thinking theoretically is a practical as well as a conceptual enterprise. Certainly, we have many theoretical resources now to help us understand our communication processes in relationships at home, at work, and via mass media. Additionally, the four trends in our social life discussed in this chapter will undoubtedly affect our communication behaviors and the process of communication in unexpected ways. Thinking about these changes is challenging, fun, and rewarding. Understanding the process of communication contributes to solving today's problems and those we will encounter in the future. As our technological expertise grows, our involvement in work merges with issues of family life, and our society ages and becomes more diverse, we will need to examine and understand the communication dynamics inherent in all these changes. Further, the more knowledge you acquire about how communication affects and is affected by social trends, the more valuable you will be to employers.

Learning about what the future holds for you can be both exciting and daunting. As you sort through the opportunities, keep an open mind. As a student of communication, your broad knowledge and skills will be attractive to employers in a variety of areas. This communication theory course is one step toward a rewarding career path. Knowing current theory, recognizing what challenges lie ahead for future theory, and applying that theory are additional steps to help you move in new directions.

Appendix
Defining Communication Theories

We have identified each theory explained in the book and have provided a brief explanation of the theory below. Consider this appendix as a chance for you to review what you've already learned from the chapter your instructor has assigned. Of course, it's important to go back to the chapter and review the specific information. We could never fully capture the richness of the theory with these short explanations. Nonetheless, these summaries should be helpful for quick reference. We present the theories using the same structure that we employed in the book.

The Self and Messages

Symbolic Interaction Theory (Mead)

People are motivated to act based on the meanings they assign to people, things, and events. Further, meaning is created in the language that people use both with others and in private thoughts. Language allows people to develop a sense of self and to interact with others in the community.

Coordinated Management of Meaning (Pearce and Cronen)

In conversations, people co-create meaning by attaining some coherence and coordination. Coherence occurs when stories are told, and coordination exists when stories are lived. CMM focuses on the relationship between an individual and his or her society. Through a hierarchical structure, individuals come to organize the meaning of literally hundreds of messages received throughout the day.

Cognitive Dissonance Theory (Festinger)

The experience of dissonance (or incompatible beliefs and actions) is aversive and people are highly motivated to avoid it. In their efforts to avoid feelings of dissonance, people will avoid hearing views that oppose their own, change their beliefs to match their actions, and seek reassurances after making a difficult decision.

Expectancy Violations Theory (Burgoon)

This theory is concerned with the structure of primarily nonverbal messages. It asserts that when communicative norms are violated, the violation may be perceived either favorably or unfavorably, depending on the perception that the receiver has of the violator. Violating another's expectations may be a strategy used over that of conforming to another's expectations.

Relationship Development

Uncertainty Reduction Theory (Berger and Calabrese)

When strangers meet, their primary focus is on reducing their levels of uncertainty in the situation. Their levels of uncertainty are located in both behavioral and cognitive realms. That is, they may be unsure of how to behave (or how the other person will behave), and they may also be unsure what they think of the other and what the other person thinks of them. Uncertainty occurs at the individual and the relational levels.

Social Penetration Theory (Altman and Taylor)

Interpersonal relationships evolve in some gradual and predictable fashion. Penetration theorists believe that self-disclosure is the primary way that superficial relationships progress to intimate relationships. Although self-disclosure can lead to more intimate relationships, it can also leave one or more persons vulnerable.

Social Exchange Theory (Thibaut and Kelley)

The major force in interpersonal relationships is the satisfaction of both people's self-interest. Self-interest is not necessarily bad and can actually enhance relationships. Interpersonal exchanges are analogous to economic exchanges where people are satisfied when they receive a fair return on their expenditures.

Relational Dialectics Theory (Baxter and Montgomery)

Relational life is always in progress. People in relationships continue to feel the push and pull of conflicting desires. Basically, people wish to have both autonomy and connection, openness and protectiveness, and novelty and predictability. As people communicate in relationships, they attempt to reconcile these conflicting desires, but they never eliminate their needs for both members of the opposing pairs.

Communication Privacy Management Theory (Petronio)

Disclosure in relationships requires managing private and public boundaries. These boundaries are between those feelings that one wants to disclose and those one wants to keep private. Disclosure in relationship development is more than revealing private information to another. Negotiation and coordination of boundaries is required. Decisions regarding disclosure require close monitoring.

Groups and Organizations

Groupthink (Janis)

Groupthink occurs when highly cohesive groups fail to consider alternatives that may effectively resolve group dilemmas. Group members frequently think similarly and are reluctant to share unpopular or dissimilar ideas with others. When this occurs, groups prematurely make decisions, some of which can have lasting consequences.

Adaptive Structuration Theory (Giddens, Poole, Seibold, McPhee)

Groups and organizations create structures, which can be interpreted as an organization's rules and resources. These structures, in turn, create social systems in an organization. Groups and organizations achieve a life of their own because of the way their members utilize their structures. Power structures guide the decision making taking place in groups and organizations.

Organizational Culture Theory (Geertz, Pacanowsky, and O'Donnell-Trujillo)

People are like animals who are suspended in webs that they created at work. An organization's culture is composed of shared symbols, each of which has a unique meaning. Organizational stories, rituals, and rites of passage are examples of what constitutes the culture of an organization.

Organizational Information Theory (Weick)

The main activity of organizations is the process of making sense of equivocal information. Organizational members accomplish this sense-making process through enactment, selection, and retention of information. Organizations are successful to the extent that they are able to reduce equivocality through these means.

The Public

The Rhetoric (Aristotle)

Rhetorical theory is based on the available means of persuasion. That is, a speaker who is interested in persuading his or her audience should consider three rhetorical proofs: logic (logos), emotion (pathos), and ethics (ethos). Audiences are key to effective persuasion as well. Rhetorical syllogisms, requiring audiences to supply missing pieces of a speech, are also used in persuasion.

Dramatism (Burke)

Life is a drama. As in dramatic action, life requires an actor, a scene, an act, some means for the action to take place, and a purpose. A rhetorical critic can understand a speaker's motives by analyzing these elements. Further, purging guilt is the ultimate motive, and rhetors can be successful when they provide their audiences with a means for purging guilt.

The Narrative Paradigm (Fisher)

Humans are storytelling animals. Narrative logic is preferential to the traditional logic used in argument. Narrative logic, or the logic of good reasons, suggests that people judge the credibility of speakers by whether their stories hang together clearly (coherence) and whether their stories ring true (fidelity). A democratic judgment of speakers exists because no one has to be trained in persuasion to make judgments based on the concepts of coherence and fidelity.

Cultural Studies (Hall)

The media represent ideologies of the dominant class in a society. Because media are controlled by corporations (the elite), the information presented to the public is necessarily influenced and framed with a profit in mind. The media's influence and the role of power must be taken into consideration when interpreting a culture.

The Media

Cultivation Analysis (Gerbner)

Television (and other media) plays an extremely important role in how people view their world. In today's society, most people get their information from mediated sources rather than through direct experience. Therefore, mediated sources can shape a person's sense of reality. This is especially the case with regard to violence. Heavy television viewing cultivates a sense of the world as a violent place.

Uses and Gratifications Theory (Katz, Blumler, and Gurevitch)

People choose and use particular media. Emphasizing a limited effects position, the media are viewed as having a limited effect on their audiences because audiences are able to exercise control over the media. Uses and Gratifications Theory is primarily concerned with the following question: What do people do with the media?

Spiral of Silence Theory (Noelle-Neumann)

Due to the enormous power of the media, the media have a lasting effect on public opinion. Mass media work simultaneously with majority opinion to silence minority beliefs on cultural issues. A fear of isolation prompts those with minority views to examine the beliefs of others. Individuals who fear being socially isolated are prone to conform to what they perceive to be a majority view. Every so often, the silent minority raises its voices into activism.

Medium Theory (McLuhan)

Society has evolved as its technology has evolved. From the alphabet to the Internet, we have been affected by and affect electronic media. In other words, the medium is the message. The laws of media—enhancement, obsolescence, retrieval, and reversal—demonstrate that technology affects communication through new technology.

Culture and Diversity

Face-Negotiation Theory (Ting-Toomey)

How do people in individualistic and collectivistic cultures negotiate face in conflicts? Face-Negotiation Theory is based on face management, which describes how people from different cultures manage conflict negotiation to maintain face. Self-face and other-face concerns explain the conflict negotiation between people from various cultures.

Standpoint Theory (Hartsock)

People are situated in specific social standpoints—they occupy different places in the social hierarchy. Because of this, individuals view the social situation from particular vantage points. By necessity, each vantage point provides only a partial understanding of the social world. Yet, those who occupy the low rungs of the hierarchy tend to understand the social situation more fully than those on top.

Muted Group Theory (Kramarae)

Language serves men better than women (and perhaps European Americans better than African Americans or other groups). This is the case because the variety of experiences of European American men are named clearly in language, whereas the experiences of other groups (namely women) are not. Due to this problem with language, women appear less articulate than men in public settings. As women create more language to express their experiences and as men and women have similar experiences, this situation should change.

Communication Accommodation Theory (Giles)

This theory considers the underlying motivations and consequences of what happens when two speakers shift their communication styles. During communication, people will try to accommodate or adjust their style of speaking to others. This is done in two ways: divergence and convergence. Groups with strong ethnic or racial pride often use divergence to highlight group identity. Convergence occurs when there is a strong need for social approval, frequently from powerless individuals.

References

Adler, R. B., & Towne, N. (2002). *Looking out/Looking in* (10th ed.). Ft. Worth, TX: Harcourt Brace.

Agne, R., Thompson, T. L., & Cusella, L. P. (2000). Stigma in the line of face: Self-disclosure of patients HIV status to health care providers. *Journal of Applied Communication Research, 28,* 235–261.

Aitken, J. E., & Shedletsky, L. J. (Eds.). (1997). *Intrapersonal communication processes.* Annandale, VA: National Communication Association/Midnight Oil.

Aldag, R. J., & Fuller, S. R. (1998). Organizational tonypandy: Lessons from a quarter century of groupthink phenomenon. *Organizational Behavior and Human Decision Processes, 73,* 163–184.

Alkhazraji, K. M. (1997). The acculturation of immigrants to U.S. organizations: The case of Muslim employees. *Management Communication Quarterly, 11,* 217–265.

Allen, B. J. (1996). Feminist standpoint theory: A black woman's (re)view of organizational socialization. *Communication Studies, 47,* 257–271.

Allen, R. L. & Hatchett, S. (1986). The media and social reality effects: Self and system orientation of Blacks. *Communication Research, 13,* 97–123.

Allman, J. (1998). Bearing the burden or baring the soul: Physicians' self-disclosure and boundary management regarding medical mistakes. *Health Communication, 10,* 175–197.

Altman, I. (1975). *The environment and social behavior.* Monterey, CA: Brooks/Cole.

Altman, I., & Taylor, D. A. (1973). *Social penetration: The development of interpersonal relationships.* New York: Holt, Rinehart & Winston.

Altman, I., Vinsel, A., & Brown, B. (1981). Dialectic conceptions in social psychology: An application to social penetration and privacy regulation. In L. Berkowitz (Ed.), *Advances in experimental social psychology* (pp. 130–145). New York: Academic Press.

Altman, K. E. (1990). Consuming ideology: The Better Homes in America campaign. *Critical Studies in Mass Communication, 7,* 286–307.

Alwood, E. (1997, October 14). The power of persuasion: The media's role in addressing homosexual issues in the future. *The Advocate,* 54.

Andersen, P. (1994). Explaining intercultural differences in nonverbal communication. In L. A. Samovar & R. E. Porter (Eds.), *Intercultural communication: A reader* (pp. 229–239). Belmont, CA: Wadsworth.

Anderson, J. A. (1996). *Communication theory: Epistemological foundations.* New York: Guilford Press.

Anderson, R., & Ross, V. (2000). *Questions of communication: A practical introduction to theory.* New York: St. Martin's Press.

Angus, I., Jhally, S., Lewis, J., & Schwichtenberg, C. (1989). On pluralistic apology. *Critical Studies in Mass Communication, 6,* 441–449.

Ardener, E. (1975). The "problem" revisited. In S. Ardener (Ed.), *Perceiving women* (pp. 19–27). London: Malaby Press.

Ardener, S. (1978). *Introduction: The nature of women in society.* In S. Ardener (Ed.), *Defining females* (pp. 9–48). New York: Wiley.

Armour, S. (2001, December 7). War of words: Free speech vexes employers. *USA Today,* p. B1.

Arnett, R. (1990). The practical philosophy of communication ethics and free speech as the foundation for speech communication. *Communication Quarterly, 38,* 208–217.

Arnhart, L. (1981). *Aristotle on political reasoning: A commentary on rhetoric.* Dekalb: Northern Illionis University Press.

Aron, A., & Aron, E. N. (1989). *The heart of social psychology: A backstage view of a passionate science* (2nd ed.). Lexington, MA: Lexington Books.

Aronson, E. (1969). The theory of cognitive dissonance: A current perspective. In Leonard Berkowitz (Ed.), *Advances in experimental social psychology* (pp. 1–34). New York: Academic Press.

Asante, M. (1987). *The Afrocentric idea.* Philadelphia: Temple University Press.

Asher, H. (1995). *Polling and public: What every citizen should know.* Washington, DC: Congressional Quarterly.

Austin, J. L. (1975). *How to do things with words.* Cambridge, MA: Harvard University Press.

Ayres, D. M., Ayres, J., & Hopf, T. S. (1995). Reducing communication apprehension among at-risk children. *Communication Reports, 8,* 178–184.

Ayres, J., & Hopf, T. S. (1989). Visualization: Is it more than extra-attention? *Communication Education, 38,* 1–5.

Ayres, J., & Hopf, T. S. (1991). Visualization: The next generation. *Communication Research Reports, 8,* 133–140.

Ayres, J., & Hopf, T. S. (1992). Visualization: Reducing speaking anxiety and enhancing performance. *Communication Reports, 5,* 1–10.

Babbie, E. R. (1995). *The practice of social research* (7th ed.). Belmont, CA: Wadsworth.

Bahrampour, T. (2002, August 13). Most deadly of the natural disasters: The heat wave. The *New York Times,* p. D5.

Baldwin, J. R., & Lindsley, S. L. (1994). *Definitions of culture: Conceptualizations from five disciplines.* Tempe: Arizona State University Press.

Bandura, A. (1977). *Social learning theory.* Englewood Cliffs, NJ: Prentice-Hall.

Banks, S. P., & Riley, P. (1993). Structuration theory as an ontology for communication research. In S. A. Deetz (Ed.), *Communication yearbook 16,* (pp. 167–196). Newbury Park, CA: Sage.

Bantz, C. R. (1992). Organizing and the social psychology of organizing. In K. Hutchinson (Ed.), *Readings in organizational communication* (pp. 90–99). Dubuque, IA: Wm. C. Brown.

Baran, S. J., & Davis, D. K. (2003). *Mass communication theory: Foundations, ferment, and future* (2nd ed.). Belmont, CA: Wadsworth.

Barnes, S. B. (2003). *Online connections: Internet interpersonal relationships.* Cresskill, NJ: Hampton.

Barnlund, D. C. (1970). A transactional model of communication. In K. K. Sereno & C. D. Mortensen (Eds.), *Foundations of communication theory* (pp. 83–102). New York: Harper.

Bavelas, J. B., Black, A., Chovil, N., & Mullett, J. (1990). *Equivocal communication.* Newbury Park, CA: Sage.

Baxter, L. A. (1983). Relationship disengagement: An examination of the reversal hypothesis. *Western Journal of Speech Communication, 47,* 85–98.

Baxter, L. A. (1984). Trajectories of relationship disengagement. *Journal of Social and Personal Relationships, 1,* 29–48.

Baxter, L. A. (1988). A dialectical perspective on communication strategies in relationship development. In S. Duck (Ed.), *Handbook of personal relationships* (pp. 257–273). New York: Wiley.

Baxter, L. A. (1990). Dialectical contradictions in relationship development. *Journal of Social and Personal Relationships, 7,* 69–88.

Baxter, L. A., & Montgomery, B. M. (1996). *Relating: Dialogues and dialectics.* New York: Guilford Press.

Baxter, L. A., & Sahlstein, E. M. (2000). Some possible directions for future research. In S. Petronio (Ed.), *Balancing the secrets of private disclosures* (pp. 289–300). Mahwah, NJ: Erlbaum.

Baxter, L. A., & Wilmot, W. W. (1985). Interaction characteristics of disengaging, stable, and growing relationships. In R. Gilmour & S. Duck (Eds.), *The emerging field of personal relationships.* Hillsdale, NJ: Erlbaum.

Beatty, M. J., & Dobos, J. A. (1992). Adult sons' satisfaction with their relationship with their fathers and person-group (father) communication apprehension. *Communication Quarterly, 40,* 162–176.

Bell, A. (1991). Audience accommodation in the mass media. In H. Giles, J. Coupland, & N. Coupland (Eds.), *Contexts of accommodation: Developments in applied sociolinguistic* (pp. 69–102). Cambridge: Cambridge University Press.

Bell, K. E., Orbe, M. P., Drummond, D. K., & Camara, S. K. (2000). Accepting the challenge of centralizing without essentializing: Black feminist thought and African American women's communicative experiences. *Women's Studies in Communication, 23,* 41–62.

Bellamy, R. V., & Walker, J. R. (1996). *Television and the remote control: Grazing on a vast wasteland.* New York: Guilford Press.

Bem, D. J. (1967). Self-perception: An alternative interpretation of cognitive dissonance phenomena. *Psychological Review, 74,* 183–200.

Bem, S. (1993). *The lenses of gender: Transforming the debate on sexual inequality.* New Haven, CT: Yale University Press.

Berelson, B. (1959). The state of communication research. *Public Opinion Quarterly, 23,* 1–6.

Berger, C. R. (1977). The covering law perspective as a theoretical basis for the study of human communication. *Communication Quarterly, 25,* 7–18.

Berger, C. R. (1979). Beyond initial interaction: Uncertainty, understanding, and the development of interpersonal relationships. In H. Giles & R. St. Clair (Eds.), *Language and social psychology* (pp. 122–144). Oxford: Blackwell.

Berger, C. R. (1982). *Social cognition and the development of interpersonal relationships: The quest for social knowledge.* Paper presented at the First International Conference on Personal Relationships, Madison, WI.

Berger, C. R. (1986). Uncertain outcome values in predicted relationships: Uncertainty reduction theory then and now. *Human Communication Research, 13,* 34–38.

Berger, C. R. (1987). Communicating under uncertainty. In M. E. Roloff & G. R. Miller (Eds.), *Interpersonal processes: New directions in communication research* (pp. 39–62). Newbury Park, CA: Sage.

Berger, C. R. (1995). Inscrutable goals, uncertain plans, and the production of communicative action. In C. R. Berger & M. Burgoon (Eds.), *Communication and social processes* (pp. 1–28). East Lansing: Michigan State University Press.

Berger, C. R., & Bradac, J. J. (1982). *Language and social knowledge: Uncertainty in interpersonal relations.* London: Arnold.

Berger, C. R., & Calabrese, R. J. (1975). Some explorations in initial interaction and beyond: Toward a developmental theory of interpersonal communication. *Human Communication Research, 1,* 99–112.

Berger, C. R., & Gudykunst, W. B. (1991). Uncertainty and communication. In. B. Dervin & M. J. Voight (Eds.), *Progress in communication sciences* (Vol. 10, pp. 21–66). Norwood, NJ: Ablex.

Berger, C. R., & Kellerman, K. (1994). Acquiring social information. In J. A. Daly & J. Weimann (Eds.), *Strategic interpersonal communication* (pp. 1–31). Hillsdale, NJ: Erlbaum.

Berger, C. R., & Roloff, M. E. (1980). Social cognition self-awareness, and interpersonal communication. In B. Dervin & M. Voigt (Eds.), *Progress in communication sciences* (Vol. 2, pp. 158–172). Norwood, NJ: Ablex.

Berk, S. (1998, December). Golden girl. *McCall's,* 18, 20, 22, 23, 24.

Berscheid, E., & Walster, E. H. (1978). *Interpersonal attraction.* Reading, MA: Addison-Wesley.

Bitzer, L. F. (1959). Aristotle's enthymeme revisited. *Quarterly Journal of Speech, 45,* 399–409.

Blalock, H. M. (1969). *Theory construction: From verbal to mathematical formulations.* Englewood Cliffs, NJ: Prentice Hall.

Blau, P. M. (1964). *Exchange and power in social life.* New York: Wiley.

Blumer, H. (1969). *Symbolic interactionism: Perspective and method.* Englewood Cliffs, NJ: Prentice Hall.

Blumler, J. G. (1979). The role of theory in uses and gratifications studies. *Communication Research, 6,* 9–36.

Blumler, J. G. (1985). The social character of media gratifications. In K. E. Rosengren, L. A. Wenner, & P. Palmgreen (Eds.), *Media gratifications research: Current perspectives* (pp. 41–60). Beverly Hills, CA: Sage.

Blumler, J. G., & Katz, E. (1974). *The uses of mass communication: Current perspectives on gratifications research.* Beverly Hills, CA: Sage.

Blumler, J. G., & McQuail, D. (1969). *Television in politics: Its uses and influence.* Chicago: University of Chicago Press.

Bochner, A. (1985). Perspectives on inquiry: Representation, conversation, and reflection. In M. L. Knapp & G. R. Miller (Eds.), *Handbook of interpersonal communication* (pp. 27–58). Beverly Hills, CA: Sage.

Bolger, N., & Kelleher, S. (1993). Daily life in relationships. In S. Duck (Ed.), *Social context and relationships* (pp. 100–108). Newbury Park, CA: Sage.

Book, P. L. (1996). How does the family narrative influence the individual's ability to communication about death? *Omega, 33,* 323–341.

Booth-Butterfield, M., Booth-Butterfield, S., & Koester, J. (1988). The function of uncertainty reduction in alleviating primary tension in small groups. *Communication Research Reports, 5,* 146–153.

Booth-Butterfield, M., & Jordan, F. (1989). Communication adaptation among racially homogeneous and heterogeneous groups. *Southern Communication Journal, 54,* 253–272.

Bormann, E. G. (1996). Symbolic convergence theory and communication in group decision making. In R. Y. Hirokawa & M. S. Poole (Eds.), *Communication and group decision making* (pp. 81–113). Thousand Oaks, CA: Sage.

Boulding, K. (1990). *Three faces of power.* Newbury Park, CA: Sage.

Bourhis, R. Y., & Giles, H. (1977). The language of intergroup distinctiveness. In H. Giles (Ed.), *Language, ethnicity and intergroup relations* (pp. 119–135). London: Academic Press.

Braithwaite, D. O., & Thompson, T. L. (2000). Communication and disability research: A productive past and bright future. In D. O. Braithwaite & T. L. Thompson (Eds.), *Handbook of communication and disabilities* (pp. 507–516). Mahwah, NJ: Erlbaum.

Branham, R. J., & Pearce, W. B. (1985). Between text and context: Toward a rhetoric of contextual reconstruction. *Quarterly Journal of Speech, 71,* 19–36.

Brashers, D. (2001). Communication and uncertainty management. *Journal of Communication, 3,* 477–497.

Brashers, D. E., Adkins, M., & Meyers, R. A. (1994). Argumentation and computer-mediated group decision making. In L. R. Frey (Ed.), *Group communication in context* (pp. 263–282). Hillsdale, NJ: Erlbaum.

Brenders, D. A. (1987). Fallacies in the coordinated management of meaning: A philosophy of language critique of the hierarchical organization of coherent conversation and related theory. *Quarterly Journal of Speech, 73,* 329–348.

Brilhart, J. K., Galanes, G. J., & Adams, K. (2001). *Effective group discussion (10th ed.).* Boston: McGraw-Hill.

Broder, J. M. (1999, July 16). A kid with a new toy (and a red face). The *New York Times,* p. A8.

Brown, P., & Levinson, S. (1978). Universals in language usage: Politeness phenomenon. In E. Goody (Ed.),

Questions and politeness (pp. 56–89). Cambridge: Cambridge University Press.

Brown, R. (1965). *Social psychology.* New York: Free Press.

Browne, M. W. (1998, June 5). Mass found in elusive particle: Universe may never be the same. The *New York Times*, pp. A1, A14.

Brummett, B. (1993). Introduction. In B. Brummett (Ed.), *Landmark essays on Kenneth Burke* (pp. xi–xix). Davis, CA: Hermagoras Press.

Budd, M., Entman, R. M., & Steinman, C. (1990). The affirmative character of U.S. cultural studies. *Critical Studies in Mass Communication, 7,* 169–184.

Budd, M., & Steinman, C. (1992). Cultural studies and the politics of encoding research. In S. A. Deetz (Ed.), *Communication yearbook 15* (pp. 251–262). Newbury Park, CA: Sage.

Burgess, E. W. (1926). The family as a unity of interacting personalities. *The Family, 7,* 3–9.

Burgess, E. W., & Locke, H. J. (1953). *The family: From institution to companionship* (2nd ed.). New York: American Book Co.

Burgoon, J. K. (1978). A communication model of personal space violations: Explication and an initial test. *Human Communication Research, 4,* 129–142.

Burgoon, J. K. (1994). Nonverbal signals. In M. L. Knapp & G. R. Miller (Eds.), *Handbook of interpersonal communication* (pp. 229–285). Newbury Park, CA: Sage.

Burgoon, J. K. (1995). Cross cultural and intercultural applications of expectancy violations theory. In R. Wiseman (Ed.), *Intercultural communication theory* (pp. 194–214). Thousand Oaks, CA: Sage.

Burgoon, J. K., Buller, D. B., Guerrero, L. K., Afifi, W. A., & Feldman, C. M. (1996). Interpersonal deception XII: Information management dimensions underlying deceptive and truthful messages, *Communication Monographs, 63,* 50–69.

Burgoon, J. K., Buller, D. B., & Woodall, W. G. (1996). *Nonverbal communication: The unspoken dialogue.* New York: McGraw-Hill.

Burgoon, J. K., Coker, D. A., & Coker, R. A. (1986). Communicative effects of gaze behavior: A test of two contrasting explanations. *Human Communication Research, 12,* 495–524.

Burgoon, J. K., Dillman, L., & Stern, L. A. (1993). Adaption in dyadic interaction: Defining and operationalizing patterns of reciprocity and compensation. *Communication Theory, 3,* 295–316.

Burgoon, J. K., & Hale, J. L. (1988). Nonverbal expectancy violations: Model elaboration and application to immediacy behaviors. *Communication Monographs, 55,* 58–79.

Burgoon, J. K., & Jones, S. B. (1976). Toward a theory of personal space expectations and their violations. *Human Communication Research, 2,* 131–146.

Burgoon, J. K., Kelley, D. L., Newton, D. A., & Kelley-Dyreson, M. P. (1989). The nature of arousal and nonverbal indices. *Human Communication Research, 16,* 217–255.

Burgoon, J. K., Manusov, V., Mineo, P., & Hale, J. L. (1985). Effects of gaze on hiring, credibility, attraction and relational message interpretation. *Journal of Nonverbal Behavior, 9,* 133–146.

Burke, K. (1945). *A grammar of motives.* New York: Prentice-Hall.

Burke, K. (1950). *A rhetoric of motives.* New York: Prentice-Hall.

Burke, K. (1965). *Permanence and change.* Indianapolis: Bobbs-Merrill.

Burke, K. (1966). *Language as symbolic action: Essays on life, literature, and method.* Berkeley: University of California Press.

Burke, K. (1968). Dramatism. In D. L. Sills (Ed.), *The international encyclopedia of the social sciences, 7* (pp. 445–452). New York: Macmillan/Free Press.

Burnett, A., & Badzinski, D. M. (2000). An exploratory study of argument in the jury decision-making process. *Communication Quarterly, 48,* 380–396.

Burrell, G., & Morgan, G. (1979). *Sociological paradigms and organisational analysis.* London: Heinemann.

Buzzanell, P. M. (1994). Gaining a voice: Feminist organization communication theorizing. *Management Communication Quarterly, 7,* 339–383.

Buzzanell, P. M., Burrell, N. A., Stafford, R. S., & Berkowitz, S. (1996). When I call you up and you're not there: Application of communication accommodation theory to telephone answering machine messages. *Western Journal of Communication, 60,* 310–336.

Buzzanell, P. M., & Turner, L. H. (2003). Emotion work revealed by job loss discourse: Backgrounding-foregrounding of feelings, construction of normalcy, and (re)instituting of traditional masculinities. *Journal of Applied Communication Research, 31,* 27–57.

Callan, H. (1978). Harems and overlords: Biosocial models and the female. In S. Ardener (Ed.), *Defining females* (pp. 200–219). New York: Wiley.

Campbell, D. T. (1965). Variation and selective retention in socio-cultural evolution. In H. R. Barringer, G. I. Blanksten, & R. W. Mack (Eds.), *Social change in developing areas* (pp. 19–49). Cambridge, MA: Schenkman.

Campbell, R. (1998). *Media and culture.* New York: St. Martin's Press.

Canary, D. J., & Cody, M. J. (1994). *Interpersonal communication: A goals-based approach*. New York: St. Martin's Press.

Canary, D. J., Cody, M. J., & Manusov, V. L. (2000). *Interpersonal communication: A goals-based approach* (2nd ed.). New York: St. Martin's Press.

Canary, D. J., & Stafford, L. (Eds.). (1994). *Communication and relational maintenance*. San Diego: Academic Press.

Carey, J. W. (1975). A cultural approach to communication. *Communication, 2,* 1–22.

Carey, J. W. (1985). Overcoming resistance to cultural studies. In M. Gurevitch & M. R. Levy (Eds.), *Mass communication review yearbook V* (pp. 27–40). Beverly Hills, CA: Sage.

Carey, J. W. (1989). *Communication as culture*. Boston: Unwin Hyman.

Carey, J. W. (1998). Marshall McLuhan: Genealogy and legacy. *Canadian Journal of Communication, 23,* 13–21.

Carlson, J. M. (1983). Crime show viewing by preadults: The impact on attitudes toward civil liberties. *Communication Research, 10,* 529–552.

Carrasquillo, H. (1997). Puerto Rican families in America. In M. K. DeGenova (Ed.), *Families in cultural context* (pp. 155–172). Mountain View, CA: Mayfield.

Carveth, R., & Alexander, A. (1985). Soap opera viewing motivations and the cultivation hypothesis. *Journal of Broadcasting & Electronic Media, 29,* 259–273.

Caughlin, J. P., Golish, T. D., Olson, L. N., Sargent, J. E., Cook, J. S., & Petronio, S. (2000). Intrafamily secrets in various family configurations: A communication boundary management perspective. *Communication Studies, 5,* 116–134.

Cavanaugh, J. P. (1999, April). Fraying relations. *Johns Hopkins Magazine,* 35–36.

Cavanaugh, J. C., & Parks, D. C. (1993). Vitality for life: Psychological research for productive aging. *APS Observer* (Vol. 2; special issue, report 2, pp. 1–2). American Psychological Society.

Chafetz, J. S. (1997). Feminist theory and sociology: Underutilized contributions for mainstream theory. *Annual Review of Sociology, 23,* 97–120.

Chaffee, S. H., & Rogers, E. M. (1997). Wilbur Schramm: The founder. In S. H. Chaffee & E. M. Rogers (Eds.), *The beginnings of communication study in America: A personal memoir* (pp. 125–148). Thousand Oaks, CA: Sage.

Chen, G. M., & Starosta, W. J. (1998). *Foundations of intercultural communication*. Boston: Allyn & Bacon.

Chen, G. M., & Starosta, W. J. (2000). *Communication and global society*. New York: Peter Lang.

Chen, T. C., Drzewiecka, J. A., & Sias, P. M. (2001). Dialectical tensions in Taiwanese international student friendships. *Communication Quarterly, 49,* 57–65.

Chesebro, J. W. (1993). Preface. In J. W. Chesebro (Ed.), *Extensions of the Burkeian system* (pp. vii–xxi). Tuscaloosa: University of Alabama Press.

Chodorow, N. (1978). *The reproduction of mothering*. Berkeley: University of California Press.

Chopra, R. (2001). Retrieving the father: Gender studies, "father love" and the discourse of mothering. *Women's Studies International Forum, 24,* 445–455.

Cirksena, K., & Cuklanz, L. (1992). Male is to female as _____ is to: A guided tour of five feminist frameworks for communication studies. In L. Rakow (Ed.). *Women making meaning: New feminist directions in communication* (pp. 18–44). New York: Routledge.

Clair, R. P. (1993). The use of framing devices to sequester organizational narratives: Hegemony and harassment. *Communication Monographs, 60,* 113–136.

Clampitt, P. G. (1991). *Communicating for managerial effectiveness*. Newbury Park, CA: Sage.

Cline, R. J. W., & McKenzie, N. J. (2000), Dilemmas of Disclosure in the age of HIV/AIDS: Balancing Privacy and Protection in the health care context. In S. Petronio (Ed.), *Balancing the secrets of private disclosures* (pp. 71–82). Mahwah, NJ: Erlbaum.

Cline, R. W. (1990). Detecting groupthink: Methods for observing the illusion of unanimity. *Communication Quarterly, 38,* 112–126.

Cohen, H. (2000). Revisiting McLuhan. *Media International Australia: Culture and Policy, 5,* 3–9.

Cohen, J. (2002, August 15). Sharing space? Share e-mail first. The *New York Times,* pp. E1, E7.

Cole, M. (1989). *A cross-cultural inquiry into the meaning of face in the Japanese and the United States culture*. Paper presented at the annual meeting of the Speech Communication Association, San Francisco.

Collier, M. J. (1998). Researching cultural identity: Reconciling interpretive and postcolonial perspectives. In D. V. Tanno & A. Gonzalez (Eds.), *Communication and identity across cultures* (pp. 122–147). Thousand Oaks, CA: Sage.

Collins, P. H. (1986). Learning from the outsider within: The sociological significance of black feminist thought. *Social Problems, 33,* 14–32.

Collins, P. H. (1989). A comparison of two works on black family life. *Signs, 14,* 875–884.

Collins, P. H. (1990). *Black feminist thought: Knowledge, consciousness, and the politics of social empowerment*. Boston: Unwin Hyman.

Collins, P. H. (1991). *Black feminist thought: Knowledge, consciousness, and the politics of empowerment.* New York: Routledge.

Condit, C. M. (1992). Post-Burke: Transcending the substance of dramatism. *Quarterly Journal of Speech, 78,* 349–355.

Conquergood, D. (1992). Life in Big Red: Struggles and accommodations in a Chicago polyethnic tenement. In L. Lamphere (Ed.), *Structuring diversity: Ethnographic perspectives on the new immigration* (pp. 95–144). Chicago: University of Chicago Press.

Conquergood, D. (1994). Homeboys and hoods: Gang communication and cultural space. In L. R. Frey (Ed.), *Group communication in context: Studies of natural groups* (pp. 23–55). Hillsdale, NJ: Erlbaum.

Conrad, C. (1993). *The ethical nexus.* Norwood, NJ: Ablex.

Conrad, C., & Macom, E. A. (1995). Re-visiting Kenneth Burke: Dramatism/logology and the problem of agency. *Southern Communication Journal, 61,* 11–28.

Cooley, C. H. (1972). *Human nature and social order.* Glencoe, IL: Free Press.

Coontz, S. (1988). *The social origins of private life.* New York: Verso.

Cooper, J., & Fazio, R. H. (1984). A new look at dissonance theory. In L. Berkowitz (Ed.), *Advances in experimental social psychology* (pp. 229–266). Orlando, FL: Academic Press.

Cooper, J., & Stone, J. (2000). Cognitive dissonance and the social group. In D. J. Terry & M. A. Hogg (Eds.), *Attitudes, behavior, and social context: The role of norms and group membership* (pp. 227–244). Mahwah, NJ: Erlbaum.

Cooper, J. M. (1996). An Aristotelian theory of the emotions. In A. O. Rorty (Ed.), *Essays on Aristotle's Rhetoric* (pp. 238–257). Berkeley: University of California Press.

Cooper, L. (1932). *The rhetoric of Aristotle.* New York: Appleton-Century-Crofts.

Cooper, T. (1989). Global universals: In search of common ground. In T. Cooper (Ed.), *Communication ethics and global change* (pp. 20–39). White Plains, NY: Longman.

Coplan, J. H. (2001). The day care dilemma. Retrieved July 31, 2002, from the World Wide Web: www.businessweek.com.

Cottrell, N. B., Wack, D. L., Sekerak, G. J., & Rittle, H. (1968). Social facilitation of dominant responses by the presence of an audience and the mere presence of others. *Journal of Personality and Social Psychology, 9,* 245–250.

Coupland, N., Coupland, J., Giles, H., & Henwood, K. (1988). Accommodating the elderly: Invoking and extending a theory. *Language in Society, 17,* 1–41.

Courtright, J. (1978). A laboratory investigation of groupthink. *Communication Monographs, 45,* 229–246.

Cox, S. A., & Kramer, M. W. (1995). Communication during employee dismissals: Social exchange principles and group influences on employee exit. *Management Communication Quarterly, 9,* 156–190.

Craig, R. T. (1999). Communication theory as a field. *Communication Theory, 9,* 119–161.

Crey, J. W. (1975). A cultural approach to communication. *Communication, 2,* 1–22.

Cronen, V. E., (1991). Coordinated management of meaning theory and post enlightenment ethics. In K. G. Greenberg (Ed.), *Conversations on communication ethics* (pp. 21–53). Norwood, NJ: Ablex.

Cronen, V. E. (1995). Coordinated management of meaning: The consequentiality of communication and the recapturing of experience. In S. J. Sigman (Ed.), *The consequentiality of communication* (pp. 17–66). Hillsdale, NJ: Erlbaum.

Cronen, V. E. (1995). Practical theory and the tasks ahead for social approaches to communication. In W. Leeds-Hurwitz (Ed.), *Social approaches to communication* (pp. 217–242). New York: Guilford Press.

Cronen, V. E., Johnson, K. M., & Lannamann, J. W. (1982). Paradoxes, double binds, and reflexive loops: An alternative theoretical perspective. *Family Process, 20,* 91–112.

Cronen, V. E., & Pearce, W. B. (1981). Logical force in interpersonal communication: A new concept of the "necessity" in social behaviors. *Communication, 6,* 5–67.

Cronen, V. E., Pearce, W. B., & Changshen, X. (1989/1990). The meaning of "meaning" in the CMM analysis of communication: A comparison of two traditions. *Research on Language and Social Interaction, 23,* 1–40.

Cronen, V. E., Pearce, W. B., & Harris, L. M. (1982). The coordinated management of meaning: A theory of communication. In F. E. X. Dance (Ed.), *Human communication theory* (pp. 67–89). New York: Harper & Row.

Cronen, V. E., Pearce, W. B., & Snaveley, L. M. (1979). A theory of rule-structure and types of episodes, and a study of perceived enmeshment in undesired repetitive patterns (URPs). In D. Nimmo (Ed.), *Communication Yearbook 3* (pp. 225–239). New Brunswick, NJ: Transaction Books.

Csikszentmihalyi, M. (1991). Reflections on the "Spiral of Silence." In J. A. Anderson (Ed.), *Communication yearbook 14* (pp. 294–298). Newbury Park, CA: Sage.

Cultural Environmental Movement. (1996). Viewers' declaration of independence. *Cultural environment monitor, 1,* 1.

Cupach, W. R., & Metts, S. (1994). *Facework.* Thousand Oaks, CA: Sage.

Cupach, W. R., & Spitzberg, B. H. (Eds.). (1994). *The dark side of interpersonal communication*. Hillsdale, NJ: Erlbaum.

Curtis, D. B., Winsor, J. L., & Stephens, R. D. (1989). National preferences in business and communication education. *Communication Education, 38*, 6–14.

Cushman, D. P., & Cahn, D. D. (1985). *Communication in interpersonal relationships*. Albany, NY: SUNY Press.

Cushman, D. P., & Pearce, W. B. (1977). Generality and necessity in three types of human communication theory: Special attention to rules theory. In B. Ruben (Ed.), *Communication Yearbook 1* (pp. 173–182). New Brunswick, NJ: Transaction Books.

Cushman, D., & Whiting, G. C. (1972). An approach to communication theory: Toward consensus on rules. *The Journal of Communication, 22*, 217–238.

Daft, R. L., & Lengel, R. H. (1984). Information richness: A new approach to managerial behavior and organization design. *Research in Organizational Behavior, 6*, 191–233.

Daft, R. L., & Weick, K. E. (1984). Toward a model of organizations as interpretation systems. *Academy of Management Review, 9*, 284–295.

Dainton, M., & Aylor, B. (2001). A relational uncertainty analysis of jealousy, trust, and maintenance in long-distance versus geographically close relationships. *Communication Quarterly, 49*, 172–188.

Dainton, M., & Stafford, L. (2000). Predicting maintenance behaviors: A comparison of relationship type, partner similarity, and sex differences. *Communication Research Reports, 17*, 171–180.

Daly, J. A. (1999, January). Communication matters. *SPECTRA, 35*, 2, 12–13.

Daly, J. A., McCroskey, J. C., & Richmond, V. P. (1977). The relationships between social activity and perception of communicators in small group interaction. *Western Speech Communication Journal, 41*, 175–187.

Dance, F. E. X. (1967). Toward a theory of human communication. In F. E. X. Dance (Ed.), *Human communication theory* (pp. 288–309). New York: Holt.

Daniels, T. D., Spiker, B. D., & Papa, M. J. (1997). *Perspectives on organizational communication*. Boston: McGraw-Hill.

Darwin, C. (1948). *The origin of species*. New York: Random House.

Dates, J. L., & Stroman, C. A. (2001). Portrayals of families of color on television. In J. Bryant & J. A. Bryant (Eds.), *Television and the American family* (pp. 207–228). Mahwah, NJ: Erlbaum.

Davidson, P. (2002, July 11). WorldCom closer to filing for bankruptcy. *USA Today*, pp. 1C, 2C.

DeFrancisco, V. (1991). The sounds of silence: How men silence women in marital relationships. *Discourse and Society, 2*, 355–370.

Delia, J. G. (1987). Communication research: A history. In C. R. Berger & S. H. Chaffee (Eds.), *Handbook of communication science* (pp. 20–98). Newbury Park, CA: Sage.

Derlega, V. J., Metts, S., Petronio, S., & Margulis, S. T. (1993). *Self-disclosure*. Newbury Park, CA: Sage.

Dervin, B., Grossberg, L., O'Keefe, B. J., & Wartella, E. (Eds.). (1989). *Rethinking communication*. Newbury Park, CA: Sage.

Dickson, F. C., & Walker, K. L. (2001). The expression of emotion in later-life married men. *Communication Quarterly, 49*, 66–71.

Diefenbach, D. L., & West, M. D. (2001). Violent crime and poisson regression: A measure and a method for cultivation analysis. *Journal of Broadcasting & Electronic Media, 45*, 432–445.

Dimmick, J. W., Sikand, J., & Patterson, S. J. (1994). The gratifications of the household telephone: Sociability, instrumentality, and reassurance. *Communication Reports, 21*, 643–663.

Dindia, K. (1994). The intrapersonal-interpersonal dialectical process of self-disclosure. In S. Duck (Ed.), *Dynamics of relationships* (pp. 27–56). Thousand Oaks, CA: Sage.

Doherty, W. J., Boss, P. G., LaRossa, R., Schumm, W. R., & Steinmetz, S. K. (1993). Familiy theory and methods. In P. G. Boss, W. J. Doherty, R. LaRossa, W. R. Schumm, & S. K. Steinmetz (Eds.), *Sourcebook of family theories and methods: A contextual approach* (pp. 313–341). New York: Plenum.

Donnelly, J. H., & Ivancevich, J. M. (1970). Post-purchase reinforcement and back-out behavior. *Journal of Marketing Research, 7*, 399–400.

Dougherty, D. S. (2001). Sexual harassment as [dys]functional process: A feminist standpoint analysis. *Journal of Applied Communication Research, 29*, 372–391.

Dougherty, D. S., & Krone, K. J. (2000). Overcoming the dichotomy: Cultivating standpoints in organizations through research. *Women's Studies in Communication, 23*, 16–40.

Douglas, W. (1990). Uncertainty, information-seeking, and liking during initial interaction. *Western Journal of Speech Communication, 54*, 66–81.

Dow, B. J. (1990). Hegemony, feminist criticism and *The Mary Tyler Moore Show*. *Critical Studies in Mass Communication, 7*, 261–274.

Downing, J. (1996). *Internationalizing media theory: Transition, power, culture*. London: Sage.

Dray, W. (1957). *Laws and explanation in history*. London: Oxford University Press.

Duck, S. (1994). *Meaningful relationships*. Thousand Oaks, CA: Sage.

duGay, P., Hall, S., Janes, L., Mackay, H., & Negus, K. (1997). *Doing Cultural Studies: The Story of the Sony Walkman*. London: Sage/The Open University.

Edelman, R. J. (1994). Embarrassment and blushing: Factors influencing face-saving strategies. In S. Ting-Toomey (Ed.), *The challenge of facework* (pp. 231–268). Albany, NY: SUNY.

Eisenberg, E. M., & Goodall, H. L. (1993). *Organizational communication: Balancing creativity and constraint*. New York: St. Martin's Press.

Elgin, S. (1988). *A first dictionary and grammar of Laadan* (2nd ed.). Madison, WI: Society for the Furtherance and Study of Fantasy and Science Fiction.

Elias, M. (1999, February 16). Work, sex and prayer in America. *USA Today*, p. D6.

Elkin, R. A., & Leippe, M. R. (1986). Physiological arousal, dissonance, and attitude change: Evidence for a dissonance-arousal link and a don't remind me effect. *Journal of Abnormal and Social Psychology, 51*, 55–65.

Elkins, J. R. (2001) Naarative theory and literary criticism. Retrieved September 11, 2002, from the World Wide Web: www.wvu.edu/lawfac/jelkins/lawyerslit/theories .htm.

Elliott, W. (1999). Personal communication. Milwaukee, WI.

Emmers, T. M., & Canary, D. J. (1996). The effect of uncertainty reduction strategies on young couples' relational repair and intimacy. *Communication Quarterly, 44*, 166–182.

England, P. (1989). A feminist critique of rational choice theories: Implications for sociology. *The American Sociologist, 20*, 14–28.

Erbert, L. A. (2000). Conflict and dialectics: Perceptions of dialectical contradiction in marital conflict. *Journal of Social and Personal Relationships, 17*, 638–659.

Esser, J. K. (1998). Alive and well after 25 years: A review of groupthink research. *Organizational Behavior and Human Decision Processes, 73*, 116–141.

Faber, R. J. (2000). The urge to buy: A uses and gratifications perspective on compulsive buying. In S. Ratneshwar, D. G. Mick, & C. Huffman (Eds.), *The why of consumption* (pp. 177–196). London: Routledge.

Farley-Lucas, B. (2000). Communicating the (in)visibilty of motherhood: Family talk and the ties to motherhood with/in the workplace. *Electronic Journal of Communication, 10*.

Fehr, B. (1996). *Friendship processes*. Thousand Oaks, CA: Sage.

Ferguson, D. A. (1992). Channel repertoire in the presence of remote control devices, VCRs and cable television. *Journal of Broadcasting & Electronic Media, 36*, 83–91.

Festinger, L. (1957). *A theory of cognitive dissonance*. Stanford, CA: Stanford University Press.

Festinger, L., & Carlsmith, J. M. (1959). Cognitive consequences of forced compliance. *Journal of Abnormal and Social Psychology, 58*, 203–210.

Festinger, L., Riecken, H. W., & Schacter, S. (1956). *When prophecy fails*. Minneapolis: University of Minnesota Press.

Ficara, L. C., & Mongeau, P. A. (2000, November). *Relational uncertainty in long-distance college student dating relationships*. Paper presented at the annual meeting of the National Communication Association, Seattle, WA.

Fisher, B. A. (1980). *Small group decision making*. New York: McGraw-Hill.

Fisher, W. R. (1978). Toward a logic of good reasons. *The Quarterly Journal of Speech, 64*, 376–384.

Fisher, W. R. (1985). The narrative paradigm: An elaboration. *Communication Monographs, 52*, 347–367.

Fisher, W. R. (1984). Narration as a human communication paradigm: The case of public moral argument. *Communication Monographs, 51*, 1–22.

Fisher, W. R. (1987). *Human communication as narration: Toward a philosophy of reason, value, and action*. Columbia: University of South Carolina Press.

Fiske, J., & Dawson, R. (1996). Audiencing violence: Watching homeless men watch *Die Hard*. In J. Hay, L. Grossberg, & E. Wartella (Eds.), *The audience and its landscape* (pp. 297–316). Boulder, CO: Westview Press.

Fiske, S. T., & Taylor, S. E. (1984). *Social cognition*. Reading, MA: Addison-Wesley.

Floyd, K., & Morman, M. (2001). Human affection exchange: III. Discriminative parental solicitude in men's affectionate communication with their biological and nonbiological sons. *Communication Quarterly, 49*, 310–327.

Foa, E., & Foa, U. (1976). Resource theory of social exchange. In J. Thibaut, J. Spence, & R. Carson (Eds.), *Contemporary topics in social psychology* (pp. 99–131). Morristown, NJ: General Learning Press.

Foa, U., & Foa, E. (1972). Resource exhange: Toward a structural theory of interpersonal communication. In A. Siegman & B. Pope (Eds.), *Studies in dyadic communication* (pp. 291–325). New York: Pergamon Press.

Foa, U., & Foa, E. (1974). *Societal structures of the mind*. Springfield, IL: Thomas.

Ford, L. A., & Crabtree, R. D. (2002). Telling, re-telling and talking about telling: Disclosure and/as surviving incest. *Women's Studies in Communication, 25*, 53–87.

Forte, J. A., Barrett, A. V., & Campbell, M. H. (1996). Patterns of social connectedness and shared grief work: A symbolic interactionist perspective. *Social Work with Groups, 19,* 29–51.

Foss, K., & Foss, S. (1991). *Women speak: The eloquence of women's lives.* Prospect Heights, IL: Waveland Press.

Foss, S. K. (1994). A rhetorical scheme for the evaluation of visual imagery. *Communication Studies, 45,* 213–224.

Foss, S., Foss, K., & Trapp, R. (1991). *Contemporary perspectives on rhetoric.* Prospect Heights, IL: Waveland Press.

Fox, S. A. (1999). Communication in families with an aging parent: A review of the literature an agenda for future research. In M. E. Roloff (Ed.), *Communication Yearbook 22* (pp. 377–429). Thousand Oaks, CA: Sage.

Frankenberg, R. (1993). *White women, race matters: The social construction of Whiteness.* Minneapolis: University of Minnesota Press.

Frejes, F., & Petrich, K. (1993). Invisibility, homophobia, and heterosexism: Lesbians, gays, and the media. *Critical Studies in Mass Communication, 10,* 395–422.

French, J. R. & Raven, B. (1959). *The bases of social power.* Ann Arbor: University of Michigan Press.

Frewin, K., & Tuffin, K. (1998). Police status, conformity an internal pressure: A discursive analysis of police culture. *Discourse & Society, 9,* 173–185.

Frey, L. R., Botan, C. H., & Kreps, G. L. (2000). *Investigating communication: An introduction to research methods.* Englewood Cliffs, NJ: Prentice Hall.

Friedrich, G. W., & Boileau, D. M. (1999). The communication discipline. In A. Vangelisti, J. Daly, and G. Friedrich (Eds.), *Teaching communication: Theory, methods, and research* (pp. 3–13). Mahwah, NJ: Erlbaum.

Frymier, A. B., & Houser, M. A. (2002). The teacher-student relationship as an interpersonal relationship. *Communication Education, 49,* 207–219.

Gallois, C., & Callan, V. J. (1991). Interethnic accommodation: The role of norms. In H. Giles, J. Coupland, & N. Coupland (Eds.), *Contexts of accommodation: Developments in applied sociolinguistics* (pp. 245–269). Cambridge: Cambridge University Press.

Gallois, C., Callan, V. J., & Johnstone, M. (1984). Personality judgments of Australian aborigine and white speakers: Ethnicity, sex, and context. *Journal of Language and Social Psychology, 3,* 39–57.

Gallois, C., Franklyn-Stokes, A., Giles, H., & Coupland, N. (1988). Communication accommodation theory and intercultural encounters: Intergroup and interpersonal considerations. In Y. Y. Kim & W. B. Gudykunst (Eds.), *Theories in intercultural communication* (pp. 157–185). Newbury Park, CA: Sage.

Garner, A. C. (1999). Negotiating our positions in culture: Popular adolescent fiction and the self-constructions of women. *Women's Studies in Communication, 22,* 1–27.

Geertz, C. (1973). *The interpretation of cultures.* New York: Basic Books.

Geertz, C. (1983). *Local knowledge.* New York: Basic Books.

George, A. L. (1993). *Bridging the gap: Theory and practice in foreign policy.* Washington, DC: United States Institute of Peace.

George, A. L. (1997). From groupthink to contextual analysis of policy-making groups. In P. 't Hart, E. L. Stern, & B. Centals (Eds.), *Beyond groupthink: Political group dynamics and foreign policy-making* (pp. 35–54). Ann Arbor: University of Michigan Press.

Gerard, H. B., & Mathewson, G. C. (1966). The effect of severity of initiation on liking for a group: A replication. *Journal of Experimental Social Psychology, 2,* 278–287.

Gerbner, G. (1969). Towards cultural indicators: The analysis of mass mediated message systems. *AV Communication Review, 17,* 137–148.

Gerbner, G. (1990). Epilogue: Advancing on the path of righteousness (maybe). In N. Signorielli & M. Morgan (Eds.), *Cultivation analysis: New directions in media effects research* (pp. 250–261). Newbury Park, CA: Sage.

Gerbner, G. (1997). PROD press release.

Gerbner, G. (1998). Cultivation analysis: An overview. *Mass Communication and Society, 3/4,* 175–194.

Gerbner, G. (1999). What do we know? In J. Shanahan & M. Morgan (Eds.), *Television and its viewers: Cultivation theory and research* (pp. ix–xiii). Cambridge: Cambridge University Press.

Gerbner, G., & Gross, L. (1972). Living with television: The violence profile. *Journal of Communication, 26,* 173–199.

Gerbner, G., & Gross, L. (1979). Editorial response: A reply to Newcomb's "humanistic critique." *Communication Research, 6,* 223–230.

Gerbner, G., Gross, L., Jackson-Beeck, M., Jeffries-Fox, S., & Signorielli, N. (1978). Cultural indicators: Violence profile No. 9. *Journal of Communication, 28,* 176–206.

Gerbner, G., Gross, L., Morgan, M., & Signorielli, N. (1980). The "mainstreaming" of America: Violence profile No. 11. *Journal of Communication, 30,* 10–29.

Gerbner, G., Gross, L., Morgan, M., & Signorielli, N. (1981). A curious journey into the scary world of Paul Hirsch. *Communication Research, 8,* 39–72.

Gerbner, G., Gross, L., Morgan, M., & Signorielli, N. (1982). Charting the mainstream: Television's contributions to political orientations. *Journal of Communication, 32,* 100–127.

Gerbner, G., Gross, L., Morgan, M., & Signorielli, N. (1986). Living with television: The dynamics of the cultivation process. In J. Bryant & D. Zillman (Eds.), *Perspectives on media effects* (pp. 17–40). Hillsdale, NJ: Earlbaum.

Giddens, A. (1979). *Central problems in social theory: Action, structure, and contradiction in social analysis.* Berkeley: University of California Press.

Giddens, A. (1984). *The constitution of society: Outline of the theory of structuration.* Berkeley: University of California Press.

Giddens, A. (1993). *New rules of Sociological method: A positive critique of interpretive sociologies* (2nd ed.). Cambridge, UK: Polity Press.

Gilder, G. F. (1994). *Life after television.* New York: Norton.

Giles, H. (1980). Accommodation theory: Some new directions. *York Papers in Linguistics, 9,* 105–136.

Giles, H., Coupland, N., & Coupland, J. (1991). Accommodation theory: Communication, context, and consequence. In H. Giles, J. Coupland, & N. Coupland (Eds.), *Contexts of accommodation: Developments in applied sociolinguistic* (pp. 1–68). Cambridge: Cambridge University Press.

Giles, H., Mulac, A., Bradac, J. J., & Johnson, P. (1987). Speech accommodation theory: The first decade and beyond. In M. L. Mclaughlin (Ed.), *Communication yearbook 10* (pp. 13–48). Newbury Park, CA: Sage.

Giles, H., & Smith, P. M. (1979). Accommodation theory: Optimal levels of convergence. In H. Giles, & R. N. St. Clair (Eds.), *Language and social psychology* (pp. 231–244). Oxford: Blackwell.

Giles, H., & Wiemann, J. (1987). Language, social comparison, and power. In S. Chaffee & C. R. Berger (Eds.), *Handbook of communication science* (pp. 350–384). Newbury Park, CA: Sage.

Glynn, C. J., Hayes, A. F., & Shanahan, J. (1997). Perceived support for one's opinions and willingness to speak out: A meta-analysis of survey studies on the spiral of silence. *Public Opinion Quarterly, 61,* 452–463.

Glynn, C. J., & McLeod, J. M. (1985). Implications of the spiral of silence for communication and public opinion research. In K. R. Sanders, L. L. Kaid, & D. Nimmo (Eds.), *Political communication yearbook 1984* (pp. 43–65). Carbondale: Southern Illinois University Press.

Goffman, E. (1967). *Interaction rituals: Essays on face-to-face interaction.* Garden City, NY: Doubleday.

Goffman, E. (1974). *Frame analysis: An essay on the organization of experience.* New York: Harper & Row.

Golden, A. (2000). What we talk about when we talk about work and family: A discourse analysis of parental accounts. *Electronic Journal of Communication, 10.*

Golden, J. L., Berquist, G. F., & Coleman, W. E. (2001). *The rhetoric of western thought.* Dubuque, IA: Kendall Hunt.

Golish, T. D. (2000). Is openness always better? Exploring the role of topic avoidance, satisfaction, and parenting styles of stepparents. *Communication Quarterly, 48,* 137–158.

Gonzalez, A., & Bradley, C. (1990). Breaking into silence: Technology transfer and mythical knowledge among the Acomas of *Nuevo Mexico.* In M. J. Medhurst, A. Gonzalez, & T. R. Peterson (Eds.), *Communication and the culture of technology* (pp. 63–76). Pullman: Washington State University Press.

Gonzalez, A., Houston, M., & Chen, V. (2000). Introduction. In A. Gonzalez, M. Houston, & V. Chen (Eds.), *Our voices: Essays in culture, ethnicity, and communication* (pp. x–xxii). Los Angeles: Roxbury.

Goode, S. (1998). They always talked on radio: Early talk of the 1930s. *Insight on the News, 14,* 18.

Gordon, G. (1982, January). An end to McLuhanacy. *Educational Technology, 44,* 39–45.

Gottman, J., & Silver, N. (1999, February). Your biggest love problem solved. *New Woman,* 85–89.

Gouran, D. S. (1998). The signs of cognitive, affiliative, and egocentric constraints in patterns of interaction in decision-making and problem-solving groups and their potential effects on outcomes. In J. Trent (Ed.), *Communication: Views from the helm for the 21st century* (pp. 98–102). Needham Heights, MA: Allyn & Bacon.

Gouran, D. S., & Hirokawa, R. Y. (1996). Functional theory and communication in decision making and problem-solving groups. In R. Y. Hirokawa & M. S. Poole (Eds.), *Communication and group decision making* (pp. 55–80). Thousand Oaks, CA: Sage.

Gouran, D. S., Hirokawa, R. Y., & Martz, A. E. (1986). A critical analysis of factors related to decisional processes involved in the Challenger disaster. *Central States Speech Journal, 37,* 119–135.

Gow, G. A. (2001). Spatial metaphor in the work of Marshall McLuhan. *Canadian Journal of Communication, 26,* 519–536.

Graham, E. E. (1997). Turning points and commitments in post-divorce relations. *Communication Monographs, 64,* 350–368.

Gray, G. W. (1964). The founding of the Speech Association of America: Happy birthday. *Quarterly Journal of Speech.*

Gray, H. (1989). Television, Black Americans, and the American dream. *Critical Studies in Mass Communication, 6,* 376–386.

Gross, T. L. (1978, June/July). The organic teacher. *Change,* 39.

Grossberg, L. (1984). Strategies of Marxist cultural interpretation. *Critical Studies in Mass Communication, 1,* 392–421.

Grossberg, L. (1986). Is there rock after punk? *Critical Studies in Mass Communication, 3,* 50–74.

Grossberg, L. (1989). The circulation of cultural studies. *Critical Studies in Mass Communication, 6,* 413–420.

Grosswiler, (1997). *The method is the message: Rethinking McLuhan through critical theory.* Montreal: Black Rose Books.

Gudykunst, W. B., Chua, E., & Gray, A. (1987). Cultural dissimilarity and uncertainty reduction processes. In M. McLaughlin (Ed.), *Communication yearbook, 10* (pp. 456–469). Newbury Park, CA: Sage.

Gudykunst, W. B., & Hammer, M. R. (1987). The influences of ethnicity, gender, and dyadic composition on uncertainty reduction in initial interactions. *Journal of Black Studies, 18,* 191–214.

Gudykunst, W. B., & Kim, Y. Y. (1992). *Communicating with strangers: An approach to intercultural communication.* New York: McGraw-Hill.

Gudykunst, W. B., & Matsumoto, Y. (1996). Cross-cultural variability of communication in personal relationships. In W. B. Gudykunst, S. Ting-Toomcy, & T. Nishada (Eds.), *Communication in personal relationships across cultures* (pp. 19–56). Thousand Oaks, CA: Sage.

Gudykunst, W. B., & Nishida, T. (1984). Individual and cultural influence on uncertainty reduction. *Communication Monographs, 51,* 23–36.

Gudykunst, W. B., & Nishida, T. (1986). Attributional confidence in low-and high-context cultures. *Human Communication Research, 12,* 525–549.

Gudykunst, W. B., & Nishida, T. (1986). Social penetration in close relationships in Japan and the United States. In R. Bostrom (Ed.), *Communication yearbook 7* (pp. 592–610). Beverly Hills, CA: Sage.

Gudykunst, W. B., Ting-Toomey, S., & Nishida, T. (Eds.). (1996). *Communication in personal relationships across cultures.* Thousand Oaks, CA: Sage.

Gudykunst, W. B., Yang, S. M., & Nishida, T. (1985). A cross-cultural test of uncertainty reduction theory: Comparison of acquaintances, friends, and dating relationships in Japan, Korea, and the United States. *Human Communication Research, 11,* 407–454.

Guensburg, C. (1999, January 6). Cooking with conscience. *Milwaukee Journal Sentinel,* pp. G1, G5.

Hackman, M. Z., & Johnson, C. E. (1996). *Leadership: A communication perspective.* Prospect Heights, IL: Waveland Press.

Hall, B. J. (2002). *Among cultures: The challenge of communication.* Ft. Worth, TX: Harcourt.

Hall, E. T. (1966). *The hidden dimension.* Garden City, NY: Anchor/Doubleday.

Hall, E. T. (1977). *Beyond culture.* Garden City, NY: Anchor/Doubleday.

Hall, S. (1980a). Encoding/decoding. In S. Hall, D. Hobson, A. Lowe, & P. Willis (Eds.), *Culture, media, language* (pp. 128–138). London: Hutchinson.

Hall, S. (1980b). Cultural studies and the centre: Some problematic and problems. In S. Hall, D. Hobson, A. Lowe, & P. Willis (Eds.), *Culture, media, language* (pp. 15–47). London: Hutchinson.

Hall, S. (1981). The whites of their eyes: Racist ideologies and the media. In G. Bridges & R. Brunt (Eds.), *Silver linings: Some strategies for the eighties* (pp. 28–52). London: Lawrence and Wishart.

Hall, S. (1989). Ideology and communication theory. In B. Dervin, L. Grossberg, B. J. O'Keefe, & E. Wartella (Eds.), *Rethinking communication: Paradigm issues* (pp. 40–51). Newbury Park, CA: Sage.

Hall, S. (1992). Cultural studies and its theortical legacies. In L. Grossberg, C. Nelson, & P. Treichler (Eds.), *Cultural studies* (pp. 277–294). New York: Routledge.

Hall, S. (1996). Cultural studies and its theoretical legacies. In D. Morley & K. Chen (Eds.), *Stuart Hall: Critical dialogues* (pp. 262–275). London: Routledge.

Hall, S. (1997). The problem of ideology: Marxism without guarantees. In S. Hall (Ed.), *Representation: Cultural representations and signifying practices* (pp. 30–46). London: Sage/The Open University.

Halpert, J., & Burg, J. H. (1997). Mixed messages: Coworker responses to the pregnant employee. *Journal of Business and Psychology, 12,* 241–253.

Hamilton, H. E. (1991). Accommodation and mental disability. In H. Giles, J. Coupland, & N. Coupland (Eds.), *Contexts of accommodation: Developments in applied sociolinguistic* (pp. 157–186). Cambridge: Cambridge University Press.

Hammersley, M. (1992). *What's wrong with ethnography? Methodological explorations.* London: Routledge.

Haraway, D. (1988). Situated knowledges: The science question in feminism and the privilege of partial perspective. *Signs, 14,* 575–599.

Harding, S. (1987). Introduction: Is there a feminist method? In Sandra Harding (Ed.), *Feminism and methodology* (pp. 1–14). Bloomington: University of Indiana Press.

Harding, S. (1991). *Whose science, whose knowledge? Thinking from women's lives.* Ithaca, NY: Cornell University Press.

Hardt, H. (1989). Between pragmatism and Marxism. *Critical Studies in Mass Communication, 6,* 421–426.

Harmon-Jones, E. (2000). An update on cognitive dissonance theory, with a focus on the self. In A. Tesser, R. B. Felson, & J. M. Suls (Eds.), *Psychological perspectives on self and identity* (pp. 119–144). Washington, DC: American Psychological Association.

Harris, L., (1980). The maintenance of a social reality: A family case study. *Family Process, 19,* 19–33.

Harris, L., & Cronen, V. (1979). A rules-based model for the analysis and evaluation of organizational communication. *Communication Quarterly, 27,* 12–28.

Harris, L., Cronen, V., & McNamee, S. (1979). *An empirical case study of communication episodes.* Paper presented to the National Council on Family Relations, Boston.

Harris, L. M., Alexander, A., McNamee, S., Stanbeck, M., & Kang, K. (1984). Forced cooperation: Violence as a communicative act. In S. Thomas (Ed.), *Communication theory and interpersonal interaction* (pp. 20–32). Norwood, NJ: Ablex.

Hart, R. P. (1997). *Modern rhetorical criticism.* Boston: Allyn & Bacon.

Hartsock, N. (1981). Political change: Two perspectives on power. In C. Bunch (Ed.), *Building feminist theory: Essays from Quest, a feminist quarterly* (pp. 55–70). New York: Longman.

Hartsock, N. (1983). The feminist standpoint: Developing the ground for a specifically feminist historical materialism. In S. Harding & M. B. Hintikka (Eds.), *Discovering reality* (pp. 283–310). Boston: Ridel.

Hartsock, N. (1998). *The feminist standpoint revisited and other essays.* Boulder, CO: Westview Press.

Hartsock, N. C. M. (1997). Standpoint theories for the next century. *Women and Politics, 18,* 93–101.

Harwood, J. (2000). Communicative predictors of solidarity in the grandparent-grandchild relationship. *Journal of Social and Personal Relationships, 17,* 743–766.

Hasse, C. E. (1909). *Ideal education for girls. Registrar of Milwaukee Downer College. Records 1852–1964.* Milwaukee Manuscript Collection L. University of Wisconsin, Milwaukee Research Center.

Hatch, M. J. (1997). *Organization theory: Modern, symbolic, and postmodern perspectives.* Oxford: Oxford University Press.

Hayden, S. (1994). Interruptions and the construction of reality. In L. H. Turner & H. M. Sterk (Eds.), *Differences that make a difference: Examining the assumptions in gender research* (pp. 99–106). Westport, CT: Bergin & Garvey.

Haynes, W. L. (1990). Public speaking pedagogy in the media age. *Communication Education, 39,* 89–102.

Hecht, M. L., Collier, M. J., & Ribeau, S. A. (1993). *African American communication: Ethnic identity and cultural interpretation.* Newbury Park, CA: Sage.

Heckman, L. (2000). [Review of the book *World without secrets: Business, crime, and privacy in the age of ubiquitous computing*] *Library Journal, 127,* 105.

Hegel, G. W. F. (1807). *The pheomenology of mind.* (J. B. Braillie, Trans.). Germany: Wutzburg & Bamberg.

Heider, F. (1958). *The psychology of interpersonal relations.* New York: Wiley.

Heinz, B. (2002). Enga(y)ging the discipline: Sexual minorities and communication studies. *Communication Education, 51,* 95–104.

Hellweg, S. A. (1992). Organizational grapevines. In K. L. Hutchinson (Ed.), *Readings in organizational communication* (pp. 159–172). Dubuque, IA: Wm. C. Brown.

Hempel, C. (1952). *Fundamentals of concept formation in empirical science.* Chicago: University of Chicago Press.

Henry, T. (1998, October 14). Girls lagging as gender gap widens in tech education. *USA Today,* p. D4.

Hensley, T. R., & Griffin, G. W. (1986). Victims of groupthink: The Kent State university board of trustees and the 1977 gymnasium controversy. *Journal of Conflict Resolution, 30,* 497–531.

Herzog, H. (1944). Motivations and gratifications of daily serial listeners. In P. F. Lazarsfeld & F. N. Stanton (Eds.), *Radio Research, 1942–1943.* New York: Duell, Sloan and Pearce.

Hetsroni, A. (2001). What do you really need to know to be a millionaire? Content analysis of quiz shows in America and in Israel. *Communication Research Reports, 18,* 418–428.

Hewes, D. E. (1996) Small group communication may not influence decision making: An amplification of socio-egocentric theory. In R. Y. Hirokawa & M. S. Poole (Eds.), *Communication and group decision making* (pp. 179–214). Thousand Oaks, CA: Sage.

Hiam, A. (1998, October). Obstacles to creativity—and how you can remove them. *The Futurist,* 30.

Hinkle, L. L. (2001). Perceptions of supervisor nonverbal immediacy, vocalics, and subordinate liking. *Communication Research Reports, 18,* 128–136.

Hirokawa, R. Y., Erbert, L., & Hurst, A. (1996). Communication and group decision-making effectiveness. In R. Y. Hirokawa & M. S. Poole (Eds.), *Communication and group decision making* (pp. 269–300). Thousand Oaks, CA: Sage.

Hirokawa, R. Y., Gouran, D. S., & Martz, A. E. (1988). Understanding the sources of faulty group decision making: A lesson from the Challenger disaster. *Small Group Behavior, 19,* 411–433.

Hirschmann, N. J. (1997). Feminist standpoint as postmodern strategy. *Women and Politics, 18*, 73–92.

Ho, D. Y. (1976). On the concept of face. *American Journal of Sociology, 81*, 867–884.

Ho, D. Y. (1994). Face dynamics: From conceptualization to measurement. In S. Ting-Toomey (Ed.), *The challenge of facework* (pp. 269–286). Albany, NY: SUNY.

Hochschild, A., Machung, A. (1989). *The second shift*. New York: Viking.

Hofstede, G. (1980). *Culture's consequences: International differences in work-related values*. Beverly Hills, CA: Sage.

Hofstede, G. (1991). *Cultures and organizations: Software of the mind*. London: McGraw-Hill.

Hopper, R., Knapp, M. L., & Scott, L. (1981). Couples' personal idioms: Exploring intimate talk. *Journal of Communication, 31*, 23–33.

Hornsey, M., & Gallois, C. (1998). The impact of interpersonal and intergroup communication accommodation on perceptions of Chinese students in Australia. *Journal of Language and Social Psychology, 17*, 323–347.

Houston, M. (1992). The politics of difference: Race, class, and women's communication. In Lana F. Rakow (Ed.), *Women making meaning: New feminist directions in communication* (pp. 45–59). New York: Routledge.

Houston, M. (2000). When black women talk with white women: Why dialogues are difficult. In A. Gonzalez, M. Houston, & V. Chen (Eds.), *Our voices: Essays in culture, ethnicity, and communication* (pp. 98–104). Los Angeles: Roxbury.

Houston, M., & Kramarae, C. (1991). Speaking from silence: Methods of silencing and of resistance. *Discourse and Society, 2*, 387–399.

Houston, M., & Schwartz, P. (1995). The relationships of lesbians and of gay men. In J. T. Wood & S. Duck (Eds.), *Under-studied relationships: Off the beaten track* (pp. 89–121). Thousand Oaks, CA: Sage.

Howell, W. S. (1982). *The empathic communicator*. Belmont, CA: Wadsworth.

Inglis, F. (1993). *Cultural studies*. Cambridge, MA: Oxford University Press.

Innes, M. (2002). Organizational communication and the symbolic construction of police murder investigations. *British Journal of Sociology, 53*, 67–68.

Innis, H. (1951). *The bias of communication*. Toronto: University of Toronto Press.

Ishii, S. (1992). Buddhist preaching: The persistent main undercurrent of Japanese traditional rhetorical communication. *Communication Quarterly, 40*, 391–397.

Jablin, F. M. (1985). An exploratory study of vocational organizational communication socialization. *Southern Communication Journal, 50*, 262–282.

Jablin, F. M. (1987). Organizational entry, assimilation, and exit. In F. M. Jablin, L. L. Putnam, K. H. Roberts, & L. W. Porter (Eds.), *Handbook of organizational communication* (pp. 679–740). Berverly Hills, CA: Sage.

Jablin, F. M., & Krone, K. J. (1987). Organizational assimilation. In C. R. Berger & S. H. Chafee (Eds.), *Handbook of communication science* (pp. 711–746). Newbury Park, CA: Sage.

Jackson, D. (2002, July 17). President shrugs at the digital divide. *Boston Globe*, p. A23.

Jamieson, K. H. (1992). *Dirty politics: Deception, detraction, and democracy*. New York: Oxford University Press.

Jandt, F. E. (2000). *Intercultural communication: An introduction*. Thousand Oaks, CA: Sage.

Janis, I. L. (1972). *Victims of groupthink: A psychological study of foreign-policy decisions and fiascoes*. Boston: Houghton Mifflin.

Janis, I. L. (1982). *Groupthink: Psychological studies of policy decisions and fiascoes*. Boston: Houghton Mifflin.

Janis, I. L. (1989). *Crucial decisions: Leadership in policy-making and crisis management*. New York: Free Press.

Janis, I. L., & Gilmore, J. B. (1965). The influence of incentive conditions on the success of role-playing in modifying attitudes. *Journal of Personality and Social Psychology, 1*, 17–27.

Jeffres, L. W., Neuendorf, K. A., & Atkin, D. (1999). Spirals of silence: Experiencing opinions when the climate of opinion is unambiguous. *Political Communication, 16*, 115–131.

Jencks, C. (1994). *The homeless*. Cambridge, MA: Harvard University Press.

Jensen, J. V. (1997). *Ethical issues in the communication process*. Mahwah, NJ: Erlbaum.

Johanneson, R. L. (2000). *Ethics in human communication* (5th ed.). Prospect Heights, IL: Waveland Press.

Jordan, M. (1998, October). Being Michael Jordan. *Vanity Fair, 118*, 120, 122, 124, 126.

Jourard, S. M. (1971). *The transparent self* (rev. ed.). New York: Van Nostrand.

Katz, E. (1959). Mass communication research and the study of popular culture. *Studies in Public Communication, 2*, 1–6.

Katz, E., Blumler, J. G., & Gurevitch, M. (1974). Utilization of mass communication by the individual. In J. G. Blumler & E. Katz (Eds.), *The uses of mass communication:*

Current perspectives on gratifications research (pp. 19–32). Beverly Hills, CA: Sage.

Katz, E., Gurevitch, M., & Haas, H. (1973). On the use of the mass media for important things. *American Sociological Review, 38*, 164–181.

Kellermann, K., & Reynolds, R. (1990). When ignorance is bliss: The role of motivation to reduce uncertainty in uncertainty reduction theory. *Human Communication Research, 17*, 5–35.

Kelly, C., & Zak, M. (1999). Narrativity and professional communication: Folktales and community meaning. *Journal of Business and Technical Communication, 13*, 297–317.

Kendell, K. (1996). Lesbian and gay family law issues update. *Lesbian News, 22*, 18–19.

Kennamer, J. D. (1990). Self-serving bias in perceiving the opinions of others. *Communication Research, 17*, 393–404.

Kennedy, G. A. (1991). *Aristotle on Rhetoric: A theory of civil discourse.* New York: Oxford University Press.

Kenny, R. W. (2001). Toward a better death: Applying Burkean principles of symbolic action to interpret family adaptation to Karen Ann Quinlan's coma. *Health Communication, 13*, 363–385.

Kephart, W. M. (1950). A quantitative analysis of intragroup relations. *American Journal of Sociology, 60*, 544–549.

Keyton, J., Ferguson, P., & Rhodes, S. C. (2001). Cultural indicators of sexual harassment. *Southern Communication Journal, 67*, 33–50.

Kieran, M. (1997). *Media ethics.* Westport, CT: Praeger.

Kim, Y. Y. (1986). *Interethnic communication: Current research.* Newbury Park, CA: Sage.

Kim, Y. Y. (1989). Communication and adaptation of Asian Pacific refugees in the United States. *Journal of Asian Pacific Communication, 1*, 191–207.

Kimberling, C. R. (1982). *Kenneth Burke's dramatism and popular arts.* Bowling Green: Bowling Green University Press.

King, G., & Hermodson, A. (2000). Peer reporting of coworker wrongdoing: A qualitative analysis of observer attitudes in the decision to report versus not report unethical behavior. *Journal of Applied Communication Research, 28*, 309–329.

Kirby, E. L., & Krone, K. J. (2002). The policy exists but you can't really use it: Communication and the structuration of work-family policies. *Journal of Applied Communication, 30*, 50–77.

Kirkwood, W. (1992). Narrative and the rhetoric of possibility. *Communication Monographs, 59*, 30–47.

Kissling, E. (1991). Street harassment: The language of sexual terrorism. *Discourse and Society, 2*, 121–135.

Klein, D. M., & White, J. M. (1996). *Family theories: An introduction.* Thousand Oaks, CA: Sage.

Klemz, A. (1977). *Blindness and partial sight.* Cambridge: Woodhead Faulkner.

Knapp, M. L. (1978). *Nonverbal communication in human interaction.* New York: Holt, Rinehart & Winston.

Knapp, M. L., Ellis, D. G., & Williams, B. A. (1980). Perceptions of communication behavior associated with relationship terms. *Communication Monographs, 47*, 262–278.

Knapp, M. L., & Hall, J. A. (2002). *Nonverbal communication in human interaction* (5th ed.). Ft. Worth, TX: Holt, Rinehart & Winston.

Knapp, M. L., & Vangelisti, A. L. (2000). *Interpersonal communication and human relationships* (4th ed.). Boston: Allyn & Bacon.

Knox, R. E., & Inkster, J. A. (1968). Postdecision dissonance at posttime. *Journal of Personality and Social Psychology, 8*, 310–323.

Kotkin, S. (2002, September 7). A world war among professors that affects jobs and resources. The *New York Times*, pp. A15, A17.

Kotler, J. A., Wright, J. C., & Huston, A. C. (2001). Television use in families with children. In J. Bryant & J. A. Bryant (Eds.), *Television and the American family* (pp. 33–48). Mahwah, NJ: Erlbaum.

Kramarae, C. (1981). *Women and men speaking: Frameworks for analysis.* Rowley, MA: Newbury House.

Kramarae, C., & Treichler, P. (1985). *A feminist dictionary.* Boston: Pandora.

Kramer, M. W., & Berman, J. E. (2001). Making sense of a university's culture: An examination of undergraduate students' stories. *Southern Communication Journal, 66*, 297–311.

Kreps, G. (1980). A field experiment test and revaluation of Weick's model of organizing. In D. Nimmo (Ed.), *Communication yearbook 4* (pp. 389–398). New Brunswick, NJ: Transaction Books.

Kreuter, M., Farrell, D., Olevitch, L., & Brennan, L. (2000). *Tailoring health messages: Customizing communication with computer technology.* Mahwah, NJ: Erlbaum.

Kubey, R., & Csikszentmihalyi, M. (1990). *Television and the quality of life: How viewing shapes everyday experience.* Hillsdale, NJ: Erlbaum.

Kuhn, T. S. (1970). *The structure of scientific revolutions.* Chicago: University of Chicago Press.

Kurtz, H. (1998, August 13). Homicide rate down, except on the evening news. *San Francisco Chronicle*, p. A8.

Labich, K. (1999, March 1). Boeing finally hatches a plan. *Fortune, 139*, 100–106.

Lambert, J., & Tomasson, G. C. (1997). Mormon American families. In M. K. DeGenova (Ed.), *Families in cultural context* (pp. 85–108). Mountain View, CA: Mayfield.

Lamoureux, E. L. (1994). Rhetorical dilemmas in Catholic discourse: The case of bishop John J. Meyers. *Communication Studies, 45,* 281–293.

Langer, E. (1989). *Mindfulness.* Reading, MA: Addison-Wesley.

Lannutti, P. J., Laliker, M., & Hale, J. L. (2001). Violations of expectations and social-sexual communication in student/professor interactions. *Communication Education, 50,* 69–82.

La Poire, B. A., & Burgoon, J. K. (1992). A reply from the heart: Who are Sparks and Greene and why are they saying all these horrible things? *Human Communication Research, 18,* 472–482.

LaPoire, B. A., & Burgoon, J. K. (1996). Usefulness of differentiating arousal responses within communication theories: Orienting response or defensive arousal within nonverbal theories of expectancy violation. *Communication Monographs, 63,* 208–230.

LaRossa, R., & Reitzes, D. C. (1993). Symbolic interactionism and family studies. In P. G. Boss, W. J. Doherty, R. LaRossa, W. R. Schumm, & S. K. Steinmetz (Eds.), *Sourcebook of family theories and methods: A contextual approach* (pp. 135–163).

Lea, M., & Spears, R. (1995). Love at first byte? Building personal relationships over computer networks. In J. T. Wood & S. Duck (Eds.), *Under-studied relationships: Off the beaten track.* (pp. 197–233). Thousand Oaks, CA: Sage.

Lee, J. (2002, August 15). As gadgets go to class, schools try to cope. The *New York Times,* pp. E1, E7.

Leeds-Hurwitz, W. (1990). Notes on the history of intercultural communication: The foreign service institute and the mandate for intercultural training. *Quarterly Journal of Speech, 76,* 262–281.

Lemert, J. B. (1981). *Does mass communication change public opinion after all? A new approach to effects analysis.* Chicago: Nelson-Hall.

Leo, J. (2001, July 23). Is there an echo? *Newsweek,* 17.

Lerner, B. H. (2002, July 23). In the death of a doctor, a lesson. The *New York Times,* p. D4.

Lesh, D. A. (2002). Hegemony, articulation, and counter-hegemonic struggle. Retrieved September 10, 2002, from the World Wide Web: www.leestreet.com.

Leung, L., & Wei, R. (2000). More than just talk on the move: Uses and gratifications of the cellular phone. *Journalism & Mass Communication Quarterly, 77,* 308–320.

Levinson, P. (1999, October 15). McLuhan for the millenium. *Chronicle of Higher Education, 48,* B10.

Levinson, P. (2001). *Digital Mcluhan: A guide to the information millennium.* London: Routledge.

Levy, M., & Windahl, S. (1985). The concept of audience activity. In, P. L. Palmgreen, L. A. Wenner, & K. E. Rosengren (Eds.), *Media gratifications research: Current perspectives* (pp. 109–122). Beverly Hills, CA: Sage.

Lewis, J., & Morgan, M. (2001). He may not be a liberal, but he plays one on TV: Imagining the ideology of President Clinton. *The Communication Review, 4,* 327–345.

Lewis, W. F. (1987). Telling America's story: Narrative form and the Reagan presidency. *Quarterly Journal of Speech, 73,* 280–302.

Lim, T. (1994). Facework and interpersonal relationships. In S. Ting-Toomey (Ed.), *The challenge of facework* (pp. 209–230). Albany, NY: SUNY.

Lim, T., & Bowers, J. W. (1991). Facework, solidarity, approbation, and tact. *Human Communication Research, 176,* 415–450.

Lin, C. A., & Salwen, M. B. (1997). Predicting the spiral of silence on a controversial issue. *Howard Journal of Communications, 8,* 129–141.

Lindner, E. E. (Ed.) (2001). *Yearbook of American and Canadian churches.* Nashville, TN: Abingdon Press.

Lingle, J. H., & Ostrom, T. M. (1981). Principles of memory and cognition in attitude formation. In R. E. Petty, T. M. Ostrom, & T. C. Brock (Eds.), *Cognitive responses in persuasive communications* (pp. 399–420). New York: McGraw-Hill.

Littlejohn, S. W. (2002). *Theories of communication* (7th ed.). Belmont, CA: Wadsworth.

Long, E. (1989). Feminism and cultural studies. *Critical Studies in Mass Communication, 6,* 427–435.

Longley, J., & Pruitt, D. G. (1980). Groupthink: A critique of Janis' theory. *Review of Personality and Social Psychology, 1,* 74–93.

Lord, C. (1994). The intention of Aristotle's *Rhetoric.* In E. Schiappa (Ed.), *Landmark essays on classical Greek rhetoric* (pp. 157–168). Davis, CA: Hermagoras Press.

Lowenthal, M. (1998, March 1). Nowhere man: How a vacation became a quest for connection. *The New York Times Magazine,* p. 84.

Lucaites, J. L., & Condit, C. M. (1985). Re-constructing narrative theory: A functional perspective. *Journal of Communication, 35,* 9–108.

Lull, J. (1982). How families select television programs: A mass-observational study. *Journal of Broadcasting, 26,* 801–811.

Lum, A. M., & Zuiderveen, M. D. (2001). The electronic medical record—barrier or bridge to effective clinician-patient communication? Retrieved September 10, 2002, from the World Wide Web: www.kaiserpermanente.org.

Lyman, R. (2002, August 25). Revolt in the den: DVD has the VCR headed to the attic. The *New York Times,* pp. A1, A13.

Ma, R. (1992). The role of unofficial intermediaries in interpersonal conflicts in the Chinese culture. *Communication Quarterly, 40,* 269–278.

Macdonald, D. (1967). He has looted all culture . . . , In G. Stearn (Ed.), *McLuhan: Hot & Cool* (pp. 56–77). New York: Dial.

MacIntrye, A. (1981). *After virtue: A study in moral theory.* Notre Dame, IN: University of Notre Dame Press.

Maisel, E. (1997). *Fearless presenting.* New York: Back Stage Books.

Mamali, C., & Paun, G. (1982). Group size and the genesis of subgroups: Objective restrictions. *Revue Roumaine Des Sciences Sociales—Serie de Psychologie, 26,* 139–148.

Marchand, M. (1989). *Marshall McLuhan: The medium and the messenger.* New York: Ticknor & Fields.

Markus, H., & Kitayama, S. (1991). Culture and the self: Implications for cognition, emotion, and motivation. *Psychological Review, 2,* 224–253.

Martin, J. N., & Davis, O. I. (2001). Conceptual foundations for teaching about whiteness in intercultural communication courses. *Communication Education, 50,* 298–313.

Martin, J. N., & Nakayama, T. K. (1999). Thinking dialectically about culture and communication. *Communication Theory, 9,* 1–25.

Martin, J. N., & Nakayama, T. K. (2000). *Intercultural communication in contexts.* New York: McGraw-Hill.

Marx, K. (1963). *The communist manifesto of Karl Marx and Friedrich Engels.* New York: Russell & Russell.

Maslow, A. H. (1970). *Motivation and personality* (2nd ed.). New York: Harper & Row.

Massey, K. B. (1995). Analyzing the uses and gratifications concept of audience activity with a qualititative approach: Media encounters during the 1989 Loma Prieta earthquake disaster. *Journal of Broadcasting & Electronic Media, 39,* 328–349.

Matheson, C. (2001). *The Simpson's and Philosophy: The D'oh! Of Homer.* Ottawa, IL: Open Court.

McBurney, J. H. (1994). The place of the enthymeme in rhetorical theory. In E. Schiappa (Ed.), *Landmark essays on classical Greek rhetoric* (pp. 169–190). Davis, CA: Hermagoras Press.

McCauley, C. (1989). The nature of social influence in groupthink: Compliance and internalization. *Journal of Personality and Social Psychology, 57,* 250–260.

McCloskey, D. (1993). The neglected economics of talk. *Planning for Higher Education, 22,* 11–16.

McCroskey, J. C. (1997). *An introduction to rhetorical communication.* Boston: Allyn & Bacon.

McCroskey, J. C., Burroughs, N. F., Daun, A., & Richmond, V. P. (1990). Correlates of quietness: Swedish and American perspectives. *Communication Quarterly, 38,* 127–137.

McCroskey, J. C., & McCain, T. A. (1974). The measurement of interpersonal attraction. *Speech Monographs, 41,* 261–266.

McCroskey, J. C., & Richmond, V. P. (2000). Applying reciprocity and accommodation theories to supervisor/subordinate communication. *Journal of Applied Communication Research, 28,* 278–289.

McGregor, G. (1995). Gender advertisements than and now: Goffman, symbolic interactionism, and the problem of history. In Norman K. Denzin (Ed.) *Studies in symbolic interaction* (pp. 3–42). Greenwich, CT: JAI Press.

McKenzie, R. (2000). Audience involvement in the epideictic discourse of television talk shows. *Communication Quarterly, 48,* 190–203.

McKinney, D. H., & Donaghy, W. C. (1993). Dyad gender structure, uncertainty reduction, and self-disclosure during initial interaction. In P. Kalbfleish (Ed.), *Interpersonal communication: Evolving interpersonal relationships* (pp. 33–50). Hillsdale, NJ: Erlbaum.

McLaughlin, M. L., Cody, M. J., & Rosenstein, N. E. (1983). Account sequences in conversations between strangers. *Communication Monographs, 50,* 102–128.

McLuhan, M. (1962). *The Gutenberg galaxy.* New York: Mentor.

McLuhan, M. (1964). *Understanding media.* New York: Mentor.

McLuhan, M. (1967). Preface. In G. Stearn (Ed.), *McLuhan: Hot & Cool* (p. i). New York: Dial.

McLuhan, M. (1984). *Understanding media* (reprint). Cambridge, MA: MIT Press.

McLuhan, M., & Fiore, Q. (1967). *The medium is the massage: An inventory of effects.* New York: Bantam Books.

McLuhan, M., & Fiore, Q. (1968). *War and peace in the global village.* New York: Bantam Books.

McLuhan, M., & McLuhan, E. (1988). *Laws of media: The new science.* Toronto: University of Toronto Press.

McLuhan, M., & Nevitt, B. (1972). *Take today: The executive as dropout.* New York: Harper & Row.

McLuhan, M., & Parker, H. (1969). *Counterblast.* New York: Harcourt, Brace & World.

McMullen, W. J. (1996). Reconstructing of the frontier myth in *Witness. The Southern Communication Journal, 62,* 31–41.

McQuail, D. (1984). With the benefits of hindsight: Reflections on uses and gratifications research. *Critical Studies in Mass Communication, 1*, 177–193.

McQuail, D., Blumler, J. G., & Brown, J. (1972). The television audience: A revised perspective. In D. McQuail (Ed.), *Sociology of mass communication* (pp. 135–165). Harmondsworth, England: Penguin Books.

Mead, G. H. (1934). *Mind, self and society: From the standpoint of a social behaviorist.* Chicago: University of Chicago Press.

Mehrabian, A. (1981). *Silent messages: Implicit communication of emotions and attitudes.* Belmont, CA: Wadsworth.

Melia, T. (1989). Scientism and dramatism: Some quasi-mathematical motifs in the work of Kenneth Burke. In H. W. Simmons & T. Melia (Eds.), *The legacy of Kenneth Burke* (pp. 156–173). Madison: University of Wisconsin Press.

Merritt, B. D. (1991). Bill Cosby: TV auteur? *Journal of Popular Culture, 24*, 89–102.

Merritt, B. D. (1997). Illusive reflections: African American women on prime time television. In A. Gonzalez, M. Houston, & V. Chen (Eds.), *Our voices: Essays in culture, ethnicity, and communication* (pp. 52–60). Los Angeles: Roxbury.

Merten, K. (1985). An essay: Public opinion—our social skin. *Journalism Quarterly, 62*, 649–653.

Meyer, J. (1995). Tell me a story: Eliciting organizational values from narratives. *Communication Quarterly, 43*, 210–224.

Meyrowitz, J. (1985). *No sense of place.* New York: Oxford University Press.

Miller, G. R. (1978). The current status of theory and research in interpersonal communication. *Human Communication Research, 4*, 164–178.

Miller, G. R. (1981). Tis the season to be jolly: A yuletide 1980 assessment of communication research. *Human Communication Research, 7*, 371–377.

Miller, G. R., & Steinberg, M. (1975). *Between people: A new analysis of interpersonal communication.* Chicago: Science Research Associates.

Miller, J. (1999, July 13). Globalization widens rich-poor gap, U.N. report says. The *New York Times*, p. A8.

Miller, R. E. (1996). *Embarrassment: Poise and peril in everyday life.* New York: Guilford Press.

Molitor, F. T. (1994). The effects of television exposure on the cultivation of AIDS-related fears: A test of a new model for predicting resonance. *Dissertation Abstracts International, 54*(7-A), 2372.

Molm, L. D. (2001). Theories of social exchange and exchange networks. In G. Ritzer & B. Smart (Eds.), *Handbook of social theory* (pp. 260–272). London: Sage.

Monge, P. R. (1973). Theory construction in the study of communication: The system paradigm. *Journal of Communication, 23*, 5–16.

Montgomery, B. M. (1984). Individual differences and relational interdependencies in social interaction. *Human Communication Research, 11*, 33–60.

Montgomery, B. M. (1992). Communication as the interface between couples and culture. In J. A. Andersen (Ed.), *Communication yearbook 15* (pp. 475–507). Newbury Park, CA: Sage.

Moore, M. P. (1997). Rhetorical subterfuge and "the principles of perfection," part II: Bob Packwood's Senate Resignation. *The Southern Communication Journal, 63*, 37–55.

Moran, R. (1996). Artifice and persuasion: The work of metaphor in the *Rhetoric.* In A. O. Rorty (Ed.), *Essays on Aristotle's Rhetoric* (pp. 385–398). Berkeley: University of California Press.

Morgan, M. (1986). Television and the erosion of regional diversity. *Journal of Broadcasting & Electronic Media, 30*, 123–129.

Morgan, M., & Signorielli, N. (1990). Cultivation analysis: Conceptualization and methodology. In N. Signorielli & M. Morgan (Eds.), *Cultivation analysis: New directions in media effects research* (pp. 13–34). Newbury Park, CA: Sage.

Morisaki, S., & Gudykunst, W. B. (1994). Face in Japan and the United States. In S. Ting-Toomey (Ed.), *The challenge of facework* (pp. 47–94). Albany, NY: SUNY.

Morley, D., & Chen, K. H. (1997). Introduction. In S. Hall (Ed.), *Representation: Cultural representations and signifying practices* (pp. 1–22). London: Sage/The Open University.

Morreale, S. P., & Vogl, M. W. (Eds.). (1998). *Pathways to careers in communication.* Annandale, VA: NCA.

Morris, M., & Ogan, C. (1996). The Internet as mass medium. *Journal of Communication, 46*, 39–50.

Morrow, L. (1998, June 1). Caught in the act of soliloquy. *Time*, 11–12.

Mortensen, C. D. (1997). *Miscommunication.* Thousand Oaks, CA: Sage.

Motley, M. T. (1990). On whether one can(not) not commuicate: An examination via traditional communication postulates. *Western Journal of Speech Communication, 54*, 1–20.

Moy, P., Domke, D., & Stamm, K. (2001). The spiral of silence and public opinion on affirmative action. *Journalism and Mass Communication Quarterly, 78*, 7–25.

Mumby, D. K. (1988). *Communication and power in organizations: Discourse, ideology and domination.* Norwood, NJ: Ablex.

Murdock, G. (1989). Cultural studies: Missing links. *Critical Studies in Mass Communication, 6,* 436–440.

Nakayama, T. K., & Krizek, R. L. (1995). Whiteness: A strategic rhetoric. *Quarterly Journal of Speech, 81,* 291–309.

Narula, U., & Pearce, W. B. (1986). *Development of communication: A perspective on India.* Carbondale: Southern Illinois University Press.

Navarro, M. (1998, July 20). Florida gives teen-age smokers a day in court. The *New York Times,* pp. A1, A14.

Neel, J. (1994). *Aristotle's voice: Rhetoric, theory & writing in America.* Carbondale: Southern Illinois University Press.

Nelson, C. (1989). Writing as the accomplice of language: Kenneth Burke and poststructuralism. In H. W. Simons & T. Melia (Eds.), *The legacy of Kenneth Burke* (pp. 156–173). Madison: University of Wisconsin Press.

Neuliep, J. W. (1987). Gender differences in the perception of sexual and nonsexual humor. *Journal of Social Behavior and Personality, 2,* 345–351.

Neuliep, J. W., & Grohskopf, E. L. (2000). Uncertainty reduction and communication satisfaction during initial interaction: An initial test and replication of a new axiom. *Communication Reports, 13,* 67–77.

Newcomb, H. (1978). Assessing the violence profile studies of Gerbner and Gross: A humanistic critique and suggestion. *Communication Research, 5,* 264–283.

Nichols, M. H. (1952). Kenneth Burke and the new rhetoric. *The Quarterly Journal of Speech, 38,* 133–134.

Nieves, E. (2002, June 27). Judges ban pledge of allegiance from schools, citing "under God." The *New York Times,* p. A1.

Nippert-Eng, C. E., (1996). *Home and work.* Chicago: University of Chicago Press.

Nishida, T. (1996). Communication in personal relationships in Japan. In W. B. Gudykunst, S. Ting-Toomey, & T. Nishida (Eds.), *Communication in personal relationships across cultures* (pp. 102–121). Thousand Oaks, CA: Sage.

Nkomo, S. M., & Cox, T. (1996). Diverse identities in organizations. In S. R. Clegg, C. Hardy, & W. R. Nord (Eds.), *Handbook of organizational studies* (pp. 338–356). London: Sage.

Noelle-Neumann, E. (1983). The effect of media on media effects research. *Journal of Communication, 33,* 157–165.

Noelle-Neumann, E. (1984). *The spiral of silence: Public opinion—our social skin.* Chicago: University of Chicago Press.

Noelle-Neumann, E. (1985). The spiral of silence—A response. In K. R. Sanders, L. L. Kaid, & D. D. Nimmo, (Eds.), *Political communication yearbook, 1984.* Carbondale: Southern Illinois University.

Noelle-Neumann, E. (1991). The theory of public opinion: The concept of the spiral of silence. In J. A. Anderson (Ed.), *Communication yearbook 14* (pp. 256–287). Newbury Park, CA: Sage.

Noelle-Neumann, E. (1993). *The spiral of silence: Public opinion—our social skin* (2nd ed.). Chicago: University of Chicago Press.

Noller, P., Feeney, J. A., Bonnell, D., & Callan, V. J. (1994). A study of conflict in early marriage. *Journal of Social and Personal Relationships, 11,* 233–252.

Nussbaum, J. F., Thompson, T., & Robinson, J. D. (1989). *Communication and aging.* New York: Harper & Row.

O'Brien Hallstein, D. L. (1999). A postmodern caring: Feminist standpoint theories, revisioned caring and communication ethics. *Western Journal of Communication, 63,* 32–56.

O'Brien Hallstein, D. L. (2000). Where standpoint stands now: An introduction and commentary. *Women's Studies in Communication, 23,* 1–15.

O'Connor, A. (1989). The problem of American cultural studies. *Critical Studies in Mass Communication, 6,* 405–412.

O'Leary, C. M. (1997). Counteridentification or counter-hegemony? Transforming feminist standpoint theory. *Women and Politics, 18,* 45–72.

O'Mara, J., Allen, J. L., Long, K. M., & Judd, B. (1996). Communication apprehension, nonverbal immediacy, and negative expectations for learning. *Communication Research Reports, 13,* 109–128.

O'Neill, J. M. (1915). The national association. *Quarterly Journal of Public Speaking, 1,* 51–58.

Oetzel, J. G., Ting-Toomey, S., Masumoto, T., Yokochi, Y., Pan, X., Takai, J., & Wilcox, R. (2001). Face and facework in conflict: A cross-cultural comparison of China, Germany, Japan, and the United States. *Communication Monographs, 68,* 235–258.

Oetzel, J. G., Ting-Toomey, S., Yokochi, Y., Masumoto, T., & Takai, J. (2000). A typology of facework behaviors in conflicts with best friends and relative strangers. *Communication Quarterly, 48,* 397–419.

Olsen, T. (1978). *Silences.* New York: Delacorte Press.

Opt, S. K. (1988). Continuity and change in storytelling about artificial intelligence: Extending the narrative paradigm. *Communication Quarterly, 36,* 298–310.

Orbe, M. P. (1998). *Constructing co-cultural theory: An explication of culture, power, and communication.* Thousand Oaks, CA: Sage.

Pacanowsky, M. E. (1983). A small town cop. In L. L. Putnam & M. E. Pacanowsky (Eds.), *Communication and organizations: An interpretive approach* (pp. 261–282). Beverly Hills, CA: Sage.

Pacanowsky, M. E. (1989). Creating and narrating organizational realities. In B. Dervin, L. Grossberg, B. J. O'Keefe, and E. Wartella (Eds.), *Rethinking communication* (pp. 250–257). Newbury Park, CA: Sage

Pacanowsky, M. E., & O'Donnell-Trujillo, N. (1982). Communicaton and organizational cultures. *Western Journal of Speech Communication, 46,* 115–130.

Pacanowsky, M. E., & O'Donnell-Trujillo, N. (1983). Organizational communication as cultural performance. *Communication Monographs, 50,* 127–147.

Pais, S. (1997). Asian Indian families in America. In M. K. DeGenova (Ed.), *Families in cultural context* (pp. 173–190). Mountain View, CA: Mayfield.

Palmgreen, P. L., Wenner, L. A., & Rayburn, J. D. (1980). Relations between gratification sought and obtained: A study of television news. *Communication Research, 7,* 161–192.

Palmgreen, P., Wenner, L. A., & Rosengren, K. E. (Eds.). (1985). *Media gratifications research: Current perspectives.* Beverly Hills, CA: Sage.

Pan, Y. (2000). *Politeness in Chinese face-to-face interaction.* Stamford, CT: Ablex.

Papacharissi, Z., & Rubin, A. M. (2000). Predictors of Internet use. *Journal of Broadcasting & Electronic Media, 44,* 175–196.

Parks, M. R. (1982). Ideology in interpersonal communication: Off the couch and into the world. In M. Burgoon (Ed.), *Communication yearbook 5* (pp. 79–108). New Brunswick, NJ: Transaction Books.

Parks, M. & Adelman, M. (1983). Communication networks and the development of romantic relationships: An expansion of uncertainty reduction theory. *Human Communicatoin Research, 10,* 55–80.

Parry-Giles, T., & Parry-Giles, S. J. (1996). Political scopophilia, presidential campaigning, and the intimacy of American politics. *Communication Studies, 47,* 191–205.

Pavitt, C., & Johnson, K. (2002). Scheidel and Crowell revisited: A descriptive study of group proposal sequencing. *Communication Monographs, 69,* 19–32.

Pawlowski, D. R., Thilborger, C., & Cieloha-Meekins, J. (2001). Prisons, old cars, and Christmas trees: A metaphoric analysis of familial communication. *Communication Studies, 52,* 180–196.

Pearce, W. B. (1976). The coordinated management of meaning: A rules-based theory of interpersonal communication. In G. R. Miller (Ed.), *Explorations in interpersonal communication* (pp. 17–35). Beverly Hills, CA: Sage.

Pearce, W. B. (1989). *Communication and the human condition.* Carbondale: Southern Illinois University Press.

Pearce, W. B. (1994). *Interpersonal communication: Making social worlds.* New York: HarperCollins.

Pearce, W. B. (1995). A sailing guide for social constructionists. In W. Leeds-Hurwitz (Ed.), *Social approaches to communication* (pp. 88–112). New York: Guilford Press.

Pearce, W. B. (1998). "Do no harm or make it better?" Some implications of transcending the false dichotomy between theory and practice. In J. Trent (Ed.), *Communication: Views from the helm for the 21st century* (pp. 325–331). Boston: Allyn & Bacon.

Pearce, W. B., & Conklin, F. (1979). A model of hierarchical meanings in coherent conversation and a study of indirect responses. *Communication Monographs, 46,* 75–87.

Pearce, W. B., & Cronen, V. E. (1980). *Communication, action, and meaning: The creation of social realities.* New York: Praeger.

Pearce, W. B., Cronen, V. E., & Conklin, F. (1979). On what to look at when analyzing communication: A hierarchical model of actors' meanings. *Communication, 4,* 195–220.

Pearce, W. B., & Foss, K. A. (1990). The historical context of communication as a science. In G. L. Dahnke & G. W. Clatterbuck (Eds.), *Human communication : Theory and research* (pp. 1–20). Belmont, CA: Wadsworth.

Pearce, W. B., & Littlejohn, S. W. (1997). *Moral conflict: When social worlds collide.* Thousand Oaks, CA: Sage.

Pearce, W. B., & Pearce, K. A. (2000). Extending the theory of the coordinated management of meaning (CMM) through a community dialogue process. *Communication Theory, 10,* 405–423.

Pearson, J. C. (1985, October). *Innovation in teaching gender and communication: Excluding and including women and men.* Paper presented at the annual conference of the Organization for the Study of Communication, Language, and Gender, Lincoln, NE.

Pearson, J. C., West, R., & Turner, L. H. (1995). *Gender and communication* (3rd ed.). Madison, WI: Brown & Benchmark.

Penman, R. (1994). Facework in communication: Conceptual and moral challenges. In S. Ting-Toomey (Ed.), *The challenge of facework* (pp. 15–46). Albany, NY: SUNY.

Perloff, R. M. (1993). *The dynamics of persuasion.* Hillsdale, NJ: Erlbaum.

Perse, E. M., & Courtright, J. A. (1993). Normative images of communication media: Mass and interpersonal channels in the new media environment. *Human Communication Research, 19,* 485–503.

Perse, E. M., & Greenberg-Dunn, D. (1998). The utility of home computers and media use: Implications of multimedia and connectivity. *Journal of Broadcasting & Electronic Media, 42*, 435.

Peterson, E. E. (1987). Media consumption and girls who want to have fun. *Critical Studies in Mass Communication, 4*, 37–50.

Peterson, I. (2002, August 14). Questions about germ scientist after Princeton anthrax finding. The *New York Times*, p. A21.

Petit-Zerman, S. (2002, Sept.–Oct.). No laughing matter. *Utne Reader*, 24.

Petronio, S. (1991). Communication boundary management: A theoretical model of managing disclosure of private information between married couples. *Communication Theory, 1*, 311–335.

Petronio, S. (1999). Translating scholarship into practice: An alternative metaphor. *Journal of Applied Communication Research, 27*, 87–91.

Petronio, S. (2000). The boundaries of privacy: Praxis of everyday life. In S. Petronio (Ed.), *Balancing the secrets of private disclosures* (pp. 37–49). Mahwah, NJ: Erlbaum.

Petronio, S. (2002). *Boundaries of privacy: Dialectics of disclosure*. Albany, NY: SUNY Press.

Petronio, S., Ellemers, N., Giles, H., & Gallois, C. (1998). (Mis)communicating across boundaries: Interpersonal and intergroup considerations. *Communication Research, 25*, 571–595.

Petronio, S., Flores, L. A., & Hecht, M. L. (1997). Locating the voice of logic: Disclosure discourse of sexual abuse. *Western Journal of Communication, 61*, 101–113.

Petronio, S., & Kovach, S. (1997). Managing privacy boundaries: Health providers' perceptions of resident care in Scottish nursing homes. *Journal of Applied Communication Research, 25*, 115–131.

Petronio, S., & Martin, J. N. (1986). Ramifications of revealing private information: A gender gap. *Journal of Clinical Psychology, 42*, 499–506.

Petronio, S., Martin, J. N., & Littlefield, R. (1984). Prerequisite conditions for self-disclosing: A gender issue. *Communication Monographs, 51*, 268–273.

Petronio, S., Reeder, H. M., Hecht, M. L., & Ros-Mendoza, T. M. (1996). Disclosure of sexual abuse by children and adolescents. *Journal of Applied Communication Research, 24*, 181–199.

Pew Research Center (2001). Wired seniors. Retrieved September 4, 2002, from the World Wide Web: www.pewinternet.org.

Philipsen, G. (1989). An ethnographic approach to communication studies. In B. Dervin, L. Grossberg, B. J. O'Keefe, & E. Wartella (Eds.), *Rethinking communication: Vol. 2. Paradigm exemplars* (pp. 258–268). Newbury Park, CA: Sage.

Philipsen, G. (1995). The coordinated management of meaning theory of Pearce, Cronen, and Associates. In D. Cushman & B. Kovacic (Eds.), *Watershed traditions in human communication theory* (pp. 13–43). Albany, NY: SUNY Press.

Phillips, D. C. (1992). *The social scientists' bestiary*. Oxford, England: Pergamon Press.

Planalp, S. (1987). Interplay between relational knowledge and events. In R. Burnett, P. McGhee, & D. Clarke (Eds.), *Accounting for relationships: Social representations of interpersonal links* (pp. 173–191). London: Methuen.

Planalp, S., & Honeycutt, J. M. (1985). Events that increase uncertainty reduction in personal relationships. *Human Communication Research, 11*, 593–604.

Planalp, S., & Rivers, M. (1988). *Changes in knowledge of relationships*. Paper presented at the annual meeting of the International Communication Association, New Orleans, LA.

Planalp, S., Rutherford, D. K., & Honeycutt, J. M. (1988). Events that increase uncertainty in personal relationships II: Replication and extension. *Human Communication Research, 14*, 516–547.

Poole, M. S. (1983). Review of *Communication, action and meaning: The creation of social realities*. *Quarterly Journal of Speech, 69*, 223–224.

Poole, M. S. (1998). The small group should be the fundamental unit of communication research. In J. Trent (Ed.), *Communication: Views from the helm for the 21st century* (pp. 94–97). Needham Heights, MA: Allyn & Bacon.

Poole, M. S., & Hirokawa, R. Y. (1996). Introduction: Communication and group decision making. In R. Y. Hirokawa & M. S. Poole (Eds.), *Communication and group decision making* (pp. 3–18). Thousand Oaks, CA: Sage.

Poole, M. S., & Roth, J. (1989). Decision and development in small groups IV: A typology of group decision paths. *Human Communication Research, 15*, 323–356.

Poole, M. S., Seibold, D. R., & McPhee, R. D. (1985). Group decision-making as a structurational process. *Quarterly Journal of Speech, 71*, 74–102.

Poole, M. S., Seibold, D. R., & McPhee, R. D. (1986). A structurational approach to theory-building in group decision-making research. In R. Y. Hirokawa & M. S. Poole (Eds.), *Communication and group decision-making* (pp. 237–264). Beverly Hills, CA: Sage.

Poole, M. S., Seibold, D. R., & McPhee, R. D. (1996). The structuration of group decisions. In R. Hirokawa & M. S. Poole (Eds.), *Communication and group decision making* (pp. 114–146). Thousand Oaks, CA: Sage.

Popper, K. R. (1959). *The logic of scientific discovery*. New York: Basic Books.

Popper, K. R. (1976). *Unended quest: An intellectual autobiography*. LaSalle, IL: Open Court.

Postman, N. (1992). *Technopoly: The surrender of culture to technology*. New York: Knopf.

Potter, W. J. (1991). The relationships between first and second order measures of cultivation. *Human Communication Research, 18*, 92–113.

Potter, W. J. (1993). Cultivation theory and research: A conceptual critique. *Human Communication Research, 19*, 564–601.

Preston, E. H. (1990). Pornography and the construction of gender. In N. Signorielli & M. Morgan (Eds.), *Cultivation analysis: New directions in media effects research* (pp. 107–122). Newbury Park, CA: Sage.

Putnam, L. L. (1989). Negotiation and organizing: Two levels within the Weickian model. *Communication Studies, 40*, 249–257.

Radway, J. (1984). *Reading the romance: Women, patriarchy, and popular literature*. Chapel Hill: University of North Carolina Press.

Radway, J. (1986). Identifying ideological seams: Mass culture, analytical methods, and political practice. *Communication, 9*, 93–123.

Radway, J. (1996). The hegemony of "specificity" and the impasse in audience research: Cultural studies and the problem of ethnography. In J. Hay, L. Grossberg, & E. Wartella (Eds.), *The audience and its landscape* (pp. 235–246). Boulder, CO: Westview Press.

Rawlins, W. K. (1992). *Friendship matters: Communication, dialectics, and the life course*. New York: Aldine De Gruyter.

Rayburn, J. D., & Palmgreen, P. C. (1984). Merging uses and gratifications and expectancy-value theory. *Communication Research, 11*, 537–562.

Real, M. R. (1996). *Exploring media culture*. Thousand Oaks, CA: Sage.

Reimer, B., & Rosengren, K. E. (1990). Cultivated viewers and readers: A life-style perspective. In N. Signorielli & M. Morgan (Eds.), *Cultivation analysis: New directions in media effects research* (pp. 181–206). Newbury Park, CA: Sage.

Remote controls: Can one do the work of many? (1992, December). *Consumer Reports*, 796–799.

Reuther, C., & Fairhurst, G. T. (2000). Chaos theory and the glass ceiling. In P. Buzzanell (Ed.), *Rethinking organization and managerial communication from feminist perspectives* (pp. 236–253). Thousand Oaks, CA: Sage.

Rhys, W. R., & Bywater, I. (1954). *Rhetoric*. New York: Modern Library.

Richmond, V. P., Smith, R. S., Heisel, A. D., & McCroskey, J. C. (2001). Nonverbal immediacy in the physician-patient relationship. *Communication Research Reports, 18*, 211–216.

Riger, S. (1992). Epistemological debates, feminist voices: Science, social values, and the study of women. *American Psychologist, 47*, 730–740.

Roberts, W. R. (1984). Rhetoric. In J. Barnes (Ed.), *The complete works of Aristotle* (pp. 2152–2269). Princeton, NJ: Princeton University Press.

Robichaud, D. (1999). Textualization and organizing: Illustrations from a public discussion process. *The Communication Review, 3*, 103–124.

Rodgers, J. E. (1999, January/February). Fascinating flirting. *Psychology Today, 36*–41, 64–65, 67, 69.

Roethlisberger, F. L., & Dickson, W. (1939). *Management and the worker*. New York: Wiley.

Roffers, M. (2002). Personal communication, Milwaukee, WI.

Rogers, E. M. (1994). *A history of communication study: A biographical approach*. New York: Free Press.

Rogers, E. M. (2000). The extensions of men: The correspondence of Marshall McLuhan and Edward T. Hall. *Mass Communication & Society, 3*, 117–135.

Rogers, E. M., & Chaffee, S. H. (1983). Communication as an academic discipline: A dialogue. *Journal of Communication, 33*, 18–30.

Roloff, M. E. (1981). *Interpersonal communication: The social exchange approach*. Beverly Hills, CA: Sage.

Rorty, A. O. (1996). Structuring rhetoric. In A. O. Rorty (Ed.), Aristotle's *Rhetoric* (pp. 1–33). Berkeley: University of California Press.

Rosenfeld, L. B., & Bowen, G. L. (1991). Marital disclosure and marital satisfaction: Direct-effect versus interaction-effect models. *Western Journal of Speech Communication, 55*, 69–81.

Rosenthal, R., & Jacobson, L. (1968). *Pygmalion in the classroom: Teacher expectation and pupils' intellectual development*. New York: Holt, Rinehart & Winston.

Rosnow, R. L. (1992). Rumor as communication: A contextualist approach. In K. L. Hutchinson (Ed.), *Readings in organizational communication* (pp. 173–186). Dubuque, IA: Wm. C. Brown.

Rowland, R. C. (1987). Narrative: Mode of discourse or paradigm? *Communication Monographs, 54*, 264–275.

Rowland, R. C. (1989). On limiting the narrative paradigm: Three case studies. *Communication Monographs, 56*, 39–53.

Rubin, A. M. (1981). An examination of television viewing motives. *Communication Research, 8*, 141–165.

Rubin, A. M. (1994). Uses, gratification and media effects research. In J. Bryant & D. Zillman (Eds.), *Media effects:*

Advances in theory and research (pp. 281–301). Hillsdale, NJ: Erlbaum.

Rubin, L. (1998, March). *Friends and kin.* Speech presented at the conference on Successful Relating in Couples, in Families, between Friends, and at Work, Tucson, AZ.

Rubin, L. B. (1983). *Intimate strangers: Men and women together.* New York: Harper & Row.

Rubin, R. B., & Rubin, A. M. (1992). Antecedents of interpersonal communication motives. *Communication Quarterly, 40,* 305–317.

Rubin, R. B., Rubin, A. M., & Piele, L. J. (1996). *Communication research: Strategies and sources.* Belmont, CA: Wadsworth.

Rubin, A. M., & Step, M. M. (2000). Impact of motivation, attraction, and parasocial interaction on talk radio listening. *Journal of Broadcasting & Electronic Media, 44,* 635–654.

Rudd, G. (1995). The symbolic construction of organizational identities and community in a regional symphony. *Communication Studies, 46,* 201–220.

Ruddick, S. (1989). *Maternal thinking: Towards a politics of peace.* Boston: Beacon Press.

Rumbough, T. (2001). The development and maintenance of interpersonal relationships through computer-mediated communication. *Communication Research Reports, 18,* 223–229.

Russ, T. L., Simonds, C. J., & Hunt, S. K. (2002). Coming out in the classroom . . . An occupational hazard: The influence of sexual orientation on teacher credibility and perceived student learning. *Communication Education, 51,* 311–324.

Ryan, E. B., Maclean, M., & Orange, J. B. (1994). Inappropriate accommodation in communication to elders: Inferences about nonverbal correlates. *International Journal of Aging and Human Development, 36,* 273–296.

Ryan, E. E. (1984). *Aristotle's theory of rhetorical argumentation.* Montreal: Les Editions Ballarmin.

Sabatelli, R. M., & Shehan, C. L. (1993). Exchange and resource theories. In P. G. Boss, W. J. Doherty, R. LaRossa, W. R. Schumm, & S. K. Steinmetz (Eds.), *Sourcebook of family theories and methods: A contextual approach* (pp. 385–411). New York: Plenum.

Sabatine, F. J. (1989). Rediscovering creativity: Unlearning old habits. *Mid-American Journal of Business, 4,* 11–13.

Sabourin, T. C., & Stamp, G. H. (1995). Communication and the experience of dialectical tensions in family life: An examination of abusive and nonabusive families. *Communication Monographs, 62,* 213–242.

Salmon, C. T., & Kline, F. G. (1985). The spiral of silence ten years later: An examination and evaluation. In K. Sanders, L. L. Kaid, & D. Nimmo (Eds.), *Political communication yearbook 1984* (pp. 3–29). Carbondale: Southern Illinois University Press.

Salmon, C. T., & Neuwirth, K. (1990). Perceptions of opinion climates and willingness to discuss the issue of abortion. *Journalism and Mass Communication Quarterly, 67,* 567–577.

Samovar, L. A., & Mills, J. (1998). *Oral communication: Speaking across cultures.* Boston: McGraw-Hill.

Samovar, L. A., & Porter, R. E. (1995). *Communication between cultures.* Belmont, CA: Wadsworth.

Sapir, E. (1921). *Language: An introduction to the study of speech.* New York: Harcourt, Brace & World.

Satir, V. (1988). *The new peoplemaking.* Mountain View, CA: Science and Behavior Books.

Schell, J. (1982). *The fate of the earth.* New York: Avon Books.

Schoeman, F. D. (Ed.). (1984). *Philosophical dimensions of privacy: An anthology.* London: Cambridge University Press.

Schramm, W. (1997). *The beginnings of communication study in America: A personal memoir.* Thousand Oaks, CA: Sage.

Schramm, W. L. (1954). *The process and effects of mass communication.* Urbana: University of Illinois Press.

Schultz, B. G. (1996). *Communicating in the small group.* New York: HarperCollins.

Schwarzbeck, C. (1999, February 7). Children build upon details of adoption tale. *Milwaukee Journal Sentinel,* p. 6L.

Schwichtenberg, C. (1987). Articulating the people's politics: Manhood and right-wing populism in the A-Team. *Communication, 9,* 389–398.

Scott, C. R., Corman, S. R., & Cheney, G. (1998). Development of a structurational model of identification in the organization. *Communication Theory, 8,* 298–336.

Seglin, J. (2002, July 21). Corporate values trickle down from the top. The *New York Times,* p. C4.

Seguin, J. (1998). *Media career guide: Preparing for jobs in the 21st century.* New York: St. Martin's Press.

Seibold, D. (1998). Jurors' intuitive rules for deliberation: A structurational approach to communication in jury decision making. *Communication Monographs, 65,* 282–307.

Seinfeld, J. (1993). *SeinLanguage.* New York: Bantam Books.

Selnow, G. (2000, October 4). Media experts says Internet is fertile ground for sowing democracy. Retrieved January 13, 2003, from the World Wide Web: www.usinfo.gov.

Seyfarth, B. (2000). Structuration theory in small group communication: A review and agenda for future research. In M. E. Roloff (Ed.), *Communication yearbook 23* (pp. 341–380). Thousand Oaks, CA: Sage.

Shanahan, J., & Jones, V. (1999). Cultivation and social control. In D. Demers & K. Viswanath (Eds.), *Mass media, social control and social change* (pp. 35–61). Ames, IA: Iowa State Press.

Shanahan, J., & Morgan, M. (1999). *Television and its viewers: Cultivation theory and research.* Cambridge: Cambridge University Press.

Shannon, C., & Weaver, W. (1949). *The mathematical theory of communication.* Urbana: University of Illinois Press.

Sharf, B. F. (1990). Physician-patient communication as interpersonal rhetoric: A narrative approach. *Health Communication, 2,* 217–231.

Sharf, B. F., & Poirier, S. (1988). Exploring (un)common ground: Communication and literature in a health care setting. *Communication Education, 37,* 224–236.

Shaw, M. E. (1981). *Group dynamics: The psychology of small group behavior.* New York: McGraw-Hill.

Shedletsky, L. J., & Aitken, J. E. (2001). The paradoxes of online academic work. *Communication Education, 50,* 206–217.

Sherblom, J. C., Keranen, L., & Withers, L. A. (2002). Tradition, tension, and transformation: A structuration analysis of a game warden service in transition. *Journal of Applied Communication Research, 30,* 143–162.

Sheriff, R. E. (2000). Exposing silence as cultural censorship: A Brazilian case. *American Anthropologist, 102,* 114–132.

Sherry, J., Lucas, K., Rechtsteiner, S., Brooks, C., & Wilson, B. (2001, May). Video game uses and gratifications as predictors of use and game preference. Paper presented at the annual meeting of the International Communication Association, Washington, DC.

Shibley-Hyde, J., & Delamater, J. D. (2000). *Understanding human sexuality.* Boston: McGraw-Hill.

Shimanoff, S. (1980). *Communication rules: Theory and research.* Beverly Hills, CA: Sage.

Shimanoff, S. B. (1994). Gender perspectives on facework: Simplistic stereotypes vs. complex realities. In S. Ting-Toomey (Ed.), *The challenge of facework* (pp. 159–208). Albany, NY: SUNY.

Showalter, E. (1997, December). The professor wore Prada. *Vogue.* 80, 86, 92.

Shuster, B. (1998, August 23). Public's fear of violence serves varied interests. *San Jose Mercury News,* p. A19.

Shutiva, C. (2000). Native American culture and communication through humor. In A. Gonzalez, M. Houston, & V. Chen (Eds.), *Our voices: Essays in culture, ethnicity,*

and communication (pp. 123–127). Los Angeles: Roxbury.

Signorielli, N. (1990). Television's mean and dangerous worlds: A continuation of the cultural indicators perspective. In N. Signorielli & M. Morgan (Eds.), *Cultivation analysis: New directions in media effects research* (pp. 85–106). Newbury Park, CA: Sage.

Signorielli, N., Eveland, W. P., & McLeod, D. M. (1995). Actual and perceived U.S. public opinion: The spiral of silence during the Persian Gulf war. *International Journal of Public Opinion Research, 7,* 91–109.

Signorielli, N., & Morgan, M. (Eds.). (1990). *Cultivation analysis: New directions in media effects research.* Newbury Park, CA: Sage.

Simpson, C. (1996). Elisabeth Noelle-Neumann's "spiral of silence" and the historical context of communication theory. *Journal of Communication, 46,* 149–173.

Smith, D. (1979). A peculiar eclipsing: Women's exclusion from man's culture. *Women's Studies International, 1,* 281–295.

Smith, K. L., & Belgrave, L. L. (1994). Experiencing hurricane Andrew: Environment and everyday life. In Norman K. Denzin (Ed.), *Studies in symbolic interaction* (pp. 251–273). Greenwich, CT: JAI Press.

Smith, P. M. (1985). *Language, the sexes, and society.* Oxford, England: Basil Blackwell.

Smith, S. L. (1998, December). The rebirth of NIOSH. *Occupational Hazards,* 30–32.

Snyder, M. (1979). Self-monitoring processes. In L. Berkowitz (Ed.), *Advances in experimental social psychology* (Vol. 12, pp. 86–131). New York: Academic Press.

Soar, M. (2000). Encoding advertisements: Ideology and meaning in advertising production. *Mass Communication & Society, 3,* 415–437.

Sorensen, S. (1981, May). *Grouphate.* Paper presented at the annual meeting of the International Communication Association, Minneapolis.

Soules, M. (2001). McLuhan: Light and dark. Retrieved March 3, 2003, from the World Wide Web: www.kitchenmedialab.org.

Sparks, G. G., & Greene, J. O. (1992). On the validity of nonverbal indicators as measures of physiological arousal: A response to Burgoon, Kelley, Newton, and Keeley-Dyreson. *Human Communication Research, 18,* 445–471.

Sparks, G. G., & Ogles, R. M. (1990). The difference between fear of victimization and probability of being victimized: Implication for cultivation. *Journal of Broadcasting & Electronic Media, 34,* 351–358.

Spender, D. (1984). *Man made language.* London: Routledge & Kegan Paul.

Spitzberg, B. H., & Cupach, W. R. (Eds.) (1998). *The dark side of close relationships*. Mahwah, NJ: Erlbaum.

Sproule, J. M. (1980). *Argument*. New York: McGraw-Hill.

Stacks, D. W., Hill, S. R., & Hickson, M. (1991). *Introduction to communication theory*. Fort Worth, TX: Holt, Rinehart & Winston.

Steele, C. M. (1988). The psychology of self-affirmation: Sustaining the integrity of the self. In L. Berkowitz (Ed.), *Advances in experimental social psychology* (Vol. 21, pp. 261–302). San Diego. Academic Press.

Steele, C. M., Spencer, S. J., & Lynch, M. (1993). Self-image, resilience, and dissonance: The role of affirmatioanal resources. *Journal of Personality and Social Psychology, 64*, 885–896.

Steiner, L. (1988, August). *Oppositional decoding as an act of resistance*. Paper presented at the annual conference of the Association for Education in Journalism and Mass Communication, Norman, OK.

Sterk, H. (1999). Personal communication, Milwaukee, WI.

Stewart, L. (1992). "Whistle Blowing": Implications for organizational communication. In K. L. Hutchinson (Ed.), *Readings in organizational communication* (pp. 442–453). Dubuque, IA: Wm. C. Brown.

Storey, J. (1996). *Cultural studies & the study of popular culture*. Athens: University of Georgia Press.

Straus, S. G. (1997). Technology, group processes, and group outcomes: Testing the connections in performance in computer-mediated and face-to-face groups. *Human-Computer Interaction, 12*, 227–266.

Street, R. L. (1991). Accommodation in medical consultations. In H. Giles, J. Coupland, & N. Coupland (Eds.), *Contexts of accommodation: Developments in applied sociolinguistic* (pp. 131–156). Cambridge: Cambridge University Press.

Street, R. L., & Buller, D. B. (1988). Patients' characteristics affecting physician-patient nonverbal communication. *Human Communication Research, 15*, 60–90.

Street, R. L., & Giles, H. (1982). Speech accommodation theory: A social cognitive approach to language and speech behavior. In M. E, Roloff & C. R. Berger (Eds.), *Social cognition and communication* (pp. 193–226). Beverly Hills, CA: Sage.

Strine, M. S. (1992). Understanding how things work: Sexual harassment and academic culture. *Journal of Applied Communication Research, 20*, 391–400.

Stroud, S. R. (2001). Technology and mythic narrative: The *Matrix* as technological hero-quest. *Western Journal of Communication, 65*, 416–441.

Sullivan, K. (1996). Rozzie and Harriet. *Gender & Society, 10*, 747–768.

Sullivan, P. A., & Turner, L. H. (1993). *The Zoe Baird spectacle: Silences, sins, and status*. Paper presented at the annual meeting of the Speech Communication Association, Miami.

Sullivan, P. A., & Turner, L. H. (1996). *From the margins to the center: Contemporary women and political communication*. Westport, CT: Praeger.

Sunnafrank, M. (1986). Predicted outcome value during initial interactions: A reformulation of uncertainty reduction theory. *Human Communication Research, 13*, 191–210.

Surber, J. P. (1998). *Culture and critique: An introduction to the critical discourses of cultural studies*. Boulder, CO: Westview Press.

Swartz, O. (1998). *The rise of rhetoric and its intersections with contemporary critical thought*. Boulder, CO: Westview Press.

Sweeney, P. (1999, February 14). Teaching new hires to feel at home. The *New York Times*, p. B4.

't Hart, P. (1990). *Groupthink in government: A study of small groups and policy failure*. Amsterdam: Swets and Zeitlinger.

't Hart, P. (1991). Irving Janis' *Victims of Groupthink*. *Political Psychology, 12*, 1247–1248.

't Hart, P. (1998). Preventing groupthink revisited: Evaluating and reforming groups in government. *Organizational Behavior and Human Decision Processes, 73*, 306–313.

Tajfel, H. (1982). *Social identity and intergroup relations*. Cambridge: Cambridge University Press.

Tajfel, H., & Turner, J. C. (1986). The social identity theory of intergroup behavior. In S. Worchel & W. Austin (Eds.), *The psychology of intergroup relations* (pp. 7–24). Chicago, IL: Nelson Hall.

Tan, A. S. (1982). Television use and social stereotypes. *Journalism Quarterly, 59*, 119–122.

Tanno, D. V., & Gonzalez, A. (1998). Sites of identity in communication and culture. In D. V. Tanno & A. Gonzalez (Eds.), *Communication and identity across cultures* (pp. 3–7). Thousand Oaks, CA: Sage.

Taylor, A., & Hardman, M. J. (2000). Introduction: The meaning of voice. In A. Taylor & M. J. Hardman (Eds.), *Hearing many voices* (pp. 1–27). Cresskill, NJ: Hampton Press.

Taylor, D. A., & Altman, I. (1987). Communication in interpersonal relationships: Social penetration processes. In M. E. Roloff & G. R. Miller (Eds.), *Interpersonal processes: New directions in communication research* (pp. 257–277). Newbury Park, CA: Sage.

Taylor, E. (1989). *Prime-time families: Television culture in postwar America*. Berkeley: University of California Press.

Taylor, J. R., & Van Every (2000). *The emergent organization: Communication as its site and surface.* Mahwah, NJ: Erlbaum.

Tedford, T. L., & Herbeck, D. A. (2001). *Freedom of speech in the United States.* State College, PA: Strata.

Thibaut, J., & Kelley, H. (1959). *The social psychology of groups.* New York: Wiley.

Thomas, J., & Johnson, K. (1999, January 30). Long-term plan shown in Salt Lake City bid. The *New York Times,* pp. A1, B16.

Ting-Toomey, S. (1988). Intercultural conflict styles: A face negotiation theory. In Y. Y. Kim & W. B. Gudykunst (Eds.), *Theories in intercultural communication* (pp. 213–238). Newbury Park, CA: Sage.

Ting-Toomey, S. (1991). Intimacy expression in three cultures: France, Japan, and the United States. *International Journal of Intercultural Relations,* 15, 29–46.

Ting-Toomey, S. (1993). Communicative resourcefulness: An identity negotiation perspective. In R. Wiseman & J. Koester (Eds.). *Intercultural communication competence* (pp. 72–111). Newbury Park, CA: Sage.

Ting-Toomey, S. (1994a). Face and facework: An Introduction. In S. Ting-Toomey (Ed.), *The Challenge of facework* (pp. 1–14). Albany, NY: SUNY Press.

Ting-Toomey, S. (1994b). Managing intercultural conflicts effectively. In L. A. Samovar & R. E. Porter (Eds.), *Intercultural communication: A reader* (pp. 360–372). Belmont, CA: Wadsworth.

Ting-Toomey, S., & Cocroft, B. A. (1994). Face and facework: Theoretical and research interests. In S. Ting-Toomey (Ed.), *The challenge of facework* (pp. 307–340). Albany, NY: SUNY.

Ting-Toomey, S., & Cole, M. (1990). Intergroup diplomatic communication: A face-negotiation perspective. In F. Korzenny & S. Ting-Toomey (Eds.), *Communication for peace: Diplomacy and negotiation* (pp. 77–95). Newbury Park, CA: Sage.

Ting-Toomey, S., Gao, G., Trubisky, P., Yang, Z., Kim, H. S., Lin, S., & Nishida, T. (1991). Culture, face maintenance, and styles of handling interpersonal conflict: A study in five cultures. *The International Journal of Conflict Management,* 2, 275–296.

Ting-Toomey, S., & Chung, L. (1996). Cross-cultural interpersonal communication: Theoretical trends and research directions. In W. B. Gudykunst, S. Ting-Toomey, & T. Nishida (Eds.), *Communication in personal relationships across cultures* (pp. 237–261). Thousand Oaks, CA: Sage.

Toulmin, S. (1958). *The uses of argument.* London: Cambridge University Press.

Tracy, K. (1990). The many faces of facework. In H. Giles & W. P. Robinoson (Eds.), *Handbook of language and social psychology* (pp. 209–226). New York: Wiley.

Tracy, K., & Baratz, S. (1994). The case for case studies of facework. In S. Ting-Toomey (Ed.), *The challenge of facework* (pp. 287–306). Albany, NY: SUNY.

Trenholm, S. (1991). *Human communication theory.* Englewood Cliffs, NJ: Prentice-Hall.

Trevino, L. K., Lengel, R. H., & Daft, R. L. (1987). Media symbolism, media richness, and media choice in organizations: A symbolic interactionist perspective. *Communication Research,* 14, 553–574.

Triandis, H. C. (1972). *The analysis of subjective cultures.* New York: Wiley.

Triandis, H. C. (1988). Collectivism vs. individualism: A reconceptualization of a basic concept in cross-cultural psychology. In G. Verma & C. Bagley (Eds.), *Cross-cultural studies of personality, attitudes and psychology* (pp. 60–95). London: Macmillan.

Tronto, J. C. (1993). *Moral boundaries: A political argument for an ethic of care.* New York: Routledge.

Trujillo, N. (1983). Performing Mintzberg's roles: The nature of managerial communication. In L. Putnam & M. E. Pacanowsky (Eds.), *Communication and organizations: An interpretive approach* (pp. 73–98). Beverly Hills, CA: Sage.

Tulmulty, K., & Gibbs, N. (1999, January 4). The better half. *Time,* 112–120, 122.

Turkle, S. (1995). *Life on the screen: Identity in the age of the Internet.* New York: Simon & Schuster.

Turkle, S. (1998). Identity in the age of the Internet: Living in the MUD. In R. Holeton (Ed.), *Composing cyberspace* (pp. 5–11). Boston: McGraw-Hill.

Turner, J. H. (1978). *The structure of sociological theory.* Homewood, IL: Dorsey Press.

Turner, J. H. (1986). *The structure of sociological theory* (4th ed.). Chicago: Dorsey Press.

Turner, L. H. (1990). The relationship between communication and marital uncertainty: Is her marriage different from his marriage? *Women's Studies in Communication,* 13, 57–83.

Turner, L. H. (1992). An analysis of words coined by women and men: Reflections on the muted group theory and Gilligan's model. *Women and Language,* 25, 21–26.

Turner, L. H., & West, R. L. (2002). *Perspectives on family communication* (2nd ed.). New York: McGraw-Hill.

Turner, M. E., & Pratkanis, A. R. (1998). Twenty-five years of groupthink theory and research: Lessons from the evaluation of a theory. *Organizational Behavior and Human Decision Processes,* 73, 105–115.

Turow, J. (2003). *Media today: An introduction to mass communication* (2nd ed.). Boston: Houghton Mifflin.

23-Year Low Spot in Crime. (1997, November 16). *San Jose Mercury News*, p. A1.

UCLA Center for African American Studies (2002). Prime time in black and white: Making sense of the 2002 Fall season. *The CAAS Research Report, 1,* 1–12.

U.S. Census Bureau (2000). Census bureau projects doubling of nation's population by 2100. Retrieved September 13, 2002, from the World Wide Web: www.census.gov.

VanLear, C. A. (1991). Testing a cyclical model of communicative openness in relational development: Two longitudinal studies. *Communication Monographs, 58,* 337–361.

VanLear, C. A. (1996). Communication process approaches and models: Patterns, cycles, and dynamic coordination. In J. H. Watt & C. A. VanLear (Eds.), *Dynamic patterns in communication processes* (pp. 35–70). Thousand Oaks, CA: Sage.

Varchaver, N. (1998, Dec./1999, Jan.). Warning: Second-hand smoke may NOT kill you. *Brill's Content,* 87–92.

Vaughan, C. E. (1998). *Social and cultural perspectives on blindness: Barriers to community integration.* Springfield, IL: Thomas.

von Bertalanffy, L. (1968). *General system theory.* New York: George Braziller.

Waldron, V. R., & Lavitt, M. R. (2000). Welfare-to-work: Communication competencies and client outcomes in a job training program. *Southern Communication Journal, 66,* 1–15.

Walker, L. (1984). *The battered woman syndrome.* New York: Springer.

Wallace, W. L. (1971). *The logic of science in sociology.* Chicago: Aline Atherton.

Wallace, W. L. (1983). *Principles of scientific sociology,* New York: Aldine.

Wallace, R. A., & Wolf, A. (1995). *Contemporary sociological theory: Continuing the classical tradition.* Englewood Cliffs, NJ: Prentice Hall.

Walther, J. (1992). Interpersonal effects in computer-mediated interaction: A relational perspective. *Communication Research, 19,* 52–90.

Walther, J. (1993). Impression development in computer-mediated interaction. *Western Journal of Communication, 57,* 381–398.

Walther, J. (1994). Anticipated ongoing interaction versus channel effects on relational communication in computer-mediated interaction. *Human Communication Research, 20,* 473–501.

Walther, J. B., & Burgoon, J. K. (1992). Relational communication in computer-mediated communication. *Human Communication Research, 19,* 50–88.

Watzlawick, P., Beavin, J. H., & Jackson, D. D. (1967). *Pragmatics of human communication.* New York: Norton.

Weaver, A. T. (1959). Seventeen who made history—The founders of the association. *Quarterly Journal of Speech, 45,* 195–199.

Wedel, T. (1994). *The spiral of silence in popular culture: Applying a public opinion theory to radio station popularity.* Master's thesis, California State University, Fullerton.

Weick, K. (1969). *The social psychology of organizing.* Reading, MA: Addison-Wesley.

Weick, K. (1979). *The social psychology of organizing* (2nd ed.). Reading, MA: Addison-Wesley.

Weick, K. (1995). *Sensemaking in organizations.* Thousand Oaks, CA: Sage.

Weick, K., & Westley, F. (1996). Organizational learning: Affirming an oxymoron. In S. Clegg, C. Hardy, & W. Nord (Eds.), *Handbook of organizational studies* (pp. 440–458). London: Sage.

Weiner, A. B. (1976). *Women of value, men of renown: New perspectives in Trobriand exchange.* Austin: University of Texas Press.

Welton, K. (1997). Nancy Hartsock's standpoint theory: From content to "concrete multiplicity." *Women and Politics, 18,* 7–24.

West, R., & Turner, L. H. (1995). Communication in lesbian and gay families: Developing a descriptive base. In T. J. Socha & G. H. Stamp (Eds.), *Parents, children, and communication: Frontiers of theory and research* (pp. 147–169). Mahwah, NJ: Erlbaum.

What is dignity? (2001). Retrieved July 31, 2002, from the World Wide Web: dignityusa.org.

What is ontology? Retrieved August 30, 2002, from the World Wide Web: www.formalontology.it/section_4.htm.

Whitchurch, G. G., & Constantine, L. L. (1993). Systems theory. In P. G. Boss, W. J. Doherty, R. LaRossa, W. R. Schumm & S. K. Steinmetz (Eds.), *Sourcebook of family theories and methods: A contextual approach* (pp. 325–352). New York: Plenum.

Whorf, B. L. (1956). Languages and logic. In J. B. Carroll (Ed.), *Language, thought, and reality: Selected writings of Benjamin Lee Whorf* (pp. 233–245). Cambridge, MA: MIT Press.

Wickham, D. (1999, April 13). Renew black studies, unfetter race dialogue. *USA Today,* p. A15.

Wicklund, R. A., & Brehm, J. W. (1976). *Perspectives on cognitive dissonance.* Hillsdale, NJ: Erlbaum.

Wiener, N. (1948). *Cybernetics*. New York: Wiley.

Willemyns, M., Gallois, C., Callan, V. J., & Pittam, J. (1997). Accent accommodation in the job interview: Impact of interviewer accent and gender. *Journal of Language and Social Psychology, 16*, 3–22.

Willis-Rivera, J. L., & Meeker, M. (2002). De Que Colores: A critical examination of multicultural children's books. *Communication Education, 51*, 269–279.

Wilmot, W. W., & Hocker, J. L. (1998). Interpersonal conflict (5th ed.). Boston: McGraw-Hill.

Windahl, S. (1981). Uses and gratifications at the crossroads. In G. C. Wilhoit & H. DeBock (Eds.), *Mass communication review yearbook* (pp. 113–132). Beverly Hills, CA: Sage.

Winsor, J. L., Curtis, D. B., & Stephens, R. D. (1996, November). *National preferences in business and communication education II*. Paper presented at the annual meeting of the Speech Communication Associaton, San Diego.

Wolf, G. (1996). Channeling McLuhan. Retrieved March 3, 2003, from the World Wide Web: www.wired.com.

Wolf, M. A., Meyer, T. P., & White, C. (1982). A rules-based study of television's role in the construction of social reality. *Journal of Broadcasting, 26*, 813–829.

Wood, J. T. (1982). Communication and relational culture: Bases for the study of human relationships. *Communication Quarterly, 30*, 75–82.

Wood, J. T. (1992). Gender and moral voice: Moving from woman's nature to standpoint epistemology. *Women's Studies in communication, 15*, 1–24.

Wood, J. T. (1992). *Spinning the symbolic web: Human communication as symbolic interaction*. Norwood, NJ: Ablex.

Wood, J. T. (1994). *Who cares? Women, care, and culture*. Carbondale: Southern Illinois University Press.

Wood, J. T. (1998). *But I thought you meant . . . : Misunderstandings in human communication*. Mountain View, CA: Mayfield.

Wood, J. T., Dendy, L. L., Dordek, E., Germany, M., & Varallo, S. M. (1994). Dialectic of difference: A thematic analysis of intimates' meanings for differences. In K. Carter & M. Prisnell (Eds.), *Interpretive approaches to interpersonal communication* (pp. 115–136). New York: SUNY Press.

Woodward, G. C. (1997). *Perspectives on American political media*. Needham Heights, MA: Allyn & Bacon.

Worchel, S. (1998). A developmental view of the search for group identity. S. Worchel, J. Morales, D. Paez, & J. Dechamps (Eds.), *Social identity: International perspectives* (pp. 53–74). London: Sage.

Worchel, S., Rothgerber, H., Day, E. A., Hart, D., & Butemeyer, J. (1998). Social identity and individual productivity within groups. *British Journal of Social Psychology, 37*, 389–413.

Wright, K. (2000). Perceptions of on-line support providers: An examination of perceived homophily, source credibility, communication and social support within on-line support groups. *Communication Quarterly, 48*, 44–59.

Wright, K. (2002). Motives for communication within on-line support groups and antecedents for interpersonal use. *Communication Research Reports, 19*, 89–98.

Yerby, J. (1995). Family systems theory reconsidered: Integrating social construction theory and dialectical process. *Communication Theory, 5*, 339–365.

Young, S. L. (1998). Where silenced voices speak out: The hidden power of informal communication networks. *Women and Language, 21*, 21–30.

Yum, J. O. (1997). The impact of Confucianism on interpersonal relationships and communication patterns in East Asia. In L. A. Samovar & R. E. Porter (Eds.), *Intercultural communication: A reader* (pp. 75–86). Belmont, CA: Wadsworth.

Zajonc, R. B. (1965). Social facilitation. *Science, 149*, 269–274.

Zanna, M. P., & Cooper, J. (1976). Dissonance and the attribution process. In J. H. Harvey, W. J. Ickes, & R. F. Kidd (Eds.), *New directions in attribution research*, (pp. 199–218). Hillsdale, NJ: Erlbaum.

Zillman, D., & Wakshlag, J. (1985). Fear of victimization and the appeal of crime drama. In D. Zillman & J. Bryant (Eds.), *Selective exposure to communication* (pp. 141–151). Hillsdale, NJ: Erlbaum.

Zimbardo, P. G., Ebbesen, E. B., & Maslach, C. (1977). *Influencing attitudes and changing behavior*. New York: Random House.

Zorn, T. E. (1995). Bosses and buddies: Constructing and performing simultaneously hierarchical and close friendship relationships. In J. T. Wood & S. Duck (Eds.), *Under-studied relationships: Off the beaten track* (pp. 122–147), Thousand Oaks, CA: Sage.

Zuengler, J. (1991). Accommodation in nativenonnative interactions: Going beyond the "what" to the "why" in second-language research. In H. Giles, J. Coupland, & N. Coupland (Eds.), *Contexts of accommodation: Developments in applied sociolinguistics* (pp. 223–244). Cambridge: Cambridge University Press.

Name Index

Stein, Robert, 186
Steinberg, Mark, 8, 163
Steinem, Gloria, 485
Steiner, Linda, 372
Steinman, Clay, 370, 373
Step, Mary, 395
Stephens, R. D., 313
Sterk, Helen, 479
Stern, Lesa, 506
Stewart, L., 34
Stewart, Martha, 120, 331–332
Stone, Jeff, 133
Straus, S. G., 405
Street, Richard, 501, 503, 504
Strine, Mary, 488
Stroud, S. R., 36
Sullivan, Patricia, 128–129, 336, 517
Sunnafrank, Michael, 166
Surber, J. P., 372
Swartz, Omar, 318
Swayze, Patrick, 211

Tajfel, Henri, 495, 496
Takai, J., 447, 457
Tan, A. S., 388
Tanno, Delores, 450
Taylor, Anita, 478
Taylor, Dalmas, 171, 172, 174, 176, 179, 181, 183, 185, 187
Taylor, J. R., 309
Taylor, Shelley, 120
Tedford, Thomas, 19
't Hart, Paul, 252–253, 254
Thibaut, John, 179, 189, 191, 197
Thilborger, C., 31
Thomas, Jo, 255
Thompson, Teresa, 185, 517
Ting-Toomey, Stella, 445, 446, 447, 448, 450, 451, 452, 453, 454, 455, 456, 457, 458, 459, 518
Toulmin, Stephen, 350
Towne, N., 172, 178
Tracy, Karen, 448, 451, 458

Trapp, R., 341
Treichler, Paula, 489
Trenholm, Sarah, 4
Trevino, Linda, 85
Triandis, Harry, 452
Tripp, Linda, 354
Tronto, J. C., 482
Trubisky, Paula, 452
Trujillo, Nick, 284
Tuffin, K., 288
Tulmulty, K., 343
Turkle, S., 37
Turner, John, 495, 496
Turner, Jonathan H., 44
Turner, Lynn H., 58, 128–129, 131, 163, 185, 336, 482, 501, 517
Turner, M. E., 254
Turow, J., 399

Vangelisti, Anita, 178, 186
VanLear, C. Arthur, 5–6
Vaughan, Edwin, 501
Vinsel, A., 187
Vogl, M. W., 511, 512
von Bertalanffy, Ludwig, 57, 295

Wack, D. L., 243
Waksal, Samuel, 331
Wakshlag, J., 388
Waldron, V. R., 34
Walker, J. R., 406
Walker, K. L., 185
Wallace, R. A., 464
Wallace, Walter L., 64
Walster, E. H., 125
Walther, Joseph, 168, 514, 515
Wartella, E., 290
Watzlawick, Paul, 6, 9, 56
Weaver, A. T., 24
Weaver, Warren, 10, 154
Wedel, T., 421
Wei, Ran, 404
Weick, Karl, 85, 292, 294, 295, 298, 299, 300, 301, 302, 303, 305, 306, 309
Weiner, A. B., 480

Weinman, Janice, 490
Welton, K., 469
Wenner, Lawrence, 401
West, M. D., 380
West, Richard L., 185, 482, 501, 517
Westley, F., 309
Whitchurch, G. G., 55
White, C., 54
White, James M., 48, 66, 67
Whiting, Gordon, 102–103, 110
Whitman, Christine Todd, 491
Whorf, Benjamin, 334
Wicklund, Robert, 127, 132
Wiemann, John, 498
Wiener, N., 48
Willemyns, M., 506
Willis-Rivera, J. L., 38
Wilmot, W. W., 163
Wilson, B., 404
Windahl, Sven, 399, 401
Winfrey, Oprah, 34
Winsor, J. L., 313
Withers, L. A., 270, 271
Wolf, A., 464
Wolf, Gary, 439
Wolf, M. A., 54
Wood, Julia, 215, 466, 471–472, 482
Woodward, Gary, 365
Worchel, Stephen, 495, 496
Wright, K., 31, 36

Yang, Shizhong, 452
Yang, S. M., 164
Yerby, Janet, 48, 49, 60
Yokochi, Y., 447, 457
Young, Stacy L., 64, 70

Zajonc, Robert, 243
Zak, Michele, 351
Zanna, M. P., 123
Zillman, D., 388
Zimbardo, P. G., 123
Zorn, Theodore, 218, 515
Zuengler, Jane, 504, 505, 506
Zuiderveen, Mark, 4

Subject Index